AF777965

The U.S. Supreme Court, 1933–1937. (Collection of the Supreme Court of the United States)

Franklin Roosevelt and the Great Constitutional War

The Court-Packing Crisis of 1937

Marian C. McKenna

Fordham University Press
New York
2002

Copyright © 2002 by Fordham University Press

All rights reserved. No part of this publication may be reproduced, stored in a retrieval system, or transmitted in any form or by any means electronic, mechanical, photocopy, recording, or any other except for brief quotations in printed reviews, without the prior permission of the publisher.

Library of Congress Cataloging-in-Publication Data

McKenna, Marian C. (Marian Cecilia), 1926–
Franklin Roosevelt and the great constitutional war : the court-packing crisis of 1937 / Marian C. McKenna.
p. cm.
Includes bibliographical references and index.
ISBN 0-8232-2154-7 (hardcover)
1. United States. Supreme Court—History. 2. Judges—Selection and appointment—United States—History. 3. United States—Politics and government—1933–1945. I. Title.
KF8742 .M356 2002
347.73′26′09—dc21 2002003885

Printed in the United States of America
02 03 04 05 06 5 4 3 2 1
First Edition

In Memoriam

This book is dedicated in loving memory to my maternal uncle John Hanfling (d. 1968). With his two brothers he operated our home farm in Westchester County and later moved with them to farm in Dutchess County. He lost his life savings in the bank failures of 1930, and in his will he left me his unredeemed gold certificates! But there was enough legal tender to acquire for my mother and me our first and only grand piano. Like many small farm operators, my uncle had disdain for the first and second AAA and most policies of his Hyde Park neighbor. He loved flowers and was an artist in growing them. Above all he was a man of conviction who chose with a careful eye the things to be remembered by.

It is within the undoubted constitutional power of Congress, for example, to overwhelm the opposition of the Supreme Court upon any question by increasing the number of Justices and refusing to confirm any appointments to the new places which do not promise to change the opinion of the Court. Once, at least, it was believed that a plan of this sort had been carried into deliberate effect. But we do not think of such a violation of the spirit of the Constitution as possible, simply because we share and contribute to that public opinion which makes such outrages upon constitutional morality impossible by standing ready to curse them.

—Woodrow Wilson, speaking on
"Government Under the Constitution"[1]

[1] An English writer, Herbert W. Horwill, published *The Usages of the American Constitution* (New York: Oxford University Press, 1925). On pp. 186–90 the book contains a discussion of "packing the Court," and this long quotation is found on p. 189. See also Woodrow Wilson, *An Old Master and Other Political Essays* (New York: 1893), p. 154.

CONTENTS

PREFACE AND ACKNOWLEDGMENTS

In the spring of 1937 *Life* magazine reported that no issue in recent years had shaken the country as did President Roosevelt's proposal of February 5 to enlarge the size of the Supreme Court to fifteen by appointing a new judge for every justice over seventy who refused to resign or retire. In proposing to increase the Court's membership to ensure pro–New Deal decisions, the president presented Congress with a momentous and serious issue. Almost overnight there began a nationwide debate on the court plan and the very fundamentals of U.S. government.

No less amazing than the boldness of the proposal itself was the manner in which the electorate rose up in wrathful protest against what it believed to be President Roosevelt's effort to "pack" the Court to validate his New Deal. No group was more outspoken than the nation's press in joining this vociferous discussion of constitutional theory and practice. The demonstration in defense of the Supreme Court amounted to nothing less than a popular tribute to its integrity and the character of its members. It was almost a vote of confidence in the Chief Justice, Charles Evans Hughes. Meanwhile, the justices went about their job without comment on the political storm of which they formed the vortex.

The subject of this book concerns that constitutional conflict between the executive and judicial branches of the government from 1933 to 1937. It occurred at a time when a rapid transformation was taking place in U.S. economic, social, political, and jurisprudential life. The very ideal of U.S. government during those years was being greatly modified. The Roosevelt era saw the beginnings of a perceptible shift of emphasis from legal to social justice and was accompanied by a waning respect for settled law. The lessening of the lawyer's influence in the community was a contributing cause of this. Some of that waning respect was directed at the courts and at substantive law. Conspicuous among these developments was widespread criticism of the efficiency of the country's judicial machinery. The law, as it was being enforced, administered, or, in many cases, unenforced and poorly administered, was being challenged, a challenge that expressed itself most vehemently in court cases, critical newspaper comment, political discourse, and congressional reaction. The times, it was thought, demanded judicial reforms of all kinds, but substantive legal reforms resisted most of the pressures. The conclusion to be drawn from the tumultuous events of the early thirties was that many different and creative remedies would have to be found and applied before the domain of the rule of law could recover the ground it had lost and could be extended further.

It would be impossible to acknowledge in this limited space all those who have assisted in my researching and writing this book, from a long line of secretaries, word processors, reference librarians, law librarians, and editors. My first obligation is owed to the University of Calgary and its Department of History, where colleagues and staff over many years have been witness to the long and sometimes agonizing process of bringing this research and its results to book form. A number of university research and travel grants enabled me to carry out research in widely scattered archives and libraries in the United States, both before and after I retired from teaching in 1996. Since then my days have been devoted to committing these research findings to paper.

Students in my classes in U.S. constitutional history at the University Calgary invariably showed an unusual interest in that most fascinating of periods, the New Deal. When we came to the court-packing episode, their enthusiasm for the subject, their research, both as undergraduates and graduates, led to useful and, at times, endless discussions. This encouraged me to do more research and write this book. Unwittingly, my Canadian students played an important role in this undertaking. I wish to thank them, if only collectively and in absentia, for their support, affection, and genuine enthusiasm for the study of U.S. constitutional history in all its many manifestations.

Completing the compilation of research was facilitated by a two-year research grant from the Social Science and Humanities Research Council of Canada. The Council's anonymous referees who vetted my grant application gave me, as a bonus, the benefit of many helpful insights, comments, constructive criticisms, suggestions, and caveats at that early stage in the project. I hope the outcome will in some measure justify their confidence in its eventual execution.

My former colleague during summers, Professor Roger Daniels of the University of Cincinnati, read and critiqued five chapters of an early draft and saved me from errors of fact and matters of style and offered valuable suggestions. While he was at Ohio State University, Professor Kermit Hall produced a thoroughgoing evaluation of a completed early draft, offering a shrewd appraisal of its strengths and weaknesses. I profited from his reading and that of subsequent reviewers of the script at a critical stage in its development. At Fordham my readers wisely asked me to shorten by about one hundred pages an already long book.

Two distinguished New Deal scholars, Arthur Schlesinger Jr. and James MacGregor Burns, somehow made time between their own multitudinous engagements, book projects, and a generally frenetic range of activities to read all or parts of the manuscript prior to copyediting. I did not expect them to agree with some of my conclusions, but Professor Burns wrote assuring me he agreed on the main points. I thank both these Roosevelt scholars sincerely for their interest in my work. I had the benefit of a short conference with G. Edward White while working at the Alderman Library in Charlottesville at a time when he was contemplating beginning a book on the New Deal Court, since published by Harvard University Press and cited in this text. Robert Cushman and Richard Friedman, two eminent legal scholars in the vanguard of revisionism of New Deal constitutional history, have been most generous in sending me the results of their prodigious research, and I thank them for it.

What could I have hoped to accomplish without the unfailing support and help in countless ways of the History Department secretariat? Without their aid, this book in all probability would not be finished yet. Joyce Woods, Violet Lake, and Wendy Amero did some of the word processing of early drafts and taught me about the mysteries of computers. When in trouble, Paul Kubicek and his expert computer department's staff came to my rescue. My heaviest debt is owed to the current support staff that includes Marjory McLean, Olga Leskiw, Karen McDermid, Carol Murray, and Brenda Oslawsky. They carried the heaviest burden and made many tasks possible, and at times even enjoyable. John King did an expert preliminary copyedit before submitting the final script to the publisher. I thank him for this and many other kindnesses. Processing the illustrations was performed expertly by Jim Burton and Dave Brown in the Photo Imaging Services at the University of Calgary.

The reception I was invariably given by the staff of Pace University's Law Library in White Plains, New York, where I have relatives, was both unexpected and overwhelmingly cordial. It seems much too feeble a gesture to acknowledge here what I owe to the personnel of that institution, whose hospitality enabled me to combine research and sporadic visits to family. The research staff at Pace, during or between semesters, performed marvelous feats producing needed books or documents. They made their fine collection available to me when I most needed it. The assistance and cooperation of Pace's reference librarians went well beyond what any visiting scholar has a right to expect. My particular thanks go to Vicky Gannon (often notified of my arrival the day before!), Marie Newman, Heide-Marie Bliss, Margaret Moreland, Greta Boeringer, and Jeanne Bonadies. They always made me feel welcome, even special. David Williams, a wizard in Database Research citation searches, pulled many a chestnut out of the fire for me, helping solve a problem, answer a question, provide a source, or give me a ride home. My thanks to all those at Pace who helped make this book possible.

On many visits to the Franklin D. Roosevelt Library in Hyde Park, New York, I became aware of how it might be possible to spend ten lifetimes researching in its staggering treasure trove of historic documents. Most of my research was done there several years ago, and most of the reference librarians who assisted me are no longer in service. I must, however, mention my appreciation for the help extended to me by Nancy Snedeker and Paul McLaughlin, who first introduced me to the collection of cartoons compiled by FDR's lawyer, Basil O'Connor.

At Fordham University Press I would like to extend my thanks to Jacqueline Philpotts and Mary Beatrice Schulte, who have done so much to further this project on so many fronts. The very idea of this book may not have been possible without their intervention. Anthony Chiffolo has been the most patient and expert of the copyeditors, ably advising me during the various stages in preparing the manuscript for the printer. The Press's Director, Saverio Procario, was from the beginning supportive, patient, encouraging, and kind. As a team, they have eased progress over my path toward the final product. For their unique blend of professionalism and collegiality, something not always found in the publishing houses of today, I extend my thanks for their faith in me and my work.

Calgary
January 3, 2002

INTRODUCTION

THIS BOOK PRESENTS a full-blown history of the New Deal in its relation to the federal judiciary, with emphasis on the origin, evolution, and fate of Roosevelt's so-called 1937 judicial reorganization bill, otherwise known as the court-packing plan. The opening five chapters of the book combine an account of the origin and implementation of some of the New Deal's social and economic legislation that transformed the United States in a difficult period in its history with the inevitable court challenges to that legislation which ensued. The resulting clash these laws encountered with the federal judiciary at all levels formed the prelude to Roosevelt's decision to "reform" the judiciary. Ultimately, it brought about the involvement of the Supreme Court in a titanic struggle with the executive.

After his stunning electoral victory in 1936, Roosevelt plunged more deeply into the game of power politics than in his first term. As a result, many of his policies, especially court-packing, caused him to make enemies of former allies, ended his ability to dominate Congress, and halted further New Deal initiatives. Effectively, 1938 brought an end to the New Deal. The court bill fight began at a stage in Roosevelt's presidency when he was at the apogee of his power. A modified version of the bill went down to a humiliating defeat six months later. The resulting decline in his leadership power and prestige, along with the immediate and long-term results of the court-packing fiasco, form a coda to this saga. In many ways, the story of FDR's court-packing scheme serves as a sobering lesson in how a popular political leader can climb to dizzying heights, but within a short time plunge to an all-time low. Roosevelt tied his political fortunes to his court bill, fought long and hard for its passage with all the considerable resources the White House could command, and in the end lost badly.

In January 1935, as a supporter of the World Court, Roosevelt was handed an earlier legislative defeat. The vote for United States membership in the court failed of the required two-thirds in the Senate, a sharp reminder of the limits of presidential power over foreign relations. This was an area in which the Supreme Court would later proclaim the president's nearly supreme might. After 1935, Roosevelt's experience—and not only with his attempts at court reform—revealed that on the domestic front, presidents can often exert even less influence over affairs than they exercise through the almost plenary powers they wield over the conduct of foreign affairs. From 1933 to 1937, Roosevelt would find that his main problems lay at home.

From the earliest period in the Supreme Court's history, presidents and Congresses have recognized that the tribunal actually has enormous power to determine the character of public policy. In the crisis atmosphere of the Great Depression, in addition to creating an alphabet soup of new government bureaus and agencies, Roosevelt and his New Deal took extraordinary actions, closing all the nation's banks, devaluing the currency, taking the country off the gold standard, canceling the gold clauses in public and private contracts, and dictating the price of gold over his breakfast tray! Capping all this was such unprecedented legislation as the National Industrial Recovery Act (NIRA) and the Agricultural Adjustment Act (AAA) in the first hundred days, during which Roosevelt's administration produced radical departures from policies and programs of past administrations. These and other initiatives involved an enormous aggrandizement of executive power. By 1935 a Supreme Court majority seemed bent on limiting that authority, denying Roosevelt powers Congress had willingly yielded to him in 1933 and 1934. The NIRA, the AAA, and nine other New Deal measures were declared unconstitutional by 1936 on such grounds as the delegation of legislative powers to the executive, revealing that an expansion of executive power, for justices that included Louis Brandeis, was a worrisome trend.

The court-packing episode had far-reaching significance. However, it remains to this day one of a few important New Deal subjects in need of an updated study. Its significance derives not only from what it has to tell us about the Constitution and the

Supreme Court in the 1930s, but for what it can reveal about the character of Franklin Roosevelt throughout one of the most intriguing periods in the history of the American presidency. It demonstrates, among other things, that Roosevelt was not the master politician historians have made him out to be, even though the New Deal era brought about substantive changes in early-twentieth-century America that altered fundamental ideas about the nation's political, social, and constitutional life.

For a long time, the New Deal literature has been lacking a scholarly study of court-packing, even though this episode caused a tumultuous upheaval in its day and left unsettling consequences in its wake. Well over half a century later, it remains a timely topic that still resonates. The narrative presented here traces the unraveling of the close working relationship between Congress and the president by the time he came out early in 1937 with his controversial court bill. This bold attempt to alter the structure and personnel of the Supreme Court—in effect amending the Constitution by circumventing ordinary procedures—provoked a pitched battle in Congress and a furious reaction in the country. The administration's attempt to ram the bill through an unwilling Congress makes an exciting and at times thrilling tale. The struggle involved all three branches of government, first pitting the president against the judiciary and then against Congress. A headstrong chief executive, accustomed to having his own way, frustrated by the Supreme Court's wreckage of much of the New Deal program, sought revenge. Congress, chafing under public criticism for acting as a "rubber stamp" during Roosevelt's first term, was now prepared to assert its independence, a development that only increased FDR's anger and frustration.

Raymond Moley, a close presidential adviser before 1936, suggested that after Roosevelt's reelection, and perhaps before, the president began to act as if he could do anything he wanted. He felt that he was the only possible man to lead the country. "I think," wrote Moley after leaving the White House, "he began to feel that way more and more, the longer he stayed in office."[1]

[1] Moley is quoted in Robert A. Wilson, *Character above All: Ten Presidents from FDR to George Bush* (New York: Free Press, 1997), 35.

One must admit that Roosevelt's serious failures of perception and vision led to the abortive court-packing scheme. The fiasco resulted, according to a recent account, from a combination of arrogance, secrecy, and ignorance. FDR, it seems, badly misjudged the generally held respect for the Supreme Court and members of the bench when in 1937, even at the height of the court-packing controversy, seven of every ten of those who had an opinion in a Gallup poll on the issue of appointing nonlawyers to the federal courts, including the Supreme Court, opposed such a development, and over 50 percent opposed the court-packing attempt.[2]

This subject deserves a fully researched, well-documented monograph, taking a close look at the political, social, and legal influences operating on the American judicial process and its constitutional development. Certain special features distinguish this study from the existing literature. It is grounded in a solid evidentiary base derived from archival sources that have been previously either unattainable, ignored, or neglected. Rich archival records have previously been unused or not used effectively. One reader of an early draft of this manuscript exclaimed: "The stuff from [Homer] Cummings's 'Secret Diary' is great." It contains much valuable material about the New Deal era neglected by most writers and confirms the central role the diarist played in shaping the original court plan. By 1934, Cummings had become one of FDR's most trusted advisers.

This fresh approach to the Supreme Court controversy modifies some previous interpretations and refutes earlier claims of a linkage between Roosevelt's reelection victory in 1936, his judicial reorganization bill, and the "1937 constitutional revolution." A key addition in this retelling of the court fight includes new evidence on the work Cummings and his handpicked Justice Department lawyers performed in researching alternative approaches to resolving the Supreme Court impasse. Their two-year "secret" investigation is explored in great detail. This background information establishes that, far from being a last-minute

[2] American Institute of Public Opinion poll, reported March 1, 1937, in Hadley Cantril, ed., *Public Opinion: 1935–1946* (Princeton: Princeton University Press, 1951), 388. Cf. Wilson, *Character Above All,* 35.

reaction to an obstructionist Supreme Court, Roosevelt's plan to limit the Court's power (and eventually to pack it) was a long time in the making. Serious thought had been given to the matter as early as remarks FDR made in his 1932 campaign. At times consideration was being given to taking away all or some of the Supreme Court's appellate jurisdiction, or its power of judicial review.

The history of litigation on New Deal laws struck down by the Supreme Court prior to 1937 is given fuller treatment and analysis here than in previous works. The case histories are deemed essential to explaining why FDR and the Court got so out of joint. Without a firm grasp of the test cases—detailing their fact patterns, the legal theories that then prevailed, their influence on the doctrinal categories in the constitutional consciousness of the individual justices, and the internal politics complicating all this—it would be virtually impossible to understand the friction that developed, why the Court's decision making took the form it did, and how Roosevelt, under pressure, reacted as he did. He was determined, by one means or another, to force a showdown with the Supreme Court. FDR and his key advisers were no innocent bystanders in this, one of the great constitutional crises in American history. By taking a blithe approach to sloppy bill drafting and a peculiar kind of "wink and nod" attitude toward the Constitution, knowing there would be judicial challenges to these laws, Roosevelt and his subordinates played a central role in precipitating the crisis.

To be fully understood, however, the controversy between the Court and Roosevelt should be seen as transcending the particular court cases involved in the buildup of tensions that preceded the assault on the nine justices. The attack was, in effect, a political broadside in the guise of an enforced retirement plan. Despite administration claims to the contrary, the court-packing bill violated Article III of the Constitution, which guarantees Supreme Court justices life tenure. Only death, voluntary retirement, or resignation can remove them. The conflict thus concerned the very character of the established constitutional order.

Like his predecessors Jefferson and Jackson, Roosevelt did not consider himself bound by Supreme Court pronouncements on social and economic matters. He urged Congress to follow a different political path, thus producing the New Deal, and laws requiring novel constitutional interpretations. Those supporting his proposal to enlarge the Supreme Court had for their obvious purpose to change the meaning and construction of the Constitution, and hence the Constitution itself. Without resort to the traditional amending process, which the democratic Roosevelt refused to trust, the Constitution was by default to be amended.

The election of 1936 had no bearing on the decisions reached by the justices in subsequent cases coming before them for review. The election victory may have suited Roosevelt's instinct for strategic timing, treating it as a catalyst for action. The court bill was finalized very soon afterward and after a long period of deliberation. The midterm elections of 1934 were almost as one-sided as that in 1936, but after them the Court showed no hesitation in invalidating New Deal legislation. Contrary to Mr. Dooley's statement, the Supreme Court did not "follow the election returns." Nor did FDR's court-packing threat affect 1937 Supreme Court decisions. The *Parrish* case was decided in December 1936, two months before Roosevelt introduced his court bill. In March 1937, when the opinion upholding a Washington State minimum wage law for women was announced, the shift from a prior position by a *single* justice, Owen Roberts, made the difference between victory and defeat for Elsie Parrish. Four justices adhered to traditional due process doctrine in minimum wage disputes. The conventional interpretation of court-packing nevertheless made the *Parrish* case the centerpiece of its "constitutional revolution" theory, giving far greater significance to this decision than it merits. It is likely that the Supreme Court lineup in the post–March 1937 cases would have occurred as it did without FDR's court-packing challenge.

The court-packing crisis has for long been a New Deal topic strangely neglected by historians. From the beginning it was preempted by journalists. Two Washington reporters, Joseph Alsop and Turner Catledge, produced the earliest account, *The 168 Days* (1938), based on hearsay and personal contacts with principals. Leonard Baker, another journalist, produced the latest book-length study, *Back to Back: The Duel between FDR and the*

Supreme Court (1967). Both works are now outdated. Despite containing valuable information, they make almost no use of original sources. Baker's work relies heavily on secondary materials and features undocumented "inside" information from sources he refused to identify.

In 1995, political historian William E. Leuchtenburg, after devoting years of work to researching in original sources, compiled a book of essays, *The Supreme Court Reborn.* But for all its merits, and they are considerable, the work fails to meet a need for a comprehensive narrative on the history of court-packing with the potential to attract not only scholars and constitutional or legal experts, but general readers as well. This and previous publications focusing on the court fight follow the conventional interpretation developed by generations of writers. The justices are portrayed as old men bearing stereotyped labels. These accounts include such prominent themes as the deliberate involvement of the Court in politics and the formulation of public policy, as well as the inclination to resist popularly mandated social and economic change. Major tenets of the conventional approach are currently under revision and subject to further erosion by the findings in this study.

In recent years, a cadre of lawyers and law professors has sought, both in law review articles and books, to provide correctives to the conventional interpretation of the Supreme Court controversy and its legacy. Barry Cushman, Peter Irons, Richard Friedman, and G. Edward White, to name a few, have been systematically chipping away at key parts of the accepted wisdom on the constitutional issues, jurisprudence, and nature of court-packing, putting a whole new face on the controversy. The older versions tried to establish a direct link between the 1936 election, the court bill, the "switch in time" theory, and "constitutional revolution" of 1937. The Supreme Court, it is true, between March and May 1937, reversed rulings on the contract clause, the commerce clause, and the due process clause. The abrupt about-face is depicted as resulting directly from the "fear of God" that Roosevelt's court bill put in the hearts of the sitting justices! This notion is reminiscent of a remark made by FDR's distant cousin, Theodore, who once boasted: "I may not know much about law, but I do know one can put the fear of God into judges!"[3] The new legal studies by Robert Cushman show that the changes that occurred in American constitutional jurisprudence stretched over a much longer period than three short months in 1937.

Roosevelt failed to recognize or appreciate the power and reputation of the institution he attacked and the institutional nature of the American system of government, with its built-in balance of power system. A well-documented record of the disarray in his administration and his failures in management, administration, and policy planning may also be symptomatic of this inability to work within the confines of the established structure not only of the federal government, but of the federal-state-local pyramid. During the crisis atmosphere of 1933 FDR was allowed to bypass or avoid many of the ordinary blockades that other presidents have to face, such as slowdowns, veto traps, gridlock, and the compromises endemic in a democratic system of governance. But he refused to accept the reality of his limitations.

The founders of the American constitutional system deliberately fashioned features and inserted them in it so as to thwart efforts by any one branch of government to encroach on the domain of another, to block rapid government responses to popular majorities, and to delay continuous follow-through on policies and programs until they could be well thought out. This essential structure has never been altered over the intervening centuries since the framers completed their work. There was nothing that even a Franklin Roosevelt, with all his alleged political skills, could do about it.

This book is a work of history, not of law. It views the changes in American society during the New Deal and the constitutional crisis of 1937 through a historian's eyes, considering their complex origins and the shifting fortunes of the principal antagonists, as in chapters 5 and 6. Where possible, it delineates the practices of the era's legal and political elites in framing laws and in molding national policy, rules, concepts, principles of law, and ideol-

[3] James Charlton, ed., *A Lawyer's Quotation Book* (New York: McGraw-Hill, 1989), 29.

ogy. The emphasis throughout this work is on politics and the sweep of changing circumstances brought on in part by the Depression, but attention is also given to evolving legal ideas and practices as they became interwoven with the politics of the day.

One further aim I contemplated when beginning this research was to try to reinstate or restore the reputation of the individual justices on the New Deal Supreme Court. They were unfairly maligned during their time by partisan supporters of the Roosevelt administration and perpetrators of its vendetta, as well as by the contemporary commentators, beginning with the authors of the book *The Nine Old Men* (1936), columnist Drew Pearson with the assistance of Robert S. Allen. Their characterization has been perpetuated to a surprising extent in conventional interpretations appearing in books and articles ever since. Pearson's caricature of the justices as "old men" was applied indiscriminately and soon found its way into common usage. The age issue was eventually exploited by Roosevelt and Cummings in their judicial reorganization bill as a rationale for court-packing.

The work of rehabilitating the justices has to a large extent been preempted in new publications by Barry Cushman and G. Edward White. Professor White demonstrates how conventional accounts of constitutional history began for the first time in the 1930s to attach labels to individual justices, whether they were appropriate or not, and soon after began to refer to judicial blocs. In his phrase, they "canonized" as "progressive" or "liberal" Justices Holmes and Brandeis while demonizing McReynolds, Butler, Van Devanter, and Sutherland as hopeless reactionaries for opposing New Deal measures. The conventional account was eventually constructed on the assumption that all nine judges, for subscribing to an essentialist view of the Constitution and their role as guardians of its text and interpretation, were so fundamentally flawed in their understanding of constitutional interpretation and the nature of judging that their modus operandi should be dismissed as "outmoded" or "reactionary." Anti–New Deal opinions were invariably caricatured as "biased."

Professor White concludes that the whole of judicial decision making in the 1930s has been distorted to fit this modernist formula, which features as its new icon "a living Constitution." He writes: "Its triumphal narratives have created a misconception of the nature of a period of great jurisprudential ferment in American legal history in which fundamentally antipathetic conceptions of the nature of law, the meaning of legal sources and the role of the judge as a constitutional interpreter were in collision."[4]

Gnawing questions may continue to underlie the origins and implementation of court-packing. Did Roosevelt fully comprehend the reverence in which many Americans held the Supreme Court, the institution on which he resolved to launch a frontal attack? With a Congress already widely considered a "rubber stamp," the public feared that he now had designs on a takeover of the judiciary. Republicans, along with many Democrats, had misgivings about Roosevelt's tendency toward consolidating power within the executive branch. It remained for the Senate and all thinking Americans to make the final determination that Roosevelt and Cummings chose the wrong plan, employed the wrong method of achieving their goal, at the wrong time, and in the end had to suffer the consequences. It is essential to the American system of government, operating under a written Constitution, that the courts retain not only their independence but the power to interpose themselves between the will of the people, represented not by transitory programs but by the Constitution, and the will of the president and legislature.

[4] *The Constitution and the New Deal* (Cambridge: Harvard University Press, 2000), 300. See especially for the development of these ideas his chapter 9, "The Canonization and Demonization of Judges," and chapter 10, "Cabining the New Deal in Time." For an exhaustive survey of the entire corpus of decision making of Justices Sutherland, Butler, Van Devanter, and McReynolds on the Court, see Barry Cushman, "The Secret Lives of the Four Horsemen," *Virginia Law Review* 83 (April 1997): 559–645.

ABBREVIATIONS USED IN NOTES

ALDL	Alderman Library, University of Virginia, Charlottesville
COHC	Columbia University Oral History Collection, Butler Library, Columbia University, New York City
CPPC	*Complete Presidential Press Conferences of Franklin D. Roosevelt.* 12 vols. New York: Da Capo Press, 1972.
FDRL	Franklin Delano Roosevelt Presidential Library, Hyde Park, New York
HLL	Harvard Law Library, Cambridge, Massachusetts
LC	Library of Congress, Manuscript Division, Washington, D.C.
MHS	Montana Historical Society, Helena
NA	National Archives and Records Service, Washington, D.C.
RG	Record Group
PPA	*The Public Papers and Addresses of Franklin D. Roosevelt.* Samuel I. Rosenman, ed., 13 vols. New York: Random House, Macmillan, Harper Bros., 1938–50.
SL	Sterling Library, Yale University, New Haven, Connecticut
UAL	University of Arkansas Library, Special Collections, Fayetteville

1

The Fifty-Fourth Attorney General

> More than anyone but the President himself, it is the Attorney General who sets the moral tone of the Administration, symbolizing its commitment or lack of commitment to impartial justice.
>
> "Ties of Attorney General to Chief," *New York Times,* January 30, 1984, A14, col. 3.

THE AMBITIOUS EXPERIMENTAL PROGRAM that Franklin Roosevelt, the brain trust, and Congress cobbled together during the famous "hundred days" special session of the Seventy-third Congress had for its aim relief for the unemployed, recovery from the depression, and reform of the economic and social order. It was the most innovative, progressive, and far-reaching undertaking the country had known since Wilsonian days, and its implementation would require support from all three branches of government. The executive department played an important role in its formulation, supervising the drafting of numerous statutes that were swiftly enacted into law by a compliant Democratic Congress. In the depths of the economic crisis, Republicans and Democrats responded to the call for action demanded by an impatient chief executive, but New Deal laws faced opposition from the third branch of government, the judiciary. It would be in the federal courts that controversy and crisis would have their origins.

The lower federal courts, dominated by Republican judges, made a regular practice of granting injunctions suspending the application of New Deal statutes. Over time this practice became widespread and menacing, prompting introduction of the phrase "government by injunction." Friction between the New Deal and the lower federal courts intensified as the latter continued to disrupt the work of the administration. For example, early in 1935 an order by Judge William I. Grubb of the Northern District of Alabama in Birmingham restrained a statute giving his court jurisdiction over all Tennessee Valley Authority (TVA) cases, effectively preventing the TVA from selling electricity to municipalities in all of Alabama.[1] The lower courts issued nearly two thousand injunctions against various government programs, many of which involved the taxes imposed on processors under the Agricultural Adjustment Act. A federal statute prohibited such injunctions, but as the attorney general told Roosevelt in exasperation, "the Courts seem to have found a way of declaring it inapplicable," and they continued to enjoin federal agencies "rather freely."[2]

Accordingly, a heavy burden of litigation would eventually fall on the Justice Department, requiring a strong hand at the helm to ensure a favorable outcome to court challenges of New Deal laws. FDR at first wanted Thomas Walsh of Montana for his attorney general, but Walsh was somewhat reluctant to give up the Senate seat he had held since 1913. Regarded highly in Washington as a progressive, a prospective "balance wheel," and an elder statesman for the new administration, the seventy-four-year-old attorney had been permanent chairman of the 1932 Democratic Convention in Chicago and one of the few chosen to join the presidential train on FDR's 1932 campaign tour of western states. During the interregnum, he held consultations with outgoing Attorney General William Mitchell in an effort to arrange a smooth transition in the Justice Department.[3]

---

[1] Senator Hugo Black of Alabama responded by introducing a bill that would have allowed a direct appeal to the Supreme Court from the federal courts when injunctions prohibiting enforcement of federal statutes were issued. Justices Brandeis, Van Devanter, and Hughes appeared before the Senate Judiciary Committee to give testimony that would lead to killing Black's bill, arguing that their Court's authority to grant review, before an appellate court heard such a case, was adequate. Roger Newman, *Hugo Black: A Biography* (New York: Fordham University Press, 1997), 209–10.

[2] Homer S. Cummings to Franklin D. Roosevelt, July 19, 1935, OF 10, Box 4, and June 2, 1936, OF 10, Box 5, FDRL.

[3] Josephine O'Keane, *Thomas J. Walsh: A Senator from Montana* (Francestown, N.H.: n.p., 1955), is a sound but undocumented biography. Walsh's role in the 1932 campaign and his views on the Justice Department are briefly described in Raymond Moley, *After Seven Years* (New York: Harper Bros., 1939), 110, 123.

Roosevelt wanted Walsh's appointment announced upon his return from a cruise in mid-February. Before sailing, he asked his trusted aide Raymond Moley to sound Walsh out on how he felt about having Felix Frankfurter, a Harvard law professor, as solicitor general. Moley later asserted: "Old Tom Walsh kept us on tenterhooks for almost a month," and although he finally agreed to accept appointment as attorney general, Walsh would not have Frankfurter, owing to his lack of practical experience at the bar. He said he did not want somebody in there "who would lose cases in the grand manner."[4]

Official Washington was in shock when it was learned that Senator Walsh suffered a fatal heart attack on the morning of March 2, 1933. Stricken in his railway compartment on the way to Roosevelt's inauguration, Walsh was returning with his wife of a few days from their wedding in Cuba. He had been planning to take her on an extended tour of the Northwest to show her the country after the inauguration. News of his death reached the president-elect by way of Associated Press reports as he was boarding a New York train that same day, en route to the nation's capital. On arrival in Washington, he hastily conferred with William Woodin, Secretary of the Treasury Jim Farley, and several others about the new situation, only two days before the inauguration. In a meeting at his Mayflower Hotel suite with Bronx County machine boss Edward J. Flynn, FDR said he was unable to think of a suitable replacement for Walsh and had just about decided to let the matter lay over until after the inauguration. The banking crisis was making it impossible for him to give careful study to another appointment.

Marguerite ("Missy") Le Hand, Roosevelt's personal secretary and close associate, attended that discussion, and at some point in the conversation she casually remarked: "Well, perhaps Homer Cummings would make a good appointment." Roosevelt hesitated, reluctant even to consider her suggestion, having already named Cummings governor-general of the Philippines. But the longer he thought about it, the more convinced FDR became

[4] Raymond Moley, *The First New Deal* (New York: Harcourt, Brace, and World, 1966), 76–77; Leonard Baker, *Brandeis and Frankfurter: A Dual Biography* (New York: New York University Press, 1986), 280.

that, at least on a temporary basis, moving Cummings to Justice would solve the problem. There are many examples of Missy's influence. Her approval or disapproval of a person or course of action was more difficult for FDR to overcome than that of anyone else, even perhaps Mrs. Roosevelt.[5] No inkling of these consultations reached newsmen, and the final decision to make Cummings the attorney general was hammered out in subsequent hotel meetings.

The press was also kept in the dark about the unrelenting campaign Cummings had been conducting in pursuit of the appointment eventually handed him by a kind fate. His maneuvering, recorded in his "Secret Diary," remained secret until long after his death. The diary recounts in minute detail the high-level contacts Cummings made and the persistent lobbying he pursued between early December 1932 and mid-February 1933, always in the hope that even after Walsh's appointment, something might go awry to change the makeup of the Roosevelt cabinet.

Advocating Cummings's appointment were Cordell Hull, future secretary of state; Joseph E. Davies, FDR's ambassador to Moscow; and Senator William Gibbs McAdoo of California. Davies offered to urge Cummings's candidacy upon Roosevelt, but told him it was "perfectly idiotic for anyone to want the office, in view of what the attorney general was going to be up against in the next few years." Supporters also included Colonel Edward M. House, close confidant of former president Wilson; Jim Farley; Breckenridge Long, a prominent Washington lawyer; and Democratic senators Key Pittman, Joseph T. Robinson, James F. Byrnes, and C. C. Dill. On a train bound for New York after the Gridiron Club dinner on December 17, 1932, one of the passengers, George A. Combs, was "full of gossip" and said Roosevelt was considering Cummings for attorney general.[6] A good many

[5] Edward J. Flynn, *You're the Boss* (New York: Viking, 1947), 125–26; Moley, *First New Deal,* 76–77. A view of Flynn as a well-meaning victim of Roosevelt's selfish and manipulating politics is found in Lyle W. Dorsett, *Franklin D. Roosevelt and the City Bosses* (Port Washington, N.Y.: Kennikat, 1977).

[6] Secret Diary of Homer S. Cummings, entry for December 18, 1932. The diary forms part of the collection of 130,000 items deposited after Cummings's death in the Alderman Library, University of Virginia, Charlottesville, by his longtime associate Carl McFarland.

people, however, were taking potshots at FDR, claiming he had no business going into a small state like Connecticut to fill such an important cabinet post—especially a state that had voted for Hoover.

In private discussions, Senators Wheeler and Dill explained that if Walsh wanted the post, they would be strong for him. Dill tried to soften the blow, saying that "if Walsh were out of the picture, he [Cummings] would have his support." Wheeler well remembered an incident at the 1932 Chicago convention when Cummings had asked to take the floor to speak against the two-thirds rule, required at that time as opposed to a simple majority to nominate a presidential candidate. Wheeler was convinced that if Cummings had succeeded in making that speech, he would have alienated southern delegates from Roosevelt. He believed it had been Cummings's intention to deprive FDR of the nomination and throw the convention open to a dark-horse candidate, perhaps himself, or someone with more appeal for non-southern delegates.[7]

A seasoned politician like Cummings could not have entertained such unrealistic ambitions. His devotion to Roosevelt, a longtime idol, makes such a theory ludicrous. Wheeler, who was destined to play a key role in the court-packing controversy, detested Cummings. He considered him a cheap politician, never trusted him, and had no use for some of his close associates. He later alleged that Roosevelt's difficulties with the Supreme Court would never have materialized if Tom Walsh had been FDR's attorney general, or if Cummings had been a better lawyer, and not always trying to make a "political case" against the Supreme Court.[8]

"Senator McAdoo came to the front for me 100%," Cummings relates, "and made more arguments on my behalf than I

[7] *New York Times,* June 26–29, 1932; Burton K. Wheeler with Paul F. Healy, *Yankee from the West* (Garden City, N.Y.: Doubleday, 1962), esp. chapter 11; Sean J. Savage, *Roosevelt, the Party Leader: 1932–1945* (Lexington: University Press of Kentucky, 1991), 109; Charles Michelson, FDR's speechwriter, recorded in his memoir that Wheeler thought he should have been offered second place on the Roosevelt ticket in 1932 "and has been grouchy about it ever since." *The Ghost Talks* (New York: Putnam, 1944), 140.

[8] Leonard Baker, *Back to Back: The Duel between FDR and the Supreme Court* (New York: Macmillan, 1967), 27.

could have thought of myself." Like many others, McAdoo doubted Walsh would accept the post if offered it. McAdoo seemed so confident Cummings would prevail that at one of their many talks he raised the possibility of changing the law with regard to the makeup of the Supreme Court so as "to get the antiquated judges off the bench." The senator wondered if a statute could be drawn up that would be constitutional. The justices, he noted, were appointed for life at certain salaries, and he acknowledged that this might raise constitutional questions.

McAdoo thought a bill could be drafted that would withstand a constitutional test if it provided, for instance, that justices retire from the bench and become "justices emeritus, as it were" after reaching the age of seventy or seventy-two. Their salaries would continue to be paid and they could sit with the Supreme Court when requested by the chief justice, "but no more than one at a time."[9] He wanted Cummings to have the matter briefed in his office, and if it could be worked out he would introduce such a bill in the Senate. He said he had talked the matter over with Governor Roosevelt, who liked the idea. "This would get rid of some of the 'old fossils,'" McAdoo added, though he said he would regret to see Brandeis get off the bench. But then, he added: "He was getting pretty well along in years and so it would not much matter."[10]

When word reached Hull that Walsh had been appointed, he seemed very downcast. He had so wanted Cummings in the cabinet. Cummings recounted: "He still thinks that things may shift around before the fourth of March and that it will be possible after all."[11] Meanwhile, he asked Hull to gather data for him on the Philippines. Both were disconsolate. In the end, "things did shift around," though not in the way anyone could have predicted. A month later, Walsh's sudden death opened the path for Cummings to realize his most cherished ambition.

Walsh's successor is one of the forgotten figures of the New Deal era. There is no full-length biography of Homer Stillé Cum-

---

[9] Cummings, Secret Diary, January 21–26, 1933, 101–2.
[10] Ibid.
[11] Ibid., February 3, 1933, 122–24.

"Homer Stillé Cummings." The 54th Attorney General of the United States (1933–1939) was paradoxically the country's chief law officer and the chief architect of the ill-fated court-packing plan.

mings, no recent article, no long essay recounting his career. A last-minute choice, he spent almost six years as attorney general, years that were among the most important and tumultuous in modern political and legal history. Handed the job of the nation's chief law officer as a temporary expedient, he had no thought of permanent tenure, no advance plans, no staff or assistants. In spite of all this, he took up his duties in the musty old building at the corner of Vermont Avenue and K Street leased by the government to house the Justice Department's headquarters.[12]

Born in Chicago, Cummings (1870–1956) was brought up in a Republican household. After graduating in law from Yale in 1893, he entered the office of Connecticut's state's attorney, Samuel Fessenden. A year later they formed a partnership (Fessenden, Carter & Cummings) in Stamford, then a small town of about five thousand. Cummings later formed a partnership with Charles D. Lockwood, a relationship that lasted until 1933 and was resumed after 1939. By 1896 Cummings was a regular Democrat, and he began his political career campaigning for William Jennings Bryan. Four years later he entered the mayoral race in Stamford, running against the Republican incumbent, Edward J. Tupper. To the surprise of everyone, including the hostile *Stamford Advocate,* he was elected in that traditionally Republican stronghold by a plurality of 104 votes, and served three terms between 1902 and 1908. After 1900 his rise in national politics was swift. He was elected vice chairman of the Democratic National Committee and in 1919 and 1920 became chairman. He served on it until 1924. During the intervening years he narrowly lost campaigns for the House of Representatives and the Senate.[13]

In 1914, Cummings began a ten-year term as state's attorney for Fairfield County, during which time he scored his greatest courtroom triumph by securing the dismissal of an indictment against Harold Israel, a vagrant accused of murdering a popular

---

[12] Groups of employees were scattered throughout several buildings in Washington until late 1934, when the Justice Department moved into its new building of some fifteen hundred offices between Constitution and Pennsylvania Avenues and 9th and 10th Streets, N.W. *The Selected Papers of Homer Cummings,* ed. Carl Brent Swisher (New York: Scribner's, 1939), xiv–xv.

[13] Hugh Russell Fraser, "Attorney General Cummings," *American Mercury,* 23 December 1934, 400.

Bridgeport priest. Despite compelling circumstantial evidence and a confession by the accused, Cummings was unconvinced of Israel's guilt and was eventually able, after conducting a private investigation, to present evidence exonerating him. The trial created a sensation and was given added celebrity by the case's inclusion in the Wickersham Report of 1931.[14] It was later dramatized in the popular 1947 film *Boomerang.*

At the 1924 Democratic National Convention in New York's Madison Square Garden, Cummings supported William Gibbs McAdoo over the more popular Al Smith for the presidential nomination. For this he incurred the implacable enmity of Smith's followers, was deprived of his place on the Democratic National Committee, and became a dead letter in Connecticut politics for the remainder of the decade.

With the onset of the depression, Cummings reentered national politics, helping to plan the strategy and tactics for Roosevelt's nomination in 1932 and acting as one of his floor managers at the Chicago convention. Although pledged to Al Smith, he delivered a rousing seconding speech for FDR, earning himself a reputation as a Democratic wheelhorse. However, as delegate-at-large from Connecticut, he overplayed his hand in an attempt to secure all the state's delegates for his hero. Without his intervention, the Democrats probably could have succeeded in claiming half, but in the end they lost them all under the unit rule.[15] Roosevelt failed to carry the state in November.

Informed of Senator Walsh's death by Joseph E. Davies on March 2, Cummings was summoned the next day to the president-elect's hotel. Roosevelt said he wanted him in the cabinet but had not given up on the idea of sending him to the Philippines, which he regarded as a more important assignment in view of the worsening situation in the Far East. Cummings was asked to serve as attorney general for a few weeks. In further talks,

[14] Based largely on forensic evidence related to the weapon found on the person of Harold Israel, whose bullets did not match the one extracted from the victim, Cummings's findings, presented to the trial judge in Superior Court, Hartford, resulted in a judgment of *nolle contendere.* Cummings, "The State v. Harold Israel," *Journal of the American Institute of Criminal Law and Criminology* 15 (May 1924–February 1925): 406–34.

[15] Wheeler, *Yankee from the West,* chap. 11.

Roosevelt hastily reviewed his various contacts with New York's banking representatives, who, as he said, "had completely lost their heads and were recommending that he do all sorts of fantastic things." The full cabinet was sworn in by Associate Justice Benjamin Cardozo in the White House Oval Room on March 4, in the presence of relatives and friends. This represented a break with tradition, the result of a personal invitation from Roosevelt to his official family and, as he told a friend, the kind of change he intended to initiate from time to time.[16]

From Cummings's first day on the job, his path as advocate and protector of New Deal initiatives was a thorny one. Roosevelt proposed declaring a bank holiday, closing all the nation's banks, but wondered if he had the constitutional authority. Did the 1917 Trading with the Enemy Act's Section 5 provide sufficient legal ground for a proclamation? After a hasty investigation, Cummings advised that the law would permit closing all banks as well as regulating gold hoarding and export. Roosevelt took immediate steps to close the banks, suspend gold exports, and issue executive orders relating to gold. Historians ever since have argued that such drastic steps were based on dubious constitutional authority, since the 1917 act, as drawn, applied exclusively to wartime.[17] Nevertheless, Roosevelt took these bold measures, confirmed in part by Congress's enactment of the Emergency Banking Relief Act of 1933. He had previously discussed this matter with the late Senator Walsh and had sought a ruling on it. Walsh advised that in an emergency the needed exercise of power would be valid.

Cummings's cooperative spirit and speedy action in the banking crisis impressed Roosevelt, and within weeks he was asked to stay on as attorney general. The Philippine assignment went to

[16] John T. Flynn, *The Roosevelt Myth* (New York: Devin Adair Co., 1965), 9.

[17] Michael E. Parrish, "Constitutional History, 1933–1945," *Encyclopedia of the American Constitution,* eds. Leonard Levy et al., 2 vols. (New York: Macmillan, 1986), 1:442–48, at 445; Alfred H. Kelly and Winfred Harbison, *The American Constitution: Its Origins and Development* (New York: Norton, 1976), 684; Michael E. Parrish, "The Great Depression, the New Deal, and the American Legal Order," *Washington Law Review* 54 (1983–84): 736; Moley, *After Seven Years,* 144–46. Former President Hoover, heeding the advice of his attorney general, hesitated to use the 1917 Trading with the Enemy Act as authority to declare a bank holiday. Moley, *The First New Deal,* 139.

Frank Murphy. Ready compliance with his chief's wishes caused some journalists to characterize Cummings as Roosevelt's "legal yes-man," while to others he was a party hack, "just another politician and not a particularly smart one at that." His real flair, they said, was for hero worship and quick enabling opinions for the administrative benefit of his idol.

Roosevelt knew exactly what he wanted in an attorney general. Too often, he complained to aides, lawyers were disposed to search for reasons why something that was necessary *cannot* be done, rather than find the means whereby it *can* be done. This, he assured them, would change. The government lawyer's job is to find constitutional ways to do what has to be done. Time and again he laid down this challenge to successive chief law officers: "If you are a good attorney general, tell me how I can do it."[18] Cummings proved to be unusually adept at accommodating his chief's requests for advice and was the ideal attorney general for a man like Roosevelt, always able to find ways that permitted him to do whatever he wanted to do. Many of his advisory opinions were oral, which in the light of history may have been fortunate for him. One journalist called him the "legal mechanic" of the administration. FDR used him as big business used corporation lawyers.[19]

Roosevelt faced another problem: the appointment of a solicitor general. The office was created by Congress in the Judiciary Act of 1870. The role of the solicitor general in the American judicial system epitomizes the tensions inherent in a system of separation of powers. As a political appointee of the chief executive and an officer of the Supreme Court, the solicitor general serves two separate branches of government and two institutions as the nation's lawyer. He maintains an office in the Justice Department as well as permanent chambers in the Supreme Court, the only attorney permitted to keep an office in its building. Occupying the two offices epitomizes the dual role the solicitor general

[18] Arthur M. Schlesinger, Jr., *The Politics of Upheaval, 1935–1936,* vol. 3 of *The Age of Roosevelt* (Boston: Houghton Mifflin, 1960), 230.

[19] John Franklin Carter, *The New Dealers, by Washington's Unofficial Observer* (New York: Simon and Schuster, 1934), 261–62.

plays, acting as a bridge between the judicial and executive departments.

As chief lawyer, the solicitor general advises and defends the interests of the government in court. His statutory responsibilities include acting as a respected adviser to the justices and as a gatekeeper, in control of and accountable for all government litigation before the Supreme Court. He is answerable to the attorney general and is in fact what he is in name—the chief law officer of the U.S. government as far as the courts are concerned.[20]

Paul Freund and, more recently, the late Justice Lewis Powell observed that the solicitor general is in many ways "a tenth justice." The other nine expect him to be impartial and nonpartisan. They need his help. He is not just an advocate for the government, but serves the justices as a resource whose briefs and arguments develop the background of the law. The justices rely on him implicitly for accuracy and integrity. His staff of assistants and batteries of government lawyers are expected to be devoted to the same ends. He represents one of the last remnants of an old tradition persisting in the formal apparel he wears when arguing for the government before the Supreme Court (morning coat or cutaway, striped trousers, and dark vest).

When he became solicitor general in 1940, Francis Biddle was advised by Felix Frankfurter to "stay out of politics." Biddle claimed that the solicitor's guide is the ethics of his profession, framed in the ambience of his own experience and judgment. The nation's law officer, he believed, has no other master to serve but his country. There were to be no political compromises, no deviations, no considerations of expediency. Patronage was outside his ken, and administration was usually reduced to a minimum.[21] But his formula hardly fits the early New Deal years.

At first Roosevelt wanted Felix Frankfurter as solicitor, and he was offered the post on March 8, 1933, with assurance that Cummings "knew all about it, admired him, and was eager to have him." This was far from the truth, since Cummings had no

[20] Rebecca Mae Salokar, *The Solicitor General: The Politics of Law* (Philadelphia: Temple University Press, 1992), 1–14.

[21] Francis Biddle, *In Brief Authority* (Garden City, N.Y.: Doubleday, 1962), 97–98.

more use for Frankfurter than he had for the late Senator Walsh. Frankfurter gave the matter some thought and consulted his wife and close friends, including Justices Brandeis and Cardozo. In the end he rejected the offer, bluntly informing Roosevelt: "I think I know the demands of that office perhaps more completely than there is reason for your knowing them. . . . I have known about the work . . . almost from the time I left law school. It is exciting and profoundly important. But if a man is to be Solicitor General he must make up his mind that it will absorb sixteen hours of his day."[22] For refusing the offer, Roosevelt privately referred to Frankfurter as "an independent pig," barely able to conceal his irritation at the rebuff.

Frankfurter and Brandeis were already showing dissatisfaction with the administration of the Justice Department. They had fairly good relations with the other government departments and agencies, but Cummings prevented any interference in the Justice Department, the one they were most anxious to influence. Both wanted Dean Acheson, a partner in the Washington law firm Covington and Burling, for solicitor general. Frankfurter forcefully argued his case with Roosevelt, but when FDR approached Cummings the reaction was immediate, violent, and adverse.

Acheson's memoirs reveal that he yearned to be solicitor general, but Cummings bore a personal grudge against him because Acheson's father, the Episcopal bishop of Cummings's Connecticut diocese in 1929, disapproved of his multiple marriages, frowned on his divorce of his second wife, and denied the complicity of the church in his marriage to Cecilia Waterbury, the daughter of a prominent Darien, Connecticut, businessman.[23] Frankfurter first declined the post, and it was at his and Bran-

[22] Memorandum of March 15, 1933, Felix Frankfurter Papers, HLL. Some years later, Cummings joined ranks with John Nance Garner and Jim Farley in their attempt to block Frankfurter's appointment to the Supreme Court. Cummings made the matter a personal issue, opposing Frankfurter in 1939 with an astonishing vehemence. Garner pressed for the importance of geographic considerations. Had New Dealers failed to mobilize support from Senator George Norris and Frank Murphy, Roosevelt might have been forced to fill the vacancy with someone else. Joseph Alsop and Robert Kintner, *Men around the President* (Garden City, N.Y.: Doubleday, Doran, 1939), 158–59.

[23] Dean G. Acheson, *Morning and Noon* (Boston: Houghton Mifflin, 1965), 161.

deis's suggestion that Acheson should have it. When Cummings refused to accept him, a frustrated Roosevelt, never known for his patience, threw up his hands and cried: "Well for God's sake, get me somebody."[24]

The nonentity finally named as the New Deal's first solicitor general was James Crawford Biggs, a sixty-year-old North Carolina trial lawyer and judge who landed the job because no other candidates were actively in the field. All assumed the post would go to Frankfurter. When it came to a showdown, there was Biggs with endorsements from the likes of Senator Josiah Bailey of North Carolina, O. Max Gardner, Josephus Daniels, and a host of state judges and past presidents of the American Bar Association.

From the outset, Biggs seemed bewildered by his new responsibilities. That he was unfit for them was demonstrated when he lost ten of the seventeen cases tried in his first fifteen months in office. He was amiable, kindly, honest, and courtly, but just plain unqualified for the job. A justice of the Supreme Court referred to him as "Serjeant Buzfuz" after a character in Charles Dickens's *The Pickwick Papers.*[25] In making an oral argument before the high bench, Biggs was publicly rebuked by the chief justice: "Mr. Solicitor General, you have talked forty-five minutes already. You had better take the next fifteen minutes telling us what you want this court to do."[26]

When a new solicitor general is appointed, he is expected to make the rounds, paying courtesy calls on each of the justices and coming back from them impressed with the expectations they have of him and his staff. Paul Freund stated: "During the early New Deal days with J. Crawford Biggs as Solicitor General . . . I think it fair to say that the Court did not have that same confidence."[27]

---

[24] Leonard Baker, *Brandeis and Frankfurter,* 283.

[25] Lincoln Caplan, *The Tenth Justice: The Solicitor General and the Rule of Law* (New York: Knopf, 1987), 13.

[26] Schlesinger, Jr., *Politics of Upheaval,* 261.

[27] Biggs was by training a trial lawyer or, as Paul Freund put it, a jury lawyer. He was known for making rather emotional arguments but had not had experience with federal law, including constitutional law, nor was his strength in appellate advocacy. Freund thought the government was not getting the kind of representation it needed; nor was the Court getting the kind of help it needed. Interview with Paul Freund, October 18, 1982, Stanley Reed Oral History Proj-

On completion of the 1933–34 term in June, the justices conveyed word to the president that Biggs should be kept from arguing in their court if the administration wanted to win any more cases before it. Justice Brandeis complained to Frankfurter that Biggs was giving a "bad impression." Assistant Solicitor General Angus MacLean was also "somewhat concerned" and promised that he "would bring the S.G. in for advice," but Brandeis wrote Frankfurter: "They haven't appeared yet." Frankfurter, a regular correspondent of Justice Stone's, made known to FDR Stone's objections to Biggs. Stone wrote: "I would like much to see you. I feel some concern as to what is happening to the Solicitor General's office. I wonder if the president realizes how important the efficiency of that office is going to be to his program." Frankfurter of course passed Stone's letter on to Roosevelt.[28]

Complaints about Cummings's staffing of the Justice Department with second-rate political appointments came from all quarters. Formerly the department had been steeped in a tradition that excluded appointment of party hacks. But as a faithful party man, Cummings was an easy target for Postmaster General Farley, who came close to wrecking the department by loading it up with "deserving Democrats." One of Cummings's worst mistakes was to appoint Pat Malloy, an Oklahoma oil man, to head the newly created Criminal Tax Division. Malloy proved to be so obvious a misfit that, under pressure from New Dealers, he was fired. "Mr. Cummings' appointments make sad reading," complained one Washington observer. "They might have gone unnoticed in the days of Harding and Coolidge, but they were wholly inadequate as individuals, and a terrible crew to unload on a Department that was soon to be confronted with some of the most complicated legal cases ever tried in the history of the government."[29]

Secretary of the Interior Harold Ickes joined the critics, complaining that Cummings's department "was simply loaded with

ect, University of Kentucky, Lexington, cited in Barry Cushman, *Rethinking the New Deal Court: The Structure of a Constitutional Revolution* (New York: Oxford University Press, 1998), 141–42.

[28] Stone to Frankfurter, May 17, 1933, OF 10, Box 27, FDRL.

[29] Carter, *New Dealers,* 261–62.

political appointees," noting that "hardly anyone has any respect for the standing and ability of the lawyers over there." Cummings was considered "a man of some ability," but Ickes concluded that he had delivered himself into the hands of the place hunters. Biggs, so obviously incompetent, stayed on as solicitor for two years, by the end of which much damage was done. Frankfurter had a long talk with Roosevelt about the situation on December 16, 1934, and reported: "The President now thoroughly understands the weaknesses of the [Justice] Department."[30]

Moley wrote that, in periods of sweeping reform, a certain amount of muddling was inevitable and tolerable, but an excess, he warned, was certain to tarnish some of the New Deal's hopeful sheen. Lawyers in the Justice Department came in for most of the criticism, but now and then the attorney general himself was the target of a full blast from the press. When the issue of applying the provisions of the Veterans' Preference Act to the Works Progress Administration (WPA) came up, an editorialist asked:

> Why does the Roosevelt Administration, with all the brains at its beck and call let itself in for legal jams like this and so many others? Why does Congress pass sloppy laws? . . . And may we not need a *legal new deal* inside the administration—an alert, aggressive and sure-footed Attorney General with a staff expertly fighting for the millions of the Government's voiceless clients—to whom these major policy measures could be submitted before they are signed into law?[31]

But Cummings had a tough skin and was quite prepared to fend off each successive assault. He came, wrote a journalist, of a Yankee breed of men who would rather go down fighting than surrender. If the Supreme Court ever began to upset New Deal legislative efforts, he would be quite capable of introducing into the soundproof chamber of that eminent tribunal "the mutter of tumbrels" and "the roar of the barricades" as atmosphere, if not argument for the New Deal's legerdemain.[32]

---

[30] *The Secret Diary of Harold Ickes,* 3 vols. (New York: Simon and Schuster, 1953–54), 1:243, 247.

[31] Undated clipping, *Washington News,* PSF 150, FDRL.

[32] Carter, *New Dealers,* 263.

In 1870, when Congress passed the act creating the Justice Department, it was designed to be both an institution in the country's legal system and an agency of the federal government. The act's avowed purpose was to save money by eliminating the expense of retaining lawyers engaged in private practice to try the increasing volume of cases and to consolidate the government's legal work under a single head. The department grew, along with the government, at an increasingly accelerated rate, expanding enormously around the turn of the century. The attorney general headed up all U.S. attorneys and law officers in the various departments, but over time he became immersed in the details of administration and preoccupied with politics. The management of a growing department left him little time for courtroom law as barrister to the Supreme Court.

In the 1930s, the Justice Department was not yet what it was to become in the 1960s under the Kennedys—that is, a major instrument of policy—but it was already beginning to move in that direction. Well before its creation, lawyers in other government departments had become firmly entrenched, and U.S. attorneys enjoyed autonomy over government litigation in the districts to which they were assigned. Departments had their own legal officers to represent their interests in court. In spite of formal incorporation in the Department of Justice after 1870, they managed to retain their independent role.

Historically, the Justice Department always had difficulty maintaining control over the legal activities of other federal departments and agencies, which, with support from their respective heads, insisted on the right to conduct their own litigation. Preoccupied with the expansion of his own bureaucracy, the attorney general had little success in counteracting this. As new boards and agencies were created, Congress gave control of litigation to their counsel. An executive order of 1918 made a new attempt to consolidate in the Justice Department the function of representing the government in the courts, but once again the slow process of disintegration set in.[33]

During the New Deal this state of affairs became a major

[33] Sewall Key, "The Legal Work of the Federal Government," *Virginia Law Review* 25 (1938): 165.

source of conflict that raged on throughout the early years. Interdepartmental quarrels were common, and formerly independent legal officers resisted consolidation under the Justice Department. The personalities and politics involved exacerbated internal differences over litigation. Alluding to the problem, Frankfurter wrote Jerome Frank, legal counsel for the Agricultural Adjustment Administration (AAA), referring to the crowd of able young lawyers in the various New Deal agencies: "Their wisdom ought to be equal to cohesion among themselves, and secure the triumph over the inevitable frictions and differences [among them]." He went on: "If all you fellows will allow your common purposes and agreements among you to be binding forces—I mean ALL of you in the various departments and agencies . . . you will have intrinsic authority."[34]

To counteract the centrifugal forces in his administration, Roosevelt arranged a viable compromise, establishing the basic pattern followed in succeeding decades. Commissions and agencies, maintaining their legal staffs for purposes of advice and planning, were allowed to conduct litigation in the lower federal courts, provided the Justice Department was given access to all information on the conduct of the proceedings. The Justice Department's monopoly, however, was reasserted at the Supreme Court level, buttressed by a series of executive orders. As a result of secret lobbying at the White House by Cummings, on June 10, 1933, FDR issued an executive order authorizing the consolidation within the Justice Department of legal divisions of all federal agencies, placing the department in full control of all federal litigation.

Roosevelt's executive order returned the conduct of nearly all the government's litigation to the Justice Department, but by no means were all of the legal functions of the United States thereby brought under a central head. Formal law offices were still retained in almost every executive department and bureau, and continued to exist as separate entities. They performed efficient services as legal advisers in the work of their own units of government. In the field of administrative law they were considered desirable, if not indispensable. And as new emergency agencies

[34] January 27, 1934, Box 12, Jerome Frank Papers, SL.

proliferated, Congress gave their lawyers authority over their own litigation, again decentralizing the legal work of the federal government. Independent regulatory agencies such as the Federal Trade Commission, the Interstate Commerce Commission, and the National Labor Relations Board were not bound by the opinions of the attorney general.

Only a handful of National Recovery Administration (NRA) cases reached the courts before 1934, and local U.S. attorneys, unfamiliar with the issues in them, permitted NRA lawyers to handle the case preparation and arguments. They had scarcely begun sifting through their complaint dockets when Cummings, in a letter to Hugh Johnson, the NRA's administrator, directed that in the future, Justice Department lawyers would "assume full responsibility for the institution and prosecution of litigation." Simultaneously, he withdrew the permission to appear in court that had previously been granted to NRA lawyers deputized as special assistants to the attorney general.[35]

Lawyers in the AAA were served with an identical order. This did not go over without cries of anguish from officials in New Deal agencies, who resented being subjected to what they considered excessive control. The executive orders were represented as economy measures, but they resulted in even larger payrolls, duplication of resources and facilities, inefficiency, and more red tape. Adding to all the other legal woes the New Deal eventually had to face were persistent interdepartmental rivalries and jealousies, generated by the dual legal structure set in place under Roosevelt.

In March 1935, J. Crawford Biggs resigned. In his place, Roosevelt appointed Stanley Forman Reed, who remained solicitor general until he was elevated to the Supreme Court in 1938. The fifty-one-year-old Kentuckian had earned two bachelor's degrees before entering Columbia Law School. President Hoover appointed him legal counsel for the Federal Farm Board, and in 1932 he moved to the Reconstruction Finance Corporation, where he served during the early years of the New Deal. Roosevelt drafted Reed to provide a legal basis for taking the country

[35] April 9, 1934, RG 9, Box 10, NA, cited in Peter Irons, *The New Deal Lawyers* (Princeton: Princeton University Press, 1982), 40.

off the gold standard, and early in 1935 he was made special assistant to the attorney general to argue the gold clause cases in the Supreme Court.

Reed proved a good, but not a great, solicitor general. He was a hardworking and generous chief, bent on improving the department staff he inherited. He brought in such capable lawyers as Tom Corcoran and Ben Cohen, kept the dour Scot Angus MacLean as assistant solicitor general, and added new legal talent from other agencies and departments, such as Robert Jackson, John Dickinson, Charles Wyzanski, and Alger Hiss—all loyal New Dealers. At the time, few were aware that Reed harbored deep misgivings about the constitutionality of parts of the New Deal program. To make matters worse, he faced a Supreme Court increasingly suspicious of both New Deal measures and Roosevelt's motives.[36]

Was the New Deal's Justice Department equipped to handle the onslaught of constitutional challenges facing it? Possibly no department, however well integrated or administered, would have had the resources to cope with the challenge that was to confront it. In an era of depression and instability, the Justice Department also had to face an epidemic of crime throughout the country and attempt to step up enforcement programs. Facilities had to be provided for handling the tax litigation transferred to it from the Treasury Department shortly after the administration came to power. The Antitrust Division had to formulate an entirely new policy, for it had virtually no antitrust litigation to handle after Congress exempted business and agriculture from the antitrust laws in 1933 in conformity with the provisions of the NIRA. There was the need to study newly enacted emergency legislation, prepare its defense before the courts, and work out the juris-

---

[36] A biographical essay on Stanley Reed by C. Herman Pritchett is in *The Justices of the United States Supreme Court, 1789–1969,* eds. Leon Friedman and Fred Israel, 5 vols. (New York: Chelsea House, 1969–78), 3:2373–98; the Stanley Reed Oral History Collection is in the University of Kentucky Library, Lexington, with his papers; Reed's reminiscences and related material in the Marquis Childs Collection are in the Columbia University Oral History Collection; the best introduction to Reed's work as solicitor general is in Paul L. Murphy, *The Constitution in Crisis Times: 1918–1969* (New York: Harper and Row, 1972).

dictional lines between the Justice Department and the new emergency agencies.[37] Cummings's lawyers were called upon to render more opinions on legal questions in a single year than had been rendered during the entire Hoover administration.

For the disarray in this vital department, Roosevelt and Cummings were responsible. Henry L. Stimson later asserted: "The President is the poorest administrator I have ever worked under in respect of the orderly procedure and routine of his performance."[38] Talking this over with Frankfurter one evening during World War II, the secretary of war (1940–45) unburdened himself. Frankfurter said he had better make up his mind that orderly procedure was not and never had been a characteristic of FDR's administration. "It has other virtues but not that." Stimson was advised to reconcile himself to "looseness of administration . . . and the inevitable frictions and conflicts resulting therefrom."[39]

In Arthur Schlesinger's account, the disarray in the Justice Department would not have mattered so much if Cummings had had an abler solicitor general than the amiable but ineffectual Biggs,[40] but under Reed problems only multiplied. A constitutional debate was emerging, centered not only on Roosevelt's quixotic monetary and banking policies, but on the more comprehensive industrial and agricultural legislation that formed the core of the New Deal. Bitter conflict between New Dealers and their opponents marked nearly all phases of Roosevelt's presidency with the exception of the war years, and the unavoidable fallout from it involved the Justice Department. Government lawyers in all agencies and departments found themselves enmeshed in a political system that imposed constraints on them and engendered recurrent conflict.

In the 1930s, the majority of government attorneys were not, ideologically speaking, New Dealers. They had no particular regard for some administration programs. Men like Reed, Wyzanski, Frank, and at times Cummings himself harbored doubts about their constitutionality. In judicial circuits where they oper-

[37] Swisher, ed., *Selected Papers,* xxiii–xxv.

[38] Diary of Henry Stimson, March 24, 1943, Henry L. Stimson Papers, SL.

[39] Joseph P. Lash, ed., *From the Diaries of Felix Frankfurter* (New York: Norton, 1974), 168.

[40] Schlesinger, Jr., *Politics of Upheaval,* 261.

ated, U.S. attorneys continued to enjoy autonomy, subject only to limited supervision from Washington. Decisions on whether to prosecute or launch an appeal were made on a case-by-case basis, with more reference to what had been done in the past than to what was needed in the future.[41]

Coordinating litigation on anything like a national scale was beyond the ability of the attorney general, who instead immersed himself in details of administration and the task of developing an internal bureaucratic structure. He spent a great deal of time and energy on reforming federal criminal law and procedure, and presided over a revision of the uniform code of civil procedure for cases in federal courts. He even found the time in 1937 to publish two books: *We Can Prevent Crime* and, with his associate Carl McFarland, *Federal Justice.*

In a recent study, Edward A. Purcell, Jr., claims that Cummings was "an enthusiastic law reformer who believed strongly in the desirability of court-made rules of procedure."[42] He based his claim on the attorney general's revival and support of an American Bar Association (ABA) bill introduced earlier that transferred authority to prescribe uniform procedural rules in actions at law in the federal courts from Congress to the Supreme Court, thus freeing the federal courts from their dependence on state practice. The bill had had the support not only of the ABA and most state bar associations, but the law schools, the legal elite, and many other groups. But the most outspoken opponent of the ABA bill was Senator Thomas Walsh, who at the time was one of the ablest lawyers on the Judiciary Committee. Deeply suspicious of the ABA and the motives of large eastern law firms, he represented small-town practitioners like his former self and wanted to retain the variegated rules of state practice.

In the Senate Judiciary Committee, Walsh, backed by other progressives, fought the bill vigorously, and when it was brought to a vote he won a ten-to-six majority for an adverse report.

---

[41] Irons, *New Deal Lawyers,* 4–5.

[42] Edward A. Purcell, Jr., *Brandeis and the Progressive Constitution: Erie, the Judicial Power, and the Politics of the Federal Courts in Twentieth Century America* (New Haven: Yale University Press, 2000), 32; Homer S. Cummings, "Immediate Problems for the Bar," *American Bar Association Journal* 20 (1934): 212.

When Cummings replaced Walsh as attorney general, however, he managed to bring the president around to backing the procedural reform bill, partly to placate business and show that the administration was concerned with the courts' needs and prestige. The Cummings bill easily passed both houses and became law on June 19, 1934.

Known as the Rules Enabling Act, the bill empowered the Supreme Court, subject to the approval of Congress, to adopt and promulgate uniform rules and forms of pleadings, practice, and procedure in actions at law in the federal courts. It authorized the Court to merge the rules with those for suits in equity, thereby creating a single form of civil action in the federal courts. Representatives of the Justice Department had been cooperating with a committee appointed by the Supreme Court in drafting and preparing such rules.[43]

While this may represent a substantial achievement, it hardly qualifies Cummings for status as "an enthusiastic law reformer." The real hero in that category, as events would show, was Judge William Denman of the Court of Appeals of the Ninth Circuit, who agitated single-handedly for a comprehensive reform of the lower federal courts. Denman lobbied untiringly for two years or more, but Roosevelt and Cummings paid little attention to his proposals until they reached the flashpoint after the election of 1936, and incubation of the judicial reorganization plan introduced on February 5, 1937, with Denman's proposals as a "by-path" to camouflage the plan's real objective.

In 1933, Cummings announced his intention to reorganize the Justice Department and spent weeks looking for someone to do the job. William Stanley was finally persuaded by his Maryland neighbor, Breckenridge Long, to take it on, but aside from shifting tax litigation from the Treasury Department and putting antitrust in a separate division, there were few signs of any reor-

---

[43] 48 Stat. 1064 (1934); Cummings to FDR, June 12, 1934, OF 5708, Box 5, FDRL. The act imposed one limitation—that the rules "shall neither abridge, enlarge, nor modify the substantive rights of any litigant." Purcell, *Brandeis and the Progressive Constitution,* 32. See also *Annual Report of the Attorney General of the U.S. for the Fiscal Year 1936* (Washington, D.C.: G.P.O., 1936), 2.

ganization. The department continued to struggle along with holdovers from Harding's "Ohio gang" still firmly entrenched, although the late Senator Walsh had been prepared to dismiss them with a stroke of the pen.[44]

As part of the executive branch, the Justice Department lawyers should have been prepared to take part in drafting New Deal legislation, but they did not. Cummings's greatest failing was his deliberate choice to exert little if any influence on White House staffers and others in drafting laws, or in trying to prevent passage of hastily or poorly drafted laws. To understand the decisions of the Supreme Court after 1935, a better grasp of the legal problems themselves and the fate of the laws moving through the lower federal courts will offer valuable clues.

In March 1937, Senator Wheeler had a long conversation with the Chief Justice. Hughes mused openly on what might have been the story of the New Deal's legislation of the past few years if, as he put it, "we had an Attorney General in whom the . . . Court had confidence." "As it was," Hughes continued, "the laws have been poorly drafted, the briefs have been badly drawn and the arguments have been poorly presented. We've had to be not only the Court but we've had to do the work that should have been done by the Attorney General."[45] The fundamental charge Hughes made here was that the justices often could find no means of upholding legislation that was so poorly drafted.

Barry Cushman asserts that there is no dearth of evidence to suggest the conclusion that the fate of at least the first New Deal can be explained by the fact that its statutes were drafted with scant attention to, and even flagrant disregard for, existing constitutional law. Never an admirer of Homer Cummings, Senator Joseph O'Mahoney, a strong New Deal Democrat, believed that many of the problems of constitutionality arose simply because legislation was so poorly drafted. In his opinion, the Justice De-

---

[44] Fraser, "Attorney General Cummings," 403–4.

[45] The quotation is drawn from the conversation he had with Chief Justice Hughes at the justice's home on March 21, 1937. See Wheeler, *Yankee from the West,* 329; Cushman, *Rethinking the New Deal Court,* 36; William Swindler, *Court and Constitution in the Twentieth Century: The New Legality, 1932–1968* (3 vols., Indianapolis: Bobbs Merrill, 1970), 2:72–73–in this volume the author discusses the Hughes's Court's response to FDR's legislative program.

partment did not do its homework. Cummings, in addition, was chiefly responsible for failing to give adequate attention to the selection and cultivation of promising test cases and for failing to see to it that the legal arguments offered in their defense were ably framed and felicitously presented.

In spite of the conventional wisdom about the New Deal Court and the narrow way in which it has been analyzed by a host of interpreters, its history during the early years is no simple tale of the interplay of politics, judicial intent, external events, and case outcomes. A mass of evidence has been presented in a more plausible analysis by Professor Cushman. The fate of New Deal laws rested on the capacity for statutory formulation, test-case fact patterns, and legal theories that would resonate with the set of doctrinal categories making up the constitutional baggage of the individual justices.

Although the New Deal Court and its history cannot be comprehended in purely political terms, politics certainly colored, publicized, and at times dominated events. As Cushman suggests, an honest effort to delineate the various dimensions and subtleties of judicial behavior and the justices' jurisprudential positions, with a more respectful attitude toward their integrity, provides a better approach than that undertaken in past studies.[46] What is also involved in this morality tale is the question of how a tradition that had generated such a formidable and plausible system of constitutional thought over so many decades underwent gradual though not sweeping transformation during the first four decades of the twentieth century.

[46] Cushman, *Rethinking the New Deal Court,* 36–37.

2

The New Deal in Court

> Who in hell cares what anybody says about them [constitutional questions] but the Final Five of the August Nine?
>
> Judge Learned Hand, quoted in Arthur Schlesinger, Jr., *The Politics of Upheaval,* 252.

WHEN CONGRESS ADJOURNED for the summer on June 16, 1933, the legislative results of the special session already pointed to a dramatic alteration in the balance of federal-state relations and a redistribution of powers exercised by Congress and the executive. As for private enterprise, laissez-faire philosophy and capitalism were to be altered by a new version of statism. Change occurred swiftly, experimentally, building on its own momentum. The resulting pragmatic approach had a strong element of relativism—the belief, as far as it could be articulated, that democracy basically was not a fulfilled system but rather a process in the state of flux, forever changing. It could not be said that Roosevelt was flagrantly unconcerned about the Constitution; he was not. But he applied to it some of that same spirit of change, of relativity, of dynamism that marked his first years in office. In his view, constitutional methods could not be reduced to fixed principles, preserved on tablets of stone.[1]

Little was heard of the Constitution as the vast New Deal juggernaut got under way. With gloom and misery everywhere, there was scant concern for the means to be employed to reach the common goal of recovery. Doubts about the constitutionality of New Deal programs were hesitantly expressed by a few, in-

[1] George Wolfskill, "New Deal Critics: Did They Miss the Point?" in *Essays on the New Deal: The Walter Prescott Webb Memorial Lectures,* eds. Harold M. Hollingsworth and William F. Holmes (Austin: University of Texas Press, 1969), 59.

cluding some of those involved in the legislative drafting process, but most were confident that the crisis would be over before the Supreme Court was given an opportunity to act. This may have been wishful thinking. According to Robert Jackson, who by then had joined the administration, serving in a variety of posts, New Dealers were inclined to ignore the problem of constitutionality, at least publicly, though they were well aware of the Court's "brooding omnipresence."[2] Two years would pass before government lawyers appeared before the high bench for the first important New Deal test case. Meanwhile, the entire issue hung suspended, with the outcome in doubt.

Historians Charles and Mary Beard believed that if cases concerning the new legislation had been appealed to the Supreme Court in 1933, the Court might have called up its positive precedents, upheld state and national legislation, and maintained a position somewhere on the periphery of the political arena, where it would have been safe from reproach or attack. "Not many laymen supposed that the Supreme Court would venture to pull down the pillars of the great fabric erected, as alleged, for the salvation of the country."[3] But this is not what happened.

Before long, anti–New Deal forces began proclaiming that the new policies and programs were undermining constitutional forms and subverting the democratic system. Roosevelt's name became synonymous with the New Deal, so he became increasingly sensitive to charges that he had malevolent designs on the Constitution and/or the American system. Not until 1941, when Judge Samuel Rosenman persuaded him to write an introduction to the 1937 volume of his public papers, did he take time to articulate his views on the role of the executive in the American constitutional system.[4] Well before that, at least a dozen New Deal laws had been put to the supreme constitutional test and had been found wanting.

The hopeful words in Roosevelt's first inaugural address had etched in the public's mind a vague outline of things to come. A

[2] Robert H. Jackson, *The Struggle for Judicial Supremacy: A Study of a Crisis in American Power Politics* (New York: Knopf, 1941), 77–78.

[3] Charles and Mary Beard, *America in Midpassage,* vol. 3 of *The Rise of American Civilization,* 3 vols. (New York: Macmillan, 1939), 257–58.

[4] *PPA,* 1937 volume, xlvii–lxxii.

year later, much of that outline had been filled in. FDR insisted in 1933 that the Constitution could meet the demands of the current crisis and expressed the hope that the normal balance between executive and legislative authority would be adequate to meet the task confronting the country and its government. But he warned that the "unprecedented demand and need for undelayed action might call for a temporary departure from that normal balance." Congress, representing a frightened people, allowed the chief executive to take center stage—a position FDR relished. He considered the Constitution capable of many differing interpretations—at least that had always been the case in the past—and hoped it would now prove elastic enough to enable the government to meet extraordinary needs "by changes in emphasis and arrangements without loss of essential form."[5] He for one did not intend to stand idly by, if that meant letting people starve "by strictly constitutional methods." If honest men could differ over the interpretation of the Bible and its meaning, then other men, equally honest, could dispute the meaning of the Constitution, which after all was not Holy Writ, traced by the finger of God.[6]

Professor Arthur Schlesinger, Jr. put it mildly when he wrote that Roosevelt was not one to regard the judiciary as sacrosanct. Over at the other end of Pennsylvania Avenue, attending to routine matters, sat the nine men in whose hands the power was lodged to undo much, if not all, that the New Dealers intended to do or had accomplished so far. Was there any substance to Roosevelt's charge that for two decades or more the Supreme Court had been successfully thwarting the common will of the majority of the American people? Had it, as he claimed, been diverting the functions and philosophy of government into channels running counter to the thought and objectives of progressive opinion and reform? If so, then as a result of its unavoidable involvement in the political process, the Court could once again become an object of reproach and perhaps of attack.[7]

---

[5] *PPA,* 1933 volume, 11–15.
[6] Wolfskill, "New Deal Critics," 59.
[7] *PPA,* 1937 volume, xlvii.

In dealing with the federal judiciary, Roosevelt initially was more restrained and subtle than his cousin TR, who during his Bull Moose days demanded the recall of state judges and judicial decisions. FDR came of age in a period of court-bashing and, according to some analysts, had as a lawyer become particularly receptive to the realist school of legal intellectual thought, which considered judges policy makers, motivated in large part by their own opinions and prejudices. This is mere speculation. Roosevelt took a direct approach, holding that the Supreme Court was and always had been in politics, more or less. He viewed the Constitution and the Supreme Court as secular, not sacred, institutions.

Judges sympathetic to the vehement conservative protest over the New Deal's interference with private property rights, traditional laissez-faire economics, and limited federal power would experience little difficulty in finding justification for striking down as unconstitutional many important New Deal statutes. But under the system of separation of powers, there was, according to Roosevelt, no reason for the judiciary to have the final word in constitutional interpretation, any more than there was for the president or Congress.

This position was taken earlier by Presidents Jefferson and Jackson, two of FDR's Democratic heroes. He was convinced that most Supreme Court decisions holding laws constitutional or unconstitutional were not, in reality, impartial interpretations of the document. The laws under review were often found to reinforce or violate some precept of the social and economic philosophy held by the justices—an idea driven home in forceful dissents by former justice Oliver Wendell Holmes. Roosevelt thought it completely unjustifiable for the men on the high bench, on critical constitutional questions, to void laws unless they were found unconstitutional beyond all reasonable doubt by an absolute majority. Critics of the Court argued that judicial review in itself was an anti-majoritarian and undemocratic method of settling outstanding constitutional questions.

Constitutional reformer Louis Boudin held that, in view of their narrow training as lawyers, judges were not well equipped to interpret social and economic questions under the Constitution in the light of modern social needs. He urged the outright abolition of the power of any court to declare any law, federal or state, invalid, while other reformers wanted to limit the federal courts to invalidating state legislation only.[8]

The concept that government has the responsibility for keeping order not only politically or physically, but economically and socially, was gradually being translated into legislation.[9] A significant shift from legal to social justice was taking place. In striking down some social legislation, justices were accused of "discovering" unconstitutionality. The epitome of this style of judging was reached in *Lochner v. New York,*[10] which voided a state law limiting the hours of workers in bakeries. The decision represented no evaluative judgment, but merely declared what the law was.[11] Usurping the legislature's authority to enact health regulations in bakeries evoked scathing criticism, as did the glaring subjectivity of Justice Rufus Peckham's ruling. In 1910, Theodore Roosevelt pointed to *Lochner* when he denounced the courts for erecting insurmountable obstacles in the path of reform.[12]

The attempt to disguise judicial lawmaking as something else stirred angry protests and anti-court sentiment. In 1916, Louis D. Brandeis charged that the unwritten or judge-made law, as distinguished from written legislation, was largely deaf and blind to urgently needed reform. Instead of interpreting the Constitution broadly, the courts applied eighteenth-century concepts of the liberty of the individual and the sacredness of private property. "Where statutes giving expression to the new social spirit were clearly constitutional," wrote Brandeis, "judges, charged with social responsibility, but imbued with the relentless spirit of individualism, often construed them away."[13]

---

[8] These arguments were used later to support the New Deal's position in its struggle with the Supreme Court. Louis B. Boudin, *Government by Judiciary,* 2 vols. (New York: William Godwin, 1932); Carl Brent Swisher, *American Constitutional Development* (Boston: Houghton Mifflin, 1943), 773–74.

[9] Louis D. Brandeis, "The Living Law," *Illinois Law Review* 10 (February 1916): 461–71.

[10] 198 U.S. 45 (1905).

[11] Alpheus T. Mason, *The Supreme Court from Taft to Warren* (Baton Rouge: Louisiana State University Press, 1958), 28.

[12] Paul Kens, "Lochner v. New York," in *Oxford Companion to the Supreme Court of the United States,* ed. Kermit Hall (New York: Oxford University Press, 1992), 510.

[13] Brandeis, "Living Law," 463–64, 466.

A traditional respect for the "priesthood of the Constitution" was usually mingled in the popular mind with an instinctive skepticism about lawyers, especially corporation lawyers. A Washington journalist touched on this popular assumption when he wrote: "The New Dealers have no designs against the Constitution, provided that it retains the elasticity of the original fabric. This elasticity has always been in evidence whenever a Philadelphia lawyer desired to drive a corporate caravan through it, but it has been remarkably rigid whenever the rights of the common man were up for consideration."[14]

Roosevelt undertook a reinterpretation—some would say an amending—of the Constitution in the light of contemporary social and economic conditions. New Deal laws affected matters of vital economic interest and broke new ground. FDR often complained bitterly that he could take few important steps without having his opponents' striking up the anvil chorus: "Is it unconstitutional?"—a phrase that greatly irritated him and one which he equated with obstructionism. The idea was further developed by Judge Julian Mack in a letter to Felix Frankfurter, who passed it on to FDR:

> There is a great danger it seems to me to arise from the constant habit which prevails when anything is opposed or objected to, of resorting without rhyme or reason to the Constitution as a means of preventing its accomplishment, thus creating the general impression that the Constitution is but the barrier to progress instead of being the broad highway through which alone progress may be enjoyed. Upon whom does the duty more clearly rest to modify and correct this evil than upon the members of our profession?[15]

Writing to Senator Josiah Bailey of North Carolina, who had sent him an encouraging note about the perceived upswing in the economy, FDR replied:

> I think you are right about the prospective advancement [in economic indices] and also that we should capitalize on it. As a matter

[14] Carter, *New Dealers,* 392.

[15] Judge Mack to Felix Frankfurter, August 28, 1934, PPF 1820, Box 9, FDRL. On this same theme, Judge Mack referred FDR to addresses by Chief Justice Edward D. White (1914) and Associate Justice John Hessin Clarke (1934) to the American Bar Association. Mack was then on the Court of Appeals for the Second Circuit (New York), where he served until 1941.

> of fact, the country is coming to realize this also, and with the realization there will be less and less attention paid to the silly cries of obstruction, destruction, radicalism and unconstitutionality.[16]

In the ensuing conflict between FDR and the Supreme Court, both sides claimed as their mission "saving the Constitution." Moley at first believed that a fundamental purpose of the New Deal was to preserve the Constitution for generations to come. But former president Hoover and a growing body of conservatives, their ranks swollen after 1934 by disaffected businessmen, were talking more and more about preserving and protecting that same Constitution from violation, if not annihilation, by the New Deal. Before long, organized groups like the American Liberty League, its successor, the National Committee to Uphold Constitutional Government, and a splinter group, the Southern Committee to Uphold the Constitution, would join the crusade—all intent on rescuing the constitutional system from imminent peril.[17]

In 1934, constitutional expert Edward S. Corwin, a professor at Princeton University, predicted that in its application of the Constitution's due process and commerce clauses the Supreme Court would eventually be forced to abandon some of its previously held doctrinal positions. He urged recognizing the plenary power of Congress in the economic realm and emphasized the need for federal regulation of business, if not the nationalization of industry in the United States. Like Roosevelt, Corwin was convinced that the individual states could not deal with the new problems of the national economy without a concentration of authority in Washington. As between the thesis of dual federalism and that of nationalism, he wrote, ineluctable forces have chosen.[18]

---

[16] August 29, 1935, PPF 2518, FDRL.

[17] On the history of the American Liberty League see George Wolfskill, *The Revolt of the Conservatives: A History of the American Liberty League, 1934–1936* (Boston: Houghton Mifflin, 1962); cf. Richard Polenberg, "The National Committee to Uphold Constitutional Government, 1937–1941," in *Journal of American History* 52 (December 1965): 582–98; the Southern Committee to Uphold the Constitution is treated in Wolfskill, *Revolt of the Conservatives,* chap. 9.

[18] Edward S. Corwin, *The Twilight of the Supreme Court: A History of Our Constitutional Theory* (New Haven: Yale University Press, 1934). In some gen-

Corwin's argument seemed to forecast the decay of judicial review. With the national government in possession of power to expend the social product for any purposes that may seem good to it, to make itself the universal and exclusive creditor of private business, with all that this would imply of control, to inflate the currency to any extent, and to go into any business whatever (a reference to TVA), what then becomes of judicial review, conceived as a system for throwing about property rights a special protection "against the mere power of numbers," and for perpetuating a certain type of industrial organization?

What indeed? countered Harvard law professor Henry M. Hart, in a generally negative review of Corwin's book *The Twilight of the Supreme Court* (1934). If judicial review is thus imperiled, and for the reasons given, the Supreme Court could yet be relied on to discover "constitutional snares" for the spending power. As a matter of fact, in decisions on TVA and the Public Works Administration, the lower courts were already discovering them; the decisions, he said, qualified or denied almost every one of Corwin's asserted powers. It was a naive assumption on Corwin's part, wrote Hart, to draw so large a practical conclusion from so abstract a premise, as if one were to find the Achilles' heel of the Court in the well-recognized power of Congress to increase its membership and to alter or take away its jurisdiction. His review concludes:

> Judgment upon the future of this particular tradition of judicial review is not so easy as this. It is bound up with judgment as to the future of American capitalism as a whole, which Mr. Corwin does not discuss, not to mention the [whole question of the] success of the Roosevelt experiment, which he seems to take for

eral observations on the Court's constitutional position under the New Deal and a searching analysis of its economic complexities, Corwin indicated the perils that lurked in judicial intervention of the old style—hence the book's title. In a review, Professor Henry H. Hart of the Harvard Law School argued that nothing is easier than to assert that Congress must have the power to do what has to be done. The arguable points are questions of degree. "In failing to accord claims for decentralization any validity whatever," Hart wrote, "Mr. Corwin . . . cut himself off from the heart of the problem." He added: "the probability is also that he has mistakenly estimated the attitude of the Supreme Court." See Henry Hart, "The Supreme Court Carries On," *New Republic* 82 (April 3, 1935), 220–21.

> granted. Nor would an illuminating estimate of the future of the Court confine itself to this particular tradition. Neither one big socialist state nor a federated union of socialized states, it must be remembered, would find it easy to dispense with a supreme judicial tribunal.[19]

In the long run and after a great constitutional upheaval, Corwin's analysis of the future of judicial review, for reasons he could not have envisioned, contained elements of validity. But neither Corwin nor Hart was able to offer revealing insights into the actual contours of the problem facing FDR and New Dealers in relation to the federal courts.

Amid a growing opposition within and outside the courts to New Deal laws, two years of depression lay between the first assaults by government lawyers on the fortress of laissez-faire jurisprudence and the final breaching of its massive walls. The cases in the long constitutional battle tested national regulatory powers over the three main components of the economy—industry, agriculture, and labor. With each government reversal, it became more apparent that the New Deal was on trial before the courts. Judges looked with increasing dismay on the broadly based New Deal approach to legislation and the attempt to increase national power over nearly all aspects of economic life. Government lawyers grew more apprehensive, sensing the rising judicial hostility. They delayed litigating New Deal measures as long as they could, but the hammer blows began to fall in 1935.

In February 1934, the Supreme Court decided two cases that indirectly involved the New Deal's future. *Booth v. United States* and *Amidon v. United States*[20] dealt with the retirement pay of federal judges. In 1919, Congress passed a law permitting any circuit or district court judge seventy years of age or over with ten years on the bench to retire with full pay for life. When Circuit Court Judge Wilbur F. Booth retired (November 28, 1931), having served continuously as district or circuit judge for more than seventeen years, his salary (and that of all federal judges) was reduced by the Independent Offices Appropriation Act of

[19] Hart, "Supreme Court Carries On," 221.
[20] The two cases were decided as one. 291 U.S. 339; 54 S.C. 379 (1934).

June 16, 1933, better known as the Economy Act (48 Stat. 283, 307). His retirement pay was reduced from $12,500 to $10,025. Charles F. Amidon was appointed February 18, 1897, as judge of the U.S. District Court of North Dakota and served continuously in that capacity to June 2, 1928, when he retired. The judges took the government to court with an argument hinging on the independence of the judiciary. Justice Owen Roberts, speaking for a unanimous bench on February 5, 1934, held that judges retiring under the 1919 act did not relinquish their office, but remained technically in service. Reducing their pensions violated Article III of the Constitution, which states that the pay of judges cannot be reduced during their tenure. A similar blow at the economy drive was struck in *Lynch v. United States,*[21] a decision invalidating Congress's repudiation of veterans' insurance privileges under the Economy Act of 1933. The opinion was assigned to Justice Brandeis.

The 1869 and 1919 laws on judges' pay were half measures at best, leaving Supreme Court justices wholly dependent on the government to determine the salary or pension they were entitled to at the time of resignation.[22] Unfortunately for Justice Holmes, who left the bench in 1932, the 1919 act and related case law did not apply to him, but the Economy Act did. Supreme Court justices could withdraw from active duty only by formal resignation, and they had to rely for their retirement pay on the good faith of Congress. Until Justice Holmes's death in 1935, at the age of ninety-four, his pension was reduced from $20,000 to $10,000 a year. He once observed that it was a good thing he had been prudent enough to lay adequate savings aside to provide for his old age!

When the chief justice approached the ninety-year-old Holmes to suggest that he retire, he was given the impression that Justices Van Devanter and Sutherland were preparing to follow him into private life if there could be no uncertainty about the salary Congress would provide them. It was apparent to Hughes that a more enlightened retirement policy for Supreme Court justices might have resulted in two members' leaving the bench, making unnec-

[21] 292 U.S. 571 (1934).

[22] Swindler, *Court and Constitution in the Twentieth Century,* 3:4–6.

essary Roosevelt's confrontation with the Court and Congress. William Swindler agreed that if Roosevelt had appreciated the simple economics of judicial retirement, an unequivocal pension law early in his administration could have averted the later crisis.[23]

Although the New Deal's legislative output in 1934 was even more substantial than that of the "hundred days," the first two years of experimentation failed to bring about recovery. Conservatives in both parties were alarmed by indications that in technical content and detail, many of the "emergency" controls over the nation's economic life, once thought to be only temporary, were being converted into a permanent system. Constitutional issues were being raised with greater frequency, and administration spokesmen had to address them as they prepared in 1934 to test their legislative accomplishments at the polls. In campaign speeches they alternated between suggesting that a new constitutional order was being born out of the "emergency" and asserting that the basic objective of the administration was to return to the fundamental, homely values in American life.[24] The president was holding off on introducing any other progressive measures until after the election—throwing out a few hints here and there, but refraining from articulating his post-election plans.

In November, the Democrats swept the field. They gained nine Senate seats, and their House majority rose from 309 to 322. Arthur Krock called the election the most overwhelming victory in the history of American politics. In only one other midterm election since the Civil War had a party in power gained seats in both houses of Congress, and not since the days of Reconstruction had any one party achieved such overwhelming majorities. As for Roosevelt, William Allen White wrote, "He has been all but crowned by the people."[25]

Just as the 1932 election had set the stage for the first New Deal, the 1934 election prepared the groundwork for the so-called Second New Deal of 1935, with its far more liberal agenda that included social security, the Wagner Act, and tax revision.

[23] Ibid., 5–6.
[24] Ibid., 27.
[25] *New York Times,* November 7, 11, 1934; *Time,* November 19, 1934.

Democrats in Congress, while protesting loyalty to the administration, were organizing a bloc including Senators Gore, Bailey, Byrd, Glass, and Clark to oppose parts of the mushrooming bureaucracy dubbed by Al Smith "Alphabet Soup." By 1934 such New Deal initiatives as the NIRA were in serious trouble. With the country in a state of economic stalemate, a political stalemate was threatening.[26] In January 1935, when the Seventy-fourth Congress convened, Roosevelt was poised to complete the task he had begun in 1933, and no one, it seemed, was there to stop him except the Supreme Court. If that occurred, there would in addition be the makings of a constitutional stalemate.

The "Hot Oil" Cases

The period of nervous calm before the storm was shattered in January when the justices handed down a ruling on one of the NIRA's code provisions. Given the Democrats' success at the polls, this anti–New Deal decision, coming just after FDR's hopeful annual message to Congress, ought to have created something of a stir. This was the first time the Court had the chance to review a major New Deal statute. This and other recovery measures would have reached the Supreme Court earlier if the attorney general had not stalled for time, seeking more favorable test cases.

The administration moved quickly after March 1933 to wrestle with the problem of overproduction in the oil industry. In the rich east Texas fields, prices had plunged to as low as ten cents a barrel and the wholesale price of gasoline hovered around two and a half cents. In early attempts to reduce production the states imposed quotas, but the oil produced in excess of these quotas—so-called "hot oil"—could be easily diverted to some part of the extensive pipeline network, rendering enforcement virtually impossible.

When attempts at persuasion and voluntarism failed, the federal government assumed responsibility for imposition and enforcement of production quotas. Congress added section 9(c) to

[26] Schlesinger, Jr., *Politics of Upheaval,* 6–7.

the NIRA's petroleum code, authorizing the president to prohibit shipment in interstate and foreign commerce of petroleum produced or withdrawn from storage in excess of the amount set by the state. The NIRA's section 3 authorized production quotas and new marketing practices mandated under the petroleum code. Roosevelt implemented enforcement of these controls in a series of executive orders.

A Petroleum Administration Board (PAB) was set up in Ickes's Interior Department to establish strategy, rules, and procedures. Ickes favored vigorous enforcement of the oil code, securing a green light from FDR to prosecute violators of regulations. As an outgrowth of his conviction that section 9(c) was not lawworthy, Donald Richberg, legal counsel for the NRA, was reluctant to resort to litigation. Ickes, always mischief-minded, reported to the president that it was a tactical mistake for General Hugh Johnson, chief administrator of the NRA, and Donald Richberg, its general counsel, to give such a clear impression of how apprehensive they were about the law's constitutionality. Richberg warned Ickes that litigation testing the validity of the oil code, particularly if it resulted in the loss of a major Supreme Court battle, would imperil the entire recovery program.[27]

In October 1933, two independent oil producers, Panama Refining Company and Amazon Petroleum Company, filed civil suits in the district court for the Eastern District of Texas, challenging the constitutionality of the "hot oil" regulations in section 9(c) (48 Stat. 195 [1933]) and the production quota provisions in the petroleum code. Their grievances were shared by most of the country's small oil producers, who regarded state and federal controls on production as inequitable.

The government won an initial skirmish on February 12, 1934, when a preliminary injunction sought by Amazon Petroleum Company in its suit against the Texas Railroad Commission was denied by a three-judge panel in federal court for the Eastern District of Texas, with Judge Randolph Bryant dissenting (5 F.Supp. 633–39). On that same day, however, Judge Bryant rejected government arguments in *Amazon Petroleum Co. v. Ryan* and *Panama Refining Co. v. Ryan* and sustained an injunction

[27] Ickes, *Secret Diary,* 1:94.

against federal officials, giving the opinion in both cases (nos. 632 and 635, 5 F.Supp. 639ff.).

With the expectation that civil suits would take a year or more to reach the high court, the government sought criminal indictments against violators of the oil code. On February 13, the day after the *Panama* and *Amazon* decisions at the trial-court level, indictments were brought against J. W. Smith and other independent oil producers. They immediately filed demurrers, which were granted by Judge Bryant, who ruled that section 9(c) was an unconstitutional delegation of legislative power to the president. He added that Smith et al. were not engaged in interstate commerce. On March 20, 1934, the government appealed the ruling, and a criminal suit was on its way to becoming the first NIRA test case to reach the Supreme Court.

Around the time Ickes was urging the government to take a test case to the Supreme Court, it was understood that PAB lawyers were to prepare briefs and argue the appeal. Initially, the attorney general had agreed, as long as his approval was not taken as a precedent. What further strained relations between the Justice Department and the PAB was the abrupt move by the attorney general two weeks later, stripping lawyers in all the emergency agencies, including the NRA, of the power to argue New Deal cases without his special permission.

Within a month of the government's petition for *certiorari* Cummings changed his mind about pursuing the Smith case, claiming that the lower-court record was sadly defective. It would, he said, prove a bad test case, risking a negative ruling. Just as the Supreme Court term was coming to a close, the case was withdrawn by the government over Secretary Ickes's protests. Cummings succeeded in convincing Roosevelt that they should move with greater caution and find more attractive cases for a test of the NIRA. Advised one editorial: "It was an open secret in Washington that the legal defense of the New Deal was in a bad way."[28]

Another opportunity opened up in late May 1934, when the Fifth Circuit Court of Appeals reversed the decrees in *Panama* and *Amazon* and ruled for the government, ordering that the bills

[28] "Planless Legal Planning," *New Republic,* May 23, 1934, 31–32.

be dismissed (71 F. [2d] 1, 8). The two companies took their case on appeal to the Supreme Court. Oral argument was set for December 10–11, 1934. Addressing the commerce issue, the circuit court made reference to the peculiar conditions governing oil production in Texas and their effect on commerce in other states, creating such a burden on it as to warrant federal regulation. In preparing their brief with the solicitor general's staff, PAB lawyers made only casual reference to the delegation question, dismissing it as of little or no consequence. The oil company lawyers, however, had argued the delegation point strenuously in the circuit court and were prepared to do so again.

Shortly before the Supreme Court heard these cases, a startling omission was discovered. In searching through the discarded record of the Smith case while preparing the government's response to the petition for an appeal in *Amazon,* M. S. Huberman, special assistant in the Justice Department, found that when the petroleum code was amended by executive order on September 13, 1933, the section providing for criminal penalties for violating the "hot oil" provisions was omitted from the official copy and was never filed in the office of the secretary of state, as was customary with certified copies of executive orders, codes, and regulations. The second paragraph of section 4 of Article III was eliminated. Only the *Amazon* case involved the oil code, thus making it necessary for the government in its response to print the applicable code provisions.[29]

Failure to give appropriate public notice of the change in section 4 had serious consequences. The persons affected, the prosecuting authorities, and the circuit court judges were all unaware of the omission. Both sides arguing in the circuit court appeal had attacked the provision that made failure to abide by the assigned quotas a criminal violation of the petroleum code, when that provision did not even exist (it was reinstated in an executive order of September 25, 1934).

The omission would probably have been found earlier if a brief in the Smith case, assigned to the PAB lawyers in Ickes's department, had been submitted in completed form to the Justice De-

[29] Sections 3 and 4 of Article III of the petroleum code provided for national control of oil production.

partment for approval. But it was not. As matters stood, the means open to affected parties in suit to determine their liabilities under the code were made not only very involved and time-consuming, but impossible to know. How could oil producers receiving regulations have guessed that certain provisions subjecting them to criminal prosecution and penalties were missing, buried in some Washington bureaucrat's desk drawer? If the Smith case had been reviewed by the Supreme Court, a successful prosecution would have had to go without penalties. *Amazon* and *Panama* were both civil suits, and were unaffected by the omission, but the error underscored the careless way federal regulations were being drawn up. When it was learned that there was no official government publication of all executive orders by which provisions of the codes were to be put in effect, sharp criticism of administration procedures resulted. Very likely they had an adverse effect on Supreme Court rulings.

The companion cases *Amazon* and *Panama* were combined for argument.[30] Government lawyers approached their task with unwarranted optimism, convinced that the oil code could withstand a Supreme Court challenge because production and distribution were clearly interstate in operation. A broad interpretation of the federal commerce power was certain to produce a decision in their favor.[31] The weak point in their case, however, was the delegation issue. Counsel for the oil companies, citing narrowly restrictive interpretations of the commerce clause found in *Hammer v. Dagenhart* and *U.S. v. E. C. Knight,*[32] claimed that oil production in Texas was a purely local activity. The main thrust of their argument was directed at the delegation issue. Section 9(c) of the NIRA laid down no guidelines or criteria limiting the executive in the orders he was permitted to issue under it.

Harold Stephens argued the "hot oil" cases for the government before the Supreme Court. He thought they had an agreement from the oil company lawyers to avoid mention of the missing segment of code regulations, but an opponent whose client had been threatened with criminal prosecution was unable to resist

[30] 293 U.S. 388 (1935).
[31] Stanley Surrey to Blackwell Smith, January 5, 1934, RG 9, Box 516, NA.
[32] 247 U.S. 251 (1918); 156 U.S. 1 (1895).

an opening: "Smith was arrested, indicted, and held in jail . . . for violating a law [with penalties] that did *not* exist."[33] Stephens then had to admit that "through an administrative error" the penalty section had been omitted. Smiles appeared on the usually solemn faces of the justices and lawyers in the Court chamber when it was revealed that a case hinging on a nonexisting section of the oil code had been sent up by the Justice Department to the Supreme Court.[34] When the embarrassing episode was reported in newspapers all over the country, reporters took full advantage of the opportunity to belittle the Justice Department in general, and Stephens in particular, implying that his lawyers were to blame for the mistake.[35]

During oral argument, Stephens was subjected to intense questioning by Justices Brandeis, McReynolds, Van Devanter, and Butler. According to Paul Freund, who attended, Stephens was interrogated many times on the publication and availability to oil companies of code regulations, the executive orders implementing them, and the steps taken thus far. The chief justice, too, concerned about the slipshod methods by which regulatory measures had been promulgated, joined the questioning. Brandeis considered the Justice Department culpable in failing to have the executive orders printed in the official record, which under ordinary circumstances was filed with the Office of the Secretary of State.[36] Ever a foe of concentrated power, he was in this case even more concerned about the delegation of legislative authority under 9(c), which permitted the executive to declare acts a crime "without findings." Recovering his poise after the grilling from the bench, Stephens tried, with the little time he had left, to focus

---

[33] Quoted in Carl Brent Swisher, "Federal Organization of Legal Functions," *American Political Science Review* 33 (1939): 984.

[34] Harold Stephens to Erwin Griswold, January 7, 1935, Box 16, Harold Stephens Papers, LC; *Washington Post,* December 11, 1934; *New York Herald Tribune,* December 11, 1934.

[35] One outgrowth of this embarrassing situation was the subsequent publication of the *Federal Register,* which contains in official form all executive orders and regulations of the government affecting the public. Erwin Griswold should get the credit for this publication.

[36] Paul Freund to Felix Frankfurter, December 11, 1934, Box 56, Frankfurter Papers, LC; Nelson L. Dawson, *Louis D. Brandeis, Felix Frankfurter, and the New Deal* (Hamden, Conn.: Archon, 1980), chap. 7; Irons, *New Deal Lawyers,* 71.

on the commerce point, emphasizing the chaotic conditions in the oil industry. But he paid virtually no attention to the delegation issue, which was allotted only 3 out of the 195 pages in the government's brief.

Lawyers—and even Supreme Court justices at times—have claimed that oral arguments do not win or lose cases and should therefore be discounted as decisive factors in their outcome. In this instance, Stephens may have been the exception that proved the rule. On his weak performance in court, Ickes commented: "It makes me sick when I think of the way Special Assistant Attorney General Stevens [*sic*] handled our oil case before the Supreme Court . . . and yet men on my legal staff think he was the best man in the whole Department to argue it."[37]

In the aftermath of the ordeal, Erwin Griswold of Harvard Law School wrote Stephens to commiserate with him: "I have been reading in the papers accounts of your troubles before the Supreme Court last Monday and Tuesday." Griswold had a special interest in the remarks attributed to the justices as to the difficulty of locating the exact text of codes, executive orders, rules, and regulations issued by the government. He had published a piece in the *Harvard Law Review* on that very question. There was as yet no such thing as a *Federal Register,* indicating long-term institutional deficiencies predating FDR and Cummings. Griswold proposed to remedy the situation with a draft statute and wanted Stephens to persuade the attorney general to make a recommendation to Congress on the matter.[38] With little help from either Cummings or Roosevelt, the proposal finally bore fruit in the much-needed publication of a *Federal Register.*

Stephens was dismayed by the way the culpability and weaknesses of his department were exploited in this episode. Worse still, there were no means of correcting the false impression it left. The Justice Department did not control publication of orders, regulations, or codes and was not responsible for irregularities in other government departments or agencies. No matter how

[37] Ickes, *Secret Diary,* 1:247; Irons, *New Deal Lawyers,* 72.

[38] Erwin Griswold, "Government in Ignorance of the Law: A Plea for Better Publication of Executive Legislation," *Harvard Law Review* 48 (1934–35): 198–213; Griswold to Stephens, December 12, 1934, Box 16, Stephens Papers, LC.

uncomfortable it made his position, however, he was not unsympathetic with the desire of the Supreme Court justices to do what they could to correct the looseness of administration on matters of importance to the public and the bar. It pained him that the impression created in the public mind was that the Department of Justice alone was at fault,[39] while the onus for the omission rested squarely on the PAB lawyers, who had only a technical relation to the Justice Department and, according to Stephens, failed to consult with its lawyers on the details of the cases they handled.[40]

It took the Supreme Court less than a month to decide the "hot oil" cases. On January 7, 1935, Chief Justice Hughes read the eight-to-one opinion holding section 9(c) of the NIRA an unlawful delegation of authority by Congress to the president. The decision focused on the delegation question. Congress could not vest in the president the authority to make laws without establishing definitive rules and clear standards under which he could act. Section 9(c) gave the executive unlimited authority to determine policy and lay down the prohibition of oil shipments in excess of orders, or not to lay it down, as he saw fit. Disobedience of his order was made a crime punishable by fine or imprisonment, or both. Hughes left untouched the question of whether Congress itself had authority to exercise the requisite power.

The commerce issue was also left undecided. Counsel for the oil companies had urged the Court to strike down the regulatory provisions in the NIRA on the grounds that production of oil was not interstate commerce and was therefore beyond the reach of congressional or executive authority. The Court's failure to address the commerce question came as a great disappointment to Stephens, who believed that the government's position on this issue was sound and felt that they were more likely to prevail on the point in this case than in some others to follow. The Court

---

[39] Stephens to Griswold, January 7, 1935, Box 16, Stephens Papers, LC.

[40] Apparently the defect in the code was discovered by the PAB's lawyers shortly after the amendment of September 13, 1933, but they had a theory, wrote Stephens, which seemed entirely untenable to him, namely, that because the error in amending the code was inadvertent, the omitted paragraph had not been legally omitted! Ibid.

did not rule on the validity of the codes, but section 9(c) and the executive order implementing it were struck down.

For the first time in its history, the Supreme Court voided legislation for unlawful delegation of power to the executive which had permitted such a situation to arise. The executive order of 1933 established no criterion to govern the president's course and required no finding by him as a condition of his action.[41] Frankfurter was unhappy about this. "What really troubled me about the majority decision," he wrote, "was the unabashed way in which they have now made finding 'in the case of delegated power' to the President a constitutional requirement." He was disappointed that Brandeis voted with the majority, but expressed none of these misgivings to him.[42] By then the law professor had changed his position on the NIRA and thought it should be allowed to expire. Brandeis, endorsing the proof sheet of Hughes's opinion, wrote on it: "Yes, Sir, complete and even the layman can understand."

In the "hot oil" cases, Justice Cardozo entered the lone dissent. He thought the Declaration of Policy in the NIRA set a reasonably clear standard for the executive, while emphasizing the magnitude of the disaster that the nation faced in 1933. But he was on weak ground in admitting that the standard "comes to us by implication" and had to be found from a view of the other sections in the act. The majority, however, could find no such relationship between the act's broad generalities and the purely discretionary powers conferred. Cardozo seemed to belittle the importance of the Court's opinion when he wrote: "There is no fear that the nation will drift from its ancient moorings as the result of the narrow delegation of power permitted by this section [9c]."

He disagreed with the argument that Congress left the matter to the president to deal with as he pleased, and expressed fear lest the separation of powers between Congress and the executive should become "a doctrinaire concept to be made use of with pedantic rigor." There needed to be an "elasticity of adjust-

---

[41] 293 U.S. 388, at 415.

[42] Frankfurter to Wyzanski, January 22, 1935, Box 118, Felix Frankfurter Papers, LC; Dawson, *Brandeis, Frankfurter, and the New Deal,* chap. 8.

ment," he argued, or a sensible approximation, in response to the practical necessities of the government, "which cannot foresee today the developments of tomorrow in their infinite variety." He concluded: "Discretion is not unconfined and vagrant. It is canalized within banks that keep it from overflowing."[43] Eight other justices, however, considered the discretion too broad and therefore an unconstitutional delegation of power.

New Dealers seemed to take the decision with equanimity, pointing to the Court's main objections to procedural defects that could be easily remedied, provided the NIRA itself were to be upheld. They cited the limited nature of Hughes's opinion. In the Justice Department, the narrowness of the decision offered some hope that in future cases the Court would seek to avoid the central issue of federal power. But critics attributed the decision in this and subsequent cases to the infirmities of the NIRA and its attempted delegation, the result of hasty and sloppy draftsmanship.[44]

Roosevelt also seemed to take the result philosophically. He came close to admitting guilt on the charge of sloppy draftsmanship when he characterized the decision as simply requiring that the New Deal effect its policies with the "correct language" and looked ahead to "a dozen or one hundred other cases where the language isn't correct yet." But whether he was willing to admit it or not, the decision in the "hot oil" cases was a serious blow to the administration, not so much because of its practical effect, which was comparatively slight, but because of what it portended. And in many ways it was a personal jolt to the president, who, with his White House staff, had closely collaborated with drafters of the NIRA during the emergency days.

One New York paper predicted that "the blank check theory of government is finished."[45] Conservatives were gleeful. Not only were they elated by the eight-to-one decision, but they confi-

---

[43] *Panama Refining Co. et al. v. Ryan et al.,* 293 U.S. 388, at 435–37, Cardozo, J., dissenting. Alpheus T. Mason and William M. Beaney, *The Supreme Court in a Free Society* (Englewood Cliffs, N.J.: Prentice Hall, 1959), 33.

[44] Mason and Beaney, *Supreme Court,* 33; Arthur Sutherland, *Constitutionalism in America: Its Origins and the Evolution of Its Fundamental Ideas* (New York: Blaisdell, 1965), 483–84.

[45] *New York Herald Tribune,* January 9, 1935.

dently expected the nullification of the entire NIRA and the rest of the New Deal. For two full years the overwhelming majority in Congress and the American public had been united in praising Roosevelt and his program. Such criticisms of him as had developed were ascribed to the "economic royalists" who were trying to protect their vested interests. But now, eight of the nine justices found part of the recovery program unconstitutional because it left the executive power element in it too unlimited. Roosevelt wanted and thought he still needed discretionary or emergency powers. Moreover, he was never fond of criticism, nor was he accustomed to hearing it from sources inside the government. But criticism was growing. Nowhere was it more evident than in the pages of the *New York Herald Tribune*. With each passing week, its editorials grew more strident:

> In the skylarking days of 1933–34, the happy administrators of the New Deal brushed aside the Supreme Court as they brushed aside Congress and the Constitution. . . . The President paid perfunctory lip service to the nation's charter of liberty. Behind the scene the whispers were loud enough to be beyond misunderstanding. Let the Supreme Court try to halt the march of the new order, according to FDR, and an act of Congress would be passed adding to its membership and packing it with enough Tugwellian jurists to overturn any conservative decision overnight.

Now, the editors exulted, "the eight-to-one decision in the Hot Oil cases has thrown this reactionary nonsense into the Potomac where it belongs."[46]

Within weeks of the Court's decision the Smith-Connally Oil Control Act passed both houses, reinstating the administration's oil policy. This law, extended to 1942, was never successfully challenged in court. Whatever damage may have been done by the *Panama* ruling was quickly repaired, but other cases were making their way up through the lower courts, and a more alarming situation involving cases testing the constitutionality of the New Deal's monetary and gold policies threatened the very fabric of the economic order.

---

[46] Quoted in "New Deal Meets Tests in Supreme Court," *Literary Digest* 119 (January 19, 1935), 5–6.

The Gold Clause Cases

By early 1935, the outlook for the administration was becoming increasingly troubling. Emergency measures designed to bring about recovery were not working. More than 10 million were still unemployed, and the country seemed to be facing the permanent condition of economic stalemate. Major actions of Congress during the "hundred days" helped plant the seeds of future constitutional challenges to Roosevelt's concept of emergency power. The gold clause cases tested the administration's monetary policy, which had dramatically altered the relationship between gold and the U.S. dollar. They were the outcome of earlier executive and congressional actions dealing with the economic crisis.

When the bank holiday was followed by the reopening of sound banks, abnormal gold exports and hoarding, according to FDR, were undermining the stability of the monetary system. Invoking the 1917 Trading with the Enemy Act, he suspended by executive order all gold exports and foreign exchange operations. The Emergency Banking Relief Act of March 1933 was rushed into law, authorizing these steps and requiring the surrender of all gold coin, bullion, and certificates to the U.S. Treasury. It was illegal to hold, sell, buy, or trade gold without securing a government license. Holders of any form of gold were forced to accept the equivalent in paper.

A major action of the special session of Congress was the Joint Resolution of June 5, 1933, which canceled gold clauses in all public and private contracts, including bonds issued by the U.S. government, relieving all debtors of their contractual obligations to make payment in gold. Finally, Congress gave the executive blanket authority to devalue the U.S. dollar with respect to gold, a prerogative that Roosevelt did not use until later. Al Smith, one of the first prominent Democrats to break with FDR, was by then editor of the *New Outlook* and wrote in its columns that New Deal monetary policies were producing "baloney dollars."[47]

---

[47] Schlesinger, Jr., *Politics of Upheaval,* 6; William Lasser, *The Limits of Judicial Power: The Supreme Court in American Politics* (Chapel Hill: University of North Carolina Press, 1988), 125. This was done in a series of presidential proclamations lowering the gold content of the dollar, eventually fixing it at 15 and 5/21 grains. Congress authorized the reduction in the Gold Reserve Act of January 30, 1934. It was later estimated that Roosevelt's gold policy shaved off about $70 billion from public and private debts.

Formal testing of this legislation eighteen months later inaugurated judicial review of major New Deal enactments. On their face they were emergency measures, such as the NIRA and the AAA, but they went far beyond the exigencies of the day, marking in effect the beginning of a whole new relationship between the people and the government and between the government and the banking system. Support of public credit was transferred to banks, while the supremacy of the government was established over the currency. FDR was given blanket authority to devalue the dollar in terms of its gold content. Retirement of gold as a circulating medium and devaluation of the currency to produce inflation made necessary passage of the Joint Resolution, voiding the gold clauses in public and private contracts. These contracts, calling for payment in a fixed amount of gold by weight, stood in the way of devaluation.

Legislation dating back to 1900 had set the standard written into the gold clause contracts. In the absence of any declaration of policy by the financial community, much uncertainty and lack of agreement prevailed on the essential nature and value of the obligation. In the little more than thirty years since its establishment, the gold standard and currency regulations accompanying it had become deeply embedded in American thought, business practices, and popular psychology. It was thought of as sacred, absolutely essential to the proper functioning of business and commerce. But FDR, for one, was convinced that gold was no sacred cow. He disagreed with those who believed that to threaten or touch it was to "profane the sanctuary of the Almighty Dollar." Though Great Britain and other countries had abandoned the gold standard, a majority of U.S. economists regarded their action as only temporary and, in any case, no guide for American policy.

In the depths of the depression, holders of gold certificates or bonds with gold clauses already found themselves in difficulty, for with all banks closed, some for good, no payment of any kind was possible. When sound banks reopened, they were forbidden to pay out gold or issue gold certificates. The executive order of April 5, 1933, called in all privately held gold on or before April 28; another order prohibited all private transactions in gold.

Within a few months, gold vanished entirely from the American marketplace.

With all transactions in gold halted by executive order, Congress faced the issue of whether or not to honor contracts containing clauses requiring payment in gold. This uncertainty took the form of speculation about whether the courts would enforce the obligation as written in the contracts, or whether Congress had the power to nullify the clauses and prevent their inclusion in future contracts. In the first session of the Seventy-third Congress the gold clauses were debated on and off. A year earlier a bill to nullify them had been introduced in the House by Representative Ed. H. Campbell of Iowa on February 8, 1933 (H.R. 14604, 72nd Cong., 2nd sess.). Similar bills were introduced in the session, but initial attempts at passage failed.

Doubts about the constitutionality of such enactments were the main stumbling block. Was the power to insert or abolish these clauses within the legitimate authority of the government? That question was answered in the Joint Resolution of June 5, 1933, and it would again be raised in some form before the Supreme Court. It is no wonder Congress was so reluctant to abrogate gold clause contracts, for they had been held enforceable by the courts ever since the decision of the Supreme Court in *Bronson v. Rodes* (177 Wallace 229) in 1868.

Fulfillment of the guarantee of payment in gold for gold certificates, railroad bonds, or Liberty bonds had always been a matter of theoretical certainty, but after March 1933 payment in gold on all these instruments was declared by Congress to be "against public policy." Prior to the changes, it had been customary to honor the obligations in such contracts by payment in gold coin "of the present standard of value." It now became impossible to honor such contracts.[48]

Twenty billion dollars in U.S. government contracts alone required annual interest payments of up to $700 million. If these obligations had to be honored, they would have drained all the gold out of the U.S. Treasury. The government quickly implemented a series of refunding operations in which billions of dol-

48 Beard and Beard, *America in Mid-Passage,* 212–14.

lars' worth of old bonds were replaced by new ones omitting the gold clauses. In most instances, payment in paper was accepted under protest; however, legal-minded holders brought suit in federal court to test the validity of the actions taken by the president and Congress, especially the Joint Resolution of June 5, 1933.

The first of these gold clause cases, *Norman et al. v. Baltimore & Ohio Railroad Company,*[49] involved private contracts in the form of railroad bonds. Norman C. Norman and plaintiffs demanded payment of a $22.50 interest coupon (old value $38.10, the difference resulting from devaluation). Most of the suits involved small amounts, but in the aggregate they represented a staggering sum at a time when the U.S. Treasury held only $4 billion in gold reserves. Plaintiffs challenged the government's cancellation of gold clauses, devaluing debts by the substitution of paper for gold. Norman won his suit in federal district court in St. Louis, and, along with a companion case,[50] it went on appeal to the Supreme Court.

Nortz v. United States[51] originated in the U.S. Court of Claims. It was a suit to recover the difference between the face value of $10,000 in gold certificates, which the plaintiff was being forced to surrender to the government, and the face value in devalued dollars. A fourth case, *Perry v. United States,*[52] involved an attempt by the holder of a $10,000 Liberty bond to recover the difference between the original gold value of the contract and its current worth in new dollars ($16,931). At issue in all four cases was the power of Congress to impair the obligation of public or private contracts containing gold clauses antedating the New Deal's currency legislation in pursuance of its monetary policies. The Supreme Court in effect was asked to determine whether the government had the power to compel acceptance of the new currency regulations in satisfaction of private and public contracts, including its own gold clause obligations in Liberty bonds.

By 1935 the nine justices fully understood that the administration's monetary policies were not working as expected, that the economy was still in the doldrums, and that its entire structure

[49] 294 U.S. 240 (1935).
[50] *U.S. v. Bankers' Trust Company,* 294 U.S. 240 (1935).
[51] 294 U.S. 317 (1935).
[52] 294 U.S. 317, at 330 (1935).

rested on a shaky base. In his intimate observations of FDR's modus operandi from 1933 to 1935, Moley found that expediency—the force of circumstances—played a greater role than was usually conceded in his decisions. "These rationalizations," he later wrote, "in turn, were to become the intellectual bridges to a silly and futile monetary policy."[53] He drew his conclusions after the fact, but Justice Brandeis, whose role in the outcome of the gold clause cases would be central, took a dim view of the policies at their inception. He wrote:

> The action on the gold clauses is terrifying in its implications. A declaration of bankruptcy, or composition, is honorable if warranted by existing conditions. But the deliberate repudiation by the Government of its own obligations, entered into freely in contemplation of the contingency which has arisen and for the purpose of dealing with it, involves an alarming application of its power. If the Government wished to extricate itself from the assumed emergency, taxation would have afforded an honorable way out.[54]

Galvanized into action by the high stakes involved in these cases, Cummings, along with Assistant Solicitor General Angus MacLean and others, became deeply immersed in the preparation of briefs and arguments. Cummings sent out the briefs to a wide cross section of the bench and bar, asking for comments. He was himself to make the opening argument for the government. When the time came, he sent Marguerite Le Hand this note:

> The gold cases will begin today. There are four of them, and the Government has filed briefs in three of the cases. I have spent so much time, day and night, on these briefs and in the preparation of my oral argument, that I begin to feel a bit like King Midas. I hope things will go along well, and I am using the presidential cuff links for the first time by way of good luck. They too are gold.[55]

---

[53] Moley, *After Seven Years,* 160–61.

[54] Brandeis to Frankfurter, June 13, 1933, quoted in *"Half Brother, Half Son": Letters of Louis Brandeis to Felix Frankfurter,* eds. Melvin Urofsky and David W. Levy (Norman: University of Oklahoma Press, 1991), 523. "Composition" is defined as an agreement between a debtor and his or her creditors whereby, in return for an immediate payment, the latter agree to take less than the full amount of the claim.

[55] Attachments included the principal brief and appendices for the president's perusal. January 8, 1935, OF 10, Box 2, FDRL. Beginning with the 1920 campaign, when he ran on the national ticket with presidential candidate James M.

Oral arguments, begun on January 8, 1935, were spread over three days. On the second day, Stanley Reed took over where Cummings left off. The constitutional issues in these cases had momentous implications, and a vague sense of what hung in the balance began to agitate Wall Street. In his rationale, Cummings placed the government's overriding power of self-preservation above what he termed "the supposed sanctity and inviolability of contractual obligations." While acknowledging that no state can impair the obligation of contracts, he tried to juxtapose against this the powers of the sovereign. One of the prerogatives of sovereignty, he asserted, is the power to coin money and regulate the currency, determining what is and is not legal tender. To deny this power in the midst of a depression, he insisted, would result in "a stupendous catastrophe . . . such as to stagger the imagination." The outcome would be chaos. If the Court should find against the government, he warned, it would risk making the United States "a cripple among the nations of the earth." Prior to answering questions from the bench, he made the unusual request of the justices to "keep the case open" in the event that the government failed to supply them with all the information necessary to sustain its position in annulling the gold clauses.[56]

The weeks following oral argument were tense ones for the administration. In the White House nerves were frayed to an unusual degree during the enforced waiting, with indications that the Court's deliberations would take a long time. The issues involved in the cases were of such magnitude as to tax the wildest flights of the imagination. Washington officialdom was more absorbed in the question of how the Court would decide than with any subject since the banking crisis. The anxiety surrounding the gold clause cases was intensified when the chief justice, in an

---

Cox, Roosevelt began holding informal gatherings of friends and advisers in his "Cuff Links Club." Members received gold cuff links inscribed "From FDR to . . ."

[56] *Norman et al. v. Baltimore & Ohio Railroad Co.,* 294 U.S. 240, at 256 (1935). Cummings's oral argument January 8 and 9 is at 251–72. See also *New York Times,* January 9, 11, 1935; Schlesinger, Jr., *Politics of Upheaval,* 256; excerpts from Cummings's argument are in Swisher, ed., *Selected Papers,* 112–20.

unprecedented action, announced on two consecutive Saturdays that the decisions would not come down the following Monday.

Administration doubts about the outcome can be measured by the nature and extent of the extraordinary contingency plans Roosevelt put in place. On January 11, 1935, responding to an order from the president, Robert Jackson, special assistant to the attorney general, advised responding to an unfavorable ruling from the Court by withdrawing the government's consent to be sued. Cummings immediately began studying the means of doing this to clear the way for remedial legislation right after the decision.[57]

Reporting on the gold clause cases to a cabinet meeting, Cummings said he felt confident that the government would win in a divided opinion. Ickes recounted:

> The Attorney General said that if the Court should decide against the Government in the gold . . . and Liberty Bond cases, the situation could be saved by Congress hurrying through a statute taking away from citizens the right to sue . . . for damages that they might claim. . . . If the decision goes against the Government, a number of big railroads . . . will be thrown into bankruptcy.[58]

The attorney general proposed that if the Court should decide against the government, the number of justices should be increased at once so as to give a favorable majority. The president, reported Ickes, had suggested this possibility to him in an interview. Ickes told FDR this was precisely what ought to be done: "It would not be the first time the Supreme Court was increased in size to meet a temporary emergency and it certainly would be justified in this case." This of course had no foundation in fact. He told the president that only a few years ago he had predicted that sooner or later the Supreme Court would become a political issue as a result of its continuous blockade of the popular will through declaring acts of Congress unconstitutional.[59]

FDR calculated that, while remedial legislation might mitigate some of the dire consequences of an adverse decision, it could

---

[57] Robert Jackson, Reminiscences, COHC; Swisher, ed., *Selected Papers,* 107. At the time, Jackson was general counsel for the Internal Revenue Service.

[58] Ickes, *Secret Diary,* 1:273–74.

[59] Ibid., 274.

not be expected to avert confusion and a chain reaction of bankruptcies. He was ready to resort to bolder tactics in his moment of desperation. On January 14 he told Secretary Morgenthau that he wanted his Treasury Department "to keep things as unsettled as possible while the Court was making up its mind." Bonds and foreign exchange rates were to be allowed to move up and down as if things were in turmoil. Then, in the event of an adverse decision, the man in the street would say, "For God's sake, Mr. President, do something!" Roosevelt added, "If I do, everybody in the country will heave a sigh of relief and thank God."[60]

Cummings, who was also present, not only agreed with Roosevelt but egged him on. Morgenthau, however, was deeply shocked and argued vehemently against this "wild scheme." The stabilization fund had been given to him by Congress as a trust, he said, and he would not use it to encourage uncertainty. In the end Morgenthau's sound judgment prevailed, but the episode illustrates the lack of it by the president and Cummings, his "legal yes-man." The exchange underscored the rising nervousness within the administration. Wall Street, unassisted by the Treasury Secretary, reacted negatively. Stock prices fluctuated wildly, reflecting increased uncertainty within the financial community.

Roosevelt insisted that Congress had the power to regulate the currency, an attribute of national sovereignty and one which the legislature and executive could not under any circumstances surrender to the judiciary. As for bondholders clamoring for payment in gold, they were in his estimation "no better than racketeers." No one holding a government bond could prove loss, since the depreciated dollar of 1935 commanded increased purchasing power over the gold dollar of 1926.

Other contingency measures were readied. In response to the crisis, FDR drafted a message recommending instantaneous passage by Congress of legislation withdrawing the right of citizens to sue the United States for more than the face value (in paper) of its bonds or obligations. He prepared a proclamation declaring

---

[60] *From the Morgenthau Diaries: Years of Crisis, 1928–1938,* ed. John M. Blum, 3 vols. (Boston: Houghton Mifflin, 1959–67), entry for January 14–15, 1935, 2:125–31; Schlesinger, Jr., *Politics of Upheaval,* 256–57.

a national emergency, empowering him to regulate all currency transactions. No payments on any contracts would be permitted for ninety days at a rate fixed by the government ($35 an ounce for gold). He would see to it that holders of bonds would get no more than their current value in depreciated dollars, no matter what the Supreme Court decided.

The administration braced itself for possible defeat in the gold clause cases, and FDR continued to draw up battle plans throughout January. He readied an executive order for Joseph P. Kennedy, chairman of the Securities Exchange Commission, authorizing him to close all stock exchanges. With help from Frankfurter he prepared for delivery a defiant radio address to the nation in which he would claim that the total amount of gold clause obligations (ca. $100 billion, with only $13 billion worth of gold in the entire world) was so staggering that it would obstruct Congress's power to regulate the currency and provide for its uniformity. Given an advance copy of this speech, Kennedy found some of the statements in it so strong that he predicted the American people would "burn the Supreme Court justices in effigy."[61] The speech referred to permanent legislation and/or a constitutional amendment as remedies to meet the situation.[62]

Included in the undelivered radio address was a proposed one-year moratorium on enforcement of all gold clause obligations over and above their value in current dollars. The speech warned that an adverse decision, if enforced, would result in "unconscionable profit" to investors, bankruptcy for many railroads and corporations, default by state and local governments, and wholesale mortgage foreclosures. While Roosevelt was prepared to say that he did not seek a quarrel with the Supreme Court, he made clear his determination to match the Court's "last word" on this "political issue" with one of his own: neither he nor Congress could stand idly by and permit a decision of the Supreme Court to imperil the nation's economic security.[63]

---

[61] Leonard Baker, *Brandeis and Frankfurter,* 316–17.

[62] Typescript in PPF 1055, FDRL.

[63] An amendment drafted by MacLean read: "Congress shall have plenary power over coinage and currency and may annul all contracts . . . heretofore or hereafter made, which may be found by Congress to obstruct the exercise of power." Various undated drafts of the speech are in ibid.

During the long waiting period, the justices, in accordance with a long-established tradition, were invited to the annual White House dinner in their honor. As they were arriving, Justice Stone was overheard to remark: "I suspect we will be as popular here as a skunk in a hen house."

When decision Monday came around on February 18, with no prior announcement by the chief justice, it was evident that a ruling was imminent. Hughes was mobbed by reporters and photographers who were waiting outside that morning as he emerged from his home to drive to Capitol Hill. Word was quickly relayed to the White House that the justices were assembling in the robing room, about to file into the Court chamber.

At noon, Roosevelt and his aides took up positions in the cabinet room, anxiously awaiting the decisions. A direct telephone line had been installed so that communication with the Court would be instantaneous. Minutes after the decision was announced, Joseph Kennedy was put through to the cabinet room where Morgenthau, FDR, and the others were huddled. He relieved the tension by reporting that the Supreme Court had ruled in the government's favor in all the gold clause cases. Kennedy took great pride in being the first to bring the news to "the Chief." With an eye on history, he dutifully recorded the day's events in his memoirs "for the benefit of his children."[64]

The chief justice wrote all three opinions in the gold clause cases, treating the two railroad cases as one. The vote in all the cases was by the narrow margin of five to four. The fiscal measures taken by the government were approved on carefully circumscribed and conditional terms. Upholding the Joint Resolution of 1933, Hughes emphasized that the Court was not concerned with the wisdom or policy behind the legislation, but with the authority of Congress to regulate the currency. Congress could invalidate provisions of existing contracts if they interfered with control of the monetary system. The bonds called for payment "in gold coin of the *present* standard." Hughes argued that the gold clauses were not "contracts for payment in gold or in bullion as a commodity, but for the general payment of

[64] Michael Beschloss, *Kennedy and Roosevelt: The Uneasy Alliance* (New York: Norton, 1980), 98–99.

money."[65] Plaintiffs could not claim that their abrogation deprived them of property without due process since there had been no confiscation, only a readjustment in the value of the dollar to bring it in line with changing economic conditions.

In *Nortz,* Hughes declared that the government was within its powers in replacing the gold certificates with other forms of currency of equivalent value. By receiving devalued dollars, holders of certificates could demonstrate no actual loss and had no right to sue in the U.S. Court of Claims. The opinion omitted consideration of whether gold certificates were an express contract between the holder and the government (even though on their face they bore the phrase "in gold payable to the bearer on demand"). Nor did the majority decide whether the Emergency Banking Relief Act, which ordered their surrender to the Treasury, took private property without the due process guaranteed by the Fifth Amendment.

However, Hughes's opinion in *Perry v. United States,* which involved the gold clauses in Liberty bonds, was very different in tone and substance from the others. The $10,000 bond at issue bore terms explicitly prescribing principal and interest payable to the holder in gold coin or bullion. Failure on the part of the government to honor this obligation, since it had borrowed money under the authority of the Constitution, was as much repudiation, with all the reproach that term implies, as repudiation by a state, municipality, or private citizen. Hughes made a distinction between the treatment of private and public contracts as construed in these cases. As it applied to the government's obligations as undertaken in selling Liberty bonds, he declared: "We conclude that the Joint Resolution [of 1933] . . . insofar as it attempted to override the obligation created by the bond in suit, went beyond congressional power." The government, he argued, could not legally and constitutionally violate its own obligations. Such action would destroy public faith and obstruct its borrowing power.[66]

At first blush, *Perry* appeared to be a defeat for the government. In a thinly veiled lecture, Hughes chided the administration

---

[65] *Norman et al. v. Baltimore & Ohio Railroad Co.,* 294 U.S. 240, at 302 (1935).

[66] *Perry v. United States,* 294 U.S. 330, at 347 (1935).

for the immorality of its conduct and reproved Congress for approving an unconstitutional resolution. But the decision did not end there. Hughes went on to assert that "despite the binding obligation on 'the conscience of the sovereign,' it would be impossible for the creditor to obtain judicial relief."

At issue from the government's point of view, however, was something more fundamental than a redefinition of constitutional doctrine. Hughes was well aware of the catastrophic effect that honoring the gold clause contracts would have on the economy. With some inkling, perhaps, of the retaliatory measures FDR had prepared for such a contingency, he ruled that the plaintiff could show no cause of action for actual damages and was not entitled to recover. With the altered (increased) buying power of the devalued dollar, no real loss could have been incurred by failing to receive what would have been the face value of the bond at maturity in pre-1933 dollars. "The action is for breach of contract," Hughes said. "As a remedy for breach, the plaintiff can recover no more than the loss he has suffered and of which he might rightfully complain. He is not entitled to be enriched."[67] This was a strange opinion. On the one hand, the Court majority accused the government of repudiating its obligations, shirking its moral duty; on the other hand, the Court majority refused to do anything about it.

The prolonged delay before the decisions came down in these cases underscored the awful dilemma in which the justices found themselves. Justice Stone was unable to go along with Hughes's reasoning on all points. He disagreed with him on two of the most fundamental issues: first, whether Congress had the power to abrogate the government's pledge in Liberty bonds; and second, the limitations that could be imposed on the government's monetary powers. In a concurring opinion, Stone could find no distinction between the obligation to honor private and public contracts. Holding government contracts valid while invalidating those between private parties was, for him, untenable. In his view, Hughes's opinion failed to face up to the fact that regulating a money contract might impair the constitutional obligation

[67] Ibid., at 354–55.

to honor contracts, public or private. Without mincing words about it, Stone considered the attempt by the majority to dictate the extent of Congress's monetary powers to be "a plain usurpation." Congress's power to regulate the currency was plenary and took priority over other sovereign powers to borrow money or grant immunity from suits.[68]

Justices Sutherland, Van Devanter, Butler, and McReynolds dissented without comment in the first three cases. Speaking through Justice McReynolds in *Perry,* they argued that the part of Hughes's opinion nullifying the Joint Resolution of 1933 was acceptable to them but insisted on applying the same reasoning on the sanctity of the gold clause obligation to both private and public contracts. Referring to the New Deal's "flippant approach to currency manipulation" and "the hastily drawn emergency legislation of 1933–4," they saw a dangerous disregard not only for financial stability but for social ethics as well. No feature of Roosevelt's recovery program was more abhorrent to them than the government's reneging on its own contractual obligations. It was bad enough to have to swallow cancellation of the gold clauses in railroad bonds, but to do it with Liberty bonds represented for them the "end of public morality."

The dissenters refused to recognize the distinction Hughes made between the issue of damages and that of congressional power. The government's claim of increased purchasing power in Depression dollars did not impress or concern them. Nor did the fact that, by 1935, the country's entire financial structure was keyed in with the newly devalued currency. To upset all this after numerous obligations, both domestic and foreign, had already been met with the new dollars might have resulted in a damaging upheaval in the economy and an avalanche of lawsuits demanding full payment in pre-1933 dollars. The four dissenters, it appears, were not concerned about the dreaded consequences facing the public as outlined in the government's arguments. McReynolds countered with one of his own: "Just men regard repudiation and spoliation of citizens by their sovereign with ab-

---

[68] 294 U.S. 330, Stone, J., concurring, at 359–61. Stone's concurrence was not nearly as harsh in its criticism of the government as Hughes's majority opinion. Submitting a concurrence in this case suggests that Stone thought the chief justice's argument was weak.

horrence. This might be only the beginning. Where would it all end?" He continued:

> We might not forget that if this power exists, Congress may readily destroy other obligations which present obstruction . . . by reducing the standard gold dollar to one grain of gold, or brass or nickel or copper or lead. [This] will become an easy possibility. . . . We think that in the circumstances Congress had no power to destroy the obligations of the gold clauses. . . . The attempt to do this was plain usurpation, arbitrary and oppressive.

McReynolds made only brief mention of the economic situation facing the country. He called the forecast of the incalculable financial disaster that would supposedly follow the Court's refusal to uphold congressional authority over regulation of the currency a "manifest exaggeration." Whatever the seriousness of a possible economic collapse, it was the result of an attempt to destroy lawful undertakings by legislative action. He concluded with these bitter words:

> Under the challenged statutes it is said that the United States have realized profits amounting to $2.8 m. But this assumes that gain may be generated by legislative fiat. To such counterfeit profits there would be no limits; with each new debasement of the dollar they would expand. Two billions might be ballooned indefinitely—to twenty, thirty, or what you will. Loss of reputation for honorable dealing will bring us unending humiliation; the impending legal and moral chaos is appalling.[69]

These remarks were received in a hushed courtroom. At their conclusion, McReynolds reportedly added extemporaneously: "This is Nero at his worst. And as for the Constitution, it does not seem too much to say that it is gone."[70]

Once the government was upheld in the gold clause cases, expressions of dissatisfaction emerged from outraged creditors, many of whom echoed the sentiments in McReynolds's irate dis-

---

[69] 294 U.S. 330 (1935), McReynolds, J., dissenting, at 381.

[70] No complete record of the extemporaneous remarks of February 18, 1935, was kept and no stenographic notes exist; but a copy of the dissent in his own handwriting is in the McReynolds Papers, Folder H-2, ALDL. A reporter's version appeared in the *Wall Street Journal,* February 23, 1935.

sent. The reaction by the justices themselves was ominous. From the tone of Hughes's stern lecture in *Perry* and the diatribe in McReynolds's dissent, it was obvious that the justices were unhappy with the decisions, and especially upset about being forced into a predicament where they had no choice. As one newspaper put it: "There was no power on earth that could unscramble the egg the New Dealers handed the Court." Justice Brandeis wrote Frankfurter: "It is a relief to have the Gold Clause case out of the way; but I feel little satisfaction with the Administration's performance. McReynolds' talk was very different from his opinion, and was really impressive, better than anything I have ever heard from him."[71] Brandeis's comments suggest he also feared that the country's constitutional foundations were being threatened.

From Harvard, Erwin Griswold wrote Justice Stone: "Someone here has expressed the conclusion . . . that the Supreme Court has held the abrogation of the gold clause in government bonds unconstitutional, nine Justices dissenting." He was most distressed by the attitude of his lay friends, who seemed to think of the decisions as "just another example of the trickiness of the law, a sort of legal mumbo-jumbo that only confirms their distrust of things legal." Stone replied: "All in all, I cannot get over the feeling that our performance in the Gold Cases was a sad one, but it is of some comfort to see how well the country has accepted conclusions which they do not understand and which no one seems to be able to explain to them."[72]

Frankfurter complimented Stone on his concurrence, but he expressed only contempt for McReynolds's dissent:

> I wish you had spoken for the Court in the Perry case. . . . As for the diatribe of McReynolds, J., I suppose that the poor fellow doesn't know that his kind of stuff does more to undermine public respect for the Constitution and for the Court than all the soap box oratory of the demagogues. If he would recall history, he would know that the Constitution has been "dead" for one hundred years.

---

[71] Editorial in *Troy (N.Y.) Evening Record,* March 1, 1935; Brandeis to Frankfurter, February 24, 1935, quoted in Urofsky and Levy, eds., *"Half Brother, Half Son,"* 562.

[72] Griswold to Stone, March 5, 1935; Stone to Griswold, March 7, 1935. Box 15, Harlan Fiske Stone Papers, LC.

> [Justice] Story, as you are the last person to be reminded, delivered several funeral orations upon it after [Chief Justice Roger B.] Taney's accession.
>
> Well, I am glad these cases are out of the way for the country was extraordinarily jittery about them.[73]

No one was more jittery about the gold cases than the president, who seemed relieved after the rulings but remained wary of the close vote. Roosevelt and his aides were sick with worry during the weeks of waiting, but there was a hint of smug satisfaction in the note FDR sent Joe Kennedy after the Court's decision: "With you, I think Monday, February eighteenth was a historic day. As a lawyer, it seems to me that the Supreme Court has at last definitely put human values ahead of the 'pound of flesh' called for by a contract." He congratulated Kennedy for being more accurate than the Associated Press in reporting the outcome of the decisions:

> How fortunate it is that [the Stock] Exchanges will never know how close they came to being closed up by the stroke of the pen of J.P.K. Likewise the Nation will never know what a great treat it missed in not hearing the marvelous radio address the "Pres" had prepared for delivery to the Nation Monday night if the cases had gone the other way.[74]

Kennedy replied that, when his planned defiance of the Supreme Court proved to be unnecessary, FDR's only regret must have been his inability to deliver his radio speech. The day after the decision, FDR wistfully read passages of the undelivered speech to Tugwell and Moley, who observed dryly that "the President better save the language for the time when NRA would be declared unconstitutional."[75]

Public reaction to the Court's decisions in the gold clause cases was mixed. Undoubtedly, the negative response had its im-

[73] Frankfurter to Stone, February 19, 1935, Box 13, ibid. In a letter of February 21, Stone wrote Frankfurter that he did not think the opinion in the *Perry* case was his (i.e., agreeable to him).

[74] FDR to Joseph P. Kennedy, February 19, 1935, in *F.D.R.: His Personal Letters, 1928–1945,* ed. Elliott Roosevelt, 4 vols. (New York: Duell, Sloan and Pearce, 1948–50), 1:455.

[75] Schlesinger, Jr., *Politics of Upheaval,* 260; Rexford Tugwell Diary, February 19, 1935, in Rexford G. Tugwell Papers, FDRL.

pact on the president and his advisers, but the administration's assumption that it had been vindicated and the self-congratulatory attitude of Cummings and Roosevelt proved distressing, especially in view of the Court's finding that New Dealers were really guilty of repudiation and bad faith in nullifying the gold clauses in Liberty bonds. Roosevelt must have realized that his monetary policies had been given a sound scolding by the Court majority. Aware of the close call, he wrote Angus MacLean, congratulating him on "the splendid work he had done in arguing the gold cases," and added: "In spite of our rejoicing, I shudder at the closeness of the five to four decisions in that important matter."[76]

In a fireside chat in March 1937, Roosevelt recalled how, in the dark days of 1933–34, in the midst of the banking crisis and with the authority of Congress, he had asked the nation to turn over all of its privately held gold, dollar for dollar, to the government. But when, almost two years later, the matter came before the Supreme Court, its constitutionality was upheld only by five to four. The change of one vote, he reminded listeners, "would have thrown all the affairs of this great Nation back into hopeless chaos. In effect, four Justices ruled that the right under a private contract to exact a pound of flesh was more sacred than the main objectives of the Constitution to establish an enduring Nation."[77]

The gold clause rulings sanctioned devaluation. They were the first cases in English or American history to render such a momentous decision. The right of Congress to devalue was taken for granted: only its effect on preexisting contracts was under scrutiny. The government's arguments before the Court and the majority opinions in the cases proceeded on the assumption that Congress could lawfully exercise the right to reduce the gold content of the dollar, with a somewhat ambiguous position on this point in *Perry*. But was this assumption historically sound?

A noted legal historian concluded that it was not. Debasement and devaluation, which are intrinsically the same, have had a long and dishonorable history. Phanor J. Eder traced that history

[76] FDR to MacLean, February 21, 1935, PPF 1055, FDRL.

[77] *New York Times,* March 10, 1937; Fireside Chat, March 9, 1937, PPA, 1937 volume, 122.

from ancient times to the present and found wanting the weightiest contention in the government's brief and Reed's closing argument—that is, that complete control of the coinage and currency is a prerogative of sovereignty. There is only one authority in English case law (and that, as it happens, was Irish) for the proposition that there is a sovereign prerogative to debase the currency. That case was cited by the Supreme Court in the *Legal Tender Cases,* the second of which was the basis on which Hughes rested part of his argument in the gold clause cases.

It would be impossible to say whether these citations are apt without reference to the history of the case or to the countervailing denial by Coke, Blackstone, Chitty, and Joseph Story of such a liberty-menacing proposition. But the Supreme Court rendered the only decision that was practical, possible, and statesmanlike under the circumstances that were forced upon it by the Congress and the president. It was the acts which caused these circumstances that needed to be subjected to the searchlight of history.

Professor Eder struck hard blows at Roosevelt's policies when he wrote: "Those actions, improvised by Congress without adequate debate, without public hearings, without submission to public opinion, in part as a rider to an Agricultural Bill, violated concrete traditional liberties in deference to newer uncrystalized concepts of social justice." However mistaken one may think the ideas underlying the Roosevelt administration's monetary legislation were, they were implemented as a necessary contribution to the social welfare. "The clash is clear between the traditional and concrete liberties of the common law, the old practical rugged honesty, the old morality of the Ten Commandments (Thou shalt not steal, Thy money shall not bear false witness) on the one side, and on the other, vague aspirations for social justice whose basic tenets had not yet been defined by any public creed." A choice had to be made, but which one would the people have chosen?

To avoid being harassed in future lawsuits and to prevent any successful action against the government, the administration pressed for remedial legislation. Cummings gave supporting testimony for the legislation (H.J. Res. 348) before the House Committee on Banking and Currency (July 10, 1935), and for S.J. Res. 155 before the Senate Banking Committee (July 17, 1935).

Their enactment eventually withdrew jurisdiction in gold clause suits with the exception of suits instituted within a limited period of time. A few cases arose within the period, and the government was successful in all of them.[78]

Railway Workers' Pension Case

Swarms of cases challenging New Deal statutes or parts of them were working their way up through the courts. By early March of 1935, a reported 389 cases were pending on the dockets in federal courts. By year's end, the Justice Department's Antitrust Division alone faced litigation in more than a thousand cases.[79] Included were challenges to wage regulation in the NIRA codes for the coal industry, to labor provisions in its section 7(a), and to the NIRA itself, along with the AAA and TVA.

The Railroad Retirement Pension Act of June 27, 1934,[80] was not part of the New Deal program, but if it were to be successfully challenged in the courts, its invalidation boded ill for the administration's pending Social Security Act. *Retirement Board v. Alton Railroad Co.* involved the validity of the Railroad Retirement Act, which prescribed a comprehensive pension scheme for workers on common carriers. The case originated as an injunctive suit in which 134 Class 1 carriers, two express companies, and the Pullman Car Company filed to restrain enforcement of the law on the ground that it was unconstitutional.[81]

The decision was adverse to the Railroad Retirement Board in the Supreme Court of the District of Columbia (October 26, 1934). A petition for *certiorari* to the D.C. Court of Appeals, filed on December 7, was never submitted to that court but went directly to the Supreme Court, where it came on for hearing on application for a temporary injunction. The provisions of the act

---

[78] Phanor J. Eder, "The Gold Clause Cases in the Light of History," Part I, *Georgetown Law Journal* 23 (March 1935): 359–88; and Part II (April 1935): 722–61. On the 1935 remedial legislation, see Swisher, ed., *Selected Papers,* 105–7.

[79] Schlesinger, Jr., *Politics of Upheaval,* 6.

[80] 48 U.S. Statutes 1283 (1934).

[81] 295 U.S. 330 (1935). Press release, October 1, 1935, RG 60, Box 83, Henry Suydam Files, NA.

that were attacked by respondents, invoking the equity jurisdiction of the Supreme Court, included the provisions for compulsory retirement, pensions, and annuities mandated for employees of carriers engaged in interstate commerce, all of which allegedly went beyond Congress's commerce power.

From the outset, Justice Department lawyers preparing the government's case wanted to forestall any complaints from organized labor about how they handled the case. In a confidential memo to Cummings, Stephens wrote: "I took pains to lay a foundation against criticism in the event we should lose the case, by inviting the cooperation of Mr. Frank L. Mulholland, counsel to the Association of Railway Labor Executives, representing the standard twenty-one railway brotherhoods, and of Mr. Herman Ekern, counsel to the Railway Employees' National Pension Association." He asked them for written suggestions regarding the argument of the case and invited each of them to lunch for consultations, hoping that prior approval of their brief and argument would provide "some safeguard against adverse publicity in the event we lose the case." In the memo, he added: "I also carried out your advice . . . that we associate Mr. Harry Shulman, counsel for the Railway Labor Board, in the argument. This I think has fairly well foreclosed possibility of serious criticism on the part of the Railway Labor Board."[82] Cummings relayed this correspondence to FDR to indicate the painstaking efforts being taken to mollify organized labor in the event of a Court defeat.[83] The exchange illustrates the defeatist mentality permeating Stephens's division. The Supreme Court heard oral argument on March 13–14, 1935,[84] with Stephens and Washington lawyer Harry Shulman representing the government. Stephens focused on the scope of the federal commerce power and the objectives sought by Congress in enacting the law. The written brief rested squarely on social and economic considerations as well as legal principles.

On May 6, 1935, in a five-to-four ruling, the Court invalidated the Railway Workers' Pension Act, with Chief Justice Hughes

[82] Stephens to Cummings, March 15, 1935, OF 10, Box 3, FDRL.
[83] Cummings to FDR, March 16, 1935, ibid.
[84] *Railroad Retirement Board v. Alton Railroad Co.,* 295 U.S. 330 (1935).

joining the minority. Justice Roberts summarized the majority opinion orally instead of reading it, because it was so long. He found the system of compulsory pensions both a violation of due process (taking property from *A* and bestowing it on *B*) and an exercise of power not authorized under the commerce clause. Pensions had nothing to do with promoting efficiency and safety on carriers in interstate commerce. The act itself was no proper form of regulation of the activity in interstate transportation, but an attempt—for social ends—to impose upon the relations between employer and employee "a means of assuring a particular class of employees against old age dependency."

In his approach to constitutional doctrine, Roberts was once characterized by Thomas Reed Powell as "sometimes here, sometimes there." In this ruling, he adopted a very narrow standard for Congress's commerce power, virtually limiting it to the transportation of goods in commerce. In view of his enlightened opinion in the milk license case *Nebbia v. New York* (1934), his defection from the liberals was unexpected, and it provided the narrow margin for the government's defeat.

Though it may have been unpalatable to liberals, his course should have come as no surprise to those familiar with his background in Philadelphia as a corporation lawyer. Throughout his years of practice, Roberts represented large corporations, including the Pennsylvania Railroad, but his colleagues insisted he was no "corporation lawyer" within the usual meaning of the term. He was, they said, temporarily employed by corporations, but "it was not a full-time job." The distinction seemed difficult for some to grasp, especially for critics of Justice Roberts's views and voting habits on the Court after 1934. Wags around this time gave Roberts the nickname "Penn," while Chief Justice Hughes was known as "Whiskers."

The ruling was a sweeping condemnation of the railway workers' pension plan. Key provisions of the Railroad Retirement Act, Roberts argued—such as combining individual railroads together in an industry-wide pension plan, extending eligibility to all employees with one year's service, compelling the collected funds to be deposited with the Treasury, and making the carriers insurers of employee contributions—all amounted to an arbitrary and unreasonable taking of employers' property in violation of due process. The Court not only held the pension plan provisions of the act in certain of its mechanical details arbitrary, unreasonable, and in violation of due process, but held the law invalid in all respects, asserting that it was beyond the power of Congress to pass *any* compulsory railway pension legislation. The whole subject of old-age pensions lay outside the federal commerce power. "The Act," Roberts declared categorically, "is not in purpose or effect any regulation of interstate commerce within the meaning of the Constitution."[85]

The minority justices who voted to uphold the law were not unanimous in their approval of the policy behind the measure. Justice Stone said privately that if he had been a member of Congress, he would have voted against it. The judgment of the Court, however, did not rest on the wisdom of the measure but on the scope of the federal commerce power.

The chief justice entered a vigorous dissent. He protested, he said, from great provocation and a deep sense of responsibility in rebutting the claims made by the majority. He began with an elaborate review of the jurisprudence relating to the commerce clause. It was within the power of Congress to enact this retirement statute. Hughes deplored the majority's denial of Congress's power to pass any form of compulsory pension act for railroad employees and accused them of going out of their way to prevent Congress from seeking to overcome their objections to the statute. The majority, by pronouncing the whole subject matter outside the scope of federal commerce power, argued Hughes, raised a barrier against all legislative action of this nature: "The conclusion thus reached is a departure from sound principles, and places a totally unwarranted limitation upon the commerce clause of the Constitution."[86]

Stephens, reporting to Cummings, complained that Roberts's majority opinion was couched in extreme terms and delivered in a manner which indicated that five justices thought the viewpoint of Congress as expressed in the statute, of the government as expressed in its argument, and of the minority as expressed in their dissenting opinion, was not only "beyond law, but beyond

[85] 295 U.S. 330, at 362.
[86] Ibid., at 374–75.

common sense." Hughes's dissent, he said, was clearly and cogently written. The consensus in the Justice Department was that it was one of the strongest the chief justice had ever written. Stephens concluded that, in view of this strong dissent, his department would be relieved of any possible criticism by labor to the effect that the case had not been properly presented. The dissenting opinion followed almost exactly "the pattern in the Government's brief and argument."[87]

The decision affected about a million railroad workers and was unpopular—except, of course, with railroad companies. Radio commentator Boake Carter asked: "One-man autocracy, or a nine man oligarchy. Which?" The president of one of the railroad brotherhoods called it "a bitter disappointment." Nor were its consequences limited to their effect on railroad workers. The extremely narrow construction of Congress's commerce power implied that it did not extend to certain matters related directly to transportation itself. In labeling any future pension law unconstitutional, it signaled forebodings of what the Court's attitude would be toward other federal statutes. If it took the same stand in disposing of cases testing social security legislation, which was then moving through congressional committees, the law would also be invalidated.

An editorial predicted that the Court would "smash any social security legislation that may be passed by Congress."[88] Senator Borah disagreed, joining those who argued that the *Alton* decision was not going to "put up any bars for the social security legislation." Administration lawyers agreed with him. In their opinion, the railway decision was no blanket injunction against all social legislation.[89]

At the administration's request, the Senate Finance Committee had heard testimony on the social security program prior to reporting the bill out. Angus MacLean tried to assure the committee that the railway pension decision would not have the effect of upsetting the social security program because the new bill was being framed on constitutional grounds different from those in the invalidated railroad pension law.

---

[87] Stephens to Cummings, May 6, 1935, RG 60, file 235460, NA.
[88] "5 to 4 Against," *Business Week,* May 11, 1935, 7–8.
[89] Undated press clipping, Box 85, Suydam Files, NA.

> Mr. Chairman and Senators, I think it must be reasonably clear by this time that there are two distinct schools of thought on the Supreme Court. They are evenly divided, 4 to 4, with one member not committed to any particular school of thought. The situation, if it is correct, imposes a considerable degree of caution on expressing an opinion about legislation of this kind.

Speaking for himself and the Justice Department, MacLean asserted that the opinion in the Railroad Retirement Act case was not decisive in its bearing on the social security legislation, and not directly authoritative, because the two dealt with entirely different constitutional questions.[90]

His view was challenged most conspicuously by Senator William King (D.-Utah), who found sections of the social security program flatly unconstitutional. Strong factions among Democrats were preparing to fight for important modifications in the program. The White House and Congress were in almost daily receipt of legal opinions measuring the chances of the social security legislation, with its old-age pension and unemployment insurance taxes, by the standards set in the Supreme Court's decision invalidating the Railroad Retirement Act. The day after the *Alton* decision, Cummings wrote the president:

> Attached hereto you will find certain memoranda with regard to the Railroad Retirement Board matter decided yesterday by the Supreme Court. The case was always a difficult one, but the form the opinions took would seem to indicate such a marked cleavage in the Supreme Court that it may be, and probably is a forecast of what we may expect with reference to any form of social legislation the Congress may enact. Apparently there are at least four justices who are against any attempt to acknowledge the power of the federal government for bettering general conditions, except within the narrowest limitations. This is a terrific handicap and brings up again matters we have previously discussed, including a proposed constitutional amendment. The very vigor of the language employed by the Chief Justice in the dissenting opinion is extraordinarily significant.[91]

---

[90] Senate Finance Committee, *Social Security Act, Confidential Hearings before the Committee on Finance, United States Senate,* 74th Cong., 1st sess., on H.R. 7260. Statement of Angus D. MacLean, Assistant Solicitor General, May 8, 1935, 31–32. Box 201, Cummings Papers, ALDL.

[91] Cummings to FDR, May 7, 1936, quoted in Swisher, ed., *Selected Papers,* 130.

Prodded into action by this reversal, the attorney general intensified efforts to explore possible counter-actions. The *Alton* decision raised the ominous prospect, if not the alarming likelihood, that Justice Roberts, by joining the four conservatives, would create a permanent majority on the Court. In his letter to FDR, Cummings conveyed the impression that he was pessimistic and more in agreement with the editorial views of *Business Week* than with lawyers in his own department, including Assistant Solicitor General MacLean.

For the first time since FDR took office, an opinion by the Supreme Court had the effect of antagonizing a powerful interest group, and one that could lobby for restrictions on the Court's power. The decision in the gold clause cases may have angered bondholders, but since most holders of government securities considered the Court a bulwark against social change, they were unlikely to support any movement to limit its powers.[92] Organized labor, however, was another matter. A gentleman from Wichita Falls, Texas, wrote Roosevelt: "I had an idea they would turn down that Railroad Pension. I told you the Rich Men always run to the Supreme Court to beat our laws. The Supreme Court is a PUBLIC NUISANCE."[93]

The administration proceeded to repair the damage by redrafting the railroad pension legislation in conformity with the Court's objections to the extent that was possible. A week after *Alton,* Senator Wagner introduced a bill (S. 2862) to promote safe and efficient service to the public in a national system of rail transportation by providing pensions and a retirement system for railroad employees. At the suggestion of Joseph Eastman, coordinator of federal transportation, another congressional resolution called for a comprehensive committee investigation of the issues in question; it was prepared to establish as a matter of fact, and not of law, that retirement legislation could promote the safety and efficiency of railroad transportation. A resolution was introduced asking the Supreme Court to grant a rehearing of *Alton,* but on June 4, 1935, it was decided that this would be

[92] William E. Leuchtenburg, "The Origins of Franklin Roosevelt's Court-Packing Plan," *Supreme Court Review* (1966): 355.

[93] May 17, 1935, RG 60, file 235460, Box 4197A, NA.

inadvisable. A Justice Department press release announced: "In view of the sweeping character of the [*Alton*] decision, it was determined that it would be unwise to attempt to secure new legislation at this session of Congress."[94]

Administration draftsmen went to work trying to salvage something out of the wreckage, and finally two complementary but separate statutes were drafted on a retirement system and the taxes to support it. Both became law in August 1935. Several preliminary test cases were brought to the trial courts but never went any higher. This legislation was superseded in 1937 by a comprehensive program of railroad workers' retirement benefits, approved by the labor lobby and all parties in the industry.[95]

Between January 7, 1935, and May 25, 1936, the Supreme Court voided more than a dozen New Deal laws. During that same period, approximately sixteen hundred injunctions against the execution of federal laws were issued by federal judges. This situation induced Al Smith to comment that the courts had begun to throw the New Deal's "Alphabet Soup" out the window, three letters at a time. Unfriendly critics of the Court called it "government by judiciary."

---

[94] Ibid.

[95] Swindler, *Court and Constitution,* 3:45.

3

Black Monday

> The NIRA was one of the less fortunate efforts of the Roosevelt administration to stimulate production and end the depression that had settled on the country . . . and lingered on through most of the 1930s.
>
> Francis Biddle, *In Brief Authority,* 22.

ROOSEVELT'S RELUCTANCE during his 1932 campaign to articulate the specifics of a plan to remedy the country's economic problems arose from the fact that, as yet, he had no plan. The dilemma in which New Dealers found themselves, for lack of any clear position on his part, was compounded by his commitment, announced in a Pittsburgh campaign speech, to balance the budget.[1] Sharp divisions within his circle of advisers, which steadily expanded into a much larger group, impeded efforts to forge a coherent economic program.

A full month elapsed during the "hundred days" with no word from the White House about the structure of its long-awaited economic recovery program. As the weeks slipped by, pressure from organized labor began to mount, culminating on April 16, 1933, with Senate passage of the Thirty Hour bill, introduced by Hugo Black (D.-Ala.). It would have barred from interstate commerce goods produced by any business whose employees worked more than six hours a day, five days a week. Labor Secretary Frances Perkins considered the bill unconstitutional, and so did some who voted for it. Roosevelt, put off by its rigidity, agreed with them, although he could hardly ignore the backing it had by lib-

[1] FDR gave respectful attention to counselors advising cutting federal expenditures. He had always believed in budget balancing, and the advice came from a wide spectrum of opinion within his party. William E. Leuchtenburg, *Franklin D. Roosevelt and the New Deal, 1932–1940* (New York: Harper and Row, 1963), 37.

eral and pro-labor groups in Congress. To his dismay, William Green, head of the American Federation of Labor (AFL), threatened a general strike if the bill were defeated in the House. Columnist Ernest K. Lindley opined: "It was revolution boiling up from the bottom."[2]

Roosevelt worked to fend off consideration of the Black bill in the House, where it remained stalled in the Rules Committee, while urging his advisers to get on with framing a recovery program. When the Black bill seemed to be gaining momentum, he began to focus more on the recovery problem, commissioning an exploratory group to lay the groundwork for a comprehensive program. A curious admixture of representatives from business, labor, and government collaborated in drafting the legislation. FDR convened a meeting at the White House of the leaders of the various groups on May 10, 1933.

These leaders were badly divided on ideology, aims, and the means of achieving the objectives in what was to become the National Industrial Recovery program. The main differences were between those who wanted a substantial public works program and advocates of government-imposed regulations with industrial codes. When someone spoke up to ask "Why not have both?" the president agreed. As the story goes, he instructed the leaders of the various factions to lock themselves in a room until they could reach an agreement.[3]

Under heavy pressure and prodded by an impatient president, the draftsmen faced a daunting task. Added to demands from organized labor, Progressives in Congress wanted strict federal regulatory controls of business and long-range planning. FDR had a keen personal interest in their point of view, for it appealed to what has been described as his progressive philosophy. His experience as president of a trade association in the 1920s had convinced him that self-regulation in industry did not work.[4] Op-

---

[2] Arthur Schlesinger, Jr., *The Coming of the New Deal, 1933–1935,* vol. 2 of *The Age of Roosevelt* (Boston: Houghton Mifflin, 1959), 95; Perkins, *Roosevelt,* 158.

[3] James MacGregor Burns, *Roosevelt: The Lion and the Fox* (New York: Harcourt, Brace, and World, 1956), 180.

[4] Bernard Sternscher, *Rexford Tugwell and the New Deal* (New Brunswick: Rutgers University Press, 1964), 309; Rexford G. Tugwell, *The Democratic Roosevelt: A Biography of Franklin D. Roosevelt* (Garden City, N.Y.: Double-

posing groups balked at including provisions for regimenting industry or objected to the failure to provide for currency inflation.

Progressives in Congress, including Senator Borah, insisted that the antitrust laws must not be suspended. The outcome, they feared, would be a "sell-out" to industry. Presidential advisers Bernard Baruch, Raymond Moley, Rexford Tugwell, and Adolf Berle, however, thought the time was ripe to end the experiment with antitrust laws and replace the goal of atomizing business with that of consolidating and controlling it. Baruch, Hugh Johnson, and FDR had experienced favorable results during World War I with the War Industries Board and wanted to adapt some of its features to a new program regulating industry in the "emergency."

The theories, goals, and methods of achieving those goals, coming from so many disparate sources, were contradictory. Roosevelt adopted a strategy designed to combine the proposals (however much they conflicted with one another), gain support for the measure from diverse groups, and offset the voting strength of dissidents, should they decide to combine against it. This would present grave difficulties and weaken operation of the recovery program. Differences worked out in the drafting process were usually at the expense of some faction such as the Progressives in Congress or the Brandeis-Frankfurter group, which was never comfortable with such features of the NIRA as the suspension of the antitrust laws.

Charles Wyzanski, the Labor Department's solicitor and one of the draftsmen, was committed to the Brandeis-Frankfurter ideology. He opposed suspending the antitrust laws and the sweeping regulations imposed on hundreds of businesses, large and small (more than five hundred codes were adopted in the first year). In his view, the NIRA crossed the line drawn in earlier Supreme Court decisions beyond which there could be no congressional interference in intrastate commerce. He considered the program, as finally drafted, so far beyond the bounds of constitutionality that it would be fatal to expose it to judicial scrutiny.[5]

---

day, 1957), 143; Daniel Fusfeld, *The Economic Thought of FDR and the Origins of the New Deal* (New York: Columbia University Press, 1956), 56–57.

[5] Irons, *New Deal Lawyers,* 23–24; Moley, *After Seven Years,* 187; Charles Wyzanski to Frankfurter, May 21, 1933, Box 150, and May 24, 1933, NRA file, Box 159, Frankfurter Papers, LC. See also his memo of May 30, 1933, ibid.

The outcome was a compromise between two divergent proposals seeking reform and recovery. One draft, in a concise two pages submitted by Hugh Johnson, provided for setting up industrial councils to write codes of fair competition subject to approval by the president. The codes were to be exempted from the antitrust laws, but monopolistic practices were supposedly still prohibited. A tough government licensing system for trade associations was to be set up with authority to regulate prices, production, and trade practices in an attempt to keep businessmen in line.

Another draft was prepared by Undersecretary of Commerce John Dickinson in collaboration with the group headed by Senator Robert Wagner (D.-N.Y.). After considerable lobbying by this team, their draft incorporated proposals to recognize trade associations, which would regulate production. Section 7a was inserted; it included vague provisions for standardized wages and hours of labor in the new codes, labor's right to collective bargaining, and elimination of child labor. A separate title of the bill authorized expenditures of more than $3 billion for a large-scale public works program.

The final legislation wove together threads from several proposals. Those most actively engaged in the drafting process included Donald Richberg, Rexford Tugwell, Hugh Johnson, Charles Wyzanski, Senator Robert Wagner, and John Dickinson. Felix Frankfurter later made clear that he had not been consulted and insisted he had nothing to do with drafting the legislation's form or administering its provisions.[6] Recovery, it was hoped, would result from the abolition of "unfair trade practices" and conformity by business and labor to code provisions, all under the benevolent eye of government. Representatives of big business, brought to Washington for the purpose, were to write their own codes and choose the personnel to administer them.

This legislation, attempting a sweeping control of the national economy under the commerce power and called the National Industrial Recovery Act, was sent to Congress on May 17, 1933, and was approved by the House within a week with only minor

[6] Frankfurter to Alfred Cohn, October 30, 1935, Box 97, Frankfurter Papers, LC.

changes. In the Senate the bill did not have such easy going. Debate centered on suspension of the antitrust laws. Progressives from both parties joined Senator Borah, who led the attack on the bill with warnings that it would confer on industry the power to control not only production but prices as well. Trade associations were poised to engage in price fixing even before the act became law. Senators scorned the testimony of Richberg before a House committee in which he baldly asserted that price fixing under the NIRA would be prohibited. Borah predicted that large industries would dominate the code-making process no matter what language the bill contained.[7] In Congress, the rush to adjourn for the summer recess swept all before it. In the Conference Committee, Borah's antimonopoly amendment was defeated by the narrow margin of forty-six to thirty-nine. On June 16, 1933, the NIRA, one of the twin pillars on which the New Deal rested its hopes for recovery, became the law of the land.

This gigantic attempt to create industrial self-government became law mainly because a great many congressmen had an almost blind faith in the president (one representative likened him to "Moses, leading his people out of the wilderness"). The idea behind the NIRA was based on a naive trust in the benevolence of business and its willingness to forego profits, even temporarily, to allow a rise in prices and wages. Roosevelt, who may once have believed that voluntary self-regulation in industry did not work, now signed on to the notion that this scheme could work in bad times and in an emergency would draw men together. Francis Biddle, a later attorney general, wrote: "That the Congress and the country should have accepted so queer an adventure in unity bore evidence of the magic of his [FDR's] wand. He had done so much already in so short a time that Americans were still 'breathless' with the accomplishments of the 'hundred days' and ready to accept new experiments."[8] Two journalists summed it up this way: "From the egg . . . produced by such a strangely collective group of parents [was] hatched the Blue Eagle. And the screeching of the . . . Eagle . . . set the tone for

[7] *Congressional Record,* 73rd Cong., 1st sess., 77, pt. 5:5239.
[8] Biddle, *In Brief Authority,* 22–23.

the first period of the New Deal," initiating a bitter conflict with the Supreme Court that dominated the second period.[9]

DOUBTERS AND DISSENTERS

The NIRA was subjected to withering criticism by Justice Brandeis both before and after its passage. On a visit to Hugh Johnson in May 1933, Brandeis told him that "NRA was bad." Johnson, himself a lawyer, already doubted whether the Supreme Court would sanction the law's edicts. Brandeis listed the reasons for his opposition: the impossibility of enforcement, the dangers presented to small industries and businesses, the inefficiency of large industrial units, and the potential for consolidation and monopoly in the absence of antitrust laws. He later reported that Johnson seemed "crushed" when these difficulties emerged within the agency for whose administration he was chiefly responsible.[10]

NRA administrators soon were experiencing "troubles galore." From Oxford, Frankfurter wrote Brandeis that it was going as badly as he had feared. That summer, they noted that reducing productivity and raising prices would prove ineffectual without a corresponding increase in purchasing power and, as Brandeis emphasized, regularity of employment. "Without all these," the justice said, "the New Deal is impossible." He charged that the NRA had a terrible record for putting people back to work. "The evidence," he wrote, "begins to indicate that the Künstücke [clever tricks], including both NRA and AAA are having the effect of retarding recovery."[11]

Brandeis was possibly the most influential of the NRA critics, and their number was legion. On April 22, 1934, he wrote his daughter: "I see little to be joyous about in the New Deal

[9] Joseph Alsop and Robert Kintner, *Men around the President* (Garden City, N.Y.: Doubleday, 1939), 36–37.

[10] Brandeis to Frankfurter, August 14, 1933, Box 28, Frankfurter Papers, LC.

[11] Brandeis to Frankfurter, July 25, 1933, February 21, 27, 1934, quoted in Nelson L. Dawson, *Brandeis, Frankfurter, and the New Deal* (Hamden, Conn.: Archon, 1980), 64–65.

measures. . . . NRA and AAA seem to be going from bad to worse." Both laws were likely to reach the Supreme Court. How many other justices, one wondered, agreed with him in opposing the corporatist philosophy behind these measures, and as jurists would they be capable of distinguishing what they liked from what they considered constitutional?[12]

Justice Brandeis never put forward any formal recovery proposal of his own (in his position, that would have been highly unethical). However, he let it be widely known that in addition to enforcement of the antitrust laws, he favored a heavy dose of confiscatory taxation and a substantial public works program. His position found no immediate favor at the White House; instead, it laid him open to charges of looking back to some bygone era of small proprietors and corner grocers and attempting to revive unworkable mechanisms. That approach, critics charged, characterized an older America where open competition and individualism reigned supreme.

Moley took full advantage of the weaknesses in the fragmented opposition, especially after Justice Brandeis's ringing dissent in an otherwise obscure Florida case in which the imposition of a tax on chain stores to right the balance with small retailers was overturned by the Supreme Court.[13] In a rebuke worthy of a Hebrew prophet, Brandeis flayed corporate monopolies as the "very negation of industrial democracy." By taxing chain stores to protect small retailers, Florida's legislature may have been merely trying to preserve competition, but its purpose could also have been a broader and deeper one. Legislators who wrote the law may have believed that chain stores, by furthering the concentration of wealth and power and promoting absentee ownership, were thwarting American ideals. After reading this passionate attack on corporate greed, Moley wrote Roosevelt of the need for government controls to stimulate and stabilize economic activity, a need that necessitated full rejection of the Wilson-Brandeis philosophy, which held that "if the U.S. could once more become a nation of small proprietors . . . and smithies under spreading

---

[12] Melvin Urofsky, *Louis D. Brandeis and the Progressive Tradition* (Boston: Little, Brown, 1981), 160–62.

[13] *Liggett Co. v. Lee,* 288 U.S. 517 (1933).

chestnut trees, we would be able to solve the problems of American life."[14]

Brandeis resented the Johnson-Moley ascendancy in determining New Deal policy and continued to heap scorn on the New Deal experiment. When opponents of the NRA, including small businessmen and consumers, clamored for a congressional investigation, agency officials were loath to give hostile members of Congress a platform from which to air their views on the recovery program. Instead, on March 7, 1934, Roosevelt appointed a National Recovery Review Board with labor attorney Clarence Darrow as counsel to investigate the effect the NRA was having on small business. The administration may have done better with a congressional investigation. The six-member board brought a predisposed hostility to their work. At the opening of the hearings, one of them announced that "if he had his way, he would blow the NRA out of the water." The majority of those who testified opposed the codes. In May and June, the board issued three scathing reports criticizing the NRA. In disgust, Brandeis wrote Frankfurter: "The NRA [Review Board] sessions have, I judge, satisfied no one, and the doubters have become more vocal." For more than a year, Brandeis repeatedly reminded Hugh Johnson that "frankly he was a'gin the Experiment." Borah was more blunt when he told him: "Hugh, your codes stink."[15]

In spite of warning signals from Wyzanski, Frankfurter, Brandeis, and others, the NRA went into effect as soon as a "blanket code" was promulgated. Jerome Frank, the AAA's general counsel, complained that Richberg, the NRA's legal counsel, never gave an opinion on anything. Frank said *he* had to do it. "Those NRA codes went through without ever having any lawyer say they were invalid under the statute. That was one reason for the debacle later."[16]

---

[14] Quoted in Irons, *New Deal Lawyers,* 21; Fusfeld, *Economic Thought of FDR,* 219–20.

[15] Tugwell, *Democratic Roosevelt,* 6; Brandeis to Frankfurter, October 30, 1933, February 27, March 18, September 19, 1934, quoted in Urofsky and Levy, eds., *"Half Brother, Half Son,"* 533, 554; Marian C. McKenna, *Borah* (Ann Arbor: University of Michigan Press, 1961), 309.

[16] Jerome Frank, Reminiscences, COHC, 29.

The rationale and constitutional basis for the NRA rested on the assumption that Congress could nationalize trade and labor practices under its power to regulate interstate commerce. In the past, the Supreme Court had sustained statutes resting on this prerogative, construing some of them broadly. There were positive commerce clause precedents that could be used to justify the regulations in codes, but there were also negative precedents that could serve to strike down the act. The Court could choose to go the negative route, in part because the statute provided for an unprecedented delegation of legislative authority to the executive. The administration's worst fears would then be realized. At the outset, however, doubts about the law's validity were set aside in favor of bold action.

Initial enthusiasm for the Blue Eagle was whipped into a frenzy in the campaign staged by Johnson, replete with parades and hoopla, but it quickly faded even before the end of 1933. That summer, compounding the problems impeding recovery, a wave of strikes hit the industrial sector and, once codes for large industries were promulgated, NRA lawyers were inundated with violations. They had to decide whether or not to replace reliance on voluntarism and public opinion with the more potent weapon of enforcement, involving litigation against violators. As Borah had predicted, small businesses were being done in by the giants. Labor and industry were in open conflict, and the cumbersome, complex, confused recovery machinery was creaking at the joints.

Neither Johnson nor Richberg had any enthusiasm for litigation as an enforcement mechanism, preferring persuasion and appeals to public opinion or patriotism, but when the volume of code violations began to mount dramatically they had to set up a Compliance Division separate from the Legal Division. By the end of 1933 it was swamped with a backlog of more than ten thousand complaints of code violations. NRA and Justice Department lawyers evaded prosecuting violations and risking a constitutional test in the courts. "One of the deepest weaknesses of the administration in Washington, ever since the Agricultural Act and the Recovery Act went into effect," noted a liberal journal, "has arisen from its fears that these laws, or parts of them, would be declared unconstitutional if allowed to be tested in the courts."[17]

Ickes prodded Johnson to take some action. "I pointed out to him," his diary relates, "that there would be more likelihood of getting a favorable opinion from the Court while public opinion for the codes was running high than after a cold sweat had begun to break out."[18] But Richberg and his aides showed no inclination to change course in those early months. Observing that previously contested laws had been swiftly subjected to a judicial test, in the spring of 1934 a correspondent asked Frankfurter: "Why can't we have a decision on the NRA?" Frankfurter's curt reply was: "Why are you so anxious for a decision until you are sure of getting the right one?"[19] Justice Stone also deplored the agitation for haste to get decisions in constitutional cases. It was more important, he said, for them to be decided correctly than in a hurry. But even Stone finally came to realize that the delays so carefully orchestrated by the administration were unusual and embarrassing. He wrote his sons: "The one NRA case that has come up has been postponed at the urgent request of the Government."[20]

Lingering doubts about constitutionality hanging over the NRA hampered enforcement. To handle noncompliance with the labor provisions of section 7a, on August 5, 1933, Roosevelt appointed members to the first National Labor Board (NLB), composed of representatives from industry and labor, with Senator Wagner as chairman. But when it came to enforcing decisions of the NLB, the Justice Department was slow to move. There was as yet no statute authorizing procedures. If, for example, a district court found for an employer, a reversal would be difficult to obtain since an appellate court would not ordinarily reverse a trial court on a finding of fact.

In a case handled by one of Cummings's assistants, Golden W. Bell, a ruling by the NLB was held "illegal, unconstitutional, invalid, even un-American." Most district judges at the time

[17] "Take the New Deal to Court," *New Republic,* November 15, 1933, 5.

[18] Ickes, *Secret Diary,* October 2, 1933, 1:101.

[19] Quoted in Alpheus T. Mason, *Harlan Fiske Stone: Pillar of the Law* (New York: Viking, 1956), 385–86.

[20] May 3, 1934, quoted in ibid.

were conservative and Republican. "They watched with skeptical and jaundiced eyes the vast jumble of executive orders issued under this New Deal law. They noted the thin and ambiguous declaration of principle in Section 7a and they were disinclined to enjoin employers whose acts they instinctively approved."[21] Moreover, the law itself was unclear, imprecise, and, as Brandeis asserted, unenforceable. Delays made enforcement officials timorous and violators contemptuous of the law. As the months dragged on, its opponents became more hopeful, interpreting vacillation as a sign of weakness.

After a series of reverses in district courts in Florida and Delaware, Cummings announced that all decisions adverse to the NRA would be appealed to the Supreme Court. A statement by a witness before the Senate's Interstate Commerce Committee that the law was "a failure and a flop" was sympathetically endorsed by four Democrats on the committee. By then it was obvious not only that section 7a was unenforceable but that the entire NRA might be toppled, either by Congress's allowing it to expire or through defeat in the courts.[22] Thomas Emerson, NRA's legal counsel in the retail field, summed up the frustrations of his and other agencies when he complained that Justice Department lawyers had done nothing except lose cases. The department, he said, was the most political branch of the administration, and its staff was filled with people who were more or less failures as lawyers or else ancient bureaucratic types.

> The Department of Justice was then at its lowest ebb of any time during the New Deal period in terms of the capacity of its personnel. Under Homer Cummings, it was a patronage agency. The lawyers, at least the ones we dealt with, were very limited in their abilities, highly political in their backgrounds, and hardly interested or capable of carrying on an effective enforcement program, particularly of Section 7 (a).

Justice Department lawyers had no particular interest in the New Deal, Emerson charged, and were completely out of sympathy with the NRA.[23] Francis Biddle testified somewhat later be-

---

[21] Biddle, *In Brief Authority,* 23.

[22] *New York Times,* March 1, 1935, 1; Irons, *New Deal Lawyers,* 228.

[23] Thomas I. Emerson, *Young Lawyer for the New Deal: An Insider's Memoir*

fore the Senate Labor Committee hearings on the Wagner Act and reminded members that in almost two years the Justice Department had brought suit in only two cases of the two dozen in which he had sought litigation on section 7a. "It is hardly necessary to labor the point that such delays as this amount to a complete nullification of the law."[24]

Meanwhile, the Justice Department was feeling strong pressure from local U.S. attorneys who did what they were expected to do—that is, prosecute code violators—but then felt abandoned when higher officials refused to appeal adverse decisions. One attorney announced publicly that he would take no more NRA cases to a grand jury until the Supreme Court ruled on the validity of the entire program. The sheer weight of cases and pressures for a definitive decision on the act's constitutionality was driving the program toward a Supreme Court challenge.[25]

A case with the potential of forcing such a test of the NRA codes was *U.S. v. Belcher,*[26] which challenged the lumber code. The defendant, William E. Belcher, owned several sawmills in the soft pine region of central Alabama. The lumber code, approved by FDR in the summer of 1933, established a minimum wage of twenty-four cents an hour and a forty-hour week. Belcher, who was in open defiance of these provisions, complained to the code authorities that compliance would force him to lay off three hundred to five hundred workers.[27] He was indicted in August 1934, charged with paying his employees seven cents an hour and working them up to forty-eight hours a week. The district court judge in the area, seventy-three-year-old William Grubb, had

---

of the Roosevelt Years (Savage, Md.: Rowman and Littlefield, 1991), 34–35. At that time, Emerson lived with Justice Cardozo's clerk, Ambrose Doskow, and heard constant reports from him that members of the Supreme Court were extremely dissatisfied with the government's arguments in the cases.

[24] Quoted in Irons, *New Deal Lawyers,* 228 and 324n6. U.S. Senate Labor Committee, *Hearings on the National Labor Relations Act,* 95–96, 74th Cong., 1st Sess. (1935). Biddle wanted the Senate to give the first NLB its own litigation powers. "The division of responsibility of relations with the Justice Department," he said, "creates chaos."

[25] *New York Times,* March 7, 1935.

[26] 294 U.S. 736 (1935).

[27] For the indictment, record of the *Belcher* case, and a chronology, see Box 159, folder 3181, Frankfurter Papers, LC.

been appointed to the bench in 1909 by President Taft and was known to be avowedly hostile to the NIRA. Aware of this, NRA lawyers asked their Justice Department counterparts to delay legal action against Belcher for several months.

Justice Department lawyers, however, were annoyed because NRA officials were the ones who initially made the unusual request to prosecute Belcher. U.S. attorneys had already begun preparing for grand jury proceedings and the trial to follow. Harold Stephens was at first more than willing to defer legal proceedings in the light of Judge Grubb's grave doubts about the constitutionality of the NIRA, but when it was no longer possible to delay action, the Justice Department and NRA lawyers again changed course. Anticipating a negative ruling by Judge Grubb, they prepared to invoke the Criminal Appeals Act of 1907, under which a direct appeal could be made to the Supreme Court of a district court order for a demurrer to a criminal indictment on a finding of the unconstitutionality of the statute involved.[28]

Government lawyers at the time were in the process of withdrawing the Smith case and taking the "hot oil" cases to the Supreme Court, while trying to persuade Belcher's lawyers to delay their client's motion to dismiss. Not until October 31, 1934, did Belcher's lawyers file their demurrer, alleging that the lumber code contained an unlawful delegation of legislative power and an unconstitutional attempt to regulate interstate commerce. They argued that the code's wages and hours provisions (which were not being contested) had no effect on interstate commerce and that due process had been denied to Belcher by imposing on him a code he had not signed. That same day, Judge Grubb sustained the demurrer and dismissed the indictment, declaring the NIRA unconstitutional on all three grounds raised by the defendant. Shortly thereafter, Belcher's counsel and U.S. attorney Jim Smith, on receiving permission from his superiors

[28] That same year, Chief Justice Hughes, with Justices Van Devanter and Brandeis, gave testimony against a bill introduced by Senator Hugo Black which provided for direct appeal to the Supreme Court from any decision by a district court, enjoining the enforcement of an act of Congress. U.S. Senate Committee on the Judiciary, *Hearings on S. 2176,* 74th Cong., 1st sess. (1935); Walter Murphy, *The Elements of Judicial Strategy* (Chicago: University of Chicago Press, 1964), 162.

in Washington, agreed to expedite an appeal to the Supreme Court, filed in early January 1935.[29]

But, with the stage set for a court test of the NIRA, Justice Department officials began questioning whether they wanted it *with this case.* Three days after the Supreme Court agreed to hear the *Belcher* case (January 4, 1935), it decided *Panama* and *Amazon.* NRA lawyers agonized over whether to allow this setback to be followed by another appeal and the risk of a second defeat. The press, meanwhile, hailed the *Belcher* appeal as a positive step, responding to a need to end the uncertainty over the NIRA's constitutionality. A *New York Times* editorialist rejoiced over the prospects for an end to suspicions that the administration was evading a clear-cut test of the NIRA.[30]

Only after doing everything in their power to scuttle it had Justice Department lawyers agreed to the appeal. Pressure to abandon the case began building soon after the appeal was filed. Oral argument was scheduled for April 8, 1935. At a cabinet meeting in early February, Cummings said that one of his concerns was the "state of the record," meaning the lack of a full trial record in the case, but he did not ask Roosevelt to intervene in the matter.[31] Frankfurter and Reed were adamantly opposed to taking the NIRA to the Supreme Court with a case like *Belcher,* which they said would be "madness." Doubting the law's constitutionality, they wanted to let it expire and be replaced by a modified program restoring competition in the economy.

Richberg, under extreme pressure from NRA lawyers, feared the complete collapse of code enforcement if he yielded to demands to withdraw the appeal, but Frankfurter ultimately prevailed in convincing Roosevelt to abandon it. On March 25, two weeks before oral argument was to begin, the Justice Department

---

[29] *New York Times,* November 1, 1934, 1, and January 5, 1935, 4. The appeal was granted on January 4, 1935, and *Belcher* went on the docket for an April hearing. *U.S. v. Belcher,* 294 U.S. 736 (1935).

[30] *New York Times,* January 7, 1935, 16. Richberg was concerned lest the high court, by taking notice of the economic conditions that had led to the NIRA's passage, would remand the case to the court below with instructions to take evidence. This would have been a partial but hollow victory for the government. Donald Richberg, *The Rainbow* (Garden City, N.Y.: Doubleday, Doran, 1936), 215.

[31] Secret Diary, February 8, 1935.

requested the dismissal of *Belcher,* owing to the absence of a full trial court record and the need to revise provisions of the lumber code.[32] The request was granted on April 4.

The dismissal came as a shock to Congress, the press, and the public. All were incensed over the decision except New Deal opponents, who rejoiced. They longed for repudiation of the entire NIRA and realized that dismissal of this case would immeasurably strengthen their position. NRA lawyers assigned to preparing the briefs and arguments were described as "heartbroken." The *New York Times* scorned the move and the "unconvincing reasons" announced for it. The dismissal left the NRA "at sea" and gave the impression that the government feared a test case. "The Roosevelt administration is now in the indefensible position of urging Congress to extend with slight modifications an act the constitutionality of which it is deliberately refusing to test."[33] The *Washington Post* reported that the administration was afraid to "face the music" and contended that dismissing the case was tacit acceptance of the lower court's opinion that the NIRA and its lumber code were unconstitutional. Code authorities saw no further point in trying to enforce the regulations, and within three days they discharged most of their employees.[34]

Congress reacted quickly. Senator Huey Long of Louisiana advised citizens to refuse compliance with NRA codes. Shortly after the dismissal, Senator Bennett Clark of Missouri, a Democrat but a bitter opponent of the New Deal, introduced a resolution asking the attorney general to reinstate the case. The motion was only narrowly defeated. Clearly, Congress considered the dismissal a serious tactical error. Withdrawal of *Belcher* was followed by a new wave of code violations. Industrialists in every field argued that if the administration could so easily sidestep a test of the codes' constitutionality, there was no reason why businesses large or small should be required to obey them. On the docket of the NRA's Compliance Division there was a reported backlog of about eighteen thousand cases of wages and

---

[32] *New York Times,* March 27, 1935, 1; April 5, 1935, 2; Justice Department press release, March 25, 1935, RG 9, Box 10, NA.

[33] *New York Times,* March 28, 1935, 20, and April 2, 1935, 20.

[34] Quoted in ibid., March 30, 1935, 1.

hours violations and another four thousand cases of unfair trade practices, all awaiting action. The enforcement office made it known that unless there was a test of the law's constitutionality, its work would be futile.[35]

Richberg, who succeeded Hugh Johnson after FDR eased him out as the NRA's administrator, now faced two unattractive alternatives: accepting an immediate court test, no matter what the circumstances, or seeing the agency collapse under its own weight. He was soon rescued from this tactical dilemma. On April 1, 1935, another case decided by the Court of Appeals for the Second Circuit in New York was destined to become the first and final Supreme Court test of the NIRA.

Never had Roosevelt been so squeezed between conflicting political forces as in the spring of 1935. Spokesmen for the U.S. Chamber of Commerce were sharply attacking his administration, while Progressives were urging him to assert bold leadership. Brandeis sent word through Frankfurter that it was "the eleventh hour." FDR, in a rare display of humility, promised that in the future he would take a firmer stand, but now, under pressure from both left and right, he appeared confused and uncertain. He pinned his hopes on Congress's willingness to give the NRA another two years of life before it expired on June 16, 1935, assuring reporters that the agency was "no little Orphan Annie, but a very lively young lady."[36]

On February 20, 1935, despite all indications of the program's failure to achieve its goals, FDR formally asked Congress to renew it for another two years. The request met stubborn opposition in both houses. When the Senate Finance Committee opened hearings on the extension, the air was so full of contention that any clear indication of what was happening was lost in the confusion.[37] Eventually Congress voted to extend the NRA in a much-modified form but for less than ten months, to April 1, 1936.

[35] Drew Pearson and Robert S. Allen, *The Nine Old Men* (Garden City, N.Y.: Doubleday, Doran, 1936), 268.

[36] Burns, *Roosevelt,* 222–23.

[37] On FDR's renewal request, see his Message to Congress, *Congressional Record,* 74th Cong., 1st Sess. (1935), Vol. 79, Part 4:2265–66, 2302–3; for the quote, see *Commonweal,* March 22, 1935, 596.

Price fixing was removed from its mandate, and industries engaged solely in intrastate commerce were exempted from its provisions. The resolution passed the Senate by a voice vote on May 14, 1935, and went to the House. It was still before the House Ways and Means Committee when the decision of the Supreme Court was handed down in the NRA test case.[38]

The penultimate case, *A.L.A. Schechter Poultry Co. et al. v. U.S.* involved the live poultry code FDR signed into law on April 18, 1934. The code established a minimum wage of fifty cents an hour and a forty-hour week in the live poultry industry. All operations covered by the code were required to maintain accurate records of sales, prices, wages, hours, and so forth. Once approved, the code, like all the others, had the full force of law and violators were subject to both civil and criminal prosecution.

Walter L. Rice, a Justice Department lawyer, knew all about the live poultry business in New York City, having argued a celebrated case against racketeering in the industry brought in Brooklyn's federal district court.[39] He later won a conviction of the Schechter brothers on nineteen counts in an indictment for violations of the code, after the defense attorneys' objections to the NIRA were overruled.[40] In the Court of Appeals for the Second Circuit, a three-judge panel sustained their conviction on seventeen of the nineteen counts. They were charged, among other things, with conspiracy to sell poultry "unfit for human consumption" (hence the "sick chicken" case), violating the code's "straight killing" provisions (to prevent favoritism, birds could not be selected preferentially from a coop prior to slaughter), selling uninspected poultry, and concealing such actions from code authorities. These were the first felony convictions under the NIRA.[41]

Judge Martin Manton of the U.S. Court of Appeals ruled that the NRA codes did not include an unconstitutional delegation of legislative power. The Schechters' trade practices were linked to

---

[38] *Congressional Record,* 74th Cong., 1st Sess. (1935), Vol. 79, Part 5:6688, 7483, 7739.

[39] The case was *Local 167, International Brotherhood of Teamsters v. U.S.,* 291 U.S. 293 (1934)

[40] *United States v. Schechter,* 8 F. Supp. 136 (1934).

[41] *United States v. Schechter,* 76 F.2d 617 (1935).

public health and were within federal regulatory power under the commerce clause. The Schechters had been convicted in district court on two counts for violating the wages and hours provisions of the code, but the appeals court reversed on these, ruling that such actions had no direct or indirect effect on interstate commerce and were beyond the reach of Congress. In his concurring opinion, Judge Learned Hand ruled that the NRA code provisions regulating hours and wages crossed the boundary separating interstate from intrastate commerce, a separation essential to preserving a viable federalism. The Schechters' slaughtering and processing operations, he said, were part of general domestic activities within the state and were therefore "as immune as they from congressional regulation." The government was upheld on the other seventeen counts.

This case had been pending since November, and neither the press, the Justice Department, nor the NRA had anticipated such a decision, which left the Schechters and the government winners, but on separate issues. Both parties could appeal to the Supreme Court. The Schechters were ready to take this final chance for acquittal. Government lawyers again found themselves in a tactical bind, since they would appear in a bad light if only the poultry company petitioned to appeal. The Don Richberg–Blackwell Smith faction in the NRA's legal offices favored launching an appeal as soon as possible, while the Frankfurter-led group, now acting through presidential aide Tom Corcoran, was reluctant to use this case to test the NIRA and favored delay. Compounding these problems, the president, to whom all looked for a decision, was off on a Caribbean cruise and could be reached only by Navy Department radiogram.

Frankfurter and others believed there would be no chance of securing approval of the NIRA until it went back to Congress for extensive revisions. With small businessmen in open rebellion and Congress in a surly mood, Frankfurter predicted that an immediate court test would prove disastrous.[42] Government lawyers were also unhappy with *Schechter* as a test case. The Justice Department would have to bring a criminal suit against Joe Schechter and his brothers, whose kosher poultry operation was

[42] Pearson and Allen, *Nine Old Men,* 268.

so modest that it made government claims of regulation in the interest of the national economy appear ridiculous. If the convictions were upheld in the Supreme Court, Joe Schechter would serve a three-month jail sentence. To send him and three other lowly Jewish poultry dealers to prison for violations of a system ignored by big business magnates was not a welcome prospect and was bound to grate on humanitarian sensibilities. New Deal legalists should have realized that. Trade practices outlawed by the code—relating to the sale of diseased chickens, selecting birds from the coop, and the like—were hardly calculated to electrify any court to the need for federal regulations.[43]

There followed a brief interval of internal fighting, a battle of wills the likes of which had not been seen before among New Dealers. Richberg fired the opening salvo on April 3, presenting his position and that of the NRA in a radiogram to the president:

> Public opinion on dismissal of Belcher case very unfavorable throughout the U.S. Result enforcement of codes generally impossible and hostility of Congress to new legislation. . . . This week federal Circuit Court of Appeals in New York has sustained indictment under another code and defendant asking Department of Justice to cooperate in bringing this immediately to Supreme Court. Prompt action will reverse general retreat and strengthen entire situation. Apparently Department acting on supposed policy not to expedite cases unless otherwise directed by the President. If you telegraph Department your desire to have earliest possible presentation of a good case to Supreme Court result will be in my opinion of extraordinary help in sustaining NRA and advancing legislation. Otherwise, present discouragement will probably destroy industrial program.[44]

Cummings was unwilling to reach a decision without FDR's express approval. Why put himself in jeopardy by making the fateful choice? Roosevelt's response to Richberg's appeal was casual. He scrawled across the cablegram: "Tell Richberg [to] talk with Cummings about expediting NRA case."[45] The following day, Frankfurter enlisted Corcoran in a frantic attempt to

[43] Ibid., 269.
[44] Radiogram to FDR, "Memoranda," Box 45, Donald Richberg Papers, LC.
[45] Ibid.

head off the appeal, despite the bad press that would result. Corcoran wired the president their counter-argument:

> F.F. called. Has learned very confidentially Cummings under urging of Richberg to silence criticism of Belcher dismissal and pursuant to wire from you intends announcing to press this afternoon that government will immediately expedite to Supreme Court a new NRA case . . . involving poultry code. F.F. suggests most impolitic and dangerous to yield to press clamor now because fundamental situation on court not changed. Further suggests you wire Cummings not to take hasty action and hold whole situation on NRA appeals in abeyance until you return.[46]

Roosevelt said he was returning the following week and suggested "we talk about NRA appeal cases first unless appeal date interferes."[47] The final date for the government to act was April 11, a week away and prior to the president's scheduled return.

Frankfurter had triumphed over his rivals in previous "palace intrigues," but he failed in this case. Events moved too swiftly and radiograms too slowly. On April 4 the attorney general announced to the press that the government would appeal the *Schechter* case to the Supreme Court. For the government, there were no good choices. Cummings was too canny a politician to ignore the firestorm raised by dismissal of the lumber case, realizing it was harming his department's and the government's credibility. Reed made a final effort to ward off the inevitable. On April 10 he requested instructions from Roosevelt as to a course of action, reminding him on April 11 how hard it would be in a case involving New York poultry dealers to show that their wages and hours affected interstate commerce. "This is the most difficult type of labor provision to maintain," he wrote, but the die was cast. That same day he filed the appeal, the Schechters having filed theirs three days earlier. On April 15 the Supreme Court granted *certiorari,* and oral argument was set for May 2. Blackwell Smith, the NRA staff, and Richberg had won their battle in spite of the formidable opposition from Frank-

[46] Corcoran to FDR, April 4, 1935, OF 466, Box 11, FDRL.

[47] Radiogram, FDR to Cummings, copies to Steve Early and T. Corcoran, April 4, 1935, OF 10, FDRL.

furter, Corcoran, and Reed, but the tactical victory saddled them with what Smith described as "the weakest possible case."[48]

Frankfurter was blamed for giving Roosevelt bad advice on the matter. "If . . . Frankfurter's protégés are to be believed," wrote Arthur Krock, "his was the delaying influence. Congress was supposed meanwhile to reconstitute NRA in modified form, thus strengthening its show of will for Supreme Court consideration." But, abandoning *Belcher,* he said, had had such a disastrous effect on the NRA and so encouraged its enemies in Congress that the *Schechter* case, "which had progressed normally through the lower courts and was not highly thought of as a test was quickly taken up, and now became a *cause celebre.*"[49]

The NIRA in Court

Stanley Reed had been solicitor general for only two months when he took on the government's argument in *Schechter.* He had had previous experience arguing before the Supreme Court, but May 27 marked his debut in his new capacity. He was joined by Richberg, who had by then ceded his role as NRA general counsel to Blackwell Smith in order to replace Hugh Johnson as NRA administrator. Richberg wanted to participate in the case, citing his familiarity with the intricacies of the code program. He feared Reed would be unable to represent the NRA before the Court, as he put it, "with the same accuracy and conviction as I might give."[50] Ultimately, it was Richberg's reputation that would suffer if they lost, not Reed's. Two years later, Arthur Krock expressed amazement that "as good a lawyer as Donald Richberg could ever have been willing to stake his legal reputation on the assumption that the government would win so narrow a test."[51]

A weak element in the government's case was the commerce issue. The Schechters' poultry came mainly from out of state, but no one could figure out how it could be proved that their

[48] Irons, *New Deal Lawyers,* 85.
[49] *New York Times,* April 16, 1935, 20.
[50] Donald Richberg, Recollections, COHC.
[51] "In Washington," *New York Times,* May 29, 1937, 24.

activity placed a burden on interstate commerce since their processing operation was entirely local. It would be virtually impossible to convince any court that their practices substantially affected interstate commerce. There was also the appellate court reversal on the wages and hours issue, another factor weakening the government's case, for this matter too was intrastate.

During oral argument on May 2 and 3, Reed spent most of his allotted time answering questions from the bench. More than once he was caught off guard, and according to reports he was "none too much at ease." A disappointed Blackwell Smith had previously urged him to strengthen the link between poultry processing and the "stream of commerce" doctrine, but he failed to do so. He also gave inadequate attention to the delegation issue, as Frankfurter had urged. A few days later, Reed sent Frankfurter a report of his performance:

> You were thoughtful to drop me a line about the Schechter brief. Unfortunately, you were quite correct in your anticipation that delegation was the "hot spot" of the argument. We had felt that Local 167 might bring Justice Butler to our viewpoint on interstate commerce, the unity of its flow, and the possibility of regulating both that commerce and its incidents, even including wages and hours.

"Local 167" refers to a case decided by the Supreme Court a year earlier—*Local 167, International Brotherhood of Teamsters v. United States*[52]—in which Walter Rice had secured the conviction of "Toots" Herbert and Joe Weiner, finding their racketeering in Brooklyn's live poultry industry in restraint of interstate commerce. Reed continued:

> Justices Sutherland, McReynolds and Butler made my life miserable by demanding to have pointed out to them the lines of the Act which laid down the definite standards for Presidential action. After what might be called a desultory bombardment on that question, in the last moments Justice Butler shifted to a barrage on Presidential findings. He wanted to know what facts the President or his delegated officers had found and how they had determined the necessity for wage and hour limitation. The argument did not close in any victorious paean, and one can only hope that the brief

[52] 291 U.S. 293 (1934).

> and an examination of the Act will persuade the Court that we are within the limits of the possibility of delegated authority.[53]

Richberg devoted more of his allotted time to the history of the NRA than to addressing the legal issues in defendants' arguments. Neither counselor distinguished himself in advocacy before the Supreme Court, but the outcome of the case would not hinge on their performance. After the Court exhausted the time allotted for questions, the justices went into conference not only to decide the fate of the NRA but to finalize the opinions in other cases in that spring term which was swiftly running its course.

May 27, 1935—"Black Monday"—was a decision day of enormous significance in American constitutional history. Three opinions delivered that day by a unanimous Court were intended to restore some balance in government procedure and set it along more orderly and constructive lines. The chief justice arranged the delivery of the cases with an eye toward achieving the maximum dramatic effect. They were read *seriatim* in order of ascending importance. There had been doubts as to the advisability of dealing three such "jolts" to FDR all at once, but Justice Brandeis, considered by some to be an unofficial representative of the New Deal on the Court, said he saw no reason to postpone any decisions "on that account" and urged that the proceedings be carried through.[54] Without ceremony, Justice Butler opened the session, reading the opinion for the Court in a case involving the New York Life Insurance Company.

It was followed by Justice Sutherland's opinion in *Humphrey's Executor v. U.S.*[55] When Reed took office, the attorney general called him in and suggested that he choose a "certain victory" for the first case he would argue before the Supreme Court. Reed looked over the list of pending litigation and selected what he considered a sure winner: Humphrey's case.[56] It went up to the Supreme Court from the U.S. Court of Claims, which did not rule on it but posed several questions for the high court.

---

[53] Reed to Frankfurter, May 7, 1935, PSF 150, FDRL.

[54] Merlo J. Pusey, *Charles Evans Hughes,* 2 vols. (New York: Macmillan, 1951), 2:742.

[55] 295 U.S. 602 (1935).

[56] Wesley McCune, *The Nine Young Men* (New York: Harper's, 1947), 61.

William E. Humphrey had been appointed to the Federal Trade Commission (FTC) in 1925, reappointed in 1931 for another six-year term, and confirmed by the Senate. The FTC Act specified that the president could remove commissioners from office for "inefficiency, neglect of duty or malfeasance in office." Humphrey held views at variance with New Deal policies, and on July 25, 1933, FDR asked for his resignation, explaining that the aims and purposes of the administration with respect to the work of the commission could be carried out most effectively with personnel of his own selection. The following month, he wrote Humphrey: "I do not feel that your mind and my mind go along together on either the policies or the administering of the Federal Trade Commission."[57] When Humphrey refused to resign, he was fired "for policy reasons" not specified in the act.

Sutherland's opinion described the FTC as charged with the enforcement of "no policy except the policy of the law." Its duties were "neither political nor executive, but quasi-judicial and quasi-legislative." Sutherland then replied to the questions posed by the U.S. Court of Claims. Did the FTC Act limit the president's removal power to the causes prescribed in it? And if so, was the limitation on the president's removal power constitutional? This was the crucial issue, and the ruling stated flatly that Roosevelt had not removed Humphrey for cause, as specified in the act. Instead of charging Humphrey with some breach of its terms, he had indiscreetly written him that "their minds did not go along together." Sutherland emphasized the distinction between positions in traditional executive departments for which the president has primary responsibility and those in independent regulatory agencies established by Congress to carry out legislative and/or judicial policy. The function of the agency, he said, is determinative.[58]

---

[57] August 31, 1933, Box 1, William E. Humphrey Papers, LC.

[58] 295 U.S. 602, at 618–19, 620, 627–28 (1935); Mason and Beaney, *Supreme Court,* 60–61; Louis Fisher, *Constitutional Conflicts between Congress and the President* (Princeton: Princeton University Press, 1985), 78–79. The bitterness of the conflict was reflected in letters Humphrey wrote to Roosevelt, quoted in William E. Leuchtenburg, "The Case of the Contentious Commissioner: Humphrey's Executor v. U.S.," in *Freedom and Reform: Essays in Honor of Henry Steele Commager,* eds. Harold M. Hyman and Leonard W. Levy (New York: Harper and Row, 1967), 287–98; for the letter of August 31, see 287. The essay treats the historical background and issues raised in the case.

An outraged Roosevelt took the decision as a personal affront, a gratuitous slap in the face by a court deliberately assailing what he considered his executive prerogative. He had relied on the earlier *Myers* case[59] in removing Humphrey and expected the Court to follow the precedent it established in upholding President Wilson's dismissal of a postmaster without the Senate's advice and consent. Roosevelt did not ask Cummings for a legal opinion, and he raised no objection. FDR instead consulted Raymond B. Stevens, who had helped draft the FTC Act in 1914, and Stevens advised that on the basis of the *Myers* opinion, he could remove Humphrey for whatever reason he wished. FDR failed to accept the distinction Sutherland drew between the executive duties of a postmaster and those of a federal trade commissioner. "The Federal Trade Commission," Sutherland argued, "cannot in any proper sense be characterized as an arm or an eye of the executive."

This decision, probably more than any other, increased Roosevelt's animosity toward the Supreme Court. The unanimity of the ruling rankled. Robert Jackson later wrote: "The opinion of the unanimous Court . . . gave the impression that the President had flouted the Constitution, rather than that the Court had simply changed its mind within the past ten years."[60] But the justices had not changed. In *Myers,* Justice Brandeis entered a dissent that ran to fifty-six pages, declaring that an unrestricted power of removal "involved an unnecessary and indefensible limitation upon . . . the power of Congress." The principle of separation of powers, he pointed out, had been adopted "not to promote efficiency, but to preclude the exercise of arbitrary power. The purpose was, not to avoid friction, but, by means of the inevitable friction incident to the distribution of the governmental power among three departments, to save the people from autocracy."[61]

At the time, the *Humphrey* ruling was considered academic

[59] *Myers v. United States,* 272 U.S. 52 (1926), in which the Court sustained by a vote of six to three the removal power of the president in a case involving a postmaster. Justice Sutherland had voted with the majority, supporting its *obiter dicta* that the removal power extended even to the members of the independent regulatory commissions.

[60] "*Humphrey's Executor v. United States,*" in Levy et al., eds., *Encyclopedia of the American Constitution,* 1:940.

[61] 272 U.S. 52 (1926), 240–95, Brandeis, J. dissenting, at 293–95.

because the "contentious commissioner" was dead. The Court ordered his back pay to go to his estate. The decision was overshadowed by the other cases decided the same day, and consequently few commentators accorded it the attention it merited. *Humphrey* raised important questions about the powers of the executive and the separation of powers. Not long after the 1930s, constitutional scholars and politicians recognized the importance and correctness of the *Humphrey* ruling, which had major implications for the exercise of executive power and reached well beyond FDR's hubris.

When he later became justice, Robert Jackson had difficulty placing the regulatory agencies in their proper locus within the three branches of government. "The mere retreat to the qualifying 'quasi,'" he wrote, "is implicit with confession that all recognized classifications have broken down and 'quasi' is a smooth cover which we draw over our confusion, as we might a counterpane to conceal a disordered bed."[62] An example of the influence of *Humphrey* occurred in 1958 when President Eisenhower was prevented from removing a Truman appointee to the War Claims Commission (WCC) for political reasons similar to those in Humphrey's ouster by Roosevelt. Eisenhower dismissed the official on the premise that the act needed to be administered with personnel of his own selection.

Congress created the commission, anticipating that it would be a short-lived agency, and made no provision for removal. The initial suit brought by the plaintiff was dismissed in the U.S. Court of Claims, but on appeal a unanimous Supreme Court reversed, ruling that the president had no power under the Constitution or statute to remove a member of the WCC. Congress's intention in establishing the commission was to ensure the freedom of its members from such presidential control. Its work had an intrinsic judicial character. Congress had explicitly rejected placing the dismissal power with the executive and could not have wanted to hang over the head of the commission "the Damocles sword of removal" for no other reason than that a presi-

---

[62] *Federal Trade Commission v. Ruberoid Co.,* 343 U.S. 470, at 487–88 (1952).

dent wanted his own man. The WCC went out of existence before the Senate could act to confirm another Eisenhower nominee.[63]

Justice Brandeis read the opinion in *Louisville Joint Stock Land Bank v. Radford,*[64] which voided the Frazier-Lemke Farm Mortgage Act of June 1934. The act permitted farmers to reacquire on reasonable terms farms lost through foreclosure proceedings, or to get suspension of such proceedings, and was designed to enable the nation's debt-ridden farmers to scale down their mortgages. The federal government was empowered to buy up farm mortgages and issue non-interest-bearing treasury notes in exchange. Farmers could avoid foreclosures by paying a reasonable rental, thus retaining their farms. Without a dissenting vote, the Supreme Court voided this measure, one of the most broadly worded laws ever put on the statute books for relief of debtors. Justice Brandeis held it in violation of the Fifth Amendment's due process guarantee of just compensation, a fundamental right of mortgage holders.

Reaction to this decision was overshadowed to some extent by the other rulings that day, but for debt-ridden farmers it had far-reaching significance. Their immediate response was to blame the Supreme Court. The act was one of the laws rammed through Congress in 1934 under threat of a filibuster, on the eve of adjournment. "Emergency" was the watchword, and lawmakers gambled on the prospect that the Supreme Court would not presume to invalidate the statute. The situation evoked the old adage: "Legislate in haste; repent at your leisure." When a revised Farm Mortgage Act was subsequently drawn up with more thought given to the constitutional issues involved, it was sustained by a unanimous Court. This case history offers compelling evidence that the Supreme Court was doing its duty, while Congress was not.

FDR never indicated any displeasure at the decision overturning the first Farm Mortgage Act. Administration spokesmen tried to emphasize that strictly speaking it was not a New Deal mea-

---

[63] *Weiner v. U.S.,* 357 U.S. 349, 78 S.Ct. 1275 (1958); cf. Mason and Beaney, *Supreme Court,* 60–61, Fisher, *Constitutional Conflicts,* 81.

[64] 295 U.S. 555 (1935).

sure, although it passed with heavy Democratic majorities and was signed into law by Roosevelt. Detaching it from the New Deal program allowed them to claim that they sustained only two, not three major defeats from a unanimous Court on May 27, 1935.[65] But the results were no less devastating.

The case everyone in the crowded courtroom had been anxiously awaiting was heard last. All eyes were riveted on the chief justice as he began reading the *Schechter* opinion at the climactic moment of that memorable Monday. As he read on, his voice grew more animated, stronger, and more reassuring about what he was saying. Hughes would have been less than human if he had not savored this dramatic moment from the center chair in history's spotlight.

A unanimous Court invalidated the entire NIRA on the ground that Congress exceeded its power under the commerce clause and had illegally delegated authority that lay outside its reach to the executive. Hughes declared section 3 of the NIRA, which outlined the code-making procedure, unconstitutional. He dismissed the government's contention that the statute should be viewed in the light of the "emergency." This part of the ruling cut like a knife through the administration's pretense of the "emergency." In his column "The Magic Is Over," William Allen White wrote: "Now the Supreme Court has declared in effect that Franklin Roosevelt is not a Messiah, that he must be circumscribed by the constitutional limitations of the presidency. . . . He can no longer hide behind emergency legislation."[66]

Hughes's opinion gave a broad definition to local activity, compared to his narrow definition of interstate commerce. Congress could regulate local activities only if they had a "direct" effect on interstate commerce. The undisputed facts, he said, "afford no warrant for the argument that the poultry handled by the defendants at their slaughterhouse markets was in a 'current' or 'flow' of interstate commerce."[67] He drew a distinction between "direct" and "indirect" effects on interstate commerce. In the

[65] *Washington Post,* May 28, 1935, 8.
[66] *Kansas City Times,* May 30, 1935, copy in PPF 1820, Box 10, FDRL.
[67] 295 U.S. 495, at 543.

Schechters' poultry operation, he concluded, the effect was "indirect," meaning that there was nothing the government could do about it. He found the entire NIRA an illegal regulation of intrastate commerce.

On the NIRA's labor provisions, Hughes summarized the ruling in these words: "It is not the province of the Court to consider the economic advantages or disadvantages of such a centralized system. It is sufficient to say that the Federal Constitution does not provide for it. . . . We are of the opinion that the attempt through the provisions of the code to fix the hours and wages of employees of the defendants in their intrastate business was not a valid exercise of federal power."[68]

The *Schechter* decision was meant to serve as a warning that the era of administrative lawmaking under loosely worded legislative grants of power and efforts to invade intrastate commerce, a field reserved to the states, was over. An editorialist called it an attempt to put a stop to the obliteration of state lines and the erection of a "federal despotism."[69]

In a concurring opinion, signed by Justice Stone, Justice Cardozo distinguished the "hot oil" cases, in which he had written the lone dissent, from *Schechter,* asserting that the legislative power delegated in the NIRA's section 9c had been precisely defined, whereas the delegated legislative power that found expression in the live poultry code was "not canalized within banks that kept it from overflowing. It is confused and vagrant." The appalling number of codes, regulating hundreds of businesses, each to be enforced through the courts, was "out of control."[70] "The extension becomes as wide as the field of industrial regulation. If that conception shall prevail, anything that Congress may do within the limits of the commerce clause for the betterment of business may be done by the President upon the recommendation of a trade association, by calling it a code. This is delegation run riot. No such plenitude of power is susceptible of transfer. . . . Nothing less is aimed at by the code now submitted to our scrutiny."[71]

---

[68] Ibid., at 550.

[69] *Washington Post,* May 28, 1935, 8.

[70] 295 U.S., at 551–53.

[71] Ibid. In approving Cardozo's dissent, Justice Brandeis noted on his copy, "This is clear and strong—and marches to the inevitable doom." Pusey, *Hughes,* 2:741.

The common-law maxim *delegata potestas non potest delegari* (power once delegated and vested in one agency—for example, Congress—cannot be delegated further) is frequently cited in constitutional law as a limitation on the legislature. One of the basic points of attack by the Supreme Court on the New Deal's emergency legislation was its unqualified vesting of power in executive departments or administrative agencies to draft and apply regulations that had the force of law.[72] The legislature, it was insisted, must set standards and guidelines for executive and administrative action, although this would not of itself validate the delegation of power if the subject of the legislation were constitutionally invalid.[73] In an age of rigidly circumscribed areas of legislative action, the Court consistently held that the power to act on certain subjects could not be delegated because Congress itself had not been given the power to act on these subjects. Well after 1937, when the Court began to define congressional competence in increasingly broader terms, the former standards by which legislative power could be delegated were also broadened.[74]

These rulings were the severest blow so far struck at the New Deal. Roosevelt's reaction mirrored the shock and disbelief within the administration. The decision of the Court in all three cases left him bewildered. He was visibly upset to find the liberal wing of the Court lined up so solidly against his program. When the news of the rulings reached him at the White House, he asked: "Well, what about old Isaiah? And where was Ben Cardozo?" "With the majority," replied one of his advisers.

How Roosevelt could have expected to get "Old Isaiah's" vote in *Schechter* is puzzling. Throughout 1933 and 1934, Brandeis and his followers had made clear to everyone, including the president, that they were opposed to "bigness," supported vigorous antitrust legislation, and decried the centralization of business

---

[72] Not only was this true of the "hot oil" and *Schechter* cases but was implicit in *Opp Cotton Mills v. Administrator,* 312 U.S. 126 (1941).

[73] As examples, authorities cite *United States v. Butler,* 297 U.S. 1 (1936), and *United States v. Rock Royal Corporation,* 307 U.S. 533 (1939).

[74] Swindler, *Court and Constitution,* 3:67–68. Representative of this transition are *Currin v. Wallace,* 306 U.S. 1 (1939), and *Bowles v. Willingham,* 321 U.S. 503 (1944), both cited in Swindler.

and government. Justice Brandeis compounded Roosevelt's dismay by stating publicly, "May 27th was the most important day in the history of the Supreme Court and the most beneficent," because the decisions the Court reached that day compelled a return to "human limitations."[75]

Nor was that all. Through Corcoran and Cohen, who came to the robing room after opinion reading ended that Monday, the seventy-eight-year-old Brandeis, visibly agitated, sent this oral message: "This is the end of this business of centralization, and I want you to go back and tell the President that we're not going to let this government centralize everything. It's come to an end." Gasping for breath, he said: "The President has been living in a fool's paradise." The three decisions just handed down by a unanimous Court, he added, meant that everything the administration had been doing must be changed. Redrafting of existing and pending legislation would be necessary. Brandeis wanted the message relayed to New Deal lawyers: "As for your young men, you call them together and tell them to get out of Washington—tell them to go home, back to the states. That is where they must do their work."[76]

The unanimity of the Court was as distressing to FDR as the character of the three opinions. Both wings of the Court joined in convicting Congress and the president of unconstitutional acts. Their verdict was that Congress had overstepped its authority in the Farm Mortgage Act, that the president had done the same in ousting Humphrey, and that both had violated the Constitution in certain phases of the NRA program.[77]

Schechter found acceptance nearly everywhere as a sound decision, though not within the administration or with organized labor. The Court had severely circumscribed the regulatory powers of the federal government. Rising prices, irritating code regu-

---

[75] Alpheus T. Mason, *Brandeis: A Free Man's Life* (New York: Viking, 1946), 620.

[76] Harry Hopkins, "Statement to Me by Thomas Corcoran Giving His Recollections of the Genesis of the Supreme Court Fight," April 3, 1939, typescript in Harry Hopkins Papers, FDRL. Cf. Schlesinger, Jr., *Politics of Upheaval,* 280; Irons, *New Deal Lawyers,* 104–5, Robert Sherwood, *Roosevelt and Hopkins: An Intimate History* (New York: Harper and Bros., 1948), 89.

[77] Eugene Gerhart, *America's Advocate: Robert H. Jackson* (Indianapolis: Bobbs Merrill, 1958), 99.

lations, regimentation, and bureaucratic confusion all served to convince the public, particularly those in small businesses, that the measure had to go. After May 27, by executive order, all NRA regulations went off the books. While vacationing on Cape Cod that summer, Justice Brandeis told newsmen that the three decisions of May 27, far from returning the country to the McKinley era, "compelled a return to human limitations. . . . The curse of bigness [whether in government or industry] has prevented proper thinking."[78]

Foes of the Blue Eagle in the House and Senate were jubilant. Senator Daniel O. Hastings (R.-Del.) was quoted as saying that the decision "destroys most of the New Deal, but unfortunately does not end the spending spree."[79] The New Deal's opponents gave thanks that the Constitution still stood, while its supporters wondered if it stood still.

Reflecting on the "sick chicken" case, Harvard's Reed Powell cautioned that, without perhaps realizing it, the Supreme Court was shoving the administration in new directions. "The waters damned by judicial restrictions on the commerce power," he warned, "may break out in unwelcome fields of taxing and spending. What seems a great victory against national regulation may prove to be a Pyrrhic one. What is called the Ship of State has other controls than those with wires to where the Supreme Court is quartermaster."[80]

Newspapers hailed the Supreme Court as the "Protector of the Constitution." The *Chicago Daily News* rejoiced that "constitutional government has returned to America." Roosevelt was more upset than he let on. He was infuriated by the overturning of the NRA, the core of his recovery program. As the news of "Black Monday" sank in, Marguerite Le Hand informed Stanley High that "the President was very irritable and troubled that evening."[81] He disagreed with the rulings, but more than that, he resented them as personal attacks.

---

[78] Mason, *Brandeis,* 620.

[79] *Washington Post,* May 28, 1935.

[80] Quoted in Schlesinger, Jr., *Politics of Upheaval,* 398–99.

[81] Diary of Stanley High, March 20, 1936, Stanley High Papers, FDRL; Leuchtenburg, "Origins of Court-Packing Plan," 356–57. On Roosevelt's indignation over the *Schechter* decision, see Clapper's Diary, February 24, 1937, Clapper Papers, LC.

Roosevelt had other reasons to be upset. The line separating legal from illegal government in the United States was, for the first time in his administration, clearly defined along a broad front, and in the opinion of many critics, it was high time for such a line to be drawn. Kenneth Davis, FDR's biographer, read the president's reaction to Black Monday's *Schechter* ruling as ambiguous, or "mixed." If he was despondent, he did not let it on in public; in fact, he seemed more than normally zestful and buoyant. The Supreme Court was not even mentioned at the White House dinner table that Monday evening.[82]

An editorial stated: "When you have set up controls throughout a nation's industries, you cannot end these rigidities without a jolt." Another concluded: "No confusion could be worse than that which has attended the futile attempt of more than 5000 administrative bodies, code authorities, committees, sub-committees and agents to supervise all business activities."[83] The writer omitted mention of the preoccupation of Justice Department and NRA lawyers with the impossible task of enforcing code compliance. All things considered, Roosevelt had led the country down a blind alley and into a bureaucratic nightmare.

In the Labor Department there was apprehension over what could be done to preserve the provisions in section 7a outlawing child labor, setting maximum hours and minimum wages, and guaranteeing labor the right to organize unions and engage in collective bargaining. The bill to extend the NRA was still pending in the House. A debate ensued over whether it would be wise to amend it to preserve its "worth-while features." The day after the *Schechter* ruling, Secretary Perkins called a conference of lawyers that included Stephens, Dickinson, John Burns (general counsel of the SEC), and Blackwell Smith. Charles Wyzanski, the Labor Department's solicitor, was overseas, but he cabled Perkins from Geneva that the text of Hughes's opinion led him to conclude that a great deal of the NRA could be salvaged. Others, including Richberg, thought so too.

But when Secretary Perkins tried to convey these views to

[82] Kenneth Davis, *FDR: The New Deal Years: 1932–1937* (New York: Random House, 1986), 516–17.

[83] *Wall Street Journal,* May 29, 1935.

FDR and ask that some consideration be given to them before allowing the extension bill to die, she found out that Cummings had gotten to the president already and had convinced him that the Supreme Court's opinion in *Schechter* was so sweeping that in effect it invalidated the entire NRA and "destroyed all hope for further congressional action along those lines." Angered over the unanimous decision, the attorney general fumed: "I tell you, Mr. President, they mean to destroy us. . . . We will have to find a way to get rid of the present membership of the Supreme Court." He recommended abandoning anything even remotely resembling the NRA and telling the country that the Supreme Court had made it impossible to have this kind of legislation.[84]

Jerome Frank disagreed with the notion that killing the NRA was the luckiest thing that could ever have happened to Roosevelt "because he had gotten himself into this box." But calling the Supreme Court ruling "fortunate" was to ignore the fact that the judicial attitude toward the NRA was linked to hostility toward Roosevelt himself, and perhaps to the rest of his New Deal legislation. Frank continued:

> The mere defeat of NRA wouldn't have been so bad but it was the spirit in which it was done, and the doctrines laid down in connection with doing it. The whole thing showed that it was going to be impossible for him [FDR] to carry out his program. Consequently, I wouldn't join with those who say that Roosevelt needed the rescue. He could have gotten rid of it [NRA]. It was one of his great mistakes. He didn't understand it. I think he came later to, but at the time he didn't.[85]

The soundness of this analysis is reflected in Roosevelt's ambiguity and irresolution on what to make of the fiasco. He refused to give up completely on the NRA and insisted to William Bullitt that its principles had to be carried out in some way. Apparently, he believed strongly in the approach and persisted in efforts to revive it.[86] Compared to the views expressed to Bullitt and others, however, Roosevelt gave very different ones to Secretary Perkins. After "Black Monday," he told her, the "whole thing

[84] Perkins, *Roosevelt,* 203–4; Schlesinger, Jr., *Politics of Upheaval,* 282, 288–89.

[85] Frank, Reminiscences, COHC, 32–35.

[86] Mason, *Brandeis,* 620.

was a mess, an awful headache." He admitted that some of the things the NRA had done were "pretty wrong," but added:

> We have got the best out of it anyhow. Industry got a shot in the arm. I don't believe they will go back to their old wage levels. . . . I think perhaps NRA has done all it can do. I don't want to impose a system on this country that will set aside the antitrust laws on any permanent basis.
>
> I have been talking to other lawyers besides Homer Cummings, and they are pretty certain that the whole process is unconstitutional and that we have to restudy and revise our whole program. Perhaps we had better do it now. So let's give the NRA a certain amount of time to liquidate. Have a history of it written, and then it will be over.[87]

The House Ways and Means Committee completed its scrutiny of the Senate resolution to extend the NRA for another ten months on the same morning the justices were filing into the Court to invalidate it. The committee had been expected to vote out the two-year extension requested by the president, but the proposal was not offered to the full House until June 6. When it was, the controls over industries engaged in intrastate commerce were omitted, as were the provisions delegating power to the president to approve, prescribe, or enforce the codes. In this revised form, it was passed by the House the next day.[88]

In the conference committee, consideration of the amendments took another week. Some Democrats expected compromise, but the Senate was not in a compromising mood. The House alterations met with opposition, and as a result no important changes were made. On June 14, 1935, Roosevelt signed a bill extending the measure in name only until April 1, 1936, when it was allowed to expire. Even before the Senate had the chance to vote on it, Robert La Follette predicted that by the end of the ten months, if not before, the NRA would be as "dead as a doornail."[89]

Frankfurter added his voice to the volume of advice descend-

---

[87] Perkins, *Roosevelt,* 203–4.

[88] *Congressional Record,* 74th Cong., 1st Sess., June 7, 1935, 8818, 8899–8900.

[89] Ibid., 9190–91, 9318–19, 9346, 9351.

ing on FDR. Two days after the *Schechter* decision, in a memo outlining his ideas "On the Issue of the Supreme Court v. the President," he offered the peculiar suggestion that more anti-administration decisions by the Court would help rather than hinder the cause. He believed that the "fighting out" of the issue between Court and president might well be postponed "until decisions in other cases accumulate popular grievances against the Court on issues so universally popular that the Borahs, the Clarks, the Nyes, and all the currents of opinion they represent will be with you, in addition to the support you have today."

He went on: "That is why I think it is so fortunate that the administration has pending before Congress measures like the Social Security Act, the Holding Company bill, the Wagner Act and the Guffey Coal bill. Go on with these. Put them up to the Supreme Court." He urged FDR: "Let the Court strike down any or all of them . . . especially a divided Court. Then propose a constitutional amendment giving the national Government adequate power to cope with national economic and industrial problems." Frankfurter surmised that that would give FDR an overwhelming issue of a positive character, arising at the psychological moment for the 1936 campaign, instead of touting mere negative issues of being "a'gin" the Court which, "rising now, may not be able to sustain . . . freshness and dramatic appeal until election time."[90] Frankfurter discussed the issue personally with his friend at the White House later that week. His argument was very strange. Why would anyone who had tried so hard to prevent *Belcher* and *Schechter* from reaching the Supreme Court so as to avert adverse rulings now want to escalate a conflict with such equanimity? Brandeis would have opposed such a scheme if only because his respect for the Court precluded any wish to see it criticized or humbled.

The May 31, 1935, Press Conference

Fear of adverse rulings had been haunting New Dealers and FDR throughout the two years it had taken for the most significant

[90] Memo, May 29, 1935, Box 98, Frankfurter Papers, LC. Cf. Dawson, *Brandeis, Frankfurter, and the New Deal,* 69–70; Moley, *After Seven Years,* 306–7; and *PPA,* 1935 volume, 200.

legislation of the "hundred days" to work its way up to the Supreme Court. After "Black Monday," the administration was thrown into confusion and disarray. Everyone waited for Roosevelt's reaction, but at first he remained silent. For four days he refrained from making any public utterance.

Moley related that some "queer stories" were circulating about what transpired in the White House during those four days. He arrived in Washington on May 30 and received a detailed account of talks Hugh Johnson and Frankfurter had held with FDR. They found him in a belligerent mood. Roosevelt told them that he would *not* take the Court's action lying down, that he would *not* stand for it, that the country was with *him,* not the Court. He swore angrily that he would bring the Court into line even if he had to "pack it" or deny it its appellate jurisdiction. The two men listened to him in astonishment.

This account is corroborated by a memo from the State Department's assistant secretary, R. Walton Moore, who later sent FDR extracts from Thomas Jefferson's letters on whether judges of the Supreme Court were invested with the exclusive authority to decide on the constitutionality of a law. The memo stated that he was sending the letters "in accordance with a request the President made shortly after the NRA decision." In a public address, Moore alluded to various suggestions for constitutional changes that were being considered but said it was understood "that as yet the President had made no recommendations."[91]

Johnson and Frankfurter tried to dissuade Roosevelt from making any public expression of his anger.[92] Moley learned that, early on May 31, Roosevelt "for hours on end" had "pumped out of Felix" technical information about *Schechter* and earlier court decisions that he was about to pass on to newsmen. Then, without a word to anyone about his intentions, he was wheeled into the oval room to hold a prearranged press

---

[91] This correspondence was received by the FDR Presidential Library in Hyde Park, New York, in a folder from the president's desk marked "Schechter Case File," OF 41, Box 48; see also OF 466, "Miscellaneous Supreme Court Decisions: Schechter Folder," FDRL. R. Walton Moore addressed graduates at the commencement exercises of the National University, Washington, D.C. A copy was sent to FDR.

[92] Joseph Alsop and Turner Catledge, *The 168 Days* (Garden City, N.Y.: Doubleday, Doran, 1938), 16–17.

"The People's Liberties in Jeopardy." A cartoon by Shoemaker in the *Chicago News,* January 23, 1937.

conference.[93] He was twenty minutes late, having made more than the usual preparations for this affair. More than a hundred members of the press crowded into the room. Frankfurter declined an invitation to attend, but his wife, Marian, sat beside Mrs. Roosevelt, who was busily knitting on a blue sock. FDR

[93] Moley, *After Seven Years,* 306–7.

asked reporters: "What's the news?" "That's what *we* want to know," was the brisk reply.

He asked them to "make this 'background'" and take some time, because he had "an awfully big subject" to cover, and it was just possible that one or two of them might not have read the twenty-eight pages of the Supreme Court decision. On his desk beside a copy of Hughes's opinion was a pile of telegrams received since Monday. He read some of these "pathetic appeals," as he called them, which came not from unemployed workers or desperate farmers, but from businessmen expressing their dismay over the prospect of renewed cutthroat competition.

"I suppose we have had about fifty different suggestions," remarked Roosevelt. "They go all the way from abolishing the Supreme Court to abolishing Congress, and, I think, abolishing the President. That is to make it complete." Turning to the implications of the NRA decision, he said it was probably more important than any Court ruling since the Dred Scott case, which helped to bring on the Civil War. "We are facing a very, very great national non-partisan issue," he said. "We have got to decide . . . whether in some way we are going to . . . restore to the Federal Government the powers which exist in the national governments of every nation in the world."[94]

The limitations placed on executive powers deeply offended him. However, he said that the ruling on delegation of legislative power to the executive was not an insurmountable problem: a revised act could be written giving definite directions to administrative or quasi-judicial bodies which the Court might find acceptable. More serious was its interpretation of the commerce clause. He took emphatic exception to Hughes's definition of what constituted "local" in relation to the poultry-processing operation. This would restrict the application of interstate commerce to everything but the shipment of goods across state lines. Various decisions in recent times, he said, had enlarged on the definition of interstate commerce; the whole tendency in them had been to view the clause in the light of modern civilization. The country was in "the horse and buggy stage" when the commerce clause was written, but the line of opinions in recent years had been more progressive.

[94] *PPA,* 1935 volume, 205, 215–16.

Throughout, the president insisted that this was no mere partisan issue, but when pressed to give some indication of where he intended to go next, whether to the right or the left, he was at times arrogant and evasive: "Don't call it right or left. That is just first-year high school language," he said. He lashed out at the Court with its "horse and buggy interpretation" of interstate commerce, but never indicated what he proposed to do in the aftermath of this setback. When asked by reporters how the constitutional questions might be resolved, he replied: "We haven't gotten to that yet."[95]

This press conference lasted for more than ninety minutes. At its close, FDR declared: "In spite of what one gentleman said in the paper this morning, that I resented the [NRA] decision, nobody resents a Supreme Court decision. . . . You can deplore a Supreme Court decision, and you can point out the effect of it. You can call the attention of the country to what the results of that decision are, if future decisions follow it."[96]

For Roosevelt, a press conference was not merely an instrumentality to accommodate reporters, or through them to inform the public and critics. It was a public relations device that could be manipulated to his advantage. His expertise as a communicator facilitated this, but he was frequently less than candid in what he communicated. The May 31 conference amounted to a dissenting opinion on the *Schechter* case delivered by the president to the nation with correspondents reduced to the role of scribes. Everything he said was to be considered "background," which meant it was to remain unquoted.

As the session drew to an end, a reporter asked: "Can we use the direct quotation on that 'horse and buggy stage'?" His exact words were: "We have been relegated to a 'horse and buggy' definition of interstate commerce." The phrase echoed a 1908 statement by Woodrow Wilson: "The Constitution was not meant to hold the Government back to the time of horses and wag-

[95] Press Conference no. 209, May 31, 1935, *CPPC,* 5:309–37; Burns, *Roosevelt,* 222–23; *Washington Post,* June 1, 1935; Schlesinger, Jr., *Politics of Upheaval,* 284–88; Alsop and Catledge, *The 168 Days,* 16–17; *PPA,* 1935 volume, 200–222.

[96] *PPA,* 1935 volume, 205.

ons."[97] Turning to his press secretary for approbation, Roosevelt replied, "I think so." Steve Early cautioned: "Just the phrase." The next day, bold leaders on front pages of newspapers all over the country carried headlines blaring: "FDR: Horse and Buggy Decision."

There were almost as many creative versions of Roosevelt's use of this phrase as there were reporters. Some historians interpreted the "horse and buggy" metaphor analogy as a New Dealer's attack on conservative judges. Knowing how vitally concerned FDR was about the implications of the *Schechter* decision for other New Deal legislation, they maintain that Roosevelt, figuratively speaking, was "thumbing his nose at the Supreme Court." At the least, he was dissenting from judges who thought that what he considered national problems could be solved by the states. Moley was convinced he further alienated those who already opposed him and left his supporters in utter confusion as to his next step.[98] The impression gained by newshawks attending the press conference was that Roosevelt had some immediate solution up his sleeve. According to Moley, FDR was conferring frequently with Corcoran and Cohen, and he apparently gave fleeting thought to a constitutional amendment. But he was not committed, and his aides were opposed to such action, insisting that the trouble lay with the Court and not with the Constitution.[99]

FDR's remarks about the Court provoked a storm of indignation in all parts of the country. In Raymond Clapper's syndicated column he reported: "Within an hour after President Roosevelt held his press conference yesterday, you could almost feel the electric excitement about Washington." Before the first newspapers hit the streets, the whole city knew that something of momentous importance had occurred. Editorial writers denounced what they considered the "scornful reference to a horse and buggy court." The general feeling was one of popular displeasure.

There were more expressions of disfavor with Roosevelt's at-

[97] Saul Padover, *The Living United States Constitution* (New York: Mentor Books, 1968), 67.

[98] Moley, *After Seven Years,* 306–7; Burns, *Roosevelt,* 222–23.

[99] Moley, *After Seven Years,* 358; FDR to Senator Pat Harrison, August 24, 1935, *PPA,* 1935 volume, 334.

tack on the Court than of anger over its ruling. As one writer put it, there were few mourners at the NRA's funeral. Polls taken that summer indicated a steady decline in Roosevelt's popularity. Senator Arthur Vandenberg declared: "I don't think the President has any thought of emulating Mussolini, Hitler or Stalin, but his utterance as I have heard it is exactly what these men would say."[100] With the exception of a few loyalists, Democrats tried to distance themselves from a leader who had made the NRA the centerpiece of his recovery program and then had the props knocked out from under him.

In the press and over the radio, commentators expressed cool disapproval and even outrage over the ill-tempered attack on a revered institution. Newsmen upbraided FDR severely, took some of his remarks out of context, and portrayed him as rancorous—furious not only with the Court's decision, but with the nine men who rendered it. The "horse and buggy" statement was attached in the public's mind not to the commerce clause, which is what Roosevelt intended, but to the Court. From May to the election in November the course taken by the Court produced in FDR a feeling of almost personal injustice.[101] The public reaction, far from being anti–Supreme Court, as he had expected, was in fact anti-Roosevelt.

In politics, timing is everything. If Roosevelt had waited until after the AAA decision to launch a verbal attack on the Court, the result might have been different, but he did not. In conversation with Harry Hopkins, Corcoran said that after his famous "horse and buggy" press conference Roosevelt was "thoroughly aroused and determined to prevent the Court from blocking what he believed to be the very fundamentals of our democracy." In FDR's view, the justices were prejudiced and delivered opinions based on their outmoded political philosophies.[102] But the main battle would not be fought yet. For the moment, any notion he may have entertained of pressing an attack on the judiciary would have to be postponed. The best he could do about the Supreme Court was to do nothing at all.

---

[100] *Washington Post,* June 1, 1935.
[101] Alsop and Catledge, *The 168 Days,* 16–17.
[102] Sherwood, *Roosevelt and Hopkins,* 89.

Over the next weeks Roosevelt held many other press conferences, but he remained noncommittal. He listened to hours of advice on how to control or reverse the damage. Congress was to remain in session throughout the summer to study other approaches to the problems raised in *Schechter* and to pass the measures on his "must" list. The resulting turn by the New Deal to the left produced a burst of legislative activity. Congress was galvanized into action by a renewal of Roosevelt's determined leadership. Before adjournment, it passed four pieces of legislation: the National Labor Relations Act (or Wagner Act), the Social Security Act, a new banking bill, and the Public Utilities Holding Company Act. Eventually added to this list was a "soak the rich" tax scheme. Secretary Perkins insisted that Roosevelt "never lifted a finger" in support of the Wagner bill, for which she herself had very little enthusiasm.[103]

Columnist Max Lerner thought FDR was relieved to have the NRA out of the way. Reflecting on the case years later, he asked: "Who was it that killed the NRA? Was it the Supreme Court by its *Schechter* decision? Or was it Hugh Johnson and Donald Richberg, through the administrative chaos within the NRA and the poor selection of a test case? Or was it the President, who might have asked Congress to put through a revised act, as he did afterward with the AAA, but who welcomed a chance to get the albatross off his neck. My own guess," he concluded, "would be a combination of all three."[104]

FDR received some unsolicited advice he may not have welcomed from Representative Martin J. Kennedy, an old Tammanyite who had served in the Albany legislature with him. Sitting in his New York City office, he told reporters that if he could get to "his pal Franklin" without being blocked by the "White House secretariat," he would like to give him some friendly counsel about the NRA and the New Deal. Using the terminology of foot-

[103] Leuchtenburg, *Roosevelt and the New Deal,* 150; Frances Perkins, Reminiscences, COHC, 138, 147; and Perkins, *Roosevelt,* 203–4. For FDR's reluctance to support the Wagner Act, see Burns, *Roosevelt,* 219; Paul Conkin, *The New Deal* (Arlington Heights, Ill.: Harlan Davidson, 1975), 62; and Irons, *New Deal Lawyers,* 230.

[104] "The Great Constitutional War," *Virginia Quarterly Review* 18 (1942): 537.

ball, he referred to Roosevelt as "the quarterback" and called on him to oust his "alleged legal wizards" from the team. The "trio of laugh backs" he had in mind were Cummings, Richberg, and Frankfurter.

"Of course," Kennedy complained, "nothing but yes men and back-slappers get to see Franklin now, but if I could chat with him, I would say, Franklin, old boy, now that your Brain Trusters and their theories have had their day in and . . . out of court, why don't you return to your Albany kitchen cabinet custom?" Richberg had been thrown for losses, and the attorney general "has been running the wrong way with the ball because the Frankfurter boys' dizzy signals on the constitutional goal confused him." He called on the president to clear out the brain trusters and legal wiseacres and get some "country constitutional lawyers and hard-headed, common sense cronies who are as anxious over the safety of the people and government as you are." He added: "We would try to be sound, Franklin, instead of like those legal wizards, whose tangled magic befuddled and stultified you and others, but failed to charm the straight-thinking constitutional eye of the Supreme Court."[105]

[105] Quoted in *St. Louis Globe-Democrat,* May 30, 1935. Copy in Box 14, PPF 1820, FDRL.

4

The Fate of the AAA

> Legislation in the United States is a digestive process by Congress with frequent regurgitations by the Supreme Court.
>
> Sir Wilmott Lewis[1]

DURING HIS YEARS as New York's governor, Roosevelt familiarized himself with farm problems. He considered it a personal as well as public obligation to find a solution to the vexing conditions that reduced agriculture to its status of one of the "sick industries" in the 1920s, plunging thousands of farmers into bankruptcy and despair during the Depression. The nation's farm families constituted more than a third of the population. They had to receive some sort of relief, or there could be no hope of recovery.

The details of agricultural policy had always fascinated FDR. In the 1932 campaign he examined many proposals and tried to listen to all sorts of views. Careful consideration was given to a domestic allotment plan developed by, among others, economist Milburn L. Wilson, a professor at Montana State College.[2] The proposal aimed at raising farm prices and income by limiting production through a combination of government taxes and price supports or subsidies to encourage self-imposed quotas by producers of farm products. Wilson maintained that the government had to offer farmers payments to take some acreage out of production. To pay for such a program, Washington would have to tax processors of farm products. In September 1932, FDR's cam-

[1] Sir Wilmott Lewis wrote for *The Times* (London).

[2] William D. Rowley, *M. L. Wilson and the Campaign for the Domestic Allotment Plan* (Lincoln: University of Nebraska Press, 1970); see also Harry C. McDean, "M. L. Wilson and Agricultural Reform in Twentieth Century America" (Ph.D. diss., University of California, Los Angeles, 1969).

paign train toured the nation's heartland, where he delivered several stirring speeches. In Topeka, Kansas, he outlined in broad, general terms and seemingly espoused the very principles of crop control through acreage reduction later written into law. The New Deal farm bill was forecast in the Topeka speech and the 1932 Democratic platform.[3]

Roosevelt's "New Deal for farmers" was embodied in the bill drafted in March 1933 by Agriculture Secretary Henry Wallace, Assistant Secretary Rexford Tugwell, Hugh Johnson, George Peek (a former farm machinery manufacturer from Moline, Illinois, soon to be the new agency's chief administrator), Mordecai Ezekial, and two lawyers—Frederick Lee, Peek's personal counsel, and Jerome Frank, a former corporation lawyer recently appointed general counsel for the Department of Agriculture. As with the NRA, the drafters framed legislation that rested on vague constitutional theories and imprecise legal foundations. The lawyers involved in the process were personally and ideologically antagonistic toward each other. The atmosphere during the "hundred days" with the writing of the farm bill was charged with a sense of urgency. In Congress the mood was anxious, confused, and impatient. No one knew what to expect, but whatever emerged from the drafting process was likely to be controversial. Angry farmers, agitating for debtor relief over more than half a century, climaxed their campaign of protest by announcing a nationwide strike for mid-May 1933.

Farm organizations, long accustomed to being heard on proposed farm bills, had no part in drawing up New Deal legislation.[4] Wallace, Tugwell, and Frank wielded most of the influence

[3] Beard and Beard, *America in Mid-Passage,* 145; Roy E. Hoffman, "Montana's Contribution to New Deal Farm Policy," *Agricultural History* 33 (October 1959): 164–66. Hoffman stresses the work of M. L. Wilson and his associates, pioneers in land-use planning, a tenant farmer purchase scheme, and the domestic allotment plan.

[4] Secretary Wallace began a series of conferences with farm leaders on March 6, 1933. The eventual farm program was outlined and was met with acquiescence by those most concerned. Gilbert Fite, "The McNary-Haugen Episode and the Triple-A," *Journal of Farm Economy* 42 (December 1960): 1084–93. The Farm Bureau, under the leadership of Edward O'Neal, exerted some influence on the Roosevelt administration in the early period, but it was soon "frozen out" by the Department of Agriculture, which became the dominant force in policy making.

in drafting enabling legislation for what became the Agricultural Adjustment Act (AAA). They insisted that it include the domestic allotment plan. A similar plan, incorporated in a bill introduced in Congress in 1932 by agrarian Republicans, had been deemed unconstitutional by Stanley Reed, then general counsel for the Federal Farm Bureau.

Tugwell, the only agricultural expert in Roosevelt's brain trust, favored comprehensive economic planning and became a strong advocate of crop reduction as a solution to overproduction. But when he tried to convince FDR that this was the course to follow, he found that Peek had already gotten to the president and convinced him that the bill should include, in addition to other provisions, his plan allowing food processors—in return for paying a tax on raw farm products—to fix prices and evade the antitrust laws. Wallace and Tugwell finally agreed to the framing of a measure incorporating both Peek's and their own features, ensuring that the bill had in it the seeds of certain conflict. On March 16, 1933, twelve days after his inauguration, Roosevelt sent the AAA to Congress, characterizing it as "the most drastic and far-reaching piece of farm legislation ever proposed in time of peace."[5]

The preamble to the act made clear that its far-reaching provisions, promising stupendous sums in subsidies to staple farmers, were designed to meet the "emergency" created by the Depression. Outlining the nature of the acute economic crisis resulting from the disparity between farm prices and those of other commodities, the "Declaration of Emergency" came close to calling agriculture "a business affected with a public interest." The crisis situation, it was claimed, burdened and obstructed the normal currents of commerce.

The first AAA derived the same stimulative force from its administrators as Hugh Johnson had given the NRA. Tugwell, Frank, Chester Davis,[6] and what one writer called "intellectual-

[5] *PPA,* 1933 volume, 79.

[6] George Peek, the AAA's first administrator, was a supporter of "equality for agriculture" within the department, but he clashed with his superior, Henry Wallace, over policy and authority. In December 1933, Roosevelt removed Peek and replaced him with Chester Davis. A power struggle within the Agricultural Adjustment Administration over the means of alleviating the farm problem was the reason for Peek's removal.

type, city-bred modernists" provided the leadership that pushed ahead to secure its broad objectives, leaving in its wake the wholesale slaughter of baby pigs and the plowing under of crops.[7] Confusion reigned as to its purpose, and with it antagonism toward its methods grew. National farm policies collided head-on with local interests. AAA leadership showed favoritism to landlords in the execution of its programs. Its policies not only failed to benefit tenant farmers and sharecroppers, especially in the South, but worked harm on them and proved devastating to the poorest of the poor.

The AAA was as sweeping and constitutionally unsound as the NRA. If anything, it was more legally and socially inventive than its counterpart for business and labor. Less important pieces of New Deal legislation were framed more carefully and rested on sounder constitutional grounds, a task made easier owing to their less ambitious scope and objectives. The AAA program was constitutionally vulnerable from the outset. A possible basis for constitutionality was the commerce clause, if interpreted broadly. The act was posited on an alternate set of broad commerce clause and taxing power precedents rooted in early-twentieth-century decisions from the Progressive Era, but the claims of authority under it were so sweeping and unqualified as to betray little concern either for constitutional limitations or the authority of the states. These could be fatal flaws in the eyes of many members of the federal judiciary, who shared few if any of the constitutional assumptions of the bill's framers and had little sympathy for the creative tactics of its implementation.[8]

In the overwhelmingly Democratic House, the bill sailed through by a vote of 315 to 98 on March 22, 1933, after only five and a half hours of debate. But constitutionalists in both houses

[7] With the slaughter of 6 million pigs, hog prices rose by 20 percent in 1934, but the rise was not attributed to the slaughter. This episode was employed repeatedly in partisan attacks on Roosevelt and Wallace. George T. Blakey, "Ham That Never Was: The 1933 Emergency Hog Slaughter," *Historian* 30 (November 1967): 41–57.

[8] Paul L. Murphy, *Constitution in Crisis Times, 1918–1969* (New York: Harper and Row, 1972), 129–31. For a fuller discussion of legal decisions concerning the government's power under the Constitution to regulate agricultural production, see Murphy, "The New Deal Agricultural Problem and the Constitution," *Agricultural History* 29 (October 1955): 160–69.

found flaws in the measure's largely unprecedented tax provisions and wanted to get their objections into the record in spite of the call for haste. House debate was limited to less than six hours—a leadership-imposed gag rule. James Beck, a House Republican from Pennsylvania and former solicitor general, delivered an impassioned speech in which he argued that the Constitution never vested in Congress any power over agriculture, a jurisdiction reserved to the states. The only theory that could provide constitutional justification for the AAA was "the suggestion of an emergency." Attacking the rationale in the measure's opening section, he declared: "Of all the damnable heresies that have ever been suggested in connection with the Constitution, the doctrine of emergency is the worst. It means that when Congress declares an emergency, there is no Constitution. It means death." Alluding to the recent grant to Hitler of emergency legislative powers by the German Reichstag, Beck drew a sinister parallel: "Chancellor Hitler is at least frank about it. *We* pay the Constitution lip service, but the result is the same."[9]

Wisconsin Progressive Robert M. La Follette, Jr., once remarked that the House had become merely a registrative body, pliant to the will of the executive because of its large numbers and the adoption of gag rules, making the Senate the only forum where the minority could be heard.[10] Lawmakers in the House contributed minimally to the constitutional debate. Action in the Senate, however, was held up for weeks, not only by lobbyists for the food processors, who objected to the tax imposed on them, but by inflationists, who argued for an expanded currency and the remonetization of silver. It took almost two months to overcome resistance to pressures by those wanting to hold the line against any inflationary schemes. In the end, the administration had to accept the Thomas Amendment, which authorized the president to devalue the dollar and issue unlimited amounts of silver-backed currency, as the price for getting the bill passed. Other amendments were added at a later stage.

Senators enjoyed the privilege of unlimited debate. The most

---

[9] *Congressional Record,* 73rd Cong., 1st sess., 77, pt. 1:666, 754–59.

[10] *La Follette's Magazine,* April 1926.

damaging attack on the constitutionality of the AAA came from Pennsylvania Republican David A. Reed, who said that Congress had no power to fix the price of farm products because agriculture had never been classified in any Supreme Court ruling as "a business affected with a public interest." Reed attacked the processing tax provision, arguing that strong constitutional precedents firmly established the rule that Congress cannot take from the pocket of *A* and put the proceeds into the pocket of *B*. The Court had held in *Loan Association v. Topeka* (1875)[11] that use of public funds to aid private enterprise "is no less a robbery because it is done under the forms of law and is called taxation." This was the same point raised by Stanley Reed when the Domestic Allotment Plan was first introduced in Congress in 1932.

Senator Reed's next objection was to the AAA's licensing provision. There was a good prospect, he warned, of due-process objections by the courts to any mandatory licensing scheme. This would eventually present AAA administrators with a dilemma over how to impose a license on every farm producer without holding prior hearings. As a stopgap measure, Jerome Frank subsequently tried to publicize the licensing requirements through press releases and on the radio, but he feared that was not enough, and he said the prospects for its working "scared him to death."[12]

Finally, Reed attacked the delegation of the taxing power to the secretary of agriculture. Beck had warned earlier that the AAA would transform Wallace into "another Stalin." As secretary, he was given uncontrolled discretion to fix the processing tax at any level. Under such delegation, Congress could authorize the president or a subordinate to tax any item at any level for any purpose. If such power could be delegated by Congress, argued Reed, lawmakers might just as well adjourn and go home for the next four years, as the German Reichstag had done. The act was not limited to transactions in interstate commerce, bringing every farmer-producer under federal regulation.[13]

On the administration's behalf, Senator John Bankhead of Ala-

---

[11] 20 Wallace 655 (1874).

[12] Irons, *New Deal Lawyers,* 135.

[13] Ibid., 117.

bama tried to rebut Reed's arguments. He conceded that the processing tax issue introduced a serious question, but predicted that ultimately the Supreme Court would uphold the "broad and plenary" powers exercised by Congress. It would remain for AAA lawyers to make good on this prediction. The senators may have realized that they were making their constitutional arguments before the wrong tribunal. Reed ventured the guess that not half a dozen senators believed the bill was constitutional. But it was much easier, he said, for his colleagues, faced with the clamor for farm relief and recovery, "to shrug their shoulders and pass the responsibility on to the Supreme Court."[14]

Under the AAA, unprecedented powers were given to the federal government—for example, the right to lease or purchase land, withdraw it from cultivation, make loans backed by land, store nonperishable crops, and enforce compliance through licensing agreements with processors. The secretary of agriculture retained final authority to suspend or revoke these agreements after a hearing, and any person found handling agricultural products without a license was subject to a fine of $1,000 a day. Never before had there been such an intricately designed and complicated program for individual participation in the application of federal law at the local level. Little had been done by FDR or anyone else to prepare the public mind for the measure. Neither farmers nor their spokesmen, for whose benefit the bill was intended, could quickly grasp all the implications of such a complex set of proposals.

Jerome Frank, as the AAA's legal counsel, found many sections of the statute unintelligible. He said Frederick Lee, Washington's legislative counsel for the Farm Bureau Federation, was just "a sloppy draftsman," although Lee had taught legislative drafting and had once headed House and Senate drafting groups. Frank was full of doubts about the possible consequences of the AAA's licensing provision, which he felt was badly worded and had been clumsily handled in the drafting stage. When he questioned any one of the sixty lawyers on his staff about sections of the AAA, he found that "nobody could make head or tail of it. It was just absurdly incomprehensible."[15]

[14] *Congressional Record,* 73rd. Cong., 1st sess., 77, pt. 1:1642, 1761; Irons, *New Deal Lawyers,* 118.

[15] Frank, Reminiscences, COHC, 69–70.

The Agricultural Adjustment Act passed both houses on May 10, 1933, and was signed into law by Roosevelt on May 12, one day before the threatened farmers' general strike. It was the last major enactment of the "hundred days." The firm regulation of agricultural production and processing implicit in the bill gave a strong indication of the administration's intention to create a planned economy, an economy of subsidized scarcity—and to some minds, a collectivist society.[16] The program was expected to raise farm income in some sectors, but the enterprise met with criticism from consumers (who were upset over higher food prices), small farmers and tenants, processors forced to pay the tax, and taxpayers. Some charged that it was not promoting good land-use practices, while others protested against its impact on the rural poor. All these groups were to some degree unhappy with it.[17] Questioning its constitutionality, Pennsylvania Republican Lester J. Dickinson later declared on the floor of the Senate that the AAA was forcing the poor folk in the country to eat dog food.

In the rush to complete action on the bill before the end of the session, few lawmakers gave much thought to matters of constitutionality. The power of Congress to lay and collect taxes was expected to provide constitutional support for the measure, but

[16] Rexford Tugwell, *The Democratic Roosevelt* (Garden City, N.Y.: n.p., 1957), 275–77; "Memo on the Origins of the AAA," Tugwell Papers, FDRL; Schlesinger, Jr. *Coming of the New Deal,* 40–41. On the AAA's passage, see Murray R. Benedict, *Farm Policies of the United States, 1790–1950: A Study of Their Origins and Development* (New York: Octagon, 1953), 276ff. Most historians have focused much of their attention on the AAA's shortcomings. Foremost among these monographs is Donald H. Grubbs, *Cry from the Cotton: The Southern Tenant Farmers' Union and the New Deal* (Chapel Hill: University of North Carolina Press, 1971). See also Gilbert C. Fite, *George N. Peek and the Fight for Farm Parity* (Norman: University of Oklahoma Press, 1954); David E. Conrad, *The Forgotten Farmer: The Story of Sharecropping in the New Deal* (Urbana: University of Illinois Press, 1965). Van L. Perkins explored the first critical year of the AAA in *Crisis in Agriculture: The AAA and the New Deal, 1933* (Berkeley: University of California Press, 1969). Theodore Saloutos, *The American Farmer and the New Deal* (Ames: Iowa State University Press, 1982), is a balanced survey of this complex subject.

[17] For a trenchant critique of the AAA, see Murray R. Benedict, *Can We Solve the Farm Problem? An Analysis of Federal Aid to Agriculture* (New York: Twentieth Century Fund, 1955).

the processing tax had the potential to raise constitutional challenges on the grounds of substantive and procedural due process guarantees. The crop reduction program (which rested squarely on contracts) could eventually raise other problems, not the least of which was how to enforce compliance.

Jerome Frank was deeply involved in the early legal battle over compliance with the AAA's licensing provisions, with particular reference to the milk industry. The secretary of agriculture had the power to issue licenses permitting processors and others to handle agricultural commodities or any competing commodity in the currents of interstate or foreign commerce. "This milk license thing," he later recalled, "gave rise immediately to numerous law suits."[18] One faction within the administration, headed by Frankfurter, counseled delay in litigation. When you are dealing with statutes, he advised, it is very important to have a body of administrative practice before you get cases involving them into the courts. He noted that Supreme Court justices considered this very important.

Justice Brandeis played a role in developing this doctrine of administrative interpretation. It affected the meaning of statutes, he said, because so many federal statutes were badly drafted. The only way to get any meaning into most of them was to have them administratively interpreted. Aware of Brandeis's views, Frankfurter cautioned New Deal agency lawyers: "Go slow on this. Don't bring your cases up, either as to interpretation or constitutionality until you've got this body of law." Frank attended one of the Washington luncheons addressed by Frankfurter. Everybody in those days thought his was the "voice of Jove," but Frank stood up and challenged him: "Well, Professor Frankfurter, that's all very nice, but what are you going to do if you are brought into court and somebody sues you? That's happening to my agency right now. I can't delay unless I just want to capitulate and let judgment be entered." According to Frank, "the distinguished professor was kind of nettled" and had no answer for him.[19]

---

[18] Frank, Reminiscences, COHC, 86–87.

[19] Ibid. Along with the Beards, Robert F. Carr insisted that New Deal leadership would have been wise to push for immediate constitutional tests of its legislation, thus avoiding the politics as well as the apprehension of the waiting

So there they were with a flood of milk license suits. In the majority of cases and under the stress of "the emergency," federal district judges in those early days sustained the AAA. "They all thought the world was coming to an end," Frank said, "and the New Deal would save it." AAA lawyers even scored some successes in notoriously conservative courts. Frank was assisted in this work by Professor Thurman Arnold of Yale Law School, but their cases had to go through the Justice Department as a result of FDR's executive orders. "That made it messy," recalled Frank, "because most of the lawyers we encountered in the Department of Justice were not very good in those days."[20]

In past cases, the Supreme Court had not played a principal role in fixing the bounds of federal power to tax and spend. Congress and the president were able to expand their powers in this area in incremental steps with general approval. The courts were called upon to ratify or nullify action in a few instances, such as in the oleomargarine and child labor cases.[21] This was the situation until the coming of the New Deal, with its innovative approach to pressing national problems and its attempts to revitalize the depressed agricultural economy.

The AAA's use of the taxing power was considered the weakest constitutional foundation for such broad-based regulations. Almost from the time the machinery was put into operation, administration experts looked to the Supreme Court for clues as to the justices' viewpoint on the matter. As early as June 17, 1934, the White House was showing anxiety,[22] and in an attempt to prevent the processing tax from being passed on to consumers, Congress was urged to pass a series of amendments.

When the Court struck down the NIRA on commerce and delegation grounds, the Department of Agriculture reacted quickly, submitting amendments that Congress passed to provide clearer standards to meet the delegation test. Another modification limited control over agricultural products to those clearly moving in

---

period. See his *The Supreme Court and Judicial Review* (New York: Farrar and Rinehart, 1942). Murphy, *Constitution in Crisis Times,* 135.

[20] Frank, Reminiscences, COHC, 86–87.

[21] *McCray v. United States,* 195 U.S. 27 (1904); *Hammer v. Dagenhart,* 247 U.S. 251 (1918); *Bailey v. Drexel Furniture Co.,* 259 U.S. 20 (1922).

[22] Memo from Chester Davis to FDR, July 13, 1935, OF 1-K, FDRL.

interstate commerce. The *Schechter* ruling also had an effect on the AAA's licensing provisions. In a precautionary move, Congress passed an amendment eliminating the word "license" and substituting "marketing order." These changes had an impact on marketing, production quotas, and price fixing.[23]

Sweeping New Deal programs and Roosevelt's dictatorial manner had stiffened and angered the Supreme Court justices, causing a judicial reaction. Justice Stone, the mildest of New Deal critics, scored Roosevelt's failure to recommend "legislation of any kind" in his 1934 annual message to Congress, characterizing it as a mere report of what he had been doing with the hope that Congress would keep hands off until he could do more. Congress's abdication of its legislative responsibilities and the concentration of power in the hands of "one man" gave Stone and many others grave concern about the political future of the country.[24]

Justice Stone disliked the AAA and said he would not have voted for it, but in correspondence he emphasized that this was not the problem judges faced: their duty was to decide whether it was constitutional for members of Congress to enact such legislation. Stone said he was preoccupied with more serious matters than whether the AAA stood or fell. Above all, he was concerned with the attitude of mind displayed by his brethren, now poised to make a determination on the validity of the AAA.[25]

Justice Brandeis also disliked the AAA. A troubling aspect of the controversy was the role he played in the period prior to any court ruling. Deeply concerned about the rural poor, Brandeis formulated a powerful argument opposing what he considered "the bigness" of the AAA. He stated his objections directly to Tugwell, Wallace, and Gardner Jackson, a spirited liberal and AAA legal counsel for consumer affairs. The justice made clear that he would have designed a very different agricultural program. He was adamantly opposed to reducing output through

[23] Murphy, "New Deal Agricultural Problem," 160; idem, *Constitution in Crisis Times,* 136 n.

[24] Mason, *Stone,* 359.

[25] Schlesinger, Jr., *Politics of Upheaval,* 473.

crop quotas. Instead, he wanted the government to buy up land and lease it for farmers to work in small tracts.

Jackson reported that when Brandeis failed to influence Tugwell, the justice began issuing dire warnings, even before the AAA went to Congress. He predicted that, if passed, it would accelerate the trend toward concentration of farm holdings in fewer and fewer hands, increasing monopoly and absentee ownership. The end result would be corporate farming. He made known he was "worried as thunder about it." Administration insiders who christened him "Old Isaiah" may not have realized how appropriate it was. Jackson discussed Brandeis's grave misgivings with Frank and Tugwell, but they made no observable impact on the AAA's direction.[26]

In the months following the AAA's passage, the effects of the program lent substance to Brandeis's misgivings. By April 1934 he decided it was time for overt threats, announcing through Jackson that he was "declaring war on the New Deal." Tugwell lost no time passing the word on to Roosevelt, who promised to see Brandeis as soon as possible "to butter him up some." According to Tugwell, the administration took his warnings seriously. Government lawyers moved quickly to postpone a pending petroleum suit, reasoning that "with Justice Brandeis feeling as he does, we ought not to take the case up."[27]

Brandeis predicted that the entire crop curtailment policy would prove disastrous, having the effect of retarding, rather than hastening, recovery. His letters to Frankfurter indicate how far he was prepared to go. Through Adolf Berle, he warned the president that he had gone along with New Deal legislation so far (the *Schechter* case had not yet been decided), but unless he could see some reversal of the "big business" trend, he would be "disposed to hold the government's control legislation unconstitutional from now on."[28] FDR wrote Berle in April 1934 that he

[26] For a critical account of Brandeis's role in the AAA debate, see Bruce A. Murphy, *The Brandeis-Frankfurter Connection: The Secret Political Activities of Two Supreme Court Justices* (New York: Oxford University Press, 1982), 139 and passim. See also Gardner Jackson, Reminiscences, COHC.

[27] Tugwell Diary, April 26, 1934, 75, Box 16, Tugwell Papers, FDRL. *Panama Refining Co. v. Ryan* was not decided until the following year.

[28] Brandeis to Frankfurter, August 1, 1933, February 24, 27, 1935, Box 28, Frankfurter Papers, LC; Adolf Berle to FDR, April 23, 1934, PPF 1306, FDRL.

would not be bullied by any Supreme Court justice: "As to our friend of the highest court, I expect to have a good long talk with him within the next few days. The difficulty is that so many people expect me to travel at a rate of one hundred miles an hour when the old bus cannot possibly make more than fifty miles an hour even when it is hitting on all eight cylinders."[29]

FDR saw Brandeis the following June. Meanwhile, AAA administrators were becoming increasingly troubled about the prospect of a Supreme Court test. That summer (1934), agency officials traveled to Cape Cod, where Brandeis was vacationing, ostensibly to discuss such problems in agriculture as monopolistic practices in the dairy industry. What they really hoped to get was some assurance that he would support the AAA when it went to the Supreme Court. This was all highly irregular. Brandeis lectured them for several hours on this and that, but Gardner Jackson took away from the meeting a sense that the justice was demonstrating a new flexibility in his position on the overall legality of the AAA. The group left Chatham convinced that he would vote for the measure if and when it came before the Court.[30]

As an intrigant, Jackson paid a heavy price. Secretary Wallace later informed him that the "purge" of "radicals" in the AA—a mass firing that included Frank, Jackson, and others—came about as a result of their "lobbying" justices of the Supreme Court regarding the AAA. There were more substantive reasons for the firings, but Wallace was convinced that they were trying to subvert his program.[31] This whole episode raises troubling

[29] FDR to Berle, April 30, 1934, PPF 1306, FDRL.

[30] B. A. Murphy, *Brandeis-Frankfurter Connection,* 142; Gardner Jackson, Reminiscences, COHC, 490–94.

[31] Gardner Jackson, Reminiscences, COHC, 584–87. Jackson and Frank, upset over the treatment of tenant and small farmers, later took up the sharecroppers' cause. Frank tried to make existence for them more secure under his Legal Division, which ruled that landowners participating in the cotton program had to keep on their land the same number of tenants residing there in 1933. The ruling infuriated AAA administrator Chester Davis, Peek's successor, who feared it would alienate planters, farm leaders, and their allies in Congress. Wallace felt he had to back Davis and "purged" Frank, Jackson, and others, ruling that planters only had to keep the number of tenants residing on their land when they signed cotton contracts. Richard D. Kirkendall, "Agricultural Adjustment Administration," *Franklin D. Roosevelt: His Life and Times: an*

questions about judicial propriety. Brandeis failed to observe even the basic strictures for the judiciary as they were then understood, including a ban on using the power of one's office to further political goals. It would have been proper for him to recuse himself, instead of participating in litigation that involved a government agency in which he had an interest, and a bill on which he had expressed strong opinions. Apparently, he had done the same thing during the Wilson administration. Such "off-the-bench opinions" as Brandeis gave before the AAA ruling came down were no more acceptable then than they would be now.[32]

The anticipated constitutional test of the AAA finally reached the courts at the end of 1935 in a challenge by a group of textile mill owners who refused to pay the processing tax on the grounds that Congress had exceeded its power. *United States v. Butler*[33] was a suit by the receivers of Hoosac Mills, a cotton-processing company in Massachusetts. The government had presented a claim to the receivers of the bankrupt company for payment of processing and floor taxes on cotton. The receivers, including William M. Butler, a former senator from the state, resisted all attempts to collect the tax and asked that the claims be disallowed. Their lawyers argued that the tax was intended to finance a program of agricultural regulation that could be controlled only by the states. The taxing and spending powers of the federal government were challenged. In spite of attempts through amendments to make the program conform to judicially prescribed standards, the taxing features of the AAA were left unaltered. Large sums in taxes were tied up in litigation. More than seventeen hundred suits were pending in lower federal courts, challenging the program of crop reduction and price fixing.[34] The entire New Deal farm policy hung on the outcome of this case.

Encyclopedic View, eds. Otis L. Graham and Meghan R. Wander (Boston: G. K. Hall, 1985), 2.

[32] B. A. Murphy, *Brandeis-Frankfurter Connection,* 142–43.

[33] 297 U.S. 1 (1936).

[34] As of August 1935, processing tax cases numbered 1,026. Another 262 cases had been filed since the Agricultural Adjustment Administration had issued its previous report. Temporary injunctions had been granted in approximately 509 cases and denied in 21. Suydam Memos, August 15, September 23, 1935, Box 85, Suydam Files, NA. Cf. Jackson, *Struggle for Judicial Supremacy,* 140.

The federal district court in Boston upheld the taxes as valid and ordered them paid, but on appeal the ruling was reversed. Taken on a writ by the government, the Supreme Court heard oral argument on December 9 and 10, 1935, in the first major case argued in its elegant new quarters. In the crowded chamber sat celebrities like Rudy Vallee and the archbishop of York, while another two thousand disappointed spectators waited outside—the largest crowd ever to seek entry to a Supreme Court session.[35]

Stanley Reed, opening for the government, appeared tense and grew ashen during his presentation. When the chief justice, McReynolds, and Van Devanter let loose with a barrage of stinging questions, Reed began to sway at the rostrum. Corcoran later recounted that Justice McReynolds, considered the most irascible of the New Deal critics, so viciously abused Reed that he became physically ill and was compelled to interrupt his argument defending the AAA. "I'm afraid I'm going to have to ask the Court's indulgence," he murmured as he sank into a chair. Deputy Supreme Court Marshal Thomas E. Waggemann rushed over to administer spirits of ammonia. In the midst of arguing a later case, Reed fainted, thus becoming the first solicitor general to collapse while arguing before the Supreme Court.

An eloquent presentation was made by George Wharton Pepper, the high-powered Philadelphia lawyer representing the cotton mills. He claimed to have lost eight pounds the week before arguing the AAA case. In a voice throbbing with emotion, he ended his peroration: "May it please your Honors, I am standing here today to plead the cause of the America I have loved, and I pray to Almighty God that not in my time may 'the land of the regimented' be accepted as a worthy substitute for the 'land of the free.'"[36]

In conference, the chief justice at first seemed to favor upholding the AAA, but five justices were unalterably opposed to it and entertained not the slightest doubt about its unconstitutionality. In a later conference Hughes joined the majority, striking down the act on the grounds that it involved an unconstitutional regula-

[35] *Newsweek* 6 (December 21, 1935), 30.
[36] Quoted in Schlesinger, Jr., *Politics of Upheaval,* 470–71.

tion of agriculture by the federal government and an unlawful delegation of legislative power to the executive (the secretary of agriculture). Six justices held the processing tax in reality part of a system for regulating production, which did not fall under Congress's taxing power. Five justices, including Roberts, agreed with Hughes on these holdings but objected to resting the case on the delegation issue. Before the final vote, the chief justice stated a willingness to have the decision rest squarely on the issue of unconstitutional federal regulation. He assigned the majority opinion to Justice Roberts.

Brandeis remained unusually silent during questioning from the bench and refused to reveal his vote until the day after the final conference. Despite all his previous vituperative remarks, objections, admonitions, and dark threats to dismantle the AAA, he participated only nominally in *Butler.* He wrote no opinion, but signed Justice Stone's dissent. Historian Bruce Murphy speculated that by then he may have recognized that his indiscreet, if not unethical, conduct involving Gardner Jackson and Berle would have "left him at the mercy of his enemies" if he had voted to strike down the AAA.[37] It is hard to accept the notion that he voted his conscience in the *Butler* case.

In a memorandum to Hughes, Stone complained that the main question in the case was decided without adequate discussion, analysis, or any consideration given to the scope of the taxing and spending powers conferred on Congress. The case turned on the coercive nature of the regulations, but Stone later asserted that the matter was not even discussed in conference.[38] "The whole history of the case," he charged, "was characterized by inadequate discussion and great haste in the production and circulation of opinions."[39]

Stone wrote a bitter dissent, concurred in by Brandeis and Cardozo. Stone had received Roberts's draft opinion on December 30, allowing him only a few days to prepare it, but the draft was ready for circulation on January 3, 1936. After reading it, Roberts complained to Hughes about its surly tone, but the chief

[37] B. A. Murphy, *Brandeis-Frankfurter Connection,* 142–43.
[38] Mason, *Stone,* 415.
[39] Schlesinger, Jr., *Politics of Upheaval,* 471.

declined to intervene and suggested he speak to Brandeis. Stone made a few changes to moderate the tone, while Roberts revised his draft in an attempt to meet some of Stone's objections. On Stone's draft, Brandeis scrawled: "I join you in a fine job." In an effort to ameliorate the tension among the brethren, Hughes tried to push matters along, but he was accused of joining the majority, not because he was convinced by their arguments, but as part of an attempt to mass the Court and preserve what prestige it had left.

At noon on January 6, 1936, in a chamber crowded with spectators, Justice Roberts read the six-to-three opinion for the Court in *United States v. Butler,* rarely glancing at the papers on the mahogany table before him. Observing the scene, Thomas Stokes wrote: "Never did a judge kill a legislative creature with more elegance and soft grace."[40] On the matter of taxation, Roberts addressed a long-neglected question—the scope of the federal spending power. The Court first had to decide whether the processors on whom the tax was levied had standing to sue and to challenge the expenditures, since they had paid a substantial part of the amount earmarked for them. The payments to farmers came from taxes levied on processors of the commodity concerned, with all of the proceeds directed to that purpose. Congress, Roberts said, could not use its taxing power as a means to an unconstitutional end—that is, federal regulation of agriculture—because it was a state jurisdiction.

The Court majority at first seemed to adopt the broad Hamiltonian interpretation of the taxing power, saying that it could be exercised for the general welfare and was not limited to the direct grants of legislative power in the Constitution. But by reserving to the Court the right to decide the boundaries of that power, Roberts's ruling eventually moved closer to the Madison-Jefferson view—that Congress is not at liberty to lay taxes for any purpose it pleases, but only to pay the country's debts or provide for the welfare of the Union. The ruling stated that the use of the processing tax to limit acreage and farm production was coer-

[40] 297 U.S. 1 (1936); Thomas L. Stokes, *Chip Off My Shoulder* (Princeton: Princeton University Press, 1940), 480–81.

cive. Congress had no power to control any phase of agricultural production which was deemed to be a purely "local activity." The justices, said Roberts, did not have to decide whether the expenditure on benefits to farmers was for the general welfare, because the AAA was a regulation of agriculture, not an expenditure. Such regulation was an unwarranted invasion of states' rights, in violation of the Tenth Amendment, and so the means as well as the ends contemplated by the act were unconstitutional.

Not until this ruling had the Supreme Court offered any detailed discussion of the nature and extent of the federal spending power.[41] It thus came face-to-face with an unresolved issue dating from George Washington's administration. In the intervening decades, several presidents followed Madison's strict interpretation of the taxing and spending power and vetoed appropriations they deemed unconstitutional.[42] Later on, however, the dominant trend favored Alexander Hamilton's broader interpretation. Such a restrictive view of the scope of Congress's taxing power as Roberts presented provoked a sharp reaction outside as well as within the Court. Cummings wrote: "In a popular government the power to decide what is for the general welfare is much safer in the hands of the representatives of the people than in . . . a permanent body having no direct responsibility to the public and serving for life."[43]

Justice Stone made a strong case for the minority of three. The intramural judicial war that had been developing since 1930 now reached its zenith with his stinging dissent. He attacked the majority view of the taxing and spending powers. Congress, he wrote, was given the power to tax and spend; surely it could do so conditionally. Federal grants of money based on conditions consistent with the national purpose seemed to him clearly within the federal spending power.

As for the notion that regulation of agricultural production was

---

[41] 297 U.S. 1, at 68 (1936). Years later, Frankfurter asked Roberts if he realized "what a door you opened in your . . . Butler decision as to the scope of the 'general welfare.'" Roberts replied: "I do realize it, and often wonder why the hell I did it just to please the Chief." November 1940, Box 171, Frankfurter Papers, LC.

[42] Mason and Beaney, *Supreme Court,* 129.

[43] Secret Diary, January 10, 1936, 11–12.

reserved to the states, Stone noted, the redundancy embodied in the Tenth Amendment ("powers not delegated to the federal government are reserved to the states") had long been conspicuous among judicial instruments for limiting national power. John Marshall, as chief justice, had shown his disdain for it when he wrote: "The Tenth Amendment, framed for the purpose of quieting excessive jealousy [among the states] which had been excited, was quite innocuous, unusable as a means of limiting the implied powers without smuggling into the Constitution's text what was not there."[44] But Marshall's task was to establish the primacy of the national government over the states at that time, so his view of the Tenth Amendment was colored by that objective.

In formulating its doctrine of dual federalism, the Court had by then developed conflicting lines of precedents on the issue of federal-state relations. Stone was concerned about the inferential sanction Hughes, in his *Schechter* opinion, had given the notion of state power and went out of his way to discredit it in his dissent. He was now willing to accept a broad extension of federal authority over agricultural production, an extension he and his brethren had been unwilling to accept over business and industry with the NRA. The distinction he made in the AAA case was evidently based on his view of a need for constitutional growth and substantial expansion in the scope of federal powers.

Stone castigated the majority for judicial usurpation, calling their opinion "a tortured construction of the Constitution" devised to arrive at a result motivated by judicial judgment of the wisdom of legislative action. While conceding that there were widely held and strongly expressed differences of opinion about the wisdom of the AAA, he insisted that no matter how a judge might view legislation in terms of policy, such views should not be permitted to influence his judgment on its validity. "Courts are properly concerned not with matters of policy, but of power." The only question at issue was: Did Congress have the power to enact the AAA?

Courts, Stone lectured, should defer to the findings of legislatures, out of which controversial statutes like this one had

[44] Quoted in Mason and Beaney, *Supreme Court,* 145–46.

emerged. Judges should be ever mindful of the awesome nature of judicial power. The executive and legislative branches are restrained by the ballot box and the democratic process, but the only check on the judiciary's exercise of power is its own sense of self-restraint. Precisely because it is unfettered, judicial responsibility should be discharged with "finer conscience and humility" than that of any other department of government. Not only did Stone try to undermine Roberts's argument, but he sharply attacked the Court's tendency to act as a third branch of the legislature: "Courts are not the only agency of government that must be assumed to have the capacity to govern."[45]

This was one of the strongest dissents registered since the Holmes era. Historian Dexter Perkins later wrote: "The language of Justice Stone went far beyond what was necessary to a resolution of the Butler case. It was in effect a severely critical commentary on the Court itself."[46] Such language, coming from a justice of high reputation, profoundly pleased the administration. "Never before," declared constitutional historian Howard McBain, "has a dissenting minority gone quite so far toward calling into question the motives of the majority . . . clearly implying that they . . . abused their judicial prerogative."[47] When Stone read this statement in the *New York Times,* he wrote McBain to enter a disclaimer: "I do not question the motives of my brethren, and did not intend to do so in the vigorous language which I used in my dissenting opinion. I do question a method of thinking which is perhaps the greatest stumbling block to the right administration of judicial review of legislation."[48]

Frankfurter wired Stone: "Despite all, History remains the ultimate tribunal. There, votes are not counted, but argument weighed and so your dissent will take its place with the great moral pronouncements of your Court."[49] He said Stone saw the problems raised in *Butler* in "the true spirit of Holmes's antisep-

[45] *United States v. Butler,* 297 U.S. 1 (1936), at 87.

[46] Quoted in Charles A. Leonard, *A Search for a Judicial Philosophy: Mr. Justice Roberts and the Constitutional Revolution of 1937* (Port Washington, N.Y.: Kennikat, 1971), 55.

[47] McBain's article appeared in the *New York Times,* January 19, 1936.

[48] Stone to McBain, January 20, 1936, Box 20, Stone Papers, LC. The letter is marked "Confidential!!"

[49] January 7, 1936, Box 13, ibid.

tic attitude" in exercising judicial review under the Constitution. "And that is why I am concerned profoundly not with temporary economic dislocations, not with New Deals or Old Deals, or with merely passing phases of American political controversy, but with those factors which are essential for the maintenance of our traditional federal system."[50]

Edwin W. Patterson of Columbia's law faculty wrote Stone, predicting that the economic situation in farming was likely to be a serious problem for many years to come and that only the future would tell whether the *Butler* decision would lead to basic modifications in the governmental structure.[51] Stone replied wryly: "When one is outvoted two to one, he should be humble and skeptical of his own judgment. Only time can tell how such profound differences should be resolved."[52]

In a letter to Stone flavored with sarcasm, Judge Learned Hand stated: "I would have understood it . . . if they [the majority] had said the general welfare clause was not the general welfare clause. But the shades of Hamilton . . . were too much for them." Though he admitted he could see their point better, he could not quite accept the gloss they had imposed. "True, we can say that you must not attach any conditions [to grants]; that's what they have said, if I understand Brother Owen. I can only answer that the power to appropriate has historically never had that limitation on it; at least I don't believe so."[53]

The *Butler* decision was followed by a sharp decline in farm prices. It aroused deep resentment in certain farm circles because, contrary to contemporary news accounts, some farmers liked the AAA program. In Ames, Iowa, the six justices who formed the majority in *Butler* were hanged in effigy. Agrarian sentiment was expressed in banner headlines in rural newspapers: "SUPREME COURT VOIDS TRIPLE A: RIGHTS OF STATES INVADED, SAYS COURT. HOLY SMOKES!"[54] The press was divided: its editorial comment triggered a lively debate

[50] Frankfurter to Stone, January 9, 1936, ibid.

[51] January 8, 1936, Box 24, ibid.

[52] Stone to Patterson, January 10, and to Walter Gellhorn, January 11, 1936, Box 24, ibid.

[53] January 9, 1936, Box 15, ibid.

[54] Quoted in Arthur M. Schlesinger, Sr., *The New Deal in Action, 1933–1939* (New York: Macmillan, 1940), 22–23.

on the merits of the AAA and speculation as to just which sections of the agricultural population it had aided.

In Congress, outbursts against the *Butler* ruling were at times vociferous. Democrats denounced the justices for usurping legislative power and substituting their individual views on basically political issues for those of the people's representatives. Senator John H. Bankhead of Alabama denounced Roberts's opinion as "a political stump speech." Governor George H. Earle of Pennsylvania charged that the Court had become transformed into a "political body" with six members committed to the policies of the Liberty League.[55]

Roosevelt was in a meeting with Secretary of War George Dern when an aide put a slip of paper on his desk with news of the decision. Leaving the oval study, Dern was asked by reporters how the president had reacted. He replied: "He just held the sheet of paper in front of him and smiled." That smile, according to a Roosevelt biographer, was significant. On this decision he would enter no dissent, no "horse and buggy" retort. The situation had gone far beyond such talk. For the time being, the press and public could quarrel over the issue. Roosevelt was preparing in one way or another to challenge the Supreme Court. His smile "was that of a fighter ready for the struggle ahead . . . of a tactician watching his opponent overextend himself."[56]

Under the *Butler* ruling the AAA continued to exist, but without the legal power or financial means to maintain crop restrictions through farm subsidies. In effect, the decision crippled the AAA. So certain were lawmakers that the Court would also invalidate the Cotton and Tobacco Control Acts that they were quickly repealed. At a private dinner party in Washington, Justice Stone told guests that after *Butler* he thought it would be very difficult for Congress to draft an alternative farm measure that would meet the objections of the Court majority. Under the limits laid down, he could not see how anything that helped farmers as much as the AAA did could be devised to withstand a legal attack.[57]

---

[55] Schlesinger, Jr., *Politics of Upheaval,* 488; *The Sun (Baltimore),* January 7, 1936.

[56] Burns, *Roosevelt,* 232–33.

[57] Soon after making this statement, Stone complained that members of the press were, without authorization, quoting his private views. After they appeared in print, he stipulated that at future private dinner functions no newspapermen were to be present.

But Stone underestimated the tenacity of administration draftsmen. Guided by Secretary Wallace and other department officials, they set to work on a bill preserving as many features of the original farm bill as possible. No sooner had the AAA ruling been digested than they began cobbling together a new program permitting the government to pay farmers benefits for reducing acreage in return for soil conservation. Within a short time, Wallace won approval for a new agricultural relief measure, the Soil Conservation and Domestic Allotment Act of 1936, which levied no taxes and paid benefits for soil conservation programs. It was rammed through Congress in an election year over vociferous Republican protests.[58]

At a press conference on January 7, 1936, the president was asked what his administration's policy would be as a result of the AAA decision. He replied: "No news on that today." Pressed by reporters who asked what he thought of the AAA ruling, he said: "We are, all of us, studying the decision." He emphasized that there were really two opinions, the majority's and the minority's,[59] but he refused to discuss the ruling's implications.

Butler caused serious practical difficulties and struck a heavy blow at the administration's fiscal projections. A week later, in another case, the Supreme Court voided the processing taxes and ordered the return of $200 million collected in taxes on processors.[60] The government was deprived of revenue previously earmarked to go into a special fund for farmers agreeing to reduce acreage. The ruling exposed the Treasury Department to recapture suits for processing taxes already paid, and courts began ordering return of the impounded taxes to their sources. As a result, the projected budget was set back by nearly a billion dollars.[61]

---

[58] Leuchtenburg, *Roosevelt and the New Deal,* 171–72; P. L. Murphy, "New Deal Agricultural Program," 160–69.

[59] Press Conference no. 264, January 7, 1936, *CPPC,* 5:756–57.

[60] *Rickert Rice Mills v. Fontenot,* 297 U.S. 110 (1936). The Court voided the processing tax provisions in the AAA and amendments of August 1935, following the *Butler* precedent. The ruling sustained a large number of injunctions (1,600) granted in district courts against payment of the tax in the interest of the processors, many of whom had already added the tax to the price of their commodities. Thus, wrote Dexter Perkins, the Court awarded some $200 million to companies not entitled to it. *The New Age of Franklin Roosevelt, 1932–45* (Chicago: University of Chicago Press, 1957), 46–47.

[61] *New York Times,* March 22, 1936.

Some limited progress was made toward recovery in agriculture during the New Deal, but as late as 1939, farmers had failed to recover from the impact of World War I and the Depression. The New Deal did very little by way of remedying the root causes of the agricultural depression with its consequent loss of foreign markets and overproduction.

Such a drastic invasion of the farm economy by the federal government as was made by the first AAA in its three years of operation produced vast problems, none more difficult than finding a constitutional base on which to rest a program. The attempt at centralization of the farm economy proved disastrous. The principal beneficiaries of this and subsequent programs were large commercial farming operations, as Brandeis had foreseen. The focus on eliminating competition and regulating production and costs primarily benefited farmers with large holdings at the expense of small operators, tenants, and sharecroppers. Many of the latter two were evicted and reduced to casual farm labor. At the same time that the New Deal paid farmers not to grow crops, unemployment increased, just as other New Deal agencies were using tax revenues to decrease it. Contemporary liberals joined in branding the AAA a sellout to the commercial farm lobby and a policy disaster.

Processing taxes were added to the price consumers had to pay for food, regardless of their income. Farmers refusing to participate in acreage reduction received no benefit payments. Critics found this to be unjustified coercion. A Gallup poll that appeared the day before the *Butler* decision revealed that a majority of Americans (54 percent) opposed the AAA. Even farm leaders hailed the decision. When in 1964 Moley solicited the retrospective views of Henry Wallace on the achievements of the AAA program, his reply, in part, asserted: "We all did the best we could in May 1933 and God was good to us and the farmer and the country when the Supreme Court destroyed the processing tax."[62]

AAA administrators were accused of overreaching in their attempt to create an economy of scarcity. Little of constructive

[62] Cushman, *Rethinking the New Deal Court,* 34–35; Moley, *First New Deal,* 261; William E. Leuchtenburg, *The Supreme Court Reborn* (New York: Oxford University Press, 1995), 98.

merit could be found in what was called "temporary" legislation seeking to improve farm income, although it provided some help to farmers. For that matter, not much can be said for the effectiveness of later legislation designed to replace the AAA. Such improvements as did come to farm income were largely attributable to nature, with its droughts, pests, crop failures, and, by 1939, war. Pressures similar to those felt by New Dealers later forced the Eisenhower administration to reverse its policy and enact farm relief measures reminiscent of much that was tried in the 1930s. But no $30 million pig-killing program was included in these relief measures for obvious reasons, though it was proposed by certain members of the president's party.[63]

Finally, farmers were not the principal advocates of this ever-expanding development of government intrusion in the farming business. One negative result was the top-heavy bureaucracy in the soil conservation agencies created by new legislation. The United States proved backward in providing farm tenants with the security that would have assured them what in Ireland is called "fixity of tenure, fair rent and free sale," or long leases, moderate cash rent, and the right to sell and own the improvements tenants made on the land. Through political action the English dealt with their tenant problem far more generously and effectively than did Americans. Well might Murray R. Benedict and other critics ask: Why were New Dealers so neglectful and so politically ineffective?

United States v. Butler and other Supreme Court decisions in 1936 hardened Roosevelt's resolve at some point to meet the constitutional impasse head-on. Rumors again circulated that the administration was about to propose a constitutional amendment. They proved to be false. FDR's frame of mind is revealed in some remarks later made by his wife: "Franklin became much troubled over the decisions that the Supreme Court was rendering." He thought "no progress was possible as long as the Supreme Court invalidated all the Congressional laws." The First Lady added: "He also felt that people become too conservative as they grow older and that they should not be allowed to continue indefinitely to wield great power."[64]

---

[63] Benedict elaborates on this critique in *Can We Solve the Farm Problem?*

[64] Eleanor Roosevelt, *This I Remember* (New York: Harper and Bros., 1949), 166.

5

Secrets and Stratagems

Oh, what a tangled web we weave,
When first we practice to deceive!

Sir Walter Scott

SPEAKING IN THE BRONX during his 1928 gubernatorial campaign, Roosevelt outlined an ambitious program of judicial reform,[1] but once he went to Albany it was supplanted by more pressing concerns related to the grave economic crisis. In the White House, however, in the spring of 1933, Roosevelt instructed the attorney general to begin work on a plan to reorganize the federal judiciary. What he contemplated was part of an overall reorganization of the executive and judicial branches of the federal government. Unlike the New Deal's ambitious legislative programs for industrial and agricultural recovery, revamping the federal judiciary was looked upon as a broadly conceived reform, incremental in development and sweeping in comprehensiveness. A wide range of ideas came under consideration much earlier in the first administration than has usually been thought.[2]

In 1945, Secretary Perkins wrote that at the outset Roosevelt had no intention of "reforming, changing or modifying the Supreme Court."[3] Somewhat later she alleged that "Homer Cummings was pushing the [Supreme] court reform plan" because he hoped to become a justice himself if it were adopted. "He was its author and instigator," she recalled, "and eventually he was the one responsible for convincing the President that it would work."[4] There is no likelihood that Cummings aspired to a seat

[1] Burns, *Roosevelt,* 104.

[2] Leuchtenburg, "Origins of Court-Packing Plan," 350.

[3] Perkins, *Roosevelt,* 331.

[4] Perkins, Reminiscences, COHC; Ted Morgan, *F.D.R.: A Biography* (New York: Simon and Schuster, 1985), 469.

on the Supreme Court. Solicitor General Stanley Reed, who worked closely with him from 1935 to 1939, attested that at no time during their association did Cummings express any desire other than to be relieved of all public duties.[5]

Judicial reform was not an issue in the 1932 campaign. At that early stage Roosevelt had no coherent program, merely a collection of proposals—some well thought out, others vague to the point of meaninglessness.[6] After the election, with his advisers, he began exploring new initiatives, among them a reform of the inside workings of the federal judiciary and the so-called judicial process. As it evolved, the plan included changing the function and eventually the composition of the Supreme Court. Roosevelt was doubtful he could rely on the Supreme Court for tolerance of his New Deal experiments.

Arthur Krock traced FDR's desire for a Supreme Court receptive to New Deal programs to a speech he delivered in Baltimore on October 5, 1932.[7] Departing from the text, he commented: "After March 4, 1929, the Republican Party was in complete control of all branches of the [federal] government—the Legislature, with the Senate and Congress, and the executive departments, and I may add, for full measure, to make it complete, the United States Supreme Court as well."[8] On that occasion, Roosevelt evidently acted on an impulse, captivated by the spirit of the moment. His departure from the prepared text was picked up by newsmen who reported that the Democratic candidate considered the Supreme Court to be under the political influence of Republicans. According to one Roosevelt aide, such a blatantly partisan remark raised a "terrific hullabaloo."[9]

Republicans saw an issue with potential for embarrassing their opponents. Representative James M. Beck, a former solicitor general, told newsmen: "The Supreme Court never has been controlled by any political party, and it saps the foundation of our government to impute to the highest court of the land a statement that, in spirit or actions it is partisan." President Hoover, cam-

[5] Stanley Reed, Reminiscences, COHC.
[6] Burns, *Roosevelt,* 144.
[7] "In Washington," *New York Times,* February 11, 1937, 22.
[8] *PPA,* 1933 volume, 837; *New York Times,* October 6, 1932.
[9] *PPA,* 1933 volume, 837; Michelson, *The Ghost Talks,* 45–46.

paigning for reelection, seized upon this opening. In Indianapolis he asked: "Does that statement express his [FDR's] intention to attempt to reduce that tribunal to an instrument of party policy and political action for sustaining such doctrines as he may bring with him?"[10]

In the aftermath, Roosevelt was charged with everything from irreverence for the Supreme Court, even sacrilege, to wanting to centralize all power in the executive branch in the event of his election. Republican-controlled newspapers editorialized on the dangers inherent in having a man of such destructive views at the head of the government. Their sharp jabs were meant to arouse suspicions that a Roosevelt presidency would bring on a confrontation with the Supreme Court. At campaign headquarters in New York, FDR's supporters wondered what could be done as damage control, but their candidate was unmoved. The day after his Baltimore speech, he told James F. Byrnes: "What I said last night about the judiciary is true, and whatever is in a man's heart is apt to come to his tongue—I shall not make any explanations or apology for it."[11] The furor subsided as the campaign moved into the final weeks. The only question left to be settled was the size of the Democratic majority.

FDR's extemporaneous remarks, however, presaged his administration's concern for the Supreme Court's role in relation to projected programs for recovery and reform. All but two of the nine justices had been appointed by Republican presidents and confirmed by Republican Senates. Justices McReynolds and Brandeis were Wilson appointees. A New Dealer commented: "Franklin D. Roosevelt came to power in 1933 with his party in the majority in both Houses of Congress. But they would have to reckon with [the] concept of judicial supremacy which had an uncertain number of devotees among the Justices of the Supreme Court."[12]

Public reaction to his Baltimore statement should have given FDR some insight into the delicate distinction between criticism

---

[10] Beck's remarks were reported in the *New York Times,* October 6, 1932; Hoover's speech of October 9 was reported in ibid., October 10, 1932.

[11] James F. Byrnes, *All in One Lifetime* (New York: Harper and Bros., 1958), 65; Michelson, *The Ghost Talks,* 45–46; *New York Times,* February 11, 1937.

[12] Jackson, *Struggle for Judicial Supremacy,* 74.

of the Supreme Court's jurisprudence and of it as a less than impartial institution. Roosevelt seems not to have sensed the depth of resentment he aroused among the justices. In 1936, during that "carnival of retribution being wrought upon New Deal legislation by the Court," Mrs. Eugene Meyer, whose husband owned the *Washington Post,* attended a dinner party at which Justice Stone was one of the guests. She expressed dismay over FDR's insensitivity to the Court's members. Stone told her that "some members of the Court, being only human, were offended by Roosevelt's conduct," a reference to the Baltimore incident, "and were going too far in venting their anger."[13]

Roosevelt's apprehension about the obstacles to his plans for the federal judiciary, and particularly the composition of the bench, surfaced in the fall of 1933. Responding to one of his inquiries, the attorney general wrote FDR: "You may recall a few days ago I spoke to you about a compilation I am causing to be prepared to indicate the political alignments now existing in our federal courts." Attached was a detailed report which, he said, "I am sure you will find exceedingly interesting. You will note that of 266 judges listed, only 28% are Democrats."[14] The 140 federal judges appointed by the three preceding (Republican) presidents constituted roughly three-fourths of the district courts and two-thirds of the appellate bench. It was not only the nine men on the Supreme Court, but this group of judges, partisan in background and conservative in judicial philosophy, who could and probably would present formidable opposition to New Deal programs.[15]

In the Western District of Kentucky, for example, Judge Charles I. Dawson ruled in favor of a coal company and against the NRA, blasting the coal code as "the boldest kind of usurpation, dared by the authorities and tolerated by the public only because of the bewilderment of the people in the present emer-

---

[13] Swindler, *Court and Constitution,* 3:14–15, Clapper Diary, July 29, 1936, Clapper Papers, LC. This exchange and later manifestations tend to confirm the statement by David O'Brien in *Storm Center: The Supreme Court in American Politics* (New York: Norton, 1986), 67, that "perhaps no other President before Nixon had as great a contempt for the Court."

[14] November 8, 1933, OF 41, Box 48, FDRL.

[15] Irons, *New Deal Lawyers,* 3.

REPRODUCED FROM HOLDINGS AT THE FRANKLIN D. ROOSEVELT LIBRARY

OF 41 Box 48 1933-1937 file 4

November 8, 1933

(41)

JUDGES OF THE FEDERAL COURTS ACCORDING TO POLITICAL AFFILIATION:

75 DEMOCRATS		186- REPUBLICANS
	Supreme Court of the United States	
4		5
	Court of Claims	
2		3
	Court of Customs and Patent Appeals	
1		4
	United States Customs Court	
5		4
	United States Circuit Courts	
2	First Circuit	2
2	Second Circuit	4
1	Third Circuit	2
	1 (?)	
	Fourth Circuit	3
4*	Fifth Circuit	1
1	Sixth Circuit	4
4*	Seventh Circuit	2*
2	Eighth Circuit	4*
1	Ninth Circuit	2
	1 (?)	
1	Tenth Circuit	3
Total, 18	2 (?)	27
	United States District Courts	
2	Alabama	1
	Arizona	2
2	Arkansas	
	California	7

* Retired
(8 Cir. 2 retired)

Judges of the Federal Courts According to Political Affiliation. (OF 41 Box 48 1933–1937 file 4, FDRL)

gency."[16] Judge Alexander Akerman, a conservative Republican who presided over the federal district court in Florida, was an avowed enemy of the New Deal and the first federal judge to hold the entire NRA unconstitutional. In a 1933 citrus growers' case, he also ruled against the AAA. Two fruit-packing companies had challenged the production quotas under the AAA's marketing agreements for the state's citrus industry. In a vitriolic opinion, Judge Akerman declared that Congress had no power to regulate agricultural production in any form; he then went well beyond this holding to denounce the New Deal as a "revolution" and an "insidious encroachment on the Constitution."[17] No wonder Justice Department lawyers decided against taking this case to the Supreme Court to test the validity of the AAA's marketing agreements.

District Judge William C. Coleman's ruling against the 1935 Holding Company Act came as no great surprise to New Deal lawyers, who claimed they could nearly always guess how any district judge would decide a case. Coleman, an unsuccessful Republican office seeker, was renowned for his anti–New Deal views. The power companies, represented by John W. Davis, a prominent corporation lawyer, were confident of victory, while government lawyers anticipated defeat. In this case, the so-called power trust was able to choose the battleground. If they could have had a choice, government lawyers probably would have

---

[16] Schlesinger, Jr., *Politics of Upheaval,* 448. The handling of cases like these was bitterly denounced by NRA lawyers, who considered it "bungling at best and sabotage at worst." Irons, *New Deal Lawyers,* 42. The Kentucky case *Hart Coal Corp. v. Sparks,* 7 F.Supp. 16 (W.D.Ky. 1934), involved a challenge to the Bituminous Coal Code. Shortly thereafter, Judge Dawson resigned from the bench to represent other coal companies in suits against the government and to reenter Republican politics.

[17] Judge Akerman's opinion in *Hillsborough Packing Co. v. Wallace,* announced orally from the bench, was reported in *United States Law Week* 1 (1933): 494. Cf. Irons, *New Deal Lawyers,* 142–44. The subsequent ruling by the Court of Appeals for the Fifth Circuit (April 1934) was inconclusive; the appeal panel held that the packing companies had failed to exhaust their administrative remedies, adding that the constitutional objections to the statute were premature because the case was not "ripe" for decision. *Yarnell v. Hillsborough Packing Co.,* 70 F.2d 435, 438–39 (5th Cir., 1934). Judge Akerman did not dismiss the suit. Justice Department lawyer Abe Fortas requested that Akerman dismiss Wallace as a defendant, substituting in his place the citrus commission chairman, I. A. Yarnell.

brought a test case in New York, where there were at least some Democratic district judges. When the utilities companies went to court to test the constitutionality of TVA, they were careful to file suit in Birmingham, Alabama, where they won the first round before Judge William C. Grubb. But when the case went to the Court of Appeals for the Fifth Circuit, made up preponderantly of Democrats, the decision was overturned. The lower-court rulings served as a bellwether, but nothing could be resolved until the constitutionality of the major New Deal laws was put to the final test with a ruling by what Judge Learned Hand called "the august nine."

Both government and corporation lawyers habitually engaged in "forum shopping," attempting to prove laws constitutional or otherwise by bringing test cases, whenever possible, before so-called friendly judges. Everyone knew that federal judges were usually former politicians, chosen by politicians for political reasons. In Roosevelt's first term, the federal bench was loaded with Republicans because so many vacancies had occurred during the three previous Republican administrations.

As Justice Stone once put it, the process of judicial selection is like a "lottery" from a pool of more or less qualified individuals. Reed Powell of Harvard Law School wrote Stone that "the selection of Supreme Court justices is pretty much a matter of chance."[18] Political association and personal friendships at times determine the selection of candidates for the Supreme Court. Over the years there has been a continuing struggle by judges and scholars to perpetuate what is now called the "myth of merit." The reality is that every appointment is political. President George Washington initiated the practice of appointing only ideological kin to the Supreme Court.[19]

---

[18] Stone and Powell are quoted in O'Brien, *Storm Center,* 47; Powell to Stone, October 9, 1928, Box 24, Stone Papers, LC.

[19] O'Brien, *Storm Center,* 44–45, 57. O'Brien argues that merit competes with other political considerations such as personal and ideological compatibility, with the forces of support or opposition in Congress and the White House, and less often with demands for representative appointments on the basis of geography, religion, race, gender, ethnicity, etc. On the general question of judicial selection, see Harold W. Chase, *Federal Judges: The Appointing Process* (Minneapolis: University of Minnesota Press, 1972); Sheldon Goldman and Thomas P. Jahnige, *The Federal Courts as a Political System* (New York: n.p.,

Six months after "Black Monday," when an incumbent's candidacy for appointment to the federal bench in Virginia was being opposed, allegedly because of his opinion upholding the NRA, Donald Richberg wrote Marvin McIntyre for the president's eyes: "It seems to me we need very badly on the federal bench a few judges . . . mentally capable of understanding and sustaining New Deal legislation, and in view of the fact that some appointments have been made of just the other kind I could hardly resist calling attention to the apparent issue in Virginia."[20] The influence of the Senate has increased in recent years on the selection of Supreme Court justices, but it is even greater on that of lower federal court justices. In the Virginia case and others, Roosevelt would not have been the first or the last chief executive to trade lower-court judgeships for legislation and/or good relations.

Throughout his presidency, Roosevelt showed no signs of doing anything different from or better than his predecessors in making appointments to the federal judiciary. Invariably, he allowed partisanship to control his appointments and, like most other presidents, made no effort to balance the Supreme Court by crossing party lines until after he had filled eight seats with Democrats. Only then did he cross the line (in 1941, during wartime) to name Stone chief justice. He was determined from the start to undo the political imbalance in the courts—by single-handedly repacking them if necessary.

The Senate, of course, has the power to reject nominees, a crucial obstacle. Nominees fall prey to partisan politics because of their political views. District and appellate court selections are made on the basis of "senatorial courtesy," a tradition begun in the 1840s whereby presidents appoint judges on the advice and with the consent of the senior senator of the president's party from the nominee's home state.[21] But when it suited his purposes, Roosevelt was wont to disregard senatorial courtesy and

1976), 47–78; and John R. Schmidhauser, *Judges and Justices: The Federal Appellate Judiciary* (Boston: n.p., 1979).

[20] January 16, 1936, PPF 2418, FDRL; O'Brien, *Storm Center,* 52.

[21] Rodney Dutcher, "Behind the Scenes in Washington," undated clipping (ca. November 13, 1935), RG 60, Suydam Files, Box 79, NA. Cummings often sought and received advice on judicial appointments from that "prince of lobbyists," former national Democratic committeeman J. Bruce Kremer of Montana, a nemesis of Senator Wheeler.

invoke the Constitution in favor of his selection. As a result, a flood of critical letters appeared in the newspapers from distinguished constitutional authorities who lined up on opposing sides of the issue to demonstrate that, like the Bible, "the Constitution can be cited by God or Satan." Unfortunately, there is no clear-cut constitutional warrant for or against the resort to senatorial courtesy.[22]

Justice Brandeis lamented to Frankfurter: "If only he [FDR] would not appoint poor judges and lawyers."[23] Charles C. Burlingham, a prominent New York lawyer, complained directly to Roosevelt about the poor quality of his appointments to the federal bench. FDR actually agreed with his friend's charge, but reminded him of how much the established bar influenced appointments.[24] He promised he would appoint better ones if people like Burlingham would find him worthy nominees: "Dig me up fifteen or twenty youthful . . . Lincolns from Manhattan and the Bronx to choose from. They must be liberal from belief and not by lip service. They must have an inherent contempt both for the John W. Davises and the Max Steuers. They must know what life in a tenement means. They must have no social ambitions. There is a job for you."[25]

After Roosevelt named Frankfurter to the Supreme Court in

[22] Beryl Harold Levy, *Our Constitution: Tool or Testament?* (New York: Knopf, 1941), 238.

[23] February 16, 1936, in Urofsky and Levy, eds., *"Half Brother, Half Son,"* 576.

[24] The president and his top advisers scaled down the list of candidates for federal judgeships to two or three on the basis of a political evaluation and, until the Reagan administration, sought informal approval by the ABA. After an exhaustive FBI investigation, a formal evaluation by the ABA was until very recently requested. O'Brien, *Storm Center,* 53. On the influence of the ABA, see Chase, *Federal Judges,* 120–64, and Schmidhauser, *Judges and Justices,* 28–33. On Roosevelt's selections for judgeships at all levels there is a dearth of literature. Scattered information can be found in Sheldon Goldman, "Judicial Appointments to the United States Courts of Appeals," *Wisconsin Law Review* 186 (Winter 1967): 206–11; Richard A. Watson, "Judging the Judges," *Judicature* 53 (February 1970): 283; Abner J. Mikva, "Judicial Selection: Casting a Wider Net," *Annals of the American Academy of Political and Social Science* 462 (July 1982): 112–24; Arthur S. Miller, "Justice without Politics," *Progressive* 38 (April 1974): 34–35; and Daniel J. Meador, "Role of the Justice Department in Maintaining an Effective Judiciary," *Annals of the American Academy of Political and Social Science* 462 (July 1982): 136–51.

[25] FDR to Charles C. Burlingham, February 6, 1936, in Urofsky and Levy, eds., *"Half Brother, Half Son,"* 576 n.

1939, Burlingham, writing to Reed Powell, referred to FDR as "The Warwick of Judge Makers." "As to Frankie's own record," he wrote, "I don't know how much he has gladly accepted political recommendations in order to have peace in the family and get votes, and how much he has been reluctant to do so. It is perfectly clear that if there had not been political considerations either on his part or on that of Farley or various Senators, we would have had much better appointments than those which he has given us."[26] Good or bad, FDR's selections for federal judgeships were seized upon as opportunities to influence national policy and confer political patronage, not forgetting that the tradition of senatorial courtesy guarantees patronage.

"There is no reason in the world why a President should not 'pack' the Court—appoint people to the Court who are sympathetic to his political and philosophical principles." Thus did Justice William Rehnquist respond to Democratic charges that President Ronald Reagan's 1984 reelection could change the direction of Supreme Court policy making. "Because justices serve for life," Rehnquist continued, "they furnish Presidents with historical opportunities to influence the direction of national policy well beyond his own term."[27] From 1933 on, there could be no mistaking Roosevelt's intentions for the federal judiciary at all three levels. He meant to infuse his political ideas and philosophy into the courts. All district and appellate court appointments would turn on the litmus test of support for the New Deal. And when the opportunity to fill Supreme Court vacancies finally arose, the test was applied even more rigorously, along with certain other conditions.

This prospect left Senator Lester J. Dickinson (R.-Iowa) apprehensive. A candidate for the presidential nomination in 1936, he spoke forcefully about "the vital issue" of who would make appointments to the high bench after November. He warned that "at the same time that the New Deal was seeking to palm off under the guise of great humanitarian sympathy an alien social and political philosophy, six of the justices . . . were past the age

[26] February 8, 1939, Box A, file 3, Thomas Reed Powell Papers, HLL.

[27] Associate Justice William Rehnquist, "Presidential Appointments to the Supreme Court," Lecture, University of Minnesota, October 9, 1984, quoted in O'Brien, *Storm Center,* 44.

of 70." By then, in almost a dozen historic decisions, the Court had repudiated much of the New Deal's basic philosophy. Addressing the Sons and Daughters of the American Revolution, the senator said: "That philosophy has been held not only repugnant to the Constitution, but to the spirit of American institutions. Congress and the executive have shown plainly their own nonchalant regard for this fundamental law, thus placing upon the Supreme Court not only the entire burden of enforcement of the Constitution, but what is even more important, of observing the spirit that underlies it."

Given the Court's makeup, Dickinson said, the next president would likely be in a position to name a majority of the justices. If Roosevelt were to control these appointments, he feared, "these new justices will be selected, as the members of the Federal Reserve Board were selected, on the basis of their personal adherence to the President and his philosophy." He asked: "Are we willing to trade liberty for an alleged economic security, under-written by the Federal government? Are we ready to exchange that self-reliance which made this nation what it is for dependence upon bureaucratic direction for all the important activities of life?" Dickinson firmly believed that the growing paternalism would not only insidiously undermine democracy itself but would strike at the very existence of the states.[28]

More and Better Judges

Roosevelt, for obvious partisan reasons, wanted vacancies on the federal bench at all levels, and after preliminary discussions he concluded that more judges were needed to handle the increasingly heavy caseload. Inquiries directed to officers in the various executive departments hinted at what he was contemplating. Early in 1934, he wrote the director of the budget: "Will you speak to me about the matter of retired pay for federal judges?"[29] Later, he asked the attorney general: "What is the status and

[28] "Supreme Court Balance in Peril," unidentified clipping, February 22, 1936, PPF 2278, FDRL.

[29] FDR to Lewis Douglas, January 8, 1934, OF 41A, FDRL.

prospects of legislation for additional district court justices in various parts of the country? Do you think many additional judges are absolutely necessary? I have my doubts."[30]

In 1933 and 1934, Roosevelt was influenced by fiscal conservatives Treasury Secretary Henry Morgenthau and Budget Director Lewis Douglas, both of whom constantly pressured him for fiscal restraint and a balanced budget. As a result, he found himself at cross purposes, since filling vacancies and increasing the number of judgeships cost money. In May 1934, Cummings solicited the advice of Chief Justice Hughes: "The President would be glad to have your views as to the necessity for the appointment of additional district judges."[31] Hughes replied that, in view of existing austerity measures, additional judgeships would have to be limited to two each for the Southern District of New York and the Southern District of California, the country's fastest-growing urban centers, where swelling court dockets were impeding the proper administration of justice. Although need could be shown for additional judgeships in five other districts, Hughes conceded that under present fiscal conditions, they would have to take lower priority than appointments for New York and California.[32] The Judicial Conference of the Senior Circuit Judges had made these recommendations along with requests for permanent—as opposed to temporary—judgeships in twelve districts, with two each for Massachusetts and New York.

Congestion and delays characterized certain districts, Hughes said, but not the district court system as a whole. The attorney general's annual report for 1934 alluded to serious delays in New York and California resulting from the failure to provide a sufficient number of judges.[33] Hughes tried to provide relief by assigning judges from other districts to those that were understaffed, but delays persisted. He told the president in December 1934 that he hoped remedial legislation for these conditions would be introduced at the next session of Congress.[34]

---

[30] February 26, 1934, OF 41, Box 48, FDRL.

[31] Cummings to Hughes, May 29, 1934, Box 8, Charles Evans Hughes Papers, LC.

[32] Hughes to FDR, May 30, 1934, ibid.

[33] The average delay before reaching trial in New York's Southern District in civil jury cases was seventeen months, while in California the average delay for all civil cases was between eighteen and twenty-four months.

[34] Hughes to FDR, December 31, 1934, PPF 7590, FDRL.

A lone but persistent voice in the drive for additional federal judges in the lower courts was raised by Judge William Denman, named by Roosevelt to the Court of Appeals for the Ninth Circuit in 1934; but even before going on the bench, Denman, dismayed at the state of the federal judiciary, had embarked on a one-man lobbying campaign for "More and Better Judges." On frequent trips to Washington he conferred with Roosevelt, the chief justice, Cummings, Justice Stone, and many others. On a visit to the White House, he told Roosevelt that the delays in litigation were indefensible and that the Judicial Conference was doing nothing meaningful about them.[35]

In April 1936, Denman sent the president a lengthy proposal ("Elimination of Delays in Federal Courts") that had previously been submitted to Justices Brandeis and Stone for their suggestions. Stone told him he was "on the right track" but wanted more details and clarification; Brandeis termed his proposal "excellent."[36] In one memo, FDR asked Stanley Reed to speak to him about Judge Denman's proposals "asking for a centralized judicial administration of the 91 Federal Courts" and "presenting the need for 50 new district judgeships."[37] It was no coincidence that FDR's 1937 judiciary reorganization plan ultimately requested *fifty* new federal judgeships.

Denman provided the president with an array of facts and statistics painstakingly amassed to support the need for more judges, but none of his proposals affected the Supreme Court. Authorization for new judgeships was a congressional matter. Serious delays, he said, resulted from Congress's failure to provide an adequate supply of judges to do the work of the courts, some of which were taking six months or longer to reach trial after joinder of issue. Why not three months? he asked. The increase in court business was creating logjams. "People do not dare go to the federal courts now," he asserted, "and the weaker fellow accepts whatever he can get from the stronger."[38]

Judge Denman also recommended appointing an administrator

[35] Leuchtenburg, *Supreme Court Reborn,* 113.

[36] Denman to FDR, May 8, 1936, Box 199, Cummings Papers, ALDL.

[37] March 11, 1936, OF 10F, Box 27, FDRL (for the original memo, see OF 41, Box 48).

[38] Denman to FDR, May 8, 1936, Box 199, Cummings Papers, ALDL.

called a "proctor" to handle the day-to-day bookkeeping—that is, monitoring the federal courts to provide a more businesslike organization of their administration. But his main target was crowded court dockets and delays before reaching trial. The effect these delays were having on both criminal and civil litigation was serious. Each day that passed between joinder of issue and trial increased the fading of memory, the disappearance of documents, the loss of witnesses and of hard evidence. Denman's proposal required the federal courts to be so reconstituted that whenever a case was ready for trial there should be a judge on hand, ready to preside without delay.

As it was, judges, overburdened with cases, yielded to dilatory practices by lawyers. There were far too many continuances, postponements, extensions, and similar tactics. Courts were overwhelmed to the point of denying justice to litigants, the result of failing to lobby Congress for the necessary relief. Denman wrote urging Roosevelt to make reform of the federal courts an issue in the 1936 campaign. He was worried that the "don't rock the boat" boys would succeed in persuading him to give up any idea of making judicial reform a platform issue in the campaign. "Your election is certain," he wrote, "but the hell of opposition you will encounter in the next four years is just as certain. The reactionaries in our own crowd will turn against us. You were never more right than in your determination that they must be bound to this reform by the platform—and never more right than in your appraisal of the country's need for a freed judiciary."[39]

Denman pleaded with Roosevelt to "go on the air" just before the Democratic convention with a summary of the situation as outlined in his reports. In early May, he again wrote to remind him that the chief justice had provided him with an opportunity: "The Chief Justice yesterday gave an opening for your [radio] talk and convention platform provision for more judges. No one can say that it is a matter of partisan politics," he added, "now that the subject has been thrown open by the great Republican justice."[40] The reference was to an Associated Press release on the May meeting of the American Law Institute, a nationwide

[39] Denman to FDR, April 25, 1936, ibid.
[40] Denman to FDR, May 8, 1936, Box 199, ibid.

organization of leaders of the American bar. In the opening address to the lawyers, Chief Justice Hughes began with a lighthearted remark: "I am happy to report that the Supreme Court is still functioning." The sedate audience cheered and applauded loudly for a full two minutes.[41]

Hughes recommended the appointment of additional federal judges to speed up disposition of litigation, and noted some improvement in the situation. In fifteen of eighty-four districts, delays of no more than six months were required to reach trial after joinder of issue. But he made no mention of situations arising *before* cases actually were brought to trial, where there were the longest delays and where the strongest argument could be made for an increase in the number of judges. Hughes concluded by urging the lawyers to cooperate with an advisory committee recently set up to prepare a unified set of rules of civil procedure in the federal district courts.[42]

That May, Denman again wrote Roosevelt to congratulate him on the overwhelming vote he had received in the California primary. "But," he warned, "what must be done in your next term! The need of the litigant for *more judges* will then be at its peak."[43] However, Roosevelt ignored Denman's proposal and, to the judge's dismay, had no intention of incorporating any of his suggestions, either in his campaign speeches or the platform.

THE ASSAULT ON THE SUPREME COURT'S POWER

Challenges to the Supreme Court's power were nothing new. In the early 1800s, Thomas Jefferson and the Democratic Republicans tried to neutralize the power of the federal courts, which had been packed by their predecessors with Federalist opponents. The instrument Jefferson used to humble the courts was impeachment—the only legal method of removing federal judicial officers. In the nineteenth century, Andrew Jackson and Abraham Lincoln experienced difficulties with the Supreme Court

[41] *New York Times,* May 8, 1936.

[42] Hughes's address of May 7, 1936, is excerpted in *Vital Speeches* 2 (1936): 543 and passim.

[43] Denman to FDR, May 8, 1936, Box 199, Cummings Papers, ALDL.

and questioned the omnipotence of the judicial branch. In 1912, Theodore Roosevelt renewed the attack, proposing the recall of state court decisions and judges. These extremes shocked members of all parties, and TR was branded a radical. But even he conceded that when the Supreme Court ruled on a question of constitutionality, its judgment had to stand. The main bulwark against such assaults was judicial supremacy, part of the legacy of Chief Justice John Marshall.

Well before the Supreme Court had an opportunity to rule on New Deal measures, key figures in the Justice Department, in deepest secrecy and on instructions from the president, began investigating methods of curbing the powers of the federal judiciary. The investigation was placed under the exclusive direction of the attorney general. In the fall of 1933, Cummings made Carl McFarland his special assistant, and vice chairman of a committee charged with "investigating proposed legislation of an important character." Research was carried on under McFarland, who reported directly to the attorney general. This work was scheduled to go over to the fall of 1934 for completion and submission, with the president's approval, to Congress in the form of a statute. The team effort was described as "a legislative project of great importance."

McFarland, at the time, held only a temporary position in the Justice Department. He was in Washington on loan from the Montana State Supreme Court, and when rumblings reached Washington of attempts to lure him back, Harold Stephens wrote to the state authorities saying he feared that "if we lose the services of Mr. McFarland, it will result in a serious problem here." In May 1934, McFarland resigned as Montana's code commissioner to stay on with the Justice Department as one of Cummings's closest associates.[44]

No one in the administration had an inkling of what was going

---

[44] Stephens to Carl MacFarland, July 8, 1933; Stephens to T. L. Calloway, Chief Justice of the Supreme Court of Montana, April 11, 1934, asked the state authorities to extend McFarland's leave of absence to facilitate *important work* in the Justice Department, Box 26, Stephens MS., LC. In interviews with him in Washington, D.C., Erwin Griswold assured the author that McFarland, of all Cummings's assistants, played the key role in researching and formulating the 1937 court-packing plan.

on behind closed doors in the Justice Department. Cummings had never been part of the brain trust or the White House inner circle. He was satisfied with his role as Roosevelt's designate to conduct work on the secret project. Proposals relating to the lower federal courts were outlined by late 1935 and remained in a fluid state well into the election campaign, but toward the end of the Supreme Court's 1936 spring term the investigation shifted into high gear. Until then, the search for a possible solution to the impasse had been only desultory.[45]

A handful of lawyers in the Justice Department put in daily work on the "secret project," and Cummings gave it his spare hours. The researchers, besides McFarland, included Alexander Holtzoff, Warner W. Gardner, and R. C. MacCutcheon, among others. Their work was not coordinated; they were informed of neither its objective nor where it was leading. One of their mandates was to explore in its historical and legal aspects the appellate jurisdiction of the Supreme Court with a view to limiting or withdrawing its power to rule on the constitutionality of acts of Congress. The investigators went back to the founding fathers and looked into other aspects of the Court's powers.

The assault on the Court's appellate jurisdiction and judicial review took the form of a two-pronged inquiry. One prong was aimed at finding some means of *limiting* the Court's power to invalidate acts of Congress, an approach Cummings favored. The other was directed toward *stripping* the Court of its appellate jurisdiction over acts of Congress or constitutional questions. Underlying this effort was a deep-seated conviction in the administration that major New Deal laws—NRA, AAA, TVA, and the Social Security Act—would not survive judicial scrutiny. In December 1935, Cummings sent McFarland a memo outlining possible action to be taken if the Supreme Court decided adversely on practically all New Deal legislation and set up "constitutional standards which cannot be met."[46] Administration insiders were anticipating the worst at the hands of the nine justices.

[45] Alsop and Kintner, *Men around the President* (Garden City, N.Y.: Doubleday, Doran, 1939), 147.

[46] December 28, 1935, Swisher, ed., *Selected Papers,* 147. Cummings's memos to McFarland for this period are in Box 210, Cummings Papers, ALDL.

Researchers for the attorney general reviewed the historical evolution of judicial review with its roots in the famous 1803 case *Marbury v. Madison.*[47] Article III of the Constitution states that the appellate jurisdiction of the Supreme Court is subject to such exceptions and regulations as may be enacted by Congress. MacCutcheon pointed out for the benefit of Cummings and prospective judicial reformers that passing on the constitutionality of acts of Congress is not, properly speaking, an exercise of the Supreme Court's jurisdiction, but is "entirely apart from it, inherent in, and integral to the judicial process," as Chief Justice Marshall had asserted. It is a necessary corollary of the admitted proposition that "the Constitution is the paramount law of the land." It followed that while Congress can withdraw jurisdiction it has conferred on the Supreme Court, this cannot be held to apply to the power of the Court to pass upon the constitutionality of acts of Congress, because Congress never attempted to confer by statute the power of judicial review on the Court. Hence, his memo concluded, "it would be a mistaken notion to assume that Congress can withdraw a power which it has in fact never conferred."[48]

With this in hand, Holtzoff sent Cummings his findings on whether Congress could deprive the Court of its power to declare statutes unconstitutional by limiting its appellate jurisdiction. In view of the limited nature of the Court's original jurisdiction as conferred in Article III, its decisions are invariably rendered in cases falling under its appellate jurisdiction. The only way the Court could be deprived of the power to decide on constitutional questions, he wrote, would be to abolish its *entire* appellate jurisdiction. The same objective, in his opinion, could *not* be achieved by abolishing the Court's appellate jurisdiction in only limited groups of cases.[49]

Would an act of Congress repealing the entire appellate jurisdiction of the Supreme Court be constitutional? asked Holtzoff. If so, would such a course be practicable? Enactment of such a statute as was being contemplated would be constitutional, said

[47] 1 Cranch 137 (1803), at 176.

[48] Memo from R. C. MacCutcheon for Holtzoff and the Attorney General, February 6, 1935, Box 199, Cummings Papers, ALDL.

[49] Holtzoff to Attorney General, February 6, 1935, ibid.

Holtzoff, and was not without precedent. This very thing had been done by the Judges' Act of 1925, which amended the Judicial Code and considerably restricted the Court's appellate jurisdiction. If it were within the power of Congress to take away part of the Court's appellate jurisdiction, it could take away all of it.[50] But to do anything so drastic, he warned, would be impracticable.

Holtzoff failed to emphasize, however, that the 1925 act, mainly the work of the justices themselves and Chief Justice Taft, was called the Judges' Act because it reflected their own efforts to limit the volume of cases they were being asked to review each term. The act gave them virtually unlimited discretion in granting or denying petitions for *certiorari.* In enacting this measure, Congress was merely endorsing the justices' proposal to limit their caseload and, as a consequence, limit their appellate jurisdiction, which Article III authorizes Congress to do. There was quite a difference between the justices' own effort to limit their caseload and attempts by Congress to deprive the Court of its prerogative of judicial review by withdrawing its appellate jurisdiction.

Holtzoff concluded that if Congress limited or abolished the Supreme Court's appellate jurisdiction, such action would approach abolishing the Court itself. The few cases that would be left for it under its original jurisdiction would render it an insignificant tribunal with little or no business to transact.[51] Any such statute as was being contemplated by the administration, if passed, was certain to be ruled unconstitutional by the Supreme Court. In any case, district and appellate courts would still be able to declare federal statutes unconstitutional, and any attempt to prevent the inferior courts from declaring statutes unconstitutional would in itself be unconstitutional under the doctrine in *Marbury v. Madison.*[52] The Constitution, as John Marshall as-

[50] Ibid.

[51] Ibid.

[52] The Department of Justice Files, NA, include memoranda touching on the power of Congress to prevent the inferior federal courts from declaring a statute unconstitutional. Cf. L. R. Clark, April 6, 1917; R. L. MacCutcheon, May 24, 29, 1935; Albert Levitt, February 23, 1935; Alexander Holtzoff, June 22, 1935; W. C. Jennings, October 25, 1935; W. W. Gardner, August 15, 1935. See also W. W. Gardner's Memo to Solicitor General Reed, January 14, 1936, RG 60, file 235773, NA.

serted, supersedes any congressional statute. To change this doctrine in order to meet any such situation as the New Deal administration was facing, Holtzoff averred, would require amending the Constitution. The amendment he proposed would require a two-thirds majority of the Supreme Court to declare acts of Congress unconstitutional and would prohibit review of congressional statutes by the inferior federal courts. Holtzoff advised that this would be a wiser course than attempting to achieve the same objective by legislation. No simple statute could obtain the desired result.

Cummings returned Holtzoff's memo, complaining that he was not entirely able to follow his "line of reasoning" and still wanting to know whether *all* the Court's appellate jurisdiction had to be taken away to reach the desired result. "Is there not some formula," he asked, "by which appellate jurisdiction dealing with constitutional questions *only* could be taken away?" He asked Holtzoff to develop this more fully.[53] Holtzoff replied that the Court's appellate jurisdiction was fixed, not only by the Constitution, but by statute. After reviewing cases involving the jurisdiction issue, he reiterated: "It would be a highly dangerous step to take away from the Supreme Court the power to determine the constitutionality of statutes, if such power remains in the inferior Federal courts, for then we are likely to be confronted by a situation where a statute might be valid in one Circuit and invalid in another." A constitutional amendment, he repeated, would be necessary to achieve the desired result.[54] There the matter stood over the next few months, during which Cummings instructed McFarland to prepare a list of all the statutes passed by Congress since 1908 that were invalidated by the Supreme Court.[55]

Following the Court's decision in the railroad pension case, Cummings wrote Angus MacLean: "Has any study been made in this office of the question of the right of Congress by legisla-

---

[53] Cummings to Holtzoff, June 13, 1935, Box 199, Cummings Papers, ALDL.

[54] Holtzoff to Cummings, June 22, 1935, ibid.

[55] The Legislative Bureau of the Library of Congress was enlisted in its preparation, which was drawn from W. C. Gilbert's *Provisions of Federal Laws Held Unconstitutional by the Supreme Court of the United States.* RG 60, file 235773–4226, NA.

tion, to limit the terms and conditions upon which the Supreme Court can pass on constitutional questions? I have seen several memoranda from time to time spelling out a theory by which the result could be achieved without a constitutional amendment."[56] Cummings made no reference to Holtzoff's memos recommending a constitutional amendment. His next sentence was startling in its implications: "My recollection is that our files will somewhere disclose briefs on the theory that the Supreme Court has *no* right to pass on constitutional questions *at all.* Of course, quite a learned document could be prepared, dealing with the historical aspects of this matter, and the way in which it has . . . developed." MacLean was told to have the matter "pretty thoroughly covered" to include "the whole question of legislation which would not exactly cut off the right of the Supreme Court to pass on constitutional questions, but . . . limit it somewhere with a view to avoiding five to four decisions."[57] Holtzoff was meanwhile instructed to frame a response to Cummings's vague and somewhat contradictory directions. It is preposterous to believe that an attorney general would even want to consider reopening the much-debated question of whether there was legitimacy in the Supreme Court's exercise of judicial review.[58]

In the late summer of 1935, Justice Department lawyer Warner W. Gardner, conducting his own research independent of Holtzoff, wrote Solicitor General Reed: "There has been surprisingly little professional discussion of the proposals by Act of Congress to limit the ability of the Supreme Court to invalidate legislation. Such discussion as has been found agrees with the conclusions set forth . . . that the power to control the appellate jurisdiction of the Supreme Court does not include the power to prescribe rules of decision or to control the Court in the exercise of its

[56] May 11, 1935, RG 60, file 235773, NA.

[57] Ibid.

[58] In the preface to a 1939 reissue of *The Supreme Court and the Constitution,* Charles A. Beard announced that he had "settled" the great controversy over the legitimacy of the Supreme Court's awesome power. The book was cited often and favorably by expert witnesses at the Senate Judiciary Committee hearings on Roosevelt's 1937 court-packing plan. The committee seems to have accepted the book as authoritative. Cf. Felix Frankfurter, "Notes on Advisory Opinions," *Harvard Law Review* 36 (1924): 1003, n. 4.

judicial power, and that the power to declare legislation unconstitutional is a matter of *judicial power* rather than of *jurisdiction.*"[59] As authorities, Gardner cited constitutional historian Charles Grove Haines and former Supreme Court justice John Hessin Clarke. Five months later he wrote: "At the outset it should be stated that the logical result of the separation of powers doctrine would seem to be that Congress has no power to control a judicial function. For the reasons stated in my memorandum of August 15 . . . I should think that the power to declare a statute unconstitutional is an inherent attribute of judicial power."[60]

It would be useless, he concluded, for Congress to remove from the district courts all jurisdiction over cases involving constitutional questions, since they could arise in any type of proceeding over which the district courts have jurisdiction. Secondly, Congress would seem to have rather plain power to provide that no inferior court could issue an injunction against the enforcement of any federal or state statute. Finally, he reminded Reed that, in spite of the language in some of the earlier cases, the Supreme Court had recently expressed doubts as to the ability of Congress to interfere with the judicial power of the inferior courts. "At the present time," he concluded, "I should think this latter doubt would present a more reliable guide to constitutional law than earlier language."[61]

Well before this, Roosevelt had begun to pursue different avenues. In a memo, he asked the attorney general: "Will you speak to me about . . . the percentage of cercerari [*sic*] applications by the Government being denied by the Supreme Court?"[62] Cummings relayed a memo from the solicitor general which, he said, "I think, answers your recent question." The memo showed that writs had been granted on government petitions in 28 cases at the most recent term of Court. In nongovernment cases, 500 petitions for *certiorari* had been filed, and 65 more were granted.[63]

---

[59] August 15, 1935, Department of Justice, RG 60, file 235773, NA.

[60] January 1, 1936, ibid.

[61] Ibid.

[62] FDR to Cummings, December 19, 1934, PSF 76, FDRL.

[63] Cummings to FDR, December 24, 1934, OF 10F, Box 27, FDRL. J. Crawford Biggs was solicitor general at the time.

The inquiry indicates a lingering interest in finding a way to curb the Court's internal decision making, presumably by an act of Congress.

The motive behind Roosevelt's inquiry became clearer in 1937 when he used information about the ratio of petitions for appeal granted to those denied to demonstrate that the Supreme Court was, in his view, arbitrarily disposing of the great majority of them. The course he was contemplating amounted to interfering with established statutory law (the Judges' Act of 1925) and the Court's internal decision making. Gardner had already told him that mandating a two-thirds vote in Supreme Court decisions would also represent unwarranted interference with the Court's power to prescribe its own rules of decision.[64] The exercise of judicial review, he said, was "a matter of *judicial power* rather than of *jurisdiction.*" Gardner, Holtzoff, and MacCutcheon were all in agreement on these points. If the president was seriously considering implementing such audacious methods as were then under investigation to curb the power of the Supreme Court, he was skating on very thin ice.

Work on the Justice Department's "secret investigation" continued while Roosevelt kept looking for ways to deal with the Supreme Court. A week after the *Butler* decision, he asked Cummings: "What was the McCardle case? I am told that the Congress withdrew some act from the jurisdiction of the Supreme Court."[65] This post–Civil War case had somehow drawn Roosevelt's attention. Cummings replied: "The case of Ex parte McCardle . . . is one of the classic cases to which we refer when

[64] Denying or granting writs of *certiorari* falls under the justices' rule-making prerogative. When Congress gave the Court discretionary jurisdiction over granting writs of *certiorari* in the Judges' Act of 1925 by substituting them for mandatory appeals, the justices developed the informal rule requiring that four of the nine must agree that a case warranted arguments, briefs, and consideration by the full Court. In the 1930s, under Chief Justice Hughes, the rule was liberally applied. Frequently three or even two justices urged hearing a case on the merits. The Court was by then acting on approximately nine hundred petitions in any given term, a great many of them frivolous. Only a small percentage, as Biggs's memo reveals, were granted. O'Brien, *Storm Center,* 191–93.

[65] *Ex parte McCardle,* 7 Wallace 506 (1869). FDR to Attorney General, January 14, 1936, PSF 185 (now 165), FDRL.

considering the possibility of limiting the [appellate] jurisdiction of the Federal Courts. This whole matter has been the subject of considerable study in this Department, and, in view of recent developments, is apt to be increasingly important. A brief analysis of the case in question [prepared for FDR by Alexander Holtzoff] is annexed hereto."[66]

The revised Habeas Corpus Act of February 5, 1867, empowered the federal courts to grant writs of *habeas corpus* in all cases in which any person was restrained or deprived of liberty in violation of the Constitution and laws. Appeals could be taken to the circuit courts and up to the Supreme Court. Upon conviction and sentencing by a military tribunal for publishing inflammatory and insurrectionary articles, William McCardle, a Mississippi editor, petitioned the U.S. Circuit Court for a writ of *habeas corpus,* contending that he had been charged and held illegally. His plea was denied and he was remanded to military custody. On appeal to the U.S. Supreme Court under provisions of the Habeas Corpus Act, McCardle's counsel contended that the military tribunal, which existed only by virtue of the Reconstruction Acts, had no lawful authority to try him. The precedent cited was a recent Supreme Court decision—*Ex parte Milligan.*[67]

Fearing that the Supreme Court justices might dare, under the Habeas Corpus Act, to declare some or all of the Reconstruction Acts invalid, the Radical Republicans in Congress moved swiftly to foreclose such a possibility by another Act of March 1868, withdrawing the Supreme Court's jurisdiction in all cases arising under the Habeas Corpus Act of 1867, which formed the basis for Reconstruction policies. This law was specifically designed to kill McCardle's case before the Supreme Court. After hearing oral argument in April 1869, the Court dismissed the appeal on the ground that the "repealer" of March 1868 had withdrawn its jurisdiction. Chief Justice Samuel Chase's ruling acknowledged that the Supreme Court held appellate jurisdiction at the discretion of Congress, which now left it without power to act in McCardle's case. The appeal was dismissed for lack of

[66] Cummings to FDR, January 16, 1936, PSF 165, FDRL.
[67] 4 Wallace 2 (1866).

jurisdiction.[68] Although he acknowledged the validity of the repealer, Chase reasserted the Court's authority in all other *habeas* cases, pointedly reminding the Radicals and the bar that the 1868 repealer did not affect jurisdiction previously exercised.[69]

What did McCardle's case have to do with the New Deal's Supreme Court problems in 1936? Roosevelt thought it held out some promise as a precedent for legislation withdrawing at least part of the Court's appellate jurisdiction. He was casting about for a means of getting back at the justices for wrecking his program. A plan would eventually evolve, but it did not include withdrawing any part of the Court's appellate jurisdiction, though this alternative was being seriously considered at that time. It was not lost on Roosevelt that the assault by Radical Republicans on the Supreme Court in 1867 and 1868 had resulted in judicial submission to political threats.

Constitutional scholars have argued that Congress cannot erode the judicial power vested in the Supreme Court under Article III through "jurisdictional nibbling" at its appellate authority, the approach Roosevelt was considering in 1936. But the extent to which Congress can affect substantive rights by jurisdictional excisions remains controverted.[70]

Concluding his analysis of *Ex parte McCardle,* as requested by the president, Holtzoff offered this advice:

> It seems to me that the foregoing cases are authorities for the proposition that the Congress may limit the appellate jurisdiction of the Supreme Court by taking away from it the power to review certain

---

[68] Stanley Kutler, "Ex parte McCardle: Judicial Impotency? The Supreme Court and Reconstruction Reconsidered," *American Historical Review* 72 (April 1867): 835–51. Full coverage is in his *Judicial Power and Reconstruction Politics* (Chicago: University of Chicago Press, 1968), 89–113.

[69] The Court reaffirmed this in *Ex parte Yerger,* 8 Wallace 85 (1869), a *habeas* appeal under Section 14 of the Judiciary Act of 1789. Yerger's case also arose out of the Reconstruction Acts. From an army prison in Mississippi, he petitioned for his freedom under a writ of *habeas corpus.*

[70] Owen J. Roberts, "Now Is the Time: Fortifying the Supreme Court's Independence," *American Bar Association Journal* 35 (January 1949): 1072–74; Kutler, *Judicial Power,* 101. For a thorough statutory analysis see Leonard G. Ratner, "Congressional Power over the Appellate Jurisdiction of the Supreme Court," *University of Pennsylvania Law Review* 109 (December 1960): 157–202.

> classes of cases. I venture to suggest, however, that these decisions do not support the inference that the Congress may circumscribe the manner in which the Supreme Court shall decide a case, after the case has been permitted to reach that tribunal. In other words, if the Supreme Court is given the power to review certain types of cases, it would hardly be valid for the Congress to direct the manner in which the case shall be determined, for example as to whether or not a statute on which one of the parties relies, may be declared unconstitutional.[71]

Holtzoff and other Justice Department lawyers couched their admonitions in diplomatic language, repeatedly warning Roosevelt and Cummings that they were venturing into dangerous territory in their search for ways to limit the power of the Supreme Court.

In early 1936, Arthur Krock astutely observed that "in the long course of American history . . . the unspecified power of the Supreme Court to set aside acts of Congress" has shown that "the instances of human frailty have been rare, the examples of self-abnegating justice multitudinous."[72] This, he concluded, was one reason why the American people have long repelled any suggestion that the system of judicial supremacy be overthrown. Throughout 1936 and 1937, most Americans continued to believe in "the purer processes of the judiciary, exalted above and made free of the ballot box, as contrasted with the acts and motives of those who must go to the polls for the offices they hold and seek to retain."[73]

The Amendment Option

Almost from the beginning of his troubles with the Supreme Court, Roosevelt found himself in a quandary over whether the situation required remedy by statute or by constitutional amendment, and whether to change the Constitution or make alterations in the Court itself. After the "horse and buggy" press conference, historian and Tennessee editor George Fort Milton wrote

[71] Memo on *Ex parte McCardle,* January 16, 1936, PSF 165, FDRL.

[72] "Nine Judges, and Nine Men, Too," *New York Times Magazine,* March 29, 1936, 7:1–2, 15.

[73] Ibid.

FDR advising that his target should not be the Supreme Court, but rather the Constitution. After all, he reminded the president, Cardozo, Stone, Hughes, and Brandeis had all voted against the NRA. Given the Constitution as it was, he added, they had no other choice. He urged Roosevelt to take the lead in a great program of constitutional reform: "That is what we need to have done. Let the Constitution be amended so that the Congress will be given power to control as well as direct effects of Interstate Commerce . . . [and] provide for an intelligent measure of delegation." He thought such a course would gain support from progressives; he did not believe there would be nearly as much support for a program based on criticism of the Court itself.[74]

Members of Congress from time to time have sought to restrain the exercise of the Supreme Court's review powers by requiring that it find acts of Congress or state laws unconstitutional only if an extraordinary majority of the justices concurred in the decision. Most of those earlier proposals required that two-thirds of the justices concur, but some of the more extreme proposals have urged that such decisions be unanimous.

The idea of one or more constitutional amendments to curb the Court, one version of which would have limited or deprived it of its authority to invalidate acts of Congress, was under investigation by the administration even before the setbacks of "Black Monday." After his badly received press conference remarks, Roosevelt refrained from making any further public comment on the Court, but he continued to ponder the implications of the judicial performance. In August 1935 he told Charles Wyzanski it was becoming clear that the judges were deciding cases on the basis of partisan political views. "Of course," he said, "if the Supreme Court should knock out the AAA, then the constitutional amendment would be the real issue. It probably will be anyway, and there will be less difficulty in phrasing it than many people think. If the Court does send the AAA flying like the NRA, there might even be a revolution."[75]

When the prospect of an amendment was aired publicly that

[74] George Fort Milton to FDR, June 4, 1935, quoted in Leuchtenburg, *Supreme Court Reborn,* 91.

[75] Charles E. Wyzanski, Jr., to Mrs. C. E. Wyzanski, August 2, 1935, quoted in Schlesinger, Jr., *Politics of Upheaval,* 453.

same month, former president Hoover called on Roosevelt to reveal any changes his administration was proposing to make to the Constitution. Looking to the approaching presidential race, Hoover wanted to flush FDR out on his plans in anticipation of making the Constitution and Supreme Court campaign issues. Roosevelt was too shrewd a politician to reveal his strategy in advance to the opposition, even if he had decided what that strategy would be. As yet, he had not. The episode might have gone unnoticed had it not been for Hoover's suggestion, as reported in the press, that there was something "un-American," something "terribly wrong" about the idea of amending the Constitution, as if it were a new thing in American politics. In view of Hoover's record in championing the only amendment ever to be repealed, a liberal newspaper commented, "it is obviously absurd for him to argue that blocking constitutional amendments for social reform will save the Constitution."[76]

In late August 1935, Roosevelt called in journalist George Creel, a contributor to *Collier's Weekly* magazine, to assist him in launching a trial balloon. He had adopted a policy early in his presidency of treating all journalists equally, but there were frequent lapses from this "gentlemen's agreement." The article, which appeared under Creel's name, included whole paragraphs dictated by Roosevelt concerning the Court problem. The piece was entitled "Looking Ahead with Roosevelt," and a key paragraph ended: "It is the deep conviction of Franklin D. Roosevelt that the Constitution was never meant to be a 'dead hand,' chilling human aspirations and blocking humanity's advance, but that the founding fathers conceived it as a living force for the expression of the national will with respect to national needs." The president acted under the compulsion of "terrific necessities," FDR had Creel write. The final paragraph stated that if the Supreme Court continued to interpret the Constitution in ways rendering "the present generation . . . powerless to meet social and economic problems that were not within the knowledge of the founding fathers, then the President will have no other alternative

[76] *New York Post,* August 1, 1935, 10.

than to go before the country with a constitutional amendment that will lift the dead hand."[77]

"Fire that as an opening gun," a grim FDR told his friend. But as Arthur Schlesinger, Jr. noted, "it was apparently only a popgun."[78] While Roosevelt expected the article to win widespread attention and perhaps criticism, it provoked almost none at all. "Nothing was more plain," observed Creel, "than the lack of public interest."[79] But that was not Roosevelt's version. "Dear George," he wrote, "those features of yours I am delighted to have and may I also tell you that I have had at least fifty people speak to me about the article. . . . It made a great stir."[80]

Around this time, Roosevelt wrote Newton Baker about a letter from him which Dan Roper had shown him: "I know you will not mind. I know also that you will not mind my telling you that I think you are entirely wrong in your thought that [a] constitutional amendment will of necessity be an issue in the next presidential campaign." He went on: "As a senator with a sense of humor remarked to me today, the Republican National Committee in secret confab searched the woods for an issue; they discarded the constitutional issue and decided in a month or two to come out in favor of the Ten Commandments, proclaiming from [the] housetops that the Democratic Party wished: a) To amend the Ten Commandments b) To add to the Ten Commandments c) To scrap the Ten Commandments. On this issue they are confident that they can sweep the country."[81]

The lack of public interest in the Creel article left the question of constitutional amendments in limbo. Roosevelt was content for it to remain there, at least until there were more Supreme Court rulings on pending New Deal measures and until he could make up his mind on how to proceed in the matter.[82] An editorialist wrote: "As President Roosevelt prepared for his four-week trip to the Pacific coast, the first major activity of the 1936 cam-

---

[77] George Creel, "Looking Ahead with Roosevelt," *Collier's,* September 7, 1935, 7–8.

[78] Schlesinger, Jr., *Politics of Upheaval,* 454.

[79] George Creel, *A Rebel in Politics* (New York: Putnam, 1947), 291–92.

[80] September 10, 1935, PPF 2610, FDRL.

[81] September 26, 1935, PPF 669 and 1717 ("Constitution"), FDRL.

[82] Kenneth S. Davis, *F.D.R.: The New Deal Years, 1932–1937* (New York: Random House, 1986), 605; *PPA,* 1935 volume, 12–17.

paign, government attorneys were bending every effort to bring before the Supreme Court the remaining cornerstones of the New Deal—the AAA, TVA, Guffey Act, and National Labor Relations Act."

This was considered a startling reversal of former administration policy, interpreted in Washington as meaning that if the Court continued to follow the line laid down in the *Schechter* decision, Roosevelt was prepared to make his campaign for reelection on a constitutional amendment authorizing the federal government to control wages, hours, and conditions of labor. Taking advantage of the lull in events, an editor reported: "The obvious way to meet it [the Court problem] is to seek a new amendment to the Constitution, affirming . . . that all business is now interstate business. . . . Amendment of the Constitution is the way out. . . . To outwit the legal sharks, it should give Congress specific regulatory power over minimum wages, maximum hours, pensions, [and] conditions of employment."[83] That, however, was far from what FDR had in mind, or what he told Newton Baker. One thing, however, was certain. The president would not permit the Supreme Court to wreck any more of his attempts to achieve reform and recovery, even if his resolve moved the country toward a constitutional crisis.

The AAA had been operating for three years and was still in reasonably vital shape when it was struck down.[84] The *Butler* case, decided in January 1936, was another irritant. Even though White House insiders as early as June 1935 expressed doubts about the AAA's constitutionality, the violence of the majority's views startled them.[85] Whether the ruling was expected, Moley and Early had all they could do to restrain FDR from speaking out. Mindful of the adverse reaction to his remarks to the press a year earlier, Early implored his boss: "Please resist. Say nothing."[86] Roosevelt took this advice. There would be no repetition,

[83] "The Week," *New Republic*, October 2, 1935, 198; for the editorial, see "The Next Amendment to the Constitution," *New York Post*, September 26, 1935. Copy in PPF 1820, Box 9, FDRL.

[84] *Washington Post,* January 7, 1936, 10.

[85] Memo from Chester Davis to FDR, July 13, 1935, OF 1-K, AAA files, FDRL.

[86] Early to FDR, January 9, 1936, quoted in Joseph P. Lash, *Dealers and Dreamers: A New Look at the New Deal* (Garden City, N.Y.: Doubleday, 1988), 276; Ickes, *Secret Diary,* 1:534.

as an editorialist stated, "of the horse and buggy nonsense, and for this courtesy toward the Supreme Court, the whole country can be thankful."[87]

Addressing a Jackson Day dinner in Detroit, FDR identified the "basic issue" before the nation as "the retention of popular government," but he remained silent about the Court. It did not go unnoticed by the press. Defending his reticence, he stated an "unwillingness to rush to judge *two* of the most momentous opinions, majority and minority, that had ever been rendered by the Supreme Court." But there was more to his silence than the apparent desire to appear patient.[88] As if to confound his Republican opponents, Roosevelt was prepared to maintain his silence indefinitely.

An editor of the *Progressive Farmer* wired: "Don't be stampeded into the politically dangerous issue of asking for an amendment to the Constitution stop Instead of amending the Constitution, the important and practical thing to do is to re-elect you and let you amend the Supreme Court stop You will almost inevitably have an opportunity to transform a liberal minority of three into a majority of five stop."[89]

The AAA's invalidation gave unusual impetus to the introduction of a flood of congressional proposals to impose restraints on judicial power by statute or amendment. In the early months of 1936, congressmen introduced more than a hundred bills designed to restrict the work of the federal courts. Legislators filled the hoppers with proposals ranging from restricting the Court's appellate jurisdiction to a constitutional amendment specifically expanding federal power over commerce, agriculture, and mining. In the spring session alone, more than forty proposals affecting the Supreme Court and its work were introduced. They dealt with the size of the Court, required a seven-to-two or unanimous vote to void legislation, and offered various retirement plans for justices. A few wanted the justices' office to be made elective, or de-

[87] *New York Herald Tribune,* January 9, 1936.

[88] *PPA,* 1936 volume, 43–44; Lash, *Dealers and Dreamers,* 265–67.

[89] The reference to a "liberal minority of three" regarded the vote in the *Butler* case. Clarence Poe to FDR, May 19, 1936, Box 225, file 5, Joseph T. Robinson Papers, UAL.

manded the impeachment of "recalcitrant judges" if they refused to resign. Hostile Democratic lawmakers accused the justices of approaching the judgment of cases with minds predisposed to oppose the administration.[90]

Proposals to limit the Supreme Court's power included requiring advisory opinions on all measures immediately upon their introduction in Congress, as well as amendments prohibiting the Court from declaring *any act* of Congress unconstitutional.[91] Congressional criticism covered a wide spectrum of opinion. Independent Senator George Norris of Nebraska told newsmen: "A constitutional amendment may be the only way out. Of course, an amendment is bound to take considerable time." That same day, however, Senator Harry F. Byrd (D.-Va.) announced that he was opposed to any amendment to the Constitution.[92] Senator Joseph O'Mahoney (D.-Wyo.) wanted Roosevelt to urge Congress to enact a law depriving the Court of its authority to declare a statute unconstitutional except by a unanimous vote. This suggestion, he said, had been enthusiastically received by Democrats at the recent Jackson Day dinner. It would avoid the delay and difficulty involved in a long campaign for a constitutional amendment.[93] Other senators and representatives seemed prepared to await the president's lead, knowing that any new legislation of this nature would be controversial and difficult. Congressional Democrats concluded that, if all efforts failed and the problem with the Court had to be handled as a national one, as FDR believed it had to be, then their only recourse was to a constitutional amendment.[94]

Moley was one of many who favored an amendment explicitly giving Congress power to legislate on national and economic

---

[90] Department of Justice, January 7, 1936, RG 60, file 235773–4226, NA.

[91] *Washington News,* January 7, 1936.

[92] *New York Herald Tribune,* January 7, 1936. Norris wanted an amendment requiring a seven-to-two vote by the Court to invalidate acts of Congress within sixty days of their enactment. He also wanted to amend the judicial code to give the Supreme Court original jurisdiction in all cases attacking the constitutionality of congressional acts so as to avoid delay in the lower courts. However, Norris failed to press for action on these proposals because "he was not sure the time was ripe." He wanted to see what public reaction would follow the AAA decision. *Washington News,* January 7, 1936; cf. Notes in Box 230, Clapper Papers, LC.

[93] O'Mahoney to FDR, January 10, 1936, PPF 1200, FDRL.

[94] Unidentified news clipping, January 7, 1936, PPF 1820, FDRL.

matters. This, he said, was implied in the Constitution's general welfare clause but was so vaguely understood that any Court majority could plausibly deny its existence. This option had been available for consideration at least since the invalidation of the NRA.[95] But Harvard's Erwin Griswold could not agree with Moley. Conveying his dismay over the AAA decision, he wrote Justice Stone: "It seems to me that this nation cannot continue with powers so narrowly circumscribed as the [Court] majority now says they are. I would much rather have developed those powers within the framework of the present Constitution than take the risk of amendments enlarging those powers along any one of several possible lines." But fortunately, he added, time heals many wounds.[96]

The personal messages sent to the president were sorted in the White House mail room, and a small sampling was placed on his desk almost daily. An Indiana correspondent wrote saying he realized that any suggestion at such a distance from a man with little power would perhaps have little value. "However," he continued, "constitutional methods are available. The simplest . . . is the speedy enactment of a law increasing the membership of the Supreme Court to fifteen. This is not unprecedented and is valid. Six of the best lawyers of the United States, added to that bench would reverse this infamy."[97] Farley wired the president the same advice following the NRA decision. "Enlarge the Supreme Court to fifteen members," he advised. "Have a bill introduced immediately."[98] But the very thought of increasing the membership of the Supreme Court elicited strong criticism. One of the nation's most influential newspapers trumpeted its disapproval in no uncertain terms: "Ideas like this one are being advanced as possible ways in which the Roosevelt administration is seeking to change the constitutional rules in order to gain a special advantage in carrying out its program."[99]

There was good reason for hesitation. Resistance to such an

[95] Moley, *After Seven Years,* 330–31.

[96] Undated letter, Box 15, Stone Papers, LC.

[97] Thomas Duncan to FDR, January 7, 1936, RG 60, file 235773, NA; a copy is in ibid.

[98] Farley to FDR via A. E. McCullough, June 12, 1935, OF 41A, FDRL.

[99] *St. Louis Post-Dispatch,* July 5, 1935.

upheaval in the federal judiciary as Roosevelt was considering would be overwhelming. Requiring a seven-to-two vote would make it possible for only three justices to prevent an unconstitutional enactment from being overturned. In cautionary memos, Justice Department lawyers alluded to the hazards of interfering with the internal mechanics and decision-making processes of the Court, which went beyond the whole question of its jurisdiction. There can be times when five-to-four or six-to-three "divided opinions" can be useful, they argued, especially when constitutional doctrines are in a state of flux.

Some believed that the difficulty lay not with the Constitution, but with the Court. They argued that either the composition of the Court had to be altered or the Court must, and perhaps could, be persuaded to change its mind. In the past, Senator Norris had been unusually critical of the Supreme Court, which he once accused on the floor of the Senate of being, for all practical purposes, "a continuous constitutional convention." He called for an amendment requiring a seven-to-two majority on the Court, later changing it to a unanimous vote, and declared: "It takes twelve men to find a man guilty of murder. I don't see why it should not take a unanimous court to find a law unconstitutional." But when it came to putting his influence behind these proposals, Norris seemed reluctant to go beyond powerful rhetoric.[100]

Two well-known British commentators intruded in the debate to declare their views on the critical constitutional issues facing the United States. In June 1935, Harold Laski, a prominent journalist and academic whose socialist ideas had once held a certain fascination for a young John F. Kennedy, entered the controversy with the publication of a pair of articles in Britain.[101] Copies of them landed on FDR's desk, and the president was so impressed with

[100] Schlesinger, Jr., *Politics of Upheaval,* 491. Frankfurter and his followers opposed the amendment approach. The attorney general vacillated and seemed to leave his position ambiguous.

[101] "Constitution of the United States—the New Problem—Supreme Court's Decisions," *Manchester Guardian Weekly,* June 1, 1935, and "Constitution of the United States—State's Rights and the Nation's Needs," ibid., June 18, 1935. Copies are in PPF 1820, FDRL.

their content that he wrote Cummings: "I wish you would read these . . . extremely interesting articles. Stanley Reed and Harold Stephens may care to see them also. Please let me have them back, as they are the only ones I have."[102]

Laski suggested an "ample revision of the foundations of the [American] Constitution." It would not be easy to secure, he admitted, because behind the attitude of the Supreme Court were ranged state authorities, jealous of their historic rights; businessmen, who looked with anger and dismay at the advance of liberalism; and an amending process as difficult as any in the constitutions of modern states. But behind all these issues he perceived a deeper conflict. Against attempts by a political democracy to use its power to promote the interests of the common man, he observed, there stands a body of vested interests that live by an obsolete social philosophy in which the rights of property are placed before the claims of the common welfare. "It is that obsolete social philosophy the Supreme Court seems determined to protect."

In Laski's view, the Constitution would have to adapt to modern economic conditions because new economic conditions would not adapt themselves to the Constitution. Such amendments as were being suggested, he said, would transfer a tremendous amount of power to Washington from the states and would reduce them in economic matters to the position of units of local government. Such a transfer would also circumscribe the domination of capitalism. "Either the Supreme Court must give way," he wrote, "or means have to be found to nullify its decisions by amendment, or otherwise."[103]

Laski predicted that "there will be grave and dramatic developments in the United States of the next decade." Alexander Holtzoff was asked by FDR to analyze and summarize the essays. He submitted an even more prophetic conclusion: "One wonders whether the *Schechter* case is not a precursor to a popular demand that Congress be endowed with power to regulate

---

[102] July 5, 1935, OF 10 F, Box 27, FDRL. Laski followed up on these articles with another piece: "The Crisis in the New Deal: The Supreme Court and Its Critics," *Manchester Guardian Weekly,* January 17, 1936, 50. Copy in PPF 1820, FDRL.

[103] Copy in PPF 1820, FDRL.

economic factors which in our complex civilization far transcend the artificial geographical boundaries of the individual states."[104]

After reading Laski's articles, Stephens told Cummings he did not share Laski's belief that changing economic and social conditions would require "some adjustment in the constitutional situation" that was likely to come in some catastrophic form. "I believe," he wrote, "that the American process of trial and error in constitutional development, which you and I have several times discussed, will meet the present exigency as it has those of the past, and without radical departure from the orderly, underlying principles of our government."[105] Cummings agreed and wrote the president: "I return herewith, as you request, the clippings from the *Manchester Guardian.* It is a very discerning analysis of the situation. The writer, however, insists [that] what has come into view is the need for the ample revision of the foundations of the Constitution. I do not believe we have quite reached that point yet."[106]

During the summer of 1936, the onetime journalist Winston Churchill, a keen observer of the American political scene, commented on the impending crisis: "This is an age in which the citizen requires more, and not less, legal protection in the exercise of his rights and liberties." Perhaps, he surmised, that was why the American administration had thus far been so restrained in its response to the offensive launched by the Supreme Court against the New Deal, and why none of the suggested constitutional amendments had been supported by it. "The challenge may come at a later date," he added, "though it would perhaps be wiser to dissociate it from any question of the age of the judges, lest it be the liberal element in the Court which is weakened."

The English, he reminded his readers, continually give new interpretation to the archaic language of their fundamental insti-

---

[104] Holtzoff memo to FDR, July 16, 1935, Box 199, Cummings Papers, ALDL; Department of Justice, RG 60, file 235773, Sec. 2, NA.

[105] Stephens to Cummings, September 9, 1936, Box 199, Cummings Papers, ALDL. Before 1936 was out, Stephens was named to the U.S. Court of Appeals for the District of Columbia. He was on the Court during the court-packing fight, but from the bench he opposed Roosevelt's plan in every discreet way he could.

[106] January 29, 1936, PPF 1820, Box 10, FDRL.

tutions. He agreed that "this is no new thing in the United States" but asserted: "The judiciary have obligations which go beyond expounding the mere letter of the law. The Constitution must be made to work." It ought not to be interpreted by pedants, and "any true interpretation of the British or the American Constitution is certainly not a chop-logic. So august a body as the Supreme Court in dealing with law must also deal with the life of the United States, and words, however solemn, are only true when they preserve their vital relationship to facts." He concluded: "It would certainly be a great disaster, not only to the American Republic, but to the whole world, if a violent collision should take place between the large majority of the American people and the great instrument of government, which had so long presided over their expanding fortunes."[107]

A conflict was in the making, but it would not, as Churchill predicted, be between the people and their Constitution. The confrontation that had been brewing for some time would set president against Supreme Court. The struggle would commence when one of the two warring parties provoked it. The Supreme Court had not yet finished reviewing New Deal measures. Alluding to this, Cummings confided to his diary something the president had told him: "Mr. Frankfurter remarked—that the Supreme Court seemed to be taking 'slow poison.'"[108]

---

[107] Winston Churchill, "What Good's a Constitution? Our Heritage of Freedom" *Collier's* 98 (August 22, 1936) 22, 39–40. Also quoted in Schlesinger, Jr., *Politics of Upheaval,* 495–96.

[108] Secret Diary, January 13, 1936.

6

Toward a Constitutional Crisis

> The American People are today moving rapidly toward a constitutional crisis of unpredictable gravity.
>
> Edward S. Corwin[1]

DURING 1936, an election year, recurring problems with the Supreme Court occupied more and more of the president's time. In a moment of exasperation he asked his attorney general: "How do you feel about going up against the Supreme Court?" Cummings replied: "It's like a golf match, Mr. President. Four down and five to play." Talking about the difficulty of presenting progressive measures to the Supreme Court, Cummings used the analogy of a nine-hole golf match: "On the fifth tee, I was always four down with five to go, and it was necessary to win the next five holes in order to get the decision." This was a reference to the five-to-four division on the Court in the gold clause cases.[2] Roosevelt liked the golf story so much that he used it in speeches at a National Emergency Council meeting in February and at the National Press Club Founders' Day dinner on March 2, 1935.[3]

By mid-1936, adverse decisions by the Supreme Court were causing resentment not only within the administration but also with affected interest groups. Organized labor was upset by the *Schechter* ruling. "Black Monday," said Cummings, "has been a bitter day for labor . . . the gains of a decade seem to be slipping away."[4] Even before the NRA decision, Assistant Labor Secretary Edward F. McGrady in March 1935 told a labor audience: "With stupid judges on the bench . . . it is up to the workers to

---

[1] Quoted in *New York Herald Tribune,* September 10, 1936.
[2] Cummings, Secret Diary, February 19, 1936.
[3] Ibid.
[4] May 28, 1935, ibid.

organize to such an extent that their economic strength will make it unhealthy for a judge to defy you."[5]

Each adverse decision produced new outbursts of hostility, but stony silence came from the White House. Shortly after Roosevelt denounced *Schechter* for putting the country back in the horse-and-buggy age, Oswald Garrison Villard, editor of *The Nation,* offered to bet anyone that the president would not again refer to the Supreme Court or the issues involved until after the election. Villard got no takers, but he would have won that bet.[6]

Critics of the Court were growing louder than its defenders. Senator James F. Byrnes of South Carolina argued that, although Republicans championed states' rights, it did not follow that the federal government had to stand by helpless to meet the social and economic problems of the day. Senator Norris joined the chorus of critics. The people, he said, could change the Congress or the executive, "but only God can change the Supreme Court." The AAA decision alienated some farmers, and its impact reached well beyond the farming community. It was a decision so broad, wrote Arthur Krock, that "few New Deal acts before the Court now seem to have any chance of being upheld."[7]

The Court had no harsher critic than its own Justice Stone, whose blistering AAA dissent won the admiration of New Dealers, who now asked: if Justice Stone is able to speak in such forceful language of a "tortured construction of the Constitution" and to ask the Court majority to use self-restraint, who could blame the administration for feeling slightly desperate?[8] Writing to a former colleague, Stone questioned his brethren's method of thinking, perhaps the greatest stumbling block to a proper administration of the judicial review of legislation. "We see it [the method of thinking] frequently enough in the . . . un-

[5] Schlesinger, Jr., *Politics of Upheaval,* 487.

[6] "Issues and Men," *Nation,* November 7, 1936, 547.

[7] This climate of opinion is fully discussed in Schlesinger, Jr., *Politics of Upheaval,* 487–88. Byrnes's speech was printed in *Congressional Record,* 74th Cong., 1st sess., Vol. 80:8747–48, June 6, 1936. Borah's speech of January 2, 1936, was reported in the *New York Times* on January 3, and Krock's comments appeared in it on January 7. Borah had earlier issued a clarion call to the American people to defend the Constitution and safeguard the Supreme Court from partisan attacks.

[8] Schlesinger, Jr., *Politics of Upheaval,* 490.

trained mind, which is accustomed to think that legislation which it regards as bad or unwise must necessarily be unconstitutional. Where there is a choice of interpretation of a constitutional provision, such a habit of thought is very likely to [choose] the interpretation which would lessen the possibility of enacting a bad law."[9] In a similar vein, he told Charles Burlingham: "You do not dislike the A.A.A. anymore than I do. I think probably not as much. That is what perhaps made me emphasize the fact that our function is not to get rid of laws merely because we don't like them. If that were the criterion, I should have been on the other side."[10]

Lessening the power to enact bad laws likewise lessens the power to enact good ones. The judgment of what is good or bad, Stone said, is essentially a legislative function and is likely to be affected by the passions and prejudices of the moment. An approach to constitutional construction such as the one the Court majority was presently taking tended to increase the "dead areas" in the Constitution, the lacunae in which no power—state or federal—exists to deal with the problems of government.[11] How long, he wondered, could any government continue to operate under this dispensation? The constitutional crisis Stone and others anticipated seemed to be heightening with each adverse decision.

A central theme ran through the opinions in which the Supreme Court majority struck down New Deal statutes. The Constitution was construed in such a way as to confine the federal government within narrow limits, at times enlarging powers of the states or private interests. This, wrote Charles A. Beard, was laissez-faire theory, and while laissez-faire might be good economic doctrine, it was not in the Constitution, and was not the doctrine of the men who framed it.[12]

FDR was convinced that the entire New Deal was threatened and would expire in an agony of five-to-four or six-to-three deci-

---

[9] Justice Stone to Howard Lee McBain, January 20, 1936, Box 20, Stone Papers, LC.

[10] January 9, 1936, Box 7, ibid.

[11] January 20, 1936, Box 20, ibid.

[12] "Little Alice Looks at the Constitution," *New Republic* 87 (July 22, 1936), 315–17.

sions. Ickes wrote: "Clearly, it is running in the President's mind that substantially all of the New Deal bills will be declared unconstitutional by the Supreme Court. That will mean that everything that this Administration has done of any moment will be nullified." Given the present Court, Cummings declared, New Deal cases would not stand much of a chance "even if the Angel Gabriel himself made the argument." Roosevelt foresaw "the shadow of portending crisis" by the late summer of 1935 and predicted that if all New Deal legislation were nullified, there would be marching farmers, marching miners, and marching workingmen throughout the land.[13]

After the AAA ruling, Cummings outlined in a letter to FDR what was for him an important policy shift. "The real difficulty is not with the Constitution," he wrote, "but with the Judges who interpret it. As long as a majority of those who have the final say in such matters are wedded to their present theories, there are but two courses open to us. We must endeavor . . . to find a way to bring helpful national legislation within the explicit terms of their decisions, or we must frankly meet the issue of a constitutional amendment." He continued:

> For the present, I think our proper course is along the former line rather than the latter. The hand has not yet been played out. If we come to the question of a constitutional amendment, enormous difficulties are presented. No one has yet suggested an amendment that does not do either too much or too little, or which does not raise practical and political questions which it would be better to avoid. If we had liberal Judges, with a lively sense of the importance of the social problems which have now spilled over state lines, there would be no serious difficulty; and the existing constitutional restraint, when interpreted by such a Court would be very salutary.

In spite of his reservations and in contradiction to his own previous advice, Cummings suggested giving thought to an amendment ("should we find we are forced to that point") that "would

[13] Ickes, *Secret Diary,* December 27, 1935, 1:495; Cummings to John Dickinson, December 28, 1935, quoted in Swisher, ed., *Selected Papers,* 147; Schlesinger, Jr., *Politics of Upheaval,* 490.

require the retirement of all federal judges, or at least all Supreme Court judges, who have reached or who hereafter reach the age of seventy. It may very well be," he wrote, "that life tenure lies at the heart of our difficulty and that there should be no such thing for any public official of any kind, executive, legislative, or judicial." In states that had such a constitutional provision, he maintained, it worked very well.

"Such an amendment," he went on, "would probably encounter less opposition than almost any other I can think of. It would have the advantage of not changing in the least degree the structure of our Government, nor would it impair the power of the Court. It would merely insure the exercise of the powers of the Court by Judges less likely to be horrified by new ideas. There may be variants of the proposed amendment which will suggest themselves as the matter is studied. For instance, it might be coupled with a provision giving to the Supreme Court explicit power to pass on constitutional questions and taking away or denying such power to inferior courts."[14]

In the light of what came later, Cummings's letter sets forth the weightiest case Roosevelt had so far received from his attorney general. Its principal approach lay at the heart of the 1937 court-packing plan—enlarging the membership of the Supreme Court by replacing or inducing retirement of justices over seventy, of whom by 1937 there were six. The final plan, however, would be implemented by statute and not, as suggested here, by constitutional amendment, a *fundamental* difference.

The advanced age of the justices had long been a topic of public comment. It was the main theme of a book entitled *The Nine Old Men,* published in 1936 by those "two Walter Winchells of Washington," Drew Pearson and Robert S. Allen.[15] Columnist Arthur Krock joined supporters of an age limit for the Court: "Probably the faults of the [judicial] system could be reduced if there were an age limit for justices who have served more than a certain number of years. Aged men often grow remote from the

[14] January 29, 1936, PPF 1820, Box 10, FDRL.

[15] For a negative review see Fred Rodell, "Justice v. Justices," *New Republic* 87 (December 23, 1936), 251.

world, are unsympathetic to change, shackled by their prejudices." The suggestion, he argued, is not radical. "It has eminent associates of the highest traditionalism and patriotism. Compulsory retirement at 75 could more easily be amended, writes one of them."[16]

In support of this, Krock quoted liberally from a book by Chief Justice Hughes in which he wrote that some judges stay too long on the bench.[17] To avoid the risk of having sitting judges unable to do their work, Hughes wrote in 1928, an age limit should be imposed, but he admitted that any age selected would of necessity have to be arbitrary, since the onset of failing mental vigor differs widely.[18] Roosevelt had no opportunity in four years in

"Nine Old Men." A cartoon depicting the stereotype of justices of the U.S. Supreme Court characterized as still living in the "horse and buggy" days, as if to endorse FDR's argument to liquidate six of them, leaving Cardozo, Roberts, and Stone. (Source: The Communist magazine *New Masses,* 1937)

[16] "Nine Judges, and Nine Men, Too," *New York Times Magazine,* March 29, 1936, 7:1–2, 15.

[17] *The Supreme Court of the United States: Its Foundations, Methods and Achievements* (Garden City, N.Y.: Doubleday, 1928). Reprinted in 1936, this was a published version of a series of lectures delivered by Hughes in 1927 in the Columbia University Blumenthal Foundation Series.

[18] *New York Times,* March 29, 1936.

office to make a Supreme Court appointment, a situation that had rarely occurred in any full presidential term.[19] Using the age of sitting judges to create vacancies—or threatening to enlarge the Court if vacancies did not occur—must have held a certain attraction for him under the circumstances, but he was about to learn that juggling the size of the Supreme Court, no matter by what device, was an unacceptable way to change the substance of its decisions.

Government attorneys were gearing up to bring before the Court the other New Deal measures—the law setting up the Tennessee Valley Authority, the Guffey Coal Act, and the National Labor Disputes Act (later the Wagner Act). Cummings intended to hurry these and other cases along as soon as the Court reconvened for the 1935–36 fall term. The government had already agreed to submit the 1934 Securities Exchange Act to a judicial test of its powers.[20] This was a startling reversal of administration policy, interpreted in Washington as meaning that if the Court were to continue along the lines laid down in *Schechter,* its decisions that winter would be uniformly hostile. The about-face was erroneously interpreted as meaning that the president was preparing to campaign for reelection on the issue of a constitutional amendment specifically authorizing the federal government to control wages, hours, and conditions of labor.

Liberty League lawyers, meanwhile, were making solemn pronouncements that the remaining New Deal measures were unconstitutional. They rallied to the defense of a Constitution that the Supreme Court was fully able to protect. The league's actions were regarded by the administration as presumptuous. It infuriated Roosevelt to watch lawyers posing as disinterested authorities on constitutional law, feeding their opinions to the newspapers. Their organization's explanatory statements indicated that they were "advocates of unconstitutionality."[21]

---

[19] President William Howard Taft named six justices in one term; Warren G. Harding named four in two and a half years.

[20] Tom Corcoran and Ben Cohen were a skillful drafting team for both the Securities Act of 1933 and the Act of 1934 that established the Securities Exchange Commission.

[21] "This Week," *New Republic,* October 3, 1935, 198. For the "liberal" views of the Liberty League, consult the three articles in consecutive issues by George

The *New Republic* thought the trouble was that in the past it had been the business of government counsel to choose good cases, get them before the courts without delays that implied a lack of confidence, argue them properly, and, if the record permitted, make the Supreme Court realize that an adverse decision on constitutionality would put an end to government activity approved by both houses of Congress, the president, and the public. Few if any of these requirements had been met in the presentation of the recent New Deal cases, especially *Schechter.*[22]

Upholding the TVA

The next important New Deal case to follow invalidation of the AAA was *Ashwander et al. v. Tennessee Valley Authority.*[23] At issue was the operation of the Tennessee Valley Authority (TVA), a government-created development corporation set up in an act of May 1, 1933. It was designed to improve navigation and flood control on rivers in a seven-state region and, through a series of dams, to generate hydroelectric power, producing cheap electricity for homes, farms, and industry. The act of incorporation gave the manufacture and distribution of electricity by the government a secondary role as a by-product, partly because New Dealers anticipated that private power companies would challenge the statute in the courts on the grounds of unfair competition.

Preferred shareholders of the Alabama Power Company challenged a contract negotiated by it with TVA and brought suit to enjoin their own company and TVA from carrying out this contract, which allowed the TVA to purchase much of the company's property and equipment, including power lines, and gave it the right to sell surplus electric power directly to consumers. Plaintiffs attacked the constitutionality of the entire TVA program as exceeding the scope of congressional power. District Judge Wil-

Soule, commencing in the October 26, 1936, issue. The lawyers volunteering for the League were to contribute their legal services in test cases involving fundamental constitutional questions—presumably to private clients only, and not as "dollar-a-year men" to the Department of Justice.

[22] *New Republic,* ibid.

[23] 297 U.S. 288 (1936).

liam Grubb granted the injunction, but the Court of Appeals for the Fifth Circuit reversed, upholding the contract. The case went to the Supreme Court, which deliberated for many weeks before reaching a decision. Government attorneys who argued the case had by then gained "wisdom" from their experience with the Court, and in their briefs and arguments they decided to deemphasize the "social experiment" aspect of TVA. They also hired themselves a very smart lawyer, John Lord O'Brian of Buffalo. He was a member of the law firm Covington and Burling in Washington. An authority on constitutional law, he argued constitutional issues before the Supreme Court for four decades and served as a legal adviser to the government from time to time in six Republican administrations.[24]

In conference, the chief justice faced the difficult task of persuading his brethren to take a narrow approach on the constitutionality issue. He tried to harmonize the disparate interests and hold dissent to a minimum. On February 10, 1936, Cummings confided in his diary: "We were all agog today in view of the general assumption that the Supreme Court would hand down its decision in the T.V.A. case. Nothing happened." Lawyers were convinced that the long delay in reaching a decision resulted from protracted efforts to conciliate the differences among the justices in the processes anterior to the final outcome.

The first issue to be settled was a technicality. Did minority shareholders in this case have standing to sue? Justices Brandeis, Stone, Cardozo, and Roberts insisted that they did not. Brandeis felt so strongly that he wrote a partial dissent on this point, arguing that courts should not interfere in the internal policy of corporations at the behest of minority shareholders. Seeing no proper cause of action, the four justices wanted to vote to dismiss, but they were blocked by four others who wanted assurances that plaintiffs would not be thrown out of court on a technicality. Hughes joined them on this point, and by a vote of five to four the Court accepted jurisdiction in the case.[25] There

---

[24] Swisher, *American Constitutional Development,* 940.

[25] Cummings wrote: "There are implications of some possible future trouble in a 5:4 split on a question of this kind, as there will probably be hereafter in cases in which the government will seek to stress the idea that stockholders ordinarily cannot in a stockholders' suit raise constitutional questions of such far-reaching character." Secret Diary, February 17, 1936.

was a line of precedents for such suits, and some justices may have realized that giving preferred shareholders the right to challenge federal statutes might strengthen their arguments in pending cases challenging the Guffey Coal Act and the Public Utilities Holding Company Act.[26]

Next, Hughes tried to get agreement on confining the issue narrowly to the contract's validity and preventing its being broadened to include the entire TVA program. He sedulously avoided testing the constitutionality of disputed aspects of TVA, showing that he had his ear to the ground. He wanted to maintain the prestige of the Court, and knew they could lower it by giving the appearance of systematic obstruction or by invalidating "a measure which had already left its indelible mark on the American landscape."[27] He managed to persuade three of the four dissidents to go along on the substantive issue, sustaining the constitutionality of the sale of electricity at the Wilson Dam where the TVA was generating power.

Curiosity was aroused because the decision was postponed so frequently. On Monday, February 17, 1936, when the decision upholding the government finally came down, bands played martial airs and factory whistles blew all over the valley. It was also a day of considerable rejoicing within administration circles, according to Cummings.[28] Roosevelt, evidently pleased, believed the justices had felt rather keenly the criticism they had been under lately. By a vote of eight to one, the Court held that the TVA had the constitutional authority to compete with private power companies in the sale and distribution of electric power to customers. Its operations were a valid activity of the federal government in aid of navigation and as an exercise of its war

---

[26] Schlesinger, Jr., *Politics of Upheaval,* 475.

[27] Dean Alfange, *The Supreme Court and the National Will* (Garden City, N.Y.: Doubleday, 1937), 229.

[28] An amusing aspect of the case occurred in New York City. When stockbrokers heard that Hughes was reading the opinion in *Ashwander,* they jumped to the conclusion that it was adverse to the government and began buying utility stocks as fast as they could get their orders filled. By the time the chief justice was halfway through the opinion, they stopped buying because they had no idea what the outcome was going to be after all. Later, when it appeared that the administration had been sustained, they made frantic efforts to get rid of the stocks they had bought less than an hour earlier. Cummings, Secret Diary, February 17, 1936.

powers.[29] Justices Brandeis, Stone, Roberts, and Cardozo concurred in Hughes's opinion.

Justice McReynolds entered the lone dissent. On the constitutional merits, he pointed out the transparency of the majority's doctrinal position. Like it or not, he said, TVA was in the power-generating business for its own sake, not as part of a military program long since abandoned. He insisted that the Court determine Congress's "real" end and evaluate the appropriateness of the means to achieve it. He went on:

> Nor do I find serious difficulty with the notion that the United States, by proper means and for legitimate ends, may dispose of water power or electricity honestly developed in connection with permissible improvement of navigable waters. But the means employed to that end must be reasonably appropriate in the circumstances. Under pretense of exercising granted power, they may not in fact undertake something not entrusted to them. Here . . . we should consider the truth of the petitioners' charge that, while pretending to act within their powers to improve navigation, the United States, through corporate agencies, are really seeking to accomplish what they have no right to undertake—the business of developing, distributing and selling electric power. If the record sustains this charge, we ought to declare and decree accordingly.[30]

Quoting from TVA annual reports, McReynolds wrote: "When we carry this program into every town and city and village, and every farm throughout the country, we will have written the greatest chapter in the economic, industrial and social development of America."[31] The reports left no doubt in the justice's mind that the government intended to enter the marketplace, displace private companies, and sell electric power. His dissent displayed an impatience with sham arguments. "Under the guise of disposition, something wholly different was to be accomplished—devotion of electric power to purposes beyond the sphere of proper federal action." Justice McReynolds was more concerned with the long-term implications of the decision than

---

[29] Built in 1916, the Wilson Dam provided power for anticipated national defense needs, including the operation of nitrate plants used in the manufacture of munitions.

[30] Opinion of McReynolds, J., dissenting, 297 U.S. 288, at 356.

[31] Ibid., at 361.

with the immediate case, however unsettling that was. The Court was a party to permitting Congress to transform a government of limited powers into one of unlimited powers.

> If under the thin mask of disposing of property the United States can enter the business of generating, transmitting and selling power as, when and wherever some board may specify, with the definite design to accomplish ends wholly beyond the sphere marked out for them by the Constitution, an easy way has been found for breaking down the limitations heretofore supposed to guarantee protection.[32]

Privately, McReynolds stated that he had not wanted to enter a separate opinion, as he had done in the gold clause cases, but he concluded that someone ought to concentrate on the real issue. George Wharton Pepper, who argued many cases against the government, thought McReynolds was right on the mark and sent a letter praising his "brilliant dissent" in *Ashwander.*[33]

The decision, wrote TVA director David E. Lilienthal, cleared away "so many of the clouds hanging over us. . . . We are given an almost incredible grant of power." Hughes was credited with making a monumental effort to wrest the Court majority from what appeared to be its anti–New Deal fixation.[34] His maneuvering in this case showed some of the same constitutional dexterity demonstrated in the gold clause cases. "Policy as well as politics in the highest court," wrote Krock, "is part of the work of the Chief Justice."[35]

FDR had been on the trail of the sprawling electrical power industry even before his years as New York's governor. Within a short span it had grown into a behemoth with an investment of about $13 billion. Developing the hydroelectric potential in the Tennessee Valley would not only curb the power monopoly but also put the government in direct competition with private enterprise. Government ownership and control of dams and power lines in seven states represents the high-water mark in New Deal efforts to implement a "planned economy." TVA was the most

---

[32] Ibid.
[33] February 20, 1936, James C. McReynolds Papers, ALDL.
[34] Schlesinger, Jr., *Politics of Upheaval,* 474.
[35] *New York Times,* March 29, 1936.

revolutionary of New Deal schemes in social engineering. Legal historian Barry Cushman believes "it was about the closest thing to socialism that the New Deal had to offer and was sustained by a nearly unanimous Court of putatively reactionary justices." Why the Supreme Court did not find grounds to declare the entire program unconstitutional is somewhat puzzling.[36] Future Congresses worked assiduously to confine this type of experiment to the Tennessee Valley. Under Republican majorities, lawmakers whittled away at its effectiveness.

The significance of the *Ashwander* ruling was captured by constitutional historian Carl Brent Swisher, who wrote that in a sense the decision, nominally the one bright spot in the Supreme Court record for the term, constituted "an embarrassment for the administration." It signaled that the Court had not set out maliciously to batter every major feature of the New Deal program and that New Deal legislation might be upheld if it could be brought within traditional lines of constitutional interpretation. Swisher concluded: "In spite of the conviction of many administration leaders that the Court had set out deliberately to sabotage their program, the line-up of decisions conveyed the suggestion that it was the program and not the Court that was wrong."[37]

Cushman stresses that there is reason to doubt the conservatism often associated with certain decisions striking down New Deal legislation, because there is reason to doubt the liberalism of the New Deal programs they invalidated. He cites such forward-looking decisions by the Court of the recent past as the ruling to uphold the Railway Labor Act (1930), *Nebbia v. New York* and *Home Bldg. and Loan Association v. Blaisdell* (1934), the gold clause cases (1935), and *Ashwander.* All of these were decided before the 1936 election and the introduction of FDR's court-packing plan. Cushman concluded: "The claim that Supreme Court jurisprudence in the 1930s was all politics, and more specifically the politics of class, is difficult to sustain."[38]

[36] In *Tennessee Electric Power Company v. TVA,* 306 U.S. 118 (1939), the Court upheld the TVA and its right to sell electricity, rejecting an attempt by state-chartered power companies to put the TVA out of business. Cushman, *Rethinking the New Deal Court,* 34.

[37] Swisher, *American Constitutional Development,* 938.

[38] Cushman, *Rethinking the New Deal Court,* 34.

The eight-to-one victory for the New Deal in *Ashwander* meant at least a temporary lifting of the pressure on the Supreme Court, offering proof that it was not totally unwilling to go along with the administration's recovery efforts. New Dealers had been trying to conciliate the Court by drafting new statutes in conformity with its strictures. With FDR's approval, if not at his urging, legal staffs made efforts to narrow the issues in the Holding Company and Guffey Coal cases, which were then working their way up to the Supreme Court.

The TVA ruling may have placated the administration in some ways, but it did serious damage to the argument that everything New Dealers were litigating would be declared invalid. The decision undermined New Deal strategy, designed to provoke a solid line of legislative invalidations by the Supreme Court in a concerted effort to arouse the country in opposition to it.[39] That had been the real intention of the Justice Department's internal policy.

Six weeks after the TVA decision, the Supreme Court struck a blow at another New Deal statute. An act of 1934 established the Securities Exchange Commission, a nonpartisan agency empowered to oversee and regulate activities of the stock exchanges to prevent fraud and manipulation. The "Truth in Securities" Act of 1933 held underwriters and corporate officers responsible for the truthfulness of a stock's registration and the conditions under which it was traded.

Jones v. Securities Exchange Commission[40] involved the validity of an SEC regulation in its investigation of a proposed stock issue. J. Edward Jones, a corporation promoter, filed a statement regarding a stock issue with the SEC and then withdrew the registration to evade an investigation already under way. By a vote of six to three, the Supreme Court upheld Jones, allowing him to withdraw his statement. The Court refrained from passing on the constitutionality of the Securities and Exchange Act of 1934, which established the commission.

Justice Sutherland's opinion impugned the methods of the

[39] Krock, *New York Times,* March 22, 1936.
[40] 298 U.S. 28 (1936).

SEC, attacking them as "intolerable" and comparing them to abuses in Star Chamber proceedings. The commission had ordered a hearing on the truth or falsity of Jones's application after it had been withdrawn. Withdrawal of an application to sell stock before it went into effect, he ruled, did not affect "any right of the general public." The SEC's action, therefore, was an arbitrary invasion of a citizen's rights. Justice Cardozo, joined by Brandeis and Stone, entered a blistering dissent: "To permit an offending registrant to stifle an inquiry by precipitate retreat, on the eve of his exposure is to give immunity to guilt, to encourage falsehood and evasion, to invite the cunning and unscrupulous to gamble with detection."[41] Cardozo mocked the majority's "denunciatory fervor," noting that the SEC had no coercive powers and could not arrest, imprison, or even punish for contempt. As for the Star Chamber analogy, he observed dryly: "Historians may find hyperbole in the sanguinary simile."[42]

There was a rationale, however, for the ruling. The majority evidently intended it as a warning to New Deal commissions and bureaus against invading the rights of private citizens. The 1934 act included no provision preventing withdrawal of an application. But from the minority's viewpoint, that argument could not be used to justify a decision whose only effect was to protect stock swindlers. Justice Stone accused the majority in *Jones* of "setting an all-time high in judicial arrogance." Privately, he said the opinion was obviously written "for morons," and added that "no trained lawyer would swallow such buncombe."[43]

A Justice Department memo titled "Suggested Treatment of Remaining Constitutional Cases before the Supreme Court" reveals how the administration plotted its litigation strategy in the spring of 1936.[44] The memo lists cases involving acts of Congress far

---

41 "Cardozo Indicts the Court," *St. Louis Star-Times,* April 7, 1936, copy in Box 7, Stone Papers, LC.

42 298 U.S. 28 (1936), at 33.

43 On the ruling, see Cummings to Roosevelt, April 6, 1936, OF 10, Box 3, FDRL. Justice Stone's remarks were quoted in an editorial in the *St. Louis Star-Times,* April 7, 1936.

44 Undated memo (ca. March–April 1936), PSF 150, FDRL. The author was not identified.

enough along in the lower courts to reach the Supreme Court in its 1936 term in approximately the following order: Public Works Administration (PWA), housing activities and land condemnation, the Guffey Coal Act, the Securities Act of 1933, Resettlement Administration, PWA municipal power plant loans, the Wagner Labor Act, and the Public Utilities Holding Company Act. Of these, the document states that the government could reasonably expect to win on the Securities Act, the PWA power plant loans, and the Holding Company Act, but "the Government can feel very certain of losing the Guffey Act, the PWA housing condemnation cases, and the Resettlement case."[45]

After the *Ashwander* decision, administration officials concluded that there was no longer "any general political benefit to be derived from a succession of decisions declaring *all* administration activities unconstitutional." New Deal strategists had once believed that political benefit could be derived from a string of adverse Supreme Court decisions. Now, however, according to the memo, "Any benefit from further decisions against constitutionality must derive from a specific, and well organized class feeling directly and specifically aggrieved."[46] The prognosis was that, of the cases expected to be lost, only the Guffey Coal case would raise a specific resentment (of coal miners). A narrow interpretation of the Wagner Act would also raise resentment among labor groups. But the loss of neither the PWA housing condemnation case nor the Resettlement case was expected to raise the resentment of any conscious class directly effected.

Indicating that there was a definite litigation strategy looking to arousing the maximum amount of group or class resentment, the next paragraph states:

---

[45] Ibid. At the cabinet meeting of January 31, 1936, the slum clearance case set for argument in the Supreme Court on March 3 was discussed. It was decided that no attempt would be made to delay or drop it. Frances Perkins was the only member present who doubted the wisdom of going ahead with this and the Resettlement case. Cummings, Secret Diary, January 31, 1936. In his diary Ickes made this gratuitous sexist comment about Miss Perkins: "but I suppose that was to be expected of a woman." Secret Diary, January 31, 1936, 1:530–32. On the New Deal housing program, see Robert M. Fisher, *Twenty Years of Public Housing* (New York: Harper and Row, 1959), and Timothy McDonnell, S.J., *The Wagner Housing Act: A Case Study of the Legislative Process* (Chicago: Loyola University Press, 1957).

[46] Undated memo, PSF 150, FDRL.

> On the other hand, since the public will again consider the Court fair to the Administration because of the TVA case, unnecessary defeats in these two cases will carry more political damage than heretofore. The bad lawyer criticism is an active and politically dangerous criticism which is being taken up even by the Administration's friends. The Guffey Act has been constantly represented in the public as of doubtful constitutionality. Its invalidation will draw no criticism that the Administration's lawyers are bad lawyers. But the same excuse of doubt honestly professed at the time of the passage of the legislation does not apply to either the PWA . . . or the Resettlement case.[47]

The memo recommended abandoning either the Louisville or Detroit low-income housing projects, neither of which was considered essential to the PWA housing program. Immediate action mooting the PWA cases was suggested; the same held for the Resettlement case. Withdrawal of the cases, both of which were considered certain to be lost, without any compensating value of public reaction against the Court, was calculated to give the administration good legal and political prospects for the remainder of the 1936 Supreme Court term.

Left-leaning critics saw Roosevelt institute the first national system of relief in the United States, however imperfect or underfunded. They had watched him begin development of the country's hydroelectric resources and make at least a halfhearted gesture at low-income housing. "In a burst of light, it occurred to them," stated an editorialist, "that it is possible to buy reforms with money, just as an individual buys groceries . . . or a ton of coal. It is a lesson that none of them will forget."[48]

Following invalidation of the AAA, administration officials noticed that public reaction to repeal of the Bankhead Cotton Control Act, the Tobacco Act, and the Potato Act showed that people approved, rather than condemned, a policy of withdrawing doubtful court cases. For administration planners pursuing a strategy obviously designed to create public disfavor toward the Court, recent developments, including the unexpected outcome in the TVA case, precipitated a "real change in external condi-

[47] Ibid.

[48] "Washington Notes," *New Republic,* August 14, 1935, 17.

tions" and justified a reconsideration of earlier Justice Department policy.[49]

Carter v. Carter Coal Company

In the aftermath of *Schechter,* a statute about whose constitutionality administration officials had very serious doubts was the Bituminous Coal Conservation Act of 1935, or the Guffey Coal Act.[50] In an attempt to rescue and stabilize the soft coal industry, draftsmen extracted the main features of the bituminous coal code from the wreckage of the NRA and revised some of its provisions to ward off constitutional objections. The law was framed by miners (including John L. Lewis's powerful United Mine Workers' Union [UMW]) and the mine operators and was submitted to Congress in August 1935 by its main sponsors, Senator Joseph F. Guffey and Congressman John Snyder, both of Pennsylvania. This "little NRA" for bituminous coal sparked a bitter political and constitutional controversy.

The statute's introductory section set forth the conditions in the ailing coal industry as partial justification for its enactment. The mining and distribution of coal throughout the United States was declared to be a business affected with a national public interest. Coal production and distribution was said to have a direct effect on interstate commerce. The law was designed to regulate trade practices, prices, and labor conditions in an industry producing the nation's single most important source of energy. Section 3 gave workers the right to organize and bargain collectively on terms of employment. It was considered essential to avoid recurring strikes or labor disputes clogging the channels of interstate commerce. Section 4 set out the substantive provisions of the act causing controversy.[51]

---

[49] Undated memo, PSF 150, FDRL.

[50] 49 Stat. 991, ch. 824.

[51] Part II of section 4 authorized the establishment of a National Bituminous Coal Commission to regulate the price at which coal could be sold in interstate commerce, and part III gave coal miners the right to organize and bargain collectively insofar as that could be guaranteed on paper. A labor board was created to adjudicate labor disputes in the coal industry. Cf. Cushman, *Rethinking the New Deal Court,* 159.

The act's two basic sections (price regulation and labor provisions) were stipulated as being wholly separable, to be administered by separate agencies. Heavy penalties were imposed on producers who refused to accept the code provisions, but cooperating producers were entitled to a 90 percent rebate on the 15 percent tax placed on the price of coal. The measure applied only to transactions in interstate commerce. Roosevelt had nothing to do with drafting the legislation, and he refused to commit himself to the Guffey Act, which was not on his "must" list at the end of May 1935. But when, on June 1, 1935, UMW officials sent out strike orders, following the invalidation of the NRA, FDR began to reconsider, and when UMW leaders again threatened a nationwide strike if the Guffey bill did not pass, he halfheartedly endorsed it.

Justice Department lawyers considered the Guffey Act unconstitutional, especially in the light of *Schechter,* and they told Cummings as much. There was even greater concern for the Wagner Act, whose labor provisions were modeled on the Guffey Act, including the precise wording of its section protecting laborers' right to collective bargaining. But the Wagner Act, also enacted in the wake of the *Schechter* decision, encountered little difficulty in Congress, passing by large majorities in both houses. The Guffey Act would not have such easy going. Even FDR doubted that, if passed, it could withstand a constitutional test, but he put these doubts aside when faced with the threat of a crippling strike.

Hearings on the Guffey Act before a subcommittee of the House Ways and Means Committee began in June 1935, focusing on the bill's constitutionality. The attorney general and solicitor general were asked to testify and offer their views on the bill's constitutionality.[52] Cummings tried to evade appearing before the committee. He was unconvinced of its law-worthiness and, as he told his diary, "could not give them much comfort on the constitutional features of the Act."[53] This was before the House

[52] On the legislative history of the act, see Ralph Baker, *The National Bituminous Coal Commission* (Baltimore: Johns Hopkins University Press, 1941). On the hearings, see 49–50.

[53] Cummings, Secret Diary, June 20, 1935. Another entry reads: "Quite a number of bills . . . would have to run the gauntlet of the Supreme Court. The

subcommittee chairman insisted on having him testify. In view of the precarious position of the bill, the president advised him to go before the committee.

In his testimony, Cummings declined giving an opinion on the bill's constitutionality, diverting attention to a line of cases that could be regarded as favorable to the principles involved in the bill and to another series that could be regarded as adverse. When pressed, he proved he could be as adroit as his chief. In view of the fact that the bill dealt with an industry whose product went to all forty-eight states, and although he did not consider it a business affected with a public interest, it would be desirable, he advised, to approve the bill—to push it through and leave the question of constitutionality to the courts.[54] Cummings found no unanimity among members of the subcommittee.

Events reached a crisis stage on July 4 when the subcommittee called on the president for his view. FDR put himself in the center of the controversy when he sent a letter to Chairman Samuel B. Hill while hearings continued. The letter, prepared by Reed and Cummings, contained only one sentence added by Roosevelt and was sent to the Hill on July 6, the same day Cummings gave his testimony.

In the letter, FDR alluded to the peculiar difficulties in the coal industry (fierce competition, overexpansion, destructive price reductions, and labor strife). Conditions in production were directly affecting interstate commerce, even though the mining of coal, if considered separate from its distribution, could be classified as an intrastate activity. The constitutionality of the bill's provisions would depend on the final conclusion as to whether

---

Wagner Bill, which I regarded as of rather doubtful constitutionality; the Guffey Coal Bill, which I thought was clearly unconstitutional; the AAA amendments, which were not in good condition to meet the constitutional test. In addition to that, there was the Social Security Act, the TVA, and quite a number of other measures of high importance." Ibid., 83.

[54] Ibid., July 5, 1935, 86; *New York Times,* July 6, 1935, 2; R. Baker, *Coal Commission,* 50; Cushman, *Rethinking the New Deal Court,* 159. Cummings surmised that even if the bill could not meet the constitutional test, there would likely be "further clarification" by the Supreme Court of the range within which legislation on topics of this kind might safely be enacted. He said the purpose was not to pass an unconstitutional bill, but to endeavor to ascertain the constitutional limits, if any, within which the government might effectively act.

production conditions directly affected, promoted, or obstructed interstate commerce in the commodity. The most controversial part of the letter was the conclusion:

> Manifestly, no one is in a position to give assurance that the proposed act will withstand constitutional tests for the simple fact is that you can get not 10 but 1,000 different legal opinions on the subject. But the situation is so urgent and the benefits of the legislation so evident that all doubts should be resolved in favor of the bill, leaving to the courts, in an orderly fashion, the ultimate question of constitutionality. A decision by the Supreme Court relative to this measure would be helpful as indicating with increasing clarity, the constitutional limits within which this Government must operate. . . . I hope your committee will not permit doubts as to constitutionality, however reasonable, to block the suggested legislation.[55]

This last sentence, added by the president, created an instantaneous furor. FDR was condemned in the press and by members of both parties in Congress. One lawmaker declared him guilty of "an impeachable offense" for deliberately flouting the Constitution and showing contempt for the Supreme Court.[56] In the letter his opponents found hard evidence of a disposition to challenge the Supreme Court. Use of the phrase "however reasonable" was considered unfortunate, even by friendly historians.[57] One biographer thought it lent plausibility to the charge that he aspired to dictatorial powers.[58] The point he tried to make was couched in an expression that was unquestionably maladroit.

Constitutional authority Edward S. Corwin sought to rescue him by trying to clarify FDR's meaning: "When . . . [he] said that doubts as to the constitutionality of the Guffey Coal Bill were 'reasonable,' he did not err as to fact, but only as to tact. He should have said that doubts as to its *un*constitutionality were reasonable, as indeed they were and still are."[59] Analysts may

---

[55] FDR to Representative Samuel B. Hill, July 6, 1935, *PPA,* 1935 volume, 297–98. A copy is in Box 14, folder 8, Burton K. Wheeler Papers, MHS. Cf. *Congressional Record,* 74th Cong., 1st sess., Vol. 79:13449.

[56] Davis, *New Deal Years,* 549.

[57] Schlesinger, Jr., *Politics of Upheaval,* 335–36.

[58] Davis, *New Deal Years,* 549.

[59] "The Schechter Case—Landmark or What?" *New York University Law Quarterly Review* 13 (January 1936): 151–90.

have agreed with Corwin, but the letter proved embarrassing. Its phrasing aroused suspicions among citizens becoming increasingly apprehensive about the prospects of a dictatorship. The episode served to reinforce well-founded fears of an impending attack on the Supreme Court.

Roosevelt regretted the language used in the letter soon after gauging public reaction to it. In the introduction to the 1935 volume of his papers, he betrayed a certain "unease of mind." In self-defense, he quoted former Supreme Court justice Bushrod Washington's "presumption of constitutionality" doctrine, as announced in *Ogden v. Saunders:* "It is but a decent respect due to the wisdom, integrity and patriotism of the legislative body, by which any law is passed, to presume in favor of its validity, until its violation of the Constitution is proved beyond all reasonable doubt."[60]

The House kept the Guffey bill bottled up in committee for another five weeks. Four of the subcommittee's seven members believed the bill was unconstitutional. In spite of this, Cummings had told them it would be enacted, as something the president desired. The White House managed to get it reported out of the full House Ways and Means Committee "without recommendation," but the struggle did not end there. In that committee, eight of the eighteen Democrats and six of the seven Republicans were opposed to the bill. Throughout early August the Democrats held secret meetings, trying to get sufficient votes to secure a favorable report. In a meeting of the full committee on August 12 they were able to get them, but only by the narrow margin of twelve to eleven, and this was only made possible by the expedient of persuading two members of the Democratic majority to withdraw their negative votes and merely answer "Present."[61]

The minority report focused entirely on the bill's unconstitu-

[60] 12 Wheaton 213 (1827); *PPA,* 1935, 298. Roosevelt often complained about the tendency of newspaper editors and columnists to take his words out of context—and in this instance, he chided them for giving a wholly false impression of the meaning behind his letter to Representative Hill. He said he considered this treatment "typical." True enough, in most accounts of this incident, only the last sentence of the letter was reported in news stories.

[61] R. Baker, *Coal Commission,* 51; cf. remarks of Representative Allen Treadway of North Carolina, *Congressional Record,* 74th Cong., 1st sess., Vol. 79:13437, quoted in Cushman, *Rethinking the New Deal Court,* 160.

tionality, arguing that stream of commerce cases like *Swift* and *Schechter* offered no precedent for the Guffey bill. In the business of mining coal, interstate commerce had not even commenced. On August 20, the final vote in the House was 194 to 168, and three days later the bill squeaked through the Senate by a vote of 45 to 37 in the "end of session rush" (Democrats held 69 of the 96 Senate seats). Despite lingering doubts about its constitutionality, the bill was signed into law on August 30, 1935.[62] Even with unrelenting administration arm-twisting and open lobbying, substantial numbers of Democrats defied the president. According to Congressman Bertrand Snell of New York, this was "the first time in the history of the country that the House passed a bill opposed by the subcommittee which wrote it, by the full committee which approved it, by the Rules Committee which brought it to the floor, and toward which the entire House organization was entirely indifferent."[63]

As Cushman pointed out, in the light of the heavy vote by which the Wagner Act passed, it seems unlikely that the votes against the Guffey Act were motivated by any general animosity toward federal regulation of labor relations. Patently, many members of Congress sincerely doubted the act's constitutionality. Their feelings were summed up by Senator Millard Tydings of Maryland, who gave this ominous forecast of the bill's future: "Like an autumn flower it will be blown away by the first winter blast of the Court."[64]

On the same day the Guffey Coal Act became law, James W. Carter, president of the Carter Coal Company, filed suit in federal court, protesting that the act was unconstitutional. He had been one of the first mine owners to speak out, denouncing the bill as "the first step in the socialization of the [coal] industry." At a board of directors meeting in Washington he moved that his

---

[62] *Congressional Record,* 74th Cong., 1st sess., Vol. 79:13666–67 and 14084. In the Senate, twenty-four Democrats joined twelve Republicans and one Farmer-Laborite in opposition to the bill.

[63] For the legislative history of the act, see James P. Johnson, *The Politics of Soft Coal* (Urbana: University of Illinois Press, 1979), 220–24; for the quote, 224.

[64] Ibid., 224, also quoted in Cushman, *Rethinking the New Deal Court,* 161.

company refuse to adopt the code, but he was outvoted (one of the board members was his father) in a prearranged maneuver calculated to force a court challenge. The next day, company lawyers filed suit in Washington's district court to enjoin their own company and prevent it from becoming a code member forced to pay the "tax" on coal.

A day later, Stanley Reed sent Marvin McIntyre a memo enclosing a petition to test the constitutionality of the Guffey Act. A copy of the petition he was about to file in federal court had been handed to him by Frederick Wood of the prestigious Wall Street firm Cravath, de Gersdorff, Swaine and Wood, who intended to bring a court proceeding immediately. Reed promptly warned the White House that "Carter's move will give us plenty of trouble," reminding FDR that Wood had represented the Schechter brothers. At first Reed asked McIntyre to advise the president that his department was considering opposing Carter's suit as premature (the tax on coal would not go into effect until November). How successful they would be was doubtful. He added: "Wood is going to shove every way he can to get a prompt decision in the Supreme Court." He thought the president would want to know about the matter.[65]

This court action had characteristics of a collusive suit. Both sides of the controversy wanted the same outcome, so there was no real issue in dispute between them.[66] Like TVA, the Guffey Act was challenged in a stockholders' suit, a procedure sometimes used during the New Deal to test the constitutionality of federal statutes. District judges by then were notorious for striking down New Deal laws and delivering stump speeches from the bench in the process. More than one hundred federal judges (over a third of the entire bench) issued upwards of a thousand

[65] Reed to McIntyre, August 31, 1935, OF 41A, Box 49, and OF 1732-Misc., FDRL. Attached to the memo was the petition, which became the case of *James Walter Carter, Plaintiff, v. Carter Coal Company, et al. Defendants.* Attorneys for the plaintiff were Frederick Wood of New York City and Richard H. Wilmer of Washington, D.C.

[66] The courts at this time allowed such suits and would take jurisdiction even if the situation were somewhat contrived, provided there was a genuine disagreement and indications that both points of view in a controversy would be fairly and fully developed. Samuel Krislov, *The Supreme Court in the Political Process* (New York: Macmillan, 1965), 44–45.

injunctions from 1933 to 1936, and lawyers naturally rushed to exploit such opportunities to the full.[67]

Companies seeking injunctions employed ingenious methods to prevent the government from coming into court to defend the challenged statute. By raising a constitutional question through friendly private suits, stockholders sued their own companies to enjoin them from obeying the law. Under present-day rules on standing to sue, such actions would not reach the Supreme Court, but these proceedings were valid in 1935—and Carter's lawyers were prepared to make the most of them.[68]

Reed, having evidently changed his mind, pushed the Carter case up to the high bench. In late December 1935, along with three companion cases coming up from the lower courts, it went on the Supreme Court docket.[69] By then, District Judge Jesse Adkins, a progressive Republican of the District of Columbia bench, had ruled the labor provisions of the Guffey Act invalid under the *Schechter* precedent, but he upheld the price-fixing machinery. Another district court judge had declared both sections of the Guffey Act valid, but Federal District Judge Charles I. Dawson in Western Kentucky found for the coal company and blasted the coal code as "the boldest kind of usurpation."[70] In view of the divergent lower-court rulings decided on constitutional grounds, Reed asked the Supreme Court to hear all four cases without waiting for decisions from the appellate courts. The Court agreed. But by the time Reed made up his mind to seek a review, enforcement of the coal code had ground to a virtual standstill. District court judges were issuing wholesale injunctions against the new Coal Commission and the Internal Revenue Service, charged with the responsibility for collecting the excise tax.[71]

Carter v. Carter Coal Company[72] gave promise of evolving

---

[67] Schlesinger, Jr., *Politics of Upheaval,* 447–49.

[68] *Pollock v. Farmers' Loan and Trust Co.,* 157 U.S. 429 (1895), and *Pollock v. Farmers' Loan and Trust Co.,* 158 U.S. 601 (1895).

[69] Irons, *New Deal Lawyers,* 249–50. Two cases involved the Tway Coal Company.

[70] Schlesinger, Jr., *Politics of Upheaval,* 448. The case referred to here was *Tway Coal Co. v. Glenn.*

[71] Ibid. See also Irons, *New Deal Lawyers,* 249.

[72] 298 U.S. 238 (1936).

into a titanic legal struggle. John Dickinson, having succeeded Harold Stephens in the Justice Department's Antitrust Division, argued the case for the government. Harvard's Reed Powell and Princeton's Edward S. Corwin worked on the briefs. Cummings wrote the president: "You may . . . be interested in knowing that Professor Corwin, confidentially, is giving us aid, comfort and assistance in the preparation of the briefs in the Guffey Act case."[73] Counting Reed's staff and Robert L. Stern, more than a dozen lawyers were involved full time in preparing the case.

Carter's team included that star of the legal profession in Frederick H. Wood. Judge Dawson, who had ruled both the NRA and the Guffey Act unconstitutional before leaving the bench, represented the Tway Coal Company. Seven coal-producing states filed *amicus* briefs supporting the regulatory measures in the Guffey Act as the only solution for the troubled and oftentimes chaotic coal industry.[74] Oral argument was heard on March 11–12, 1936. In summing up, Judge Dawson said: "Coal mining is just as much a local activity as is farming and manufacture." Assistant Attorney General Dickinson cited the essence of the current dispute between the administration and Supreme Court: "The issue of federal power is here at stake . . . there lurk within the Constitution crevices through which federal power may have sifted away."[75] Dickinson made an able presentation of the government's case. Constitutional historian Leonard Levy considered *Carter* the strongest New Deal case yet heard by the Supreme Court. But internal memos indicate that the Justice Department did not share his confidence. Neither did the president and attorney general.

Dickinson conceded that the "tax" on coal was a penalty, designed to coerce acceptance of the code, under the *Butler* precedent. His strategy was to abandon the tax argument in order to rescue at least one of the act's remaining provisions, relying on the separability clause in section 15. He drew attention to the

[73] February 3, 1936, PPF 1820, Box 10, FDRL.

[74] 298 U.S. 238 (1936), at 269–77. The states were Indiana, Ohio, Illinois, Kentucky, New Mexico, Washington, and Pennsylvania.

[75] "Back to the Constitution," review by Thurman Arnold of Edward S. Corwin's *The Commerce Power versus States' Rights* (Princeton: Princeton University Press, 1936), in *New Republic,* December 12, 1936, 222.

seven coal-producing states that filed *amicus* briefs in support of the government. His argument rested squarely on the federal commerce power, exercised for purposes affecting the nation as a whole in matters with which the states could not individually deal.

It took sixty-eight days—the longest period the justices ever deliberated over a New Deal statute—for the Supreme Court to decide the fate of the Guffey Act. On May 18, 1936, the long-awaited ruling was announced. A headline next day read: "The Court Splits in an Unusual Fashion 5–1–3."[76] The opinion and dissent, with oral arguments and briefs, take up a hundred pages in the *U.S. Reports.* Justice Sutherland's opinion struck down the wages and hours provisions of the act, even though they had not yet gone into effect and were not at issue, on the grounds that they exceeded the scope of federal power under the commerce clause.[77] Insofar as the act delegated to a majority of coal producers, rather than to the government, power to fix hours and wages for employees of other coal producers, the provision was an arbitrary enactment in violation of the due process clause of the Fifth Amendment. Failure of the Court majority to affirm the Carter Company counsel's contention that the wage-fixing provisions also infringed liberty of contract was, according to Cushman, a conspicuous omission.[78]

With Justice Roberts casting the crucial vote, a five-man majority found the entire Guffey Act unconstitutional. Since the price-fixing provisions were intimately joined with its labor provisions, they were inseparable and therefore unconstitutional. Anticipating a court challenge, the draftsmen had deliberately inserted section 15 to enable one section to stand if another were struck down. Sutherland announced the rule was "against the

[76] *New York Herald Tribune,* May 19, 1936, 1; *Washington Star,* May 19, 1936.

[77] The actual issue presented in government briefs and arguments concerned only that part of the act which dealt with price stabilization and fair trade practices.

[78] The failure of Justice Sutherland, who wrote the opinion in the 1923 case *Adkins v. Children's Hospital,* to cite the precedent in *Carter* gave rise to the inference that the refusal here to mobilize liberty of contract doctrine was a concession to Justice Roberts. Cushman, *Rethinking the New Deal Court,* 93.

mutilation of a statute." He came in for much criticism for disregarding the explicit intention of Congress. William Wiecek wrote: "The Court in effect told Congress that it did not mean what it said it meant."[79]

Justice Sutherland's opinion reiterated the states' rights argument advanced by Wood. He admitted the coal industry was in dire straits but was unpersuaded by the emergency rationale for the enactment. He denied that the dislocations growing out of the struggle between employers and workers over wages, working conditions, and the right to collective bargaining resulting in labor strife affected interstate commerce in any direct way. The Constitution's general welfare clause was limited to the powers enumerated in Article I. "Nothing is more certain than that beneficent aims, however great or well directed, can never serve in lieu of constitutional power." He could find no authority for Congress to legislate in respect of these general purposes, unless it be found in the commerce clause.[80] And it could not be found there, because the evils in the coal industry were local evils over which the government had no legislative control. The Tenth Amendment, he argued, reserves control over all labor matters to the states. "All the controversies which formed the object of the Act to regulate and minimize are local controversies which at common law fall under 'domestic relations.' Such effect as they may have on commerce, however extensive, is only secondary and indirect, and thus beyond congressional control."[81] Finally, the opinion attacked the tax on coal as a "penalty," citing *Butler.* If the act, with its labor and price-fixing provisions, could not be upheld, then, said the majority, the "tax" must fall with them.[82]

Chief Justice Hughes's split opinion held that the labor provi-

---

[79] William M. Wiecek, *Liberty under Law: The Supreme Court in American Life* (Baltimore: Johns Hopkins University Press, 1988), 137.

[80] 298 U.S. 238 (1936), at 291–97.

[81] Ibid., at 309–10. Justice Sutherland relied on an 1895 antitrust case *U.S. v. E.C. Knight Company,* 156 U.S. 1 as precedent for this "indirect effect" limitation on the federal commerce power, although by that time it was considered by most lawyers and law schools as repudiated. This famous case determined that the Havemeyer Sugar Trust, in control of 98 percent of the country's sugar refineries, was neither in violation of the Sherman Antitrust Act nor a combination in restraint of interstate trade, because manufacturing was not commerce.

[82] 298 U.S. 238 (1936), at 289.

sions had to fall as beyond the scope of the federal commerce power, but he disagreed with Sutherland's logic on other points. He upheld the price-fixing provisions on coal moving in interstate commerce and would have been prepared to take Congress at its word on the separability question. The Court was obliged, he said, to give full weight to Congress's clearly signified intent.[83] Justices Cardozo, Brandeis, and Stone dissented on both grounds.[84] The vote was six to three to invalidate the act's labor provisions and five to four to strike down the entire statute.

Justice Cardozo's dissent noted that 97 percent of the coal produced by the Carter Company was shipped to other states. He agreed that mining, if considered simply as production, did not constitute interstate commerce, but he believed its relation to that commerce could be such that, for the protection of the one, there was need to regulate the other. In a reversal of his *Schechter* denunciation of the regulatory provisions in the NRA's codes as "delegation run riot," he now claimed that the rights of coal producers did not include "the right to persist in this anarchic riot."

He favored sustaining the Guffey Act's price-fixing provisions. As for the labor provisions, he said they were being prejudged and were not "ripe" for decision. Carter was asking for a decree to restrain a provision of the statute even before it went into operation. "What the code will provide as to wages and hours of labor, or whether it will provide anything," he wrote, "is still in the domain of prophecy. The opinion of the Court begins at the wrong end. To adopt a homely form of words, the complainants have been crying before they are really hurt."[85]

The three dissenters took an expansive view of the commerce power, which, they said, "should be as broad as the need that

[83] Separate opinion of Hughes, C.J., 298 U.S. 238 (1936), at 320.

[84] In a summary, Holtzoff broke down the voting in *Carter* in the Supreme Court and lower federal courts as follows: seven judges in all ruled the wages and hours provisions of the act unconstitutional, while one judge (Elwood Hamilton of Kentucky), a recent Roosevelt appointee, voted to uphold them; and on the price-fixing regulations, eight judges voted in favor of their constitutionality, while only one held them invalid. Memo for the Attorney General, re: Constitutionality of New Deal Cases, July 26, 1936, Box 199, Cummings Papers, ALDL.

[85] Opinion of Cardozo, J., dissenting, 298 U.S. 239 (1936), at 341.

evokes it." The decision reinforced the administration's belief that the majority's narrow view and alleged anti-labor and anti–New Deal bias determined the outcome. Notably, administration spokesmen scrupulously refrained from admitting or revealing what Justice Department lawyers, the attorney general, and the president had believed all along—that there was the taint of unconstitutionality to the Guffey Act—a fact that alone would justify the Supreme Court's decision, however clumsy its reasoning.

In a press release, Cummings stated: "It should not be overlooked that the opinion of the three dissenting Justices, and the separate opinion of the Chief Justice, constitute the first clear expression by members of the Supreme Court upholding the constitutionality of price fixing for commodities moving in interstate commerce. Important, also, is the statement . . . of Mr. Justice Cardozo that the prevailing opinion leaves the pricing provisions open for consideration in the future."[86]

The dissents in *Carter* accentuated the sharp division in the Court and the conflicting approaches to reviewing acts of Congress, especially in the case of social and economic legislation. In *Carter* the majority showed its willingness to face the issue of constitutionality, while the minority avoided meeting it wherever possible. Above all, the Court majority attempted to make Congress toe the line, while the minority went out of its way to give acts of Congress a wide berth with every benefit of every doubt.[87]

Minimum Wage Legislation

The last case decided in the Supreme Court's 1936 spring term involved minimum wage legislation for women and raised the question of whether states had a power denied to the federal government. The controlling precedent was the 1923 *Adkins* decision, which struck down a federal statute establishing a District of Columbia board empowered to set minimum wages for women and minors.[88] Frankfurter, counsel for the plaintiff, de-

[86] May 18, 1936, PSF 185, FDRL.

[87] "When Should the Court Decide?" Bertram Benedict, Editorial Research Reports, May 19, 1936, Box 230, Clapper Papers, LC.

[88] *Adkins v. Children's Hospital,* 261 U.S. 525 (1923).

fended the statute as a legitimate exercise of congressional power to protect public health, morals, and the general welfare in the District of Columbia. In a five-to-three ruling, Justice Sutherland rejected the "Brandeis brief" submitted by Frankfurter, which tried to show the relation between low wages and child neglect, broken homes, disease, and prostitution. Justice Brandeis did not participate in the decision.[89]

Invoking the freedom of contract doctrine, the Court ruled that women enjoyed the same rights to contract for work as men, no more and no less. Having gained the vote, they were entitled to no special status. They had a constitutional right to work for whatever wage they pleased. Employers, said the majority, should not be subjected to wage floors. According to an editorial: "The feature of this statute which perhaps more than any other puts upon it the stamp of invalidity is that it exacts from the employer an arbitrary payment for a purpose and upon a basis having no causal connection with his business or the contract or the work the employee engages to do."[90] A statute requiring an employer to pay the equivalent of the value of services rendered, said Sutherland, would be understandable, but the law in question violated due process guaranteed by the Fifth Amendment. The *Adkins* ruling effectively voided all similar state laws and remained the classic expression of the identification of laissez-faire economics with constitutional rights until 1937.

During the 1920s, when Frankfurter was asked by the National Consumers' League to draft a model bill for New York State, he teamed up with Ben Cohen to draft a law they hoped would be looked on more favorably by the Supreme Court than the one overruled in *Adkins.*[91] Referring to this new bill, Mary Dewson wrote Harold Ickes: "Every word of it was written with the Supreme Court of the United States in mind."[92] At the time, however, Frankfurter warned league members that it would be "foolish beyond words . . . to be hopeful that a changed Court or changing times would make for a liberal outlook . . . and a rever-

[89] For a more thorough analysis of *Adkins,* see Cushman, *Rethinking the New Deal Court,* 66–70 and passim.

[90] "The Minimum Wage Case," *New York Times,* June 2, 1936.

[91] Liva Baker, *Felix Frankfurter* (New York: Coward McCann, 1969), 179.

[92] June 14, 1933, National Consumers' League Papers, LC, quoted in ibid.

sal of the 1923 decision." He assured them that there was no right to any such hope "under the leadership of Hughes, let alone the others." In spite of his forebodings, they gambled that the new laws, introduced in legislatures of eight states and passed by six, including New York, would somehow fare better with the Court and initiate a new line of decisions.[93]

One of the Court's chief objections to the D.C. law had been its failure to take into account the principle of value for service rendered. According to this, some work is of such a menial nature that it may not be worth the minimum wage, and if forced to pay it, employers could suffer an enforced denial of property or, if pressed, might eliminate these jobs. During times of depression, many businesses and factories were forced to shut down, unable to meet the fierce competition. The laws enacted on the Frankfurter model were based on reasonable value for service rather than on the cost of living. A fair wage was defined as one reasonably commensurate with the value or class of service rendered.[94]

Not one of these statutes was tested in the courts prior to 1935, but in that year New York's law was challenged by John Tipaldo, the proprietor of a Brooklyn laundry. He had been indicted for paying female workers less than the $12.40 per week provided by law and for covering up this violation with false time-book entries. He was sent to jail to await trial on a charge of forgery. In March, the New York Court of Appeals, in a four-to-three decision, declared the New York law indistinguishable from the one in *Adkins,* and therefore unconstitutional.

Six weeks later, the Supreme Court heard oral argument in a review of the New York law.[95] Henry Epstein, the state's solicitor general, and Dean Acheson, arguing for the National Consumers' League, tried to show that the state law was distinguishable from the D.C. statute invalidated in 1923, but their brief did not specifically ask the Court to overrule *Adkins.* Their arguments fell on barren ground. Although Stone, Brandeis, and Cardozo considered *Adkins* bad law and wanted to overrule it, Justice Roberts

[93] Frankfurter to Josephine Goldmark, January 10, 1933, ibid.; F. Perkins, *Roosevelt,* 202–3.

[94] Minimum wage scales in the laundry and hotel industries were not adopted until after a board had carefully investigated the relevant facts.

[95] *Morehead v. New York ex rel Tipaldo,* 298 U.S. 587 (1936).

disagreed, arguing that the Court ought not to reach out for issues that were not before it. He found the New York law indistinguishable from the one in *Adkins.* Hughes was ready to agree that the New York law could be distinguished, but Roberts cast the deciding vote, making the five-man majority which held that the New York statute was not in any material way distinguishable from the law invalidated in *Adkins.* Because that precedent had not been challenged, the Court majority was required to strike down the New York statute.[96]

Justice Butler's majority opinion was at first based narrowly on distinguishing the two statutes, but the circulation of a biting dissent by Justice Stone so infuriated him that he decided to broaden the opinion, moving from the technical point to a bold defense of freedom of contract as enunciated in *Adkins.* "The right to make contracts about one's affairs," he wrote, "is part of the liberty protected by the due process clause. In making contracts of employment . . . the parties have equal rights to obtain from each other the best terms they can by private bargaining." The New York statute was a denial of the freedom embodied in the Fourteenth Amendment's due process clause and was therefore null and void.

The dissents of Hughes and Stone were concurred in by Brandeis and Cardozo. Hughes found the New York law a reasonable exercise of the state's police power and distinguishable from the D.C. statute. He could find nothing in the Constitution denying to states the power to protect women workers from exploitation by avaricious employers. Stone went on the attack in a fierce diatribe against the majority. Why, he asked, should a contract of employment be considered too sacred a subject for regulation? "It is difficult to imagine any grounds, other than our own personal economic predilections, for saying that the contract of employment is any the less an appropriate subject of legislation than are scores of others in dealing with which this Court has held that legislatures may curtail individual freedom in the public interest."[97] "There is grim irony," he wrote, "in speaking of the freedom of contract of those who, because of economic neces-

[96] Ibid., at 604–9.

[97] Opinion of Stone, J., dissenting, ibid., at 633.

sity, give their services for less than is needful to keep body and soul together. If this is freedom of contract, no one ever denied that it is a freedom which may be restrained, notwithstanding the Fourteenth Amendment, by a statute passed in the public interest."[98] He added: "The Fourteenth Amendment has no more embedded in the Constitution our preference for some particular set of economic beliefs, than it has adopted, in the name of liberty, the system of theology which we may happen to approve."[99]

Commenting later, Stone wrote that while he agreed that the distinctions pointed out by the chief justice were valid, he nevertheless thought that the ruling should be placed on broader grounds, namely, that due process had nothing to do with wage regulation, at least wherever there was a serious legislative problem presented. But for the time being, the will of the five-man majority prevailed and in October the Court denied a motion for reargument of the *Tipaldo* case.[100]

In a survey of 344 newspaper editorials, Arthur Schlesinger, Jr. identified only 10 that approved of the *Tipaldo* decision—and these were primarily from textile towns. Nearly sixty papers, including the *Baltimore Sun* and other conservative organs that hardly ever had anything good to say about the New Deal, called for a constitutional amendment to counter the Supreme Court's intransigence.

Some of the "Tory" newspapers (as FDR labeled them) remained silent, while a few actually condemned the Morehead decision. Stanley High wrote the president: "I think it is significant that the New York *Herald Tribune,* which heretofore has hailed every one of the Supreme Court's adverse decisions with editorial glee, passed up this morning's with no editorial comment whatsoever on yesterday's decision. . . . Is it possible that they recognize that there can be too much of a 'good thing' and that this—more than any previous decision—may solidify opinion in favor of an amendment?"[101] Franklyn Waltman's column called the opinion one of the best political breaks Roosevelt and

[98] Ibid., at 632.
[99] Ibid., at 636.
[100] Stone to Youngsters, April 1, 1937, Stone Papers, LC.
[101] June 2, 1936, PSF 185, FDRL.

New Dealers had received in many months, potentially "the turning point in the entire controversy over the Supreme Court and the necessity for amending the Constitution."[102]

Laymen could perhaps understand how the Supreme Court might have found poultry processing in *Schechter* a local operation that could not be regulated under the federal commerce power, and there were legalistic, but comprehensible, grounds for the decision annulling the AAA. But the New York minimum-wage decision was difficult to comprehend, even by a lawyer's mind. Four justices, including the chief, found the New York law valid and the power involved clearly within the state's jurisdiction.

The slender margin of defeat again raised the issue of presumption of constitutionality. If the rule stood that all reasonable doubt had to be resolved in favor of a statute's constitutionality, and at the same time only five justices could overrule the act, who was to say that its violation of the Constitution had been proved beyond all reasonable doubt? What did this say about the integrity and good judgment of the "four honorable colleagues" in dissent? Not only that, but if the power to fix minimum wages did not reside in the federal government, and could not be found in the states, with their right to provide for their own citizens, where then was the power to enact such laws?

This decision represented the first serious crack in the Court's armor, threatening its power to nullify laws. *Tipaldo,* more than any previous New Deal case, raised the issue of how to lessen that power in order to avoid "government by judicial oligarchy." A New York editorial concluded: "This question may be dodged by both parties in the 1936 election campaign. But it is the next fundamental issue for the American people to meet and work out. We do not see how old judicial gentlemen . . . can forever be permitted to override the will of the people as expressed through the people's own elected Legislatures, Congress and President."[103]

The decision, wrote Frankfurter, left him numb. "The five con-

[102] "Politics and People," *New York Herald Tribune,* June 2, 1936.

[103] "Another 5–4 Conservative Decision," *New York Daily News,* June 2, 1936, copy in PPF 1820, Box 10, FDRL.

"The Majesty of the Law." The cartoon ridicules an elderly judge peering at a pinhead, as if searching for technicalities. To this day, the law and lawyers are accused of searching for loopholes. (The New York Public Library)

servative justices constituting the majority have demonstrated anew the versatility, or at least the resources of unreason and folly."[104] He wrote FDR: "And what am I to reply to Frank Buxton of the Boston *Herald* who calls me up and asks, 'Is it true that the President bribed Butler and his four associates to decide the minimum wage case for him the way they did?'"[105]

Frankfurter wrote Charles Burlingham: "Can it be so, or is it a hoax? Is my copy of this morning's *Times* just a leg pulling, or is the following sentence from the leader . . . what was printed in every copy?" 'It is not doubtful that in the course of nature the complexion and personnel of the Supreme Court will be so changed that minimum wage laws will be decided to be valid without altering our Constitution.'" He asked: "Can it be, after all, that Chief Justice Hughes was right when he said: 'We are under a Constitution, but the Constitution is what the judges say it is.'" The letter concluded: "Do ask your old friend Rollo Ogden whether he will not allay the anxiety of at least one law professor who owes a conscientious duty to his students to make them understand what the Constitution really is. What is it?"[106] Robert Jackson later wrote Morris Ernst: "The Constitution is what the judges say it is, and now it appears that they can't make up their minds what to say. What then is the Constitution in such a case?"[107]

The president expressed dismay over the *Tipaldo* ruling in a few carefully chosen words. At a press conference on June 2, 1936, he borrowed a phrase from an editorial in the *St. Louis Star-Times,* calling the vacuum created by the Supreme Court at all levels of government a "legal no-man's land." When asked if, in view of the Court's series of opinions about New Deal objectives, he could see any way in which these objectives could be reached within the framework of the Constitution, he declined to answer, but merely advised the American people to read all three opinions—that of Justice Butler, of Hughes, and Stone's dissent—"because it is the combination of the three that . . . made one fact fairly clear . . . the existence of a 'no-man's land,'

[104] Frankfurter to Stone, June 2, 1936. Frankfurter Papers, LC.
[105] June 9, 1936, PPF 1440, FDRL.
[106] June 9, 1936, Box 13, Stone Papers, LC.
[107] November 23, 1936, Box 29, Robert H. Jackson Papers, LC.

as defined by the present majority of the Court, where no government can function, whether state or federal." "How can you meet that situation?" a reporter asked. Again, Roosevelt sidestepped the question: "I think that is about all there is to say about it."[108] His measured words only created more suspicions that he was preparing to raise the constitutional issue in the presidential campaign.

More than one Roosevelt opponent, including his Dutchess County neighbor Hamilton Fish, a congressman (R.-N.Y.), predicted that the constitutional issue would be in the 1936 campaign, whether Roosevelt put it there or not. The *Tipaldo* decision was going to cost Republicans a million votes in November, he said, unless they themselves took over the leadership and demanded a constitutional amendment. His estimate of lost votes was too low. In the popular mind, Supreme Court decisions nullifying New Deal–type laws were now being looked upon as "Republican" decisions, not so much because the Court was partisan, although FDR certainly believed it was, but because so many Republicans supported the Court and seemed to share its philosophy.

One thing was certain. Republicans would not be the ones to force the issue of Supreme Court reform, nor would they be able to compel the president to reveal more about his plans on the matter than he desired. They would have to bide their time, to wait and see. As for Roosevelt, the dilemma facing him in the approaching campaign was clearly outlined in this editorial passage: "What does the President want? He wants to be pushed. He knows that he can carry on his program, in the future, only through laws acknowledged by the Court to be valid. But he doesn't want to open himself to the charge that he is trying to upset the Constitution or the Supreme Court. It is better strategy, politically, to let a universal popular exasperation set the forces of reform in motion."[109]

---

108 *PPA,* 1936 volume, 191–92.

109 "No Man's Land," *St. Louis Star-Times,* June 5, 1938, copy in Box 7, Stone Papers, LC.

7
Landslide

> I don't think it would have made any difference what kind of campaign I made as far as stopping this avalanche is concerned. That is one consolation you get out of a good licking.
>
> Arthur Schlesinger, Jr.,
> *The Politics of Upheaval* (p. 643)

"WE WILL WIN EASILY next year," Roosevelt told members of his cabinet late in 1935, "but we are going to make it a crusade." His reelection campaign took off prematurely on January 3, 1936, with the annual State of the Union message. Breaking with tradition, he decided to address the joint session of Congress in the evening to maximize reaching a radio audience with millions of prospective voters. The decision was made over protests from several lawmakers. All that day, discussions turned on the proper attire for the unprecedented occasion—should it be dinner jackets, full dress, or perhaps even morning coats? Exasperated by persistent inquiries from the Protocol Division, FDR told aides he had just about made up his mind to tell them that since the proceedings would take place in the evening, everyone should come in their pajamas.[1]

The reception on the president's entry to the House chamber was tumultuous. After the din of applause died down, he began his address by reviewing the worsening international situation, artfully tying it in to the theme of autocracy at home and abroad. "The old crowd," he warned, was scheming to return to power by masquerading under the Constitution. Moley, who had worked on an earlier speech draft, wanted a more conciliatory tone toward business and a call for a constitutional amendment explicitly enlarging Congress's power to legislate for the general

---

[1] Burns, *Roosevelt,* 266; Cummings, Secret Diary, January 3, 1936; Davis, *New Deal Years,* 603.

welfare. FDR rejected his advice and delivered the more aggressive text prepared by Corcoran and Rosenman. Referring contemptuously to men of wealth, he charged:

> They seek the restoration of their selfish power. . . . They steal the livery of great national constitutional ideals to serve discredited special interests. The principle that they would instill into government if they succeed in seizing power is well shown by the principles which many of them have instilled into their own affairs: autocracy toward labor, toward stock-holders, toward consumers, toward public sentiment. Autocrats in smaller things, they seek autocracy in bigger things.[2]

The message resembled a campaign speech. Was it the opening gun in the election battle of 1936? It showed FDR's mastery of the grammar of vituperation. The message offended not only members of the business community, but public opinion on the left and right. The president was condemned in the press for speaking not as a statesman, but as a "pure politico," transforming what was supposed to have been a reasoned report on the state of the nation to a political diatribe.[3] Nevertheless, the volume of mail flooding the White House was largely positive.

With his legal advisers, FDR continued to struggle with the problem of how to deal with the Supreme Court, casting about for some effective method to break the blockade of New Deal legislation. Liberals were growing impatient with his "heads or tails" vacillation on whether to make constitutional reform the supreme campaign issue. A journalist concluded: "The Court nonetheless embodies the real urgency of the immediate future."[4] Some Roosevelt followers were pressing for an all-out assault on "the citadel of the judiciary."

Advice poured in to the White House from all quarters. One memo headed "Blank advised" was from Justice Brandeis, who made a fetish of routing anonymous advice through various channels to the president in a futile attempt to preserve at least the appearance of judicial discretion. It cautioned: "(a) do not attempt any legislation with the open support of the President

[2] *PPA,* 1936 volume, 8–18, 14.

[3] *New Republic* 85 (January 15, 1936), 270–71.

[4] Max Lerner, "A Garland of Posies," *New Republic* 84 (September 11, 1935), 136–37.

relating to the size or function of the Supreme Court at this session (b) [George] Norris and [Hiram] Johnson best situated and best qualified to undertake a program of lower court reform."[5] W. F. Wiley, a *Cincinnati Enquirer* editor, informed FDR: "One real issue of the campaign is the preservation of the American system of government as guaranteed by the Constitution of the United States." The president agreed, and replied: "That is why I am voting for myself," hoping that Mr. Wiley would, too.[6]

Wheeler wanted Norris to head the drive for an amendment, considering him the only public figure distinguished enough to attract the necessary support. Norris was not interested. Edward Corwin and Dean Acheson only clouded the issue, saying privately that they favored an amendment but speaking out publicly against one. After the nominating conventions that summer, Acheson told members of the Maryland bar at a meeting in Atlantic City that amending the Constitution "would only substitute new for old uncertainties."[7] Corwin, a thoroughgoing conservative, was anxious to preserve the constitutional system. He feared that any amendment which was agreed on in order to meet the present problem might have to be so sweeping that it would destroy the Supreme Court as an arbiter between the states and the nation.[8]

Later in the campaign, a well-known commentator observed: "The Democrats realize how hard it would be to make even the most scrupulously drawn amendment look like anything but a grant of tyrannical power; hence their reluctance to get off the fence, uncomfortable as it is to sit upon." He mentioned that another possible course would be to enlarge the membership of the Supreme Court, but this, he wrote, "need hardly be regarded as a serious possibility in the immediate future; it would be too obviously a cowardly move."[9]

Not everyone grasped the subtlety in attempts at amending the

---

[5] June 22, 1936, PSF 165, FDRL.

[6] W. F. Wiley to FDR, October 5, 1936, PPF 1717, and FDR to Wiley, October 6, 1936, PPF 259, FDRL.

[7] *New York Herald Tribune,* July 5, 1936, PPF 2278, FDRL.

[8] Arnold, "Back to the Constitution," *New Republic* 88 (December 16, 1937), 222.

[9] Frederick Lewis Allen, "Behind the Campaign," *Harper's* 173 (October 1936), 476.

Constitution, which amounted to an admission that the invalidated New Deal measures were in fact unconstitutional and required changes in the document. John Dickinson asserted: "There is no substitute for wise and enlightened [judicial] interpretation. Without it, the possibility of amendment is but a barren hope." Corwin noted: "Whatever the amendment, we must still trust the Court . . . to correct its own errors." No wording was likely to win the backing of a majority of pro-amendment forces, and any amendment that was approved would inevitably undergo review by the justices. Trying to solve the Court problem by amendment seemed not only elusive, but downright irrelevant.[10]

That the Court issue would not figure in the approaching campaign became clear on an evening in late May when FDR told Moley: "There's one issue in this campaign. It's myself, and people must be either for me or against me." Roosevelt's way of delaying decisions on tactical matters was to play up the presidential personality. He spoke of "specific issues" as "details" in which he was not at that stage interested, but sooner or later he would be pressed to make policy decisions about these "details," and be forced to decide once and for all whether to make a campaign issue of his opponents' potential weapon—the Constitution as interpreted by the Supreme Court majority.[11] Even before the nominating conventions, Republicans were sending the president pointed signals. Charles Curtis, vice president under Hoover, predicted a vigorous campaign and informed the press that the Supreme Court's NRA decision would make a good talking point in the upcoming battle: "It's one of the outstanding issues. The Republican Party has always been in favor of doing things according to the Constitution. The other people haven't been so successful."[12]

FDR appeared eager to answer the Republican challenge, but

[10] Dickinson and Corwin are quoted in Schlesinger, Jr., *Politics of Upheaval,* 492.

[11] Moley, *After Seven Years,* 342; Schlesinger, Jr., *Politics of Upheaval,* 577–78; Davis, *New Deal Years,* 632; Burns, *Roosevelt,* 269–71. The latter study gives a lucid account of how FDR dithered over tactical problems, shifting back and forth between conducting a defensive campaign, resting on his record, and a more aggressive, partisan approach. By early May, as Landon's campaign began to take off, he had decided to follow the partisan direction.

[12] *Jefferson City (Mo.) Tribune,* May 30, 1936, copy in PPF 1820, FDRL.

Farley, designated to manage his campaign, told him he would only be looking for trouble if he did. "Mr. President," he said, within hearing of Secretary Perkins, "the people of the United States don't understand it [the problem of the Supreme Court]. You could not possibly get a sufficient excitement among the people about it."[13] Farley could recall only one occasion when he had been consulted on the matter: "Late in February, 1936, Roosevelt called me [to a meeting] at the White House for a general review of the political situation. In its course he expressed annoyance with the courts, particularly the Supreme Court." McIntyre, Early, and Hall Roosevelt, FDR's brother-in-law, were also present, as was former congressman Charles West.

The president said: "I've been thinking that it would be a good idea if we could appoint fifty Federal judges to hold office for about five years. They would hold roving commissions which would permit them to operate in sections of the country where they could be helpful. What do you think?" Neither Farley nor McIntyre liked the idea, but Early and West seemed receptive to it. McIntyre thought they should get the chief justice to propose the appropriate legislation. Roosevelt agreed to enlist Cummings to try to persuade Hughes to make the proposal. Farley concluded: "I have often thought this was the germ of the Supreme Court packing plan, which he [FDR] was to give Congress a year later."[14] Of course, he knew nothing about the clandestine work going on in the Justice Department. In researching the Supreme Court problem, reform of the lower federal courts was given scant attention, although it was later featured in Roosevelt's judicial reorganization bill. There is ample documentary evidence to confirm that throughout 1935 and 1936 various methods to limit the power of the Supreme Court constituted the main focus of the investigation.

Since the disappointing results of the trial balloon FDR had launched in *Collier's Weekly,* there had been the *Butler, Carter,* and *Tipaldo* rulings, each of which antagonized various interest groups and provoked angry denunciations of the justices. FDR

---

[13] Perkins, Reminiscences, COHC.

[14] *Jim Farley's Story: The Roosevelt Years* (New York: Whittlesey House, 1948), 60–61. This was actually a rehash of the proposal Judge William Denman had been advancing in a one-man crusade for "More and Better Judges."

was convinced that the high court was no longer a truly judicial body but rather "in politics," and in it primarily as a tool of big business. But he also feared that the public would not rally behind him if he attacked the Court and proposed radical judicial reforms, shifting power to the legislature or the executive. Such a strategy might invite public disapproval if he resorted to such tactics during the campaign, as his Republican opponents urged. This could destroy the momentum he enjoyed toward his triumphal reelection in November.[15] To members of his inner circle he hinted that the Court would be dealt with once the election was won, but with a campaign facing them, he demanded maintaining the strictest secrecy on the matter.

Evidence of FDR's determination to act can be found in the intensified work at the Justice Department. A select few continued to explore various approaches to the Court problem throughout the campaign.[16] Until the end of the Supreme Court's 1936 spring term, one that Justice Stone called "the most disastrous in its history," the search had been desultory, but during that critical summer, as the campaign heated up, the team in Justice accelerated its efforts. Secret orders went out to an expanded group of constitutional and legal experts, including Edward Corwin of Princeton and William Draper Lewis of the American Law Institute, to join the select few investigators.[17]

Hoping to seize the initiative, Republicans organized an early campaign. Their candidates included Senator Arthur M. Vandenberg of Michigan, Governor Alfred M. Landon of Kansas, Senator William Borah of Idaho, and Frank Knox, conservative publisher of the *Chicago Daily News.* Landon led in the popularity ratings, and by the time the delegates convened in Cleveland on June 9, 1936, Vandenberg and Knox had fallen behind. Knox made known his availability for second place on a Landon ticket. Only Borah stayed in. Landon was nominated on June 11 on the first ballot, with 918 votes to Borah's 19.[18] When the results were

[15] Davis, *FDR: New Deal Years,* 633.

[16] Joseph Alsop, Box 50, Joseph Alsop Papers, LC.

[17] Alsop and Kintner, *Men around the President,* 20.

[18] Eugene H. Roseboom, *A Short History of Presidential Elections* (New York: Collier Books, 1967), 193.

announced, the hall erupted in a sea of banners, the band struck up "Oh! Susannah" (the campaign theme song), and every delegate sported a sunflower, the Kansas state flower.

Landon opened his campaign for the presidency with a national radio broadcast in which he proclaimed himself a "constitutional liberal."[19] Columnist Ray Clapper, an early supporter, warned Landon against waging a "Hearst-like" campaign: "After all, Roosevelt is still popular—he either has an actual majority or something very close to it. But I think it is a strength that has some flimsy underpinning—it is held to him by fear of having the old crowd thrust back upon the country." Many people, he said, were swallowing Roosevelt's mistakes, his poor follow-through, his wastefulness, and the "cheap politics" that marred so much of his administration, solely because they could see no alternative that would save the better things for which he stood. He predicted that if it were to be a choice between Roosevelt and reaction, the country would take Roosevelt.[20] Clapper was counting on the margin of shifting votes, sympathetic to some of Roosevelt's known objectives but critical of the means used to reach them. He estimated that as many as 5.5 million new voters might swing the balance to Landon if he could only establish in the public mind that he stood for something besides "giving big business the bridle again."[21]

Late in the campaign and even after the election it became fashionable to make Landon the butt of jokes, but in June 1936 he was no joke to Democrats. Characterized even by fellow Republicans as somewhat colorless and a poor speaker, he proved demonstrably capable. He was a more effective campaigner than they expected and more liberal than his party. Roosevelt thought he was the weakest choice his opponents could have made, but the nation's leading newspapers disagreed, as did Ickes, who called Roosevelt's assessment "absurd" and warned Farley in mid-July that Roosevelt would lose the election.[22] Ickes disliked both candidates, calling Landon a man of mediocre ability and complaining that Roosevelt was "too cocksure of himself," un-

[19] Schlesinger, Jr., *Politics of Upheaval,* 524–33.
[20] Clapper to Landon, May 6, 1936, Box 48, Clapper Papers, LC.
[21] Ibid.
[22] Ickes, *Secret Diary,* July 18, 1936, 1:638–39.

willing to take advice from competent men. "FDR surrounded himself," he grumbled, "with men like . . . Hopkins and Tugwell, plus a lot of lesser lights."[23]

Frankfurter shared some of Ickes's misgivings. In late summer he visited Landon at his home in Topeka, and after lunch one day they talked for several hours. "Landon is not the smartest man in the world," he later told FDR, "but I think possibly he has more qualities which might appeal to the rank and file of the voters than any other Republican possibilities except Borah." He believed Borah could carry more agricultural states than any other Republican but doubted that eastern party leaders would stand for his "unorthodox money ideas." Landon assured his visitor that he agreed with many of the principles underlying the New Deal but thought the administration of them was "horrible."[24]

Eventually, Roosevelt received a cautious endorsement from the *New York Times* on the grounds that he would prove to be the "insurance" against radicalism of the sort that the United States had most to fear. But leading columnists like Walter Lippmann of the *New York Herald Tribune,* in supporting Landon, saw no great differences on issues between the two major parties. Both would accept what the Supreme Court had allowed to remain of the New Deal. He faulted Roosevelt for unnecessarily alienating business and establishing a personal, faction-ridden government. Landon, if elected, would in all probability be held in check by a Democratic Senate, wrote Lippmann, and would be more likely to forge a government of "national union."[25]

While keeping an eye on developments in the Republican camp, FDR began to consult more frequently on legal matters with the attorney general. At a session devoted to a postmortem on the invalidated Guffey Coal Act, Cummings assured him that the substitute bill being drafted would likely be upheld by the

---

[23] Booth Mooney, *Roosevelt and Rayburn: A Political Partnership* (Philadelphia: Lippincott, 1971), 71. This phase did not last, especially after Roosevelt asked Ickes to go on the campaign trail to make a series of speeches urging his reelection.

[24] Frankfurter to FDR, n.d., PSF 150, FDRL.

[25] In his daily column "Today and Tomorrow," Lippmann reiterated these and other themes throughout the campaign. Mooney, *Roosevelt and Rayburn,* 74.

Court in the light of the split opinion in *Carter.* The outcome, he said, would depend on the vote of Justice Roberts. As they were conferring, a secretary brought a memo from FDR's aide, Stanley High, and placed it on the president's desk. In it, High expressed disappointment with the Court's recent anti–New Deal decisions. Anticipating the campaign tactics the Republicans were likely to use "if they had the wit to employ them," he feared they could prove very embarrassing to the Democrats. He recommended a counter-procedure that, if adopted, would raise the constitutional issue in the campaign quite prominently. Recent Court decisions had taken so much vitality out of New Deal measures, he maintained, that the administration would be virtually compelled to explain to the voting electorate what they proposed to do about it.

Cummings had to agree that the points High made were "so plausibly stated that they made quite an impressive argument." But when Roosevelt asked him what he *really* thought, he replied that "the premises were wrong and the conclusion unwarranted." Always sensitive to any perceived criticism of his work and perhaps resentful of High's interference, Cummings saw the memo as a reproach to his department and its "bad lawyer" image. He reminded the president that each adverse decision (e.g., the AAA and Guffey Coal Act rulings) left the door open to remedial legislation that was quickly drafted to meet the Court's objections. The government had been upheld in the gold clause and TVA cases, and other New Deal measures had survived scrutiny. The government's spending powers in measures establishing the PWA and WPA had gone practically unchallenged.[26] Cummings was confident that better-drafted legislation could withstand the constitutional test, even with the present Court.

Roosevelt ignored High's suggestions. Cummings reassured him that the chances of disaster overtaking them in November

---

[26] Cummings, Secret Diary, May 19, 1936, 109–10. Stanley High, a smooth-mannered young man recently added to the White House secretariat, had a religious background. According to one Roosevelt biographer, it prompted him to supply the president with what his more irreverent White House aides called "inspirational messages." In this case, High tried to steer his boss toward a more honest, less deceitful path than the attorney general and FDR wanted to pursue. Burns, *Roosevelt,* 266.

were very remote. At that stage, he said, he opposed any shift in tactics, "always a dangerous procedure." Despite advice from High, Tugwell, Moley, and others, Roosevelt was against turning the campaign into a referendum on the Constitution, the Supreme Court, or the amendment issue.

By mid-1936 only Moley remained from the conservative wing of Roosevelt's original brain trust, and he would not last long. There were serious differences between him and FDR on campaign strategy and over FDR's failure to counter opposition attacks on the latter's alleged dictatorial aspirations and readiness to subvert the Supreme Court and the Constitution. Moley considered Roosevelt's approach no exercise in political strategy, but rather a sign of growing megalomania. "Was it really his plan," he asked, "to secure a blank check from the American people, a mandate not to the party or platform, but to himself, enabling him to do anything he wanted to do?" For months he had watched with growing anxiety as the New Deal veered to the left. But he stayed on until one night in June when, in a small gathering of his cronies, FDR taunted Moley about his "new conservatism." An angry quarrel ensued, and that ended the old, historic relationship.[27]

Roosevelt said repeatedly that the people were with him and that whatever he wanted they would also want.[28] Having told himself this so often, he obviously came to believe it, because it enhanced his self-image.[29] The death that April of his old friend, adviser, and former secretary Louis M. Howe left a void in Roosevelt's life that was never filled. "Franklin is on his own now" were among the last words spoken by the gnomelike figure who had directed the 1932 campaign. Steve Early told Ickes that, with Howe's death, Roosevelt would have to plan his own reelection strategy, make every important policy decision himself, and direct the campaign in its every phase. The platform would be dictated from the White House.[30]

---

[27] Moley, *After Seven Years,* 339–40; Burns, *Roosevelt,* 265.

[28] Lash, *Dealers and Dreamers,* 264 and passim; Moley, *After Seven Years,* 339–40.

[29] Clarence Poe to FDR, May 19, 1936, Box 225, Joseph T. Robinson Papers, UAL.

[30] Lash, *Dealers and Dreamers,* 264 and passim; Davis, *FDR: New Deal Years,* 628, 632.

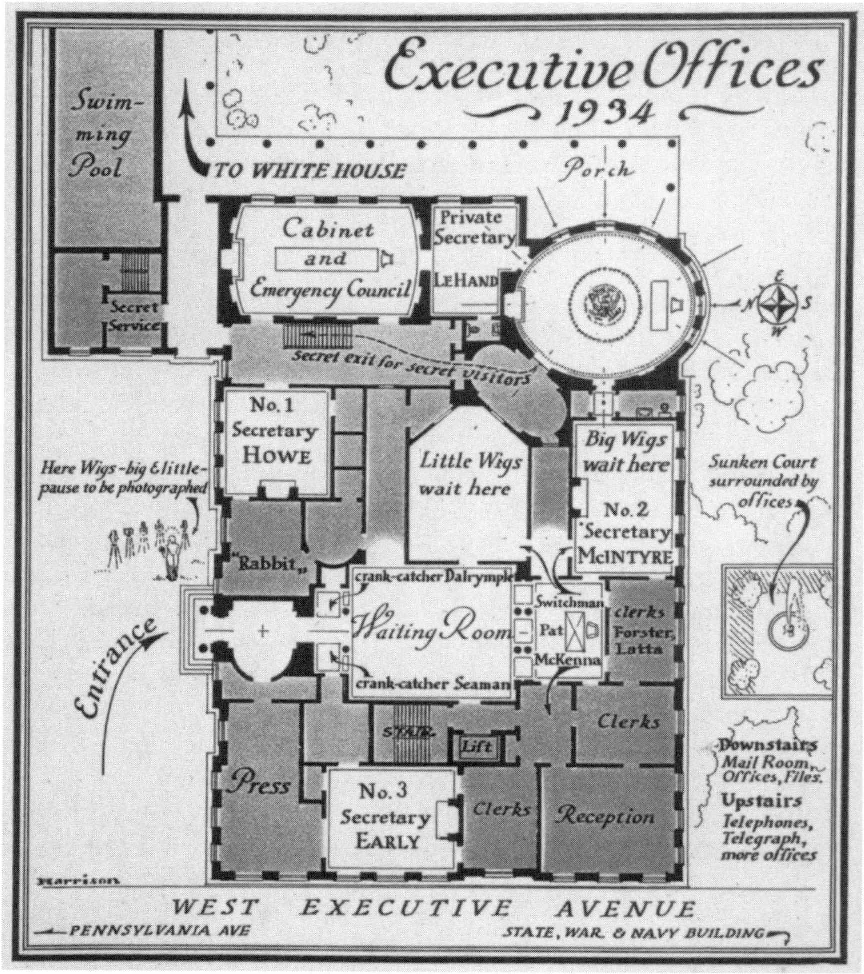

Executive Offices of the White House, 1934. "The vibrant heart and busy brain of the New Deal was in the Executive Offices." The floor plan shown here first appeared in *Time,* December 17, 1934. In the remodeling completed that year, President Roosevelt gave himself a circular office in this new (west) wing, closer to the White House. Louis Howe's office remained vacant for almost two years after his death. (*Life,* January 4, 1937, p. 37)

Mrs. Roosevelt believed that after Howe's death her husband never had another adviser who, while remaining completely loyal, was also willing and able to expose him to all the possible pitfalls in any intended course of action. "Consequently," she wrote, "after Louis' death Franklin frequently made his decisions without canvassing all sides of a question."[31] By then it is highly unlikely that any aide could have exerted much influence over him. During Howe's yearlong illness, Roosevelt already had begun to distance himself from his old mentor.

At the Cleveland convention, the Republican platform reversed the historic position of the party to issue a call for states' rights. It praised the work of the Supreme Court and gave organized labor a plank endorsing its right to form unions and engage in collective bargaining. Child labor, sweatshops, and starvation wages, it stated, could be eliminated "within the Constitution as it now stands." But Landon, eager to depart from the position of the Court majority in the recent *Tipaldo* ruling, sent a telegram to the delegates in Cleveland in which he stated that he favored a constitutional amendment allowing the states to regulate wages, hours, and working conditions for women and children if it proved impossible to control these matters through the states, or in case such legislation could not be lawfully enacted "within the Constitution as it now stands."[32]

Landon impressed voters throughout the country by boldly stating his position on this and other planks in the Republican platform. This move put him somewhat to the left of his party and caught Democrats by surprise. They were startled that a candidate would be so courageous as to propose a constitutional amendment. A columnist noted: "This was the bold, brave act which the Roosevelt administration had so far avoided by maintaining a painful silence."[33] Administration insiders were counting on more adverse decisions by the Supreme Court like the unpopular *Tipaldo* ruling to help their cause. They feared that

---

[31] *This I Remember,* 167–68.

[32] Murphy, *Constitution in Crisis Times,* 151 n; Republican National Committee, *Text Book of the Republican Party* (Washington, D.C.: n.p., 1936), 33, 121.

[33] Beard, "Rendezvous with the Constitution," *New Republic* 88 (September 2, 1936), 92.

their advantage might be lost if a substantive remedy such as the one organized labor was calling for should be included in the Republican platform to counteract the Court's record over the past two years. But everyone knew that any amendment would be difficult to frame and dangerous to defend.

The Democrats met in Philadelphia's Municipal Auditorium from June 23 to June 27 in what was described as "a ratifying affair" since both platform and candidate were predetermined.[34] FDR dominated the proceedings throughout, passing on the major speeches to be delivered and making all the main decisions. Preconvention maneuvering to abolish the century-old two-thirds rule for nominating resulted in a successful vote, easily carried on the convention floor. Bennett "Champ" Clark, whose father had been a victim of the rule in 1912, had the honor of moving adoption of the majority rule.[35] Just as important as the convention proceedings were the preconvention activities, during which most of the important determinations were made.

In the weeks before the convention, the platform had become a source of controversy. After the *Tipaldo* ruling, Democratic leaders were no longer certain that forces pushing for a constitutional amendment on labor's demands could be confined to committee and kept off the floor of the convention. Prominent among these forces was a militant labor bloc. The White House was making every effort to keep the amendment issue out of the news before the convention. In a June 2 editorial, Arthur Krock wrote that "the impression among Democratic politicians persists that an amending proposal can be kept out of the platform, as the President desires," but between June 2 and the convention the situation remained volatile. Some hard and agile thinking would be required, wrote Krock, to keep the party from making what some of its leaders believed would be a great tactical mistake.[36] Three days before the convention opened, Cummings wrote FDR:

[34] Roseboom, *History of Presidential Elections*, 193.

[35] Burns, *Roosevelt,* 271–72. Southern delegates, for whom the rule had been initiated, put up a desultory fight. They were won over by a promise of increased representation for their section.

[36] "In Washington," *New York Times,* June 2, 1936.

> There seems to be a growing conviction amongst our friends that the Democratic Platform should contain some affirmative statement dealing with a Constitutional Amendment. No doubt, it is true, that the way has been opened for such a course, by the recent decision in the minimum wage case, and the action of the Republican Party and Governor Landon with reference thereto. The primary difficulty, however, seems to be that if we attempt to deal specifically with this problem we must go so much further than the Republican Platform, or its candidate, that an entirely new situation is apt to be created which may shift the emphasis of the campaign.

In a cabinet meeting, Roosevelt had warned of the perils in formulating a platform along traditional lines "with specific planks on this or that." However, Cummings said he had no doubt that many groups, especially labor, would want to be heard by the Resolutions Committee at Philadelphia on the subject of an amendment and feared "they may have some drastic suggestions to make." The letter went on to say:

> Should it be necessary to have a specific plank . . . the matter of approach is fully as important as the subject. With that contingency in view . . . I enclose a rough draft which you may . . . find interesting. An amendment to the Constitution of the type suggested would, I think, assure us of success in any litigation involving any essential New Deal legislation.[37]

The draft amendment attached contained a verbose recital of grievances deriving from the Court's creation of "a lawless No-Man's Land." Some passages strongly resembled those in Krock's column of June 2. Underlined for Roosevelt's benefit, one sentence read: "Should *a clarifying amendment* be necessary to assure judicial approval of these essential purposes, we favor the adoption of an amendment which would protect the rights of the States to enact legislation with respect to maximum hours, minimum wages, employment of minors, sweatshops," and so forth. He explained: "The words (so) underlined have the advantage of not closing the door to the thought that perhaps, after all, an amendment *may not be necessary.* They also convey the thought that what we are seeking to obtain is judicial sanction

[37] Cummings to Roosevelt, June 20, 1936, PSF 76, FDRL.

and . . . all that is needed is a clarifying amendment. The clause, you will observe, uses the word 'favor' instead of 'pledge.'"[38] This ambivalent proposal, perhaps designed to obfuscate the issue, shows Cummings at his wily best.

The drafters of the Democratic platform faced a quandary: What, if anything, should be said about recent Supreme Court decisions that were supposedly impeding the New Deal's recovery and nullifying its reform measures? Judge Rosenman, one of those in charge, thought this was the most pressing issue of all. The ticklish Supreme Court problem could be handled by a plank calling for a constitutional amendment broadening Congress's power over the economy, by silence on the whole matter, or by a resort to generalities—assuming, of course, that no plan had as yet been formulated.

Roosevelt was cool to the idea of *any* constitutional amendment, having said as much on a swing through the Southwest while the convention was in progress. In a speech in Little Rock, he repudiated the idea that an amendment to the Constitution was required in view of the negative decisions of the Supreme Court. All that was necessary, he stated, was a reinterpretation of the Constitution—though he neglected to explain how the conservative majority on the Court was to be brought around to this point of view.[39] He may not have realized that support for a constitutional amendment, at least within Democratic Party ranks, was not as widespread as was believed.

Many hours were spent on the amendment issue at White House meetings prior to the convention. FDR asked Cummings and Richberg to prepare the plank on the Supreme Court, and Judge Rosenman was asked to rework their proposals and incorporate them in a draft. Cummings's plank reaffirmed the Democratic Party's devotion to the Constitution: "We believe that the Constitution, as it now stands, when correctly interpreted, affords adequate authority for the attainment of these legitimate ends [of economic and social reform]. . . . Should a clarifying amendment be necessary to assure judicial approval of these essential pur-

[38] Ibid. (italics are mine)

[39] *PPA,* 1936 volume, 199–200; "This Week," *New Republic* 87 (June 24, 1936), 1.

poses, we favor the adoption of an amendment." He appealed for an end to "the lawless judicial No Man's Land" in which neither states nor the federal government could act for what was believed to be the general welfare. But Cummings feared that the final paragraph of his proposed plank might lay them open to attack for making "an apparent criticism of the Supreme Court."[40]

Richberg's plank also included the phrase "a clarifying amendment," implying that the Constitution already gave Congress all the power it needed but that the Supreme Court justices were either too obtuse or too perverse to interpret its meaning accurately. Richberg reportedly pulled his draft out of his pocket at a White House meeting with FDR, Rosenman, and High. Its wording differed only slightly from Cummings's draft, an indication that they were in continuous communication, collaborating on a final wording. The Richberg/Cummings proposal caused a momentary rumpus, but in the confusion it went in.[41] However, as Moley related in his memoirs, that was not the end of the matter.[42]

Late on the afternoon of June 25, as Roosevelt was putting the final touches to his acceptance speech, he gave Corcoran and Moley revised copies of the draft platform which had already been dispatched to Philadelphia. This, he told Moley, was something he had composed in his study "with his eyes fixed on the ceiling." "I saw, as I read it," Moley states, "that it was remarkable for more than its curious origin." It was also susceptible of more varying interpretations than most other documents of its kind. At dinner that evening with Corcoran and Cohen, on the terrace of the Shoreham Hotel, Moley mentioned that the platform seemed to commit the Democrats to a constitutional amendment permitting Congress to exercise wider controls over commerce than it had in the past.

"It was as though I'd threatened to drop a bomb on their

---

[40] Cummings to FDR, June 20, 1936, PSF 76, FDRL. For background on this, see Samuel I. Rosenman, *Working with Roosevelt* (New York: Harper and Row, 1952), 102–3.

[41] Schlesinger, Jr., *Politics of Upheaval,* 581–82; cf. D. Johnson and K. Porter, *National Party Platforms, 1840–1972* (Urbana: University of Illinois Press, 1973), 362.

[42] Moley, *After Seven Years,* 346–47.

heads," he relates. They hastily reread the draft plank on the Constitution. "Yes, indeed," they cried. It did propose a "clarifying amendment" if various problems could not be effectively solved by legislation within the Constitution. "That," they exclaimed, "was suicidal." Along with the rest of the group associated with Frankfurter, Corcoran and Cohen believed there was no need for an amendment. It was their theory that with the Court reconstituted, and with the proper amount of "judicial legerdemain," anything the president wanted might be achieved without an amendment.[43]

Witnessing their agitation, Moley was amused. They bolted their dinners and rushed off—Cohen to send a memo to the president urging changes in the plank on the Constitution, Corcoran to make frantic attempts to find Senator Alben Barkley and Stanley Reed to urge them to change the plank. These efforts failed. The plank stood as it had come from the president, along with the rest of the platform—except for one change made by the Resolutions Committee. On Friday evening, Roosevelt turned once again to drafting his acceptance speech, which Moley thought had been finished the previous afternoon.[44]

As expected, reaction to the platform draft at Philadelphia revealed a strong undercurrent of resentment among some delegates, who opposed injecting a proposal for a constitutional amendment, making it a possible issue in the campaign.[45] The final result was a compromise. When Roosevelt found out that seven of the twelve members on the Resolutions Committee were in favor of a flat declaration for an amendment, he intervened personally to ensure that such a course was "conditional." And at the urging of Senators Bailey, George, and Walsh, Cummings's phrase "a judicial No Man's Land" was deleted, as were all references to the Supreme Court. Democratic spokesmen tried to reassure reporters that the amendment plank in the platform "was in no way intended as a criticism of the Supreme Court."

In its final wording, the platform reflected a major decision on Roosevelt's part. Beset on all sides with conflicting advice, he

---

43 Ibid.
44 Ibid.
45 *New York Times,* June 24, 1936.

chose the method of generality. He refused to accept Cummings's clause, "which would protect the rights of the states." Asserting that the problems they faced were all national problems beyond the power of the individual states that demanded national action, the platform went on cautiously to state that the Democratic Party sought and would continue to seek to meet national problems through legislation within the Constitution, but "if these problems cannot be effectively solved by legislation within the Constitution, we shall seek such clarifying amendment as will assure to the legislatures of the several States and to the Congress of the United States, each within its proper jurisdiction, the power to enact those laws . . . necessary in order adequately to regulate commerce, protect public health and safety, and safeguard economic security. Thus we propose to maintain the letter and spirit of the Constitution."[46] Platforms, as all politicians know, do not win elections; candidates do. After the election, however, the platform would come back to haunt Democrats and the second-term president.

The convention's keynote speaker was Senator Alben Barkley of Kentucky. As the president's front man, he struck hard blows at the Supreme Court for its wholesale slaughter of New Deal laws. His speech had been approved in advance by Roosevelt with a few changes. The tour de force, appealing to the delegates' emotions, aroused them to a fever pitch. When he asked: "Is the Court beyond criticism?" or "May it be regarded as too sacred to be disagreed with?" the huge crowd roared back: "No! No!"

Barkley spoke of greatly needed laws to rescue farmers, laborers, and businesses from distress—laws passed by Congress only to be cast aside by the "rigors of legal technicality" and the application of antiquated economic predilections in interpreting the Constitution. In spite of his vituperative rhetoric, Barkley claimed he was not making an attack on the Supreme Court. "As an institution," he insisted, "I respect it," but when four justices say that a law does not violate the Constitution, it relieves the

[46] *Documents of American History,* ed. Henry Steele Commager, 6th ed. (New York: Appleton-Century Crafts, 1958), 540; *New York Times,* June 27, 1936; Johnson and Porter, *National Party Platforms,* 362.

public of any obligation to underwrite the infallibility of the five whose views prevail. In criticizing the Court, Barkley went no further than to call for a new interpretation of the Constitution. He asked for no amendment, in spite of the platform. "If, in the future," he hinted, "further amendments should become necessary to enable the people to work out their destiny, and protect their fundamental rights, or to overcome some archaic interpretation never intended by its framers, I doubt not that the people will face that duty with the calm intelligence which has guided them in the past."[47] Roosevelt, apparently, would do nothing about it, nor would the Democrats. The people would do the job.

On June 27, Roosevelt was renominated by acclamation.[48] He flew to Philadelphia and that evening delivered a barefisted acceptance speech to more than a 100,000 boisterous Democrats at Franklin Field Stadium. Barkley's address had hammered away at the Supreme Court but left the Constitution and the mythology surrounding it untouched. Roosevelt touched it "with the brush of an angel's wing."[49] He said nothing about the Supreme Court or its decisions, but talked instead about faith, hope, and charity. His ecstatic supporters listened to a vigorous assault on the "forces of reaction," the keynote of the campaign:

> These economic royalists complain that we seek to overthrow the institutions of America. What they really complain of is that we seek to take away their power. Our allegiance to American institutions requires the overthrow of this kind of power. In vain they seek to hide behind the Flag and the Constitution. In their blindness they forget what the Flag and Constitution stand for. Now, as always, they stand for democracy, not tyranny; for freedom, not subjection; and against a dictatorship by mob rule and the over-privileged alike.[50]

FDR opened his formal campaign at the end of September with a speech to the New York Democratic Convention in Syracuse.

---

[47] For the text of Barkley's address, see the *New York Times,* June 25, 26, 1936; cf. Beard, "Rendezvous with the Constitution," 92–94.

[48] Cummings insisted on making one of the fifty-six seconding speeches, despite a presidential order that administration members were to do nothing of that kind. Roosevelt may have waived the ruling. Ickes, *Secret Diary,* 1:632.

[49] Charles A. Beard, "Rendezvous with the Supreme Court," *New Republic* 88 (September 2, 1936), 93.

[50] *PPA,* 1936 volume, 230–36; *New York Times,* June 28, 1936.

He emphasized the alleged improvement in the economy since 1932. Democrats not only took credit for a dramatic change for the better under Roosevelt but argued that old abuses had been eliminated and confidence restored. Against this optimistic rhetoric, the Republicans' claim that the Constitution and the American way of life were in danger fell flat.[51] Landon rarely referred in his speeches to the Supreme Court, leaving it to others. His supporters repeatedly called attention to the alarming possibility that if Roosevelt won a second term he would make one or more appointments to the Supreme Court. Bainbridge Colby, secretary of state under Wilson, predicted that a Roosevelt administration would nullify the Constitution. In Detroit, Senator James A. Reed of Missouri convened a conference of newly organized "Jeffersonian Democrats" who declared themselves against the Roosevelt ticket.[52] A popular campaign slogan was: "Life, Liberty and Landon." At Republican rallies all over the country his followers sang

> Alf Landon learned a thing or two,
> He knows the right solution,
> And in the White House he will stay
> Within the Constitution.[53]

In June, attacks from both left and right intensified and brought a sudden drop in Roosevelt's popularity. Some of the most vituperative rhetoric came not from the stump, but from the nation's leading newspapers. In fifteen of the most populous cities, newspaper alignment was 71 percent for Landon, measured by circulation figures.[54] Nor were attacks on FDR confined to editorials denouncing him or the New Deal. In a letter to the editor of the *Boston Transcript,* Dawes Eliot compared Roosevelt's treatment of the Constitution to the kaiser's scornful reference to the Versailles Treaty as "just a scrap of paper," and characterized Con-

[51] Roseboom, *History of Elections,* 197.

[52] The Jeffersonian Democrats split away from the New Deal in the spring of 1936 and were thus given an opportunity to make speeches against Roosevelt under their own auspices, rather than those of the Republican Party or the Liberty League. They were even rumored to be considering setting up a third party.

[53] Quoted in Stefan Lorant, *The Glorious Burden: The American Presidency* (New York: Harper and Row, 1968), 613.

[54] Roseboom, *History of Elections,* 198.

gress as "a tool of the Executive." Instead of observing the will of the people, Eliot charged, lawmakers yielded to the will of the president. With such a supine Congress, one of the three bulwarks of the American democratic form of government was gone. At the Philadelphia convention, he wrote, the promise had been made that the Constitution would be amended "if necessary." Did this mean "if necessary to constitutionalize Roosevelt's own acts"? The Supreme Court was denounced at the convention. Why? "Because it did not uphold the President . . . in his high-handed actions, but stamped them as unconstitutional." Thus another bulwark was threatened. "What have we left?" Eliot asked. "Only the polls in November."

Landon supporters attacked the administration on all fronts, particularly for reckless spending and waste on makeshift projects, antagonism toward big business, erratic monetary policies, and alleged disregard of the Constitution. New Dealers were accused of coddling socialism and even communism. In reply to a Florida judge who had written him about such charges a year earlier, FDR assured him that the people who talked of communism and constitutionalism were making no headway, "because our citizenship understands that this Government is not communistic and that it intends to proceed under constitutional forms."[55]

Following the convention, Roosevelt went on a two-week fishing cruise on waters off New England, leaving campaign organizers to grapple with the thousand and one details of winning an election. In mid-July, early polls showed Landon gaining unexpected strength. Ickes grumbled: "Meanwhile, the President smiles and sails and fishes and the rest of us worry and fume."[56] In late summer, the White House announced plans for a series of presidential trips to drought- and flood-stricken areas of the country, billing them as "non-political," but that fooled no one. Not until October did FDR make half a dozen campaign speeches in which he assiduously avoided mentioning the Constitution or Supreme Court.[57]

---

[55] Hon. Armstead Brown of the Florida Supreme Court to FDR, July 2, 1935, and FDR to Brown, July 6, 1935, OF 41A, Box 48; see also PPF 2669, FDRL.

[56] *Jim Farley's Story,* 63ff.; Ickes, *Secret Diary,* July 18, 1936, 1:639.

[57] Swisher, *American Constitutional Development,* 941; Pusey, *Hughes,* 2:750; Mason, *Stone,* 439.

Once the president began making hard-hitting speeches, Landon's momentum began to falter. The Democratic campaign train made a swing through the West, where FDR's speeches conspicuously omitted any reference to future plans for extending the New Deal. Foreign policy was almost completely ignored. Toward the campaign's close, in what appeared to be an act of desperation, Republicans tried to use the Social Security Act to embarrass FDR, attacking it as a "pay reduction" measure in a time of economic hardship, which it was. The tax on wage earners was regressive. Employers enclosed in workers' pay envelopes warnings of the dire consequences they could expect in the event of a Democratic victory in November. The threat worked against Republican candidates.

Roosevelt wound up his campaign in late October with a ten-day tour of northeastern cities, a bastion of Democratic strength. Huge crowds lined the streets, at times making it difficult for the motorcade to pass through. In Connecticut cities, it had difficulty making its way through the thick blockade of onlookers. A dejected Ray Clapper wrote William Allen White: "The Kansas Governor's campaign seems to have disintegrated into a rather sad affair, which is a great disappointment to me. It was the Milwaukee Social Security speech which finally unsold me. . . . On top of all that, the constant harping on Roosevelt's undermining the American system of government adds a grotesque capstone to an unworkable and contradictory group of specific policies." Of FDR, he wrote: "He is far from perfect, but you have to take one or the other, and on the whole I would dislike to see his general policies scrapped for what the Republicans propose."[58] A disillusioned Clapper abandoned Landon and backed FDR.[59]

The climax of the campaign came on the last day of October with Roosevelt's speech before a wildly boisterous crowd that jammed New York's Madison Square Garden. Compared to previous rhetoric, his words that night took on a sharper edge, hardened in both tone and content. Stung by Republican criticisms, which had also become increasingly harsh in tone, Roosevelt

---

[58] October 23, 1936, Box 48, Clapper Papers, LC.

[59] After the election he wrote Landon: "I wish you had gone my way more because I don't like the picture which the election leaves. It is a little terrifying." November 4, 1936, ibid.

went on the attack, directing his fire not at Landon directly but at the "forces of selfishness and greed" that he claimed stood behind the Republican party. Raking over the old "enemies of peace"—the business and financial monopoly, speculators, bankers, war profiteers, and so forth—who had begun, he charged, to consider the government a mere appendage to their own affairs, he flung out this challenge: "Never before in all our history have these forces been so united against one candidate as they stand today. They are unanimous in their hate for me—*and I welcome their hatred.*" He had difficulty continuing above the roar of the crowd that greeted his words: "I should like to have it said of my first Administration," he continued, "that in it the forces of selfishness and lust for power met their match." Cheers more raucous again interrupted him. "Wait a moment," he demanded. The din slowly subsided. "I shall like to have it said of my second Administration that in it these forces met their master."[60]

These remarks outraged the president's opponents. One of their spokesmen, Bainbridge Colby, replied in an address to the Women's Patriotic Congress. After seeing an advance copy of Colby's speech, Marvin McIntyre, FDR's secretary, sent a message to the assistant secretary of the navy, instructing him to withdraw the marine band from participating in the program! Colby returned the president's words in kind. "It was indeed a shocking spectacle for a President to make of himself, a constitutional president of a constitutional democracy who has no power save such as is conferred on him by the Constitution which he has taken an oath to preserve and defend, to obey and not transgress."

Colby referred the audience to an article published in a recent issue of the *London Observer* titled "The Psychology of Dictatorship: Stalin and Roosevelt" by the Swiss psychiatrist Carl Jung. "I have just come from America," Jung wrote, "where I saw Roosevelt. Make no mistake, he has the most amazing power complex, the Mussolini substance, the stuff of a dictator absolutely."[61] Colby commented:

[60] *New York Times,* November 1, 1936.

[61] Jung traveled to Cambridge, Massachusetts, in September 1936 by invitation to participate in the tercentenary celebrations of Harvard University. As an alumnus, Roosevelt was there, and they may have met on that occasion.

> Well, this is precisely the judgment which the people of the U.S. have reached. The American people may not be eminent psychologists, but they are very observant . . . they see what they see, and they know what's what, and they know something which even goes beyond the knowledge of an eminent Swiss scientist, they know that the President of the U.S. cannot be a dictator unless he destroys the Constitution; they know that a constitutional President cannot even aspire to dictatorial powers unless he harbors in his breast a willingness and an intention to overthrow the Constitution.

Colby outlined what he called the "approach shots" to dictatorship: one can be recognized when a president becomes impatient with the independence of the judiciary or the separate and distinct rights of persons of the legislative branch of government and seeks to gather up all power unto himself. These, he said, are "steps in the direction of tyranny, and dictatorship is only another name for tyranny," and the American people "will have nothing to do with tyranny or dictatorship . . . or aims at either, or a step, even a short one, in their direction." If a president cannot satisfy his ambition within the Constitution, Colby argued, he need not look to the American people for any support in his effort to satisfy it outside of and at the sacrifice of the Constitution. "This has been tried—but it has always failed and covered those who tried it with obloquy and disgrace."

Colby urged the president not to be angered by his failures. "Someday he will be grateful for them." He went on to recite them: failure to enlarge the powers of his office beyond constitutional limits; failure in his efforts to discredit the Supreme Court; failure to foment popular impatience with its impartial and correct decisions; and finally, failure to destroy the power, so dear to the American people, of state and local government. "The tragedy, however, of President Roosevelt's past," he concluded, "is that, if reelected, he proposes to renew these efforts, to persist in his endeavor to be an undemocratic and unconstitutional President." In a parting shot he said: "Landon's election will terminate once and for all an administration which the great Democratic Senator from Virginia, Mr. Carter Glass has repeatedly denounced as a disgrace to the nation."[62]

---

[62] Bainbridge Colby, "On the Constitution," November 2, 1936, address to the Women's Patriotic Congress, copy in PPF 876, FDRL. Roosevelt instructed

"The Liberty League's Pseudonyms for the New Deal." A cartoon by Rolun Kirby, *New York World Telegram,* November 12, 1935. (President's Personal File, Box 10, FDRL)

Roosevelt's overwhelming electoral triumph added an aura of invincibility to a president who had assumed mythical proportions even before the end of his first term.[63] He took 60.8 percent of the popular vote[64]—a margin exceeded only once in all presidential

---

Marvin McIntyre to get a copy of this speech and a transcript of his own remarks in Madison Square Garden for purposes of comparison.

[63] Although FDR was victorious in all but two states, even in his triumph he was chagrined by his failure once again to carry Dutchess County and Hyde Park in upstate New York. He never stopped hoping for the support of the home folks.

[64] Lyndon B. Johnson's 61.1 percent of the popular vote in 1964 was only

elections since 1820—and his plurality of more than 11 million votes was the largest ever recorded in electoral history. Democrats held 333 of the 435 House seats and added 6 more in the Senate, raising their majority to 75 of 96 seats. The landslide victory represented a resounding popular endorsement of the president, the Democratic Party, and the New Deal. Never since have Democratic successes at the polls reached such spectacular levels as in 1936. It was easily overlooked that Landon polled nearly a million more votes than Hoover in 1928 and carried eighty-seven more counties. Although he won only eight electoral votes, Landon received a greater percentage of the popular vote than had either John W. Davis in 1924 or James Cox in 1920. Roosevelt's popular vote, an impressive 27 million, approximated Harding's in 1920.[65]

At a press conference on November 6, Roosevelt was asked: "Now that the election is over, will you discuss your attitude toward amending the Constitution to carry out the purposes of the New Deal?" His reply was: "Why spoil another happy day?" When another reporter asked, "Mr. President, do you contemplate waiting until you get Supreme Court decisions on the remainder of the New Deal measures before drafting new legislation?" he again shrugged off the question, quipping: "Oh, let's make this a holiday."[66] The troubles with the Supreme Court were momentarily put aside. They could be dealt with later. A rare example of common sense on the matter came from the defeated candidate, who wrote Clapper: "Both politicians in Congress and big business, Governors and Presidents, have been relying too much on supreme courts to stop legislation that ought to be threshed out on its merits on the legislative floor."[67]

Roosevelt, meanwhile, was inundated with congratulatory messages, one of which came from Cecilia Cummings:

---

slightly more decisive than Roosevelt's 1936 landslide. Ronald Reagan carried every state but one (Minnesota) in 1984.

[65] Cushman, *Rethinking the New Deal Court,* 234–35; William E. Leuchtenburg, "Election of 1936," in *The History of American Presidential Elections, 1789–1968,* ed. Arthur M. Schlesinger, Jr., 5 vols. (New York: McGraw Hill, 1971), 3:2843.

[66] Press Conference no. 325, November 6, 1936, *CPPC,* 8:146–47.

[67] November 16, 1936, Box 48, Clapper Papers, LC.

> Dear Mr. President: . . . Homer is like a child—he is so pleased . . . about Connecticut [which went for Roosevelt]. . . .
>
> Of course, I cast a very definite vote for you, but I cast just as definite a vote against Mrs. Landon and her harp. The thought of that "flower of American womanhood" draped around a harp in the East Room made me violently ill. Some one remarked I needn't worry as, no doubt we wouldn't be invited to see her. But I disagreed and said it would be just the thing they would invite us to hear. Can you imagine "Oh Susannah" being twanged out by Mrs. Landon with every third note sour? . . .
>
> You know how happy we are. I am visiting in Greenwich among the Republicans, but they are strangely silent.[68]

Later that month, Ickes recalled: "The President seemed very happy yesterday. He talked a lot about the election and its implications. He spoke of the fact that he now had an absolutely free hand without the danger of being charged with having broken campaign promises." At subsequent cabinet meetings there was a good deal of discussion about the Supreme Court. Ickes sensed that Roosevelt was getting ready to move on that issue and hoped that he would. Stanley Reed, sitting in for the attorney general, related the news of Justice Stone's illness. Stone had contracted a virulent strain of amoebic dysentery after returning from a holiday in Mexico and would be off the bench for months, struggling to regain his health. The president interrupted to quip that he expected Mr. Justice McReynolds would still be on the bench when he was 105. Reed reminded him laughingly that the justice appeared to be in the best of health.

Roosevelt instructed Reed to move ahead as rapidly as possible with test cases involving the constitutionality of New Deal legislation. He expected these laws to be struck down and, according to Ickes, was looking forward to that as the basis for an appeal to the people for judicial changes over the heads of the justices on the Court. "I am keen myself," wrote Ickes, "that this question should be raised and I hope to be able to take part in that fight, if and when it comes."[69] He did not have long to wait. In the final weeks of November and December, messengers were seen

[68] November 5, 1936, PSF 76, FDRL. Connecticut, which Hoover carried in 1932, went for FDR in 1936.

[69] Ickes, *Secret Diary,* November 7, 1936, 1:705.

scurrying back and forth between Cummings's office and the president's, carrying the work of McFarland's team to the White House and returning with FDR's "chits" (small slips of paper) with his pithy comments and suggestions to aides and subordinates.

But before there would be any movement on that front, the president sailed off on a "goodwill tour" to South America to attend "an extraordinary Inter-American Conference" at Buenos Aires, the result of his invitation to the twenty-one Latin American states. The objective was to find ways, in view of the worsening international situation, to ensure the peace and security of the Western Hemisphere. When he boarded the USS *Indianapolis* at Charleston on November 18, the president's baggage included several thick briefing books prepared by Cummings and his aides. They contained all the constitutional amendments ever proposed by lawmakers to overcome judicial obstruction of congressional legislation, along with "expert" commentary on each. The largest of them included all bills proposed in Congress to curb the power of the Supreme Court, also with commentary. At every port of call along the way, additional material Cummings thought he ought to see awaited the president.

In the weeks prior to sailing, Roosevelt maintained almost daily contact with Cummings, issuing instructions on what should be done during his absence. Each discussion ended with the same command—"Go back, work on it, and come up with results." Cummings, using a private entrance to the oval room, came and went unnoticed.[70] Their meetings were kept a secret even from close Roosevelt advisers Corcoran, Rosenman, and Reed. But once on the high seas heading for South America, the president found limited time for study, which gave way to deep-sea fishing, sunning, swimming, poker games, and relaxation after a month of campaigning.[71] There were far more pleasant distractions on that "happy ship" which he would have had to forego for the sake of Cummings's dull briefing books. During most of the twelve-thousand-mile voyage, Roosevelt, temporarily at least, was able to put the Court problem out of his mind.

---

[70] Joseph Alsop manuscript, draft no. 4, Box 50, Alsop Papers, LC.
[71] Davis, *FDR: New Deal Years,* 655–56.

8

Roosevelt's Revenge

> The conjunction of a grave political and economic emergency, an assertive and popular President, and a strong-willed judiciary, provided . . . the ingredients for a constitutional conflict of major dimensions.
>
> John D. Lees, "The President and the Supreme Court: New Deal to Watergate" (BAAS Pamphlets in American Studies 3, p. 11. British Association for American Studies, Durham, U.K.: 1980)

AFTER HIS REELECTION in 1936, Roosevelt said that "1937 was the year which was to determine whether the kind of government which the people had voted for in 1932, 1934 and 1936 was to be permitted by the Supreme Court to function." Frustrated by the Supreme Court's decisions declaring so much New Deal legislation unconstitutional, Roosevelt, after wavering for a long time, was poised to go on the attack. The only question left undecided was which weapons to choose. Harvard economist John Kenneth Galbraith once claimed that there are two kinds of politicians: those who evade battle and those who invite it. Inviting it can sometimes earn a loyalty not given to other politicians, whose instincts are for evasion, accommodation, appeasement, or retreat. But for those who find real pleasure in the contest, as FDR did, there is always the risk that strategic retreat or defeat might leave them vanquished, leaderless, and exposed.[1]

From mid-December 1936 on, Roosevelt attended directly, almost exclusively, to the Supreme Court issue. During the campaign, Republicans had warned that, if elected, he would pack the Supreme Court. Democrats felt that to preserve the rest of the

---

[1] Roosevelt, as quoted in Alfred Steinberg, *Sam Rayburn: A Biography* (New York: Hawthorn Books, 1975), 143; for Galbraith, see *The New Deal: Fifty Years After,* ed. Wilbur J. Cohen (Austin: University of Texas Press, 1984), 12.

New Deal agenda, something had to be done about the judicial blockade, but they seemed willing to leave the mode of action to their leader for some future determination.[2]

The search for a feasible plan dragged on, but Roosevelt had to give some attention to the preparation of three messages to be delivered within two weeks in January: the State of the Union message, his second inaugural address, and the message accompanying a bill to reorganize the executive department.[3] Corcoran, who had carried a heavy burden for the president during the campaign, was now one of his principal speechwriters, helping High, Rosenman, and Richberg in drafting these state papers. They knew nothing about the handful of insiders in the Justice Department carrying on Cummings's "secret investigation."

This became clear when Corcoran visited Moley in New York after the election. Moley raised the amendment issue, which, despite its inclusion in the party platform, had scarcely been mentioned since June. He regretted that Roosevelt had deliberately avoided any discussion of the constitutional issue in the campaign. Changing the subject, Corcoran referred to a new book he had just read about the Supreme Court by Drew Pearson and Robert S. Allen. Proof sheets were sent to the White House in advance of publication. *The Nine Old Men* was a sensational exposé, featuring lurid and even libelous personal attacks on certain justices. Corcoran spoke with great enthusiasm about it. Some justices must be "ease[d] out," he said. Asked how they proposed to do that, he mentioned a possible pension law or age limitation. Moley remarked wryly that any age limitation on the justices would force Justice Brandeis off the bench at once. Countering with a non sequitur, Corcoran said that the book he was talking about "gave Brandeis a complete bill of health."

"You'll have a hard time drafting a law embodying the specific likes and dislikes of this book's authors, won't you?" Moley asked. Ignoring this, Corcoran said: "After all, Van Devanter and Sutherland are the only ones we need to get at." Within the White House inner circle these two justices were considered the backbone of the anti–New Deal Court, although the *New York*

---

[2] Swisher, *American Constitutional Development,* 941.

[3] There was a budget message and several other items to prepare over the next weeks.

Times's own survey for the 1936 term had indicated that Van Devanter "had stood with the Roosevelt forces nine times and against them three times." Nevertheless, it too characterized him as "always a conservative" and "a thorn in the administration's side when it came to decisions on New Deal measures."

Had it occurred to Corcoran, Moley asked, that whether the membership of the Court were changed or not, the White House would have to honor the implied promise to appoint Senate Majority Leader Robinson to the Court? Earlier, Roosevelt, through an intermediary, had conveyed his intention of putting Robinson on the Court.[4] Corcoran's response to that was extraordinary: "I've learned a lot about politics from being down there. When a politician makes a promise, he knows that he is not binding himself, and the man to whom he makes the promise knows it too. That is one of the things you've got to learn. There aren't any binding promises in politics. You just know that the strongest side wins." As he listened, Moley believed he was witnessing a curious phenomenon. "Tom," he wrote, "had been, figuratively speaking, stricken with a rare occupational ailment. He was falling to the ground from the sheer weight of the new power and responsibility that he was carrying."[5]

In mid-December, Solicitor General Reed, who was uninformed of what was going on in his own department, was asked to make a comprehensive study including various suggestions "by which the legislature might . . . lessen its vulnerability to the constitutional views of the majority of the Court." The study was being prepared, Reed told Cummings, "so that if, as and when the President brings the matter up again, we would have this background. It was suggested at the first Cabinet meeting after the election that we should be thinking about it." The matter, he added, "has been handled confidentially and I have my copy of the memorandum under lock."[6] An earlier memo by Justice Department law-

[4] The intermediary was Jim Farley, who contacted Senator Robinson. See also G. Edward White, *The Constitution and the New Deal* (Cambridge: Harvard University Press), 293, and for the survey of the 1936 Term, see *New York Times,* May 19, 1937, 1, 18.

[5] *After Seven Years,* 353. The meeting took place on November 13, 1936.

[6] Stanley Reed to Attorney General, December 19, 1936, RG 60, 235773, NA. Cummings had been the first to suggest putting all communications in the form of memoranda. The president, from the beginning, accepted the idea.

yer Warner W. Gardner ("Congressional Control of Judicial Power to Invalidate Legislation") had been sent to Roosevelt aboard the USS *Indianapolis* on his return from South America.[7]

Gardner's formula suggested that Congress "might increase the number of Supreme Court justices, in order to obtain a judiciary more of whose constitutional views are attuned to the contemporary development of the society which is governed by the Constitution." He explained: "It would be necessary to add either three or perhaps as many as nine or ten new justices, according as one evaluated the likelihood of antagonizing the present liberal justices to a point where they would retaliate by voting against the constitutionality of legislation." He then offered six formidable objections to this solution, including "the superficial character of the remedy," but said it was the only one that was "certainly constitutional." Ultimately, he thought the choice had to be made between a constitutional amendment and increasing the size of the Court, but "only the former of these two alternatives would seem to offer a permanent solution."[8]

Reed's memo analyzed, classified, and appraised suggestions thought to have some element of feasibility in solving the Court problem. His study served chiefly to clear the air by pointing out all the impossibilities or pitfalls in the way of trying to achieve the desired end. The five-part document was useful mainly as background for decisions affecting a plan Cummings and Roosevelt devised soon after its submission. The lawyers in Reed's office who helped frame the memoranda were extremely pessimistic about the practicality of any of these proposals once all the legal and political objections to them were taken into account.[9]

In late November, Reed asked Corcoran and Cohen to prepare additional memoranda on the Court situation, specifically requesting drafts of constitutional amendments "in case of need." Roosevelt had long ago abandoned this approach, but Reed, like Frankfurter, was inclined to believe the president still favored,

[7] Warner W. Gardner to the Attorney General, December 10, 1936, ibid. Copies of a great many memos were sent to the president; nearly all of them were lost in a fire in Warner Gardner's home at 2700 Tilden Street, Washington, D.C. A copy is in Box 226, Frankfurter Papers, LC.

[8] Ibid.

[9] Swisher, *American Constitutional Development,* 941.

among all the proposals for a solution, a constitutional amendment. A proposal Reed supported, similar to several introduced in Congress, would have permitted an unchallengeable reenactment by Congress of any law invalidated by the Court on constitutional grounds. Congress would have to override such a decision by a two-thirds majority, or by a simple majority after an intervening election. A similar proposal would have enabled Congress to validate state laws rejected by the Court.[10] This approach faced enormous political obstacles. Frankfurter, among others, knew this, but he also saw "the need for constitutional reform" in the wake of what he called the Court's "dismal performance in 1936." He had urged confrontation, but not the method finally chosen by the president.[11]

Cohen would have given the president authority by amendment to appoint as many additional Supreme Court judges as would be necessary to replace those over seventy years of age, ensuring a liberal majority. This plan would not have permanently increased the size of the Court, whose membership would return to nine as justices over seventy left the bench. When Cohen showed it to Roosevelt, according to Corcoran, he dismissed it, instructing that all amendments had to clear Cummings's office. "Ben got nowhere," Corcoran reported. Cohen forwarded the draft proposal to Frankfurter with this message: "After working hard to show that it is impossible to draw up such amendments, I have found it harder to sit down and draft them myself. But I am sending you the result. . . . You can act as *advocatus diaboli.*"[12]

Roosevelt meanwhile had been reading several books on the origins of the Constitution, including Jonathan Elliot's edition of the debates in the 1787 Constitutional Convention. He consulted or corresponded with constitutional experts Charles A. Beard,

---

[10] Kenneth S. Davis, *F.D.R.: Into the Storm: 1937–1940* (New York: Random House, 1986), 52.

[11] Frankfurter to Reed, December 14, 1936, Reed to Frankfurter, December 17, 1936, Frankfurter to Cohen, December 17, 1936, Box 170, Frankfurter Papers, HLL, cited in Michael E. Parrish, *Felix Frankfurter and His Times: The Reform Years* (New York: Free Press, 1982), 266–67.

[12] Quoted in Lash, *Dealers and Dreamers,* 292.

Edward Corwin, and Howard Lee McBain.[13] Before FDR left for South America, his aides had tried to discuss various proposals to cope with the Court problem, realizing that something had to be done, and quickly. On his return, they submitted the first draft of the annual message, in which they had tried to outline the whole problem but made no attempt to suggest a method of attacking it. "Leave the whole thing very general for now," Roosevelt told them. "Let's just point up the need and when we get ready we'll submit the solution. I'm not quite ready yet."[14]

Cummings, meanwhile, had been reading proof sheets for a series of articles prepared by Corwin for the *Philadelphia Record* that dealt with the Supreme Court, the Constitution, and proposals for reorganizing the federal judiciary.[15] The remedies he suggested were contradictory. One article argued that the resort to amendments was not the answer, while another stated that amendments might be needed. In the final article, one sentence stood out: "No reform could be better adopted than the requirement to be laid down by an act of Congress, or, if necessary, by constitutional amendment, that no Judge may hold office under the United States beyond his seventieth birthday." (Corwin is credited with formulating the age-limit provision incorporated in the original court bill.) Stanley Reed, to whom advance proof sheets had also been sent, wrote: "I wonder whether you overemphasize the possibility of requiring retirement at seventy. It seems too small a thing to justify a constitutional amendment." Corwin replied:

> I was glad to get your comments on those articles—I believe that my age limit proposal, if adopted, may have considerable effect. It

---

[13] FDR may have taken heed of Beard's advice: "Assuming . . . that anybody . . . really wanted to know something about the Constitution and the Supreme Court, before blowing his kazoo, how would he proceed? That is to go back to the original sources, printed and unprinted, that are related to the formation and development of the Constitution. At the gateway stand the three huge volumes containing the record of the convention of 1787, edited . . . by Max Farrand. These must be supplemented by Elliot's debates in five volumes, and by innumerable papers unearthed by recent scholarship." Quoted in Beard, "Little Alice Looks at the Constitution," 315.

[14] Rosenman, *Working with Roosevelt,* 140–41.

[15] OF 41, Box 48 (now 116), FDRL.

> might not get more liberal judges, but it would assure a more rapid replacement of the Bench. Today Jefferson's complaint is well justified: "Few die and none resign."—indeed, the statement might be made stronger. Also, such a reform would be apt to turn the attention of the appointing power more frequently to the faculties of the great law schools where superior talent is apt to emerge at a much earlier age than in practice at the bar.[16]

Referring to amendments, Corwin wrote: "As to the difference between two-thirds [the majority required in both houses of Congress to propose] and three-fourths [the majority of state legislatures required to ratify]—I think that might be very material. Besides, an amendment may be defeated by an adverse majority in one house of the 13th legislature. Also, the Senate is subject to party leadership at Washington in a way the state legislatures are not." As for his age-limit proposal, he concluded: "I believe it could be validly accomplished by an act of Congress, unless it were to apply retroactively."[17]

Corwin's suggestions reached Cummings and Reed at a propitious time. FDR had been wrestling with court-packing as a method on and off, but he recognized (and feared) its limits as a taboo. He needed some underpinning principle to legitimate it, and found it in Corwin's formula relating new Supreme Court appointments to the ages of sitting justices. If it were adopted, the administration could try to exploit what it perceived as a growing popular resentment toward aging justices on the bench.[18] Rosenman, one of the president's principal aides, knew FDR was leaning heavily toward this solution. Even as aides continued into January working on the annual message, the Justice Department team was moving ahead, drafting a judiciary bill and presidential message to accompany it. On one draft, Roosevelt scribbled in pencil: "Are House and Senate to be in session on February 5

---

[16] Reed to Corwin, December 3, 1936, and Corwin to Reed, December 16, 1936, RG 60, file 235868, NA. When Roosevelt finally secured appointments to the Court, three of them (Felix Frankfurter, William O. Douglas, and Wiley Rutledge) were drawn from law schools. This was part of his effort to expand the field of recruitment for justices. Of the three, only Frankfurter went directly from the lecture hall to the bench.

[17] Corwin to Reed, December 16, 1936, ibid.

[18] Leuchtenburg, *Supreme Court Reborn,* 115–19.

for message at noon?" Judge Rosenman tells us: "We knew nothing of this at the time."[19]

The Breakthrough

Roosevelt pored over suggestions, memos, and information, much of it from the Justice Department, warning against using the very method and strategy he ultimately adopted. His speech files contain a wealth of items clearly defining the dangers he faced.[20] But he could no longer delay deciding which of many proposals to choose. Shortly before Christmas, Cummings wrote: "I am bursting with ideas anent our constitutional problems, and have a plan I would like to talk over with you when you have the time"[21]

A breakthrough occurred in late December. Normally, the Roosevelt family spent Christmas at Hyde Park with the president's mother, but in 1936 they celebrated the day at the White House, enjoying what the press called an "old fashioned affair." Cummings telephoned FDR on December 26 to say he was ready to discuss the constitutional question with him whenever he cared to. They met that same afternoon at five in a conference that lasted over two hours, interrupted only by the president's son James, who brought them tea and toast. Cummings had revealed nothing about "his plan" until he arrived that day, loaded down with thick sheaves of documents and heavy briefing books. Details of the meeting were minutely recorded in his "Secret Diary," evidently with posterity in mind.[22]

Cummings had spent Christmas Eve in his office working on the constitutional problems encountered by the administration over the years. He had been endeavoring to formulate a policy that would warrant submission to his chief. "Manifestly," he told Roosevelt, "we are confronted by a rather serious situation." Cases not yet before the Supreme Court "in an official manner,"

---

[19] *Working with Roosevelt,* 140–41.

[20] PPF 1820, FDRL.

[21] December 22, 1936, PSF "Supreme Court" folder, FDRL.

[22] Entries for December 26, 1936, 185–97; cf. Alsop Notes, Box 53, Alsop Papers, LC.

he said, were in serious peril.[23] The problem called for statesmanship of a high order. "I have, however, a plan . . . taking shape in my mind," he said, "and it is somewhat novel." It would not be free from objection, but he considered it the most practical way of dealing with the matter, less open to challenge than almost any other scheme he could think of.[24]

Roosevelt brought up his forthcoming annual message. Coinciding as it did with the end of his first term, even though he would succeed himself, he thought that in the future there would be quite a number of one-term presidents. The annual message, therefore, "needed to be very general." Perhaps he could be more specific in his second inaugural address. Returning to "reflections on the Constitution," he told Cummings to proceed with what he had in mind.

There followed a long-winded review of the trend in recent Supreme Court decisions. Cummings said he was going back to fundamentals and "trying to diagnose our troubles before seeking to apply a remedy." The minority opinions of recent days, which had followed a liberal viewpoint, would have afforded them all the relief they needed, if they had been the majority opinions. The real difficulty was with the manner in which the Constitution was being interpreted—or, as he believed, misinterpreted. Roosevelt reportedly urged: "Go on. You are doing good. I wish I had a stenographer present so that this could be taken down." They should therefore dismiss any thought of amendments and focus on the other aspect of the matter, the personnel of the Court. Alluding to rumors that Justices Sutherland, McReynolds, and Van Devanter were contemplating retiring at the end of the Court term, Cummings feared that waiting for that to happen would take them to the end of the congressional session, after which there would be further delays, congressional elections, "and the fat would be in the fire again." He did not believe delay was a risk worth taking. What was chiefly required was speed.

As to strategy, Cummings recommended taking a bypath,

[23] The litigation referred to here included cases testing the constitutionality of the National Labor Relations Act, the Holding Company Act, and the Social Security Act.

[24] Cummings, Secret Diary, December 26, 1936.

bringing up Judge Denman's proposals for additional judges and reform of the lower federal courts. Too little attention was being given to the plight of litigants in these courts. He reiterated Denman's arguments for "more judges," but Denman had never mentioned or advocated any enlargement or changes in the Supreme Court. Roosevelt had asked Cummings to speak to him about Denman's proposals immediately after the election. Referring to his correspondence with Denman and the judge's letters to Hughes and the Honorable Martin E. Manton "re need of additional judges and reorganization of the Federal Courts," the president said he had written Denman from aboard his "Special Campaign Train," thanking him for his letters and expressing the hope that they would get some congressional action on courts in the fall.[25] Clearly, Judge Denman's proposals played only a minor role, or none at all, in plans for dealing with the Court problem until late into December.

After wandering down this bypath, and without indicating why he was doing so, Cummings then turned to a different matter. He recounted what President Taft had written in his book *Popular Government,* in which he pointed out that there was a defect in the constitutional system whereby federal judges were not required to retire when they reached the age of seventy, and were "loath thoroughly to investigate cases where such work involves real physical endurance," but Taft could see no way of meeting the situation except by a constitutional amendment. The attorney general also mentioned a suggestion which had been made that the retirement privileges extended to the bench might be withdrawn when judges declined to retire at seventy, but then he had to agree with Taft that such a plan would be in the nature of a reprisal and would not be looked upon with favor. In fact, it would probably fail of its purpose.[26]

The Taft observation led Cummings to make some reflections on packing the Court. Playing devil's advocate, he reprised some

---

[25] Memo from FDR to Attorney General, October 19, 1936, OF 41, Box 48, FDRL.

[26] William Howard Taft, *Popular Government: Its Essence, Its Permanence and Its Perils* (New Haven: Yale University Press, 1913), 158–60; Cummings, Secret Diary, December 26, 1936; cf. Leuchtenburg, *Supreme Court Reborn,* 124.

of the general objections to court-packing. "While we were probably unduly terrified by a phrase," he said, "nevertheless there was a discernible and substantial objection in the country to making a deliberate addition to the Supreme Court bench for the purpose of meeting the present situation." But, he then argued, if the federal judiciary as a whole were to grow in numbers, there was no particular reason why the Supreme Court should not grow also. Alluding to the backlog of cases in the federal courts, he linked it to criticism of the Supreme Court for declining to grant *certiorari* in a great number of instances.

Cummings came finally to the core of the plan he had in mind when he recommended passage of a "brief statute" providing in substance that when any federal judge, including Supreme Court justices, attained the age of seventy and had served on the bench for ten years, but had not resigned, the president should appoint, with the Senate's consent, an additional judge. Such a plan, he ventured to guess, had never been brought to the attention of the president before. He produced a mass of statistics to demonstrate how the whole scheme would work in practice. In district and circuit courts, the age rule would affect twenty-five sitting judges, but if the statute were enacted there was no telling how many of them would retire. If they failed to retire, they would be supplemented by an equal number of judges. All district and circuit court appointees would be roving judges. If such a statute, "very simple in its terms," could be pushed through quickly and new appointments made ready, Cummings believed the whole thing could be over within sixty days! The excitement aroused by it, in his opinion, would eventually subside, and the job would be done.

Six new appointments to the Supreme Court would be available if no justices over seventy chose to retire. Cummings thought they could afford to take their chances on a maximum of fifteen justices. With three liberals already on the bench, the plan would give them a majority of nine out of fifteen (he was evidently counting on no retirements). They could then look forward to decisions of a progressive nature and would probably get all they would actually need to carry out their social program. Mistakes, he admitted, could be made and the entire plan could miscarry, but generally speaking it seemed to him fairly sound.

Roosevelt agreed and immediately began discussing strategy, timing, and ways to put the plan into effect.

Cummings said he had called in Stanley Reed to explain the plan to him, "just to get his reaction and under seal of strictest confidence."[27] Roosevelt seemed to favor introducing the age requirement in a separate measure, leaving increases in judicial personnel for later treatment, and using a "try and see" approach to learn whether "a good many judges" would choose to retire. But Cummings insisted on linking the two parts of his plan to ensure that, by increasing personnel in the lower courts and swelling the number of cases to be disposed of, more of a burden would fall on the Supreme Court, requiring its enlargement. The bill, he argued, "would simply extend the general recommendation on the lower federal courts to include the Supreme Court, where the need for increased personnel was demonstrably as great as in the lower courts." Although the two parts of Cummings's plan were inextricably linked, it was made clear from the way he presented his case to the president that "reform" of the lower federal courts was a mere diversion, a secondary consideration, a subterfuge. The real target of the plan was enlargement of the Supreme Court.

If this is an authentic account of that fateful meeting, and it is the only one we have, it demonstrates that Cummings, with several motives in mind, masterminded the contours of the evolving court plan, worked out the method, and sold the full package to the president. Earlier that December, Roosevelt had attempted to launch another trial balloon in an article dictated to George Creel for *Collier's Weekly,* which hinted broadly at the option he was preparing to take in dealing with the Court.[28] But when it failed to produce the expected reaction, he was more inclined to accept Cummings's intricate scheme to treat the Supreme Court problem in the guise of a judicial reorganization, applying mainly to

[27] Reed's reaction was only lukewarm. He admired the reference to Chief Justice Taft as an authority on retiring superannuated judges from the bench, implying that he, like Taft, preferred a constitutional amendment. Cummings, Secret Diary, December 26, 1936, 192–93.

[28] George Creel, *Rebel at Large: Recollections of Fifty Crowded Years* (New York: Putnam, 1947), 294; idem, "Roosevelt's Plans and Purposes," *Collier's,* December 26, 1936.

the lower federal courts. This Cummings-Roosevelt proposal they called a reorganization; its opponents labeled it court-packing.[29] The most important, though unstated, reason for the exercise, as Cummings's diary reveals with such disarming candor, was to counteract negative rulings by the Supreme Court in New Deal cases, with the prospect of more to come. To win out over their adversaries, Roosevelt and Cummings wanted the dissident justices neutralized or replaced.

The only solution they were able to come up with was the resort to court-packing, a proposition Roosevelt had initially disdained. Even now he hesitated, knowing that it violated taboos. The plan was conceived in secrecy and disguised as a reform of the federal judiciary, meant to divert attention from the push for more favorable rulings. The method chosen was said to have historical precedent.

Judge Denman was not consulted. Without his knowledge, his lower-court reform ideas were appropriated and manipulated to serve ends to which he may have objected. That he did not participate in any of these discussions is evident from a letter to Stephens four days after the December 26 meeting: "I have been looking for a chance to come on and stir up the movement for reorganization of the Federal Bench and the adequate staffing of at least the District Courts. Have you heard any discussion of such a project as part of the Administration's program?"[30] Stephens, then a judge on the D.C. Court of Appeals, replied that he knew nothing of "any definite Administration project for reorganization of the Federal Bench and adequate staffing of the district courts."[31] Denman was never let in on the big secret.

The State of the Union Message

As Roosevelt worked on his annual message, lawyers over at the Justice Department, behind locked doors, were drafting a court

[29] Schlesinger, Sr., *New Deal in Action,* 46. The particular formula decided on at the December 26 meeting harked back to 1869 and a similar proposal, confined to the lower federal courts, which passed the House but failed in the Senate.

[30] December 28, 1936, Box 12, Stephens Papers, LC.

[31] December 31, 1936, ibid.

bill, its framework already chosen. The Supreme Court, according to FDR, was obstructing the national will and impeding the social progress on which the New Deal was predicated. The "reactionary" members of the Court, he concluded, would remain on the bench as long as life remained in them, for the sole purpose of blocking his reform programs. He had grown impatient with judicial vetoes and the frustration of his objectives.

On Tuesday, January, 5, FDR read a preview of the annual message to his cabinet and congressional leaders. Without mentioning it by name, he raised the Supreme Court issue adroitly, emphasizing the cordial and effective cooperation that existed between the legislative and executive branches. Politely but firmly, he invited the judiciary's cooperation, making clear that the function of legislating should be left to Congress, where the Constitution intended it to be. Pointedly, he said that while the legislative and executive branches would continue to meet the demands of democracy, the judicial branch was also asked by the people to do its part in making democracy successful.

His remarks seemed to be addressed more to the nine justices than to Congress. He made a plea for the fundamental law to be construed in such a way as to make possible the social and economic reforms for which the New Deal stood. A key passage stated: "Because all of us believe that our democratic form of government can cope adequately with modern problems as they arise, it is patriotic as well as logical for us to prove that we can meet new national needs with new laws consistent with an historic constitutional framework clearly intended to receive liberal and not narrow interpretation." There followed a veiled warning to the Court: "Means must be found to adapt our legal forms and our judicial interpretation to the actual present national needs of the largest progressive democracy in the world."

Democratic leaders in Congress—especially Senator Robinson, Chairman Ashurst, and Speaker Bankhead, all of whom had declared for a constitutional amendment to meet his aims—were surprised when he continued: "During the past year there has been a growing belief that there is little fault to be found in the Constitution . . . as it stands today. The vital need is not an alteration of our fundamental law but an increasingly enlightened view with reference to it." Ickes interrupted to ask whether that meant he was closing the door on a possible constitutional amendment as completely as he seemed to be doing. Wallace echoed his inquiry. Roosevelt insisted the message was not closing the door on any method that it might be necessary to employ to put the Supreme Court in its place: it merely indicated that no amendment was needed, although one could always be resorted to. It seemed to Ickes and Wallace that he did close the door, but they could do no more than raise the point.[32] Everyone except Cummings seemed bewildered, wondering what it all meant and where it was leading. They waited to hear more, but Roosevelt ended the reading with no further explanation.

FDR read his message word for word, incorporating material contributed by Cummings, who later wrote: "He [FDR] seemed to take especial pleasure in these passages because he looked over at me knowingly every time he came to one. I think . . . the tactics of the President are well calculated to bring about the result he has in mind. Indeed, he is proceeding more or less along the lines I discussed with him . . . at the White House."[33]

Roosevelt entered the House chamber on January 6, formally attired in striped trousers, morning coat, and vest, or what one writer called his "high Tory church clothes, a slightly vainglorious touch of assertive ego . . . more pronounced in the gray cutaway." The assemblage cheered, shouted, chanted, and applauded for a long interval before he could speak. All wondered if he would mention the Supreme Court or its decisions. They were not disappointed.[34]

Sharp barbs at the Supreme Court were sprinkled throughout his remarks. To each, Roosevelt gave added emphasis in clipped phrases and stronger intonation. "The statute of NRA has been outlawed. The problems have not. They are still with us." Jabs at the Supreme Court were greeted with loud and long applause and were cheered wildly by the Democrats. "Rebel yells greeted the President's first crack at the Court," wrote a Washington correspondent, indicating that "at least the noisier members of Con-

[32] Ickes, *Secret Diary,* January 10, 1937, 2:32.

[33] Cummings, Secret Diary, January 5, 1937; he refers here to the White House meeting of December 26, 1936.

[34] Alsop and Catledge, *The 168 Days,* 39–40.

gress were tired of having their work undone by five or six gentlemen appointed back in the distant past."[35]

Passages written by Corcoran contained muffled warnings to the justices that unless they fell into step, their powers would be curbed. Roosevelt said that difficulties had grown out of the Constitution's interpretation but, rightly considered, it could be used as an instrument of progress and not as a device for prevention of action. He suggested it would be worthwhile to read its Preamble and Article I, which confers legislative powers on the Congress. "With a better understanding of our purposes, and a more intelligent recognition of our needs as a nation, it is not to be assumed that there will be prolonged failure to bring legislative and judicial action into closer harmony."

Weeks later these words sparked an angry debate on the House floor between William P. Connery, Jr. (D.-Mass.), and Robert Luce (R.-Mass.):

> *Mr. Connery.* "Mr. Speaker, did not the President in his message refer to the Supreme Court in terms substantially that he would like to see the . . . Court give a more enlightened interpretation of the Constitution . . . ?"
>
> *Mr. Luce.* "The word he used was "intelligent."
>
> *Mr. Connery.* "That he would like to see the Supreme Court give an intelligent interpretation of the Constitution . . . ?"
>
> *Mr. Luce.* "Yes. Does the gentleman approve such language in an address to our most honored institution?"
>
> *Mr. Connery.* "In my judgment the Supreme Court is as human as anybody else."[36]

Congressman Luce announced: "As for myself, I was amazed and alarmed when I heard that proposal, for I have never heard more dangerous words spoken within the walls of this Chamber, never heard a doctrine that threatened to do more to undermine

[35] *New York Times,* January 7, 1937; *Washington News,* January 7, 1937, Box 59, Clapper Papers, LC.

[36] *Congressional Record,* 74th Cong., 3rd sess., Vol. 81, pts. 1 and 2:278, January 18, 1937. What neither congressman could have known was that aides tried to get FDR to substitute "enlightened" for wanting to see the Supreme Court give a more "intelligent" recognition of "our needs as a nation." The argument dragged on for a full day, but FDR did not change the wording.

the Republic than that which was implied in this language [Applause]."[37]

Roosevelt's phrase "intelligent recognition" was construed as an intentional affront to the justices. "A better understanding of our purposes," a thing clearly being sought by the president from the Court, was suspect. Critics noted that a better understanding of the executive's purpose does not change the Constitution, which both he and the Court were sworn to uphold. The inference was that the Court, in interpreting the Constitution, was obliged to pay attention to the purpose of the laws, when in fact the Court is obliged, to the best of its ability, to interpret the Constitution as it is written.

In his *Adkins* dissent, Justice Holmes, with customary pithiness, made clear that "the criterion of constitutionality is not whether we believe the law to be for the public good."[38] If this had been the case, New Dealers would have lost Stone's and Brandeis's dissent in *Butler.* And yet here was the chief executive in effect demanding that the Court take into account *his* purposes, as opposed to the constitutionality of legislation. It might as reasonably have been said that Congress and the president should have had a better regard for the Constitution.[39] Later, Cummings wrote: "I suspect . . . that there will be a diversity of opinion in the newspapers as to exactly what he [FDR] has in mind. I think, however, they cannot have much doubt that he must have some definite plans in mind."[40]

Much but not all the response to the message was negative. A couple from Wisconsin sent FDR congratulations: "Belatedly you are finally taking up the challenge of the Judiciary. Hope you and Congress will put them in the place the Constitution says they belong. Whenever we want ex-corporation lawyers to

[37] Remarks by Robert Luce, ibid., 277. He pointed out that when George Washington delivered his first annual message to Congress, there had been a formal reply by the Senate and House after the fashion of the British Parliament. James D. Richardson, ed., *A Compilation of the Messages and Papers of the Presidents, 1789–1897,* 10 vols. (Washington, D.C.: By Authority of Congress, 1899), "First Annual Address, January 8, 1790," 1:65–70.

[38] *Adkins v. Children's Hospital,* 261 U.S. 525 (1923).

[39] Merlo J. Pusey, *The Supreme Court Crisis* (New York: Macmillan, 1937), 68.

[40] Secret Diary, January 6, 1937, 2:4.

make the laws of the land we will elect them."[41] Senator Ashurst, caught off guard on the constitutional amendment issue, vaguely characterized the presidential message as "apples of gold in pitchers of silver."[42]

A seething rage had been building in Roosevelt for a long time. The November landslide had swollen an already substantial ego. He was more cocky, aggressive, vindictive, vengeful, and determined to punish those who had defied him. He would bring the Supreme Court low. The 1936 triumph gave him a launching pad from which to make the long-delayed attack on the Court, and in moving against it he claimed he would be acting on the command of the American people. But would he? By remaining silent on this issue throughout the campaign, he made the first of many tactical blunders. If the lack of public understanding of the constitutional issues involved was as serious as Farley claimed, FDR's duty as president was to try to educate the public by exploring in campaign speeches possible ways of overcoming the Court's obstruction. He did not do this. To have done so might have enabled him to claim that his election victory included a mandate to move directly against the Supreme Court.[43]

Senator Carter Glass, the peppery old Democrat from Virginia, pointed out that such a claim only made a mockery of Democratic Party government. To lay title to a mandate from the people, the Supreme Court would have to have been an issue in the campaign. The people had certainly not been asked for any such mandate and were given no hint of the drastic legislation to follow. They were deliberately kept in ignorance of FDR's purpose and led to believe that, if his aims could not be achieved within the limits of the Constitution, he would seek a "clarifying amendment" to resolve the problem. Republican opponents asked him over and over during the campaign to confirm or deny that he planned to move against the Court. He not only ducked the specific question but skirted the entire constitutional issue. If anyone so much as hinted that control of the Court was an objec-

[41] Mr. W. A. Genetts to FDR, January 6, 1937, PPF 200, Box 38, FDRL.
[42] Quoted in *Time* 29 (January 18, 1937), 14.
[43] Davis, *FDR: New Deal Years,* 633.

tive, the insinuation was vigorously denied. This may have been "good politics," helping him roll up a massive electoral majority, but it also meant FDR had no mandate to act against the Supreme Court.[44] That fact was to dog his footsteps along the rough path ahead.

Professor Laurence Tribe of Harvard Law School cast doubt on whether Roosevelt had a mandate to restructure the Supreme Court even when vacancies occurred, as they eventually would. "Our winner-take-all system does not give the substantial minority anything resembling the control of the president for 40% of the time," he wrote. "Yet there seems no sound reason why the person chosen by just 60% of the voters—what we call a landslide—should be allowed 100% of the time to select Supreme Court judges, and perhaps a full Court majority, reflecting his views alone." This could become a matter of particular concern when a candidate winning only 39 percent of the popular vote was in a position to name three or four justices. In Tribe's analysis, the point remained strong even if a candidate won by a landslide, "because the size of the avalanche is irrelevant to the question whether the President had a mandate to re-make the Court in his own image."[45]

Only the election of FDR in 1936, according to Tribe, could be said to have given the victor such a mandate, because that was "the one campaign in which Supreme Court appointments surfaced as a major issue" and in which the victor won by a mandate-sized margin. But Tribe failed to take into account the personalized nature of Roosevelt's sweep in 1936 ("The sole issue [in the campaign] is myself," as he told Moley). Supreme Court appointments did *not* surface as a major issue, certainly not with Democrats, although Republicans saw with alarm the possibility that, if Roosevelt won a second term, he would make several appointments. If a president is elected on such a constitutionally extraneous platform as "prosperity, patriotism and personality," Tribe stated, the electorate has not given him a blank check to redirect the Supreme Court, because the campaign did

[44] Senator Glass's remarks are quoted in Pusey, *Supreme Court Crisis,* 66–67; cf. Burns, *Roosevelt,* 287.

[45] *God Save This Honorable Court: How the Choices of Supreme Court Justices Shape Our History* (New York: Random House, 1985), 134.

"1936 Election Post Mortem." A cartoon by Ord, *Chicago Tribune,* February 16, 1937.

not draw on that particular account.[46] For FDR, the whole problem did not concern filling vacancies. He was too impatient, too unwilling to wait for attrition by retirement, resignation, or death to open the way for appointments. He seized upon court-packing instead.

January 6, 1937, marked the first time any president, addressing Congress, so sharply criticized the judiciary. The entire speech had the tenor of an appeal to the Court to put aside its prejudices. The message was cast in such a way that FDR did not "let the cat out of the bag" about his court plan, but it allowed those with ears sharp enough to hear the animal meow. After hearing the speech, Breckenridge Long, a Washington lawyer, went home and read through a printed copy twice. There was no intimation of any specific plan, but to Long it was plain that FDR had something definite in mind. Congressman Harold Knutson (R.-Minn.) found the message disturbing and wondered if Roosevelt would attempt to "pack" the Supreme Court. "There is no limit on the number of judges that may be appointed to the Supreme Court," he wrote, "and by adding two or three he could easily secure control of the judiciary. Would he go that far?"[47]

Of all the members of Congress applauding so vigorously on January 6, Representative Hatton Sumners, the courtly chairman of the House Judiciary Committee, really believed what his ears told him. He saw at once that something like a court bill must be coming, and in an effort to derail it he promptly revived his judiciary retirement bill.[48] Ickes believed the country was poised at the opening of an era in which the powers of the Supreme Court would be more strictly limited than they had ever been in the past.[49]

There was another unique and highly noticeable feature of that event. The justices of the Supreme Court, formally garbed in the black robes of their office, traditionally attended the joint session

---

[46] Ibid.

[47] Breckenridge Long Diary, January 6, 1937, Breckenridge Long Papers, LC; Knutson to Elmer E. Adams, January 11, 1937, Adams Papers, Minnesota Historical Society, quoted in Leuchtenburg, *Supreme Court Reborn,* 127–28.

[48] Alsop and Catledge, *The 168 Days,* 39–40. Sumners's bill (H.R. 2518), introduced in the House on January 11, 1937, was referred to his Judiciary Committee.

[49] Ickes, *Secret Diary,* January 10, 1937, 2:32.

to hear the annual message, filing into the House chamber to take front-row seats with members of the cabinet. Not a single one attended that session, apparently having received advance warning of what was to come.[50] Later, FDR casually mentioned to Ickes that, although members of the Court were invited, not one of them showed up. He suspected they had gotten a "tip" about the contents of the speech (perhaps from Corcoran). Cummings wrote: "In any event, I am sure they were more comfortable where they were than they would have been had they been present." Clapper commented: "The Supreme Court was too busy with its argument in the Palace of Justice to go over and hear a rougher one."[51] They had no inclination to sit in the House chamber listening to insults.[52]

Roosevelt's message was hardly likely to carry much weight with the justices. They knew by heart what was in the Preamble and Article I of the Constitution. The Court had long regarded the Preamble as only a declaration of pious hope and conferred no power on the federal government. Moreover, the NRA ruling, which the president had singled out for scorn, happened to concern one New Deal measure that no member of the Court, liberal or conservative, could find constitutional.

That Roosevelt felt a strong antagonism toward the Supreme Court surprised no one. That he was now gearing up for an open declaration of war on the judiciary was becoming apparent and gave cause for concern, if not shock. It was the main reason for an undercurrent of suspicion throughout the remaining weeks of January that a bold move against the Court was imminent.[53] And when it finally came, Roosevelt fully intended that it would take Congress and everyone else by surprise.

Cummings arrived for a White House meeting with the president on January 7, while he was still at lunch with Richberg. They discussed the impact of the annual message and then examined a

[50] Cummings, Secret Diary, January 6, 1937. This was not the only occasion on which Supreme Court justices failed to attend a president's annual message. It occurred in 1986 and again in 2000.

[51] *Washington News,* January 7, 1936.

[52] Leonard Baker, *Back to Back,* 20–21.

[53] Ibid.

counter-proposal by Richberg—a statute requiring the retirement of Supreme Court justices when they reached the age of seventy. Roosevelt read the draft to Cummings, who found it open to serious constitutional objections: "The difficulty," he said, "is that it seems to run afoul of the constitutional authority that lies at the basis of life tenure." Roosevelt agreed. They argued over the matter for some time, during which Richberg put up a stout defense, but to no avail.

As Cummings tells it: "I then handed the President the draft of a proposed bill along the lines of our previous discussions. He went over it and expressed great satisfaction with it." Minor changes were suggested, and Cummings agreed to have the bill redrafted. This meeting marks the real genesis of the court plan. They discussed questions of timing, who was to be consulted in the matter, and various approaches to be taken. Roosevelt wondered whether it should be brought to the attention of the cabinet. Cummings doubted it would be useful. FDR was now firmly committed to the project and asked for material to include in his inaugural address with strong arguments in support of the plan. Later that afternoon, Cummings met with Reed, McFarland, and Gardner regarding "the re-draft of the law affecting the judicial set-up."[54]

Over the next weeks, activity in the White House was feverish. Justice Department lawyers, with the framework less vague, were drafting a judiciary bill behind locked doors. The bill went into its fifth draft on January 5 and its eighth in mid-January.[55] Senator Robinson told the press that he favored a constitutional amendment to solve the Supreme Court problem. Legislation by itself, he said, would not be sufficient without broader constitutional power. In his annual message, Roosevelt had stated the exact opposite—that the difficulty was *not* with the Constitution, but with its interpretation by the justices.

A few days before the inauguration (January 20), Cummings went to the White House for another long session with Roosevelt. During that meeting, he related that in casting about for a means by which to reconstruct the Supreme Court and while research-

[54] Ibid.; Cummings, Secret Diary, January 7, 1937.
[55] The edited drafts are in Box 199, Cummings Papers, ALDL.

ing his new book, *Federal Justice,* he had come across a proposal made in 1913 and again in 1914 by then–attorney general McReynolds, a Wilson appointee. In his annual reports for those years, McReynolds had recommended that when any judge of a federal court other than a justice of the Supreme Court failed to retire at the age (seventy) provided by law, the president, with the advice and consent of the Senate, could appoint an additional judge to preside over the affairs of the court and have precedence over the older one. "This will insure at all times the presence of a judge sufficiently active to discharge promptly and adequately the duties of the court."[56]

McReynolds specifically exempted the Supreme Court justices from his proposal, but Roosevelt and Cummings ignored this important exception. They thought they had found a clever solution to their problem, and one no less attractive because it would permit them to hoist FDR's judicial nemesis by his own petard. They took great relish in the fact that, although proposed in a different form, a court plan similar to theirs had originated with the crusty old justice. When presented with the facts of McReynolds's long-forgotten proposal, Roosevelt, both interested and bemused, called it "the answer to a maiden's prayer." Of course, Cummings wrote, "it had to do with the matter at hand, and was very pat."[57]

THE SECOND INAUGURAL

January 20, 1937, dawned cold, gloomy, and wet. It rained steadily all day—a chilling downpour, which at times sluiced down

[56] *Annual Report of the Attorney General* (Washington, D.C.: 1914), 10; McReynolds had made the same recommendation in his Annual Report for 1913, 5; James Edward Bond, "James Clark McReynolds: I Dissent," unpublished MS, 96–97, ALDL.

[57] Cummings, Secret Diary, January 17, 1937; Alsop and Catledge, *The 168 Days,* 36; Moley, *After Seven Years,* 358; Burns, *Roosevelt,* 297. Moley thought the president chose his particular plan in order to embarrass Justice McReynolds. He was obviously swayed by the fact that the plan could be traced back to his archenemy in a policy recommendation concerning retirement of lower federal court judges only because of age. John McCraw, "Mr. Justice McReynolds and the Supreme Court, 1914–1941" (Ph.D. diss., University of Texas, Austin, 1949), 265.

in torrents. Despite the inclement weather, Roosevelt insisted on holding the inaugural ceremony on the east steps of the Capitol, as planned. This was the first inaugural ever held in January, following ratification of the Twenty-second Amendment to the Constitution, which went into effect in 1933, too late for Roosevelt's first inaugural.

The most dramatic incident of that occasion was the oath taking, when the bearded chief justice, personifying the judicial branch of the government, faced an assertive, at times defiant chief executive. They stood eyeing one another grimly on the platform. Hughes asked, with steadily mounting emphasis, whether he would "preserve, protect and defend the Constitution of the United States." With equal emphasis and with a strong voice, rising in volume as he spoke, the president repeated the entire oath, as he had done in 1933. Like Hughes, he spoke slowly, giving emphasis to the words "*preserve, protect* and *defend* the Constitution of the United States."[58]

Later, FDR told Judge Rosenman that as he spoke the words of the oath he longed to cry out, "Yes, but it is the Constitution as *I understand it,* flexible enough to meet any new problem of democracy—not the kind of Constitution *your Court* has raised up as a barrier to progress and recovery."[59] Ickes noted in his diary: "What the Constitution was to the Chief Justice was not the Constitution to the President, at least in some very vital particulars. And that poses the question that is becoming more clamorous in this country today. . . . Just what is the Constitution of the United States? Is it what five of nine Justices of the Supreme Court say it is, or is it what the President and millions of Americans believe it to be?"[60]

The address indicated that FDR was still wearing his campaign uniform. It was short, taking up a mere six pages in his published papers. There was only one oblique reference to the Supreme Court: "The essential democracy of our Nation and the safety of our people depend not upon the absence of power, but upon lodg-

[58] Ickes, *Secret Diary,* January 24, 1937, 2:52; Stephen Early to Ambassador Joseph E. Davies, January 25, 1937, Stephen Early Papers, Box 3, FDRL; Burns, *Roosevelt,* 291.

[59] Rosenman, *Working with Roosevelt,* 141.

[60] *Secret Diary,* January 24, 1937, 2:52.

Oath-Taking, January 20, 1937. A picture for the history books. It shows Chief Justice Hughes (left) administering the oath of office to the president on January 20, 1937, at ceremonies inaugurating him for his second term. The man in the center is Supreme Court Clerk Charles E. Cropley. Ten days later FDR asked Congress for the power to appoint six additional justices to the Supreme Court for every active justice, including Hughes, over seventy. (*Life,* March 8, 1937, p. 35)

ing it with those whom the people can change or continue at stated intervals through an honest and free system of elections. The Constitution of 1787 did not make our democracy impotent."[61] He hinted at what was stated more boldly in his annual message—that all agencies of popular government should use effective instruments in advancing the common good.[62] The address, well received by the rain-drenched crowd, was subdued and more statesmanlike than his annual message. It gave no hint of any plan to counteract obstruction of the administration program by the Supreme Court majority.

The Court had invalidated main parts of a less radical program than the one New Dealers had in mind. They now wondered how they could expect to carry on to achieve the liberal agenda and larger goals of a "second New Deal." The inaugural address gave no answer. Richberg, who wrote a substantial part of the

[61] *PPA,* 1937 volume, 2.

[62] Ibid., 5; Ickes, *Secret Diary,* January 24, 1937, 2:52–53.

address, was stung by critics who complained that it was not specific enough and lacked punch. FDR struck a militant note when he said: "I see one third of a nation ill-housed, ill-clad, ill-nourished."[63] It was a gloomy picture painted for the audience, but he promised that the gloomy conditions he outlined would be painted out. The promise made of a serious commitment to end poverty in America, however, was to receive less attention in his second term than it had in the first. The next six months would be consumed by a bitter constitutional battle over his court-packing bill.

Much of the press reaction to the inaugural address was unfavorable, especially in the South where most of the "ill-clad, ill-housed and ill-nourished" lived, and where sensitive editorialists accused FDR of pointing invidiously to their region as "one third of the nation." Disappointed by the poor reception of the speech he had helped to draft, Richberg broke his silence and told Clapper that Roosevelt had a number of bombshells he was getting ready to throw which would astound the country. He said FDR was in an "audacious mood," was even thinking of enlarging the Supreme Court, and was determined to put the Court in its place. "He will go ahead even if many people think it unwise." The president, he added, "was sore about the coverage of his address and intends to crack down on the press about it."[64]

Early recounts what took place the evening of FDR's second inaugural. He telephoned the president at about 9:30, having been asked to check out and let him know the press reaction to his address. Early gave him a favorable report. Then he asked FDR if he would like to hear a recording of himself delivering his inaugural address. He said he would like that very much. About ten minutes later he found that the major broadcasting companies had recorded the inaugural ceremonies and were rebroadcasting them. He listened in, thanked Early, and then said: "You can't guess what I am doing." He had had a nice dinner,

[63] *PPA,* 1937 volume, 5. This part of the address was taken from a letter written by Stuart Chase to the *New York Times.* Roosevelt received an advance copy of the letter, and on his request, the *Times* withheld its publication so he could use the material in his address. He did this with permission, but without attribution either to Chase or to the newspaper.

[64] Richberg to Clapper, January 20, 1937, Box 8, Clapper Papers, LC.

but all the family and guests had gone off to the inaugural concert and left him alone. "Playing with your stamps?" Early ventured. "That's right," he said, laughing. Early found it rather a welcome contrast to the inaugural evening four years earlier. They had brought about such changed conditions that the chief could sit alone in the White House study on a Wednesday evening, with nothing more to do than toy with his stamp collection.[65]

After the inauguration, Cummings wrote: "I *think* it was this

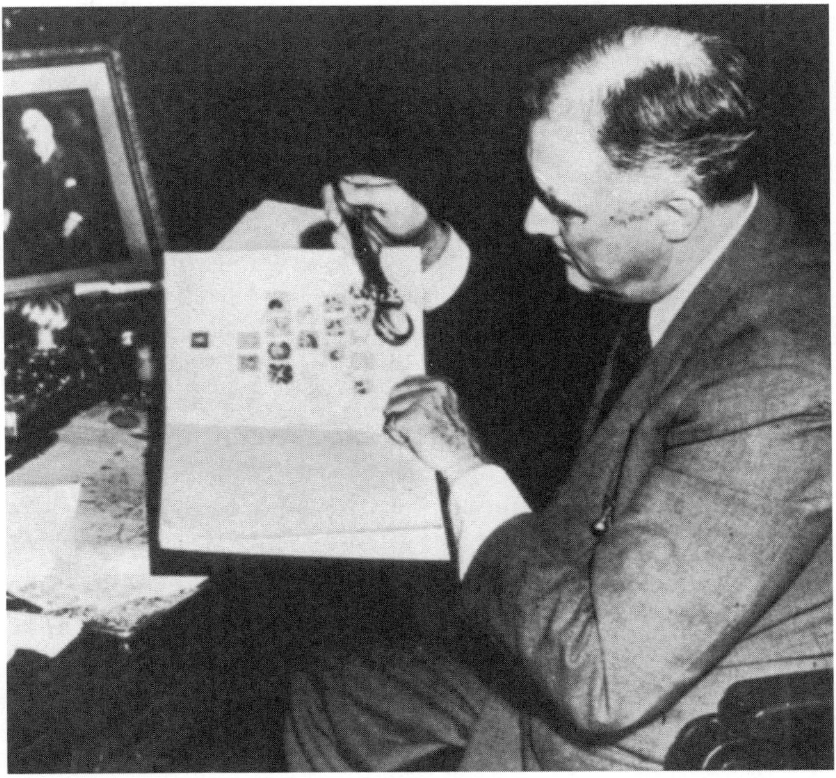

President Roosevelt in his Hyde Park study, working on his stamp collection in 1937. He began the collection as a child, and throughout his life, scarcely a day went by that he did not spend some part of his time with his stamps. (Franklin D. Roosevelt Library, Hyde Park, N.Y.)

[65] Stephen Early to Joseph E. Davies, January 25, 1937, Box 3, Early Papers, FDRL.

day [January 24] that the president told me he had had a talk with [John L.] Lewis on the [court] plan and the latter agreed to support it, and thought it better than the amendment plan. The President also told me he had tried it on Tommy Corcoran and the latter agreed it would work. . . . [FDR] had informed [Charlton] Ogburn [AFL legal counsel] and the latter was immediately favorable."[66] Ogburn, who helped draft the National Labor Relations Act, had seen Roosevelt on December 28, 1936. Only days later Ogburn wrote, saying how eager he was to develop further with him the subject of their conversation. He wrote again in mid-January: "I think the power for this legislation is in the Constitution, and we do not need an amendment. But even if we did, this is not the time, as a matter of tactics, either for you or for the American Federation of Labor to advocate the necessity of an amendment."[67]

Considering Roosevelt's fetish for keeping his court plan secret, it comes as a surprise to learn that he told two labor leaders, Corcoran, and God only knows who else details of the plan before its formal announcement, while refusing to divulge any information about it to members of his cabinet and the congressional leaders who would be expected to push it through the House and Senate. He withheld it from his chief adviser on constitutional matters, Felix Frankfurter. Writing him on another matter in mid-January, he mentioned casually that he had a court plan but could not reveal it yet. "Very confidentially, I may give you an awful shock in about two weeks. Even if you do not agree, suspend judgment and I will tell you the story."[68]

It was a Roosevelt custom to invite a bevy of his favorite Hollywood stars, along with other guests, to a White House luncheon to celebrate his birthday (January 30). That evening his guests, who included actress Jean Harlow and her escort, Robert Taylor, attended the annual birthday ball. But for the luncheon that day the president made apologies to his guests to preside at a lun-

[66] Secret Diary, January 24, 1937, 2:13.

[67] Charlton Ogburn to FDR, January 18, 1937, PPF 3794, FDRL.

[68] January 15, 1937, in *Roosevelt and Frankfurter: Their Correspondence, 1928–1945,* ed. Max Freedman (Boston: Little, Brown, 1967), 377–78; Davis, *FDR: New Deal Years,* 47.

cheon in the study upstairs, while his wife entertained downstairs in the state dining room. Present at the working luncheon were Cummings, Reed, Richberg, and Judge Rosenman, who had been summoned from New York by phone the night before and told that it was urgent. Rosenman had no idea why he had been sent for, "but was [ready to be] as helpful as possible."[69]

After lunch, the president read drafts of a supporting letter for his bill by Cummings, the text of the court bill, and the message to Congress to accompany these documents.[70] No implicit or explicit reference was made to the real reason for the legislation—nullification by the Supreme Court of New Deal laws. FDR was keen to have his message rank among the nation's great state papers. Doubtful that Cummings was capable of recasting it, he asked Richberg to contribute his expertise. According to a Justice Department lawyer, Richberg at first reacted to these three documents with "extreme political fear and shock."[71]

Rosenman learned for the first time that day about FDR's court proposal, which Cummings had already discussed with Reed and Richberg. The legislation dealt mainly with Judge Denman's scheme to expedite cases in lower federal courts by increasing the number of district and circuit court judges, employing a proctor, and shifting incumbent judges from areas where pending cases were minimal to districts that were "congested." Of greater interest was the provision to increase the number of federal judges, including Supreme Court justices, to a total of fifty to be added to the bench, ostensibly to increase efficiency.

Rosenman, Reed, and Richberg were much troubled by the indirect approach in the bill, letter, and message, recognizing the transparent attempt to disguise the plan as a means of increasing efficiency in the courts, while the real purpose was to pack the Supreme Court with justices who would approve New Deal measures. Richberg and Reed questioned the emphasis placed on

---

[69] Cummings, Secret Diary, January 30, 1937. Cf. Davis, *FDR: New Deal Years,* 47–48. Judge Rosenman, among others, helped draft the annual message and the second inaugural address.

[70] The original draft of the accompanying message is in PPF 1820, FDRL.

[71] Donald Richberg, *My Hero* (New York: Putnam's, 1954), 221–22; Leuchtenburg, *Supreme Court Reborn,* 125. It was later said of the message that "Cummings prepared the first draft but Richberg added the venom."

crowded dockets. They saw the plan as a deliberate attempt to mislead or deceive the public about important constitutional and national issues—the same disingenuous approach taken during the election campaign to withhold public discussion of the Court and Constitution.

How, they wanted to know, would Congress and the public be persuaded that the principal concern with the judiciary had now all of a sudden become its inefficiency? Would it not be advisable to state openly the real reason for the proposed legislation? They questioned the wisdom of the approach in the message and letter, but their arguments were dismissed. The president reminded them sternly that he had waited long enough to do something about the Supreme Court and had finally decided to act. He intended to go all out for court enlargement. With his temper rising, he referred all further criticisms to the attorney general. Cummings was immovable. This plan had gotten a completely favorable response from the president. Priding himself on his part in its formulation, he refused to admit that any indirection was being practiced and insisted that the situation was *exactly* what FDR's letter said it was.

Judge Rosenman redrafted the message to Congress, which the president said lacked "punch." All agreed that it needed editing and polishing. Alexander Holtzoff contributed some material to it, as did Cummings. Day and night they pored over the documents, passing drafts around, considering length, phrasing, evidence—subjecting every nuance to sharp scrutiny.[72] Cummings assigned lawyers to gather statistics on the Supreme Court's denial of *certiorari* and the ages of federal judges, without ever telling them why this information was wanted, or giving any of them enough to do so they could piece together what was going on. Rosenman was called in only when the draft message was delivered to the White House.

Once assigned his task, Judge Rosenman asked whether he could consult Corcoran on the draft. Hesitating at first, Roosevelt said: "Yes, but keep him out of any conferences, and for God's sake, don't tell Cummings."[73] The enmity between Corcoran and

---

[72] Alsop Notes, Box 53, Alsop Papers, LC.

[73] Rosenman, *Working with Roosevelt,* 147; Davis, *FDR: New Deal Years,* 53; Alsop and Catledge, *The 168 Days,* 43–47. Drafts of the presidential message

Cummings had become acute. At one point in their labors, the two collided head-on. Corcoran had no part in the preparation of the special message and was denied all knowledge of the court bill's content until the last minute.[74]

On the afternoon of February 2, Richberg, Rosenman, Reed, and Cummings again met with Roosevelt and the old arguments were resumed. Roosevelt complained that the draft message still lacked "pep," and Rosenman was told to do a complete rewrite. They argued over whether the increase in the number of Supreme Court judges was to be temporary or permanent. Cummings insisted the increase should be permanent, and Roosevelt shared his view. Irving Brant, chief editorial writer for the *St. Louis Star-Times,* a staunchly pro–New Deal paper, later wrote Corcoran that this was a serious mistake, as was fixing the number of Supreme Court membership at fifteen.[75]

The delicate question of aged and infirm justices was introduced in the final draft, which laid more stress than did earlier ones on the stamina deficiency and conservatism of elderly jurists. Roosevelt added a few final touches. The new draft showed no improvement over the old ones. Presidential aides renewed their plea for a direct attack on the Court's conservative decisions, but noting FDR's rising anger and stubborn defense of the chosen course, they fell in line. At a final three-hour session on February 4 the finishing touches were put on the draft message. Even at that late date Cummings was still not sure Roosevelt would go through with it. If he did, the Court's nine justices would be made acutely aware of the contempt in which they were held by the president.

---

are in the "Message to Congress on the Judiciary" folder, Judge Samuel I. Rosenman Papers, FDRL.

[74] Davis, *FDR: New Deal Years,* 52–53.

[75] Brant to Corcoran, February 18, 1937, Box 190, Thomas Corcoran Papers, LC. "I am sorry that the court proposals provide for permanent additions to the Supreme Court and specify the number fifteen. It gives the opposition something to shoot at. I am going to write an editorial on a matter to which no attention has been paid—the overworking of the justices in the writing of opinions (not including Van Devanter). That, I believe, might justify a permanent increase in the court to eleven." The aspect of permanence also met resistance from Richberg, and the whole matter was not settled until the next day when the four men held another five-hour session with the president.

Tuesday evening, February 2, the White House East Room was ablaze with lights for the annual dinner held in honor of the Supreme Court justices. The affair was reminiscent, wrote two journalists, of the Duchess of Richmond's ball on the eve of the Battle of Waterloo. Actually, they wrote, "it topped the Duchess's celebrated rout by being given on the eve of a great battle by the commander of one side" for his adversaries.[76] As usual, it was an elaborate affair. The guest list of nearly ninety included Mrs. Woodrow Wilson. Justice Stone, who was ill, and Justice Brandeis, who rarely attended evening functions, were absent. At the table, there was much animated conversation sprinkled with humor. The chief justice was in an unusually jovial mood, but the jollity barely concealed a certain indefinable tension in the air. Upon the retirement of the ladies, Justice Van Devanter moved to the head of the table to sit beside the president, joining Hughes in bantering exchanges.

Four men who stood off to the side, observing the goings-on (Richberg, Rosenman, Cummings, and Reed) noticed that the tension was especially acute. Watching Roosevelt with Hughes, the four exchanged knowing glances, their expressions communicating knowledge of a shared secret. They spoke in whispers. Wishing the secret were out, Cummings told Rosenman that he was decidedly uncomfortable. "I felt," he confessed, "too much like a conspirator." Nor was Roosevelt, for all his show of relaxed affability, fully at ease. He revealed this to Rosenman while his wife greeted the arriving guests in the West Hall, prior to the dinner. When earlier he served the usual pre-dinner cocktails to intimates in his study, he displayed telling signs of post-decision anxiety, using almost precisely the same words over and over: that he had to act *now* on the Supreme Court problem. Any further postponement was impossible: "Unpleasant as it is, I think we have to face it."[77] All the same, he was more than a bit nervous about it.

Poised at last to launch his court plan, Roosevelt was deter-

[76] Alsop and Catledge, *The 168 Days,* 64; Davis, *FDR: New Deal Years,* 62.

[77] Rosenman, *Working with Roosevelt,* 155; Davis, *FDR: New Deal Years,* 62–63. FDR had been urged to delay launching any plan until the Wagner Act cases were decided, but he rejected the idea. Word of his court plan had begun to leak out, and speculation on it was getting closer and closer to the mark.

mined to put it in the most dramatic setting possible. At a White House reception on February 4, he teased some of the guests—newspapermen among them—casually remarking that "there will be big news tomorrow," but laughingly rejecting all pleas to reveal what that news would be.[78] For dinner that evening, the president went to the Georgetown home of his son James and wife, Betsy Cushing. Other guests included Grace Tully, Marguerite Le Hand, and Tom Corcoran. The "secret" with its general content was known to all present and was the sole topic of conversation. Corcoran reportedly speculated on the terrible effect it was going to have on "Old Isaiah," and supposedly received "the Boss's OK" to go to the Court the next day and warn him of what was coming.[79]

Robert Sherwood narrated a somewhat contradictory account. Corcoran, he writes, was not able to discuss the matter with the president until the next morning (February 5), though he had tried earlier to caution him against using statements in his message which he was sure were wrong (e.g., crowded court calendars). It was then, writes Sherwood, that Roosevelt told Corcoran to advise Brandeis at once, "to soften the blow." All agree on what followed. Corcoran crashed the robing room of the Court around noon on February 5, as the justices were about to file into the chamber. He spoke with Brandeis as they moved toward the parted velvet curtain. Justice Brandeis thanked him and asked him to thank the president for informing him, but said that he was unalterably opposed to his bill and believed he was making a very great mistake.[80]

---

[78] *New York Times,* February 6, 1937, 8:2.

[79] Rosenman, *Working with Roosevelt,* 156.

[80] Sherwood, *Roosevelt and Hopkins,* 89–90; Davis, *New Deal Years,* 632 n. 37.

9

A Storm of Fury

> Much to Roosevelt's surprise, his Court reorganization plan aroused a storm of fury. He was accused of trying to pack the Court.
>
> Gerald D. Nash[1]

FEBRUARY 5 was the day chosen by Roosevelt for his "big surprise"—an unveiling of his court plan. On the previous evening, cabinet and congressional leaders were summoned to the White House by telephone to an urgent meeting the following morning. "The matter to be discussed," they were told, was "highly confidential."[2] Morgenthau and Hull were out of town, but Vice President Garner, Senate Majority Leader Robinson, Speaker Bankhead, House Majority Leader Rayburn, and the House and Senate Judiciary Committee chairmen, Hatton Sumners and Henry F. Ashurst, were there. A special press conference was to follow this meeting. Arriving early, Ray Clapper noticed the long line of official cars in the White House driveway, an indication that "something big" was unfolding. No cabinet meeting was scheduled that day. The atmosphere was tense, but a few newsmen thought the excitement "concerned new wages and hours legislation and a possible constitutional angle to that."[3]

White House secretaries had been notified to report for work at 6:30 A.M. and were busily preparing hundreds of mimeographed copies of Roosevelt's message, his bill, and Cummings's letter for the meetings. The documents were distributed at places around the cabinet table. When Roosevelt was wheeled in at 10 A.M., he announced after a genial "Good morning" that he

---

[1] *The Crucial Era: The Great Depression and World War II, 1929–1945* (New York: St. Martin's Press, 1992), 66.

[2] Ickes, *Secret Diary,* February 6, 1937, 2:64–65.

[3] Clapper Diary, February 5, 1937, Box 8, Clapper Papers, LC.

wanted to read excerpts from a message he was sending to Congress in an hour, calling for reorganization of the federal judiciary in a bill incorporating proposed reforms. He outlined the contents of Cummings's letter supporting the legislation, emphasizing the need for an increased number of federal judges to lessen heavy caseloads and speed up the litigation process, thus eliminating crowded court dockets, postponed trials, and justice denied by long delays.

No congressional leader had been given advance notice; all were completely unprepared for this bold stroke, especially since they had not seen or heard of any of the documents before them. Roosevelt said he had very little time and did not ask for comments. He was due to meet the press in less than half an hour. Announcing his purpose to reorganize the judiciary, he gave a brief explanation of the documents' contents, read a few passages from the message, and asked them to discuss none of it until it was made public. The message and bill would be sent at noon to Capitol Hill.

The president told them that he had considered legislation governing court procedures, particularly along the lines of requiring that the Supreme Court could not declare a law unconstitutional except by a two-thirds or three-fourths majority. However, he feared that such a law would be ruled unconstitutional and "we would be left just where we are." He had also considered, but put aside, amending the Constitution. "Give me ten million dollars and I can prevent any amendment to the Constitution from being ratified by the necessary number of states," he said. While the "economic royalists" were giving the impression that the proper way to proceed was by amendment, they were preparing, he said, to defeat any amendment if at all possible. After a brief discourse on the need for his proposal, Roosevelt abruptly ended the meeting. He asked them to leave the documents on the table and then wheeled himself off to meet the press.[4]

If TV cameras had been in the low-ceilinged cabinet room that morning, they would have captured some startled expressions on the faces of those around the table. Ickes left word portraits revealing his impressions. The faces were a study in mixed emo-

[4] Davis, *New Deal Years,* 63–64; Alsop and Catledge, *The 168 Days,* 66.

tions. Ickes, of course, was elated, having urged the president to move against the Court for some time. Cummings wore the expression of a Cheshire cat, sitting back in his chair, twirling his pince-nez and seeming unconcerned but obviously pleased with himself as the one real insider in the unfolding drama. Congressman Sumners said nothing but seemed pleased when the president endorsed his bill to retire Supreme Court justices at full pensions on reaching the age of seventy.

Congressional leaders sat immobilized, momentarily stunned. Robinson, obviously upset, blushed crimson, and with deep concern all over his face, stared down at the tabletop. He gave a feeble sign of approval. Garner and Rayburn spoke not a word during the entire discussion. Ickes noted: "This is the first time that I have ever seen him [Garner] at a Cabinet or any other meeting sit entirely silent. What this might mean, I do not know." The face of Speaker Bankhead, father of actress Tallulah Bankhead, was especially interesting to watch: "It appeared to me," Ickes wrote, "to be distinctly 'pokerish.' There was no expression to indicate how his mind was working." Senator Ashurst sat straight in his chair, staring up at the ceiling, murmuring that the method proposed by the president was better than his own idea of an amendment.[5] On the drive back to the Capitol, Chairman Sumners announced: "Well, boys, here's where I cash in."[6] Never comfortable with the New Deal, he considered Roosevelt's latest plan the last straw. His subsequent refusal to cooperate with the administration was to make Rayburn's job much more difficult.

The Press Conference

At 10:55 A.M. the president was wheeled into his office, where over a hundred members of the press corps had been waiting. He said he had a "somewhat important matter" to take up with them and asked that it be held in strict confidence until the bill and

[5] Ickes, *Secret Diary,* February 6, 1937, 2:66; cf. Alsop and Catledge, *The 168 Days,* 65–67.

[6] Sumners would later have something to say in extenuation of his provocative remark.

message involved were released in accordance with the wording on the press copies, or until they were read in the Senate or House, whichever came first. "Copies will be given to you as you go out," he said, and "don't anybody go out until that time. (Laughter)."[7] One reporter quipped: "We brought our lunches." Roosevelt said: "That's all right. I am glad you did."

He began by announcing: "We have come to the very definite conclusion that there is required the same reorganization of the Judiciary as . . . recommended . . . in the case of the Executive branch of the Government." He read brief excerpts from Cummings's letter, and when he came to the part about delays in court trials—so interminable that to institute suit was to "embark on a life-long adventure"—he got laughs in which he joined.[8] He stressed the "simple fact" that the personnel of the federal judiciary was insufficient to meet the business before them. In the past fiscal year, he related, the Supreme Court had declined without opinion to hear 717 of the 867 petitions presented for review. "That," he emphasized, "is a tremendously important fact." Hence, the clear necessity for an increase in the number of judges, including the Supreme Court justices. He offered no other reason.[9]

Throughout the monologue, Roosevelt's voice seemed tense, betraying inner excitement. In reading lines, he attempted to wring the most laughs possible out of newsmen with swipes taken at the Supreme Court. When he mentioned how, during the early days of the Republic, justices were required to "ride Circuit," he interjected that "riding Circuit in those days meant riding on horseback. It might be called a pre–horse and buggy era." He got another laugh. "That is not in the message," he added with mock solemnity, provoking general hilarity.[10] Roosevelt seemed to be asking reporters to applaud the perfection of his scheme and its nicely calculated indirection.[11] At times he seemed out of breath, taking quick, short gasps as he read.[12]

[7] Press Conference no. 342, *CPPC,* 9:130; see also *PPA,* 1937 volume, 35–50.

[8] Press Conference no. 342, *CPPC,* 9:131–32.

[9] Davis, *New Deal Years,* 64; *PPA,* 1937 volume, 41.

[10] Press Conference no. 342, *CPPC,* 9:135.

[11] Ibid., 139; Alsop and Catledge, *The 168 Days,* 67; Davis, *New Deal Years,* 64.

[12] Clapper Diary, February 5, 1937, Box 8, Clapper Papers, LC.

When he came to the question of aged or infirm judges, Roosevelt looked up to add, "a subject of delicacy and yet one which requires frank discussion," provoking more laughter. No pension or retirement allowance had been provided for federal judges by Congress until 1869, but, he said, it was not much of a solution.[13] It found a well-entrenched tradition among judges to cling to their posts, in many instances far beyond their years of physical or mental capacity. Their salaries were small. No alternative had been open to them except to attempt to perform the duties of their office "to the very edge of the grave." That phrase brought louder laughter, and when he added, "I am talking about 1869," the room exploded in mirth.[14]

Admitting that some judges retain to an advanced age full mental and physical vigor, he added that those not so fortunate are often unable to perceive their own infirmities. Here he interjected: "They seem to be tenacious of the appearance of adequacy." He pointed out that that quotation was "from a very important judge . . . you will have to find out who said it. I am not going to tell you." His teasing reference was to Chief Justice Hughes's *History of the Supreme Court* (1928).[15] The voluntary retirement law of 1869, he insisted, was only a partial solution and had not proved effective in inducing aged justices to retire on a pension.

The president then summarized four major recommendations made in his bill, claiming that his proposals did not raise any issue of constitutional law. When he finished, Roosevelt was asked if he intended to deliver his message to Congress person-

[13] Senator Charles Sumner of Massachusetts introduced S.R. 44 on March 23, 1869. 41st Cong., 1st sess. (1869).

[14] Press Conference no. 342, *CPPC,* 9:138.

[15] *PPA,* 1937 volume, 41–42. During sessions drafting the message to accompany the court bill right up to February 4, FDR and his aides debated whether to include the Hughes quotation, the legislative history of the Act of 1869, and references to the bill that passed the House based on proposals in 1913 and 1914–15 by then–attorney general McReynolds and his successor. Included in the president's speech material were excerpts from "Was the Supreme Court Packed by President Grant?" which as Cummings thought "the President might find helpful if he comes to the point of explaining why the present plan is the best." Cummings to FDR, February 4, 1937, PPF 1820, Box 2, FDRL. See also Annual Reports of the Attorney General for Fiscal Years 1936 and 1937 (Washington, D.C.: 1936, 1937).

ally. He said it would be read by a clerk in about half an hour.[16] "Just for background," a reporter asked, "is this intended to take care of cases where the appointee has lost mental capacity to resign?" FDR snapped "That is all." There were no more questions.[17] Later, he remarked that it was the most "jubilant press conference he had ever had."[18]

As the message was being read by the clerk of the House, it was simultaneously broadcast to the nation over stations WABC and WJZ. Vice President Garner laid the message before the Senate to be read and ordered it to be printed, with accompanying papers, in the *Record.* The bill was later referred to the Judiciary Committee and printed as a Senate document.[19] While the message was being read, Garner stepped down from the dais where he was presiding, walked to the rear of the chamber, and stood at the door of the cloakroom, holding his nose with one hand and vigorously shaking his thumb down with the other. The gesture was difficult for anyone on the Senate floor to miss and could be taken by some as an omen of things to come. In the evening newspapers headlines blared: "ROOSEVELT ASKS POWER TO REFORM COURTS" and "INCREASING SUPREME COURT TO 15 JUSTICES." On the New York Stock Exchange, the markets registered steep declines on all fronts.[20] Within hours, court-packing crowded everything else off front pages, the *New York Herald Tribune* devoting seven of its eight front-page columns to Roosevelt's proposal.[21] The cloakrooms in both houses of Congress were abuzz as knots of legislators exchanged views, trying to come to grips with the startling development.

[16] Press Conference no. 342, *CPPC,* 9:146–47.

[17] Davis states that after the press conference the president lingered to answer or adroitly parry several questions. *New Deal Years,* 64. In fact, he did not do this. Excited correspondents questioned him. "Was that message the reason for the special cabinet meeting?" one asked. "Yes," the President replied, "I did exactly what I did here. As soon as I finished I came in here. There was no discussion. There would have been no change even if there had been a cabinet discussion." There was no discussion with newsmen either after he had finished his long presentation, interrupted only by laughter or comment.

[18] Alsop and Catledge, *The 168 Days.* 66.

[19] *New York Times,* February 6, 1937, 1.

[20] Ibid., 8:2.

[21] February 6, 1937, 1.

"Aiming High–Too High." A cartoon by Herblock in the *Syracuse Herald,* January 8, 1937.

Roosevelt's news fell like a bombshell on a Congress that thought it had already experienced the ultimate in surprises with his message on reorganization of the executive branch. Suddenly and without warning, he "cut through the tangle of proposals" by legislators, lawyers, and private citizens with a broadax message asking for passage of a statute to effect drastic court reforms.[22] A few savants had anticipated the move, predicting its terms fairly accurately. On January 7, a month before the plan's revelation, the Scripps-Howard chain's Washington bureau informed its news agencies: "An increase in the Supreme Court's membership—if necessary—is being considered by the Administration. . . . President Roosevelt's forthright stand against amendment of the Constitution was interpreted by many as pointing toward an eventual decision to use the big stick."[23]

Columnists Drew Pearson and Robert Allen had predicted that the president was about to surprise the nation with a request to add six justices to the Supreme Court. Roosevelt took a perverse delight in keeping press and public ignorant of his plan until February 5, but it could not entirely escape notice by alert columnists, who had prophesied that such a move was coming. In May 1936, Rodney Dutcher wrote: "You can mark it down as a strong possibility that sometime within the next year there will be a move to add more than nine justices. By a simple act of Congress, the President would be enabled to appoint additional members of the Court." In October 1936, Irving Brant hinted in an editorial that "immediately after the election attention is going to focus on the Supreme Court as never before." Given these predictions, it is somewhat surprising that FDR's coup came as such a shock to so many.[24] His move immediately became the subject of national attention—or more accurately, the eye of a political cyclone.[25]

After the bombshell exploded, the chief justice was reminded by a correspondent (as if he needed to be) that "the Supreme Court is *not* answerable to a *mere* President who comes and goes

[22] *New York Times,* February 6, 1937, 1, 8:2.

[23] Copy in Box 233, Clapper Papers, LC; see also Leuchtenburg, *Supreme Court Reborn,* 287.

[24] Leo C. Rosten, *The Washington Correspondents* (New York: Harcourt Brace, 1937), 143, 383. Rodney Dutcher is quoted in *Editor and Publisher,* February 13, 1937, 2; Irving Brant of the *St. Louis Star-Times,* October 15, 1936, is quoted in Mason, *Stone,* 793; cf. Herbert Little, *Washington Daily News,* January 7, 1937.

[25] Charles S. Hyneman, *The Supreme Court on Trial* (New York: Atherton Press, 1963), 53–54. Cf. Burns, *Roosevelt,* 293.

at a nation's whim. . . . He didn't and couldn't put you into power—and I hope you will use your great minds, [and] all your knowledge of legal procedure to defeat this shocking action of this country's [chief] executive to belittle you and *us* and make us puppets of a man's whim. Fight him, and the Lord be with you." The writer wondered why everyone seemed so afraid of the president's clever way of paying back anyone who differed with him. Congress, she said, "either gives in or resigns itself." Just one body—the Supreme Court—had held itself entirely aloof from "the scourge of the Mis-Deal."[26]

Viewed in the light of its main objective of enlarging the Supreme Court, the judicial reorganization plan was an assault on an independent judiciary, provoking a bitter, prolonged controversy. Opposition came from within the Court itself, from Congress, from the press, and from an outraged public, regardless of class, region, or party affiliation. Bar associations, state governments, community groups, and countless citizens joined in the debate.

The Supreme Court's Reaction

Most directly affected by the proposal were the nine justices. Constrained by their traditional role, they had to remain silent, taking no part in public discussion of the measure. In spite of this, their reaction to Roosevelt's bill was closely observed. Shortly after noon on February 5, as the justices listened to oral argument on a New Jersey Teachers' Tenure Act, Elmore Cropley, clerk of the Court, was handed a sheaf of papers by a White House messenger. Without waiting for arguments to end, he slipped through the curtain behind the dais and handed Hughes the mimeographed papers. Copies were distributed to the other justices as Hughes continued reading his.

The lawyer arguing at the rostrum was baffled by the disturbance on the dais. Hughes broke in to question him about teachers' salaries and then continued reading. Roberts, stroking his chin, thumbed through the pages rapidly, stopping to study one

[26] Beatrice Wilson to Charles E. Hughes, February 6, 1937, Box 168, Hughes Papers, LC.

passage intently. Van Devanter, scanning his copy, remained expressionless. Butler and Roberts exchanged glances and chuckled, as if enjoying some item. Staring at the sheets, Brandeis switched on his desk lamp and began to read. All wore grave expressions, but Van Devanter's "was actually grim."[27]

Making his customary visit to the Court on February 8, Clapper found that although it was decision Monday, the atmosphere was unusually subdued. No opinions were delivered that day. The chief justice appeared outwardly cheerful, but the orders were issued in the wrong sequence and, when it was announced that they were on file in the clerk's office, reporters had to wait nearly an hour until they were ready. To Clapper, it looked like a "sit-down strike." Veteran Court watchers said they had never witnessed such an irregular day. The press room clerk, with for-

"Marvin McIntyre's Reply to 'the Boss.'" A cartoon by Berryman in the *Washington Star,* March 10, 1937.

[27] Stokes, *Chip Off My Shoulder,* 68–71; cf. *New York Times,* February 6, 1937; Burns, *Roosevelt,* 294–95.

givable hyperbole, exclaimed: "My God, the Court is punch drunk!"[28]

Visiting the classical Marble Temple a few days later, a journalist observed that the new building, breathtaking in its scale and lavish space, housed a relatively small court chamber. The marble pillars flanking the raised table at which the justices sat would prevent any elongation of it. Government architects, carpenters, and stonemasons were in for some awful headaches if any structural changes ever had to be made, since the room had been especially designed and built for nine—and only nine—justices.[29] So remote were these judges that, according to George Creel, any Washington correspondent who succeeded in discovering *anything* that went on behind those sacred portals, no matter how trivial, would in all likelihood be hailed as worthy of a Pulitzer Prize.[30] The Supreme Court, the institutional embodiment of the Constitution and American law, stood aloof, its justices silent but grimly united in their determination to fight off Roosevelt's assault.[31] To shield them from invasion by a voracious press, on February 6 the Court's marshal issued an order barring reporters from entering the bronze doors leading to the justices' private offices unless by authorized appointment.

Despite being off-limits in their new quarters, the justices were not isolated from public opinion. Thousands of letters and telegrams on the new bill poured in to the mail room each day, nearly unanimous in their opposition.[32] Justice Brandeis received thousands of messages from women, children, lawyers, judges, doctors, farmers, and grocery clerks, expressing their dismay. Ninety percent were against the president's proposal.[33] Chief Justice Hughes heard from worried admirers who pleaded with him not to waver under fire or resign under pressure. "Do not desert

[28] Clapper Diary, February 8, 1937, Box 8, Clapper Papers, LC.

[29] George Carroll in *New York Evening News,* February 11, 1937, Box 168, Hughes Papers, LC.

[30] "If the Court Pleases," *Collier's,* May 8, 1937, 26.

[31] E. Kimbark MacColl, "The Supreme Court and Public Opinion; A Study of the Court Fight of 1937," (Ph.D. diss., University of California, Los Angeles, 1953), 102–3.

[32] Pusey, *Hughes,* 2:753.

[33] Mason, *Brandeis,* 624.

us," one wrote. "Please hold the Court—hold the Fort. Even if you are old and tired, you can't quit now for three years." A fearful Nebraska housewife wanted Hughes to acknowledge receipt of her letter so that she would know whether it was delivered—"[Postmaster General] Farley may censor the mail."[34]

Would the justices give way before the assault by the chief executive? The threat to their independence was deeply resented, but not to the point of open defiance. On February 8 a United Press International (UPI) bulletin hinted that something was afoot, noting that the justices had been closeted in conference for hours the previous Saturday. In a radio broadcast, Lowell Thomas predicted that a rash of resignations was coming. The justices may have considered mass resignations, but if the idea

"The Turnabout." *Tampa Tribune,* c. February 15, 1937. Courtesy of the *Tampa Tribune* archives.

[34] MacColl, "Supreme Court and Public Opinion," 95–96.

ever crossed their minds, it was dropped out of fear that Roosevelt would relish the chance to make nine appointments. According to a less plausible rumor making the rounds, "the Supreme Court will now recommend to Congress that the presidency be enlarged to three persons, because the duties [of the office] are too arduous for Mr. Roosevelt."[35]

The justices received messages from well-wishers like a woman who wrote: "We hope that the five wise and able men of the Supreme Court [there were actually six over seventy] will overlook the inference that they are past their usefulness. We hope that for the sake of the American people they will stick to their posts. The thinking people of this country know well the motive for this sudden and drastic move."[36] The brethren exchanged personal views in private. During their weekly conferences, always held in secret, they avoided discussing the president's bill. According to Hughes, Brandeis and Stone held many private talks on the subject, and undoubtedly other justices did too.[37]

Congressional Reaction

When Roosevelt's bombshell burst upon Congress, the startled lawmakers learned for the first time what was expected of them—giving him power to appoint up to six new justices to the Supreme Court and forty-four judges to the lower federal courts. The bill put a halt to all injunctive proceedings involving constitutional issues until federal lawyers could be heard, provided for speedy appeals of all constitutional cases, and included the appointment of a proctor or administrator to oversee lower-court dockets to prevent cases from piling up. Cummings claimed that

---

[35] Paul Mallon, "News behind the News," *Washington Evening News,* February 8, 1937. In response to the radio announcement, Floyd G. Wolven wrote Hughes: "Please, Sir, don't do that." February 8, 1937, Box 168, Hughes Papers, LC.

[36] Caroline Kent to the Editor, *New York Herald Tribune,* February 6, 1937.

[37] Hughes, "Autobiographical Notes," typescript in Hughes Papers, LC.

these ideas originated in the Justice Department,[38] but in actuality they came from Judge William Denman.

The big question was: How much opposition to the bill would develop in Congress, where its fate would be decided? White House agents operating in shifts could not by their own efforts enact the proposal. FDR's first tactical error was the failure to consult congressional leaders. "The very men . . . expected to wage the administration's fight . . . [in] Congress did not even see the battle plans until after the war had been declared."[39] They learned of it only an hour before it was announced to the press. Just three weeks earlier, Roosevelt had assured Garner and Robinson that, at that session, there would be only several appropriation bills for Congress to consider.[40] FDR lost the support of men like Speaker Bankhead, who strongly resented being excluded from discussions on such an important matter. Clapper observed: "The President has put his leaders in a ridiculous light."[41]

In his first term Roosevelt had consulted regularly with party leaders on important initiatives, but in this case he insisted on almost conspiratorial secrecy. Why did he spring his plan so suddenly on Garner and Robinson, who would have to manage the bill in the Senate; on Ashurst, chairman of the Senate Judiciary Committee, who only weeks earlier, in a public speech, had denounced court-packing as a "prelude to tyranny," hotly denying that Roosevelt had any plans for doing it; or on Rayburn and Farley, who would have to rally the party faithful to accept the scheme if they valued their political hides?[42]

By 1937, FDR had evidently come to believe he no longer needed to consult anyone. Shortly after the president's landslide victory in 1936, Senator Hiram Johnson predicted: "I think that Roosevelt during the next session will give free rein to his imagination. There will be nobody to stop him, and but a few to pro-

---

[38] Mallon, "News behind the News," *Washington Evening News,* February 8, 1937.

[39] MacColl, "Supreme Court and Public Opinion," 165.

[40] Robert Caro, *The Years of Lyndon Johnson: The Path to Power* (New York: Knopf, 1983), 560.

[41] Stokes, *Chip Off My Shoulder,* 465; Clapper, "Along the Potomac," *Review of Reviews* 105 (March 1937): 29–31.

[42] Leuchtenburg, *Supreme Court Reborn,* 127.

test. He will really feel that he has been given a mandate by the people to do as he pleases, and there will be enough people in Congress anxious to truckle to him, that will enable him to do just as he desires."[43]

After the February 5 announcement, Farley asked: "Boss, why didn't you advise the senators in advance that you were sending them the Court bill?" He replied: "Jim, I just couldn't. I didn't want to have it get out prematurely to the press." Disclosure, he said, would have given his opponents an extra advantage.[44] This explanation is nonsense. The plan had been worked out to the last detail by Cummings and FDR, and seeking advice would have resulted in criticism that would prove embarrassing. So neither Garner nor Robinson nor anyone else in Congress was to be admitted to the secret. Two journalists concluded: "The carelessness of congressional feelings was carried so far that the President and Cummings were determined to attach a copy of the bill to his message, as though to suggest that congressional erasure of the merest comma would not be allowed."[45] Compliance with the president's wishes, they said, had become automatic. At his February 5 press conference, however, FDR denied this: "That bill . . . as I explained to the Chairmen of the Judiciary Committees of the House and Senate just now, is merely something for them to work on, as in any other case when any bill goes in. It is simply . . . to save them the trouble of trying to put the language together."[46] But this version strains credibility.

The bill was formally introduced in the Senate by Henry Ashurst on February 8, just as it came down. Struck by the omission of a title, the record clerk notified the White House that he was anxious to have one for S.R. 1392. Hearing nothing, he went ahead and, "just to classify it," gave it the title "A Bill to Reorganize the Judicial Branch of the Government." Ashurst wrote FDR, wanting to know if that was all right with the White House,

---

[43] Hiram W. Johnson, Sr. to Hiram W. Johnson, Jr., November 15, 1936, quoted in Richard Lowitt, "Only God Can Change the Supreme Court," *Capital Studies* 5 (Spring 1977): 9.

[44] *Jim Farley's Story,* 73.

[45] Alsop and Catledge, *The 168 Days,* 48.

[46] *PPA,* 1937 volume, 45.

or if there was any suggestion. In pencil, the president OK'd the memo and the bill's proposed title.[47]

A strong cadre of Senate opponents to the bill quickly formed. The floor debate led off with sharp criticisms directed at the provision for enlarging the Supreme Court. Even before the issue reached the floor, it had touched off oratorical fireworks. On occasion the cry of dictatorship had been raised, and opponents now openly accused the president of trying to wreck the judiciary. Garner and Robinson both realized the bill would be no "pushover." As for ramming it through, that task fell to Robinson. Meanwhile, the no's were gathering strength.

Senator Arthur H. Vandenberg (R.-Mich.) charged angrily that behind Roosevelt's fine words a foul intent was evident: "I most emphatically do not agree to packing the Supreme Court," he said, "no matter how adroitly the proposal be described in a multitude of words." Bertrand Snell (R.) of New York stated that the administration, having already destroyed the economic stability of the country, apparently would not be content until it had destroyed its judicial stability as well. To Senator Warren Austin (R.-Vt.), the president's message was "a most ostentatious quest for power to pack the Courts."[48] Reserving comment, Borah viewed the proposal "with grave alarm." Senator McNary (R.-Oreg.) said he was giving it careful study, for it involved "the transfer to the President of greater powers over the judiciary than had ever before existed."[49]

Roosevelt's message and bill had a somewhat warmer reception in the House. Minutes after the clerk finished reading, Maury Maverick of Texas, one of a radical new breed of Democrats that the 1934 elections sent to Washington, snatched a copy of the bill, scrawled his name across the top, and dropped it in the basket of legislative proposals. Having urged judicial reform for months, he had introduced only a day or two earlier three bills to curb the Supreme Court. His grandfather refused to brand

[47] Vince Price, Clerk of the Senate Judiciary Committee to FDR, February 6, 1937, and reply by "K" (Kanee—Roosevelt's secretary), OF 41, Box 48, FDRL.

[48] *New York Times,* February 6, 1937, 8:2.

[49] Ibid., 9:2.

While he was seated in front of the Capitol, with the marble façade of the Supreme Court building in the background, the granite profile of Idaho's Senator William E. Borah is outlined as he pondered the president's audacious court-packing proposal. Washington could expect his eloquent voice to be raised against it. (*Life,* February 22, 1937, p. 15)

his cattle, and thus made the family name a synonym for a political or any other kind of wanderer from the herd. The young San Antonio congressman embraced the idea that democracy is "liberty plus economic security." He once claimed: "We Americans want to talk, pray, think as we please, and eat regular."[50]

Reflecting House sentiment, a member wrote: "Honestly, this beats me. He [FDR] just was not fair to his party (if they only knew it) and not decent to the people when he did not disclose this kind of a plan. The folks might want it, I don't know. We were entitled to know about it, I mean the voters. . . . There isn't even an excuse of an 'emergency' for it. As a matter of fact, he told us on the first day of the session that the 'emergency' is practically over."[51]

In public, Robinson said the plan was "in no sense a violent innovation," but in private he referred to it as "pretty raw." Loyal Democrat Joseph Guffey of Pennsylvania, described as "the first of the liberal bosses," called it "a splendid solution." But doubtful Democrats like Schwellenbach of Washington, Logan of Kentucky, and Overton of Louisiana wanted to reserve judgment. McAdoo was waiting for the Senate hearings. Congressional opinion on the proposal began to crystallize within the first few weeks.[52]

Passage by the House, with its four-to-one Democratic majority, was considered certain.[53] Battle lines were forming, but not in the way Roosevelt anticipated. It was no surprise when Carter Glass, Harry F. Byrd, and Josiah Bailey flared up in opposition to a bill that Glass termed "an outrage on constitutional morality." The seventy-nine-year-old Virginian announced to the press: "I shall oppose it with all the strength that remains to me," but he added despondently, "I don't imagine for a moment that it will do any good."[54]

---

[50] Mooney, *Roosevelt and Rayburn,* 66.

[51] Edward H. Rees (R.-Kans.) to W. A. White, February 16, 1937, White Papers, LC.

[52] To gauge individual senators' reaction, the *New York Times* sent each of them telegrams: "We will appreciate it if you will wire collect your position on the President's proposed Judiciary changes, especially where they affect the Supreme Court." Telegram to Senator McAdoo, February 7, 1937, Box 430, William Gibbs McAdoo Papers, LC.

[53] *New York Times,* February 9, 1937, 4:3.

[54] Quoted in Mooney, *Roosevelt and Rayburn,* 66.

Hiram Johnson belonged to a group of Senate Progressives and had gone along so far with many of Roosevelt's ideas. But after conferring with Borah, the old veteran of the 1919 League of Nations fight announced: "The issue, stripped of all its verbiage, seems to be plain: Shall the Congress make the Supreme Court subservient to the Presidency?" For him the implications were so grave that he could do but one thing, "that is, to the limit of my capacity, oppose this extraordinary legislation."[55]

Within a week the court plan was causing serious divisions and unhappiness in the Senate, "from the leadership down to the most junior member."[56] Joseph O'Mahoney observed that what support there was for the bill derived from loyalty to the president rather than enthusiasm for its provisions. Of ninety-six senators, seventy-five were Democrats whose loyalty Roosevelt was counting on. Nebraska's Independent, Senator George Norris, caused a stir when he told colleagues: "I am not in sympathy with the plan to enlarge the Supreme Court."[57] A longtime champion of court reform, Norris had been loudly critical of some of the Supreme Court's New Deal decisions.

After making his public statement, Norris was called to the White House for a talk. FDR tried to convince him that "court enlargement" was the only feasible scheme. Norris doubted it was the best or even a viable scheme. He admitted that some action was called for and agreed to say or do nothing in public against the plan, at least for the moment, but his cool reception had a damaging effect on attempts to win liberal support for the bill. Norris preferred a constitutional amendment. In a UPI dispatch in April he was reported as saying he saw no merit in the president's plan.[58]

---

[55] Ibid. Others to defect included Frederick Van Nuys (D.-Ind.), who was later read out of his states's Democratic Committee; Ellison D. Smith (D.-S.C.); and Guy Gillette (D.-Iowa), an anti–New Dealer Roosevelt later labeled a Copperhead. They were joined by conservative Democrats Tom Connally, Bennett Champ Clark, Edward Burke, David Walsh, Walter George, Royal Copeland, Peter Gerry, and at least a dozen others. Charles Andrews of Florida and Richard Russell of Georgia assumed a more moderate position and merely advocated adoption of Sumners's bill allowing Supreme Court justices to retire at seventy with full pensions.

[56] *New York Times,* February 14, 1937.

[57] Burns, *Roosevelt,* 298.

[58] Davis, *Into the Storm,* 65; Richard C. Lowitt, *Norris: Triumph of a Progressive, 1933–1944* (Urbana: University of Illinois Press, 1978), 185–90; Alsop and Catledge, *The 168 Days,* 95–96, 185–90.

There was widespread misunderstanding of the Roosevelt-Cummings plan and confusion over what would be the consequences. Robinson told reporters on February 9 that changing the size of the Court would be only temporary: "Any increase above nine in the membership of the Court can exist only as long as there are judges eligible for retirement. When judges retire, the number is reduced by the number retiring. The purpose is always to keep nine members on the Court who are under retirement age."

When newsmen asked about this, Roosevelt snapped: "Look up the bill." Looking, they found that subsection A proposed to add a new judge for each sitting justice over seventy, while subsection B said that "the number of judges of any Court shall be permanently increased by the number appointed under the provision of Sub-section A." Robinson's remarks landed him in trouble with the Justice Department. Henry Suydam rushed to the White House. Failing to find Early, who was at a funeral, or McIntyre, he left them memos about the number of phone calls received from the press that day asking about Robinson's statement. One memo read: "Mr. Suydam says the Senator is entirely incorrect."[59]

Robinson may have been confused, but he was not the only one. Three days before the bill's announcement, Richberg, Cummings, Reed, and Rosenman had debated for hours about last-minute changes on this very question of whether an increase in Supreme Court justices was to be temporary or permanent. Cummings wrote: "Apparently, Mr. Richberg had not understood that the bill provided for a permanent increase rather than a temporary one." The next day Cummings sent FDR a memorandum "in opposition to the proposed alteration in the bill making change temporary." The group met again at another four-hour session that same day, and Cummings reported: "The plan of the bill as originally drafted was retained."[60]

At the outset, FDR was expected to win his fight. Few thought his iron will could be thwarted by Congress. A business journal

---

[59] February 9, 1937, Suydam Files, Box 87, NA; cf. Mooney, *Roosevelt and Rayburn,* 91.

[60] Secret Diary, February 2–3, 1937. If as astute a lawyer as Richberg could misinterpret the bill's meaning, it is little wonder that Robinson found difficulty with it. Many others did also, as became clear in the Senate hearings.

"A Message to Six of the Nine." A cartoon by Pease in *Newark* (N.J.) *News,* February 6, 1937.

predicted: "The boys will not be able to take it when he turns on the heat."[61] Roosevelt derided Democratic defecters like Wheeler for dividing the party. It was actually his court plan—and the loss of trust resulting from the misrepresentation and deceit accompanying it (the false claims about crowded court dockets and the attack on aging justices)—that brought desertions, distrust, and doubts about Roosevelt's leadership. Senator O'Mahoney

[61] This was the opinion of six seasoned reporters in *Nation's Business,* April 1937, 36.

later wrote a friend: "I am very much inclined to the opinion that this marks the beginning of the party realignment . . . I predicted . . . to you long before the election as a very likely development during this term."[62] Something indeed was happening to the grand coalition that had carried Roosevelt to his thumping victories in 1932 and 1936.

The violent reaction to the president's bill and his refusal to wait for deaths or resignations on the Court tended to distract public attention from the political consequences of the move. Democrats and "irregulars" found themselves embroiled in a dispute with Roosevelt. Their open hostility marked the first serious break between the administration and liberal elements in both parties. Columnist Arthur Krock considered this one of the two most important political consequences of FDR's proposal to change the majority viewpoint of the Supreme Court.[63]

A second was that Republicans now had a focal point for effective opposition to a popular leader and dominant congressional majorities. The issue promised a resuscitated and more militant opposition in a Congress where Republicans were hopelessly outnumbered, and put new hope in members of their National Committee. Knowing they could not overcome the president in a straight party fight, they decided to tread carefully and plot their strategy. The Liberty League, moribund after the 1936 election, was not revived. Both liberals and conservatives were sincere in their belief that a constitutional amendment was the only way to settle the problem. Roosevelt soon found himself aligned against not only Republicans and conservative Democrats, but liberals and Progressives on whose support he thought he could count.

Opposition strength was reflected in the readiness, only a week or so after the plan's announcement, with which congressional Democrats began seeking compromise. Through intermediaries, they tried to encourage one or two justices to retire, as they seemed ready to do in 1933. There was renewed interest in Sumners's judicial retirement bill, pending on the House calendar. If

[62] O'Mahoney to Tracy McCraken, March 6, 1937, quoted in Gene M. Gressley, "Joseph C. O'Mahoney, FDR, and the Supreme Court," *Pacific Historical Review* 40 (1971): 191.

[63] "Two Results of Supreme Court Argument," *New York Times,* February 10, 1937, 22:C5.

it became law, justices might take advantage of an opportunity to retire. That would give FDR one or two appointments to make, instead of the six he was asking for.[64]

Senator Key Pittman of Nevada, no liberal, was nevertheless a staunch Roosevelt loyalist who supported compromise. Writing to Cummings, he reiterated what he had already told the president—that he intended to back him in reforming the judiciary: "I feel, however, that you should be apprised of the sentiments I hear expressed by Senators":

> Several of them who are very strong supporters of the President deplored the fact that the . . . procedure with regard to the Supreme Court is subject to the construction that it is actuated by a desire to punish the Court, and at the same time [allow the President to] . . . immediately appoint so many additional Justices to the Court that his views with regard to the . . . Constitution will be adopted by the Court. And this construction has already been placed upon it in a number of editorials in the press of the country.[65]

Reform would come more easily, Pittman said, if the president were willing to accept a Court of eleven members, allowing other provisions with regard to retirement after the age of seventy to take effect at some future time—perhaps twelve months after passage of the enactment.

The Nevada senator thought such a procedure would result in a broader construction of constitutional questions submitted to the Court. "It might prevent decisions by a 5 to 4 majority, and eliminate the danger of deadlock by reason of the prolonged illness of one member, preventing decisions."[66] He thought the law should provide (as Sumners's bill did) for retirement of aged justices at full pay. Some might be "responsive to the opinion of Congress" and retire within a reasonable period, "even if nature did not assist in such adjustment." Finally, he said: "Such . . . legislation would remove all arguments to the effect that the President is attempting to pack the Court, while many grave con-

---

[64] Ibid., February 9, 1937, 4:C3.

[65] February 8, 1937, Box 199, Cummings Papers, ALDL.

[66] The illness of Justice Stone, causing his absence from the Court between November 1936 and February 1, 1937, resulted in many four-to-four rulings and deferrals of decisions until he was able to return to the Court.

stitutional questions are pending." He expected no expression of opinion from Cummings regarding the matter and emphasized that his letter was "entirely personal."[67]

Pittman's plan, though it was left unstated, would have relieved Democrats of having either to desert their leader or to fight opponents whose arguments many considered legitimate. Promoters of compromise were badly misguided, however, if they thought Roosevelt would listen to them or settle for half a loaf. His well-known disdain for the views of Congress could be measured by his speedy rejection of them. It was becoming a rare occasion when he conferred with Congress at all.

Public Reaction

From the start, Roosevelt's court proposal met vigorous public opposition. Opponents amply demonstrated their capability of exerting pressure on Congress. Arguments were heated and at times violent. Clapper said he could not understand the hysterical outcry over FDR's plan, considering the fact that it closely resembled one recently introduced in New Zealand that had encountered little or no resistance. But the American public still regarded the Court as the guardian of the Constitution, aloof from politics. The proposal was denounced for perverting the Constitution, undermining judicial integrity, and destroying judicial independence.

The mail pouring in to congressional offices ran nine-to-one against. Senator Ashurst received a thousand telegrams a day, and his staff experienced difficulty in even opening all the letters. Hiram Johnson received thousands of letters on some days, as did Senator Andrews, who announced that it was impossible to read even a third of his mail regarding the Supreme Court, much less try to answer it. His staff had to work nights and Sundays. Snowed under by thirty thousand letters and telegrams, Senator Royal Copeland's office was totally disorganized. He admitted

[67] Pittman to Cummings, February 8, 1937, Box 199, Cummings Papers, ALDL.

sardonically that he was "now fully informed of the wishes of his constituents."[68]

Bewildered by the protests flooding his office, Senator McAdoo was urged by one constituent to vote against the bill and support an amendment with the effective date January 1940, "if change is really for the good of the country."[69] He was reminded that many senators were well past "the new dead line of seventy years," but their mature judgment was still vitally needed. FDR's attack, the writer said, lowers the public's opinion of all courts and "bids for the supreme power of one man."[70] Another writer asked: "Now that the Supreme Court issue has come out into the open, won't you vote to put the question of change up to the people? This seems a very fair request in view of the fact that Congress is no longer a deliberative body." In congressional mail, two recurring themes—abdication of authority by Congress and Roosevelt's insatiable appetite for power—permeated the messages and letters coming in from all parts of the country.

"President Roosevelt has done some fine things," wrote a Californian, "but I am surprised, disappointed and chagrined this morning when I read that he wants to pack the Supreme Court. We admit it has some faults but can you name any government official or department of government which is without fault, even without serious fault?" He went on: "To add more judges to the Supreme Court or the Circuit Courts would simply create more government jobs, more expenses to the already huge government expenditures, and MORE TAXES. Why not let business have a chance to recover? THE LAST CONGRESS WAS A RUBBER STAMP. What will this Congress be? Isn't this another step to more power and eventual dictatorship?"[71]

---

[68] *Washington Star,* February 7, 1937; *Washington Daily News,* February 7, 1937, 2. For Ashurst, see *St. Joe (Mo.) Observer,* February 26, 1937. Cf. William E. Leuchtenburg, "Franklin D. Roosevelt's Supreme Court Packing Plan," in *Essays on the New Deal,* ed. Harold H. Hollingsworth and William F. Holmes (Austin: University of Texas Press, 1969), 77.

[69] L. C. Stribling to McAdoo, February 7, 1937, Box 430, McAdoo Papers, LC.

[70] A. B. Scheele to McAdoo, February 5, 1937, ibid.

[71] W. W. Lindsay, Los Angeles, to McAdoo, February 6, 1937, ibid.

Press Reaction

When the court bill became public, there began one of the great debates in American constitutional history. No group joined the vociferous discussion of law, constitutional theory, and practice with more vigor and intelligence than the pundits of the nation's press–those political experts who in regular columns under their own names spoke their views on vital questions. As a result of the press coverage that Roosevelt's astounding initiative received, and their commentary over a period of six months, they proved that the United States in that era was by no means poor in the matter of alert and intelligent journalistic brains.

The court bill seemed to be the biggest news story of the decade. Within minutes of its announcement, the press wires across the country were cleared of all other news. Editorial writers rushed to their typewriters, reporting staffs were assigned to ferret out every feature, detail, and picture angle, cartoonists were sent to their drawing boards "to blast or applaud," and front pages all over the country were recast. Few stories rivaled its domination of news coverage.

For its day the news of Roosevelt's "big surprise" spread with amazing rapidity. Ticker tape machines carried it to newsrooms and boardrooms all over the country and flashed it to the floors of the stock exchanges with the result that stock prices plunged. It spread in banner headlines across front pages of every newspaper in the land.

The alarm of the independent press that in normal times supported Roosevelt was typified by the *New York Times,* which declared: "Cleverness and adroitness in dealing with the Supreme Court are not qualities which sober-minded citizens will approve." Frank E. Gannett, the multimillionaire owner of a chain of newspapers that still bears his name, sent out this statement to every American newspaper:

> President Roosevelt has cleverly camouflaged a most amazing and startling proposal for packing the Supreme Court. It is true that the lower courts are slow and overburdened, we probably do need more judges to expedite litigation but this condition should not be used as a subtle excuse for changing the complexion and under-

"(To furnish the Supreme Court Practical Assistance)." Cartoonists had a field day with their comment, largely critical of President Roosevelt's "court-packing" plan. This one was drawn by Elderman of the *Washington Post,* February 6, 1937.

> mining the independence of our highest court. Increasing the number of judges from nine to fifteen would not make this high tribunal act any more promptly than it does now, but it would give the President control of the Judiciary Branch.

Gannett concluded: "The President is mistaken if he thinks he can conceal his real purpose of packing, influencing and controlling the Supreme Court by confusing that objective with a long dissertation on the slow action of our various courts."[72] He sent out thirty-five thousand letters, appealing to newspaper publishers and "leading Americans" to organize committees and bombard Congress with protests.

A Scripps-Howard editorial writer made clear that because the president's political purpose "sticks out like a sore thumb," he must accept the responsibility for returning the controversy to the realm of emotion.

Clapper's boss, Deak Parker, head of the Scripps-Howard chain's Washington bureau, visited Roosevelt shortly after he sent his bill to Congress. He said he thought it would have been better to have put the proposition straight out on its merits, instead of dressing it up. Roosevelt replied: "I wasn't trying to be clever. I never thought the Supreme Court thing would be seized upon. I was interested in the judiciary reform program and scarcely gave the Supreme Court thing a thought. I didn't think I was being clever about it." In his diary Clapper wrote: "Of course, that's hooey, because the whole project was based on what to do about the constitutional court impasse."[73]

William Randolph Hearst, owner of another large newspaper chain, sent telegrams to all his editors, ordering them to kill a vicious editorial by Jimmy Williams on the president's judiciary proposal. The *Washington Times*'s editor was instructed not to use it under any circumstances. Hearst added: "I do not wish to crusade in this matter. Print the news of the debate on both sides without editorial comment."[74]

---

[72] *Life,* March 22, 1937, V. 12, no. 12, p. 62; February 6, 1937, Box 199, Cummings Papers, ALDL.

[73] Clapper Diary, February 8, 1937, Box 8, Clapper Papers. When Cummings was asked the same question, Clapper reports, "his version says that the reform angle came in late in the discussion."

[74] The informant on this was Earl Godwin. William D. Hassett, a Roosevelt aide, learned of the order from him "in strictest confidence." Hassett Memo to Early, February 15, 1937, PSF 165, FDRL.

Hearst aside, a barrage of protests against the plan spread from coast to coast. From the heartland, William Allen White, editor of the *Emporia (Kans.) Gazette,* fired an opening salvo:

> Adroitly, the President is proposing to pack the Supreme Court. Flouting the democratic process of open discussion . . . [he] revealed in the long campaign no inkling of his plan. . . . His silence then, in this morning's light, was a little more than insincere. . . . In a world challenging democracy, in a day when tyrants, appearing as demagogues, crying out against predatory wealth, have shattered Europe's democratic institutions, this court message of the President's seems strangely like the first looming American symptom of danger. Surely Mr. Roosevelt's mandate was to function as the President, not as *Der Fuehrer.* . . . How long will the people be fooled?[75]

White ended with a somber warning: "Relish the idea or not, there are strong indications that America is headed toward a dictatorship. It can only be prevented if the people rally around this fundamental issue of maintaining the integrity of our courts."[76]

George R. Holmes of the International News Service's Washington bureau had a canny appreciation of FDR's ability to turn on the heat and predicted that he would get his program through "if he bears down hard enough." J. Fred Essary of the *Baltimore Sun* saw no chance of defeat in either house: "The President happens to have too much power for the opposition to overcome. It is power in terms of patronage, of prestige, and of vast sums of money. The Senate may bolt . . . but I doubt it." Raymond P. Brandt of the *St. Louis Post-Dispatch* agreed. Roosevelt would succeed if he turned on the political heat, dangling patronage before recalcitrant members, but Brandt anticipated considerable opposition from both judiciary committees, packed as they were with "old-time lawyers." The public could expect powerful debates in the Senate, whose ninety-six members "were wont to think of themselves as constitutional authorities."[77]

---

[75] "Topics of the Day," *Literary Digest,* February 13, 1937, 1.

[76] Ibid. Irving Fisher, a Yale economist and finance authority, wrote the president urging him to stifle "all this fear of an American dictatorship" by issuing a declaration that he would not accept a third term. There was no response. *New York Times,* February 28, 1937, 34.

[77] Assorted news clippings in Box 168, Hughes Papers, LC. See also Box 199. Cummings Papers, and *Editor and Publisher,* February 13, 1937, 1.

FDR explained what he had in mind along the lines of turning on pressure in a talk with Farley a week after the bill went to Congress:

> This is very important to me; it's something that affects the heart of my program. I'll keep them here all year to pass it, if necessary. I must pass it at this session. I want you to help. . . . I'm going to have Senators and Congressmen down in groups and explain what this means. We must bring the Court in step with the New Deal. . . . First off, we must hold up judicial appointments in states where the delegation is not going along. We must make appointments promptly where the delegation is with us. Where there is a division, we must give posts to those supporting us. Second, this must apply to other appointments as well as judicial appointments. I'll keep in close contact with the leaders.[78]

The role public opinion would play in the great debate was largely ignored by most journalists, but William K. Hutchinson, chief of the International News Service's Washington bureau's Senate staff, predicted: "If the fight is long, to such an extent that the opinion of the country can be registered (which I expect to be adverse), then . . . the Senate will defeat the Court bill. However, it is doubtful now, with the odds favoring the President."[79]

Even some liberal journals were caustically critical. An *Oakland Tribune* editorial branded Roosevelt's request for six more justices, ostensibly to speed up decisions, a challenge to the American form of government: "Stripped of all disguising phraseology it is a bold attempt to pack the Supreme Court. . . . If a single executive were suddenly to be given the power to name six new justices, the door would be open to dictatorship. Regardless of the intent of this reorganization plan, it is, in effect, a club over the Court, which is told it must support the New Deal legislation or be made over into a body that will." The editorial continued:

> Congress has already abdicated to the Executive. During a period of four years this body has passed many bills recommended by the President without reading and in some instances before they have

---

[78] The talk took place on February 11, 1937. *Jim Farley's Story,* 73–74.
[79] Ibid.

> gone to print. . . . When the President urged the high court to be more liberal in its interpretations of law there was no . . . hint that he was about to follow up with a proposal aimed at ending its effectiveness. . . . Although the President has an overwhelming majority in Congress, it does not seem possible that his Democratic supporters there can support so marked a deviation from the paths of constitutional government.[80]

In the forefront of antagonists stood the *New York Herald Tribune*'s editorial trio of Walter Lippmann, "sick at heart," branding the plan "the greatest crisis in seventy years"; Dorothy Thompson, who abhorred it; and Mark Sullivan, who wrote: "We are going down the road to fascism." David Lawrence wrote that the tragedy of what was happening was that "Mr. Roosevelt has become too much enveloped in partisan passion." If the Supreme Court goes, he asserted, all other U.S. institutions will begin to crumble one by one. In his heavily documented arguments, he was supported by Franklyn Waltman and Frank Kent of the *Baltimore Sun.* Westbrook Pegler, a little out of his depth, adopted "an attitude of suspicion." Roosevelt supporters included Jay Franklin, unexcited but cogent; Heywood Broun, half-serious, half-humorous; and Clapper, who day after day gave some of the best arguments for the court plan. The greatest phrase-maker of them all was Hugh Johnson, still smarting from the "Dred Schechter decision" but now a daily columnist, "delighted to be back in the thick of battle again."[81]

Writing in the *Baltimore Sun,* Frank Kent observed:

> No one knows definitely . . . the three men with whom and with whom alone Mr. Roosevelt told friends he had cooperated in formulating this comprehensive scheme for bending the courts to the New Deal will, though it is quite certain none of them is a member of Congress.
>
> This, however, is sure—the man who wrote the message, drafted that bill and set the stage with his statistics was a lawyer of learning, experience and ability. From the White House angle he did a

[80] *Oakland Tribune,* February 6, 1937, Box 168, Hughes Papers, LC.

[81] *Nation,* March 6, 1937, 253. See assorted clippings in Box 199, Cummings Papers, ALDL. Veteran reporter Frank Kent was managing editor of the *Baltimore Sun.* His column was syndicated in over a hundred newspapers. See also Walter Lippmann's column "Today and Tomorrow," for "Change by Usurpation," *New York Herald Tribune,* February 11, 1937.

fine piece of literary work, the cleverness of which, it is hard to exaggerate.[82]

The Bar Associations

State bars and the American Bar Association lost no time registering disapproval of the court plan. Ickes noted: "The bar associations are lined up against the President, as might have been expected."[83] McAdoo added sourly: "The bar is as a rule the most conservative force in America . . . and it announced with a finality of judgment its opposition to the President's bill and message without giving due consideration to the arguments pro and con."[84]

Historian Henry Steele Commager made a stronger case when he wrote that the dignity, prosperity, and influence of the legal profession is one of the most striking phenomena of American culture. In no other country, he asserted, have lawyers occupied a comparable position or played a comparable role. All but ten American presidents to 1937 were exposed in varying degrees to legal training, including FDR. Nowhere, thought Commager, has the law been more faithfully cultivated, more assiduously studied. The law school, like the constitutional lawyer, is an American institution. "This influence, so pervasive and so powerful, was, naturally enough, a force for conservatism, for law is by its very nature conservative, and most of its disciples gladly share its nature." From the days of Jefferson's "assault on the judiciary" to Franklin Roosevelt's court-packing plan, almost every liberal at some time found it necessary to attack the misuse of the judicial prerogative.[85] But conservatives, with few exceptions, lined up in solid defense of an independent Supreme Court and the Constitution as the bulwark of American democracy.

---

[82] February 7, 1937. Copy in Box 199, Cummings Papers, ALDL. Roosevelt misled "friends" by mentioning "three men" when in fact there were many more, but none were in Congress. Kent was one of the rare commentators who, without naming him, congratulated Cummings for his part in the scheme.

[83] *Secret Diary,* March 15, 1937, 2:93.

[84] McAdoo to Thomas Storke, February 10, 1937, Box 430, McAdoo Papers, LC.

[85] *The American Mind: An Interpretation of American Thought and Character since the 1880's* (New Haven: Yale University Press, 1950), 364–66.

One by one, the state bars fell in line in opposing the court plan. The New Jersey bar condemned the proposal and named a committee of forty to work for its defeat. Fewer than a dozen of its 450 members supported the plan.[86] The St. Louis bar, in a resolution passed by a vote of 232 to 14, declared that "in dealing with cases in which the existence of legislative power is in question, it is for the Court to determine only whether the Constitution grants such power."[87] Utah's state bar declared its opposition to FDR's plan, as did Colorado's. Wilson McCarthy, a lawyer friend of Stephens's, told him: "I think it would be fair to state that eighty percent of the lawyers of the country are against his proposal. . . . Personally, I should be very much surprised if the President, with all of his friends is able to put this across."[88]

Legal critics charged Roosevelt with "smooth evasion" for remaining silent on the plans for a court-packing bill in the 1936 campaign and called the whole scheme "an intellectually dishonest procedure." Its dishonesty became even more evident when further facts were revealed. Justin Moore speculated that in November, if not earlier, the president must have had in mind some proposal similar to the one now before them but he had intentionally refused to submit it to the judgment of the people. The Democratic Party under Roosevelt "has had altogether too many subterfuges," wrote Moore. Campaigning on one platform and then substituting some other program was unacceptable. "For the life of me," Moore continued, "I can not see how the appointment of six additional judges is going to remedy the situation."[89]

A former law partner of Stephens's commented: "I do not know who advised the President with respect to his [court] program. In my opinion the advice is not only unsound and fraught with great danger to our American system of government, but . . . if carried out, will seriously impair the President's position in history as a democratic leader."[90] Stephens told a Utah lawyer:

[86] *Literary Digest,* February 11, 1937.

[87] *St. Louis Star-Times* editorial, n.d., Box 7, Stone Papers, LC. The pro–New Deal editor, Raymond Brandt, ridiculed this assertion, comparing it to Justice Roberts's so-called "slot machine" theory in his *U.S. v. Butler* opinion.

[88] March 1, 1937, Box 26, Stephens Papers, LC.

[89] Justin Moore to Stephens, February 18, 1937, Box 16, ibid.

[90] Frank Holman to Stephens, February 23, 1937, Box 29, ibid.

"I have never been so deeply disturbed since I have been at the bar and in public life as I am over this thing. I think it goes to the very roots of our civilization."[91]

The Federal Bar Association issued a vicious condemnation of Roosevelt's "ambitious program to aid in modernizing the courts." At a New York meeting on February 17, its president, Henry Ward Beer, fought hard for the administration but was shouted down. Even in defeat, Beer continued to believe Roosevelt was succeeding in making the country "Federal court conscious."[92] New York City's bar association issued a majority report roundly denouncing the court reforms; Simon Rifkind, Senator Wagner's law partner, wrote a minority report. A pro-Roosevelt member noted: "The old banker-lawyer reactionaries, who represent about one tenth of one percent of the population of the country, made their usual . . . attack upon the President. In fact, Judge [Samuel] Seabury went so far as to say that the President was guilty of trying to obtain his program through false pretenses."[93]

Louisiana's bar held a referendum on the "main issue," the question of enlarging the Supreme Court, and there was overwhelming disapproval by its respondents to the court plan. Senator Pittman notified Roosevelt that the Nevada bar had adopted a resolution asking its congressional delegation to oppose the judicial reform program. Judge George S. Brown, a leading Reno lawyer, wrote Pittman recounting their reasons for opposing the program.[94]

The ABA sponsored wide use of the radio. Senators Connally, King, and Burke, all Democrats and members of the Judiciary Committee, went on a national hookup and calmly reviewed the outstanding New Deal cases, demonstrating how the Court's decisions had been beneficial to the national welfare, and not detrimental. King was the senior Democrat on the committee.

ABA members in a referendum voted seven-to-one against the

---

[91] Stephens to Monte Appel, February 23, 1937, ibid.

[92] Henry Ward Beer to FDR, February 11, 1937, PPF 3375, FDRL.

[93] Beer to Marvin MacIntyre, February 25, 1937, ibid. The reports were issued at a special meeting on February 24 in New York City.

[94] Pittman to FDR, February 19, 1937, PPF 1169, FDRL. The results in Louisiana were announced in the newspapers on March 1, 1937.

bill, and twenty-five thousand lawyers who were not members voted four-to-one against. ABA president Frederick H. Stinchfield took to the airwaves with "Why Lawyers Would Save Our Supreme Court." He appointed a special five-member committee to coordinate opposition activities. They set up a Washington office staffed with volunteer lawyers ready to assist opponents of the bill. Senator Burke took advantage of their offer to suggest establishing a permanent research staff for Congress. Senior partners and some of the brightest young men from the country's largest law firms were assigned to a revolving staff. They supplied the opposition with valuable ammunition for use in the approaching Senate hearings.[95]

Administration Strategy—First Phase

Initial administration strategy for winning passage of the court bill called for action in the House, but immediately that move ran into trouble. The bill was blocked by Chairman Sumners, who was determined to kill it if it ever came before the Judiciary Committee. At one time a powerful Texas prosecutor, by the 1930s Sumners had grown sour on life and people in general. "He was not young in spirit," according to Lady Bird Johnson. When he learned that Rayburn was trying to help Roosevelt on his court plan, that brought an end to a long friendship.[96]

Speaker Bankhead sent FDR a handwritten note informing him: "I have acquainted James [Roosevelt] with some developments on Judicial Reform that I feel you should know about—I think it quite important for you to ask Hatton Sumners . . . to see you *alone* at as early a moment as possible."[97] On February 8, Early assured Clapper that no more than fifteen Democrats would vote against the bill in the Senate, that its leaders were "all right," but that "Sumners on the House side was all wet." Alerting FDR, Early wrote:

---

[95] On Stinchfield's activities, see OF 41A, FDRL; Alsop Notes, Box 53, Alsop Papers, LC; Alsop and Catledge, *The 168 Days,* 123.

[96] D. B. Hardeman and Donald C. Bacon, *Rayburn: A Biography* (Austin: Texas Monthly Press, 1987), 223.

[97] PSF 187, FDRL.

Smiling Representative Hatton Sumners, Chairman of the Judiciary Committee, was supposed to start pushing the president's Judicial Reorganization program through the House in early February. But "Hattie" had other plans. (*Life,* February 22, 1937, p. 15)

> You might know before luncheon today, that Hatton Sumners held an "off the record" conference with newspapermen this morning. . . . He was savage in his attack upon your proposal. He called it "infamous." He refused to let himself be quoted. . . . One of the newspapermen present just telephoned me and said that Sumners gave the proposal "hell, specifically and generally." This, of course will lead the press into writing more and more stories about bitter opposition by congressional leaders.[98]

---

[98] Clapper Diary, February 8, 1937, Clapper Papers, LC; Early to FDR, February 8, 1937, PSF 186, FDRL.

Sumners was called to a White House meeting with FDR, Wagner, and Ashurst at which he was persuaded to make no more public remarks on his position for the time being, leaving some hope that he might change his mind. He did not. Privately he continued to express his disdain.

By mid-February, Sumners had a majority on his committee against the bill. If hearings had been held, they would have been dominated by opponents. The bill could be reported to the full House by the committee only if compelled to do so, either by a discharge petition signed by 218 members to relieve the committee of any further consideration of the measure or by a vote to suspend House rules, which required a two-thirds majority. Neither move was considered wise by Bankhead and Rayburn. They felt confident they could bulldoze the bill out of committee and ram it through the House despite an unfavorable report, but it would be at a cost of so much ill will that final passage in the House, after Senate action, would prove impossible.[99] Chances for a victory in the Senate, given that body's factions, would be seriously impaired, and possibly destroyed.[100]

With Chairman Sumners refusing to endorse the bill, Bankhead and Rayburn finally convinced Roosevelt, not without difficulty, that the Senate should take it up. On February 18 the administration made the public announcement that the Senate would be the first to consider the court bill. Senator Robinson was determined to ram the bill through. The fight would center on the provision to increase the number of Supreme Court justices, but he was sure the other parts of the bill would pass easily if they were voted on separately. He knew they were a subterfuge designed to make the bill more palatable. Hearings before the Senate Judiciary Committee were to begin the second week in March.

Sumners's obstinacy at once enraged FDR and proved contagious among members of his committee. If within a week after February 5 a vote had been taken in the Judiciary Committee, the bill would have been defeated in the House by a majority of five.[101] Sumners's stand forced a major shift in White House

[99] Mooney, *Roosevelt and Rayburn,* 89.
[100] Davis, *New Deal Years,* 73.
[101] Ibid., 71.

strategy. The usual order on any administration bill is action in the House, then the Senate. Roosevelt was already paying a heavy price for failing to take party leaders into his confidence before announcing the court plan. Ignoring their counsel not only deprived him of a useful sounding board but left Democrats feeling disgruntled over having been excluded from the decision-making process on a matter of such importance.

Meanwhile, Sumners would not wait for senatorial action. His strategy was to carve FDR's court bill up into separate bills and kill its main objective. On February 10 the House passed his judicial retirement act by a vote of 315 to 75. But just as he was preparing for debate on a bill allowing the government to intervene in federal court cases when the constitutionality of a congressional act was at issue, Speaker pro tem Rayburn, acting on direct orders from the White House, moved for an adjournment. Roosevelt would not tolerate having his plan cannibalized.[102]

Both sides in the contest faced formidable obstacles. The opposition had the daunting task of overcoming the indomitable will of a popular president and huge Democratic majorities in Congress. Roosevelt's strategy was damaged as the consequence of his own failings. Having refused to prepare the public mind for his move, he met stiff resistance from the electorate and fervent opposition from congressional leaders. Prompt and effective maneuvers by the opposition alerted legislators and the public to the fact that the bill was in trouble.

Senate opponents sought a leader, preferably from among Democratic ranks. When Senator Wheeler of Montana declared against the plan, they found the man they were looking for. His press release stated: "The usurpation of the legislative function by the courts should be stopped. But to give the executive the power to control the judiciary is not giving the law-making power back to the branch of government to which it rightly belongs, but rather is increasing the dangers inherent in the concentration of power in any one branch."[103]

In his press statement, Wheeler said the bill was an unconstitu-

---

[102] Earl Canham, *Christian Science Monitor,* February 11, 1937.

[103] February 13, 1937, Box 8, Wheeler Papers, MHS.

tional grab for power by the president and would result in destroying the Supreme Court as an institution. The senator's willingness to defy Roosevelt and assume leadership of his opponents was a serious blow to the administration. An outspoken critic of the Court, Wheeler for long had wanted to solve the problem of what he called its arbitrary decisions and conservatism, but he was adamant in opposing the method adopted by FDR. A liberal with impeccable credentials, he had supported nearly all important New Deal legislation and would be a formidable adversary. The senator never liked the highly personalized Roosevelt presidency. Confronted by the court bill, he was certain that it implied a fundamental alteration in the balance of power, shifting the advantage to the White House.

By opposing FDR, Wheeler knew he was consigning any future he had in Democratic politics to oblivion. When he asked his wife, Lulu, for her advice, she reinforced his determination. She despised Roosevelt for his deceitfulness and, like other Washington wives, was outraged by his blatant public appearances and scandalous behavior with Marguerite Le Hand.[104] Mrs. Wheeler's advice to her husband was a variation on Admiral Farragut's order: "Damn the torpedoes. Full speed ahead."

Roosevelt counted on young Bob La Follette of Wisconsin to rally the liberals and recruit left-leaning Independents in the Northwest. But Wheeler won over Senators Gerald Nye, Lynn Frazier, and Henrik Shipstead (a Farmer-Laborite from North Dakota) to the opposition before La Follette could get to them. The smear campaign waged against Wheeler was ineffective. He was called an ingrate, a closet Tory, a disgruntled office seeker, and worse. Roosevelt spent half an hour urging Myron W. Thatcher, the leader of a minority wing of the Farmer's Union, to go to Montana with Senators Nye and Frazier to "build a fire under Wheeler,"[105] but such tactics only succeeded in alienating many of the state's people.

From long years in Congress, Wheeler knew every twist and

[104] Wheeler, *Yankee from the West,* 320–22.

[105] On Wheeler's leadership role in the Supreme Court fight, see Marian C. McKenna, "Prelude to Tyranny: Wheeler, F.D.R., and the 1937 Court Fight," *Pacific Historical Review* 62 (November 1993): 405–31, at 417; cf. Alsop and Catledge, *The 168 Days,* 119.

turn of the legislative game and was capable of employing brutal tactics if they promised to produce results. The senator was impervious to blandishments from the White House conveyed through emissaries Michelson, West, and Corcoran. He was invited to dine with the president to "talk over the issue." He told Michelson, who had delivered the invitation, "Charley, I've just given out a statement opposing the packing of the Court, so the President ought to save the plate for someone who persuades more easily."[106] Wheeler relished a good fight, especially against a proposal with Cummings as its principal author.

Over the radio, Wheeler warned that the bill would transform the Supreme Court into a weapon whose use "would be dictated only by the conscience of the wielder." His followers could have no cause to doubt his liberalism. "The court plan is not liberal," he told them. "A liberal cause was never won by stacking a deck of cards, by shifting a ballot box, or by packing a court." At a private luncheon in Senator Robinson's office for Manuel Quezon of the Philippines, John Garner was reported to have paid Wheeler the ultimate compliment when he reached around the table, thumped him on the back, and said, "Burt, you're a real patriot. The day is coming when we'll have to go down to the White House and tell the President so."[107]

Wheeler lost no time putting together an organization and strategy to do battle, allowing few openings and little opportunity for flanking movements or diversions. His steering committee included Peter G. Gerry, second in command, and Senators Van Nuys, Bailey, Clark, Connally, Byrd, Glass, Burke, and Tydings. Throughout that winter and spring, they carried the fight to the towns and cities, to rural areas, to the Senate floor and cloakroom, to social gatherings, over the radio, and on the lecture platform. Wheeler related:

> Our steering committee met secretly every day in the Capitol hideaway to alter strategy in the light of shifting events. Our intelli-

[106] Wheeler, *Yankee from the West,* 320–22; Michelson, *The Ghost Talks,* 178.

[107] Raymond Brandt, *Washington Evening Star,* April 21, 1940. According to the report in *The New York Times* for July 23, 1937, this incident took place some time during the first week of March, 1937. Cf. MacColl, "Supreme Court and Public Opinion," 211–12.

> gence network was unexpectedly reinforced by reports from inside the administration forces . . . relating who was weak on their side and who seemed to be weakening on our side. I never knew for certain why . . . it could even have been done with the consent of Senator Joe Robinson, the majority leader, in the hope that building up the opposition to the bill would force the President to back down and compromise. Actually, Robinson had no more stomach for the court-packing scheme than we did; he dutifully led the fight for it because he was Senate Democratic leader and it was believed FDR had promised him a seat on the Supreme Court.[108]

The Conspiracy of Silence

Senator Borah said he got some of his biggest thrills assisting Wheeler in devising their strategy in this game of congressional warfare. William K. Hutchinson, a Washington correspondent for the International News Service, maintained that Borah masterminded the strategy for the Senate rejection of FDR's court bill. That overstated the senator's role, but he did help formulate the bipartisan strategy that ultimately led to the bill's defeat. He even placed the fight on court-packing on a plane above the battle over U.S. entry into the League of Nations, because it involved the independence and integrity of the federal judiciary, and with it the preservation of democracy in America.

Borah's notes, dictated to Hutchinson, describe the major steps in the opposition's campaign[109] and indicate that behind the scenes he worked hard at keeping their efforts on target. Closeted on February 6 with McNary and Vandenberg, he emphasized that with all Republicans in the Senate lined up against the bill, it could be defeated only with Democrats' votes. They realized that too vigorous opposition might encourage wavering Democrats to close ranks with his supporters and rally behind their leader. Defeat of the bill could be attained by remaining on the sidelines, allowing the Democrats to fight among themselves. The "con-

---

[108] Wheeler, *Yankee from the West,* 323.

[109] *News Articles on the Life and Work of Hon. William E. Borah,* a pamphlet by William K. Hutchinson ordered to be printed in the *Congressional Record* by Senator Frederick Van Nuys, February 29, 1940, 76th Cong., 3rd sess., S. Doc. 150 (Washington, D.C.: Government Printing Office, 1940), 10.

spiracy of silence" among Republicans was anything but popular. Keeping politicians quiet anywhere at any time is no easy matter. Yet, Borah warned that if they failed, they stood to lose the "greatest issue of the century," one that could wreck the Democratic Party and Roosevelt with it.

Landon, among others, found it difficult to resist the urge to speak out. Court reform was to be his topic in an address to the New York Republican Club on February 9, but a few senators convinced him to tear up his speech and replace it with what turned out to be a tribute to Lincoln.[110] Hoover was most difficult of them all to silence. He argued that by failing to seize this issue, Republicans were passing up a golden opportunity. It would be better, he said, for the party to be beaten out in the open, in a knock-down, drag-out fight, making a record on which future victories could be based, rather than to pursue such a devious strategy. Dissenting Democrats would win the credit for any good results that might accrue from voicing their opposition.[111]

As he was putting the final touches to a radio address denouncing court reform in doomsday terms, Hoover was told by phone about the meeting of senators. He asked sharply: "Who was there?" Borah, McNary, and Vandenberg were no favorites of his and would not sway him with their advice. He did not even recognize their claim to leadership in the party. Finally, he agreed to cooperate, owing to the efforts of columnist Mark Sullivan and John Callan O'Laughlin, two close friends. But his patience lasted less than two weeks. On February 20 he delivered a blistering radio address entitled "Hands Off the Supreme Court."[112] Congressman Clifford Hope (R.-Kans.) wrote:

> Of course, the big fight back here all along has been to keep our enthusiastic Republicans out of the picture. I was sorry that Hoover made his speech. It was a good one, but came at the wrong time. A Republican Senator was telling me no later than yesterday that two Democrats that they could otherwise count on were still pretty

[110] *New York Times,* February 13, 1937.

[111] Ibid., April 9, 1937.

[112] The speech was reprinted in Herbert Hoover, *Addresses on the American Road, 1933–1938* (New York: Scribner, 1938), 228–36; cf. Alsop and Catledge, *The 168 Days,* 98–100.

> much on the fence and were saying that Hoover's speech made it . . . hard for them to come out and oppose the President's plan.[113]

Hope concluded: "Their own convictions must be a little weak to let a thing like that influence them, but nevertheless the only way this thing is going to be stopped is in the Senate and one or two votes may be the margin on the final showdown. I thought Alf [Landon] handled the situation just right in New York. It was undoubtedly a great temptation to him to say 'I told you so,' but he restrained himself most nobly."[114]

With few exceptions, Republicans demonstrated remarkable self-discipline in maintaining their strategy of silence. Republican National Committee chairman John Hamilton, however, soon found it difficult to raise funds for a party that had virtually been erased from the political map. When he initiated a series of radio broadcasts in May to satisfy Republicans that their party still existed, he met immediate resistance from strategists who insisted that comment on the judicial reform bill, even after months of debate, would be premature. Hamilton was persuaded to limit the broadcasts by omitting the court bill as a topic of discussion.

The effectiveness of "the conspiracy" became a matter of debate. Some have concluded that it has been exaggerated. Republicans were faulted for failing to provide responsible opposition or formulate some alternative to FDR's proposal. In the most critical legislative battle of the New Deal era, Republicans were accused of "ducking the issue" rather than raising a clear cry of criticism. Political scientist Karl Lamb viewed their conduct as "an amazing admission of impotency."[115] But most journalists disagreed. Two contemporary writers concluded: "Probably no single thing annoyed administration strategists . . . [as much as the] conspiracy of silence. Confronted for once by silent Repub-

[113] Hope to Don Berry, an Indianola, Iowa, editor, February 26, 1937, Box 1, folder 18, Don Berry Papers, Iowa State University Library, Ames. The author is indebted to Professor Richard Lowitt of Norman, Oklahoma, for this letter, which he came across in the course of his own research and brought to my attention.

[114] Ibid.

[115] "The Opposition Party as Secret Agent: Republicans and the Court Fight," *Papers of the Michigan Academy of Arts, Science and Letters* 46 (1961): 539–50.

licans . . . the Democratic leaders were deprived of the irritant they had most relied on to give fervor and cohesion to their forces."[116]

Other activities by Republicans who were against the court plan were carried through and may have had more effect than silence. Party headquarters became a resource center for opponents, regardless of affiliation. Republicans played the game of "silent partner" with skill. The only test of this political strategy was the pragmatic one. It worked. What did it matter if defeat of the bill were to be credited to dissident Democrats rather than Republicans? If the strategy succeeded, there would be plenty of credit to be shared by all.

Democratic opponents of the court plan feared they could not defeat FDR's bill without offering an alternative, and they began looking for a substitute. This was a touchy issue. Roosevelt would block any substitute for the plan offered by the recognized leader of the party. Borah advised his Democratic colleagues to "Agree to nothing." They were to speak of amendments "in the vaguest of terms." He reminded them of how in the League of Nations fight Senator Lodge's reservations had torpedoed Wilson's proposal. Borah had warned Lodge that the league's opponents would never agree on anything. The league would be defeated on its merits. Reservations were a diversion. "Well, in this fight," Borah told them, "you'll soon learn that Roosevelt hasn't anything like the prestige that Wilson enjoyed. Wilson was regarded as a Messiah; Roosevelt [is regarded] only as a Santa Claus. Wilson had a tremendously popular issue. Roosevelt has one which is unpopular. . . . We'll defeat him on the merits."[117]

No alternative solution was advanced by either side in a manner that would allow for a meaningful debate and public choice. Nearly every opposition senator had his own solution. Borah wanted jurisdiction over social legislation reserved to the states by alterations in the Fourteenth Amendment; O'Mahoney's amendment required a two-thirds majority for the Court to invalidate an act of Congress; Wheeler's amendment would allow

---

[116] Alsop and Catledge, *The 168 Days,* 100.

[117] Hutchinson, *News Articles,* 12.

Congress to override a judicial veto; and Burke wanted a fixed retirement age for judges. As matters then stood, it was to be the Roosevelt plan or nothing.

Administration Strategy—Second Phase

Although his plan faced growing opposition, Roosevelt appeared outwardly confident and imperturbable.[118] "The people are with me," he repeated over and over like a mantra. As for strategy, he said he was "holding his fire. Let the opposition blow itself out and then move in." Cabinet members were restrained while he waited to use Cummings to make their case before the Senate Judiciary Committee. He would not go to the country. "There was nothing like that in the picture so far," Early reported. He thought "it was bad stuff to go over the head of Congress, and he had never seen it win." That was used only in the most desperate situations. Clapper told his diary that if Roosevelt ever went to the country on this, "we will all know . . . he is really worried."[119]

A California judge wrote Cummings: "I hope the [president's] message will be read in full by the citizenry, but I find my friends talking from the headlines. There are many not bothering to reason deeply, who close the case with their opposition to tinkering with the Constitution and the Court." If the message could be given to the people through the medium of a fireside chat, he said, it would be better understood.[120] At a press conference in early February, FDR was asked if he would discuss the court plan in a fireside chat. With one word, "No," he dismissed the query as if the thought had never entered his head. "The quarterback . . . had called his play. He was fully confident that he would score."[121] But not all his supporters shared his confidence.

[118] George Carroll, "F.D.R. Very Confident," *New York Evening News,* February 11, 1937. Copy in Box 126, Hughes Papers, LC.

[119] Clapper Diary, February 8, 1937, Box 8, Clapper Papers.

[120] District Judge Albert Lee Stephens to Cummings, February 6, 1937, Box 199, Cummings Papers, ALDL.

[121] George Carroll, "F.D.R. Very Confident," *New York Evening News,* February 11, 1937. Copy in Box 186, Hughes Papers, LC.

Behind the scenes FDR exuded personal charm, using his influence and persuasion on doubtful legislators. They were called in for frank, private talks and perhaps some arm-twisting. Roosevelt entertained the notion that a senator was like a nervous horse, "needing only a little gentling to make him obedient." Before the end of the second week of the court fight, Roosevelt told Farley he would have to convert many Democratic senators himself. He called in to the White House Norris, Pittman, McAdoo, Dieterich, Wagner, O'Mahoney, King, Van Nuys, Burke, Connally, Harrison, and Byrnes. O'Mahoney canceled his appointment, while Burke, Van Nuys, and King responded with great reluctance. He asked for no commitments, but rather expected to get some. He got very few. In fact, one senator gave him an unexpected condemnation of his bill, with a blunt warning that he was courting defeat in Congress. On this occasion FDR failed to laugh off the idea, as was his habit. He merely stared straight ahead with a fixed gaze as the angry senator stormed out of the room.[122]

The president preferred to take no active role in the fight, at least not until after returning from his Warm Springs vacation in the second week of March. But the delay gave his opponents an opportunity to expose the real motives behind his plan, which had little to do with crowded court dockets, aging jurists, or denial of justice to the masses. The only thing on his agenda was an address at a fund-raiser on March 4, a Victory Dinner at which he planned to make no mention of court reform. But this could change as the storm of fury against his bill intensified.

On a visit to the Justice Department, Clapper asked Cummings why the administration had decided to spring its plan on the country at that time. The attorney general said they wanted to submit it early in the session; it took time to get such a measure through. The bill contained a clause putting it into effect thirty days after its enactment in order to give the justices time, after its passage, to resign, thus requiring no enlargement of the Court. Justices, said the attorney general, might want to wait and see if the bill passed before leaving the bench. But if they chose to

[122] Alsop and Catledge, *The 168 Days,* 91–92; *Christian Science Monitor,* February 11, 1937.

remain, Cummings warned, they and not the administration would be responsible for enlarging the Court. Their strategy was to maneuver the Court into determining its own size. They wanted the legislation to go through early enough to permit nominations to go to the Senate at that same session.[123]

By launching the plan early in February, Cummings assured Clapper, they were saving a lot of people the trouble of working on alternative plans. Roosevelt wanted to get his proposal out so that others would be dropped. Senator Minton and two dozen members of a House-Senate bloc had just finished drafting a bill requiring a seven-to-two vote for Supreme Court decisions, an indication of how far out of touch with FDR Minton was. They needed to get this "troublesome matter" cleared up so that Congress could focus on other New Deal legislation and shape it, knowing that it would be put up to an enlarged Supreme Court holding views resembling those held by Justices Stone, Cardozo, and Brandeis. That, he insisted, was all the administration wanted, not dictatorial power.[124]

A lot of second-guessing was going on about how the Supreme Court would vote in the next round of cases. News stories picked up on the "perfect timing" of Roosevelt's dramatic move to rejuvenate the Court, especially in view of the distinct possibility that it might strike down the Wagner Labor Act. This, he believed, would result in Congress's losing no time in enacting his judicial reforms. Rulings in pending cases testing the constitutionality of the National Labor Relations Act were expected sometime after March 15. Adverse decisions, some thought, would cause a repetition of the furor following the outlawry of the NRA and AAA, as one New York evening paper outlined this scenario:

> The President and the few select advisers with whom he secretly molded his court policy believe invalidation would cause such popular resentment that Congress would have to act. The political precision with which the White House launched its proposal puts the New Deal in a win-win position whichever way the Supreme Court votes on the Wagner Act. If killed and administration strat-

---

[123] Clapper Diary, February 8, 1937, Clapper Papers.

[124] Ibid.

egy proves flawless, as is hoped, the howl will be so loud that the nine justices will find things happening fast in their marble palace.[125]

Clapper learned that Roosevelt had strategic reasons for his decision to turn the heat on the Court before a ruling on the Wagner Act. That, he wrote, "may be the key decision which will indicate whether the New Deal objectives can be pursued without a change in the Constitution."[126] The press was not the only source predicting defeat of the Wagner Act. Professor Reed Powell of Harvard Law School wrote: "With or without early changes in the composition of the Supreme Court, we have ahead of us the possibility and even the likelihood that important statutes now on the books will be condemned . . . by judicial action. The recent condemnation of the labor provisions of the Coal Conservation Act makes it almost certain that the Wagner Labor Act will be denied application to manufacturing concerns by six votes and possibly by nine."[127]

District Judge Wilbur ("Bill") Clark of Newark, New Jersey, agreed that the end result would be unanimous rejection of the Wagner Act so far as it applied to manufacturing establishments, but the reaction would then be the recognition that the real trouble was with the Constitution and *not* the Supreme Court. "Brandeis," he said, "interprets the Constitution learnedly and liberally, and yet here (as in *Schechter*) he finds the present Constitution an insurmountable obstacle. You couldn't pack against a man like Brandeis."[128] Roosevelt and his supporters were counting heavily on a judicial veto of the Wagner Act and an outraged public opinion to save the day for the court bill, but that was another bad miscalculation. The outrage would be directed against the president and his court bill, and not the Supreme Court itself.

The steering committee assigned to getting the bill passed was an informal group known as the White House general staff. The

[125] *New York Evening Journal,* February 11, 1937.

[126] *Washington Evening News,* January 7, 1937, Box 59, Clapper Papers, LC.

[127] The reference was to *Carter v. Carter,* 298 U.S. 238 (1936). "The Next Four Years: The Constitution," *New Republic,* January 13, 1937, 319.

[128] Clark to James Roosevelt, February 17, 1937, Box 79, Jackson Papers, LC.

members were all intimates of the president. They included Corcoran, who drove their agenda ahead of what party members at times were willing to follow.[129] In this role of "hatchet man" he was charged with bringing whatever amount of pressure was necessary to win over doubtful lawmakers to their side in the Supreme Court fight. For nearly all practical purposes he acted as Roosevelt's chief of staff. Joseph Keenan, special assistant to the attorney general, had distinguished himself for prosecuting kidnappers. Corcoran and Keenan were jointly assigned to lobby the Senate. They doled out charm, patronage, and threats. Corcoran's strong-arm tactics and brash behavior limited his effectiveness. Keenan, the more affable of the two, was shrewd and hardheaded, but legislators trusted him more than his overzealous partner.

Charles West, a White House informant and lobbyist, worked the House, a task assigned to him in 1936. Robert Jackson, another special assistant to the attorney general, was in several places at once, arguing the administration's case in public forums. He was to testify at the forthcoming Senate hearings. Jackson's effectiveness was not limited in spite of his well-known disagreement with the method used to sell the bill and to certain policy differences with Roosevelt and Cummings.

Roosevelt's oldest son, James, served during this period as the president's personal secretary. He was to be his father's eyes, ears, and legs at functions and distant meetings which FDR could not attend. He reported to him on staff activities and tried to assuage his loneliness. This arrangement was made over loud protests from the inner circle and from Mrs. Roosevelt, who foresaw the pitfalls awaiting their son, soon to become an object of derision, charged with nepotism and incompetence. The job took a heavy toll on his none-too-robust physical condition. He became a victim of powerful congressional factions and was used by them as a pawn in attempts to pressure his father.[130] The group

---

[129] Jordan A. Schwartz, "Thomas G. Corcoran: The Fixer," *The New Dealers: Power Politics in the Age of Roosevelt* (New York: Vintage Books, 1994), 141.

[130] Alsop and Catledge, *The 168 Days,* 84–85; interviews with James Roosevelt, Corona del Mar, California, May 10–11, 1990. Beginning in January 1937, James was assigned "odd jobs." He began as assistant to Executive Clerk Rudolph Forster but soon moved into Steve Early's office, and Early took over the office of the late Louis Howe. James soon became FDR's personal secretary,

held almost daily sessions at which reports were studied, strategy formulated, and tactics adopted. Members reported individually to the president, who exercised direct control. When differences arose, it fell to James to report both sides of an issue to his father, leaving the decision up to him.

A great amount of energy was consumed in polling lawmakers. Long before it was made public, Keenan reported: "O'Mahoney definitely opposed. Thinks it is a grave error. Believes that the fact that some of the judges may have imposed their economic views on other branches of the government does not provide an adequate excuse for doing indirectly what the Constitution prohibits doing directly, causing men to retire at seventy." Connally and King announced their opposition to the press. When Senator Neely reported that Carl Hatch (D.-N.Mex.) was for the bill, Keenan asked Neely to get Hatch on the phone, which he did, only to find that Hatch was "showing a great deal of doubt about the main provisions of the measure"—appointment of so many new judges and the dilemma that would be created if older ones failed to retire.[131]

An internal memo to FDR indicated the meetings were used to wield the patronage weapon:

> 1. Senator Richard M. Russell.—4:10 P.M. Marion Allen, his closest friend. [The senator] wants him appointed Collector of Internal Revenue, now held up because of Senator George's opposition. Needs general buttering up. Might discuss possibility of making him sole patronage approver [in Georgia].
>
> 2. Senator [Prentiss M.] Brown of Michigan.—4:40 P.M. I understand he is desirous of coming along, but needs to be strengthened, and I think a general discussion on the Party's future and a feeling that you were personally putting it up to him to be one of your lieutenants would do the trick. Also enclosed, some of his campaign remarks.[132]

An informal House poll conducted by Charles West and Representative Fred Vinson (D.-Ky.) resulted in a majority for the bill,

---

the first president's son to hold such a job since Andrew Jackson employed his foster son Andrew Jackson Donelson. *Time,* January 11, 1937, 1.

[131] Keenan to Cummings, February 9, 1937, Box 200, Cummings Papers, ALDL.

[132] Undated and unsigned memo to FDR, Box 38, James Roosevelt Papers, FDRL.

with indications that it could be brought up to two-thirds "by more extreme forms of pressure."[133] Some freshman Democrats who had ridden into office on FDR's coattails in 1936 were openly opposed or noncommittal. Balking on the first major legislative initiative of the president's second term indicated widening cracks in the party. Southern Democrats, though slow in making their opposition known, included many conservatives and some moderates who were preparing to bolt. Roosevelt's policies on deficit spending for relief, as well as his handling (or mishandling) of the sit-down strikes then plaguing industry, were unpopular with southern senators. Garner disagreed with FDR on these policies, as did influential senators like Pat Harrison of Mississippi and James F. Byrnes of South Carolina. They were no longer willing to do any heavy lifting for FDR on his court-packing bill.[134]

In mid-February, Treasury Secretary Morgenthau told Roosevelt he gave his court plan no more than a fifty-fifty chance of passing the Senate.[135] Eighteen Senate Democrats held dinner meetings periodically at the Maryland home of Millard Tydings and acted as a tightly knit steering committee directing the opposition forces. The group included Wheeler, George, Van Nuys, Burke, Gerry, Bailey, Clark, Connally, King, McKellar, and Copeland.[136]

A Senate poll taken on February 19 showed roughly thirty senators definitely committed to the bill, another thirty opposed, and thirty-four undecided, with one seat vacant. All but two of the undecideds were Democrats. Roosevelt still had two tactical advantages: his personal popularity and the widespread belief that something had to be done to break the judicial logjam and solve the Supreme Court problem. The president's bill was the only plan before them. Over the long run it would be wavering Democrats—eager to avoid committing themselves on such an unpopu-

---

[133] Alsop and Catledge, *The 168 Days,* 92; Robert J. Steamer, *The Supreme Court in Crisis: A History of Conflict* (Amherst: University of Massachusetts Press, 1971), 211. The author states that "an informal poll taken on February 19 showed that a majority of 100 House members supported the president's bill."

[134] Alsop and Catledge, *The 168 Days,* 130–32.

[135] Leonard Baker, *Back to Back,* 47.

[136] Alsop and Catledge, *The 168 Days,* 103–4.

lar issue but anxious to resolve the problem and avoid a schism—who would hold the balance of power.

Opponents of the plan had strategic advantages of cohesion and unity of direction which the administration's supporters lacked. The White House general staff harbored sharp internal divisions over policy. Cummings and Roosevelt tried to maintain the indirect approach they had devised to divert attention from court-packing. Cummings stubbornly insisted on following his bypath that spoke of crowded court dockets, delays, the need for more judges, and the volume of *certiorari* petitions denied by the Supreme Court.

Corcoran, Cohen, and Jackson, picking up on the argument Richberg and Reed had made prior to the plan's unveiling, tried to induce Roosevelt to take a more direct approach and attack the Court's narrow reading of the Constitution's commerce and due process clauses. The president, they said, should have the courage to acknowledge his real objective and stand behind his reason for court-packing: obstruction by an intransigent Court majority. With the opposition winning popular support, they wanted him to put the emphasis where it belonged, on the Supreme Court features of the bill, its primary purpose. They warned all would be lost if Roosevelt continued to follow the strategy he and Cummings laid out. Roosevelt balked.

Speakers on both sides of the court issue frequently took to the airwaves. Cummings delivered a major address on February 14.[137] Reaction to his message was largely negative, if not hostile. Ickes wrote: "The Attorney General went on the air Monday night . . . on behalf of the Court program. He made a pretty good speech, but I did not think it was particularly telling."[138] Cummings's mail was by and large unfavorable. A Connecticut man wrote:

---

[137] *New York Times,* February 15, 1937. A copy of the address, "The President's Proposals for Judicial Reorganization," February 14, 1937, is in Box 200, Cummings Papers, ALDL, along with a fourteen-point analysis of the criticisms the bill elicited. Excerpts are in Swisher, ed., *Selected Papers,* 149–52. The speech, broadcast over WABC, was recorded by Audio-Scriptions, Inc. on four aluminum double-faced discs that could be played on any phonograph.

[138] *Secret Diary,* 2:75.

> I heard your speech . . . and to me it seemed a little far-fetched. It is what lawyers call poorly prepared. You tried to make a case, but like some of the Government cases that went before the Supreme Court, you could not put it across. If you think the average man who reads the papers and who does some thinking is behind the President's plan, you are badly mistaken. I know of no measure that has been so widely and adversely discussed than this attempt to expand the Court with a lot of hand-picked justices. It may go through, but I doubt it.[139]

Comparing Cummings's speech to Wheeler's radio talk of March 10, a citizen from Damascus, Ohio, wrote: "I listened last evening to the speech by Hon. B. K. Wheeler, and I thought what a difference between it and the one you made. You echoed Parrot-like what your master wanted you to say. You try misrepresentation and subterfuge to accomplish what WE THE PEOPLE will not NOW or any other time submit to—the packing of the Court. You know as Attorney General that the way you are trying to change the Court is not the American Way. If you do know it, you are not fit to hold this position."[140] A Brooklyn man echoed similar sentiments: "How does it feel to be Roosevelt's stooge?"[141]

From Milwaukee came this condemnation: "Your feeble effort to justify the expansion of the Supreme Court was indeed childish and unworthy of a man occupying the position of trust that you do. How some of you asses attain the heights in public life . . . is a mystery to the average layman. But politics is politics. While senility is quite apparent, one must give you credit for knowing on what side of the bread to spread the butter. Your chieftain has you under superb control. Your exit will be awaited with pleasure."[142]

Reports of the speech in the press were equally harsh. David Lawrence expressed shock over Cummings's admission that the

---

[139] T. G. Bracken to Cummings, February 16, 1937, Box 199, Cummings Papers, ALDL.

[140] R. B. Watters to Cummings, March 11, 1937, ibid. A transcript of Wheeler's speech is in Box 16, folder 7, Wheeler Papers, MHS.

[141] James B. Andrews to Cummings, March 11, 1937, Cummings Papers, ALDL.

[142] The letter, signed "Mystified," was dated March 11, 1937, ibid.

real purpose of the plan was to pack the Court.[143] It was unjust to Progressives who opposed the plan, he wrote, to use such pejorative terms as "hysterical voices" and "insensate clamor." It was hitting below the belt to make the justices resign if they didn't want the Court's size increased. Cummings's speech was characterized as insulting and offensive, and his argument on "immorality" was termed "deplorable." A *Washington Star* editorial accused him of betraying his position as the nation's nonpartisan chief law officer by his "special pleading for a measure to make it possible to sustain unconstitutional laws." The unfriendly *Washington Post* charged that "like his chief, he has no regard for the American system of government," tossing the amendment process aside and rendering the system of checks and balances inoperative.[144]

Carter Glass attacked both the speech and the speaker: "The country is in infinitely greater need of an Attorney General than of additional judges on the Supreme Court." He told reporters that the speech was "the most evasive, disingenuous and misleading statement that he had ever read on any grave public problem." Glass characterized the six prospective new appointments as "judicial wet nurses for six of the present members of the Court." A former law partner told Harold Stephens: "The bar is criticizing Cummings severely for his complete change of front and for the irreconcilable inconsistencies between what he said in his Annual Report of 1936 and what he said in the letter which he gave the President for publication."[145]

Cummings, on a golfing vacation in the South, was slated to make another speech on March 8 at the *Washington Evening Star* forum. He planned to expand on earlier criticisms of the bar for

---

[143] *Baltimore Sun,* February 16, 1937, ibid.

[144] *New York Herald Tribune,* February 16, 1937; editorial in *Washington Post,* February 16, 1937; *Washington Star,* February 17, 1937; all in ibid.

[145] List of Criticisms of Speech by Attorney General Cummings, February 15, 1937, Box 200, Cummings Papers, ALDL; Senator Carter Glass, who was seriously ill, rose from a sick bed later to deliver a radio address broadcast nationwide on March 29, 1937, entitled "Constitutional Immorality." On Glass's speech, see Rixey Smith and Norman Beasley, *Carter Glass: A Biography* (New York: Longman's, Green, 1939), 374–79. The full text of the speech is on 496–510. See also, on Cummings's address, Monte Appel to Harold Stephens, February 18, 1937, Box 29, Stephens Papers, LC.

failing to support liberal legislation. The Justice Department's Henry Suydam, deputy to Solicitor General Reed, wired him suggesting that the forum would be an inappropriate venue for him to renew his earlier remarks.

> You would appear to be aligning yourself with the National Lawyer's Guild [an offshoot of dissenting lawyers] in its dispute with the American Bar Association and . . . against the background of your radio speech of February 14 on Court reform, you might be exposed first to the criticism of having attacked the Court, and second of having attacked the Bar. I am afraid that all sorts of implications would be read into such a speech in view of the Court issue being so hot and of Senate hearings starting the morning after your broadcast.[146]

Suydam wanted him to cancel the speech or select a less controversial subject such as prison reform. Cummings wired back, agreeing to postpone the speech: "A colorless address at this time worse than useless."[147] Lawyers in the Justice Department feared that the attorney general's public utterances were proving more of a liability than an asset to the debate.

Throughout February the president remained silent, waiting for his opponents to talk themselves out. Then, he said, he would move in, make a few speeches, and carry the day. But the delay was a costly mistake. The opposition had time to consolidate and strengthen its position. Aides pleaded with Roosevelt to make a move, but he refused, allowing the situation to worsen. He finally was forced to abandon the old strategy for a new battle plan.[148]

When Cummings returned to Washington, he found to his chagrin that the indirection he and FDR favored had been put aside. During his absence Corcoran and Cohen had undermined his position and his "intimate" rapport with Roosevelt. They held him responsible for getting them into the mess in which they now found themselves. Jealousies and suspicions swirled around Roosevelt's inner circle, poisoning relations among members of his

---

[146] February 25, 1937, Suydam Files, Box 79, NA. A public announcement gave the opening date of the hearings as March 9, 1937, but they were postponed one more day on account of Roosevelt's scheduled fireside chat.

[147] February 26, 1937, ibid.

[148] Alsop and Catledge, *The 168 Days,* 107–10.

team even before the battle with the Supreme Court had advanced beyond the first month.[149]

Hatton Sumners's judiciary retirement bill, having passed the House without amendment, went to the Senate, where it was approved on February 26. It became law on March 1. Under it a justice of the Supreme Court, instead of resigning, could retain his office but retire from active service. This measure is considered one of the oddest sideshows in the entire history of the Supreme Court fight. It had been offered in a previous session of Congress, when Sumners saw the probability that the Court would run into trouble. Sounding out the situation in 1936, he learned that Justices Sutherland and Van Devanter were considering retiring, but uncertainty about salary provisions for justices was holding them back. Although full pensions until death were already in effect, they had reason to fear that Congress might again impose the salary cuts Justice Holmes and others had to take under the Economy Act of 1933. They did not want to become subject to the income tax, and would have done so under existing law with loss of their judicial status.[150] Sumners designed a bill preserving their judicial status, establishing the new category of "retired justice," which retained certain minor judicial functions. If they retired, as opposed to resigning, they would in a sense still be members of the Court; thus their compensation could not be reduced by law, nor would they be subject to the income tax.

This earlier bill sailed through committee and on to the House floor, only to have this delicately conceived plan upset by a filibuster led by Sumners's fellow Texan, Tom Blanton, who insisted that no man, *not even a Supreme Court justice,* deserved

[149] Ibid., 109.

[150] The Supreme Court in *Miles v. Graham,* 268 U.S. 501 (1925), held that income taxation of a federal judicial salary was an unconstitutional diminution of compensation. The case was argued shortly after Justice Stone went on the Court. He joined Holmes and Brandeis in voting against the immunity of the judges' salary from income tax. Holmes and Stone decided not to record a dissent. The same principle had been laid down in *Evans v. Gore,* 253 U.S. 245 (1920). Stone later came to regret his action in *Miles v. Graham;* it put him, he said, on record as being in support of the majority decision. Mason, *Stone,* 790 n.

more than his own annual honorarium of $10,000. That left the matter unresolved at the end of 1936. Sumners revived his bill in January 1937, hoping to get it through both houses with the retirements over and done with before Roosevelt could make his move. But it was just a little too late to head off FDR's plan introduced on February 5, a very different kind of measure for retiring justices.[151]

In a House speech, Sumners said that Supreme Court justices electing to retire would be cooperating with their government. No justice need fear any loss of respect if he were to retire.[152] He was responding to remarks by Senators Hiram Johnson and Edward Burke, who, during a debate on February 26, charged the administration with trying to lure justices from the bench. Johnson declared: "Any Supreme Court Justice who would retire at this particular time would not be the sort of individual for whom I would have the greatest respect,"[153] and Burke expressed similar sentiments, only in more bitter terms. Under prodding from Senator Robinson, Johnson added: "When the Justices are sought to be removed in another way, if any one of them should seek retirement by virtue of the bait that is being held out to them, I would have very little respect for him." He said he favored passage of Sumners's bill, but "not at this particular time." A bewildered Robinson wrote Raymond Robbins: "One of the strange complications pertaining to this subject is found in the position taken by the so-called progressive bloc in the Senate."[154]

Roosevelt was always happy when he found himself in a good fight. "What a grand fight it is going to be!" he told his friend

---

[151] Alsop and Catledge, *The 168 Days,* 40–41.

[152] Draft of speech, March 2, 1937; cf. clipping in *Austin American,* March 3, 1937, OF 41, Box 2, FDRL.

[153] *Congressional Record,* February 26, 1937, 75th Cong., 1st Sess., Part 1, 1644. Johnson said he would support retirement of any justice when there was no bait held out to him, no lure in any law that was enacted, and when he could retire without any suggestion of being driven off the bench by other legislation. Senator Pat McCarran of Nevada pointed out that if the bill they were then dealing with had been a law during the past ten or fifteen years, "in all probability the atmosphere which the able Senator from California speaks of would not exist at all." He chided Johnson for putting something into the measure that did not belong there. Ibid., 1645.

[154] February 27, 1937, Robinson Papers, UAL.

George Creel. "We need everything we have got to put in it."[155] The editors of a liberal journal wrote: "The President is having the fight of his life on the Supreme Court issue and from all evidence—the time of his life."[156] The barrage trained on his proposal from almost all quarters brought out submerged character traits in him—belligerency, stubbornness, and vengefulness. As any good commander might do in the midst of a battle, he and the general staff finally decided it was time to bring up the heavy artillery. He endorsed Sumners's bill. Some newshawks erroneously credited FDR with masterminding the strategy that produced the bill, as the first phase in a more comprehensive court plan. However, Sumners's bill was his own, and was designed to undercut any need for FDR's court bill.

Yet to come were two major public addresses Roosevelt, with his aides, was preparing for March 4 and 9. They would be followed by Senate Judiciary Committee hearings. Almost daily the president's men threw up to him the precarious state of New Deal measures, as if to underscore their argument that unless the Supreme Court entrenchments were blasted out, the entire future of his second administration's legislative program was imperiled.

---

155 Quoted in Burns, *Roosevelt,* 298.

156 Editorial, "Is It to Be Buchanan?" *New Republic,* March 6, 1937, 255.

10

Some Bad Miscalculations

> Intoxicated with success, Roosevelt . . . attacked a venerable American institution. Overly sure of himself, he had made mistake after careless mistake. His potency had gone to his head. Learned pundits quoted Lord Acton: Power tends to corrupt, and absolute power corrupts absolutely.
>
> James MacGregor Burns[1]

AFTER PUBLIC ANNOUNCEMENT of the president's court bill, it was attacked and harshly criticized from all quarters. Within weeks it was encountering rough sledding. Prominent public figures who spoke for it over the airwaves included Senator Robert La Follette, Jr.,[2] followed in mid-February by Homer Cummings and Senator Sherman Minton (D.-Ind.). Although it was still official administration policy to adhere to the efficiency approach in Roosevelt's message to shift attention away from court-packing, Democratic spokesmen began making direct attacks on the Court for invalidating New Deal legislation. They asked their listeners to deluge Congress with telegrams and letters to offset the many thousands received by lawmakers from citizens who opposed FDR's sweeping plan to reshape the Supreme Court "with more liberal-minded men."

In mid-February a staff writer for the *New York Times*'s Washington Bureau reported: "Conservative Democrats . . . especially those in the Senate, gagged at the [court] proposals. . . . Many of them maintained a prudent silence, waiting to see how the cat

---

[1] *Roosevelt,* 313.

[2] For excerpts from La Follette's NBC radio address of February 13, 1937, see *Vital Speeches of the Day,* 2:312–13. The full text is in the Jerome Frank Papers, SL.

of public opinion would jump."[3] Two days later the same paper noted:

> On the showing of informal polls that the Administration's judiciary reform bill may hang on the decision of less than a dozen senators, President Roosevelt and the forces identified with him, particularly organized labor, intensified their efforts to insure its passage as a prerequisite to further New Deal legislation. . . . The opposition strategists in the Senate were . . . making preparations for one of the stiffest legislative battles of recent years. They were making no particular effort to dig into the dwindling reservoir of unpledged senators, leaving that to the weight of the letters and telegrams still coming in from all parts of the country.[4]

The controversy became so heated that the American Institute of Public Opinion, which had accurately forecast the 1936 election results, decided to conduct an extended series of polls. Movement on the court issue was tracked chiefly by this institute, the brainchild of George Gallup. Polls on February 8 and 15 gave the plan a 47 percent approval rating. Thereafter, weekly opinion samplings were divided equally—45 percent for or against and 10 percent undecided.[5] Analysis of the ballots revealed that some sentiment for court reform derived from a tendency to follow Roosevelt's leadership, regardless of the legislation proposed. Writing Senator Borah, Representative D. Worth Clark of Idaho confirmed this: "Frankly, I think at the moment the rank and file of our Idaho people are in favor of the President's plan. The man in the street does little thinking on the subject, and is for whatever the President is for."[6]

An informal poll of senators, taken around the same time, indicated that thirty-two favored the proposal, twenty-eight were opposed, with thirty-five uncommitted. Ninety percent of the public

[3] *New York Times,* February 17, 1937.

[4] Ibid., February 19, 1937.

[5] These figures are from a Gallup poll for the week of February 15, 1937. Frank V. Cantwell, "Public Opinion and the Legislative Process," *American Political Science Review* 40 (October 1946): 926.

[6] February 24, 1937, William E. Borah Papers, LC. In the ballots referred to (nos. 68, 69, and 72) the "No Opinion" tally was 11 percent, 10 percent, and 9 percent, respectively. Burns agrees that there was a solid core of New Dealers and a group of senators who went along with the bill, largely out of personal loyalty to the president. See his *Roosevelt,* 301.

was on record, while only 63 percent of senators took a definite stand. The president, convinced he had a popular mandate, wanted the pressure of public opinion to push his proposal through, but the expected public support was not forthcoming. As sentiment became increasingly hostile, a handful of senators sat on the fence, watching public opinion swing behind the opposition.

The next stage in the battle—what two journalists called "trench warfare"[7]—began on February 19 when debate on the bill opened in the Senate. Chairman Ashurst of the Judiciary Committee, mindful of his previous public statement in the campaign ridiculing the idea that the president would dare to enlarge the Supreme Court, said: "The man who attempts to be consistent in his public service may end up consistent indeed, but may never accomplish anything else."[8] In the opening debate, administration spokesmen went on the attack. McKellar and Minton repeatedly took to the floor to savage the opposition, including the Supreme Court justices. Replying two weeks later to Senator Wheeler, Governor Phillip La Follette of Wisconsin acknowledged: "Of course the President's proposal will affect the decisions of the Supreme Court. It was intended to do exactly that."[9]

Conflicting signals emerged from the Roosevelt camp. His supporters were advised not to rush the bill through after all. "Think things over," FDR told invited visitors.[10] Conferring with a steady stream of dissenters, he sought to woo them with flattery and soft words. There was less blustering or browbeating; the new strategy was aimed at letting matters "settle down and simmer for awhile." The lull would allow him "to work on doubtful senators." But his monthlong public silence permitted opponents to recruit new support, solidify ranks, and harden their resolve. As Farley noted, they made the most of this opportunity, and it was certainly good politics.[11]

Every senator, newspaper correspondent, and strategy adviser

---

[7] Alsop and Catledge, *The 168 Days,* 106.

[8] *Congressional Record,* 75th Cong., 1st Sess., Part 1, February 19, 1937, Vol. 81:1411.

[9] *Christian Science Monitor,* March 2, 1937.

[10] Ibid., February 17, 1937.

[11] *Jim Farley's Story,* 77; Alsop and Catledge, *The 168 Days,* 109.

had his own set of figures showing the current lineup on the issue. An opposition Democrat told Borah that there were already forty-two against the bill.[12] Data from another source had 37 percent against and 40 percent for. Of the 19 percent undecided, 48 percent were against, 46 percent were in favor, and the rest were determined fence-sitters.[13]

Despite the breadth and intensity of the opposition, Roosevelt seemed confident, although Farley later recounted that he was tormented by doubts. When George Creel told him the battle was lost, FDR angrily produced a Corcoran poll to prove him wrong. Looking it over, Creel found among the list of supporters at least ten senators whom he knew to be against the bill. "But he [FDR] again insisted that I did not know what I was talking about. . . . He exuded the confidence that had its base in a conviction of indisputable power."[14] William Allen White suggested to Senator Arthur Capper (R.-Kans.) that a group of progressives get together to fight the court bill. There was no apparent necessity for such action, Capper replied. He said he was sure "the bill was already licked, although it may yet be modified or a constitutional amendment may be submitted."[15]

During the critical weeks of March, popular support for the court plan began slowly but steadily to ebb, and White House strategists became alarmed. They were too well aware of the fallout from FDR's adroit attempt to conceal his motives, playing false with the people. In letters to friends, Robert Jackson said the Cummings-Roosevelt court proposal seemed "in many respects unsatisfactory." It did not deal with the main problem, the kind of decisions that the Court had been making. He supported the bill as a means to counter the views of conservative justices, who, "while honest enough, are entirely closed to any argument that this age may advance as to constitutional interpretation. . . . I think . . . they are creating some damn bad precedents which will plague us for years."[16]

---

[12] Borah to W. A. White, February 24, 1937, White Papers, LC.

[13] *Christian Science Monitor,* February 25, 1937. The poll was taken on February 23, 1937.

[14] *Rebel at Large,* 294.

[15] February 26, 1937, White Papers, LC.

[16] Jackson to John G. Curtis, February 22, 1937, Box 79, Jackson Papers, LC.

Alone among the inner circle, Jackson had the courage to disagree openly with FDR on more than one point. Expressing his concerns, he wrote the president: "I have returned from some time among the plain people and regret to report to you that, in my opinion, support is not increasing for your court reform but rather decreasing. This, I think, is distinctly due to the terms in which the problem is approached." He thought the public could not be expected to understand the significance of *certiorari* denied. "To begin with they do not even know what certiorari is, and in the second place, they believe the courts review too many cases anyway."[17] Nor could they comprehend calendar congestion. Alluding to Cummings's letter, he added: "Nobody ever yet went into a fight with a set of statistics." Instead of talking about cases the Court would not take, he urged, "let us talk about the cases they did take—how they have gone out of their way in the Railroad Retirement Board case to prohibit Congress from ever enacting a [pension] law . . . according to the Chief Justice's dissenting opinion." He believed the people would support the proposal if they understood that "this is a fight to make the court a contemporary and nonpartisan institution."[18]

Slow to react, or to admit he was capable of making a major blunder, Roosevelt finally had to abandon once and for all the duplicitous stratagem in his message in favor of a blunt, hard-hitting attack on the decisions of the Supreme Court. Jackson is credited with encouraging a more straightforward approach. He made his case directly to the president and Stanley Reed at a luncheon on February 25, a meeting arranged to get agreement on his appearance as a witness at the hearings. Jackson outlined his disagreement with the "old-age and overworked judges" rationale and served notice that he intended to testify on the real reason for the bill.

Roosevelt was urged to end his silence and speak out about the need for this legislation. "Knowing that I had an appointment," Jackson wrote, "Thomas Corcoran and Mr. Oliphant urged me to impress upon him [FDR] the necessity of speaking at once. I waded into it and told him I was afraid public sentiment would

[17] Jackson to FDR, February 22, 1937, Box 29 (now 79), ibid.
[18] Ibid.

form against him in his absence [during a two-week Warm Springs vacation]. . . . I pointed out that his original message did very little to arm . . . [supporters] for a discussion." The president made no commitment, but within days a fireside chat was announced by the White House for March 9.[19]

After meeting with FDR, Jackson joined the general staff to help orchestrate the change in tactics.[20] He feared that "sentiment against the bill would crystalize unless Roosevelt spoke out," and if his speech were to have any influence, it had to be delivered promptly. There were already indications that sentiment was solidifying against the plan. The most powerful weapon in their arsenal—a direct appeal by the president—was needed. Changes in strategy called for an administration endorsement of labor's Non-Partisan League at a rally on March 8, an extensive trip through the South by Farley to drum up support for the judicial program, and a direct attack on the Court's opinions by Jackson in the Senate hearings.[21]

Early drafts of the Victory Dinner address had to be scrapped. Corcoran, Rosenman, Richberg, and Cohen went to work on a speech dealing with the "real mischief," the decisions which, as a studied and continued policy, had been coming from the Supreme Court over the past three years.[22] The original court plan's rationale, masquerading as judiciary reform, lasted little more than a few weeks. Within a month of its announcement, Roosevelt went before the public and made a complete about-face, talking earnestly, at times belligerently, about the dire need to change the direction of Supreme Court decision making. The surge of protest had had its effect—stripping his proposal of its "efficiency" facade and showing it for what it was, an attempt to pack the Court.

---

[19] Stephen R. Alton, "Loyal Lieutenant, Able Advocate: The Role of Robert H. Jackson in Franklin D. Roosevelt's Battle with the Supreme Court," *William and Mary Bill of Rights Journal* 5 (Summer 1997): 563. Alton cites Jackson's unpublished Autobiography, 115–17, which is in Box 188 of the Jackson Papers, LC.

[20] MacColl, "Supreme Court and Public Opinion," 212–13.

[21] *New York Times,* March 8, 1937.

[22] *PPA,* 1937 volume, lxv. Jackson was one of several aides who contributed suggestions for the March 9 speech. Autobiography, 117, cited in Alton, "Loyal Lieutenant," 564.

The Democratic Victory Dinner

On March 4, Washington's Mayflower Hotel was the scene of the main dinner at which FDR was the speaker. The resplendent gala was a $100-a-plate affair, $95 of which went to the Democratic National Committee to help pay off the party debt. Before thirteen hundred Democrats, Roosevelt delivered the "fighting speech" prescribed by his strategy group. An estimated 500,000 attended similar affairs in eleven hundred cities across the country.[23] They were attended by party bigwigs, state and local officeholders, would-be officeholders, lobbyists (who could write off the tab on expense accounts), dignitaries of one sort or another summoned by special invitation, and nobodies, whose sense of importance was somehow enhanced by attending. The throng of notables included Walter P. Chrysler, AFL president William Green, Frances Perkins, and Madam Director of the Mint Nellie T. Ross.[24] The latter two were among the few female guests: most Democrats were unwilling to pay $100 to feed their wives.[25]

At Newark, New Jersey, the guest speaker was Hugh Johnson. He caught the spirit of the occasion, declaring that the dinners were backed by a big enough election triumph to justify "serving stewed elephants as a main course." The Mayflower diners ate their way through terrapin soup, pompano, breast of capon, and *nougat quarante six* (Maine and Vermont excluded).[26] When the levity and rattle of china ceased, the diners abandoned their whistling and convivial war whoops to settle down to hear what Roosevelt had to say. They heard for the first time an admission of the real reason for his court bill.

He spoke of a "distinguished member of Congress" who had visited him about national problems in general and the judiciary

---

[23] Roosevelt's address was beamed to all the other dinners that evening over a telephone link.

[24] Missouri-born Nellie Taylor Ross, after having succeeded her husband as the elected governor of Wyoming (1925–27), served as vice chairperson of the Democratic National Committee in 1928 and vigorously supported Roosevelt in 1932. He appointed her in 1933 director of the mint, a position she held until 1952.

[25] *Time,* March 15, 1937, 14.

[26] Ibid.

in particular. Roosevelt told him he had a great ambition in life. By no means was he satisfied with having twice been elected president with large majorities. By this time, he said, his visitor was "sitting on the edge of his chair," expecting announcement of a third term from his own lips. Roosevelt then repeated what he had said in a recent interview: "I do not want to leave it [the nation] to my successor [on January 20, 1941] in the condition in which Buchanan left it to Lincoln."[27] He enjoyed playing this game of "cat and mouse" about his aspirations for a third term. Some, however, were not easily fooled. Later that month, Senator Minton described this encounter with Roosevelt's Oyster Bay relative:

> My dear Mr. President:
>
> At supper last night I had the pleasure of sitting beside your "adoring" Cousin Alice [Longworth]—She has you measured already for your shirt—brown sleeves, black body and red tail. Notwithstanding her confidence in her ability to forecast your future action because of her knowledge of your character I bet her forty to ten you would not be a candidate or be drafted in 1940. Now I don't mind losing my senatorial toga or my political life following you, but I can't afford to lose forty dollars—so don't run out on me.[28]

The senator—a future Supreme Court justice—lost the bet as well as his toga.

Trying to justify his proposal, Roosevelt complained about how impossible it was to ensure the success of American democracy with an obstructionist Court, which he compared to one of three horses pulling the national plow: "If three well matched horses are put to the task of plowing up a field where the going is heavy, and the team of three pull as one, the field will be plowed. If one horse lies down in the traces or plunges off in another direction, the field will not be plowed."[29]

He condemned the justices' use of legal technicalities to veto

---

[27] *PPA,* 1937 volume, 115. FDR gave Krock this exclusive interview. *New York Times Magazine,* February 28, 1937, 1. The backlash from other journalists created embarrassment for both FDR and Krock, not to mention Steve Early.

[28] March 22, 1937, PSF 188, FDRL.

[29] *PPA,* 1937 volume, 115.

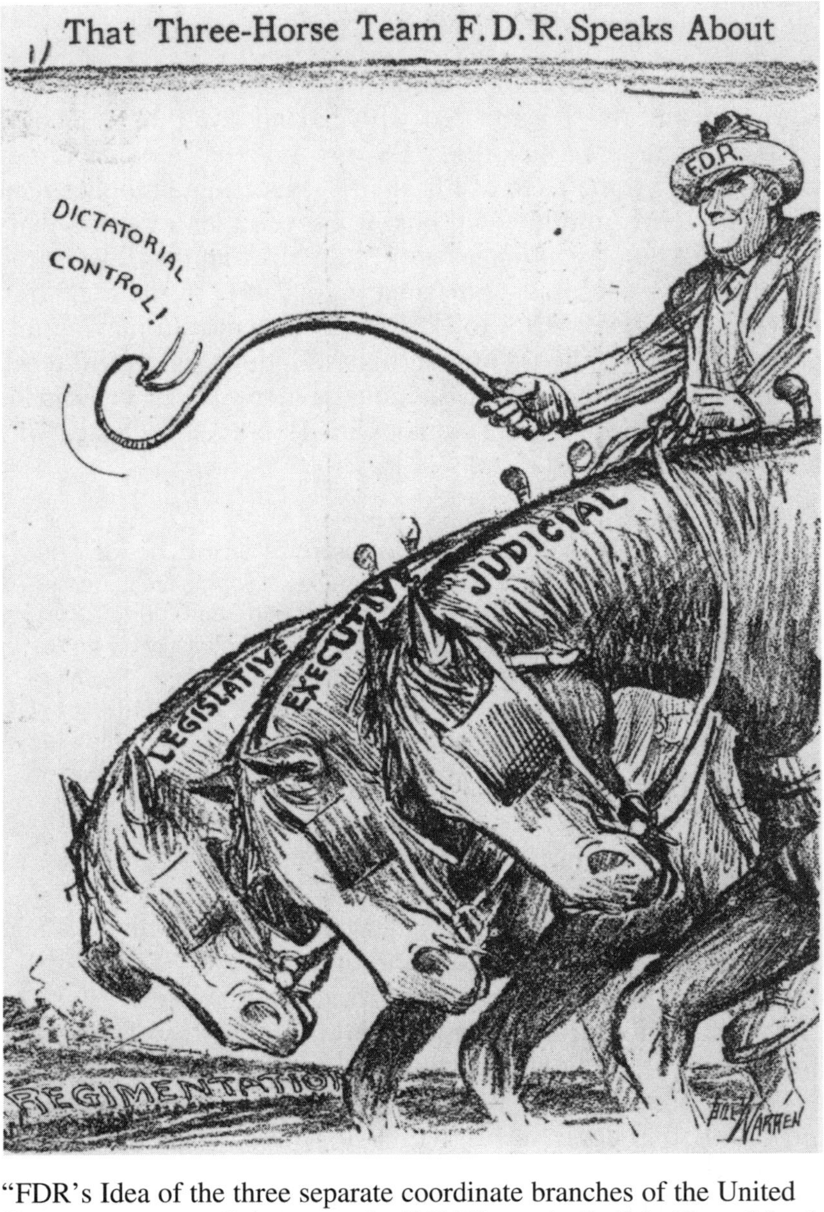

"FDR's Idea of the three separate coordinate branches of the United States government." A cartoon by Bill Warren in *Buffalo News,* March 12, 1937.

key measures such as the AAA. "Neither individually nor as a party can we postpone and run from that fight on the advice of defeatist [Liberty League] lawyers. But I defy anyone to read the majority opinion invalidating the A.A.A. and tell us *what* we can do for agriculture in this session of the Congress with any reasonable certainty that what we do will not be nullified as unconstitutional."[30] He wanted complete partisan loyalty on his bill, warning that if the party could not move along with the times and peoples' needs, it would die as had the Ice Age animals. Despite all the cheers and thunderous applause, there was no assurance that all Democrats were willing to heed his warning.[31]

Roosevelt reminded his listeners of how the administration had made efforts to raise wages, reduce hours of labor, abolish child labor, and eliminate unfair trade practices. "And what happened?" he asked. "You know who assumed the power to veto, and did veto that program." In attempts to extend the Tennessee Valley project to the Ohio and other valleys, he complained, the lower courts had not hesitated to paralyze its operations by sweeping injunctions. "The Ohio River and the Dust Bowl are not conversant with the habits of the Interstate Commerce Clause. But we shall never be safe . . . until we have somehow made the Interstate Commerce Clause conversant with the habits of the Ohio River and the Dust Bowl."[32] The Court majority rendered the states as powerless as the federal government to touch the problem of hours and wages. It pleased the "personal economic predilections" of a majority, he charged, that "we live in a Nation where there is no legal power anywhere to deal with its most difficult practical problems—a No Man's Land of final futility."[33] Reviewing judicial vetoes of New Deal measures, he accused the Court of usurping legislative power.

FDR ended by calling for immediate action on his court bill. "If we would keep faith with those who had faith in us, if we would make democracy succeed, I say we must act—NOW!" It was a good pragmatic formula that could lead almost anywhere. Four years earlier, following his first inaugural, it had led to the

[30] Ibid., 117.
[31] Ickes, *Secret Diary,* March 6, 1937, 2:88–89.
[32] Ibid., 119.
[33] Ibid., 118.

NRA. In 1937, the people were left with no idea where it would lead over the next four years.

In Judge Rosenman's opinion, "the Victory Dinner speech did not win the popular support for his [court] plan that the President expected." The backing he sought to arouse in this speech and the one to follow lacked stability and depth. It simply disintegrated as the long fight wore on. His advisers overestimated FDR's powers of persuasion with the public.[34] A Gallup poll measuring the speech's impact indicated that opponents of the bill dropped from 48 to 47 percent, while those in favor of it climbed slightly from a low of 41 percent. But closing a margin of seven or eight percentage points would prove illusory.

Press reaction to the speech was mainly hostile, although not as savage as that to the court bill itself.[35] The *Christian Science Monitor* found no evidence that it had any appreciable effect on senators, except to stir the wrath of opponents. On the Senate floor, Wheeler declared: "I regret that the President had to influence the passions of the people with the implications that the Supreme Court was to blame for the 'Dust Bowl' and Ohio floods."[36] The *St. Louis Post-Dispatch* called the address "a savage attack on one of the three coordinate branches of the government."[37] The *Nation* considered FDR's recent interview with Arthur Krock a more serious discussion, more carefully reasoned than the Victory Dinner speech. Its militancy lent fuel to the charge that he would brook no interference with his court plan. "The President spoke like a man with his back against the wall—like one of those incredible cavaliers out of [Alexander] Dumas—as a swordsman . . . trapped and surrounded by the mercenaries of his enemies."[38]

New Yorker magazine refuted a claim that the court plan's opponents were the same crowd as those opposed to the New Deal. "This is balderdash. The opposition to his plan to bring the judi-

---

[34] *Working with Roosevelt,* 158; Burns, *Roosevelt,* 302.

[35] Burns, *Roosevelt,* 299–300; Alsop and Catledge, *The 168 Days,* 71–72.

[36] *Christian Science Monitor,* March 8, 1937.

[37] Quoted in ibid.

[38] "Roosevelt on the Radio," *Nation* 140 (March 13, 1937), 284; Krock interview, *New York Times Magazine,* February 28, 1937, 1.

ciary into line is from people who care not about property . . . or profits, and their old Lincoln limousines, but who care about their freedom from authority. . . . Mr. Roosevelt has turned into an Eagle Scout whose passion for doing a good turn every day has at last got out of hand."[39]

New Dealers were dismayed by the failure of the speech to "catch fire." Neither Roosevelt's remarks nor his mellifluous radio voice could convince the public of his court program's urgency, nor did it put to rest talk of his craftiness and the intention to establish a dictatorship by indirection. Listeners questioned his sincerity. After Senator McAdoo spoke over CBS on March 5 in support of the court bill, he was bombarded with letters from irate constituents. One wrote:

> Speaking of Mr. Roosevelt, you close your speech by saying: "He can be trusted to use the power of his great office for the advancement of democracy and for the welfare of the people of the United States." I do not think he can be trusted. We have never had another President whose oath of office was so shredded and tattered as his and whose word was so little respected by friend and foe alike. If Grover Cleveland were President he could and would be trusted as an honest man. He might be mistaken—as he was regarding the tariff—but his honesty was never questioned to my knowledge. Such is not the case now.
>
> Mr. Roosevelt has admitted—since you made your speech—that his purpose in enlarging the Supreme Court is to put men there who will see as he sees regarding his New Deal policies. By their help he intends to amend or abrogate the Constitution and he has ADMITTED IT. Therefore all you say to the contrary falls to the ground.
>
> If you have taken an oath as Senator to preserve, protect and defend the Constitution of the United States you cannot in honor and honesty work for or vote for his bill for its passage and his use of the power it will give him will *destroy* the Constitution. I can't think that you are willing to accompany him down the dark road of history which will judge of this matter upon its merits. Who is he and what is he that he should force you to accept such a fate? Senator McAdoo, I hope you will reconsider your position toward that bill. Let the Supreme Court alone. The labor situation looks

[39] *New Yorker,* March 13, 1937, 11.

> as if it will lead to another civil war. We will need the Court and Constitution then.[40]

Ironically, it had been Senator McAdoo who was one of the earliest and most enthusiastic supporters of enlarging the Supreme Court prior to Roosevelt's first administration. He had planted the idea in Cummings's mind before he held a cabinet post.

Cartoonists had a field day with the reference to the three-horse team. Chief Justice Hughes received a copy of one labeled "an insult to the Supreme Court." A letter to the editor stated:

> Well, Roosevelt's second oath to uphold the Constitution has evidently "gone with the wind," along with his last one. He says in

"A Novel Reaction to the three-horse metaphor." A cartoon by Thomas, *Detroit News,* March 15, 1937.

[40] At the request of Senator Ashurst, McAdoo's radio speech went in the Appendix to the *Congressional Record,* 75th Cong., 1st sess., February 17, 1937, vol. 81. Homer Moore of Bosque Ranch, Santa Barbara, California, to McAdoo, March 1, 1937, is in Box 431, McAdoo Papers, LC.

> effect, "I want to be boss of the Courts just as I am boss of Congress." Now, is what we have down there in Washington a real Congress of men of honor and decency, or just Roosevelt's flea Circus hopping around dizzily at his command?
>
> Norris seems to have taken his slap in the face as an old man unfit mentally and liked it, but [Senators] Glass and Borah have a little more backbone. More power to those men who are still using the brains God gave them instead of borrowing Roosevelt's.[41]

At a Victory Dinner in Raleigh, North Carolina, Senator Millard Tydings (D.-Md.), a bitter foe of the court plan, was the main speaker. Without mentioning Roosevelt, he spoke of Hitler, Mussolini, and undermining a nation's institutions. The inferences were clear to all. His remarks were deeply resented by some of the listeners, including Roosevelt's old boss, former Navy Secretary Josephus Daniels. They were so offended that they began immediately to lay plans for another dinner to offset the effect of Tydings's violent attack. The senator, intending to become a candidate to succeed himself in 1938, could expect no support from the party organization.[42] Before leaving for Warm Springs, FDR told Ickes, who was to deliver the principal speech at the second dinner, to "take Tydings' hide off and rub salt in it." In private, Tydings continued to assert that FDR not only aspired to become a dictator but was working assiduously toward that end.[43]

The Fireside Chat

In view of the importance he attached to his court bill, Roosevelt decided to devote the entire fireside chat of March 9 to it. Like the previous one, this talk would dwell on judicial obstruction as a disease, the court bill as a cure. On each draft Roosevelt made changes, deletions, and additions, working as hard as he had on

[41] Unidentified news clipping, Hughes Papers, LC.

[42] Ickes, *Secret Diary,* March 15, 1937, 2:91, 95–96. Ickes later complained that the *Washington Post* carried only an inch on his Raleigh speech on an inside page. The *Washington Herald* carried nothing at all.

[43] Ibid., 95.

the second inaugural address.[44] He stated his case against the Supreme Court more boldly, but at times he sounded defensive. In this, the first radio address of his second term, he reminded listeners that in 1935 the Court had upheld his gold policy by the narrow margin of five-to-four. The change of only one vote, he said solemnly, "would have thrown all the affairs of this great Nation back into hopeless chaos." He urged that, with the dangers of 1929 again becoming possible, national laws were needed to complete his recovery program in time to avoid another breakdown in the economic system. "The Courts have cast doubts," he charged, "on the ability of the elected Congress to protect us against catastrophe by meeting squarely our modern social and economic conditions."[45]

Returning to an earlier metaphor, he charged that only two of the three-horse team were pulling in unison. "Those who have intimated that the President of the United States is trying to drive that team overlook the simple fact that the President, as Chief Executive, is himself one of the three horses. It is the American people themselves who are in the driver's seat . . . who want the furrow plowed . . . who expect the third horse to pull in unison with the other two."

He accused the Court majority of assuming the power to pass on the wisdom of acts of Congress and to approve or disapprove of the public policy written into these laws.[46] Quoting from Justice Stone's *Butler* dissent, which characterized the majority opinion as "a tortured construction of the Constitution," he mentioned that two other justices (Brandeis and Cardozo) agreed with him. He accused the majority of "reading into the Constitution their own personal economic predilections," and if the legislature were not left free to choose the methods of solving the problems of poverty, subsistence, and health of large numbers of people, government would be rendered impotent. "In the face of these dissenting opinions," he asserted, "there is no basis for the claim made by some members of the Court, that something in the Constitution has compelled them regretfully to thwart the will of

[44] Davis, *New Deal Years,* 73–74.
[45] *PPA,* 1937 volume, 122–23.
[46] Ibid., 124–25.

the people." He added: "It is perfectly clear that as Chief Justice Hughes has said: 'We are under a Constitution, but the Constitution is what the Judges say it is.'"[47]

At last owning up to the real reasons for submitting his court plan, he stated: "We have . . . reached the point as a Nation where we must take action to save the Constitution from the Court, and the Court from itself." He called the Court a "super-legislature" and accused the justices of reading into the Constitution words that were not there and were never intended to be there, amending the Constitution by the arbitrary exercise of their judicial power. They were denying the existence of facts that were universally recognized.

On the age issue he stated it was public policy "to provide for a flow of younger blood into the judiciary"—judges who had "personal experience and contact with modern facts and circumstances under which average men and women have to live and work." It was so much in the public interest to maintain a vigorous judiciary, he said, that he was encouraging the retirement of elderly judges by offering them a life pension at full salary.[48] Why, he asked, leave the fulfillment of this public policy to chance or make it dependent upon the desire or prejudice of any individual judge?

To widespread accusations that he was seeking to "pack" the Court, he responded on a note of rising anger: "If, by that phrase 'packing the Court' it is charged that I wish to place on the bench spineless puppets who would disregard the law of the land, would decide specific cases as I wished them to be decided, I make this answer: that no President fit for his office would appoint, and no Senate of honorable men fit for their office would confirm, that kind of appointees to the Supreme Court."[49] The vehemence in his intonation came over the airwaves.

---

[47] Ibid., 125–26. Cf. Mason, *Stone,* 444.

[48] He seems here to be taking the credit for Sumner's judicial retirement bill. The justices' full salary was $20,000. He might have added mention of complaints he received about the exemption from the income tax, along the lines of a recent telegram message from a concerned citizen: "Federal judicial salaries are exempt from income tax because of the constitutional provision that salaries shall not be 'diminished' during the term of office of a federal judge. . . . The grocery bills of average folks have a tendency to diminish with their salaries." Wesley Disney to FDR, March 6, 1937, OF 41, Box 48, FDRL.

[49] *PPA,* 1937 volume, 129.

By the end of their first term practically every former president had been able to make at least one appointment to the Supreme Court.[50] "Such a succession of appointments," FDR averred, "should have provided a Court well balanced as to age. But chance and the disinclination of individuals to leave the Supreme bench have now given us a Court in which five Justices will be over seventy-five years of age before next June and one over seventy. Thus a sound public policy has been defeated." He proposed in the future to provide by law assurances against an ill-balanced Court, and if such a law established a precedent, it would be a desirable one.

Part of the president's talk outlined his reasons for discarding a constitutional amendment as an approach to the problem. It would take months to ratify, if the wording could be agreed upon, and could then easily be defeated by majorities in the legislatures of thirteen states, where powerful economic and political interests were in control. He concluded:

> Like all lawyers, like all Americans, I regret the necessity of this controversy. But the welfare of the United States, and indeed of the Constitution itself, is what we all must think about first. Our difficulty with the Court today rises not from the Court as an institution but from human beings within it. But we cannot yield our constitutional destiny to the personal judgment of a few men who, being fearful of the future, would envy us the necessary means of dealing with the present.[51]

These fireside chats often drew millions of listeners and were considered one of FDR's most formidable weapons. But in this case the result was different. Any direct attack on the Supreme Court was doomed to fail because from the outset it had been founded on a false premise. The "big lie" in the message of February 5 had done its work. Using old age, overwork, and crowded dockets as reasons for judicial reform fooled no one. This belated admission of the real motive behind his plan exposed Roosevelt to charges of "unvarnished hypocrisy." The frank avowal of the subterfuge came too late.

---

[50] Taft had five appointments, Wilson three, Harding four, Coolidge one, and Hoover three.

[51] *PPA,* 1937 volume, 130.

These two radio addresses revealed a psychological approach common to FDR aimed at stirring up latent public fears. The fireside chat made a direct reference to the "dangers of 1929 . . . again becoming possible" within a year or two, using the worsening economic conditions as a scare tactic. FDR considered this approach one of the basic determinants of public opinion. *New York Times* editor John Finlay asked "Where is the crisis?" and reproduced segments of annual reports submitted by the secretaries of agriculture, commerce, and labor, and by Harry Hopkins, relief czar, none of which made any mention of a crisis. Instead, they gave glowing accounts of the nation's progress toward recovery and stability. "From what source," he asked, "is the pressure so great as not to be able to wait for a constitutional amendment?"[52]

According to John Spargo, FDR's appeal as "a party politician to party politicians" was in poor taste: "That speech, as I wrote him, was deplorable from every point of view. I am confident that he will live to regret his utterance whereby he lowered the great dignity of his office. Nor does it seem to me that it does the President any injustice to prefer the formal message to his 'fireside chats' to the nation by radio."[53] Walter Lippmann ridiculed Roosevelt's abrupt change of strategy: "All his words about one-third of the nation being ill-housed and undernourished . . . is so much hooey." He questioned the propriety of assuring the American people that such deep-seated social ills could be cured in one or two years. "The President's quarrel with the Supreme Court," he added, "has no real relation to the power of the administration to prevent a[nother] crash."[54]

A more favorable report surmised that Roosevelt had no intention of packing the Court with "spineless puppets." "He simply proposed to return the Court to its historic place [in our system of constitutional government] and to save the Constitution from hardening of the arteries."[55] But a California editor argued: "Mr. Roosevelt does not like the hardening of judicial arteries caused by an overdose of his NRA, AAA and other New Deal cocktails.

---

[52] March 10, 1937.
[53] Stephens to John Hessin Clarke, March 24, 1937, Stephens Papers, LC.
[54] *New York Herald Tribune,* March 11, 1937.
[55] *New York Times,* March 10, 1937.

He would like to soften these arteries with an acid dose of Mr. Roosevelt's justices."[56]

There was little indication that the two March addresses changed anything. Robert Jackson later claimed that none of the speeches during the court fight did much to convince people to change their minds about the proposal. The president, however, seemed confident that his speeches had done the trick, and he went blithely off on his Warm Springs vacation. From Georgia he telephoned Farley to boast: "All I had to do was to deliver a better speech and the opposition will be beating a path to the White House door."[57] Instead of making decisive gains, the administration was losing the battle for public opinion and majorities in Congress.

The Senate Hearings

Hearings on S. 1392, the bill to reorganize the federal judiciary, began on March 10 in the spacious marble caucus room of the old Senate Office Building. Chairman Ashurst and his committee members filed in just before 10:30 A.M., accompanied by the first witness—the attorney general—and members of his staff. Cummings's prepared statement claimed the president's bill was in response to problems resting on four pillars: an impossible situation created by the reckless use of injunctions to restrain the operation of federal laws; the presence on the federal bench of aged and infirm judges; crowded court dockets, leading to delays in the lower federal courts and putting a heavy burden on the Supreme Court in reviewing petitions to hear appeals from lower courts; and the need for an effective system to infuse new blood into the federal judiciary. Throughout Cummings adhered to the indirect approach he instigated, as was expected.

He cited statistics: 15,000 pages of briefs were filed in the Supreme Court during the 1935 term, along with 35,000 pages of record and 869 petitions for *certiorari,* a total of 344,232 pages.

[56] *Redlands (Calif.) Daily Facts,* March 10, 1937.

[57] *Jim Farley's Story,* 79; Alsop and Catledge, *The 168 Days,* 113; Robert Jackson, Reminiscences, COHC, 444–45.

"P.S.—'Furthermore, We Don't Like the Court's Decisions.'" A cartoon by Jim Cassel, *Brooklyn Daily Eagle,* March 14, 1937.

A justice would need to work ten hours a day, seven days a week and read 122 pages an hour to review all these documents. "It would be like reading *Gone with the Wind* before breakfast every morning," the attorney general added.

On infirm judges, he quoted from Chief Justice Taft's book published in 1913, alleging that on reaching the age of seventy, men lose their mental and physical vigor. He quoted Theodore Roosevelt on the same subject. The court bill, Cummings said, was not designed to enslave the judiciary but merely to rejuvenate the machinery, speed justice, and give the Court men with a fresh outlook who would refrain from infringing on the powers of Congress. The president's bill, he assured them, would restore a proper balance to the government machinery.[58]

At question period, Senator Borah asked: "With respect to your complaint relative to 5 to 4 decisions, or law made by one vote by a court of 9, what guarantee will you have that the same situation won't exist with a court of 15, and by a vote of 8 to 7?" Cummings admitted that if the Supreme Court reached fifteen members, "we would be just where we are now." After a few more questions, Borah gave up and left the room.[59] Warren Austin pressed Cummings on his assertion that it would be difficult, if not impossible, to ratify an amendment to the Constitution in sufficient time to obtain the needed results. The Vermont senator reminded him that the Twenty-first Amendment had been ratified in only nine and a half months. Senator Hugo Black later congratulated Cummings on doing an excellent job before the committee, "especially in dealing with the Senator from Vermont."[60]

More than a hundred members of the press covered Cummings's session. Even those reporters who believed the president's plan to be wrongheaded—and that probably included most of them—credited Cummings with giving a facile performance. Maintaining his composure even in the face of hostile cross-ex-

---

[58] Senate Judiciary Committee, Reorganization of the Federal Judiciary, *Hearings on S. 1392 before the Senate Committee on the Judiciary,* 75th Cong., 1st sess., 3 vols. (Washington, D.C.: Government Printing Office, 1937), 1:4–12 (hereafter cited as *Hearings*).

[59] Report of Joseph O'Mahoney over NBC, March 10, 1937, summarizing evidence produced at the Senate hearings. A copy is in PPF 1200, FDRL. The White House strategy group was not satisfied with Cummings's reply, and in a memorandum for Senator Neely advised that in the forthcoming testimony by Robert Jackson, if the question came up again, the answer should be framed along this line: "That of course there will be no guarantee, nor can there be any . . . that the same situation might not possibly prevail. There is no attempt in this proposal directed at the independence of the judiciary. . . . [H]owever, what is being suggested is that under the proposal of the President, the personnel of the Supreme Court now and in the future be chosen in a manner that will bring it more in harmony with . . . the popular will and needs so that it will become coordinate with and not obstruct the legislative and executive branches of the Government." Memo, March 11, 1937, Box 657, James Roosevelt Papers, FDRL.

[60] Relayed to the Attorney General, March 11, 1937, Box 200, Cummings Papers, ALDL.

aminers, he leaned back, occasionally swinging the swivel chair from side to side. He answered deftly—some thought a little too deftly. Newsmen were reminded of the weekly press conferences he used to give in which embarrassing questions were deflected with wisecracks.[61] Recent critics, including Jackson's biographer, Stephen R. Alton, maintain that Cummings's appearance had very limited success at best. The original "inefficiency" rationale to which he doggedly adhered had been discredited. Committee members were angered by his approach, and few, if any, were persuaded by his testimony.[62]

The incoming mail gave a mixed reception to Cummings's efforts to sway the senators. An Iowa citizen, having read two separate reports of his testimony, wrote: "Your own words are in substance: The President seeks to appoint liberal judges to approve laws passed by [a] presidentially controlled legislature, regardless of what those laws are and . . . how they may effect my liberties and rights . . . and rights of my state. As one lone voter of many millions, I am prepared to say to you that I and they will never consent to such one-man rule. Have you any other correct name for it?" The writer accused Roosevelt of failing to keep promises he had made "in self-written party platforms and . . . speeches and in his oath of office," and asked: "Are you presuming that a majority is now going to believe that promises of benign rule with such power are going to be kept? If so, you and the President and all his supporters in this move are less astute and politically cunning than had been presumed."[63] The writer astutely predicted that the more the real purposes of this campaign were discussed by the president and his advisers, the stouter would be the resistance to it.

Another critic wrote: "In reading reports of your testimony given yesterday . . . I came across the remark . . . that it would be a strange appointing power and . . . administration that did not appoint men (as Supreme Court justices) sympathetic to the administration." With a touch of sarcasm, the writer said she supposed the decisions of Justices Stone and Brandeis, of which

[61] *Bridgeport (Conn.) Post,* March 11, 1937.

[62] Alton, "Loyal Lieutenant," 570; Davis, *New Deal Years,* 75.

[63] H. J. Rodgers to Cummings, March 11, 1937, Box 199, Cummings Papers, ALDL.

FDR approved, were "the living and breathing reflections of the economic opinions" of Presidents Coolidge and Hoover. "I respectfully submit that, unless the President, assuming he is granted the power, appoints to the Bench men pledged to agree with him and therefore 'spineless puppets,' no man on earth can predict how they will act in specific cases." As to congestion and delay in the federal courts, she described the current situation in Missouri, her former home:

> A newly created Federal judgeship there was vacant for over a year, and appointment was made only a few days ago, after the Pendergast Senator from the Western part of the state [Harry S. Truman] announced his intention to support the Court-packing bill. Who is delaying the work of the Courts if not the President, when he delays appointments for political motives? . . .
>
> Another thing—you say that your voice is seldom raised against the wishes of the great masses of the people. It is being so raised on this court-packing issue, and the best evidence of the truth of this assertion lies in the activities of the Administration itself. If the election "mandate" was a blanket authorization to make the Supreme Court what the President thinks it is, with an eye on the next election, why is Mr. Farley dashing about putting on pressure from his vast patronage machine? Why are individual congressmen, who have shown evidence of having a little respect at least for their oaths of office, being subjected to every possible inducement and threat to bring them into line? Why all this shifting from one line of attack to another, in public addresses?[64]

The writer asked: "If the 'great masses of the people' are willing to let Mr. Roosevelt be the Court, why is he finding it such uphill going to get a law passed? One might almost begin to believe that Mr. Roosevelt is afraid to give the people a chance to express their opinions as to whether this scheme, designed ostensibly to achieve the aims they advocate, will not defeat those aims and wreck democracy."[65]

The writer of this letter could not have known how parlous the situation was in staffing the federal bench outside her former home state of Missouri. The dockets of thirty-four district courts

---

[64] Mary Wright Aber, New York City, to Cummings, March 11, 1937, ibid.
[65] Ibid.

were in arrears on July 30, 1936, but in only four of these courts were the judges over seventy years of age. Walter Lippman reported that there were as of February 1937 nine vacancies in the federal courts which Roosevelt had not filled. A full year had elapsed during which he failed to fill the two vacancies in the Seventh Circuit Court of Appeals, and he took nearly eight months to fill the vacancy in the Third Circuit. Into the bargain, he had not as yet filled four district judgeships created by Congress in June 1936. As the lady made clear in her letter, he took a year to fill a vacancy in Missouri and a year to fill one in her adopted state of New York. What was he waiting for? In some cases he was waiting for the local politicians to agree on candidates, and in others he was holding up the patronage plums until after the election. Under his proposed court plan, FDR could have named only two additional judges in the ten district courts most congested. "By this time," wrote Lippman, "the claims that the object of the scheme is to expedite justice has become too hollow to impress anyone."[66]

Robert Jackson was the administration's next witness. Unlike Cummings, he used the direct approach favored by White House advisers. In a prepared statement, he advised the senators that his testimony would be a little different from that of the attorney general. Whereas Cummings had stressed the age issue and heavy caseloads that required this legislation, Jackson said he believed the judicial crisis stemmed from the Court's assumption of a judicial veto over state and federal legislation.

He argued that the current controversy reflected divisions within the Court, often referred to as a split between liberals and conservatives. The serious ideological differences among the justices impaired the Court's prestige and ability to function. Neither Congress nor the president had sought the present dissension, nor had they in any manner interfered with the judicial function, "and neither has failed to obey any decision of the Court." A majority of justices, he said, had made it apparent that the great objectives of the administration and this Congress offended their deep convictions and that the methods of this day violated their conception of good government.

---

[66] "The Flight from Democracy" in "Today and Tomorrow," syndicated column reproduced from *News Leader,* February 17, 1937.

Jackson rehashed, with telling effect, predictions by the justices of "impending moral chaos," fear that "the Constitution is gone" (McReynolds in the gold clause cases), characterization of the SEC as a "star chamber" (Sutherland in *Jones v. SEC*), and accusations that the Congress and the executive had coerced farmers (*United States v. Butler*), deprived women of their freedom of contract (*Morehead v. Tipaldo*), and despoiled the states. All these charges, in his view, indicated an implacable, although unquestionably sincere, opposition to the use of national power to accomplish the policies so overwhelmingly endorsed by voters.[67] The current crisis was the outgrowth not of a single decision of the Court, but of a series of decisions that indicated a certain mind-set on the part of the majority. He defended an increase in the Court's size as a method of bringing the elective and non-elective branches of the government into a proper coordination. "Changing the size of the Court has never deprived it of independence or prestige."[68]

Jackson gave an able presentation of the administration's case, putting its position on sounder ground than before.[69] He was partisan, as expected, and as his opponents would be, but he gave an impression of pressing the administration's cause while arguing in terms of the national interest. Jackson was the strongest advocate among the government witnesses, offering a more convincing defense of the bill than anyone else. A journalist referred to his testimony as "a landmark in judicial history. . . . Nothing abler and clearer than the . . . Jackson statement has emerged from the entire debate, and nothing that will better stand the test of time."[70]

The administration team of Senators Neely, Dieterich, and McGill, assisted by Corcoran and Keenan, directed the hearings. They selected witnesses, timed the order of their appearance, and

[67] *Hearings,* 1:47–48.

[68] Ibid., 37–51, statement of Robert H. Jackson at 40–43. For fuller coverage of Jackson's testimony and an able presentation of the ensuing critique of it, especially that by Walter Lippman, see Alton, "Able Lieutenant," 570–86.

[69] Ernest Cawcroft to Robert Jackson, March 11, 1937, Box 29, Jackson Papers, LC.

[70] Editorial, *Nation* 144 (March 20, 1937), 309.

coached them in advance of testifying. Joseph Alsop later noted: "There was scarcely an administration witness whom the [opposition's] legal researchers had not caught in some sort of inconsistency, even before he came to the stand."[71] Within the committee itself there was no leadership on the administration side. Hugo Black might have provided it, having had the background to rival Connally's or Borah's skill at cross-examination, but he left it in January to chair the Committee on Education and Labor. Administration strategists failed to anticipate his potential for work on the Judiciary Committee.

Those in favor of the bill were Ashurst, Neely, Logan, Dieterich, Hughes, Pittman, Norris (still pushing his substitute amendment), and McGill. Opposed were King, Van Nuys, Burke, Connally, Borah, Austin, Steiwer, and O'Mahoney, frantically searching for a substitute. Hatch and McCarran were as yet undeclared. The trio of Burke, Van Nuys, and Connally directed opposition strategy and managed the hearings. They made an admirable team. Burke had deserted the administration over the Holding Company Act, and he aligned himself with conservative Democrats. In leading the fight, he defied the party organization.[72] He was firmly committed to defeating the bill, acting with the tenacity of a bulldog and the determination of a bloodhound. Connally had an unbroken record of Democratic orthodoxy until he rejected the president's court bill.

The administration team, led by Corcoran, marshaled an impressive array of witnesses—deans of law schools, legal experts, labor leaders, and farm lobbyists. Prior to their appearance, the opposition scrutinized their past record. At the hearings they were subjected to exhaustive questioning (Farley called it "heck-

[71] Alsop and Catledge, *The 168 Days,* 123; Alsop Notes, Box 50, Alsop Papers, LC.

[72] Those who talked admiringly of Senator Burke's great courage in opposing the administration were not always aware of the fact that a powerful wing of the Democratic Party in his home state of Nebraska was anti–New Deal. If Burke had been motivated purely out of regard for his own future, he would have behaved as he did. And this was not the case with Burke alone. There were at least a dozen other states in which the Democratic organization was in a state of incipient revolt against the New Deal. "Mr. Roosevelt's fate on the Supreme Court issue is being decided in part at least on the basis of petty parochial squabbles." Editorial, "The Success Story of Senator Burke," *New Republic* 91 (May 26, 1937), 72.

ling") and exposed to the sarcasm of Connally, the hounding of Burke, and attacks by their colleagues. Questioning consumed as much time as actual testimony.

Corcoran had his own ideas about managing the hearings. Well before the appearance of any witnesses, he wanted to speed up the process, assuming that all necessary arguments could be intelligently presented on any measure before a committee in two weeks. Everything that could be said, had been said; the rest was repetition. All that mattered, he said, was pressure. But even he had to admit that the pressure advantage was with the opposition, since it had a favorable press and plenty of money.

Corcoran and Keenan tried to get Chairman Ashurst to limit the hearings to two weeks for presentation of their case by each side, but when the suggestion was put to Burke, Van Nuys, and Connally, they balked. They could not agree with Corcoran and Keenan on anything, not even the time of day.[73] After two weeks of testimony, fewer than half the government's witnesses had been heard. Burke suggested they take more time. The opposition was not yet ready with its case and would welcome the delay. Corcoran and Keenan suspected a deliberate attempt to drag the hearings out. With help from Ashurst, the opposition was in effect conducting "a subterranean filibuster." It allowed them to gain strength by exposing the bill as a bald attempt by the president to secure a compliant judiciary.

When Corcoran asked Ashurst to urge his committee to limit the hearings by resolution, he replied: "I cannot get the Senators to agree. I can never get them to agree to do that." The senator enjoyed conducting this clandestine campaign against the bill. When Ashurst received a letter from a constituent praising his "heroic stand" on the president's bill, he is said to have replied, "Which stand?"[74]

An exasperated Corcoran abruptly ended negotiations and decided to call no more witnesses. It was a tactical mistake, allowing the opposition to drag the hearings out indefinitely. The court bill had been submitted to Congress in early February to avoid

---

[73] Alsop and Catledge, *The 168 Days,* 122.

[74] Alsop Notes, Box 53, Alsop Papers, LC; Alton, "Loyal Lieutenant," 586–87; Leonard Baker, *Back to Back,* 149–51, Alsop Notes, Box 50, Alsop Papers, LC.

this danger. The sooner it was debated, the more easily it could be won. FDR's own team was outsmarted by the friendly, smiling Senators Burke and Ashurst and an endless queue of witnesses. The hearings had little value for the administration side, for as Leonard Baker concluded, "No new friends were won" by them.

The Cruelest Stroke

While the administration was calling witnesses, opposition strategists were readying theirs, laying the groundwork for "the cruelest stroke" of the court fight.[75] From the start they had wanted to bring the justices into the battle, knowing how incensed they were over the president's attempt to force compliance from them. To a man, the brethren were ready to use all the weapons at their disposal to ward off the frontal assault on their integrity, character, authority, and independence. At steering committee meetings, in cloakroom discussions, and in daily gatherings, opposition senators explored all aspects of the problem, but they could come up with no means of involving the justices. The brethren scrupulously maintained public silence, appearing calm and detached. Privately, of course, they were distraught.

It would be out of character to join in an unseemly political debate. Justice McReynolds, self-consciously dignified but the most anti–New Deal of the nine, broke his silence with an offhanded remark. Addressing the annual Phi Delta Theta fraternity dinner in Washington in mid-March, he named no names but imputed poor sportsmanship to the president: "I have taken an oath to do justice to the best of my ability. . . . I try to protect the backwoodsman in the hills of Georgia as well as the man of wealth in the mansion on Fifth Avenue. . . . The evidence of good sportsmanship is that a man who has had a chance to present a fair case to a fair tribunal must be a good sport and accept the outcome."[76]

He presumed that this impromptu remark would be "off the

[75] Typescript of draft MS, 124, Box 50, Alsop Papers, LC.
[76] *Literary Digest,* March 27, 1937, 4.

record," but it was taken down and reported in the press. A stormy reaction followed. For intruding in the debate he received abusive letters and postcards calling him a "sour puss," an "old crab," and "public enemy No. 1." One writer advised him to "get the hell off the bench as fast as you can." Another reminded him that "the people always kill their tyrants in the end."[77] McReynolds's clerk tried his best to spare the justice by intercepting the more abusive postcards, but he felt obliged to deliver sealed letters. The irascible jurist took each day's mail to his study, read the letters, and then burned them on a silver tray. After completing this exercise he went out for his daily walk. For weeks the suite of offices reeked with the acrid smell of burnt paper.

George Fort Milton, editor of the *Chattanooga News,* wrote Cummings: "I really think that McReynolds has done you a great service. He has compressed the issue as to the Court into a single sentence. . . . Of course the whole issue is that the present Supreme Court is *not* a 'fair tribunal.' I don't believe you can hammer on this too hard." Milton advised:

> Take McReynolds at his word, point out how basically unfair is the adoption into Court decisions of his economic and social prejudices. That is, his and those of the other hidebound three. . . . Actually, you are having to make your appeal to one man—to Roberts. Instead of being a Court of nine justices uncommitted in advance, four are always adversely committed and unless you can win one generally agreeing conservative, there is no chance.[78]

McReynolds's remarks angered Roosevelt. Their mutual contempt for each other was well known. The justice's intrusion was not exactly what opponents of the bill were looking for, but it emboldened several of them to approach the chief justice and formally request that he testify at the hearings.

A delegation headed by Wheeler, including Senator William H. King, the senior Democrat on the Judiciary Committee, and Warren Austin, representing its Republican members, called on Hughes on March 18 and urged him to testify, emphasizing Roosevelt's assertions about the justices' incapacity to do the Court's

[77] Bond, "McReynolds: I Dissent," 98.
[78] March 17, 1937, Box 199, Cummings Papers, ALDL.

work. The chief justice at first seemed receptive to the idea of appearing if he were accompanied by at least one other justice, preferably Brandeis owing to his standing as a Democrat and liberal. But the next day he told King and Wheeler that "there was a strong feeling that the Court should not come into the controversy in any way." However, if the committee desired particular information on any matter relating to the actual work of the Court, he would be glad to convey it in writing, giving the facts.[79] Having consulted Justice Brandeis in the matter, Hughes had been advised to decline all invitations to go before the committee.

A few days before Wheeler was scheduled to testify as the opposition's first witness, he received a letter and three-page memo from Professor Douglas Johnson of Columbia University, a geologist with no legal training.[80] Johnson had been a personal adviser to President Wilson at the Paris Peace Conference in 1919. He wanted to draw Wheeler's attention to the fact that the arguments in Roosevelt's message of February 5 constituted a grave misrepresentation of the facts, namely, his charge that the Supreme Court was being forced by the sheer necessity of keeping up with its business to decline without even an explanation to hear 87 percent of the cases presented to it by private litigants. And (as Cummings testified) that the Court could keep abreast of its work only by shirking some of the intolerable burden thrown on it by the hundreds of thousands of pages it had to read and digest.

Since these arguments were calculated to do serious damage and impair the prestige of the Supreme Court "in order to create support for the President's dangerous proposals," Johnson urged that the true facts be brought to the public's attention more fully and forcefully than had yet been done. As sources for these facts Johnson referred to testimony before congressional committees, the reports of these committees, and the congressional debates on the Judges' Act of 1925. Such information could be given to

[79] Memoranda of Hughes's telephone conversations with Senators King and Wheeler, Box 8, Hughes Papers, LC.

[80] March 18, 1937, Wheeler Papers, MHS. Professor Johnson may well have been the unsung hero of "the cruelest stroke."

the Judiciary Committee more quickly and easily "by some member of the Supreme Court."

> If the facts could be brought out by having one of the younger and liberal members of the Supreme Court answer questions before the Committee, that would perhaps be even more effective. But you are the best judge of what is practicable and wise. It seems to me important, however, to have the effect of the Attorney General's testimony offset by facts. Arthur Krock reports in the New York *Times* that this testimony, and that of Mr. Jackson have helped the President's cause greatly by giving those Senators and Representatives who think the President is wrong, but do not want to oppose him, some legal support for going along with him in this venture.

Johnson was upset because "someone has misled the President into a flagrant misrepresentation of the facts. Had he taken the precaution of examining into the work of the Supreme Court before charging it with a denial of essential justice, he would have found the real situation to be very different."

Before passage of the Judges' Act of 1925, the Court had been compelled to hear a great many cases that were wholly without merit.[81] Pursuant to that act, the declared policy of the peoples' representatives in Rule 38, subsection 5, indicated in a general way the types of cases in which the Court will grant application for a hearing. Under this procedure, which still prevails, every petition for a hearing receives the individual attention of every justice and is acted on favorably if four of the nine in full conference agree. Under Hughes the Court had proved more than generous in granting many applications that probably should have been denied. The reason why so many applications had been rejected had nothing to do with the Court's ability to keep abreast of its work. Rejections were the result of the defective nature of the applications. "A surprising number of the applications, by

[81] Many applications were brought for the obvious purpose of delaying the execution of justice; many involved no federal question; many others involved only questions of fact already passed on by a jury and an appellate court; many involved questions of law so well settled as to require no further consideration; and many others involved questions of local law about which the local circuit courts of appeal knew quite as much as, if not more than, the members of the Supreme Court. Ibid.

their utter lack of merit and by their failure to lay any foundation for the granting of the writ, are discreditable to the lawyers who draw them." Johnson cited the Solicitor General's Report of 1936: "A very large majority of the cases on the appellate docket do not possess sufficient merit to warrant consideration."[82]

This letter and memo may well have played a part in the tangle of events that followed. The arguments Johnson so cogently outlined in these two documents supplied sufficient ammunition to destroy utterly the original rationale for the court bill. As it was, the work of demolition would be carried out by the chief justice himself.

Determined to arm himself with some positive expression from members of the Court, Wheeler visited his friend Justice Brandeis, knowing the eighty-one-year-old jurist was grievously offended by the court plan and opposed it as an unacceptable political attack on the independence of the judiciary, no matter how the administration tried to disguise it. He was equally opposed to having the chief or *any* justice appear before the Judiciary Committee.[83] But at the same time, he wanted the committee to have the facts on the work of the Court and the efficient conduct of that work. The justices had to remain silent on questions of policy and the actual content or purpose of the bill, but Brandeis agreed with Hughes that the procedural issues raised by FDR's proposal provided them with an opening. He advised Wheeler to telephone Hughes from his apartment and request that he put in writing a public denial of the charges laid against the Court. With some trepidation Wheeler put the call through, emphasizing where he was calling from. Hughes agreed to write a letter but asked for more time to prepare it.

On Saturday, March 20, Wheeler visited Hughes at his home to explain that the committee wanted his letter as an opening salvo in the opposition's case the following Monday. Reluctantly, the chief justice agreed to the deadline. He said he would take care to note in the letter addressed to Wheeler: "The Justices

[82] Ibid.

[83] Mason, *Brandeis,* 626; Dawson, *Brandeis, Frankfurter, and the New Deal,* 140–45; Leonard Baker, *Brandeis and Frankfurter,* 153.

of the Supreme Court took no part in the discussion of the measure, save as I dealt with the state of the business of the Court."[84] Hughes called in his clerk, and they assembled the necessary data to support arguments against the charge of inefficiency. When completed, the letter was shown to Brandeis and Van Devanter and then copied with a final paragraph indicating their approval. Hughes later wrote that he had no time to consult the other justices. The letter was handed to Wheeler that Sunday afternoon. "The baby is born," Hughes reportedly remarked, breaking into a broad smile.[85]

On Monday, Wheeler exploded his bombshell. After giving his brief testimony before the committee, he took from his pocket the Hughes letter. The senators were stunned as he began reading it, presenting the case for the Court by its chief. It described the state of its dockets and gave a cold, statistical analysis of the disposition of cases over the preceding six terms, scotching any allegations that the Court was not abreast of its work. It said: "When we rose on March 15 (for the current recess) we had heard argument in cases in which certiorari had been granted only four weeks before—February 15."

The clash of opinions turned on the Court's handling of the thousands of petitions it received for review. Hughes cited the Solicitor General's Report for 1936, which stated: "There is no congestion of cases upon our calendar." The report, of course, amply corroborated Hughes's statement and was cited in Professor Johnson's letter. Hughes retraced the history of this matter, explaining: "We have been able for several terms to adjourn after disposing of all cases which are ready to be heard." He gave such a lucid explanation of the system by which the petitions were handled that any disagreement with his contention would be impossible.

---

[84] Charles Evans Hughes, *The Autobiographical Notes of Charles Evans Hughes,* eds. David J. Danelski and Joseph S. Tulchin (Cambridge: Harvard University Press, 1973), 304. The original of these notes, cited throughout, is in Hughes's biographical files, Box 181, Hughes Papers, LC. They were written sometime between November 1941 and the end of 1945.

[85] The full text of the Hughes letter to Wheeler of March 21, 1937, is in "General Correspondence," Box 8, Hughes Papers, LC. See also Appendix C in the Adverse Report (June 2, 1937) of the Judiciary Committee of the Senate on bill S. 1392. S. Rept. 711, 75th Cong., 1st sess. (Washington, D.C.: Government Printing Office, 1937), 38.

"Chief Justice Hughes's Letter Makes Its Mark." A cartoon by Carmack in the *Christian Science Monitor* (Boston), March 23, 1937.

Turning to the need for additional judges to expedite the work of the lower federal courts, Hughes reminded the committee that the Judicial Conference of the Senior Circuit Judges, which convened regularly, had met before the beginning of the October term in 1936. It considered the needs of all districts and circuits most carefully and recommended additional judges whenever this was found necessary. Regarding the president's request for an increase in the number of justices, Hughes wrote that apart from any question of policy, which was an exclusively legislative question that he would not discuss, an increase in personnel would not promote the efficiency of the Supreme Court, but would impair it so long as the Court acted as a unit. "There would be more judges to hear, more judges to confer, more judges to discuss, more judges to be convinced and to decide. The present number of justices is thought to be large enough so far as the prompt, adequate and efficient conduct of the work of the Court is concerned." As for suggestions (made by Cummings and others but not part of the bill) that the Court consider cases by sitting in divisions, he stated emphatically that that would be in clear violation of the Constitution's provision in Article III "that there be one Supreme Court."[86]

Hughes had good reason to resent the attack on the Court's conduct of its work. On becoming chief justice, he had tried to meet the problem of increasing pressures on its docket, primarily through skillful use of the *certiorari* process. He took it upon himself to read and summarize all the petitions that came to the Court, weeding out those that could be easily disposed of and putting them on a separate list before each Saturday conference, at which he tried to allocate about three minutes for discussion of each petition. Since he was so well prepared in advance on their content, his views were rarely challenged. This use of power did not, as was assumed by the administration, restrict access to the Court by petitioners. In fact, Hughes expanded the Court's scrutiny of petitions *in forma pauperis* to a point where *habeas corpus* arguments by prisoners became an important part of its docket.[87]

As G. Edward White has shown, Hughes used similar adminis-

---

[86] This was later characterized as an advisory opinion by Hughes. He was roundly criticized for it, even by some of the brethren, especially Justice Stone.

[87] G. Edward White, *The American Judicial Tradition: Profiles of Leading American Judges* (New York: Oxford University Press, 1976), 212–13. Descriptions of Hughes's method and style as chief are quite remarkably consistent. See, for example, Pusey, *Hughes,* 2:676; Felix Frankfurter, "Chief Justices I Have Known," *Virginia Law Review* 39 (1953): 883; Edward McElwain, "The Business of the Supreme Court as Conducted by Chief Justice Hughes," *Harvard Law Review* 63 (1949): 5; and Frankfurter's "The Administrative Side of Chief Justice Hughes," *Harvard Law Review* 63 (November 1949): 1, 3.

trative techniques in the internal consideration of cases before the Court. He came to conference prepared to the hilt, opened discussion of each case with a short but comprehensive review of the issues, barely tolerated debate, and actively discouraged requests for more time to study or reflect on an issue. Justice Stone for one resented the haste with which some cases were dispatched, and sometimes Hughes's brethren mocked his zeal for efficiency. A few saw his practices as attempts to impose his own views on them.[88]

At the first opportunity, when all the justices were assembled, Hughes, according to his own account, described the circumstances surrounding the letter to Wheeler and his inability to consult them all for lack of time. He hoped they approved of his action. Several of them spoke up at once, saying they did; others seemed to him to acquiesce. "No justice," he records, "either then or later expressed any contrary view . . . nor throughout the period when the bill was before the Senate did I hear that any of the Justices were in any way dissatisfied with my action."[89]

A year later, however, a journalist claimed that "certain justices" had not approved of Hughes's course and that a quarrel was narrowly averted by "the forbearance of those who felt that the . . . action had been unwarranted." In the margin of his copy of the author's *Harper's* article, Hughes wrote: "Matter brought up in conference—& no objection to letter voiced. On the contrary, there appeared to be emphatic approval." Justice Stone was assumed to be the source for the article.[90]

Throughout the entire court battle, Stone's position was some-

---

[88] White, *American Judicial Tradition,* 212–13.

[89] Hughes, "Autobiographical Notes," 305 n, Box 181, Hughes Papers, LC.

[90] Ibid. See also Marquis Childs, "The Supreme Court Today," *Harper's* 176 (May 1938), 587–88. A copy with Hughes's marginal notes is in his papers. His biographer makes the case for Stone's collaboration with Childs, who often accompanied Stone on his daily walks. Mason, *Stone,* 451–55. When the article first appeared, columnist Ray Clapper phoned each of the justices, none of whom would comment. But he was able to talk to Hughes, who told him: "I am in a rather delicate position if I say it [the article] is accurate," but he pointed out one thing that was inaccurate. "At end of piece is something about letter I wrote to Wheeler during court fight. And brethren supposed to have been indignant at some statements I made. If any of them have anything on their chests, they have concealed it very well." Clapper Diary, May 10, 1938, Clapper Papers, LC.

what ambivalent. He opposed the court plan, disliked FDR's legislative approach, and abhorred the president's tactics, but he reiterated in letters to friends that the Court had itself to blame for the crisis. In presenting his proposal, FDR had given no hint of wanting to stem the tide of anti–New Deal decisions. He put forward his bill on the ground that elderly jurists blocked the efficient dispatch of the Court's business. "You can rest assured," Stone wrote a friend, "that those who assert that age has affected the work of the Supreme Court, or that it does not do its work with the highest degree of efficiency of any Court in the world, cannot get to first base." He deeply resented the president's recklessness in dragging the Court into politics. "Between ourselves," he wrote, "the recent proposals about the Supreme Court are about the limit. To see it become the football of politics fills me with apprehension."

More than anything, however, Stone wished to avoid personal involvement "in this explosive political struggle." It was deeply distressing to him that Roosevelt drew some of his "best ammunition" for his fireside chat of March 9 from his dissents. He did not want to see the Court lose any of its powers, but he could find no satisfactory solution to the current problem except in the character of the judges appointed to the bench. But he ignored his own strictures on neutrality by urging editor Irving Brant, a close friend and confidant, to try to sell Roosevelt a modified court reform plan, compelling justices by constitutional amendment to retire at the age of seventy-five.[91]

Stone said he learned about the Hughes letter to Wheeler when he read it in the newspapers. Was he chagrined that he had not been consulted in its preparation? Obviously he bridled at the implication that the chief had the approval of the entire Court for his statements, but at the time he remained silent. Not until long after did he deny having approved of the letter. In 1939 he acknowledged to Frankfurter: "I should perhaps have put the matter in the proper light at the time, but it did not occur to me that such an expression of opinion would, in the circumstances, be attributed to members of the Court who were not consulted, and

[91] Stone to Irving Brant, April 20, 1937, and Brant to Corcoran, April 22, 1937, relaying this proposal, quoted in Mason, *Stone,* 444.

it seemed undesirable that . . . members should, at that stage of the . . . controversy, be subjected to any additional publicity."[92]

The justice's protestations are unconvincing. He could not have it both ways. He had to choose between standing behind the courage of his convictions (thus having to face publicity) or remaining silent so as to avoid jeopardizing the Court's position in the fight over the bill. He had ample opportunity to express his disapproval of the letter in conference. At other times he had allowed himself to be drawn into the fight. He continually fed his journalist friends Irving Brant and Marquis Childs confidential information about the Court and justices. His belated disclaimer in no way undercuts the veracity of Hughes's account as given in his *Autobiographical Notes.* Refusing to speak out publicly, Stone unburdened himself in private conversations and letters. This somewhat two-faced position made him useful to both sides in the controversy.

In spite of his equivocation and idiosyncratic character traits, Stone made one of the strongest cases of anyone except Hughes against the court bill. He was well aware of the strong conviction in some circles that the Court had misused its powers, but he also sensed the widespread popular feeling that correction of the situation could be secured in a way that would not look so much like "expecting the Supreme Court to get its law from Presidential messages." Endorsing a wise aphorism of Lincoln that nothing valuable can be lost by taking one's time, he emphasized that such drastic reforms as Roosevelt sought were unnecessary:

> Mistakes in the development of the law have a way of rubbing themselves out in time, and if we have made mistakes . . . as most institutions do, I have no doubt that time will correct them long before the country will come to any major disaster. . . . Time irons out a great many difficulties, and I have no doubt that the Court situation would have righted itself if the president could have possessed himself in patience for a reasonable time.[93]

[92] When Frankfurter's revised casebook on federal jurisdiction and procedure appeared in 1939, it contained a note on Hughes's letter implying that it represented the position of all the justices. Stone wanted to enter his objections, hence a letter dated December 29, 1939, in what he described as a prearranged correspondence. Mason, *Stone,* 452 n.

[93] Stone to Irving Brant, February 26, 1937, and Stone to Grosvenor H. Backus, March 3, 1937, both quoted in ibid., 445.

The Hughes letter had a devastating effect on the administration's case. It exposed the vulnerability of Roosevelt's message and Cummings's testimony with its withering factual refutation. Mentioning no names, the chief justice proceeded point by point to rebut the administration's claims, striking down the procedural arguments for judicial reform designed to conceal their real purpose. The letter gave a great boost to the opposition's case, completely destroying the specious contention that there was a need for additional justices. The initial indirection that Hughes exposed may have been tacitly abandoned in the presidential addresses of March 4 and 9, but in the public mind it was still fresh. The effect of the letter was "to show up for good and all as utterly hollow the smooth propositions with which the President had offered his bill. The opposition's gain in the debate was tremendous."[94]

Never before—at least not since James Monroe's administration—had a chief justice taken such an active role in a public controversy. Hughes could not escape adverse criticism for his intervention. Controversial though his intrusion may have been, as a New York paper reported, it struck with authority and suddenness, taking the administration completely by surprise.[95] Roosevelt was furious with Hughes for "playing politics" in the matter, and his anger grew with the realization that he had been outfoxed.[96] And as a recent study shows, Roosevelt had no one but himself to blame for the effectiveness of the letter.[97] It was his message and bill that politicized the Court as had almost nothing else in all its long history.

Harold Ickes, not usually generous with praise of opponents, paid the Hughes maneuver the ultimate tribute when he wrote: "This episode proves again the mistake in going to court with a weak case." He referred to the president's special message on judicial reform, which was almost entirely based on the proposi-

[94] Alsop and Catledge, *The 168 Days,* 127.

[95] *New York Times,* March 23, 1937.

[96] Burns, *Roosevelt,* 302–4; Leonard Baker, *Back to Back,* 162; Alsop and Catledge, *The 168 Days,* 127; Nathan Miller, *F. D. R.: An Intimate History* (New York: New American Library, 1983), 401. Ickes quoted Corcoran as saying in May 1937 that "Hughes had played a bad hand perfectly." *Secret Diary,* 2:145. Robert Jackson called Hughes "a superb leader in power politics" in the great tradition of John Marshall. *Struggle for Judicial Supremacy,* viii–ix.

[97] Alton, "Loyal Lieutenant," 588 n.

tion that "we needed more Federal judges, because, on account of old-age and decrepitude, we haven't enough able-bodied judges to keep up with the work of the courts." Rarely critical of FDR, he went on to say: "He abandoned this ground some time ago, but shrewdly Hughes chose to fight his skirmish where we were the weakest. . . . [Hughes] said he also believed that all the other members of the Court would agree with the position he had taken. Although the letter carefully negatives any suggestion that the Court was discussing the broad, general policy involved, the whole thing has the appearance of a unanimous Court opposing the President's plan."[98] In essence, Wheeler made the chief justice and his two senior colleagues (Brandeis and Van Devanter) the first witnesses against the court plan.

The role played by Hughes in this affair enraged Frankfurter, who wrote Brandeis: "As for the Chief—I have long written him down as a Jesuit—I deplored his letter and certainly its form."[99] To Roosevelt (and others) he was even more outspoken. "*That* was a characteristic Hughes performance—part and parcel of that pretended withdrawal from considerations of policy, while trying to shape them, which is the core of the mischief of which the majority have so long been guilty. That [Justice] Brandeis should have been persuaded to allow the Chief to use his name is a source of sadness to me that I need hardly dwell on to you."[100]

Whatever the "mischief" involved, it had been done and could not be undone. Robert Jackson candidly acknowledged that the Hughes letter gave a great boost to the opposition side, and believed that it "pretty much turned the tide" against the president's proposal.[101]

---

[98] *Secret Diary,* 2:103.

[99] *New York Herald Tribune,* March 31, 1937, Box 28, Frankfurter Papers, LC.

[100] Frankfurter to Roosevelt, March 30, 1937, Box 28, Frankfurter Papers, LC. To Charles Burlingham, Frankfurter wrote: "The less you say about his {Hughes] letter to Senator Wheeler the better, because it is indefensible on several scores." He complained that Hughes had been disingenuous in saying there was not enough time to consult other justices, and had grossly violated the settled practice against giving advisory opinions. He claimed he had talked pretty plainly to Brandeis about this, but whether he actually did is doubtful. June 9, 1937, quoted in Freedman, ed., *Roosevelt and Frankfurter: Correspondence,* 392, 402.

[101] Jackson, Reminiscences, COHC, 441; quote is in Alton, "Loyal Lieutenant," 588.

11

The Senate Hearings

> Such a precedent [as the court bill] established by so great a man as the President would have in it the germs of a crisis far more serious than any now envisaged from the present difficulty.
>
> Erwin N. Griswold, *Hearings,* March 30, 1937, II, Pt. 4, 767.

THROUGHOUT MOST OF MARCH AND APRIL, the hearings on the court plan at times resembled a historic public sideshow. "This is a very refreshing discussion of the beginnings of our Constitution. Besides, if we weren't doing this, we might be doing something a damned sight worse." So spoke courtly Henry F. Ashurst, chairman of the Senate Judiciary Committee, which by the beginning of April had rounded out its fourth week of hearings, listening to a distinguished assortment of the plan's opponents. In the magnificence of the Senate's marble caucus room, the daily meetings played to a full house. Roughly three hundred inquisitive citizens crowded into half of the cavernous chamber, straining to see over each other's heads and hear what came over the crackling loudspeakers set up among the room's marble pillars.[1]

The old game of jockeying for an advantageous political position was being played out behind the scenes with a raw display by the bill's supporters of arm-twisting and the use of patronage, tempting the doubtful with favors within the gift of the administration. Rush Holt, one of the youngest senators, reported that for fourteen months he had not been consulted even once about appointments to his state. "I got nothing," he said, "not even a janitor." But immediately after Roosevelt submitted his court

[1] *Time* 29 (April 12, 1937), 16.

plan, Holt was called to a meeting with Assistant Attorney General Joe Keenan, the president's Senate lobbyist. Keenan, in a very generous mood, wanted to know if Holt was interested in suggesting someone for a federal judgeship in West Virginia. Holt tells us: "He did not exactly say 'I am going to give you a judge for your vote.' I hope he did not think I was that dumb, but I knew what he meant, and he knew I knew."[2] These tactics repelled other Democrats like Senator O'Mahoney of Wyoming, who had not yet publicly declared against the president's bill, but soon would. Describing the situation in early March, he stated: "The whole mess smells of Machiavelli and Machiavelli stinks."[3]

Both sides worked on the undecided senators—the crop of fence-sitters FDR called "the real problem." He told Farley: "We have to get these fence sitters back in the barnyard." He said he was sending "Tommy the Cork" and Joe Keenan around to "turn up the heat on the opposition."[4] The bill's slow progress seemed not to worry the president, who said he was feeling great and was ready to do battle. But he was severely criticized by Democrats for going on vacation at such a critical phase in the struggle. In his absence, morale among his supporters deteriorated with an accumulation of setbacks, including more defections by southern Democrats. Senator Walter George of Georgia, who had helped write the party platform in 1936, now charged Roosevelt with repudiating that document.

By April, chances for the bill's passage appeared to be almost nil.[5] Key constituents of the New Deal coalition either refused to support it or damned it with faint praise. Labor and the farm bloc, two of the most powerful lobbies in Washington, were expected to help push FDR's plan along in the light of the 1935–36 Supreme Court decisions. Poll results for the week of March 22

---

[2] Ibid., 17. Senator William H. Dieterich (D.-Ill.) was originally noncommittal on the bill, but subsequently he got a morsel of patronage in the form of a federal judgeship, and by early April he was becoming downright surly toward the opposition in the hearings. To those witnesses whose answers did not suit him, the tone of his retorts was rough.

[3] O'Mahoney to Thurman Arnold, March 8, 1937, quoted in Gressley, "O'Mahoney, FDR, and the Supreme Court," 191, 197; *Jim Farley's Story,* 80.

[4] *Jim Farley's Story,* 77–78.

[5] Burns, *Roosevelt,* 302–3.

“Opening the 1937 Baseball Season.” A cartoon by Herbert Johnson in the *Saturday Evening Post* (Philadelphia), April 24, 1937.

indicated that opposition to court-packing had begun a steady climb, uninterrupted until the bill's final defeat. Testimony by opposition witnesses in the hearings before the Senate Judiciary Committee helped solidify the negative response.[6]

Defections by Farmers and Organized Labor

The depressing reality for FDR was that farm support failed to materialize. Farm organizations and their accredited lobbyists in Washington opposed the court plan.[7] FDR promised farm leaders that the AAA would be revived as soon as the judicial reform bill passed. They were invited to the White House and courted, but few took the bait. Edward O'Neal of the politically powerful Farm Bureau Federation was one of the few supporting the plan, but his endorsement came with the clear understanding that he spoke only for himself. Bureau leaders remained silent. Federation members strongly opposed the bill and wanted nothing to do with it. The most Roosevelt could hope for was to prevent any overt campaign against the bill.[8] Eventually, however, farm organizations mounted just such a campaign.

The National Grange, which had supported Landon in 1936, was even less helpful than the Farm Bureau Federation and declared it had doubts about the wisdom of the president.[9] When Grand Master Louis J. Taber sent an anti–court bill resolution to the thirty-five state masters for endorsement, four were opposed, one abstained, and the rest lined up solidly behind Taber. His resolution, released in late February, bitterly denounced the bill as a threat to constitutional liberties. He was joined in opposition by E. E. Everson of the more radical Farmers' Union, whose members managed to resist the blandishments of Agriculture Secretary Wallace.[10] The National Cooperative Council, a pro-

[6] Cantwell, "Public Opinion," 928.

[7] Ickes, *Secret Diary,* 2:104.

[8] Alsop and Catledge, *The 168 Days,* 116.

[9] *Time* 29 (March 1, 1937), 12.

[10] E. E. Everson of the Farmers' Union, Louis Taber and Fred Brenckman of the Grange testified in opposition to the court plan in the hearings before the Senate Judiciary Committee.

gressive association of farm cooperatives, polled its membership and found a large majority opposed to the court plan.

As pressure mounted, by mid-April, meetings held in farm communities all over the country reached millions. Statewide federations supplied members with literature and speakers and urged them to write their congressmen to defeat the court bill. Not even the American Cotton Cooperative Association was agreeable. Henry Wallace went into the South to talk to farm leaders, hoping to bring them around. New Deal spokesmen made a big issue of the AAA decision and emphasized "the great things" the administration had done for agriculture in the past four years. The message was: "You owe it to us."[11] But organization members acted as though there had never been an AAA decision. Discussions dragged on for another six or seven weeks, at the end of which the farm bloc generally remained cold on the proposition.

Their angry reaction confirmed that farmers in all but a few pockets of the country were unwilling to support enlarging the Supreme Court. Even the Farm Bureau's Ed O'Neal showed a certain coolness toward the plan when he remarked: "Whatever action [is] taken will be by the state bureaus individually." After a reporter reminded him of the invalidation of the AAA, he replied prophetically: "Yes, but the Court changes its mind sometimes. And then again, maybe we can change the farm program to fit the Court."[12]

Perplexed by these disclosures, Secretary Wallace had to revise his optimistic assessment of the previous weeks. Lamely, he told a press conference: "Farmers are naturally conservative and slow about a thing like this. Most farmers, until the AAA decision knew very little about the Supreme Court."[13] Roosevelt urged lawmakers to appeal directly to their farming constituents for support. In a radio talk, Representative James Pope (D.-Idaho) warned farmers that they could expect no further agricultural aid unless something resembling the president's proposal was enacted.[14] But like other citizens, farmers were attuned to

---

[11] Alsop Notes, Box 53, Alsop Papers, LC.

[12] *Christian Science Monitor,* February 24, 1937.

[13] *New York Times,* February 25, 1937.

[14] Ibid., February 26, 1937.

the currents of feeling sweeping the country—respect for the Supreme Court, fear of labor unrest, concern for law and order, and protection of property rights.[15]

If farm support evaporated, there was still labor, the New Deal's trump card, to be depended on. Had there not been so much unwarranted confidence in the White House, notice might have been taken around this time of the fact that labor support for court reform was not strong. Fearful that the Supreme Court would invalidate the Wagner Labor Act, which was then before it, leaders John L. Lewis, Sidney Hillman, and Major George L. Berry all announced to the press that they approved the president's plan 100 percent. William Green followed suit for the AFL. But the court fight was scarcely two weeks old when the widening gulf between the two wings of organized labor began having an adverse impact on administration hopes for solid labor support. With the AFL locked in "trench warfare" with the CIO, labor rallies organized by the administration fell apart.[16]

AFL journals paid scant attention to the doings in Washington. In time even CIO journals showed indifference to the court battle. The administration endorsed the activities of the Non-Partisan League, labor's most vocal political organization, in return for support of the court bill. Publicly, however, FDR tried to remain neutral, knowing the league was closely identified with the CIO. He had to avoid alienating either faction, for he needed both groups' support in his drive to reorganize the judiciary. No measures were taken by the administration for or against the CIO's militancy and participation in sit-down strikes. As a consequence, no effective labor pressure could be brought to bear on most Democratic lawmakers as long as Roosevelt refused to take a stand on the sit-down strikes.

Vice President Garner was infuriated by Roosevelt's failure to come down hard on labor militants to stem the spread of sit-down strikes crippling the automotive industry. He wanted them condemned publicly, since they were embittering relations between the administration and conservative Democrats in Con-

[15] Burns, *Roosevelt,* 303–4.
[16] Ibid., 302–3; cf. *Time* 29 (March 1, 1937), 12.

gress. Garner confronted FDR before he left for Warm Springs, Georgia, and thought he won a promise that if the situation deteriorated, the administration would take drastic action. Roosevelt was kept fully informed that the strikes were growing more violent, but he took no action. By the end of March nearly 100,000 autoworkers were out on strike in the Detroit area alone. A frustrated Senator James Byrnes (D.-S.C.) introduced an amendment to a new Guffey Coal bill about to reach the Senate floor, protesting the strikes.[17] When it was blocked, a resolution was introduced censuring sit-down strikers.[18] This crisis, as much as the court fight, brought Roosevelt hurrying back to Washington.

The president thought the battle was coming along in good shape and considered the chief danger the defeatist attitude of the vice president. "It appears that Garner talks down in the mouth to his drinking cronies," Ickes wrote, "and the President is afraid that it will have such a bad effect on [Senate Majority Leader] Joe Robinson that one of these days Robinson will agree to a compromise [on the court bill] without even consulting him about it."[19] Garner's disaffection, labor's internecine warfare, and FDR's ambivalence on labor militancy all worked to the advantage of the court bill's opponents. Adding to the administration's woes, Senator Robert Wagner (D.-N.Y.), whose name was almost synonymous with the New Deal, refused to support the court bill, remaining silent for months. Not until July 1937 did he privately agree to support a compromise.[20] His silence did much to thwart labor's support of the original court bill.

On his father's orders, James Roosevelt telephoned Charlton Ogburn, a New York labor lawyer, urging him to suggest to Rep-

---

[17] The House passed the new Guffey-Vinson Coal Control Bill, imposing a tax on coal sales by producers who did not subscribe to a coal code fixing minimum coal prices. The new bill omitted the labor provisions that had caused the old Guffey bill to be invalidated. *Time* 29 (March 22, 1937), 13.

[18] Alsop and Catledge, *The 168 Days,* 59, 115–17, 131; Burns, *Roosevelt,* 302–3; Pusey, *Hughes,* 2:753; Leonard Baker, *Back to Back,* 86–88. For coverage of the labor unrest in Detroit, see J. Woodford Howard, "Frank Murphy and the Sit-Down Strikes of 1937," *Labor History* 1 (Spring 1960): 103–40.

[19] *Secret Diary,* April 3, 1937, 2:108.

[20] *The American Politician,* ed. John T. Salter (Chapel Hill: University of North Carolina Press, 1938), 116–23. Wagner's refusal to take a public stand on the court bill was motivated partly by fear of raising public opposition to his $3 billion housing bill.

resentative William Connery and Senator Hugo Black that "we have *got to have a united front on labor legislation.*"[21] FDR notified Labor Secretary Perkins that the wages and hours legislation would have to wait.[22] A *New York Times* editor on March 21 queried: "How much can the President be blamed?" Arthur Krock assured readers that FDR was quietly using his influence to get an amicable settlement between the CIO and General Motors and endorsed Governor Frank Murphy's efforts in Michigan to restore labor peace and preserve law and order. According to Krock, peace would be restored on the labor front only if the president, using his personal prestige, issued a public statement. No statement came from the White House.

Some blamed continuance of the strike epidemic on the Supreme Court, not the president. At an American Labor Party rally in New York, Robert Jackson charged that "the conservative majority of the Supreme Court must share the blame for the current industrial unrest." He lumped the justices together with major industrialists, characterizing them as "nothing better than corporation lawyers in black robes."[23] On January 11, 1937, the Court of Appeals for the Ninth Circuit in San Francisco had been the latest of the federal courts to declare the National Labor Relations Act unconstitutional. With its fate undecided by the Supreme Court, employers in industry were openly defying collective bargaining efforts of the CIO, and the strikes became more serious. On March 17 Senator Robinson complained that nearly every one of the newly organized institutions of the government rested under a legal cloud. He referred to the SEC, PWA, TVA, the Social Security Board, and the National Labor Relations Board. Justice Department lawyers appeared to be uncertain about what powers, if any, they had to enforce the Wagner Act.

One of the administration's witnesses, Ferdinand Pecora, justice of New York's Supreme Court, easily made headlines by raising the prospect that if sit-down strikes reached the propor-

[21] FDR to James Roosevelt, March 27, 1937, PPF 3794, FDRL (italics are mine).

[22] Perkins, *Roosevelt,* 207.

[23] *Christian Science Monitor,* March 17, 1937; *New York Times,* March 25, 1937.

tions of a national crisis, they might become one of the "big guns" behind the drive for revising the Court. He accused investment bankers of a "sit-down" against the Securities Act of 1933, utilities executives with torpedoing the Holding Company Act, employers for failure to obey the Wagner Act, and asked: "How can you expect the working men and women to be religiously reverent of the letter of the law when the mighty and powerful who want the rest of the community to consider them models act this way toward the law?"[24]

When he returned from Warm Springs on April 1, Roosevelt closeted himself with Garner, Bankhead, Robinson, and Rayburn for an update on the court bill. At a White House luncheon that day with Farley and Senator Black, the talk centered on the progress of the fight. "All we have to do," said FDR, "is to let the flood of mail settle on Congress. You just wait and see." He assured them that although their opponents were having the better of the argument at the moment, the bill would come to the Senate floor and pass. Farley agreed, but he thought it might take longer than the president expected. Black cautioned that the opposition was "most determined" and would exercise every means of delay, knowing that their only hope lay in avoiding a vote. "We'll smoke 'em out," said Roosevelt. "If delay helps them, we must press for an early vote."[25]

The Hearings

Meanwhile, hearings on the court bill ground on. Senator Borah told newsmen: "We know what they [the witnesses] are going to say, and I think the mind of every Senator is already made up. If any minds aren't made up, they won't be by any arguments heard by the Committee."[26] Borah's cynicism was not shared by senators in both camps who believed that the time and effort devoted

[24] *Hearings,* 1:338ff.; *Time* 29 (March 29, 1937), 14–15. Pecora was a chief inquisitor in the banking investigation of 1933–34.

[25] *Jim Farley's Story,* 78–79.

[26] *New York Times,* March 14, 1937. Borah absented himself from most of the hearings, except for the opening session and an occasional appearance.

to hearings would prove beneficial when the issue came up for a vote. At least two committee members were still undeclared.

Opposition forces, having gained the upper hand, were determined to keep it even if the hearings dragged on for another month. Critics called for the resignation of the attorney general. A Frank Kent editorial bore the caption "He Should Resign" and was explicit: "Among the things that have been said by Carter Glass and others since his plan to control the judicial branch of the Government was revealed by the President, is that the country needs a new Attorney General very much more than it needs a new Supreme Court. The recent letter of [the] Chief Justice . . . lends substance to that statement."

Kent was referring to the Virginia senator's response to a challenge by the attorney general. In a radio speech over a nationwide network, Cummings had asked: "What is the real objection [to the president's plan]? Those who wish to preserve the *status quo* want to retain on the bench judges who may be called upon to veto progressive measures."[27] Glass retorted: "The country is infinitely greater in need of an Attorney General than of additional judges of the Supreme Court, of judicial wet nurses for six of the present members of the Court." Kent again reminded readers that the Hughes letter categorically disproved statements made in the president's message about the Court and its work—statements based on information furnished to him by the attorney general.[28]

Even without the Hughes letter, the allegations in the president's message were refuted by the record (the attorney general's annual report for 1936, the written testimony of Roosevelt's friends James Landis and Felix Frankfurter, statistics on cases heard and the character of cases left unheard). Once these allegations were abandoned, no one repeated them. Not one of them was or could be sustained. Hughes's letter was not really needed

[27] Typescript of February 15, 1937, radio address, Box 200, Cummings Papers, ALDL.

[28] Frank Kent, "The Great Game of Politics," *Baltimore Sun,* March 28, 1937. He said Roosevelt owed the opposition an apology, or at least a retraction, coupled with a rebuke of Cummings. Either course would have weakened FDR's position and injured his pride. For the Glass quote, see "National Affairs," *Time* February 22, 1937, 12.

to shoot them down, but it was effective as an authoritative statement on the Court's position. Kent concluded:

> The President has been weakened in his fight and embarrassed before the country—or anyhow [he] should be. Under the circumstances, the resignation of the Attorney General would seem to be indicated. . . . It is a difficult thing for a man such as the President to confess he made a mistake, particularly in connection with as historic and sensational an indictment as that contained in his message about the Court. He was left in the awkward position of having to abandon the charges, while failing to retract them, not a pretty position for any man, whether a President or private citizen, to occupy.[29]

Drawing the president's attention to Kent's editorial, Cummings expressed outrage: "No doubt you have seen this grossly libelous article. Much the same tactics are being employed in other quarters." Press Secretary Early was asked: "Will you speak to me about this? F.D.R." On the chit Early penciled: "Did—April 6. File."[30] Cummings was subjected to another stinging rebuke from Senator Wheeler for giving Roosevelt misinformation. Wheeler ridiculed the idea of creating six new judges "to meet the needs of the time." Reacting angrily, Cummings issued a press release:

> At no time has the President been supplied with "erroneous information" in re the docket of the Supreme Court. At no time has the President or the Attorney General made any statement to the effect that the Supreme Court is not up with its docket. Everyone who knows anything about the situation is aware of the fact that the Supreme Court is up to its docket. Those who reiterate this assertion as if it had any bearing on the present controversy, are speaking of something totally irrelevant. The question is not whether the Court is up with the docket, but by what means it keeps up with the docket, and whether the burden that it must sustain is too great to warrant the careful consideration [to] which these petitions [for *certiorari*] are entitled and whether the assistance by the appointment of additional judges is indicated.[31]

---

[29] Kent, *Baltimore Sun,* March 28, 1937.

[30] Ibid.; Cummings to FDR, April 3, 1937; FDR to Early, n.d., PPF 186, FDRL.

[31] Typescript of March 22, 1937, Box 200, Cummings Papers, ALDL.

Senator Edward R. Burke (D.-Nebr.), who once described the president's bill as "the most direct attack on the independence of our judiciary which the country has ever seen," took the lead in conducting the hearings for the opposition. With Senator Tom Connally, he held the edge in effective cross-examination of witnesses. Robert Jackson was subjected to an intense grilling on his and parts of Cummings's testimony, depriving it of much of its force, although his examiners insisted they were not "trying to create trouble between him and his boss." In one exchange Connally asked him whether in the last analysis the effectiveness of the court plan would not depend on the kind of justices to be appointed. Jackson sidestepped giving a direct answer, but on Connally's insistence he admitted: "That is largely true."[32]

Administration witness Justin Miller, a former law dean of Duke University and before that of the University of Southern California, was asked by Senator Burke whether, if none of the six justices eligible to retire did so within thirty days after the bill became law, the membership of the Court would reach and remain at fifteen unless Congress passed some other kind of legislation. Miller said he was not sure, but understood that the number "may shift between nine and fifteen, according to the number of men who resign." O'Mahoney asked: "Have you not read the bill?"[33] Miller then had to admit that the bill could provide for a permanent fifteen-member Court. Senator Burke complained that he had a hard time reconciling what was in the bill with the statements in the president's message.

Miller propounded the theory that throughout the federal court system older judges delivered by far the greater number of decisions nullifying federal laws. This provoked Senator O'Mahoney, who asked: "Have not some of the most advanced and liberal of our decisions been written by the older judges?" Miller replied: "Occasionally that has been true . . . [but] the old man with the young mind is the exception."[34] Less than a week later

---

[32] *Hearings,* 1:62–63.

[33] Ibid., 1:139.

[34] Ibid., 137–38. Miller was further embarrassed when Alice Longworth, sitting in the audience, passed a note up to Senator Van Nuys with a question for the witness. The senator said: "I have received a note from a member of the audience. Would you mind answering it? 'Could you tell us the average age of world dictators when they come into power?' Said Miller, 'No, I could not.'" Also quoted in *Time,* March 29, 1937, 14.

his argument lost much of its force when Roosevelt appointed sixty-eight-year-old Robert L. Williams to the Court of Appeals for the Tenth Circuit. In four years the president had filled nine federal judgeships with men over sixty. William Denman, noted for spearheading reform of the lower federal courts, was sixty-three in 1935 when FDR appointed him to the Ninth Circuit.[35]

Reacting to criticism of his appointments, Roosevelt shifted position. A lawyer wrote, recalling a meeting he had with FDR when he was governor of Arkansas, informing him that his name was before the Senate for appointment to a vacant judgeship in the U.S. District for Arkansas. He had learned meanwhile that the president would nominate no one over the age of sixty (he was sixty-five). If officially advised of such a rule, the lawyer said, he would immediately withdraw his name from consideration. FDR wrote: "While the rule to which you refer is not like the laws of the Medes and the Persians, nevertheless, it is a matter of policy to bear in mind the proper retirement age of Federal Judges . . . fixed by statute at seventy years, following ten years of service on the bench. Other things being equal, the preference is of course given to persons below the sixty year mark."[36] But the president did not always practice what he preached.

After observing the hearings for two weeks, columnist Paul Mallon thought he detected a "great hidden power" evident in their conduct. Whenever witnesses testified for the opposition, cross-examiners seemed to know everything he or she had ever written and could even cite page references. This was especially marked when Moley testified. Behind the scenes, witnesses were carefully researched and coached on what answers to give to which questions. It was evident to Mallon that "the G-men have moved in," and the man in charge was Joe Keenan.[37] A Justice Department agent overheard a conversation on the Senate lobby tele-

[35] *Christian Science Monitor,* March 25, 1937; MacColl, "Supreme Court and Public Opinion," 251. In 1953, Judge Denman, at eighty-one, showed no sign of even considering retiring from the bench.

[36] J. M. Futrell to Roosevelt, May 12, 1937; FDR to Futrell, May 20, 1937, PPF 1055, FDRL.

[37] *Washington Evening Star,* March 26, 1937. "G-men" was the contemporary term for "government men"—the FBI.

phone in which the caller demanded of a senator: "Get that list of opposition witnesses out of Senator Burke right away." The senator said he had tried and failed, but the caller persisted, "and in a way that few government officials care to employ against U.S. senators."[38]

Pro–court bill witnesses were examined in the Justice Department offices on what they were prepared to say. Opponents of the bill proved unrelenting during cross-examination. Professor Corwin, blushing, confessed under pressure that only a year ago he had said that there were serious objections to "packing" the Court. Leon Green was forced to admit that he had discussed his arguments beforehand with lawyers in the attorney general's office. Mallon charged that the department "was doing little else lately . . . except trying this case." Opposition witnesses were aided by the handful of volunteer lawyers provided by the ABA from private firms. But no law firm in the country could command the resources available to the U.S. Justice Department.[39]

Corcoran later claimed that White House strategy had been bungled from the start. There was no line of adequate communication between the executive offices and congressional leaders. FDR stayed away from Washington for long intervals. Corcoran accused Keenan and West of "incompetence and disloyalty,"[40] while he himself made more than his share of costly blunders. His brash behavior and heavy-handed tactics did not sit well with old-time Senate Democrats and only increased the friction between Congress and the White House. Keenan was detested by Corcoran, so much so that harmonious teamwork between them was virtually impossible.[41]

Justice Stone was unimpressed by the administration's witnesses for the court plan or by the plan itself. He opposed adding more justices to the Court by political maneuver, fearing it would "decrease faith in the constitutional decisions of the Court just at the moment when they become worthy of faith." A decline in judicial prestige could already be detected in the testimony of

---

[38] Ibid.
[39] Ibid.
[40] Sherwood, *Roosevelt and Hopkins,* 90.
[41] Alsop and Catledge, *The 168 Days,* 82–83.

those favoring the bill. Stone was chagrined that men "who by training and experience are qualified to speak, should need the reminder to act like scholars and not like politicians." The testimony of court-packing advocates (Edward S. Corwin, Leon Green, Justin Miller, Thomas F. Konop, and Charles Grove Haines) "simply boiled down," said Stone, "to the proposition that they did not believe in a Constitution, or in those orderly processes through which alone a Constitution can function."

The justice was particularly distressed over "the antics of men who ought to know better . . . who seem to think that because the Court has made some mistakes, that they ought to be corrected by another and graver one." He lamented: "I am beginning to think that all my life I have greatly overestimated the capacity of the human mind to deal with novel problems." To a Columbia colleague he confided pessimistically: "It almost makes you wonder whether the democratic form of government can permanently endure, and whether we will not ultimately go the way . . . so many European countries seem to be going now."[42]

In early April, FDR wrote Frankfurter; "Is there no way in which you can slip into town and to the White House unobserved—any time after April twelfth? You are dead right in keeping—for the moment—wholly out of the hearings. As you know, we are carrying out the dignified process of keeping still and watching each new witness damn the proposal and offer a new remedy. My last count runs to over two hundred amendment proposals and over one hundred legislative proposals." He concluded: "It is quite clear that the utter confusion of our opponents among themselves means success for us, even though it [a vote] may be deferred until June or July. The opposition has daily epilepsy because 'we are keeping our shirts on.'"[43] Frankfurter re-

---

[42] Stone to Grosvenor H. Backus, March 20, 1937, Box 13; Stone to his sons, March 30, 1937, Box 27; and Stone to Young B. Smith, April 12, 1937, Box 27; all in Stone Papers, LC. See also Mason, *Stone,* 445–46.

[43] April 5, 1937, PSF 150, FDRL. While on the Harvard Law faculty in 1937, Frankfurter was a frequent adviser to the president but refrained from endorsing the court plan. In his estimate, the Court had brought this crisis on itself. During the court fight he provided considerable behind-the-scenes advice and assistance to the president, but he maintained a public pose of neutrality on the question and reiterated to his closest friends that he had no role in the affair.

plied: "As for managing a visit—I shouldn't think that would be very difficult. I might stay either with Butler, J., or McReynolds, J.—that would make my visit wholly constitutional."[44]

On April 1, Keenan sent Cummings a "confidential" memo "re the Court Reorganization bill":

> We have informed Senator Ashurst that we are not going to present any more witnesses until the opposition has closed. They have served notice that they are going forward until April 13. Our thought is that the public interest in these hearings is not being sustained, and that it is proceeding on to a sort of drivel, and that when the opposition rests we will then go forward with a few governors and our documentary proof, and possibly have Mr. Reed or someone else, as suggested, close the matter out. We feel that nothing has been lost in the interim, since Senator Robinson felt it would be a mistake to close the hearings without being assured of enough votes to bring the bill out of committee.
>
> Senator Robinson was informed of the situation tonight, and Senator Ashurst seems to feel that in the long run it is the best strategy.[45]

Corcoran's and Keenan's haste in closing off the administration's case proved to be a tactical blunder that enabled the opposition to dominate the hearings and headlines for the next four weeks.

He was even prepared, if asked, to remain deceptive before the Senate Judiciary Committee at the hearings when he was named by FDR to the Supreme Court in 1939. His part in the episode is told in *Roosevelt and Frankfurter: Their Correspondence, 1928–1945,* edited by the Canadian-born journalist Max Freedman, 376–406. For the statement he prepared for use before the Senate Committee, see p. 15. See also Frankfurter's letter of March 30 and FDR's reply of April 5, 1937, Frankfurter Papers, LC. The late author J. Anthony Lucas told the writer that when, as an honor student at Harvard he went to see Frankfurter in Washington to discuss his Honor's Thesis, which compared the English custom of packing the House of Lords with FDR's court-packing plan, the justice, exasperated, exclaimed, "If that's what they're teaching you these days at Harvard they ought to be horse whipped." He refused to answer any questions about the 1937 episode and summarily threw the young student out of his office.

[44] April 8, 1937, ibid.

[45] April 1, 1937, Box 200, Cummings Papers, ALDL. In a postscript, Keenan added: "We seem to be losing the support of Senator Hatch. Indeed, unless we can change him, he is definitely against us." Hatch was one of the committee's "undecided" Democrats.

Burke produced a steady stream of witnesses, including a delegation of Texas politicians, representatives from various patriotic societies, farm spokesmen, lobbyists, leaders of almost all religious denominations, and journalists.

Keenan's action may have been triggered by damaging testimony the previous afternoon. Dorothy Thompson, the doyenne of New York columnists and wife of the novelist Sinclair Lewis (author of *It Can't Happen Here*), had recently written:

> No people ever recognize their Dictator in advance. He never stands for election on the platform of dictatorship. . . . Since the great American tradition is freedom and democracy, you can bet that our dictator, God help us! will be a great democrat, through whose leadership alone democracy can be realized. And nobody will ever say "Heil" to him, or "Ave Caesar," nor will they call him "Führer," or "Duce." But they will greet him with one great big, universal, democratic, sheeplike blat of "O.K., Chief! Fix it like you wanna, Chief! Oh Kaaay!"[46]

Testifying before the committee, Thompson stated: "The President's plan may be legally constitutional, but it is not politically constitutional. It strikes at the Supreme Court and Constitution in the most radical and drastic fashion imaginable, because it proposes to switch the Supreme Bench into line with the current political majority." That, she emphasized, had been frankly admitted by the president in his metaphor about the three-horse team. "What it [the bill] proposes to create is a court whose eyes are fixed, not upon the Constitution, and upon the whole body of existing law, but upon the White House and the ruling majority in Congress. It proposes to make the Supreme Court the instrument of that majority . . . [and] suggests that its [the Constitution's] framers were in confusion about the functions of society, the State and the Government."[47]

Throughout his cross-examination of witnesses, Senator O'Mahoney took every opportunity to harp on the theme of economic or political concentration of unharnessed government power in Washington. When Thompson presented her impressions of European totalitarianisms, he questioned her closely.

---

[46] Quoted in "Judiciary," *Time,* March 1, 1937, 10.

[47] *Hearings,* March 31, 1937, 2:858–84, at 862.

Cooperating fully, she assured the committee that wherever there was a concentration of economic power, a totalitarian state was sure to follow. In the battle over court-packing, she added, some believed that what was needed was "less rage and more ratiocination," but as far as she was concerned, "We should all yell to high heaven."[48] Her remarks were welcomed by some members of the committee and given extensive coverage in the press.

Administration strategists tried but failed to bring the hearings to a close without the consent of Chairman Ashurst. As long as any doubt remained about public sentiment toward the bill, opposition members wanted to continue calling witnesses. Senator Robinson agreed and said that only when they could be certain that public support for the bill was forthcoming would they agree to end the hearings. Senator Van Nuys, who had once suggested bringing all nine justices before the committee, reported that as of April 2 there were forty-two Senate votes against the proposal that could absolutely be counted on. Technically it would take forty-nine to defeat the bill, but it was rare for the full Senate membership to be present for a recorded vote. Forty-five would be enough to defeat it.[49] Hints began to circulate that it would never be brought out of the committee, which was still evenly divided, with two senators undeclared, if not undecided. Persuasive testimony by opposition witnesses was expected to bring over at least one, possibly both. These two (Democrats) were actually opposed to the measure but hoped their vote would not be necessary.[50]

Senator James M. Hughes (D.-Del.), a supporter of the bill, moved on April 8 to discontinue the hearings, but the chairman's objection in the matter was controlling. The opposition had invitations out for at least forty more witnesses, including represen-

[48] Ibid., 858–84.

[49] Frederick Van Nuys to Harold Stephens, Box 8, Stephens Papers, LC.

[50] Ibid. So far, the most significant converts were two members of the Judiciary Committee, Senators Logan of Kentucky and Hatch of New Mexico. Logan described his dilemma when he exclaimed: "I don't like this plan at all. But I can see no alternative. I cannot find a better one." Hatch had also been leaning reluctantly toward the president's plan, but after hearing testimony from Dean Young Smith he announced his readiness to "go whole hog" for Smith's plan to submit an amendment. Logan surrendered before the hearings ended. *Time,* April 5, 1937, 12–13.

tatives from the Daughters of the American Revolution, Veterans of Foreign Wars, and law schools, indicating several more weeks of testimony. Chairman Ashurst, who was expected to lead the Senate floor fight for the administration's proposal, was accused of inconsistency and even admitted to the soft impeachment. When the charge resurfaced early in April, he said he now considered himself dean emeritus of inconsistency, and was conferring degrees rapidly upon some witnesses who had appeared before the Committee.

Erwin Griswold's Testimony

One of the highlights of the hearings was the testimony by Erwin Griswold, a Harvard law professor and former Justice Department tax expert. He made headlines with his provocative statement:

> There are at least two ways of getting rid of judges. One is to take them out and shoot them, as they are reported to do in at least one other country. The other way is more genteel, but no less effective. They are kept on the public payroll, but their votes are cancelled. Such a precedent [as the court bill] established by so great a man as the President would have in it the germs of a crisis far more serious than any now envisaged from the present difficulty.[51]

Before testifying, Griswold attended a briefing session during which opposition senators told him that as matters then stood,

[51] *Hearings,* March 30, 1937, 2:760–800, at 767. Griswold had served under J. Crawford Biggs during his turbulent tenure in the Justice Department. Stone and Brandeis had commended him for his tax work. Brandeis told Frankfurter: "H.L.S. [Stephens] did well to get Erwin Griswold." Brandeis to Frankfurter, August 14, 1933, quoted in Urofsky and Levy, eds., *"Half Brother, Half Son,"* 528. Griswold was dean and taught at Harvard Law School until 1967, when President Lyndon Johnson named him solicitor general. He continued in that office until President Nixon's term. James Landis succeeded him as dean of the Harvard Law School after leaving the chairmanship of the SEC.

Senator Dieterich, inclined to grunt at witnesses, snapped at him: "Do you think there's much difference between shooting judges and retiring them?" "A great deal," replied the professor. "As I have said, retiring them or canceling their votes is much more genteel." *Time,* April 12, 1937, 17. Senator Burke, who occasionally clashed with the bumbling Dieterich, went so far as to say: "His questions do more good [for the opposition] than any I could ask." Ibid.

the president's bill was sure to pass in some form. Therefore his testimony would have the potential of producing modifications or amendments that might lessen the constitutional damage the bill would effect. Griswold needed no coaching. He came to Washington fully prepared and later called the briefing session "an eye opener."[52] He told the writer it was his distinct impression that Carl McFarland, more than anyone else except the attorney general, played a major role behind the scenes in formulating the 1937 court bill.

Griswold's remarks, which largely regarded that section of the bill providing for an enlarged Supreme Court, were divided into two parts. The first he considered "the least material" of the two, but it was actually more significant than he may have imagined. It directly rebutted one of the main arguments advanced in favor of the bill, namely, the suggestion that it was in complete accord with the Constitution and historical precedent. Griswold conclusively repudiated Roosevelt's specious claims about the applicability of precedents in Congress's previous changes in the size of the Court. This had not yet been disputed elsewhere. Griswold stated: "It seems to me worthwhile to attempt to show that this argument, like so many of the others . . . offered in support of this measure, is quite without substance." The second part of his testimony concerned his views on the merits of the bill.

The professor challenged the assertion that an increase in the size of the Court in the manner proposed by FDR had occurred six times before in its history. This history, he said, did not lead to the conclusion that these occasions had anything to do with the present case. His systematic examination of the six changes made in the past and the circumstances under which they had been made took on a wholly different light in his recounting. The resulting analysis proved damning to the administration's cause, demolishing the argument based on historical precedent in one hour.

After Jefferson's election in 1800, the last Federalist Congress, in its dying days, passed a new Judiciary Act (1801) that reduced the Supreme Court from six members to five and relieved the justices of riding circuit. When the Jeffersonian Democrats took

---

[52] Interview with Erwin Griswold, November 30, 1989, Washington, D.C.

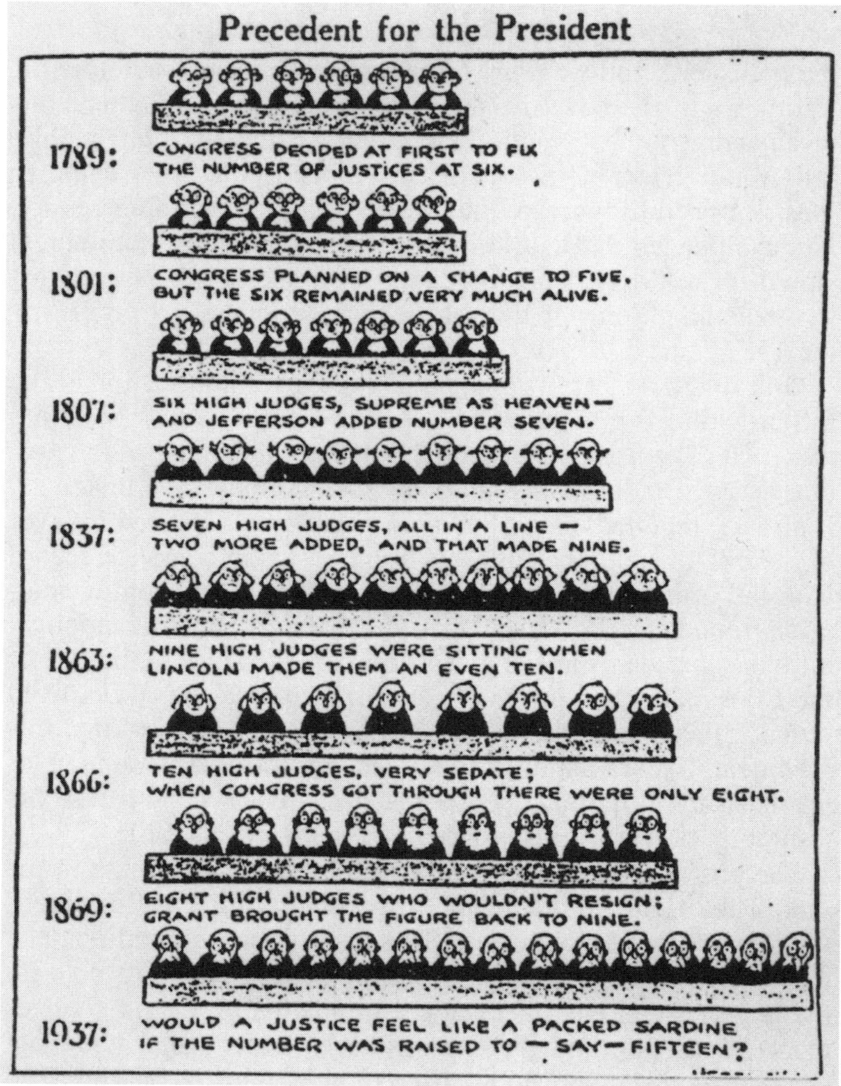

"A Parody on the Precedents at the Senate Hearings." A cartoon by Herblock, 1937.

over the entire statute was repealed, circuit riding was restored, and the number of justices was left at six. This, Griswold emphasized, furnished no basis for comparison with the 1937 bill. There was no attempt at an increase, yet FDR's supporters used it as a precedent. The next two changes in the Court's size (1807 and 1837) were the result of population expansion into Ohio,

Kentucky, Tennessee, and the Midwest, requiring additional justices to hold court in newly created circuits. The number was increased from six to nine.[53] As the country grew, new circuits were needed for the conduct of judicial business. Obviously, there was no precedent here.

The increase in 1863 was similar. The annexation of California and purchase of the Oregon Territory had long required creation of a new circuit and another justice of the Supreme Court to come from it for an area covering the entire West Coast. Congress raised the number of justices from nine to ten, the highest ever. This was not "packing" the Court in the sense in which that term was applied in 1937 and later. Neither was the next change, in 1866, which reduced the number from ten to eight. A further reduction to seven during Reconstruction was contrived by Radical Republicans to prevent President Andrew Johnson from filling any vacancies during his term.

A law of 1869 restored the number of justices to nine, where it has remained ever since. By 1937, that had occurred long enough ago for most people to consider the size as having been set by the Constitution itself. It was feasible in 1869 to set the number of justices and circuits at nine and not increase them thereafter, because in that year Congress lightened the circuit duties of justices, eliminating those duties entirely in 1891.[54]

Under the 1869 law, President Grant was allowed to make one appointment at the next session of the Senate in December. That month Justice Grier resigned, giving Grant two appointments to make. One nominee (Edwin Stanton) died before going on the bench, and a second (Ebeneazer Hoar) was not confirmed. That left Grant with the same two vacancies, but a few hours before he named Justices Bradley and Strong to the Supreme Court, its decision came down against the government in the *First Legal Tender Cases.*[55] Grant knew the position of his two new nomin-

[53] It was this proposed change that elicited the oft-quoted remark of Justice Story: "I verily believe, if there were 12 judges, we should do no business at all, or at least very little." *Hearings,* 2:762.

[54] Robert Scigliano, *The Supreme Court and the Presidency* (New York: Free Press, 1971), 52.

[55] *Hepburn v. Griswold,* 8 Wallace 603 (1870). In it the Court ruled that greenbacks issued by the Union government during the Civil War were not legal tender in payment of public or private debts, and the Act of 1862 was therefore unconstitutional because it applied to contracts made before its passage.

ees on the legal tender question but went ahead and appointed them nevertheless. These two were not even his first choices, but he was accused by his enemies of "packing the Court" to get a reversal in a decision that did not come until a year later.[56]

The vacancies Grant filled were not created so that he could appoint men to the high bench whose views might affect the outcome of a decision in a pending controversy, as was the case in 1937. He may have had private information on how his prospective nominees would rule and in due course saw the earlier decision overturned, but it was not "packing" to fill vacancies that occurred under the usual circumstances. No additions were made to the Court, so Grant's actions cannot properly be called court-packing. Griswold emphasized that never in the past had Congress increased the number on the Court because it or the president wished to influence or affect the Court's decisions.

In spite of well-established historical facts, administration spokesmen persisted in using the Grant "precedent," distorting it to their advantage. Justice Department lawyers researched Grant's appointments for use in speeches, documents, and press conferences. This was the end of the precedents, since the Court number had not changed since 1869. At their most, said Griswold, the previous changes did not hold a candle to the present proposal. Not one of them added more than two judges, and only once had as many as two been added to the Court.[57] To this day the charge of court-packing, as generally understood in American politics, concerns efforts—through means that are considered unconstitutional or otherwise improper—to increase the size of the Supreme Court in order to influence its decisions.[58]

Griswold recounted the episode in Jefferson's first administra-

---

[56] *Second Legal Tender Cases,* 12 Wallace 457 (1871). A year later the Court overruled *Hepburn* by a five-to-four vote. Justices Bradley and Strong joined Miller, Swayne, and Davis to form the majority.

[57] *Hearings,* 2:761–63.

[58] The stigma of court-packing would be attached to an appointment in which a justice committed himself to vote in a certain way, once placed on the Court, but there is no evidence that such a pledge was ever sought by a president, including Grant. Nevertheless, it was one ground upon which his appointment of Justice Joseph P. Bradley in 1870 was denounced as court-packing, even though Grant had a vacancy to fill. On this see Charles Fairman, "Mr. Justice Bradley's Appointment to the Supreme Court and the Legal Tender Cases," *Harvard Law Review* 54 (May 1941): 1142 and passim.

tion during which he had problems with a Federalist Supreme Court that he inherited but did not like and wanted to get rid of it. The method he chose was removal of justices by impeachment. An attempt was made to drive Supreme Court Justice Samuel Chase off the bench. It was a total failure, defeated in part by members of his own party. "There seems to me to be in this a very real and significant precedent," Griswold warned, "leading to the rejection of the present proposal."[59]

Turning finally to the merits of the court bill, rather than "the hollow arguments" advanced by its advocates, Griswold was in a good position to offer hands-on testimony, having taken a part in litigating more than a thousand government cases in the Supreme Court while working in the Justice Department until the late summer of 1934. He attributed much of the administration's current difficulty with Supreme Court decisions to hastily and sloppily drafted emergency legislation "which left much to be desired." He recalled instances in his own experience in which he himself had made repeated efforts to obtain certain needed changes in legislation, to have bills modified so as to eliminate constitutional flaws in anticipation of court challenges. But, as he told committee members, time and again these efforts had been "impatiently spurned."

Quoting from one of Justice Brandeis's earlier opinions,[60] Griswold stated that the Constitution's framers did not adopt the doctrine of separation of powers to promote efficiency, but to preclude the exercise of arbitrary power. "The purpose was not to avoid friction, but by means of the inevitable friction . . . to save the people from autocracy." Our system of government, he assured them, would be changed if this bill went through. "We would then have established the potential dominance of the executive branch of the Government." The president's aims in advancing his court bill, he said, were irrelevant; the future was the real issue. Break down the barriers that have protected the independence of the Supreme Court, he warned, and they "will be open for the first man who would be a dictator."[61]

---

[59] *Hearings,* 2:764.
[60] *Myers v. United States,* 272 U.S. 52 (1926).
[61] *Hearings,* 2:767.

Other opponents of the president's bill had the committee's ears for the remaining weeks of the hearings, scoring heavily in these innings for the plan's foes. Moley had been out of Roosevelt's favor for some time and had turned to journalism after resigning from his post in the administration, but for a short period thereafter he was an unofficial adviser on tough questions. His editorials increasingly diverged from administration policies. He jumped at the opportunity to go to Washington as an opposition witness before the Judiciary Committee to administer "an extra and unneeded black eye to the President's Court plan."[62]

That same quality of dispassionate logic which had characterized Robert Jackson's testimony for the bill worked for the opposition when Dean Young B. Smith of Columbia Law School gave his testimony. He made his ideas seem simple, plausible, and attractive. The soft-spoken Georgian had been a lifelong Democrat, voted for FDR, and agreed that the federal government needed more power. But he pointed out that if six new Roosevelt justices were to accept the interpretation of the Constitution's welfare clause that the president had articulated in his latest fireside chat, there would be virtually no limit to the government's powers.

Smith made these main points: FDR's plan would undermine the independence of the judiciary, impair the people's confidence in the Supreme Court, and effect fundamental changes in the national government without consulting the electorate. He favored a constitutional amendment providing for a mandatory retirement age for justices of seventy or seventy-five, allowing the present justices to leave the bench gradually, and wanted a fixed number on the Court. He proposed to let the president have a chance to have his way, but by a national referendum, not legislative fiat. Like Griswold, he was much less concerned about the president's purpose than about the prospect of changing the whole federal system without allowing the people to have anything to say about it. "It is their right to have a say."

Cleverly calling Roosevelt's bluff in his arguing that an amendment could easily be blocked by the reactionaries in only thirteen states, Smith noted: "If, as has been claimed, the elec-

[62] Dawson, *Brandeis, Frankfurter, and the New Deal,* 119.

tion returns last November were a mandate to bring about these reforms, there should be no difficulty in obtaining an amendment expressly authorizing them." When Senator Logan raised the final objection, that rich and powerful men might defeat such an amendment, he grinned with relief when the dean declared: "Those same people could only carry two States in the last election, Senator. We beat them then, and I think we can beat them easily now."[63]

President Harold W. Dodds of Princeton accused FDR of inventing a scheme by which he hoped to control opinions of the Supreme Court, and warned that Americans were opposed to appointing men to the bench under such coercive conditions. "Shall the President be empowered," he asked, "to fix the color of the Supreme Court to his liking?" Once granted, the power could not reasonably be denied to later presidents, and probably would not be.[64] Dodds's best thought was to turn the whole problem over to an independent commission. Other legal authorities followed, nearly all of whom reiterated the same objection—that the court plan would leave the road open to dominance over the other two branches of the government by the executive. New York District Judge John Knox warned senators that they should not confuse liberalism with party loyalty.[65]

Charles C. Burlingham, dean of the New York bar and a friend of the president's, testified for the opposition, arguing that the fundamental question before the American people was whether the Supreme Court was to be independent or controlled. After a brief survey of the history of an independent judiciary, he said: "With this . . . background it is astonishing that anyone who understands the fundamental principles and framework of our Government can fail to see what a blow the President's proposal strikes at the independence of the Judiciary." He said FDR had been led into a "great blunder" from which he should withdraw. Burlingham believed Roosevelt would be the last man in the world to claim he was a great lawyer. He had to rely on others to advise him as to the Constitution and the law. The president, he

[63] Quoted in "National Affairs," *Time,* April 5, 1937, 12–13; *Hearings,* 1:715–50, at 730 and passim.

[64] *Hearings,* 1:617–41, at 619.

[65] Ibid., 2:1377–98, at 1380.

charged, had been lured into a "shabby enterprise" by his advisers. "I regret that his advisers have abandoned principle for expediency."

Words failed this witness in expressing his opinion of Cummings. He quoted Shakespeare ("He is alone, the Arabian bird") to describe how unique the attorney general was. "I cannot think of more than one other Attorney General in our history—I will not name him or help anyone to identify him—who would not have resigned his office rather than condone or have any part . . . in such a shabby enterprise." The witness seemed to enjoy himself throughout more than three hours of testimony and repartee with committee members. They appreciated his allusions to Shakespeare, such as one on the mysterious authorship of the president's plan: "How now, oh mole, that works so fast in the ground?" A court of fifteen, he claimed, would be "disastrous," recalling sad tales told to him by John Bassett Moore and Charles Evans Hughes about their work with fifteen members on the Permanent Court of International Justice in the Hague. "It takes forever to get through with a case," he asserted. "They [the judges] forget about it [the issue] before they ever reach it [the decision]."

It was hardly the decent thing "to push the old men off the bench," said the outspoken lawyer. Burlingham cited the case in the 1860s of Justice Robert Grier, who retired from the Court and then attended his successor's funeral. "That was desirable often," he added, "but it had never happened before." The previous November, with others, he had conferred with FDR on a constitutional amendment to deal with the Supreme Court's adverse decision in the New York minimum wage case. The president argued that "an amendment was not necessary. The desired end could be accomplished by interpretation." Not until February 5, 1937, he said, did they find out what he had meant by "interpretation."[66]

The noted historian James Truslow Adams testified that in the last 150 years the Supreme Court had done a remarkable job of "wangling" new meanings out of the Constitution to take into account modern conditions, but it had reached a point where the

[66] Ibid., 1041–73.

Court could not wangle any more without the assistance of a constitutional amendment. Tracing the historical background of FDR's court plan, he introduced into the discussion a novel point that seemed to impress the committee members. He portrayed the Supreme Court as one of their own best defenses against pressure groups.[67]

The hearings were extended another ten days, but toward the end of April it was certain that the bill would be reported out unfavorably. Chairman Ashurst predicted that it would be voted on by the full Senate in mid-July. If it did not pass, he added for public consumption, "an outraged public opinion would demand its passage at the next session of Congress."[68] A general sense of weariness permeated participants as the hearings came to an end on April 23. At one of the last meetings only nine senators put in an appearance. After spending time on Capitol Hill, Edwin Canham wrote: "Opposition leaders are very confident they have a majority of votes against the President's proposal as it now stands."[69] He considered the testimony in favor of the court plan "less significant" than expected. The arguments seemed to have had little effect. "True, the administration had paraded an array of respectable legal minds before the Committee in favor of its plan, but the supporting testimony was not so impressive."[70] Observers agreed, however, that if they accomplished nothing else, the hearings were of great value in educating the public on the basic principles of the democratic form of government.

Few if any new friends were made for the president's reforms. No brilliant arguments in the bill's defense were voiced to sway the votes of waverers. In four weeks, the opposition brought seventy witnesses to the hearings to help their cause. In spite of Roosevelt's vehement denials, their testimony confirmed that the purpose behind the bill was to stack the Court with his puppets.[71] Nothing more of a startling nature was revealed about the administration's intentions, but they were clearly spelled out, stripped of sophistry, and laid bare for all to see. Opposition legislators

---

[67] Ibid., 1077–1115.

[68] *New York Times,* April 29, 30, 1937.

[69] *Christian Science Monitor,* April 24, 1937.

[70] Ibid., March 23, 1937.

[71] Leonard Baker, *Back to Back,* 149–51.

looking for arguments to take back to their constituents could make use of much of the testimony to underscore the president's obvious design to dominate the judiciary.

The longer the hearings dragged on, the stronger the case they built against the administration's plan became. Burke and Wheeler used the hearings as a delaying tactic. Time was the enemy, not the ally, of the court bill. Enough senators were already pledged to speak against the measure to prevent a floor vote by talking it to death in a filibuster. Senate and House members alike were upset over the administration's obsession with this bill, which was blocking consideration of all other legislation. It was believed that a filibuster at some stage in early summer could get rid of it.

While the opposition was losing him votes in the Senate, the president maintained his outwardly confident demeanor. His young lieutenants tried to warn him of the perils they faced, but he brushed them aside: "Give the opposition plenty of rope," he laughed, "and they'll hang themselves."[72] Many of his supporters hoped he would withdraw the bill, allow it to lay over to the next session, or at least agree to some sort of compromise. Against these strong currents the administration forces were prepared to carry the trench warfare in Congress underground. At the moment there existed what appeared to be deadlock.

However, there were other possible scenarios. The circumstances that had produced the impetus for the court bill in the first place could change. In fact, this was about to happen toward the end of March. The ground had already been prepared for it in December 1936, but for the time being at least, these maneuvers would have to remain a well-kept secret.

[72] Frederick Lewis Allen, "Hughes Checkmates the President," *Nation* 144 (May 29, 1937), 610.

12

No Real Mischief

> I had believed a year ago, and still believe, that the desirable way out of this blockade of the powers of Congress is for the Supreme Court to correct its own errors. But the essence of such a correction is time.
>
> Irving Brant, *St. Louis Star-Times,* March 20, 1937

ROBERT MARSHALL, a friend of Justice Cardozo's, while visiting him in his Washington apartment on March 21, 1937, performed a somersault in his hallway to demonstrate to his housekeeper the robust condition of his health, upon which the justice, observing the feat from his study door, remarked: "It might be helpful if you would come down and teach some of my colleagues to do that in their judicial decisions." During their conversation Cardozo told Marshall that "his main objection to the President's court program was the unwieldiness of fifteen members, which would ruin the discussion of cases. Even nine members," he said, "was too many."[1]

From the beginning of the Supreme Court battle, Roosevelt and his advisers had counted on opposition from liberals and conservatives, but they failed to consider the power of the Court itself to undermine their cause. The justices had already intervened publicly in an effort to preserve the Court's independence with Hughes's letter to Wheeler. A new Court majority could abandon laissez-faire constitutionalism and permit both state and federal governments to play a larger role in directing national economic life. The new outlook could mark a turning point not only in the battle over Roosevelt's reform plan but also in the future course of twentieth-century constitutional history.[2]

---

[1] As told to George S. Hellman and quoted in his *Benjamin N. Cardozo: American Judge* (New York: Russell and Russell, 1940), 253.

[2] Leuchtenburg, *Roosevelt and the New Deal,* 237.

Morehead v. New York ex rel. Tipaldo

Minimum wage legislation in the United States lagged at least twenty-five years behind that of other countries such as Australia and New Zealand. In 1909 the National Consumers' League, a social reform organization designed to improve working conditions for women and children, launched a campaign that produced a series of minimum wage laws. The first of these was enacted by Massachusetts in 1912, followed in 1913 by Washington State. Around the same time Oregon passed a similar law, approved by the Supreme Court in 1917 by a four-to-four vote.[3] Within a decade thirteen states passed such bills. In a 1923 case testing a 1918 federal statute establishing a board empowered to fix the minimum wage for women hospital workers in the District of Columbia, the Supreme Court invalidated the law.

Adkins v. Children's Hospital[4] was decided by a vote of five-to-three. Justice Brandeis did not vote because his daughter had for some time been agitating for such laws. Justice Sutherland's opinion held the 1918 federal law in violation of the liberty of contract guaranteed by the due process clause in the Fifth Amendment. He argued that "freedom of contract is . . . the general rule and restraint the exception."[5] The liberal *New York World* blasted the *Adkins* decision as "a guarantee of the working girl's right to starve."[6] The impact of this classic expression of laissez-faire doctrine reached well beyond the District of Columbia. State minimum wage laws were struck down by the courts or went unenforced.[7] Washington State's law of 1913 remained on the statute books, but for years it was regarded as a dead letter.

The onset of the Depression stimulated a revival of state mini-

---

[3] Justice Brandeis helped write the briefs before going on the Supreme Court and could not vote in the case.

[4] 261 U.S. 525 (1923). Justices Taft and Holmes filed dissents.

[5] Ibid., at 545.

[6] The *New York World* reproduced a cartoon by Rollin Kirby from the magazine *Survey* (May 1, 1923, 164) depicting Justice Sutherland handing down the decision to a woman worker over the caption: "This decision affirms your constitutional right to starve."

[7] In 1925, an Arizona minimum wage law and in 1927 a similar Arkansas law were struck down by the Supreme Court, based on the *Adkins* precedent.

mum wage laws, considered justifiable under the exceptional circumstances. New York's working women, paid as little as seven or eight dollars a week, slept in subways, unable to afford adequate food and lodging.[8] The new laws were carefully drawn in an attempt to overcome the Court's objections to the 1918 federal statute. The National Consumers' League enlisted Felix Frankfurter and Benjamin Cohen to draft a model bill for New York State, signed into law in 1933.[9] Reformers hoped the Supreme Court would look favorably on the new statutes for women and children, laws that took into account the "value of service rendered principle" favored by Justice Sutherland in his *Adkins* opinion but absent in the District of Columbia law.

By 1935, a case was working its way up through the lower courts to test the validity of New York's law. Joseph Tipaldo, manager of the Spotlight Laundry in Brooklyn, was hauled into court for failing to pay his women workers the minimum wage and falsifying his payrolls to indicate that he had. His lawyers argued for his release by the warden of the city prison (Frederick L. Morehead) on a writ of *habeas corpus,* claiming that New York's law was unconstitutional under the *Adkins* precedent. The Supreme Court for King's County denied the writ,[10] but on March 4, 1936, the New York Court of Appeals reversed, overturning the state's minimum wage law and ordering the dismissal of all charges against Tipaldo. Less than two weeks later, New York filed an appeal to the Supreme Court.

At conference the required four votes granting the appeal were cast by Justices Cardozo, Brandeis, Stone, and Hughes. Roberts later claimed that when his turn came to speak, he said that he saw no reason to hear the case unless the Court was prepared to reexamine and reverse *Adkins.* The question of whether to consider or overrule that precedent, he said, had not been presented by plaintiffs in their briefs and arguments. There was no agreement with his objection from the other justices, and the writ of *certiorari* was marked "granted."[11] The implication was that a

[8] *New York World Telegram,* March 1, 1933.

[9] *New York Times,* May 2, 1933.

[10] 156 Misc. 522; 282 N.Y. Stat. 576.

[11] Owen Roberts's Memorandum to Felix Frankfurter, November 5, 1945, in Felix Frankfurter, "Mr. Justice Roberts," *University of Pennsylvania Law Review* 104 (December 1955): 314–15.

legal technicality prevented Roberts from voting to hear the New York case.

New York's brief in the Supreme Court hearing contended that a minimum wage law was a valid exercise of state police power to protect the health and welfare of women workers. It would not be necessary for the Court to reverse *Adkins,* for the two statutes could be distinguished. In oral argument, Tipaldo's lawyer claimed that the state's police power did not extend to fixing the price of labor. He made the point that New York's highest court had found the 1933 law basically similar to the statute outlawed in *Adkins.* Justice Roberts later claimed that plaintiff's argument seemed to him "disingenuous and born of timidity" in disclaiming a need to overturn. He was unwilling to put a decision on any such grounds.[12] His position was in agreement with the ruling of New York's Supreme Court. He could find nothing in the record to substantiate any alleged distinction between the facts in the two cases. At conference he had said so, adding that he took New York at its word: the state had not asked that *Adkins* be overruled.

The Supreme Court's decision in *Morehead v. New York ex rel. Tipaldo*[13] was announced on June 1, 1936, at the end of the term. A five-man majority, speaking through Justice Butler, could find no meaningful difference between the New York and District of Columbia statutes. Both violated the liberty of contract safeguarding the equal rights of employer and employee to bargain over wages. The *Adkins* ruling and the reasoning on which it rested clearly showed that the state was without power by any form of legislation to prohibit, change, or nullify contracts between employers and adult women workers as to the amount of wages to be paid.[14] Hughes and Stone entered spirited dissents. The chief justice accepted New York's contention that its law could be upheld without overturning *Adkins.* Justice Stone made a strong plea for judicial restraint, urging the Court to face

[12] Ibid.

[13] 298 U.S. 587 (1936).

[14] Ibid., at 604–14. In *obiter dicta,* Butler rebuked New York for enacting such a statute and claiming to have rectified the defects of the earlier federal statute struck down in *Adkins.*

up to the reality of the Depression. Pointedly, he accused the majority of following their personal economic predilections in striking down the law.[15]

Tipaldo was the most bitterly criticized Supreme Court decision of the 1935–36 term. Two weeks earlier the Court had voted to prohibit the federal government from regulating wages in the coal industry,[16] but *Tipaldo* caused a fiercer public outcry than previous rulings on New Deal legislation.[17]

At his press conference, Roosevelt accused the Court of creating a judicial "no-man's land" where neither federal nor state governments could legislate.[18] Republican presidential candidate Alfred M. Landon implied that this time the Court had gone too far.[19] But William L. Ransom, leader of the American Bar Association, addressing the graduates of Albany Law School, found nothing necessarily wrong with a "twilight zone" in which no government—state or federal—could invade an area of economic and personal freedom.[20] On June 23, 1936, New York asked for a rehearing of *Tipaldo,* claiming that in the original brief and petition it had asked for consideration of the *Adkins* ruling. The issue remained in dispute until the Supreme Court convened for the fall term, and on October 12, 1936, New York's request was denied without comment.

A month after the November election, by a vote of four-to-four (with Justice Stone absent) and without opinion, the Supreme Court affirmed a New York law forcing employers to contribute to an unemployment insurance fund.[21] In *Railroad Retirement Board v. Alton Railroad* (1935), which involved federal pensions for railway workers, Justice Roberts had objected to several pro-

---

[15] Ibid., at 619–29.

[16] *Carter v. Carter,* 298 U.S. 238 (1936).

[17] *New York Times,* October 18, 1936.

[18] Press Conference no.300, June 2, 1936, 7:280–81.

[19] *New York Times,* June 7, 1936; *New York Herald Tribune,* June 3, 1936; *Newsweek,* June 13, 1936, 12.

[20] William L. Ransom, June 4, 1936, quoted in Robert R. Nichols and Joseph H. Baccus, eds., *Selected Articles on Minimum Wages and Maximum Hours* (New York: 1936), 204–7.

[21] *W. H. H. Chamberlin, Inc. v. Andrews et al.,* 299 U.S. 515 (1936). Cf. *New York Times,* November 9, 24, 1936.

visions of the Railway Labor Act, including pooling of employers, but in *Chamberlin* Roberts had no objection to the pooling of employers aspect of New York's unemployment insurance law, joining Brandeis, Cardozo, and Hughes in upholding it. This apparent change of heart attracted little attention at the time. The newspapers almost missed it. Was the Supreme Court already hinting at judicial reversals? If so, did anyone think Justice Roberts was ready to repudiate his own doctrines or to make a clean break with his position of the two previous years? The answer would come in early spring.

West Coast Hotel Company v. Parrish

On the same October day that the Supreme Court denied a rehearing of *Tipaldo,* it agreed to review another state minimum wage case. Elsie Parrish had been employed as a chambermaid at the Cascadian Hotel in Wenatchee, Washington, at $12 a week. Under the state's 1913 minimum wage law for women, she was entitled to receive $14.50 for a forty-eight-hour week and demanded the rate mandated by law—amounting to $216.19 in back pay. When the hotel offered to settle for $17, Mrs. Parrish spurned it and went to court. Almost any lawyer at the time would have advised that she did not have a chance of winning. The Washington statute dated from 1913 and was no New Deal measure.

In November 1935 the presiding judge of Chelan County's Superior Court rejected her claim, stating that the ruling *Adkins* precedent was binding on every court in the land. On April 2, 1936, however, the Washington Supreme Court took a different view, upholding the Washington law and ordering payment of all back wages.[22] The West Coast Hotel Company, which owned the Cascadian, appealed to the Supreme Court. The petition was considered by eight justices at conferences between October 5 and October 10, 1936 (Stone was still absent). Justice Roberts voted with three others to hear the case. The brethren were so startled

[22] *New York Times,* October 13, December 17, 1936.

by his vote that one of them was overheard to whisper: "What's the matter with Roberts?"[23]

Little notice was taken of the *Parrish* case when it was first docketed.[24] The facts were hardly distinguishable from those in *Tipaldo.* Why would four justices agree to hear *Parrish* so soon after that ruling? In 1945 Justice Roberts attempted to explain why he voted as he did. Unlike the New York case, *Parrish* explicitly asked the Court to review the *Adkins* precedent and overrule it. "Thus," he stated, "I was confronted with the necessity of facing the soundness of the *Adkins* case."[25] Lacking this explanation in 1936, contemporaries had to wonder, "Why now?" Had the Court majority undergone a change of heart? Legal advisers of the Consumers' League were so sure of the hopelessness of the outcome that they did not even bother to file an *amicus* brief for the defendant.[26]

Eight justices (absent Stone) heard oral argument in *Parrish* on December 16 and 17, 1936. Lawyers for the hotel owners contended that the *Adkins* and *Tipaldo* precedents clearly established that both state and federal minimum wage laws were unconstitutional.[27] The lawyer for Mrs. Parrish argued that the law under consideration fell within the state's police power to fix minimum wages for women workers, and that the Constitution permitted reasonable wage regulation for the public welfare.[28]

After hearing oral arguments, Roberts met with Hughes to announce that he would vote to uphold the Washington statute. The chief justice reportedly was so overjoyed that he felt like throwing his arms around the burly associate justice. Rumors—unfounded, it turned out—flew around that Hughes had persuaded Roberts to

---

[23] Memo, Owen Roberts to Frankfurter, November 5, 1945. Under the ruling of the Court below, the Washington law would have continued to operate even if the Supreme Court had refused to grant *certiorari* in *Parrish.*

[24] On January 3, 1937, the *New York Times* announced five cases of importance that would come before the Supreme Court when its new term opened the next day. It gave top billing to the *Parrish* case, testing the constitutionality of a Washington wage law similar to the New York law struck down by the same Court just seven months earlier.

[25] Memo, Owen Roberts to Frankfurter, November 5, 1945.

[26] *New York Times,* October 18, 1936.

[27] 300 U.S. 380 (1937).

[28] Ibid., at 382–85.

vote as he did to stonewall Roosevelt's attempt to pack the Court, but there is not a shred of evidence to support this claim. The source for it was the author Fred Rodell, who alleged that Hughes, anticipating or perhaps even knowing of Roosevelt's court plan as early as December 1936, persuaded Roberts to uphold the wage law.[29] This allegation was far-fetched. Both Hughes and Roberts vehemently denied this slander on their judicial integrity. The early collapse of public and congressional support for FDR's court bill and the chronology in the *Parrish* case reinforce their denials. What Hughes did anticipate at the time—that New Dealers would portray the shift by Roberts as a capitulation to the threat of court-packing—was borne out.

On December 19, 1936, the vote in conference was four-to-four to uphold the 1913 law, ensuring that the rulings of the Washington Supreme Court and the New York Court of Appeals would stand.[30] Stone's illness kept him away until February 1, 1937; his vote to affirm could be counted on when he returned. Not wishing to leave a weak affirmation of the lower court's decision by an evenly divided vote, Hughes got the justices to agree to hold the case over until Stone could rejoin them to cast his vote. A few days after Stone's return, Roosevelt's message and bill went to Congress. Hughes realized that if the justices ruled favorably in *Parrish* right away, it would convey the impression that they were bowing to the political threat of court-packing. Thus they delayed announcing the decision until a more propitious time.[31] For weeks the Court maintained an ominous silence which observers in some quarters called "a sit-down strike."

[29] Fred Rodell, *Nine Men: A Political History of the Supreme Court from 1790 to 1955* (New York: Random House, 1955), 149.

[30] Hughes cited the four-to-four vote at conference as having taken place "shortly before Christmas." See his "Autobiographical Notes, 1930–1941," 31, Box 181, Hughes Papers, LC; Pusey, *Hughes,* 2:757. Alsop and Catledge were made aware as early as 1938 that the vote without Justice Stone had taken place before the announcement of Roosevelt's court plan, though they mistakenly believed the first vote had taken place in January, 1937, rather than in December, 1936. *The 168 Days,* 140.

[31] Pusey, *Hughes,* 2:757. Not until March 1 of 1937 did the Court deliver another decision of any national significance, and then only the expected five-to-four ruling to uphold a section of the gold clause resolution of 1933, a decision that, according to Yale economist Irving Fisher, "sets the New Deal free to manage its own currency." *Christian Science Monitor,* March 2, 1937.

Few days in the Supreme Court's history have been as dramatic as decision Monday, March 29, 1937, a week after Hughes's letter was read to the Senate Judiciary Committee. The long-awaited decision in the Washington case was announced to a jam-packed courtroom. An overflow crowd of four thousand Easter week visitors lined the steps of the building and corridors outside, unable to gain admission.[32] Robert Jackson, Stanley Reed, and James W. Morris, Justice Department lawyers, sat at the government counsel table or preempted front-row seats as Hughes began reading the five-to-four opinion. For them it was "a moment never to be forgotten." The chief justice's strong voice resounded through the chamber on a note of triumph. He was reversing the Court, but not himself.[33]

The economic conditions that had supervened since the *Adkins* decision in 1923, Hughes said, made it not only appropriate but imperative that in deciding the *Parrish* case the subject of a minimum wage should receive fresh consideration. "What can be closer to the public interest than the health of women and their protection from unscrupulous and overreaching employers?" In each prior case the violation alleged by those attacking minimum wage regulation for women was deprivation of freedom of contract. What is this freedom? he asked. "The Constitution does not speak of freedom of contract. It speaks of liberty and prohibits the deprivation of liberty without due process of law. In prohibiting that deprivation the Constitution does not recognize an absolute and uncontrollable liberty." Regulation that is reasonable in relation to its subject and is adopted in the interests of the community, he said, is due process.[34]

The liberty the chief justice wished to safeguard was that which requires the protection of the law against the evils menacing the health, safety, morals, and welfare of all the people. The exploitation of a class of workers who are in an unequal position with respect to bargaining power and are thus defenseless against the denial of a living wage was not only detrimental to their health and well-being, but placed a direct burden for their sup-

[32] *New York Times,* March 30, 1937.
[33] Jackson, *Struggle for Judicial Supremacy,* 207–8.
[34] *West Coast Hotel v. Parrish,* 300 U.S. 379 (1937), at 391.

port upon the community. In many industries women wage earners were not free agents in an economic sense, and as a practical matter they could exercise no freedom of contract, even if they had the right in a constitutional sense. The ruling held out the possibility that other varieties of labor legislation could be sustained in the future: "The community may direct its law-making power to correct the abuse which springs from [employers'] selfish disregard of the public interest."[35]

His blunt conclusion: "The case of Adkins should be, and it is overruled." The judgment of the Washington Supreme Court was affirmed. Nor did Hughes have any difficulty repudiating the *Tipaldo* precedent. His dissent in that case had aimed a broadside at the doctrine of freedom of contract.[36] The contention of the minority in 1936 was now the law of the majority in 1937. In sustaining the Washington law, Hughes neatly sidestepped *Tipaldo*. The Court, perhaps out of deference to Justice Roberts, did not reverse that ruling. Nor would it be correct to call *Parrish* a surrender to the New Deal. Minimum wage laws were nothing new, having preceded the New Deal by several decades. The views enunciated by Hughes as law in the Washington case were ones he had espoused over a long period. The *Parrish* decision represented the culmination in an ongoing struggle against a doctrine that predated his earlier tenure as an associate justice.[37]

Speaking for the minority in its first open defeat since 1935, Justice Sutherland's dissent reiterated his *Adkins* doctrine enunciated fourteen years earlier—that a minimum wage for women violated their constitutional right to freedom of contract. Summing up deeply held tenets in a judicial philosophy stretching back over a long career, he said the Constitution gave the Court an obligation to protect the liberty of the individual. He warned the new majority that the judicial function did not include the

---

[35] Ibid., at 399–400.

[36] Alsop and Catledge, *The 168 Days,* 142; Mason, *Stone,* 456; Ickes, *Secret Diary,* 2:107; Pusey, *Supreme Court Crisis,* 51–53, makes no suggestion that Hughes changed his doctrinal position in *Parrish.*

[37] Richard D. Friedman, "A Reaffirmation. The Authenticity of the Roberts Memorandum, or Felix the Non-Forger," *University of Pennsylvania Law Review* 142:6 (June 1994): 1940–53. Cf. Cummings's Memorandum to the President on *West Coast Hotel v. Parrish,* March 29, 1937, Box 201, Cummings Papers, ALDL.

power to amend the Constitution under the guise of reinterpretation. "If the Constitution . . . stands in the way of desirable legislation," he declared, "the blame must rest upon that instrument and not upon the Court for enforcing it according to its terms. The remedy in that situation, and the only true remedy—is to amend the Constitution."[38]

Sutherland struck back at Stone for his scathing rebuke of the majority in his *Butler* dissent, which called for judicial restraint and an end to imposing the justices' own social or economic predilections on constitutional interpretation. "This whole notion of self restraint," Sutherland argued, was both "ill-considered and mischievous" and belonged to the domain of "will and not of judgment." A judge's task is to expound the meaning of the Constitution according to his own best—most conscientious and informed—convictions. For him the doctrine of freedom of contract remained in force; intervening circumstances (the Depression) had altered nothing. The meaning of the Constitution does not change with the ebb and flow of economic events.[39] His dissent was an eloquent plea for a judicial philosophy now falling down under the weight of new economic circumstances and political realities.

Having expressed a year earlier the same views adopted by the new majority, Justice Stone felt vindicated. He had maintained all along that due process had nothing to do with wage regulation. It was a bit much, he said, to hear the chief justice declaring that "if such laws [as Washington's] have a reasonable relation to proper legislative purpose, and are neither arbitrary nor discriminatory, the requirements of due process are satisfied."[40] Stone thought the chief should have assigned the majority opinion in *Parrish* to one of his brethren (himself?), perhaps Cardozo, whose *Tipaldo* dissent was more consistent with it.

The same day the Court decided *Parrish,* Justice Brandeis wrote Frankfurter: "Overruling Adkins must give you some satisfaction," to which Frankfurter responded: "It is characteristi-

[38] 300 U.S. 379 (1937). Cf. Joel F. Paschal, *Mr. Justice Sutherland: A Man against the State* (Princeton: Princeton University Press, 1951), 202. Justice Sutherland was appointed to the Court by President Harding in 1922.

[39] 300 U.S. 379–80 (1937).

[40] Ibid., at 398.

cally kind of you to think of the aspects of the Washington minimum wage case that would give me some satisfaction, but, unhappily, it is one of life's bittersweets and the bitter far outweighs the sweet."[41] Following the *Parrish* ruling, Frankfurter wrote FDR:

> And now, with the shift by Roberts, even a blind man ought to see that the Court is in politics, and understand how the Constitution is "judicially construed." It is a deep object lesson—a lurid demonstration of the relation of men to "the meaning" of the Constitution. This behaviour (in the light of the outrageous misrepresentation by Butler of the scope of the issues in the Tipaldo case, confirmed as late as October, i.e. in denying the petition for rehearing) comes on *top* of the Hughes letter. . . . I have absolutely dependable editorial friends on the other side who tell me that some foolish folk (enemies of yours) are doing their damnedest to make me attack the Court so as to start a new line of attack on your proposal. They miss their guess. I shan't help them to divert the issue from the misbehavior of the Court. There are various ways of fighting a fight.[42]

In the Senate, a jubilant Senator Robinson hoisted both brawny fists above his head in the victory sign and broke into the floor debate to announce in his Arkansas drawl the news of the *Parrish* ruling: "I would like to refer to the fact," he told them, "that the Supreme Court has reversed itself in the Adkins case and probably in the New York wage case."[43] Newspapers everywhere told the story in bold headlines: "MINIMUM WAGE LAW CONSTITUTIONAL"; "THE SUPREME COURT SWITCH DUE TO ROBERTS."[44]

The decision in *Parrish* had far-reaching consequences, the most immediate of them being that Mrs. Parrish, by then a forty-three-year-old grandmother, was awarded her $216.19 in back pay. The case produced a rash of new state minimum wage laws and a lively debate in Congress. Eventually it paved the way for federal minimum wage legislation, which became common over

---

[41] Brandeis to Frankfurter, March 29, 1937, and Frankfurter's reply, March 31, 1937, quoted in Urofsky and Levy, eds., *"Half Brother, Half Son,"* 594.

[42] March 30, 1937, PSF Box 150, FDRL.

[43] *New York Times,* March 30, 1937.

[44] Ibid., 1.

time. Justice Roberts, who had always hewed to a narrow definition of judging, never fully explained his vote, but his 1945 memo included the reason he gave for upholding the Washington law. In *Parrish* the Court was asked to consider the *Adkins* decision. Roberts did consider it, found it wanting, and voted to overrule it. In his *Autobiographical Notes* Hughes wrote: "The President's proposal had not had the slightest effect on our decision," a statement we must accept as largely true. The record shows that Roberts's change of mind, whatever its cause, came almost three months before Roosevelt's court proposal was introduced. By announcing the decision a month later, the Court had to take a roasting for appearing to retreat under fire.[45]

Ickes wrote: "The Supreme Court yesterday did a complete somersault on the question of minimum wages for women. . . . Hughes delivered the opinion and used language which, if it had been adopted earlier by the Supreme Court and consistently followed, would probably have prevented the strained relation that now exists between the . . . Court . . . and the legislative and executive branches." He referred to the other decisions the New Deal had won the previous day, but added that "the breath-taking one was the minimum wage case."

Ickes did not know what effect the ruling would have on the court fight, but wrote: "It seems to me that it is an admission on the part of the Supreme Court of charges that we have made to the effect that it hasn't been following the Constitution, but has been establishing as the law of the land, through Supreme Court decisions, the economic and social beliefs of the judges of that Court." The effect, he predicted, "will be to weaken the prestige of the Court in public estimation, because when it was under fire, the Court ran to cover. For my part, I would have had more respect for the Court if it had gone down fighting and snarling after the manner of Justice McReynolds. Hughes and Roberts ought to realize that the mob is always ready to tear and rend at any sign of weakness."[46]

What need is there for court reform, the media wanted to

[45] Hughes, *Autobiographical Notes,* ed. Danelski, 311; *Christian Science Monitor,* March 30, 1937.

[46] *Secret Diary,* March 30, 1937, 2:105–6.

know, now that it appears the Court has reformed itself? This was the greatest threat so far to the president's hopes and expectations for his bill. Frances Perkins noted: "By late spring of 1937 the President's plan was encountering rough sledding. Much of its support faded when the Court reversed itself on the minimum wage question." Two weeks later, an informal poll of senators disclosed that a majority would vote against the court bill. According to Perkins, the change in the lineup in the Court majority, which made it possible for it to sustain modern social legislation, was undoubtedly due to many factors, but she singled out "the discreet management of Chief Justice Hughes [which] greatly contributed to the change. The President persisted in his support of the plan, however, and a serious rift began to develop within the Democratic majority."[47]

Finally, the *Parrish* ruling had a decisive impact on public opinion. Polling data in the first week of April showed that support for the court plan went into a sharp decline from which it never recovered,[48] dropping from a high of 45 percent in the week after *Parrish* to a low of 31 percent by May 17. The average citizen now saw no need to coerce the judiciary to secure New Deal legislation, and those Democrats who had been certain the president's plan would be enacted were now beginning to wonder. From mid-April to the end of May the Supreme Court would reverse its position on other legislation. The next tower to fall would be a series of anti-labor decisions with a test of the 1935 National Labor Relations Act's constitutionality.

Long after March 29, that decision day would be known as "White Monday." Although the Court failed to announce its eagerly awaited Wagner Act ruling, not only did a majority uphold the minimum wage, but in *Virginian Railway v. Federation* (300 U.S. 515) it unanimously upheld the collective bargaining provisions of a revised Railway Labor Act, amended in 1934. This was the model from which the Wagner Act was drawn. But as everyone knew, the railways were so indisputably engaged in interstate commerce and thus subject to congressional regulation

---

47 *Roosevelt,* 207.

48 Cantwell, "Public Opinion," 931.

"Humpty Dumpty's 1937 Dilemma." A cartoon by Bruce Russell, *Los Angeles Times,* March 29, 1937.

that the decision gave no real clue as to how the Court would treat the pending cases testing the Wagner Act.[49]

That same day, in *Wright v. Vinton Branch* (300 U.S. 440), the Court sustained the amended Frazier-Lemke Act, which provided relief to farm debtors. The law corrected certain features a unanimous Court found objectionable in the first Frazier-Lemke

[49] The company challenging the Railway Labor Act had wanted to bargain with a company union of its shop employees, despite the fact that the majority of them had voted for representation by a wing of the AFL.

Farm Bankruptcy Act, invalidated on "Black Monday" in 1935.[50] Back then a Kentucky farmer named Radford lost his farm under a law which, in Justice Brandeis's opinion, deprived mortgagees of their property rights without due process. The amended law allowed farmers to declare bankruptcy and keep their farms by having them appraised at their current market value, paying this sum to their creditors within five years. The 1937 decision permitted a Virginia farmer named Wright to keep his farm by paying his mortgagee "a reasonable rent" over three years. It indicated a willingness to permit a broader interpretation of the due process clause. Its political effect may have lessened the resentment farmers felt toward the Court. A New Deal historian concluded: "But the most extraordinary development in the struggle was the series of Supreme Court decisions which made labor and, to a lesser extent, farmers lose a part of their obvious immediate interest in the appointment of new liberal Supreme Court justices."[51]

Roosevelt under normal conditions should have been elated by these decisions. In public at least, he took that pose. They confirmed his point that the Constitution needed no changes if the Supreme Court properly interpreted it. At a press conference he was asked: "Mr. President, do you think the Supreme Court is curing itself?" He shot back this reply: "I don't think there is any news on it. To tell the honest truth, I haven't even had the time to read the opinions. I have the printed opinions on my desk."[52] He distrusted the wily chief justice, who was proving to be his equal as an adversary. FDR believed Hughes was capable of persuading Roberts to change sides, not because "he found new meaning in the Constitution" or "discovered a concern for social justice," but because it would contribute to the defeat of his bill. He viewed the strong dissent by four justices with some apprehension. What was to prevent Roberts from swinging back to his original alliance? At another press conference, FDR, bor-

[50] *Louisville Bank v. Radford,* 295 U.S. 555 (1935).

[51] Basil Rauch, *A History of the New Deal, 1933–1938* (New York: Creative Age Press, 1944), 276–77.

[52] Press Conference no. 356, March 30, 1937, *CPPC, New York Times,* March 31, 1937.

rowing a phrase from White House aide Ed Roddan, charged that the Court-imposed "no-man's land" created by the *Tipaldo* case had now been replaced by "Roberts' land."[53] The *Parrish* ruling, in his view, was another indication of how the legality of legislation and the fortunes of millions of Americans could be determined by the whim of a single justice.

Robert Jackson, with Justice Stone's absence from the Court in mind, had alluded to this in testimony before the Senate Judiciary Committee: "When the decision of crucial constitutional issues may turn on the death or illness of a single Justice, it would seem that our constitutional progress is governed by a blind fate instead of by human reason. For a Justice . . . to know that even a temporary indisposition may turn the course of a Nation's history must add to the ordinary anxieties about health. Nobody, no matter where his sympathies lie or what his views of constitutional doctrine may be, can view this situation with composure."[54]

Defeats, and even government victories by five-to-four decisions, were unacceptable in Jackson's view. "A state of the law which depends on the continuance of a single life or upon the assumption that no Justice will change his mind is not a satisfactory basis on which the Government may enter new fields for the exercise of its power. . . . Government defeats which keep it out of the exercise of power for an indeterminate time, which may be reversed after a single death, or resignation, or change of mind, is not a stable basis upon which any administration or any Congress can permanently renounce power."[55]

The Wagner Act Decisions

After *Schechter* outlawed the NRA and section 7a, Congress responded on July 5, 1935, by enacting the Wagner-Connally National Labor Relations Act, also known as the Wagner Act, for its principal author. Referred to as "labor's Magna Charta," the

---

[53] Press Conference no. 360, April 13, 1937, *CPPC,* 9:260–61; cf. PPA, 1937 volume, 153–55.

[54] *Hearings,* March 11, 1937, 1:48.

[55] Ibid.

NLRA outlawed unfair labor practices, including interference by employers with employees in forming unions, and guaranteed labor's right to organize, join unions, and bargain collectively with employers, who were now forbidden to give financial support to company unions.[56]

Carefully crafted to withstand scrutiny by the Supreme Court, the law established a substantial connection between the regulations it imposed and interstate commerce. Section I, outlining the policy behind the law, was rewritten after *Schechter* to specify the burden placed on interstate commerce by labor unrest. The policy statement attributed the discord in industry to the denial of workers' rights, which the act was designed to secure. In *Carter* the government had argued that coal strikes would burden not only the interstate commerce of the immediate employers, but the intrastate rail system and many other industries dependent upon coal. The Wagner Act's drafters believed that a strong showing could also be made under it for employers in manufacturing. But would the Court be prepared to reverse its 1936 *Carter* decision?

Early in 1937, a Clapper editorial predicted that a case testing the validity of the Wagner Act "may be the key decision which will indicate whether the New Deal's objectives can be pursued further without a change in the Constitution."[57] A month later an editorial congratulating Roosevelt on his "perfect timing" in moving to rejuvenate the Supreme Court suggested that "nine justices might strike the blow [invalidation of the Wagner Act] that will force Congress to lose no time in enacting judicial reform."[58] When and if that occurred, the result would be a furor worse than that following the outlawry of the NRA.

In a diary entry in June 1935, Cummings noted: "Quite a number of bills . . . have to run the gauntlet of the Supreme Court. . . . The Wagner Bill, which I regarded as of rather doubtful

[56] Under the new act, no less than 340 company unions were broken up. Membership in unions grew rapidly, particularly in the unorganized mass-production industries, until in 1941 it reached 10.5 million. By then, the newly created National Labor Relations Board had handled 33,000 cases affecting more than 7 million workers.

[57] *Washington Evening News,* January 7, 1937, Box 59, Clapper Papers, LC.

[58] *New York Evening Journal,* February 11, 1937.

constitutionality, the Guffey Coal Bill, which I thought was clearly unconstitutional, the AAA amendments, which were not in good condition to meet the constitutional test . . . and which would have to be strengthened to give them any chance at all. In addition to that, there is the Social Security Act, the TVA, and a number of other measures of high importance."[59] Neither the Justice Department nor the White House had much confidence in the Wagner Act's prospects. Even its author had doubts that it could be upheld under the precedents established in *Schechter* and *Carter.*

If the NLRA were to be struck down, the administration expected the uproar to be so loud that the justices would once again be subjected to blistering criticism. District Judge Wilber Clark of Newark, New Jersey, as early as mid-February, had expressed concern in a letter to James Roosevelt and forwarded to Robert Jackson: "I am particularly worried," he wrote, "about the outcome of the Wagner Labor Relations case. . . . I think that the Supreme Court will unanimously reject the Wagner Act in so far as it applies to manufacturing establishments (Jones and Laughlin case) and will divide (6–3) and to sustain on the associated press and trading cases." Would it not be better, he asked, to anticipate such a decision on the Wagner Act?[60]

In the lower federal courts, cases testing the Wagner Act were brought by the NLRB against employers engaged in transportation, communication, and manufacturing. The courts of appeals sustained the law as applied to companies engaged in interstate transportation and communication, but they deemed themselves bound by *Carter, Schechter,* and *Butler* to hold that the act did not extend to manufacturing. On January 11, 1937, the Court of Appeals for the Ninth Circuit in San Francisco was only the latest of the lower courts to declare the act unconstitutional. Injunctions, meanwhile, paralyzed enforcement of the law. Weeks stretched into months, but there was no sign from the high court that it was ready to render a decision. Uncertainty characterized the long litigation period. Neither labor, industry, agriculture, nor the government knew what was or was not legal.

---

[59] Secret Diary, June 20, 1935, 83.

[60] February 17, 1937, Box 79, Jackson Papers, LC.

The first five cases to reach the Supreme Court[61] were argued together, beginning on February 8, 1937. The major constitutional issue in each case was Congress's power to encourage union organization and collective bargaining. A ruling was expected around mid-March. During the waiting period, nerves became frayed in anticipation. A New Yorker, grown impatient by the delay, wrote the attorney general: "Being lambasted in all directions, wouldn't you think that they [the nine justices], supposedly servants of the people, would get a faint inkling that the great majority of the people wishes to heaven they would retire—the one sensible, certain way of ending this expensive disturbance. But, no sir, they sit, and apparently sulk. They refuse to hand down vitally important decisions while the country waits—and suffers."[62]

On Monday, April 12, two weeks after *Parrish,* the Supreme Court announced its decisions in the five NLRA cases. The chief justice, looking very solemn but quite chipper, having celebrated his seventy-fifth birthday the day before, cast a quick glance at the jam-packed courtroom as he took the center chair. After the other justices filed in and the "Oyez" was called, Hughes gave a brief nod toward the right end of the bench where Owen Roberts, the youngest of the nine, took up some papers and began to read: "In this case we are to decide whether the National Labor Relations Act . . ." Spectators who had camped out on the Court's portal since dawn to get seats felt rewarded. At last the fateful decisions on the disputed Wagner Act, which had generated so much speculation and controversy, were announced.[63]

In *Associated Press v. N.L.R.B.* (301 U.S. 103) the issue was the discharge of newsman Morris Watson by the AP for union activity. Roberts ruled that the AP was engaged in interstate commerce and that collective bargaining among newspaper employees did not interfere with freedom of the press. On the latter

[61] The five cases were *Virginia and Maryland Coach Co. v. N.L.R.B.,* 301 U.S. 58; *Associated Press v. N.L.R.B.,* 301 U.S. 103; *N.L.R.B. v. Jones & Laughlin Steel Corp.,* 301 U.S. 1; *N.L.R.B. v. Friedman–Harry Marks Clothing Co.,* 301 U.S. 58; and *N.L.R.B. v. Fruehauf Trailer Co.,* 301 U.S. 149: all 1937.

[62] Ernest Boyles to Homer Cummings, March 11, 1937, Box 199, Cummings Papers, ALDL.

[63] *Time* 29 (April 19, 1937), 14.

point Justice Sutherland entered a dissent for the four conservatives, but the major issue of whether the act would be valid for other industries was not settled. The opinion on the commerce clause issue was unanimous. Roberts moved on to *Virginia and Maryland Coach Co. v. N.L.R.B.* (301 U.S. 58), ordering the company, which operated buses moving across state lines, to reinstate its employees discharged for engaging in union activity. The company's business was so obviously interstate that the vote was unanimous in favor of the defendant.

Chief Justice Hughes read the majority opinions in the three remaining cases brought against manufacturers (steel, trailers, and clothing). They contained the gist of the matter. Their operations in relation to interstate commerce seemed to be "indirect," if not remote. Were they subject to the Wagner Act's provisions, obliged to obey the orders of the National Labor Relations Board to restore discharged employees and to refrain from intimidating them against joining unions? In *N.L.R.B. v. Jones & Laughlin Steel Co. et al.,*[64] the most important ruling, a narrow majority adopted a broad interpretation of the commerce clause, allowing Congress to regulate industrial labor relations and opening the way for further expansion of its authority in this field. Hughes's discussion of the commerce power was cast in his most magisterial style and was consistent with the long sweep of his career, going back to his former tenure as an associate justice. He discarded the old distinction between "direct" and "indirect" effects on commerce (accepted by Roberts in *Carter*), replacing it with Cardozo's contention in his *Carter* dissent, measuring the extent of the effect on interstate commerce. In that case Cardozo had stated that "the question is necessarily one of degree."[65]

---

[64] 300 U.S. 1 (1937). The Court's finding in the two other cases—*N.L.R.B. v. Friedman–Harry Marks Clothing Co.,* 301 U.S. 58 (1937), and *Associated Press v. N.L.R.B.,* 301 U.S. 103 (1937)—were also significant. In the former the respondent clothing firm was a small intrastate operation whose production could not have had more than a negligible effect upon interstate commerce, and yet in his opinion the chief justice emphasized the interstate character of the clothing industry at large and ignored the actual effect production had upon commerce in this case. In the latter it was held that the labor relations of newspapers and press associations were also subject to regulation by the NLRB. On the same day the Court also upheld the application of the Wagner Act to a trailer manufacturer in *N.L.R.B. v. Fruehauf Trailer Co.,* 301 U.S. 49 (1937).

[65] *Carter v. Carter Coal Co.,* 298 U.S. 238 (1936), Cardozo, J., dissenting, at 317–41.

In the steel case, Hughes conceded that although production itself could be local, it might to some degree affect interstate commerce. In *Schechter* he had argued that the effect of the poultry-processing operation was so remotely related to interstate commerce that control of labor conditions in that business was beyond federal authority. However, critics of all three NLRA opinions on manufacturing could well ask: Was the chicken-processing operation less related than the business operations of a small clothing manufacturer (Friedman–Harry Marks), whose market was almost entirely local, or those of a steel plant or trailer manufacturer?

Hughes and Roberts had been part of the six-man majority that rejected the labor relations provisions of the Guffey Coal Act in *Carter,* but they now joined Cardozo, Brandeis, and Stone in upholding the Wagner Act. "We think it is clear that the National Labor Relations Act may be construed so as to operate within the spirit of constitutional authority." In the steel case, Hughes stated, employees have as clear a right to organize and select their representatives for lawful purposes as the respondent (Jones & Laughlin) has to organize its business and select its own officers and agents.[66] Sounding almost like a New Dealer, Hughes wrote: "When industries organize themselves on a national scale, making their relation to interstate commerce the dominant factor in their activities, how can it be maintained that their industrial labor relations constitute a forbidden field into which Congress may not enter when it is necessary to protect . . . commerce from the paralysing consequences of industrial war?" Union activity, he claimed, was often an essential condition of industrial peace. Refusal to negotiate was one of the most prolific causes of strife and therefore a proper subject of judicial notice.

The decision in the steel case consigned the bar of constitutionality to a lower level, but not without bitter protests from the four-man minority. Justice McReynolds, acting as their voice, gave answer in tones loud enough for all to hear: "The idea has been advanced that this is legislation intended to prevent strikes and thereby prevent impeding commerce. Let me read a few lines from the Act itself: 'Nothing in this Act shall be construed so as

---

[66] *N.L.R.B. v. Jones & Laughlin Steel Corp.,* 301 U.S. 1, at 43–44.

to impede or diminish in any way the right to strike.' So I think we can start with the idea that the Labor Board Act is not one to prohibit strikes." He went on to state that a private owner was being deprived of the right to manage his own property by freely selecting those to whom his manufacturing operations were to be entrusted. "We think this cannot lawfully be done in circumstances like those here disclosed."

The four dissenters did not understand how the new concept could apply and were skeptical about its future, because in their view it had no logical stopping place.[67] "Old McReynolds was sore as hell," reported Congressman Maury Maverick of Texas, "speaking like he seldom speaks, gyrating like . . . Congressmen and Senators do on the floor, and poking his pencil angrily at the crowd, as he shouted his opinion, without reading it, and his speech was a good deal different from the written one."[68]

On April 13, 1937, a newspaper headline proclaimed: "SUPREME COURT UPHOLDS WAGNER LABOR LAW. HAILED BY FRIENDS AND FOES OF BENCH CHANGE." The landmark Wagner Act cases broke the logjam of narrow precedents and forecast a new era in the labor relations of U.S. industry. Thereafter no company covered by this law could refuse to bargain collectively with its employees, fire them for joining a union, force a company union on them, or interfere with their union-organizing activity, at least in theory. "To Labor, to industry, to politics, the outcome would be momentous." For example, the Amalgamated Clothing Workers' Union was involved with the southern employer in the *Friedman–Harry Marks* case. Under the ruling in that case, employers would now be required to deal with it.[69]

The five-man majority concurred heartily with Hughes's opinions in the three manufacturing cases. "Admirably done," commented Brandeis. "Yes, Sir, a magnificent opinion," noted Cardozo on the proof sheets.[70] The chief relished a reputation for

[67] Charles C. Curtis, *Lions under the Throne* (Boston: Houghton Mifflin, 1947), 175.

[68] *A Maverick American* (New York: 1937), 336.

[69] *New York Times,* April 13, 1937, 1.

[70] Andrew Kaufman, *Cardozo* (Cambridge: Harvard University Press, 1998), 526, relates: "Cardozo was delighted at Hughes's return to the broad Commerce Clause fold."

liberal views, while at the same time doing everything in his power to tighten the reins on the New Deal. His brethren recognized the extraordinary combination of leadership qualities he possessed. Only Justice Stone was wary. These early signs of change on Roberts's part were for him unconvincing. He had witnessed sudden conversions before. Moreover, he resented the assignment of three of these opinions to Hughes himself. They belonged rightfully to Justice Cardozo, whose *Carter* dissent had spelled out the basic ideas expressed by the new majority.[71]

In upholding the Wagner Act, the Court not only validated the most favorable law ever won by American labor so far, but so broadened the interpretation of interstate commerce that the main doubt in later cases would become not so much what was included under the controlling power of the national government, but what was not. In the first few years after *Jones & Laughlin* there was a flurry of court challenges as companies searched for loopholes in its doctrine, but none was found.[72] In 1941, when the Court upheld the 1938 Fair Labor Standards Act (also called the wages and hours bill), it approved a sweeping redistribution of power from the states to the federal government.[73] Thereafter, cases testing the constitutionality of the NLRA virtually disappeared from the Supreme Court's docket.[74]

The Wagner Act rulings were victories for labor, the New Deal, and the Democratic Party, but at the time their impact on FDR's court plan seemed more important than their bearing on future labor relations or constitutional law. The three five-to-four decisions gave the government the broad powers it wanted over interstate commerce, but they dealt a crushing blow to the court bill.

---

[71] Mason, *Stone,* 813. Irving Brant, an admirer of Stone's, agreed: "The three liberals are not being allowed to speak for the Court because the two liberals-by-compulsion fear what they might say, or begrudge them credit for their consistent stand. The Chief Justice controls this." *St. Louis Star-Times,* April 13, 1937. (The "liberals by compulsion" were apparently Hughes and Roberts.)

[72] See, for example, *N.L.R.B. v. Fainblatt,* 306 U.S. 601 (1939); *Santa Cruz Fruit Packing Co. v. N.L.R.B.,* 303 U.S. 453 (1938); and *Consolidated Edison v. N.L.R.B.,* 305 U.S. 197 (1938).

[73] *United States v. Darby Lumber Co.,* 312 U.S. 100 (1941).

[74] C. Herman Pritchett, *The American Constitution* (New York: McGraw Hill, 1959), 248.

Its proponents were deprived of one of their strongest arguments—that the justices were thwarting the will of Congress and the people. Senator Robinson did not rejoice for long, knowing these decisions would cost him votes. His lukewarm backers were now likely to team up with the opposition, claiming that, with a liberal majority on the Court, the president had achieved what he wanted. This new situation would make it very difficult for Robinson to keep his Democratic colleagues, especially the moderates, in line.

On the same day the Court startled the nation by validating the Wagner Act, Farley telephoned FDR to find him exhilarated. "We did it!" he chortled. "I am very, very pleased. You ought to see Homer Cummings, who's sitting with me now. He looks like the Cheshire cat that swallowed the canary." He went on: "I am convinced now more than ever that the proposals for reform of the Court are warranted. It's the same four justices who have dissented all along that are against me this time." Farley also phoned Senator Wagner to congratulate him. Though he had been the bill's author, he had misgivings about its constitutionality and was surprised by the decisions, having fully expected them to go the other way. Farley suggested: "Maybe the Court was doing a little electioneering against the court-packing plan in the decisions."[75]

Opponents of the court plan, many of whom had also opposed the Wagner Act, now applauded the Supreme Court rulings. At his April 13 press conference, FDR joked sarcastically that he was having a "perfectly grand time" reading the *New York Herald Tribune* editorial hailing the Wagner Act as "A GREAT DECISION." To exploit the irony in the situation, he had instructed Steve Early to resurrect that same paper's editorial of September 21, 1935, in which it had warmly endorsed the National Lawyers' Committee of the Liberty League opinion that the Wagner Act was "thoroughly unconstitutional." He cautioned that these NLRA decisions were limited to specific cases. There was no indication as to how the Court would treat others, or whether it would take the same view of federal power to regulate wages and

[75] *Jim Farley's Story,* 79–80; Clapper Diary, April 13, 1937, Box 8, Clapper Papers, LC.

hours than it did with collective bargaining. Reporters were left with no indication that he would even consider pulling out of the court fight.[76]

The effect of the Wagner Act decisions on public opinion was the reverse of that following the *Parrish* ruling. The administration made some temporary gains by raising the cry that these reversals, suddenly favorable to the New Deal, proved that the Court was composed of men "who must be made to see the error of their ways." While this argument had some immediate effect, it was not powerful enough to alter the downward trend in public opinion. By the week of April 19 the "No" vote rose three percentage points while the "Yes" vote sank.[77]

The Social Security Act Cases

In the spring of 1935, as Roosevelt was emerging from a period of indecision, he was jolted into action by two major developments: the U.S. Chamber of Commerce announced that it would no longer cooperate with the New Deal, and that May the Supreme Court invalidated the NRA in the *Schechter* case. Reacting vigorously, Roosevelt denounced both capitalists and the Court in vitriolic terms. The Social Security Act (SSA) was one of five important pieces of new legislation presented to Congress in June 1935. The others were sweeping reform measures urged by liberals and progressives alike. The SSA formed the centerpiece of the New Deal's evolving social welfare program.

Some 26 million workers and 2.7 million employers in 1937 had been paying taxes toward unemployment insurance and old-age annuities since the first of the year. Not only at the outset, but over the whole course of its existence, the Social Security Act of 1935 has been a fertile source of constitutional litigation. In one of the first of many court challenges, the U.S. Circuit Court of Appeals in Boston ruled two-to-one that this important New Deal law was unconstitutional. Several other courts, however, had from time to time refused to restrain by injunctions the

[76] Press Conference no. 360, April 13, 1937, *CPPC,* 9:260–61.
[77] Cantwell, "Public Opinion," 929–30.

collection of Social Security taxes. The first important case to reach the Supreme Court was filed by Charles C. Steward Machine Company, one of two hundred Alabama companies that had failed to obtain injunctions in the lower courts restraining the government from collecting the levies. The company, which had eight employees, brought suit against Harwell G. Davis, Alabama's Collector of Internal Revenue, for the recovery of $46.14.

Six weeks after validation of the National Labor Relations Act, the Supreme Court upheld the SSA by invoking a broad view of congressional power to tax and spend in pursuit of the general welfare. In *Steward Machine Company v. Davis,*[78] the act's cooperative federal-state unemployment compensation scheme was narrowly sustained by a vote of five-to-four as a legitimate congressional exercise of the power "to lay and collect taxes" to provide for the general welfare. In a companion case, *Helvering et al. v. Davis,*[79] seven justices agreed that the federal old-age retirement benefits program was well within the purview of Congress's taxing and spending power.

In *Steward,* the plaintiff challenged the SSA's unemployment compensation provisions, which imposed a payroll tax on employers and directed the tax receipts to be paid into the general revenue. To offset part of the tax, the act granted employers a credit for taxes paid to a state unemployment fund if they conformed to federal benefits and solvency requirements. State funds were to be held for safekeeping by the secretary of the treasury and invested in federal government securities to build a trust fund. In briefs and oral arguments, the plaintiff invoked *United States v. Butler,* which had invalidated AAA price support provisions that had enabled the secretary of agriculture to contract with farmers to reduce agricultural production in exchange for payments funded by a federal tax levied on farm commodity processing. Lawyers for Steward argued that the unemployment taxation scheme, like the agricultural price support provisions in the AAA, exceeded Congress's power to tax because it infringed upon the Tenth Amendment's reservation to the states of power not delegated by the Constitution to the federal government.

[78] 301 U.S. 548 (1937). See Barry Cushman, "The Secret Lives of the Four Horsemen," *Virginia Law Review* 83 (April 1997), 559–645, at 561–62.

[79] 301 U.S. 619 (1937).

The *Steward* majority, including Hughes and Roberts, upheld the unemployment compensation scheme, the tax on employers, and a provision for grants to states adopting unemployment compensation laws. The Court described unemployment as a "problem . . . national in area and dimensions." Many states had wanted to develop their own unemployment compensation programs but feared economic competition from states without such plans. Hence a federal tax was necessary to enable states to accomplish their general welfare goals. Justice Cardozo's ruling opinion distinguished *Butler* on two grounds: the unemployment tax proceeds in the SSA could be used for the "general welfare" because they were not earmarked for any special group, and the unemployment compensation plan did not infringe upon state prerogatives because state participation in the cooperative program was entirely voluntary. He denied that the tax provisions were an attempt to coerce the states or to invade their reserved powers. Cardozo gave a ringing endorsement of the federal taxing power, which he held to be as comprehensive, except for specific constitutional limitations, as that of the states.

In *Helvering,* Cardozo upheld the statute's old-age pension and benefits provisions, citing the *Butler* precedent ("Congress may spend money in aid of general welfare"). In its permissive, rather vague interpretation of the term "general welfare," *Steward* (and its companion case, *Helvering*) seemed to repudiate the *Butler* ruling's view that Congress, while exercising its power to tax for the general welfare, is required by the Tenth Amendment to eschew regulation of matters historically controlled by the states. The Court majority now held that providing for old-age security would help promote the general welfare. The discretion to make such decisions, Cardozo argued, was not confined to the courts: "The discretion belongs to Congress, unless the choice is clearly wrong, a display of arbitrary power, [and] not an exercise of judgment."[80]

In the Social Security cases, Chief Justice Hughes approved of

[80] Ibid. He agreed that the payroll tax was an excise tax levied within Congress's jurisdiction, that crediting 90 percent of the proceeds to employers in states requiring payment of a similar tax was a valid use of the federal tax, and that states were not being coerced by the legislation into adopting the unemployment compensation scheme. Cushman, "Four Horsemen," 563–64.

the exercise of the government's spending power, as he had in a general way favored the expansive general view of its power in *Butler.* In that case, however, he had voted against the particular exercise of the federal taxing and spending power there at issue—an aspect of the first AAA that appeared coercive to him. But the Social Security cases were much stronger ones for the government, or so they appeared, not only to Hughes and Roberts, but to Van Devanter and Sutherland as well. The latter two justices, the more moderate of the four dissenters, joined Cardozo's majority in *Helvering* to uphold the old-age benefits of the SSA. They also explicitly agreed with most of Cardozo's analysis in *Steward* upholding the unemployment relief program, and dissented in that case only because they regarded the deposit of state funds in the U.S. Treasury as an abdication of federal power.

Steward is noteworthy for its sympathetic appraisal of joint federal-state welfare ventures. In his ruling, Justice Cardozo amply demonstrated that the competitive pressures of a national economy would make it increasingly difficult for states to perform traditional welfare functions without the national uniformity made possible by federal assistance and regulation.

The battle over Roosevelt's judiciary reform plan raged on throughout May while the Court issued its chain of revisionist decisions. Probably nothing in the entire battle did so much to undermine the court bill as the change of front by the Supreme Court itself. In the public's mind, Roosevelt's chief complaint against the Court collapsed. After the initial concession on an expanded federal authority in the minimum wage area, the new majority in the NLRA and Social Security cases proceeded to broaden the permissible areas of federal regulation to such an extent that Professor Edward Corwin of Princeton termed the result a "Constitutional Revolution." He vastly overstated the case. The new position taken by the court majority was more the result of the shift by Roberts than of any other factor. Contemporary comment dubbed the sudden about-face "the switch in time that saved nine."[81] The expression, whatever its origin (Abe Fortas,

[81] The phrase has also been attributed to Thomas Reed Powell, Harvard law

Paul Freund, or Corwin himself), is inane and grossly inaccurate. The questions that need to be asked are, "Why did Roberts change his vote," and "To what extent, if any, was the change the result of political pressure?"

It must first be made clear that Roberts did not dominate the Court. He controlled no one's vote but his own, no one controlled his, and he did not seem to have significant persuasive power over his brethren. After March 1937 he exercised a certain degree of leverage in the Court's decisions because his vote or that of Hughes was needed to form a majority. It may never be possible to explain with any degree of exactitude why Roberts voted as he did in these cases, though a great amount of ink has been spilled in the attempt. In 1946 Hughes's biographer, Merlo Pusey, asked him to account for Roberts's vote in the Washington minimum wage case. His reply, as Pusey reports, was: "Who knows what causes a judge to decide as he does? Maybe the breakfast he had has something to do with it."[82]

Professor Laurence Tribe of Harvard Law School speculated that whatever motivated Roberts to vote as he did, he was influenced neither by public reaction to the Supreme Court's rulings of 1935–36 nor by the election returns of November 1936, and certainly not by the court-packing threat of February 1937. His change of mind preceded the latter two events. In Tribe's analysis, Roberts should at least be given the benefit of our assuming that he simply changed his mind, or attitude, or both.

To some extent, Roberts's behavior defies understanding. He was timid and his views were not as well settled as Hughes's. In retrospect, they appear to have been considerably more idiosyncratic. His doctrinal positions seemed to change over time, and even within a short span he acted in ways that might appear to the casual observer to be inconsistent. This perceived inconsistency, however, may only mean that Roberts was moved by factors that appeared more important to him than to others. Admittedly, his conduct in the two minimum wage cases was strange. Later ex-

---

professor. It seems more characteristic of the latter than the former. It was also used in a letter by Professor Corwin, but that does not prove he originated the phrase.

[82] "Justice Roberts' 1937 Turnaround," 1983 *Year Book,* The Supreme Court Historical Society, Washington, D.C., 102, 106.

planations for it do not hold up well under the searchlight of historical scrutiny. But there is good reason to believe that his vote in *Parrish,* though not in *Tipaldo,* reflects previously held substantive views.

In the "Autobiographical Notes" the chief justice put together at a later date, substantial parts of which were published in book form, he stated: "It has been insinuated, and some have made, I understand, a direct charge that the Court during the pendency of the President's bill, and for the purpose of defeating it, changed front." The reference was aimed in particular at the two cases, *Parrish* and *Jones & Laughlin,* which upheld the NLRA. Hughes made very clear that the notion that either of these cases, or any other, was influenced in the slightest degree by the president's threat to reorganize the Court was utterly baseless.[83]

Throughout this and subsequent phases of the court-packing fracas, it was acknowledged, even by his supporters, that Roosevelt played his hand badly, and that Hughes played his with consummate skill. Neither in *Jones & Laughlin* nor in *Parrish* did Hughes choose to overrule previous anti–New Deal decisions. In *Jones,* with little explanation, he merely said that *Carter* was "not controlling." By this approach he demonstrated the talent that was wasted in 1916 when he lost the presidency to Woodrow Wilson. "He was the one man in the New Deal years who took President Roosevelt to the mat and won."[84]

The attack on Roosevelt's court plan, as Ickes, Corcoran, and many others agreed, was brilliantly managed, with the chief organizing the "nonpolitical" justices in a superb nonpolitical defense of their role. "At the same time," according to John Roche, "the Court seems to have taken a fresh (and of course non-political) look at some of the Constitution's objective requirements. The Wagner Act was held up against the commerce power by the chief justice and found to fit. Like General Douglas MacArthur, Hughes never retreated—he firmly advanced to the rear, sowing the countryside with legal land mines as he went. In short, the Court took evasive action, and thus undermined the President's case."[85]

---

[83] Hughes, *Autobiographical Notes,* ed. Danelski, 311–12.

[84] John Roche, *Courts and Rights: The American Judiciary in Action* (New York: Random House, 1966), 113.

[85] Ibid.

13

Searching for Compromise

> If there was no compromise and the bill failed, then it is difficult to foresee the accomplishments of any aims of the administration.
>
> Senator Joseph O'Mahoney to Tracy Mckraken, March 6, 1937, O'Mahoney Papers

FOR THE COURT BILL, by the beginning of May 1937 "the handwriting was on the wall," in Jim Farley's words. The president, undaunted, seemed oblivious to the possibility of defeat and was unwilling even to consider compromise.[1] In 1941, in the preface to his *Public Papers and Addresses,* Roosevelt attempted to create a far different impression from the one Farley and others left behind. "Time and time again during the fight," he wrote, "I made it clear that my chief concern was with the objective. . . . The exact kind of legislative method to accomplish the objective was not important. I was willing to accept any method proposed which would accomplish that ultimate objective—constitutionally and quickly. I received, however, no reasonable guarantee or assurance that some other definite method would obtain Congressional approval. Rumors of compromise were plenty; but never a definite agreement or offer."[2]

This explanation is open to question, and a further statement by the president appears to have even less basis in fact: "The best legislative advice which I could get from the Congressional leaders was that my own suggestion would ultimately be approved. That is the reason why no so-called compromise was ever submitted by me to the Congress; that is why it was necessary to persist in the plan originally proposed."[3] The actual re-

[1] *Jim Farley's Story,* 84.
[2] *PPA,* 1937 volume, lxv.
[3] Ibid., lxv–vi.

cord of events throughout May and June reveals a far different story. Except for a few die-hards in the Senate, the "leaders" to whom FDR referred recommended either delay, withdrawal of the bill, or compromise.[4]

No one in Congress or anywhere else had any sure notion of Roosevelt's thinking on the matter of compromise.[5] Possibly he was not as adamant on the subject as he pretended to be, or as Farley made him out to be. Few senators believed he was impervious to the idea. Edward Canham reported: "Leaders in Congress suspect President Roosevelt will have to compromise on the plan, but they don't know what lines events will take."[6] Speculation was rife that if the Supreme Court should decide to uphold the Social Security Act, the bottom would fall out of FDR's unwillingness to adjust his program.[7]

The Supreme Court justices did not appear to be overly disturbed by the possible outcome of Roosevelt's proposal. They disliked him as much as he did them. His move was no more than what could be expected from him. The really angry men were the so-called liberal justices. Laying violent hands on the Supreme Court was not their idea of liberalism. On the issue of court-packing, Chief Justice Hughes and his brethren were more united than they had been on anything in years. More ominously, liberals everywhere were weighing in.

For more than two years, liberals had been complaining that either the Supreme Court or the Constitution had to be altered to carry out the New Deal's social and economic agenda. Stripped of its disguise, FDR's original court bill was revealed as a mere means of attaining a temporary end—putting enough New Deal justices on the bench to ensure that the rest of his program would not be invalidated. When Senator Ashurst tried to convince skeptics of the "mildness" of the president's plan, as have some recent historians, it proved almost too much for liberals of the day to stomach.[8] They wanted much more than a temporary victory;

---

[4] MacColl, "Supreme Court and Public Opinion," 419–20.

[5] *Christian Science Monitor,* May 9, 1937, quoted in ibid.

[6] Ibid., May 4, 1937.

[7] Ibid., May 17, 1937.

[8] *Time* 29 (March 1, 1937), 10; cf. David M. Kennedy, *Freedom from Fear: The American People in Depression and War, 1929–1945* (New York: Oxford University Press, 1999), 331.

they sought permanent judicial reform, making it easier in the future for the government to take such social and economic steps as they championed.

As a result, liberals began scouting around for compromise proposals. Amid endless discussions, lawmakers chewed over the arguments, jockeying for position. The theme of most talk was the chance for compromise, preferably by constitutional amendment. Seizing on Roosevelt's stated aim—getting young blood on the bench—Senator Burke's amendment would have allowed justices to retire with full pay at seventy, and required them to do so at seventy-five. This idea, suggested earlier by Hatton Sumners, did not have much appeal for liberals, who could point to Holmes, retired at ninety, to Hughes, still going strong at seventy-five, and to Brandeis, widely revered at over eighty.

Senator Norris's proposal, which would require a seven-to-two majority vote by the Court to hold a law unconstitutional, was going nowhere. It conflicted with the internal rule-making powers of the Court and would have been struck down if passed as a statute. An amendment giving the government power to regulate labor, industry, and agriculture—or whatever it took to achieve New Deal aims—was a dead issue. It transferred so much power to the federal government that it would have completely destroyed states' rights. The Wheeler-Bone resolution, which would endow Congress with veto power over Supreme Court decisions by a two-thirds vote after an intervening election, would have had the effect of amending the Constitution, but only by upsetting the delicate balance existing among the three branches of government in favor of the legislature. Some of the court bill's opponents offered to support a constitutional amendment giving the federal government powers the Court had denied it if FDR would give up his plan. He refused, and by his intransigence on this and all other options he succeeded in alienating a considerable portion of his liberal following. For the first time in his presidency, Roosevelt found himself confronted by a formidable and articulate opposition.

Would-be peacemakers continued to urge compromise. Senator Key Pittman proposed a constitutional amendment to set Court membership at a permanent and unconditional fifteen, thereby avoiding retirement pressure on sitting justices. Said

Senator Vandenberg of the Pittman proposal: "It might have been a good compromise once, but the President's last speech made all compromise impossible."[9] The opposition was settling in for a fight to the finish.

After the Wagner Act decisions, even FDR's close White House aides began losing confidence in the bill's chances for passage and counseled retreat. Corcoran, Cohen, and Jackson urged the president to shift strategy, allowing the bill to lay over to the next session, since it was unlikely to pass in the current one. Corcoran was eager for delay if only they could get Roosevelt to go along. Lawmakers were anxious to move ahead on other New Deal legislation.[10] Corcoran's objective was to win over farm and labor support with the lure of new programs in exchange for more vigorous backing of the sagging judicial reforms. He believed opposition to the bill might be weakened by a long period of inactivity. This strategy could pave the way for passage of a wages and hours bill and win the support of labor. Aides warned FDR that "the sword of Damocles is hanging over our heads."

"The searing hot winds of danger were beginning to blow about Roosevelt's Court plan." He faced defeat from a Congress that he supposedly owned, body, votes and soul.[11] A filibuster in the middle of a legislative session (i.e., in April or May) almost always blew itself out and was not to be feared, but a filibuster at the end of a legislative term was risky. If the Senate failed to vote on the court bill until late July or early August, politicians wanting to avoid committing themselves on the plan one way or another could simply move for an adjournment and go home. In fact, they would resemble wild horses stampeding in all directions if a motion to adjourn *sine die* were to be offered.

Delaying the bill, however, could ruin the chance for a filibuster. If one took place at all in the current session, it would come

[9] *Time* 29 (March 22, 1937), 16. The speech to which the senator referred was the fireside chat of March 9, 1937. Some optimists still hoped that the whole issue could be sidestepped or would go away with passage of the Sumners-McCarran bill, permitting Supreme Court justices to retire at seventy with full pay. It passed the Senate by a vote of seventy-six-to-four, and the president signed it into law on March 1, 1937.

[10] Alsop Notes, Box 53, Alsop Papers, LC.

[11] "Washington Notes," *New Republic* 91 (May 12, 1937), 15.

in late summer when everyone wanted to escape the heat of the capital. Roosevelt, however, insisted on his "carrot before the donkey" approach and showed a complete lack of interest in delay or pushing any other legislation while the court bill was before Congress. Measures Democrats wanted to see passed in that session languished, from a new farm bill to "little TVA's."[12] Experienced observers predicted that constructive measures set for action at that session, such as low-cost housing, executive reorganization, crop insurance, and relief of farm tenancy, would have to go by the board. Only two major measures were enacted during that session—a new Guffey Coal bill and a Neutrality Act. Both were revampings of earlier statutes. The Senate was in session only sixty-one of the one hundred days it could have met, averaging less than three hours' work per day.[13] The House did little better.

Roosevelt's advisers failed to sway him, even after the Social Security Act was upheld. Senate Majority Leader Robinson, who favored compromise but not delay, was utterly opposed to letting the bill go over to the next session and refused to cooperate with them. The old Senate warhorse knew more than Corcoran or Cohen did about the disruptive effect of letting legislation hang fire, risking loss of interest. He clung to the slender hope that the Court (or Roberts) would switch again. Failing that, he refused to allow any delay of the bill. Win or lose, he would fight on. Senate leaders seemed to have a deep-seated dislike for unfinished business.[14] So Corcoran had to resume shuttling between the White House and the halls of Congress on his lobbying mission. Roosevelt was so confident that things were going along "swimmingly" that when Farley talked with him April 19 in a bedside conference, the court plan was barely mentioned.[15]

---

[12] The administration's wages and hours legislation was finally ready by the second week in May, by which time Roosevelt was being implored to submit it to Congress without waiting for the Supreme Court issue to be settled. The bill and message went to Congress on May 20, 1937. *PPA,* 1937 volume, 210–13.

[13] *New York Times,* May 9, 1937; *Time* 29 (May 17, 1937), 15.

[14] Alsop Notes, Box 50, Alsop Papers, LC; Alsop and Catledge, *The 168 Days,* 199. Cummings, the true author of the bill, was initially opposed to compromise, a position stemming from pride of authorship. He was part of the reason why compromise was delayed for so long, according to Alsop and Catledge.

[15] *Jim Farley's Story,* 80.

In mid-April Robinson announced that the White House had won almost everything it wanted. While opposing delay, he was well aware of the perils the administration faced in a Congress whose members were anxious to move on to other business. At that stage he began to press for compromise. He told White House lobbyist Joe Keenan: "The thing to do is to settle this . . . right now. This bill is raising hell in the Senate. Now it's going to be worse than ever, but if the President wants to compromise, I can get him a couple of extra justices tomorrow. What he ought to do is say he's won, which he has, agree to compromise to make the thing sure, and wind the whole business up."[16]

When Keenan relayed his views to the general staff, emphasizing "how worried Joe was" about the future, Corcoran, James Roosevelt, and others pooh-poohed his report. "Dear old Joe," they said, has a tendency to be a "defeatist." They argued they had no positive proof that the bill would lose many votes by the Court's turnabout. Corcoran, Cohen, and Jackson opposed compromise, equating it with defeat. Any revised bill that passed now, they said, would make future decisions by the Court the responsibility of the administration, but two extra justices would not likely produce "a dependable bench." The time could come when a Supreme Court of eleven might render an unpopular decision, and then the whole sorry business would be thrown back in the president's face. As Jackson put it, "If you're going to pack a court at all, you've really got to pack it."[17]

Those favoring compromise pressed on. The hearings were winding down, winning friends for the opposition with each new witness and gaining favorable publicity for their views. Wily Chairman Ashurst's delaying tactics were paying off. Covertly he was doing everything he could to defeat the bill, while insisting in public that there would be no compromise: "I have never heard of a man retreating when he is winning."[18]

The events of April marked a decisive shift in the character of the court fight. No longer was it Roosevelt against the Old Guard Court—the fight now was between him and Congress. Validation

---

[16] Leonard Baker, *Back to Back,* 182; Burns, *Roosevelt,* 304.
[17] Alsop and Catledge, *The 168 Days,* 159.
[18] *New York Times,* April 14, 1937.

of the SSA took the Court as an institution even farther removed from the struggle, but not all of its members.[19] In May and June, Chief Justice Hughes made a number of speeches thinly disguised as assaults on FDR's court proposal. In "informal remarks" to lawyers at the fifteenth annual meeting of the "strictly non-political" American Law Institute, he was expected to mention the work of the Supreme Court, but it was not until the last 150 words of his speech that he remarked that the Court was up-to-date in its work. He ended with a ringing appeal for an independent judiciary:

> The success of democratic institutions lies in the success of the processes of reason as opposed to the tyranny of force. Between these society must choose. If society chooses the processes of reason, it must maintain the institutions which embody these processes. Institutions for the exercise of the law-making power and for the execution of laws must have their fitting complement in institutions for the interpretation and application of laws . . . through a competent and independent judiciary. The firm and true administration of justice is thus the primary concern of civilized society.

Vigorous applause greeted his remarks. Commenting acidly on the speech, columnist Irving Brant wrote: "The processes of reason, in the case of Chief Justice Hughes, are the processes of reaction, but unlike his fellow reactionaries, he has not the stamina, or the bad judgment, to hold to them against heavy odds."[20]

By the end of May it was clear that the Roosevelt forces did not have the votes to pass the bill. Five different Senate polls taken around that time produced the same result—defeat. Newspapers hostile to the president's bill reported forty senators for, including two Independents, and forty-five against, including twenty-eight Democrats, with ten Democrats uncommitted.[21]

---

[19] Burns, *Roosevelt,* 305.

[20] Charles Evans Hughes, "Reason as Opposed to Tyranny of Force," May 6, 1937, a speech delivered at the annual meeting of the American Law Institute, Washington, D.C. Text is in *Vital Speeches* 8 (May, 1937), 458ff. Cf. MacColl, "Supreme Court and Public Opinion," 429. Excerpts from the speech and a short history of the ALU are in *Time* 91 (May 17, 1937), 72–73.

[21] Editorial Research Reports, May 10, 1937, Box 230, Clapper Papers, LC. One newspaper violently hostile to FDR at that time was the *New York Times.* On this question see Allan Nevins, *Herbert H. Lehman and His Era* (New York: Scribner's Sons, 1963), 188, 193.

Chairman Ashurst was heard in the halls of Congress humming an old southern tune: "Massa's in the Cold, Cold Ground."[22] Opponents of the bill, fearful that FDR would somehow manage to pull it through, were reassured by a New York journalist that "even if Congress should pass the law remodelling the Supreme Court, the . . . Court could always declare the law unconstitutional, what with all the practice it has had lately."[23]

On April 28, three powerful Democrats on the Senate Judiciary Committee—Carl A. Hatch, Pat McCarran, and Joseph O'Mahoney—publicly announced their opposition to the president's bill, based on testimony in the hearings.[24] After hearings ended on April 23, the committee had gone into executive session the following Monday to prepare for a vote and draft a report. The lineup, formerly eight for the bill and seven against, with three wavering, was now ten for and eight against casting their vote for an adverse report.[25]

For months Senator O'Mahoney had been flaying the administration, demanding a constitutional amendment, but by mid-April he concluded that this tactic was doomed, especially after a visit to the White House with Professor William Z. Ripley, a Harvard economist. A few days before making his public announcement, O'Mahoney was invited to visit FDR. The senator considered it a last chance to make him see the wisdom in compromise. The president wanted to try and smooth things over to win the senator's support.

Seated before his desk, FDR's visitors asked him why he refused to compromise when he had the liberal majority he wanted on the bench. He replied that a five-to-four majority was not enough. He wanted a Court that would "cooperate" with him. To their utter amazement, he stated that a close relationship between the executive and the judiciary had to be established. He wanted six new justices on the Court, men who would be "friendly and

[22] Leuchtenburg, *Supreme Court Reborn,* 145; *New York Herald Tribune,* June 5–10, 1937; *New York Times,* June 4, 7, 1937.

[23] *New Yorker* 13 (March 6, 1937), 13.

[24] *New York Times,* April 29, 1937, 1, 10.

[25] The opposition senators were King, Van Nuys, Burke, Connally, Borah, Austin, and Steiwer.

approachable," with whom he could confer from time to time on his "great plans for social and economic reform."

The president recounted how, as governor of New York, he had operated that way with the judges on the Court of Appeals. It had worked out very well. (This kind of broad discretion was then allowed under New York's constitution.) Where great questions were involved, FDR thought it was in the public interest to have the judiciary and executive work things out together rather than to have them at cross-purposes, forced to endure long intervals of uncertainty between legislative action and the Court's reaction. Early in his first term he said he had called Hughes to the White House and told him how much he would like to cooperate with the Supreme Court. He thought the consultative relationship between them would be helpful. Hughes rebuffed the overture, saying coldly: "Mr. President, I must remind you that the Supreme Court is an independent branch of the government." Roosevelt did not understand this attitude. At a much later date, when he repeated this entire conversation to Senator Wheeler, FDR said: "You see, he wouldn't cooperate."

Hearing this, O'Mahoney and Ripley were aghast. Could it be that this president knew so little of the country's constitutional structure and its history of an independent judiciary? Should they, then and there, have given him a lesson in the doctrine of separation of powers? Upon leaving the office they compared notes, for neither could believe he had heard what he thought he had heard.[26]

Earlier in the battle, Keenan had tried to warn Cummings that they could expect defections, and he specifically mentioned Senators O'Mahoney and Connally as likely opponents of the president's bill. Cummings laughed at the suggestion, and an irritated Keenan set out to prove his point. O'Mahoney was then lying ill in his apartment at the Wardman Park Hotel. Keenan phoned Farley, an old friend of the senator's, and asked him to check out his position. A week or so later O'Mahoney rang up Keenan to

[26] Gressley, "O'Mahoney, FDR, and the Supreme Court," 196; Alsop and Catledge, *The 168 Days,* 16, 154–56; Mooney, *Roosevelt and Rayburn,* 67. A provocative analysis of Roosevelt's exchange with Ripley and O'Mahoney is in F. Alan Coombs, "Joseph Christopher O'Mahoney: The New Deal Years" (Ph.D. diss., University of Illinois, 1968), 257–58, cited in Gressley, 196 n. 45.

say he had learned that there was some question about how he stood on the court bill. Well, he said, he would be glad to tell him where he stood. He considered it obnoxious, undemocratic, and an insult to the Senate. He would never stand for it.[27] In a later radio speech he denounced the measure as "an utterly futile gesture" and "an extremely dangerous innovation." He warned the administration that it would be the most tragic mistake in the history of the liberal movement in the country if this bill should pass.[28]

Senator Hatch, also demanding compromise, suggested setting the judicial age limit at seventy-five to allow the appointment of a single coadjutor justice in any one year. The proposal was turned down by the White House. Senator McCarran of Nevada had once favored expanding the judiciary, but on closer examination of FDR's plan he became concerned about its implications for the courts and potential for increasing executive power. He shifted into neutral. His wavering made him an unknown quantity on the Judiciary Committee and enhanced his influence with the bill's advocates. McCarran went home to Nevada to determine the depth of public sentiment among his constituents. When he learned it was heavily against the president, that tipped the balance in favor of his final decision, announced at the end of April. Anticipating the important vote about to take place in the Judiciary Committee, he addressed a mass rally in Philadelphia, explaining his belated decision.[29] Nevada was flooded with twenty thousand reprints of the speech—a copy for almost every voter in the state. For the first time in his long career, his stand won Republican as well as Democratic support.[30]

---

[27] Alsop and Catledge, *The 168 Days,* 86–88.

[28] The speech of May 5 was reported in the *New York Times* on May 7, 1937.

[29] A group calling themselves "The Defenders, Inc." or "Citizens' National Supreme Court Protective Committee" held their meeting in the Philadelphia Academy of Music on May 10, 1937, to protest the court bill. Besides McCarran, speakers included Senator Peter G. Gerry, Wheeler's whip on his Steering Committee; Senator Royal S. Copeland of New York; and Judge John A. Knox. The proceedings were carried nationwide over the radio, shown in newsreels, and reported in the press. The chairman of the Pennsylvania division of the committee was Owen Wister, better known as the author of the well-known novel *The Virginian.*

[30] *Literary Digest,* February 13, 1937, 7; *New York Times,* February 8, 1937; Jerome E. Edwards, *Pat McCarran: Political Boss of Nevada* (Reno: University of Nevada Press, 1982), 76.

In a letter to its membership, the director of the group sponsoring the rally explained that the Senate Judiciary Committee, then in executive session, was closely divided on the court bill. "The present hope is that the bill will be reported unfavorably by a vote of ten to eight." The mass protest was deliberately timed to be held at that critical stage in the committee's deliberations. Organizers believed it might prove to be a "determining factor" in defeating "those who wanted to sabotage the Court, and with it, the Constitution."[31]

McCarran expected his party's leaders to exact their revenge for his independent stand and deprive him of patronage. These fears were realized on May 16 when Jim Farley, in reply to a reporter who asked how the court battle was going, denounced McCarran and O'Mahoney for their perfidy: "When Senator O'Mahoney comes round for help on a sugar bill, his conscience won't be bothering him then, will it? Neither will Senator McCarran's when he wants something for his state. It's all in the point of view."[32] Farley's remarks, supposedly "off the record," were reported in the press. He later wrote that this was one of only two occasions during nearly eight years in Washington when a statement he made "off the record" was published. The press interpreted his remarks as a threat. They had the effect of making McCarran even more rigid in his opposition to the bill and less amenable to compromise. Farley later admitted: "It taught me a powerful lesson in holding my tongue."[33]

The announcement of the defection by three Democrats at that stage created a sensation. The White House may have expected desertions by O'Mahoney and perhaps McCarran, but not Hatch. Their stand ensured that the court bill would be reported out of committee unfavorably. In one final effort to head this off, FDR summoned Chairman Ashurst. In his diary the senator left this account of the session:

> Eff Dee leaves tomorrow for a two-weeks' fishing cruise in the Gulf of Mexico. At the White House today the mercury of his manners towards me registered zero as he suggested that his bill

---

[31] L. M. Bailey, April 30, 1937, Box 172, Hughes Papers, LC.

[32] *Jim Farley's Story,* 88.

[33] Ibid.; Edwards, *McCarran,* 77.

> for judicial reorganization be reported from the Senate Committee on the Judiciary *without recommendation* and he handed me a memorandum containing some data he desired should be used in such proposed Report. He requested me to show the memorandum to Senator Robinson . . . which I did during the afternoon and upon exploring the situation, Senator Robinson and I ascertained that to report the bill without recommendation was not feasible.
>
> I was not surprised this evening when a "Friendly Voice," nameless here, came over the telephone warning me that Eff Dee believes that I have killed his judicial reorganization bill by Fabian tactics and by delay and postponement in that although he submitted his plan to the Senate on February Fifth, last, I did not commence the hearing . . . until March Tenth and then strung the testimony out.
>
> Beyond doubt my refusal to pass his judicial reorganization bill through the Senate has alienated him from me and has also damaged my prospects for re-election to the Senate [from Arizona] in 1940.[34]

In mid-May a liberal journal editorial commented: "The administration could almost certainly have forced a report without recommendation, or at worst, a report with minor concessions to the opposition. But the President and his aides, with hefty majorities in both houses, were too proud to yield. They thought they had nothing to worry about."[35]

At the end of April, Roosevelt went off on his fishing cruise. He was no sooner gone than Corcoran, Cohen, and Jackson resurrected the scheme to delay consideration of the court bill at least until the end of the session. The plan was approved by West and Keenan. At the same time, another scheme to save the situation was being developed by congressional leaders, who were naturally resentful of Roosevelt's failure to consult them prior to submitting his bill. They were led to believe that even at that stage

[34] Henry Fountain Ashurst, *A Many Colored Toga: The Diary of Henry Fountain Ashurst,* ed. George Sparks (Tucson: 1962), 571–72. The original is in the University of Arizona Library in Tucson. Quoted in Leonard Baker, *Back to Back,* 193–94. In early February when the court bill was first introduced, the administration lacked a majority of votes on the Senate Judiciary Committee and was always uncertain if it could get a favorable committee report.

[35] "Washington Notes," *New Republic* 91 (May 12, 1937), 15–16.

their advice was unwanted. Congressional leaders were out of touch with the president for most of April. While he was angling for tarpon on the bright southern waters, they could stand the inaction no longer.[36]

In early May a small group that included Senators Harrison, Barkley, and Robinson invited James Roosevelt to a luncheon in the private office of Colonel Edwin A. Halsey, secretary of the Senate. Robinson, acting as spokesman, told their guest that the situation was hopeless. If his father insisted on holding out for his original bill, he would be beaten. The bill, Robinson added, with all the bitterness it had aroused, was "raising hell with the Democratic Party." He pleaded with James to make his father see that he was courting defeat. They would handle the bill themselves, and Robinson promised they would do all they could for it. James was asked to carry their message to his father personally before he returned to Washington. Robinson reportedly said: "Mr. Roosevelt, you tell your poppa that he'd better leave this whole thing to us to get what we can out of it. We'll do our best for him."[37]

James may have been convinced already that the court plan was "dead on arrival," as he later told the author, but he was aware of his father's strong belief that the congressional leaders in his own party were "defeatists," a view that had some currency in the White House at the time. An adviser recalled how exasperated FDR had been back in September after spending an entire afternoon at Hyde Park trying to convince congressional bigwigs that they were headed for an electoral victory in November. He had given up, he told his son, on trying to humor such proven pessimists. Basically, the president did not care what the congressional leaders wanted him to do.

The next day James called a meeting attended by Corcoran, West, Roddan, Early, Keenan, Michelson, and Cummings. To his surprise, they agreed with the leaders on the Hill and urged him to deliver their message without softening it in any detail. A few even tried to reach Roosevelt by phone, but were told he was at

[36] Alsop and Catledge, *The 168 Days,* 202; Alsop Notes, Box 50, Alsop Papers, LC.

[37] Alsop and Catledge, *The 168 Days,* 203.

sea. James was to fly to Galveston to meet the ship, but to avoid bad publicity he decided to board the presidential train at Fort Worth. Farley met the train at Indianapolis after it had made several stops on a tour of Texas. The general staff left that meeting more optimistic than they had been for some time. Corcoran felt that he could now promote his plan to postpone the bill at least until the end of the session.

Cummings lingered to have a private talk with James. Members of the inner circle became suspicious, thinking that the attorney general, as the bill's author, wanted it to pass without changes and would try to persuade James to ignore congressional advice, or at least soften its impact. Cummings, it appears, was not as averse to compromise as formerly, so long as the principle of their bill was preserved with its lower-court features, to which there was little or no objection. But he did not make his position known to either FDR or his son, James.

On joining the presidential train, James and Farley found that FDR would not even consider compromise. When they reminded him that the Senate was so evenly divided on the issue that Garner might have to cast the tie vote, he snapped: "Well let him do it." Farley counseled the president to consider the possibility that if he tried to ram the bill through he might succeed in doing that but would lose out in the end by splitting the party beyond repair. This provoked the surprising retort: "And good riddance too." Roosevelt reportedly gazed out the window of his private railroad car and murmured, almost as if to himself: "This is what comes from telling them I would not be a candidate again." With all the finality at his command, he assured them that he would not withdraw as much as an inch and would accept no compromise.[38]

When the presidential train rolled in to Union Station on May 14, not one member of the Seventy-fifth Congress was on hand to meet it. FDR returned from his southern fishing trip to a sullen Congress near open revolt. He was in a truculent mood. That same afternoon, one by one, he called in Senate Majority Leader Robinson, Speaker Bankhead, and House Majority Leader Rayburn (who reported that the president had on his fighting clothes). He informed them that the fight would continue. When

[38] Ibid., 203–4; *Jim Farley's Story,* 81–82.

they objected, he only laughed at their fears and insisted on putting the bill at the top of his legislative "must" list. Rayburn, accused of being ignorant of what was going on in his own district, was subjected to ridicule. Roosevelt boasted that he had just visited Texas and, after talking with precinct committeemen, was as certain as ever that the people were behind him on the court bill. The president left them with the clear impression that they could and should get him his bill, but if they failed, he would then be obliged "to take the issue to the country in 1938, or even in 1940."

The press was waiting as the leaders emerged from the meeting. Robinson, deeply irritated, dictated a statement for reporters in which he said the chief item under discussion had been the court bill. The whole matter had been gone into in great detail: "I see no prospect at this stage of any adjustment or agreement." Did "adjustment" mean compromise? he was asked. It did. Could "at this stage" mean that the president might compromise later? Robinson barked: "Strike out 'at this stage.'" The battle would go on. He predicted a close vote in the Senate, with a "fair prospect" that the bill would pass. He tried to defend the Seventy-fifth Congress, claiming that it was well up on its work in regard to general legislation.[39]

At the next cabinet meeting, FDR said: "The thing to do to sell the Court plan is to hit them hard—mow down the opposition." The people, he assured them, like a good battle. Ickes wrote that he had never seen the president so full of fight.[40] But all the bravado and tough rhetoric could not obscure the fact that the bill was mired down on Capitol Hill. In spite of the grievances some lawmakers had against the Court, Congress had no appetite for a plan to alter it. In his column Krock wrote that the president by his intransigence severely threatened the effectiveness of Robinson's leadership. "Compromise is the backbone of political tactics," he observed, adding: "Robinson is not a happy man."[41]

When Rayburn saw the president on House business, he mentioned that mail from his Texas district was running heavily

---

[39] Alsop and Catledge, *The 168 Days,* 204–5; *New York Times,* May 15, 1937; *Time* 29 (May 24, 1937), 9.

[40] *Secret Diary,* 2:141–42.

[41] "In Washington," *New York Times,* May 18, 1937.

against his court proposal. He hoped Roosevelt would take the hint and drop his bill. As they talked, FDR's demeanor swung from boredom to irritation. Finally, Rayburn exploded: "Looky here, Mr. President. By God, I'm talking to you. You'd better listen."[42]

To turn the tide of battle, White House staffers worked out a new scheme, advising FDR to return action on the bill to the House. Back in February, when Rayburn asked Chairman Sumners of the House Judiciary Committee to introduce the bill, "Hattie" refused and accused his friend Sam of kowtowing to Roosevelt. Eventually Representative Fred Vinson of Kentucky was persuaded to introduce a slightly altered version of the original bill, which would have to clear Sumners's Judiciary Committee.

Roosevelt took the matter up with Bankhead and Rayburn. The way to get around Sumners's roadblock, he suggested, was with a discharge petition to get the bill out of committee. The signatures of 218 members was required to enable House leaders to bring the bill to the floor for a vote. Bankhead and Rayburn listened patiently, but they then told FDR flat out they would have nothing to do with his proposal. Rayburn was furious at this attempt "to make the House do the administration's dirty work," as he put it, and in a needless battle. Roosevelt strategists were forced to turn once more to the Senate.[43] The president was powerless before the resistance he experienced from the Democratic House leaders.

Another stunning blow fell on advocates of the court plan with the announcement on May 18, 1937, of Justice Willis Van Devanter's retirement from the bench, effective June 2, a day after the end of the Court term. The justice first broke the news to a seventy-one-year-old Washington reporter whom he had befriended. John T. Sutter had been filing stories for the Associated Press about the Supreme Court, its decisions, and their impact for many years. That Tuesday morning he was asked to drop by

---

[42] Alfred Steinberg, *Sam Rayburn: A Biography* (New York: Hawthorn Books, 1975), 144–45.

[43] Ibid.

the justice's apartment at 2101 Connecticut Avenue, N.W., before going to his office. Hurrying over by taxi, Sutter was told that the justice was about to send the president a letter announcing his retirement. He was handed a copy of the letter, which would be released to the press soon after it reached the White House by special messenger. "Be sure to come and visit me on my farm," the justice called after the excited newsman as Sutter rushed off to file one of the biggest scoops of a long career.[44]

The letter reached the White House at 9:45 A.M. and was brought to the president's bedroom, where FDR was propped up by pillows in bed reading the morning papers. Attached to the letter was a copy of Sumners's bill, "An Act to Provide for Retirement of Justices of the Supreme Court."[45] Van Devanter was the first justice to retire from the Court under Sumners's bill. He would thus be permitted to serve as a "reserve judge" until his death in 1941. Roosevelt scribbled a reply in pencil, extending his good wishes and inviting the justice to visit him at the White House before leaving Washington for the summer. But the retiring justice was not addressed as "My dear Willis."

Senator Borah and Hatton Sumners, close friends of Van Devanter's, had conspired to hasten the retirement on at least five occasions in the weeks before the announcement. Borah told Wheeler the justice was ready to retire, provided it would not interfere with the opposition's struggle in the court fight. A faction headed by Senator Burke, seeking unconditional victory over the president, tried to prevent *any* resignations or retirements while the battle raged over the bill. Borah and Wheeler took a slightly different approach, believing that a retirement or two would weaken the president's case. Their scheme was to turn the justice's desire to leave the bench to their advantage. The maneuver was planned and timed in minute detail. Van Devanter's letter reached Roosevelt on May 18, the same day the Senate Judiciary Committee reported out his court bill unfavorably.

Conferring with Senate colleagues, Wheeler had asked how

---

[44] Leonard Baker, *Back to Back,* 225–26.

[45] H.R. 2518 authorized the president, on notice of a retirement, to appoint a successor, but stated that "such Justice of the Supreme Court so retired may nevertheless be called upon . . . to perform such judicial duties, in any judicial circuit . . . as such retired Justice may be willing to undertake."

"The Justice was not alone in his retirement." A cartoon by Rolun Kirby in the *New York Times,* May 18, 1937.

they felt about Van Devanter's move. There followed a heated debate in which a senator asked: "Why in hell should we sacrifice our political lives making this fight to save the Court if [its] members . . . haven't enough guts to stand up under a little fire?" Borah argued that a retirement at that time was a good strategic move that would deprive the president of one of his main arguments for his bill—that in four years he had not had a single high

Chief Justice Hughes (right), photographed with retiring Justice Willis Van Devanter, Washington, D.C., June 1, 1937. (Collection of the Supreme Court of the United States)

court appointment. Despite the divisions over strategy, Borah won out and got word to Van Devanter (they lived in the same apartment building). But when the justice conveyed the decision to his brethren, he ran into another storm of protests. He did his best to quiet their fears simply by saying "Borah favors it."[46]

[46] William K. Hutchinson, *News Articles on the Life and Works of Hon. William E. Borah* (Washington, D.C.: G.P.O., 1940), 12–13. This resistance by members of the Supreme Court is consonant with the refusal by Chief Justice

Before the justice's official announcement, Wheeler reportedly contacted the White House through West to advise of an anticipated vacancy on the Court. The time was ripe, he said, to compromise, and he suggested the president announce himself satisfied with appointing a replacement as long as he got court reform, preferably in the form of the Wheeler-Bone amendment allowing Congress to override Supreme Court decisions by a two-thirds vote after an intervening election. He hinted at the possibility that Justice Sutherland also wished to retire. Wheeler got nowhere. FDR regarded him as the blackest of traitors, one who should never be allowed to use his influence with any such maneuver.[47]

For the day or so they had to wait for official confirmation of Van Devanter's decision, White House staffers hoped Wheeler's news was untrue. They saw right away that a retirement meant that whether or not the court bill was delayed until the next session, Senator Robinson would have to be named to the Supreme Court with no offsetting appointments. It was widely understood that he had been promised he would fill the next vacancy. As for Roosevelt, by then he was becoming a shade less confident. While still circling around his problem, he was now at least ready to admit it was there.[48]

Van Devanter's decision opened a new phase in the battle over the court bill. Robinson would have to face wholesale desertions by moderate Democrats in his shaky coalition. Drastic judicial reform no longer seemed pressing. Jackson wrote to a Dallas friend: "Of course, the argument is now being made that it is not necessary to enact the law because the Court has become liberal. If there is anything that proves the justification of the President's criticism of the Court, it is this conversion."[49]

Hughes to accede to Herbert Hoover's efforts to persuade Justice Brandeis to resign from the bench early in the court fight. Nor would Hughes permit attempts to be made to persuade any of the other justices to resign or retire, even though there were signals that several of them, Van Devanter and Sutherland in particular, were interested in leaving the bench once their retirement pay was secured. Leonard Baker, *Back to Back,* 228.

[47] Alsop Notes, 124, Box 50, Alsop Papers, LC.

[48] Ibid., 127.

[49] Jackson to Judge Harry P. Lawther, May 26, 1937, Jackson Papers, LC.

With the vacant seat, Robinson hoped to realize a lifelong dream of going on the Supreme Court. He had always hated the ordeal of running for public office.[50] Farley had assured him that he could expect to be named to the Court for leading the president's forces in the Senate. The timing of the retirement, however, coupled with Roosevelt's alleged commitment to Robinson, caused great consternation in the White House, among liberals, and even among some moderates.

The original bill called for infusion of younger blood on the Court, and Robinson was sixty-five. Age was a touchy issue, and its inclusion in the bill offended many staunch New Deal supporters. Brandeis, in his eighties, was still one of the most liberal men on the Court. Democrats charged that FDR merely used the age issue as a convenient vehicle for adding six new members to the bench in an attempt to camouflage the real issue of packing. Roosevelt faced an awful dilemma. If he appointed Robinson, the mask of younger blood would again be exposed. In fact, the age issue had already lost most of its force. Administration spokesmen tried to soft-pedal it in response to the furor it caused. Old "Arkansas Joe" was characterized by many liberals as a southern conservative at heart. Once on the bench, he could not be counted upon by them to support their agenda. The appointment undoubtedly would look like what it was—a political payoff.

For reasons of their own, Robinson's Senate colleagues wanted him on the Court. It was taken for granted that the vacancy would be his. Their intention was to embarrass the president as much as possible. On the morning following Van Devanter's announcement, Senate colleagues crowded around Robinson's desk in the first row, pounded him on the back, shook his hand, and addressed him as "Mr. Justice." Headlines proclaimed: "May 19 Was Distinctly Robinson Day."[51] Borah, Glass, and others wrote FDR enthusiastic letters urging the appointment. Hints were circulated that if for some reason Roosevelt refused to appoint Robinson, an open revolt would follow with Senate refusal to confirm any other nominee.[52]

---

[50] Ickes, *Secret Diary,* 2:144; Burns, *Roosevelt,* 304.

[51] *Baltimore Sun,* May 20, 1937. Cf. "Court Plan Dead but Not Buried," *Literary Digest* 33 (May 29, 1937), 3.

[52] Borah to FDR, May 19, 1937, copy in Robinson Papers, UAL; "Robinson Boomed for Appointment," *Washington Herald,* May 20, 1937, 1; Marvin H. McIntyre to Kenneth McKellar, May 28, 1937, Robinson Papers, UAL.

Asked by reporters what impact Van Devanter's resignation would have on his court bill, FDR crisply replied: "I have no news on that subject today."[53] Reporters soon learned that there was plenty of news to be had. Legislators waited for the public's reaction, while the people expected their representatives to act. The deadlock was broken when public opinion crystallized. Surveys indicated that the "No" vote had climbed so that by June 7 opponents of the court bill had polled more than 50 percent.[54]

At another press conference, Roosevelt was asked if he intended to confirm the Senate's nomination of Senator Robinson. He laughed. It was nice of Roosevelt, wrote one of them, to laugh at any reference to Robinson, who by then had developed into something of a sore subject at the White House. On May 21 FDR told newsmen he had given "no thought" to the appointment of Van Devanter's successor. The announcement, which was far from the truth, had a depressing effect on Robinson and his supporters.[55]

The day Van Devanter's letter reached him, Senators Byrnes and Harrison visited Roosevelt to discuss the Robinson appointment and the matter of his successor as majority leader upon his elevation to the bench. Pat Harrison and Alben Barkley were the two main contenders for the leadership post. There was talk, they said, that the Senate would refuse to confirm any other appointee to the Court if Robinson's nomination were not forthcoming.[56] Farley feared that removal of Robinson from the Senate, where he was vitally needed, would create an insurmountable handicap.[57] Farley also said that Roosevelt could have had a two-justice bill in April with little trouble, echoing Robinson's earlier boast, but by the end of May the opposition had gained enough strength to make any compromise doubtful. He argued that Robinson should have been appointed; as a political maneuver it

[53] *New York Times,* May 19, 1937, 18; Clapper Diary, May 18, 1937, Box 8, Clapper Papers, LC.

[54] Cantwell, "Public Opinion," 931.

[55] *Baltimore Sun,* May 22, 1937.

[56] *Washington Post,* May 22, 1937. At the beginning of March, a magazine reported that Senators Harrison, Byrnes, and even Robinson, although still loyal to their leader, gave indications that at heart they were only lukewarm in support of his court bill. *Time* 29 (March 1, 1937), 12.

[57] *Behind the Ballots* (New York: Harcourt Brace, 1938), 332.

would have been an excellent way to end the congressional session, "leaving a good taste in everyone's mouth."[58]

Roosevelt left Robinson hanging—to wonder and worry. His inaction increased the sour relations with the Senate. Robinson was insulted by FDR's treatment and resolved that unless he made the first move, the senator would refuse to deal with him. Two full weeks elapsed at that critical stage in the struggle with no communication between the two. Some believe a compromise might have been worked out if FDR had made the appointment. Instead, Robinson and his followers grew more embittered and the president lost more support.[59]

At ten o'clock on Tuesday morning, May 18, the eighteen-member Senate Judiciary Committee filed into the old Senate Caucus Room to vote on the administration's court bill. Borah made certain that as they prepared to vote they were all informed of Justice Van Devanter's retirement, which had become official only about fifteen minutes earlier. The closed session began with a series of votes on motions in the form of amendments by Democrats in an attempt to deliver at least something of his bill to FDR. The first was Logan's amendment, which authorized appointing to the Supreme Court an additional justice for each incumbent over seventy-five, with no more than one in any calendar year (besides Van Devanter, four justices—Brandeis, Hughes, McReynolds, and Sutherland—were seventy-five or older). The amendment, which Logan intended to offer again on the floor of the Senate in the hope of saving the bill, was lost ten-to-eight. During the closed session Logan offered numerous compromises, including one to postpone the effective date of the legislation until after Roosevelt left office, but as he later lamented, "the conservatives wouldn't accept anything."[60]

Opponents of the bill—with the exception of Senator Hatch—held their ranks against any other compromises. Norris's motion that the bill be reported out favorably was defeated ten-to-eight.

[58] *Jim Farley's Story,* 86.

[59] James A. Farley, Private Memorandum, May 20, 1937, James A. Farley Papers, LC; Michaelson, *The Ghost Talks,* 181; Alsop and Catledge, *The 168 Days,* 213–14.

[60] Leonard Baker, *Back to Back,* 236.

Dieterich's motion that the committee issue a report "without recommendation" was also defeated ten-to-eight. Finally, McCarran offered his motion calling for submission of an adverse report, with a recommendation that "the bill not pass." It was adopted by a vote of ten-to-eight.[61]

Administration proponents lost every motion on the court bill. The news reportedly gave the White House a jolt, although the results must have been expected. In effect, the committee recommended defeat of the president's bill, thus forcing Robinson to go up against an overwhelmingly Democratic committee which he himself had appointed less than six months earlier. After the vote the committee took up consideration of the report being prepared by their staff for submission to the full Senate in the next weeks. A draft document was approved by a vote of ten-to-eight. A final report would not be released until the first week in June.

On May 19 headlines hailed the events of the previous day: "COURT COMPROMISE SEEN ALTHOUGH F. R. IS MUM."[62] Meanwhile, Robinson and other congressional leaders threw their support behind the Logan compromise. Maintaining a noncommittal attitude on future plans, FDR waited for a more complete picture of public reaction to swift-moving events before making any decision about strategy. But events were taking on a momentum of their own.

Senate Democratic leaders now openly displayed a willingness to accept a compromise on the court bill. Senator Logan informed committee members, who in turn informed their colleagues, that Democratic leaders favored "something along the lines of his proposal." All the administration's supporters on the Judiciary Committee except Pittman backed the Logan compromise. They had no idea what the president's attitude was, but they assumed that Robinson stood with Logan. "Half a loaf," Logan added, "is better than none at all."[63]

---

[61] Voting with the majority for the adverse report were Senators King, McCarran, Hatch, Van Nuys, Burke, Connally, O'Mahoney, Borah, Austin, and Steiwer. Only the last three were Republicans. In the minority were Senators Neeley, Logan, Dieterich, Pittman, Hughes, Norris, McGill, and Chairman Ashurst.

[62] *Philadelphia Public Ledger,* May 19, 1937, 1.

[63] Ibid.

As often happens, press reports on May 19 revealed more embarrassing news than the administration wanted made public. The next day the White House advised press associations that there was not a word of truth in an Associated Press story in a Washington paper to the effect that the president was being urged by close Senate advisers to withdraw his court bill or reduce his request to two additional justices. Milo Thompson, chief of the AP's Washington bureau, was given this notice by telephone.

Roosevelt sent for Senator Gerald Nye (D.-N.D.), who reportedly had joined the opposition. The next day Nye sent out a circular letter to his constituents which said in part: "I cannot see how one could possibly support the President's proposal without first abandoning every care about the future of our Democracy and representative government."[64] The resort to direct handling of waverers, for which Roosevelt supposedly possessed such flair, had no effect on Senator Nye or on many another Democrat.

Matt McGuire, a subordinate in Keenan's office, sent a memo by special messenger to James Roosevelt on May 18, informing him that "at Mr. Keenan's suggestion, two newly drafted bills had been prepared with reference to the associate justices of the Supreme Court." The first authorized the president to name four additional justices to the Court, all of whom, if possible, were to be nominated from judicial circuits unrepresented by justices presently holding office. This bill made the appointments mandatory. The memo stated: "This is the one concerning which there has been some doubt raised as to its constitutionality." The second, designated "precatory"—that is, voluntary in nature—was an attempt to achieve the objective of the first bill constitutionally. The purpose of both bills was to provide ultimately for an associate justice from each of the ten judicial circuits. Adding the chief justice, who was not affected by this requirement, would have made a court of eleven.[65] The two new bills followed in substance provisions of a compromise measure introduced earlier in the Senate by Charles M. Andrews (D.-Fla.).

Before the Judiciary Committee released its adverse report,

---

[64] Gerald Nye to F. H. Gibbens, May 21, 1937, James Roosevelt Papers, FDRL.

[65] McGuire to James Roosevelt, May 18, 1937, ibid.

Keenan called on Henry Ashurst to discuss prospects for submitting a minority report. Corcoran had also talked to the senator about it. Keenan, however, pretended to know nothing of Corcoran's visit. Ashurst expressed the strong conviction that to submit a minority report would be a mistake. He said he would be unable to get all those who had voted the bill out to approve such a report.

Keenan said he thought they were in much better shape than was being reported in the press, and that from his contacts he counted forty-seven votes "pretty firmly" in their corner, including Prentiss Brown of Michigan. But Ashurst countered: "Of course we are definitely and completely beaten; the only question is how to accept the defeat." There was absolutely no chance for either passing the bill or even getting it brought up for a vote, and the chairman added that Keenan and others representing the administration had not the slightest inkling of the real feeling of senators.[66] Corcoran and Keenan continued pressing Ashurst and members of his committee, but it came to nothing. At the time they had a draft of a minority report, and in very strong terms, but Ashurst managed to wiggle out of doing anything about it. "I can't get the Senators to agree," he complained. "Each Senator is his own master."[67]

Meanwhile, the Justice Department was completing work on a draft compromise. On June 1 Stanley Reed wrote Cummings: "Attached is a copy of the revision of the Judiciary bill which has been furnished by congressman Fred Vinson, and will be introduced by him, on his own responsibility, today or tomorrow." His bill raised the age for mandatory retirement to seventy-five and required a minimum of ten years on the bench. One additional justice could be appointed in each calendar year.[68]

---

[66] Memorandum of a conversation between Keenan and Ashurst, May 22, 1937, Judicial File, ibid. Prentiss Brown was one of the freshman Democrats elected to Congress in the Democratic sweep of 1936. He was a leader of the faction of freshman Democrats who had difficulty with the compromise bill. From the outset they had looked for ways they could be saved from voting for a scheme they found repugnant and which they knew outraged many of their constituents.

[67] Alsop Notes, Box 53, Alsop Papers, LC.

[68] Reed to Attorney General, June 1, 1937, Box 199, Cummings Papers,

As finally drawn, the "compromise" authorized the president to appoint a new justice for each sitting justice who was seventy-five and declined to retire, but it omitted the condition requiring ten years on the bench. The authorization in the new bill was permissive and not mandatory, as it was in the original bill. Only one such appointment could be made in any calendar year. Thus, as a Boston editorialist pointed out, the president would be free to distinguish between justices over seventy-five according to his personal judgment, and "to provide or not to provide a 'wet nurse' for one of them each year as he saw fit."[69]

In a discussion between Corcoran and Hopkins at Warm Springs two years later, Corcoran told Hopkins, who penciled it in a corresponding memorandum: "We missed a compromise when that could have been accomplished—Cummings and Richberg were advising the President to stand pat although neither of them had any influence in the Senate and in fact completely misjudged the sentiment of that body." Corcoran was disgusted by the fact that Cummings had gone off on a holiday in the middle of the fight, as did Roosevelt. He concluded: "I don't believe we would have won the compromise. . . . A grand idea was lost by . . . bad political strategy."[70]

ALDL. At that stage, five justices would have been over seventy-five before June 1937: Hughes, Sutherland, McReynolds, Brandeis, and Van Devanter. Justice Butler was over seventy.

[69] Editorial, "No Compromise At All," *Boston Herald,* July 12, 1937. Another section of the compromise bill gave the chief justice virtually unlimited power to move circuit and district judges around the country. This provision received little public attention. The original bill limited the transfer by the chief justice to judges "hereafter appointed," but the so-called compromise bill eliminated that restriction.

[70] Harry Hopkins Memo, 1939, quoted in Sherwood, *Roosevelt and Hopkins,* 89–90. Hopkins added a footnote stating that "Tom C. and Ben Cohen did what they could," but Cummings and Richberg were jealous of all other legal advice "and kept Tommy at arm's length." The original, written in longhand and dated April 1939 is in the Harry Hopkins Papers, FDRL.

14
Showdown

> On April 12, [1937,] the Court upheld the Wagner Act with three decisions: . . . With these developments, widely interpreted as a capitulation by the Court, the strength of the President's forces waned, although he insisted on a showdown.
>
> David A. Shannon, *Twentieth Century America,* 2:198

SENATOR ROBINSON figured there was one possible way he might prevail over the opponents of the court bill—by turning the congressional fight into an endurance contest. Columnist Mark Sullivan reported: "Some of the President's partisans say he'll win on the court issue as soon as he gets the help of a powerful ally, namely hot weather, when Congressmen want to go home. . . . The White House is air conditioned; the homes of Congressmen are not, and Washington in summer is a very hot climate."[1] The District of Columbia was characterized as "sub-tropical." In a memoir, Noel Coward recalled sweating through steamy tropical forests and crossing burning deserts, but never in any of the equatorial hells he visited had he ever sweated as he did in Washington. "The pavement felt like nougat," he complained, and the slightest exertion soaked him to the skin.[2]

The thought of being trapped in the capital during July and August was enough to make lawmakers, even those with strong constitutions, quail. A third of the senators were over sixty. Each year, residents who could afford to do so fled for relief to the mountains or seashore, but lawmakers had to remain in the

[1] "Where Is the New Deal Heading?" *New York Herald Tribune,* May 16, 1937, 2:1; *Detroit Free Press,* July 11, 1937, 2:1.

[2] *Present Indicative* (Garden City, N.Y.: Doubleday, Doran, 1937), 219–20. On Washington's summer climate, see *New York Times,* May 10, 1937, 1:7, and July 15, 1937, 1:5; cf. *Washington Sunday Star,* July 10, 1937, A1:5.

steamy district where the thermometer sometimes hovered around eighty-two degrees at midnight, not to mention the humidity. In mid-June Roosevelt wrote Colonel House: "The Congress suffers from the usual off-year combination of heat, the jitters, and dissension among themselves. I hope they will pass the major measures and go home by the end of August."[3]

The president, who apparently held Congress in low regard, if not contempt, took his frustrations out on the White House staff and his wife. In her daily column "My Day," Mrs. Roosevelt mentioned her husband's irritability and complaints about the bland food served to him. Her candor landed her in trouble, as revealed in a letter to her daughter Anna: "Pa is both nervous and tired. The court hue and cry has got under his skin. I thought stupidly his little outburst of boredom on meals was amusing and human and used it in my column & it was taken up by papers and radio and [went] over the ticker to Steve [Early] . . . and [the] Judiciary. Got hate letters and Pa was furious with me."

Vice President Garner reproved her, saying she must learn to recognize things that are personal and should not be mentioned or else none of them would dare talk to her. "He thought I should apologize to Father," she told Anna. "I did, before McDuffie [his valet] Monday night before leaving, as I couldn't see him alone & Pa answered irritably that it had been very hard on him and he would certainly say nothing more to me on any subject! So, it has become . . . very serious . . . and I am grieved at my poor judgment and only hope it won't be remembered long. Will I be glad when we leave the W.H. and I can be on my own!"[4] At the time, Roosevelt began experiencing symptoms of hypertension, which became a long-term health problem.

The fight, originally begun to curb the Supreme Court, was no longer only that. The contest now lay between Roosevelt and his Democrat opponents in Congress. Theirs was a position of great strategic advantage. The outcome may have been uncertain, but there could have been no doubt about what was at stake—control

---

[3] FDR to House, June 16, 1937, PPF 222, FDRL; cf. "Washington Notes," *New Republic,* June 2, 1937, 99.

[4] Eleanor Roosevelt's column "My Day" for February 10, 1937, mentioned her husband's crankiness. The letter to her daughter dated March 3, 1937, is in the Anna Halsted Papers, Box 57, FDRL.

of the Democratic Party and the president's leadership. A journalist thought that a court bill satisfactory to a majority in Congress could be written in a few hours. That was an exaggeration. But the Supreme Court was no longer the main issue; that was whether Senators Wheeler, Burke, Glass, and other Democrats on the opposition side would prevail over the president. They saw a chance to humble their leader and found the prospect exhilarating.[5]

Roosevelt was vulnerable. Loyal Democrats realized that if he were to face defeat, or even give the appearance of defeat by Senate irreconcilables, it was doubtful whether his followers could ever again be relied on to support his initiatives. Democrats Prentiss Brown of Michigan, Charles O. Andrews of Florida, and John H. Overton of Louisiana searched with renewed vigor for a way out. But when it came to a showdown, Roosevelt was certain he would find these and other waverers behind him on his court bill. And if he ever felt an inclination to call a halt to the struggle, there was the promised appointment of Robinson to consider. Honoring it would not only undermine his stated objective of bringing younger blood to the Court, making a joke of his original rationale for judicial reform, but it would also alienate any liberal support he had left.[6]

Robinson's hopes of going on the Supreme Court dated from the Hoover administration, when friends urged his appointment to the next vacancy.[7] In return for getting much of the early New Deal program passed into law, often without changing anything sent to the Hill from the White House, the senator was assured that the appointment was "in the bag." At lunch with FDR on June 18, 1937, a month after Van Devanter's announcement, Farley and Cummings endorsed naming Robinson, and Roosevelt reportedly agreed. As it was then understood among professional politicians, such a discussion amounted to an ironclad agree-

[5] *New Republic* 91 (June 2, 1937), 99.

[6] The promise to Robinson had been given, and so irrevocably that Roosevelt asked Senate Minority Leader Charles L. McNary, a close friend of Robinson's, for assurances that the appointment would not be opposed. He could be sure, McNary told him, of virtually every Republican vote, and he would move to confirm the nomination himself without even referring it to the Senate Judiciary Committee for consideration. *New York Times,* May 20, 1937.

[7] *Washington Evening Star,* May 20, 1937.

ment. The next morning Farley telephoned Robinson to break the news, addressing him as "Mr. Justice" and advising him "to sit steady in the boat, . . . not rock it, and all would be well."[8] Naturally, Robinson interpreted this as a definite presidential commitment.

FDR feared he had no choice but to appoint the Senate leader and perhaps accept the compromise Robinson had been discussing with others.[9] But the very idea of having to act under prodding from senators, many of whom were avowed enemies, was something he could not have found easy to stomach. When the appointment had been urged earlier by Byrnes and Harrison, after Van Devanter's announcement, Roosevelt was infuriated, suspecting they had been sent by Robinson to force his hand on the issue. He still believed the court bill would command comfortable majorities in both houses. Additional justices were more necessary than ever, so why back down? Why not delay making the appointment, if it had to be made at all, at least until additional justices became available to offset it?[10]

The *New York Times* listed Robinson as a possible appointee, along with Wagner and Reed. The guessing game would go on until August. But the actions of his Senate colleagues and the way they were reported in the press indicated that Robinson headed the list, ranking far above others in public opinion. Front-page headlines in the *Arkansas Gazette* announced: "SENATOR ROBINSON MAY BE SOUTHWEST'S FIRST HIGH JUSTICE."[11]

Unlike Cummings's clandestine campaign to be named attorney general, there was nothing coy or secretive about Robinson's quest for a seat on the high bench. In fact, his candidacy would have been impossible to conceal. Nearly everyone in the know in Washington was aware that he wanted the appointment, and almost as many expected him to get it right away. His supporters feared that any hesitancy on their part would make it easy for the

---

[8] Alsop and Catledge, *The 168 Days,* 66; *Jim Farley's Story,* 86.

[9] Davis, *Into the Storm,* 86.

[10] Joseph Alsop and Turner Catledge, "The Ghost of Senator Robinson," *Saturday Evening Post* 210 (September 25, 1937), 44.

[11] "Court Plan Dead but Not Buried," *Literary Digest,* May 29, 1937, 3; *New York Times,* May 19, 1937; *Arkansas Gazette,* May 22, 1937.

president to pass him by and nominate someone else, even before a Robinson boom could get off the ground.

In the weeks to follow, Roosevelt listened to many cautionary voices, including some powerful ones, opposed to naming Robinson. Robert Jackson spoke of the merriment it would cause in Washington after FDR's initial attack on the Court, using the age issue. He warned: "I think it would be a great mistake for you to pack the Court, and accept additional memberships on it, if you have got to make Joe Robinson one of them. There is only one excuse for packing the Court, and that is to change it. You're very likely not to change anything and you will have all the odium of having packed it and being laughed at besides."[12]

A week or so after Van Devanter's announcement, Roosevelt, while cruising the Potomac on the *Sequoia,* remained on deck one warm Saturday night, after the other guests had retired to their cabins. Alone with Henry Morgenthau, he asked: "If Brandeis resigns, whom do you think I should appoint to succeed him? Landis or Frankfurter?" Giving it some thought, Morgenthau said he considered Landis the better choice. "Frankfurter would rate a more popular opinion," mused FDR. Morgenthau agreed, but believed the public would have more confidence in Landis. "Well," said the president, "I think I would have a terrible time getting Felix confirmed." Morgenthau concurred, adding that one of the troubles with Frankfurter was that he was over-brilliant. He then brought the conversation around to the immediate problem at hand—the Van Devanter vacancy and the expectation that Robinson would succeed him. "What are you going to do about Robinson?"

"I cannot appoint him," replied Roosevelt.

"Why not?"

"Because he is not sufficiently liberal."

"I am certainly glad to hear you talk that way," said Morgenthau. "The things you have done and talked to me about in the last ten days have encouraged me tremendously, because after all, I am a reformer."

On the matter of appointing Robinson, Roosevelt said: "If I had three vacancies, I might be able to sandwich in Joe Robin-

[12] Gerhart, *America's Advocate,* 116–17; Leonard Baker, *Back to Back,* 249.

son." But he said he had no idea who, if anyone, was going to retire after Van Devanter.[13]

Liberals, convinced of Robinson's conservatism, distrusted him and put strong pressure on Roosevelt to bypass him. One journal commented: "Robinson is a pleasant and even relatively superior party politician, but it is obvious that he has neither the true liberality of outlook nor downright intellect to qualify him for the Supreme Court in the crucial times through which we are passing."[14]

Editorialists emphasized that it would be a disheartening blow to progressives, in the thick of the court fight, to learn that its result would be the appointment of a man like Robinson to fill the first vacancy since the fight began. "They hardly expect Justice Van Devanter to be replaced by a friend of the Arkansas planters and utility magnates, for in that case it would be difficult to detect any change at all in the complexion of the Court." Roosevelt, they argued, had a moral responsibility to appoint a truly liberal justice of intellectual stature, commensurate with the issues the Court would be called upon to decide. "Robinson's appointment would be a defeat in principle of everything the Supreme Court bill was designed to obtain."[15] The editorials attacked Robinson not as a person, but as a type. The *Nation*'s editors tried to soften the harsh observation by urging that, if a Robinson appointment had to be made, it should be "sandwiched in between two liberals," an option Roosevelt mentioned in his midnight dialogue with Morgenthau.

Meanwhile, acting as if the seat were already his, Robinson wrote a friend: "Without a single dissenting vote, fellow senators have expressed themselves as favorable to my succeeding Mr. Justice Van Devanter." He discounted possible opposition from brain trusters in the White House, saying that they were just as enthusiastic for his appointment as were his fellow senators.[16]

---

[13] Henry S. Morgenthau, Jr., *Diaries,* Book 69, 308–9, FDRL; also quoted in Leonard Baker, *Back to Back,* 249–50.

[14] "Robinson Will Not Do," *Nation* 144 (May 29, 1937), 607–8; *New Republic* 91 (June 9, 1937), 314–15.

[15] *New Republic* 91 (June 9, 1937), 314–15.

[16] Senator Robinson to Dr. M. F. Dickinson, June 1, 1937, Robinson Papers, UAL.

Roosevelt vacillated on appointing Robinson or anyone else to the vacancy. "Chance," wrote Mark Sullivan, "which sometimes favors Roosevelt, may bring a condition which would point a way out." He referred to the possibility of another vacancy on the Court, which could mean appointing, along with Robinson, someone more acceptable to liberals and New Dealers. The suggestion, as it turned out, was prophetic in the sense that chance—or some would say fate—would eventually release Roosevelt from what was regarded as an unavoidable commitment. But the outcome was very different from the one Sullivan had in mind. As the weeks passed, with no announcement from the White House, talk of a possible successor to Van Devanter died down.[17]

The crippling events of May, which had dampened any hope of the bill's passage, were reflected in the mood in the Senate. Every poll taken in that body by administration agents forecast certain defeat.[18] Ending the standoff with Robinson, Roosevelt finally capitulated. Forced at last to face the reality of impending defeat, he sought some face-saving way out. If self-pride had not prevailed he might have been capable of a more direct, generous gesture. Instead, he refused to approach the majority leader personally and ordered his son James to arrange a meeting.

A reluctant Robinson at first protested that to outsiders it would look as if he were a supplicant, coming to the White House hat in hand, asking for a Supreme Court appointment. But in Robinson's Senate office, James handed him the telephone and by prearrangement he was put through immediately to FDR, who

[17] *Washington Evening News,* May 25, 1937; Editorial Research Reports, May 10, 1937, Box 230, Clapper Papers, LC. Behind the scenes, the Justice Department, which could not publicly acknowledge its support for a compromise, was nevertheless preparing a draft for one. Reed wrote Cummings: "Attached is a copy of a revision of the Judiciary bill which has been furnished by Congressman Fred Vinson, and will be introduced by him on his own responsibility today or tomorrow." June 1, 1937, Box 199, Cummings Papers, ALDL. Vinson's was a version of the Hatch proposal, raising the age for mandatory retirement to seventy-five for Supreme Court justices and requiring a minimum of ten years on the bench. Only one appointment was allowed in any calendar year.

[18] *New York Herald Tribune,* June 6, 1937, 24:1; June 10, 1937, 5:1; *New York Times,* June 5, 1937, 1:1; June 6, 1937, 1:8; June 7, 1937, 6:1;

coaxed, cajoled, and tried to assure him that no one would believe a Senate majority leader would go to the White House asking for a Supreme Court seat. Finally, Robinson agreed to a meeting, but the very next day a White House press release announced that the meeting was called at the senator's request![19]

During the two-hour session, Robinson bluntly told Roosevelt that his six-judge bill was dead and that any substitute measure adding new justices to the bench would face major obstacles. He had counted the votes. All along, he charged, the White House crowd had been relying on faulty information and vain hopes. There would be no ifs, ands, qualifications, or any prospect that the situation could be reversed. At last a member of his own team told FDR what he did not want to hear.

Robinson received permission to work out a feasible settlement. Corcoran, Keenan, and Jackson were released from managing the congressional forces. The question of Robinson's court appointment came up indirectly toward the end of the meeting. FDR reportedly said: "If there is to be a bride, there must be bridesmaids, at least four of them," his only reference to the current vacancy. In other words, he wanted at least four more justices. Robinson informed him that a compromise was being worked out that contained the "principle" in the original bill, but appointment of coadjutor justices would be limited to one or two a year. This compromise, he said, had been "kicking around" for several weeks before being formally presented. New Dealers, especially Jackson, did not take very kindly to it, but Roosevelt told Robinson to go ahead with the best solution he could work out.[20]

Rejuvenated, Robinson left feeling better than he had for weeks. He alone would cobble together a compromise which, as things stood, was a condition for his appointment. At least he had the go-ahead, unencumbered, to work out a solution to the administration's difficulties. This sign of the president's confi-

[19] *New York Times,* June 4, 1937; James A. Farley, Private Memorandum, July 13, 1937, 2, Farley Papers, LC; *Jim Farley's Story,* 86; Alsop and Catledge, *The 168 Days,* 214–16.

[20] *Jim Farley's Story,* 86; Ickes, *Secret Diary,* 2:153; Leonard Baker, *Back to Back,* 231–32; Davis, *New Deal Years,* 86.

The President holding a serious talk with his Senate Majority Leader Joseph T. Robinson of Arkansas. The two discuss FDR's court-packing strategy. The senator was promised a seat on the Supreme Court if the scheme won.

dence in him was gratifying and would, he believed, move the Senate to an affirmative vote.

As Robinson emerged on the White House steps that evening, reporters asked him about the bill to enlarge the Supreme Court. "The measure," he replied, "will be proceeded with and . . . action will be taken on it during the present session." Aside from provisions relating to the Supreme Court, other features of the bill were to be regarded as of vital importance. "It is felt that during the last few months some changes have occurred which modify the situation, but there still exists the necessity for the injection of new blood into the Court." Robinson hinted at a compromise, implying that amendments to the original bill might come from administration sources, and that one source might be himself. He announced that he was not a candidate for the Van Devanter vacancy, adding that it had not been discussed.[21]

At a press conference the next morning, Roosevelt finally conceded his willingness to accept a compromise but told reporters it was just "plain silly" to think that court reform had been abandoned, as some newsmen had assumed. Reform was going through "without question." Newsmen learned for the first time, however, of the possibility of compromise on the number of justices to be appointed to the Supreme Court.[22]

FDR's decision to yield created a whole new situation. It gave opponents of the court plan a new worry. They now feared that some Democrats, to avoid an open break with the president, might be ready to accept a milder court bill. Serious thought would have to be given to a filibuster—a last-ditch tactic to defeat a bill with less than a majority of votes. Everything now seemed to depend on Robinson and his parliamentary skills. After years on the Hill a number of colleagues were under obligation to him for various favors. He could at times be overbearing and intimidating in attempts to convince reluctant senators to go along. A leading newsmagazine noted: "Just as an expectant mother commands a certain ethereal prestige above other women, so Joe Robinson, as an expectant Justice of the Supreme Court, has become, since Justice Van Devanter's retirement a sort of Super-senator with a prestige all his own among his colleagues."[23] Would the majority leader, through the sheer force of his personality, be able to get those uncommitted votes that could mean the difference between victory and defeat? It was nearly certain that without Robinson, Roosevelt would be undone.[24]

---

[21] *New York Times,* June 4, 6, 1937; *Time* 29 (June 14, 1937), 11.

[22] *New York Times,* June 5, 1937.

[23] *Time* 29 (June 14, 1937), 11.

[24] Leuchtenburg, *Supreme Court Reborn,* 150; Frank Kent, "The Great Game of Politics," *Baltimore Sun,* July 31, 1937.

The old warhorse threw himself body and soul into the cause, looking for a proposal that would be acceptable to a winning majority. In a preliminary maneuver, he decided to introduce any revisions as a series of amendments to the original bill. His task was made more difficult by the president's delay in accepting a compromise. A Gallup poll on June 7 showed a reduction from 45 to 35 percent among those favoring the court bill, while its opponents increased from 45 to 50 percent, with the undecided up from 10 to 15 percent. Support for the bill in Congress plummeted. Members were more reluctant than before to allow any changes in the formal composition of the Supreme Court. Nor did anything happen to halt, much less reverse, this trend. The ensuing events only encouraged it.[25]

Among administration insiders there was more disagreement than consensus about framing a new proposal. In early June, labor's Non-Partisan League told members of Congress to refuse all compromise and fight on to the end. According to their executive committee, they intended, if necessary, to take the issue of court reform into the 1938 election. Without consulting Roosevelt, their executive took a position against compromise. Their action reflected remarks the president had made in May, when he reportedly told the congressional leadership: "Give me the bill, or the issue." Some advisers still wanted a postponement of the court bill, to be reintroduced at the next session and, if defeated, taken to the electorate in 1938.[26]

Charles O. Andrews, an elderly Florida Democrat elected to the Senate in 1936 from that state's supreme court, wanted to enlarge the Court's membership to eleven, requiring each justice to represent one of the ten judicial circuits, with the chief justice "at large." Andrews had introduced this proposal in the Senate as a constitutional amendment on March 23, 1937. It was one of the more favorably received compromises, meant to replace the original bill and designed to make the Court more representative geographically and nationally. In the Court's past history, twenty-two states had never been represented on it.[27]

---

[25] Cantwell, "Public Opinion," 931.

[26] *New Republic* 91 (June 16, 1937), 156.

[27] *Congressional Record,* 75th Cong., 1st sess., Vol. 81, 2616.

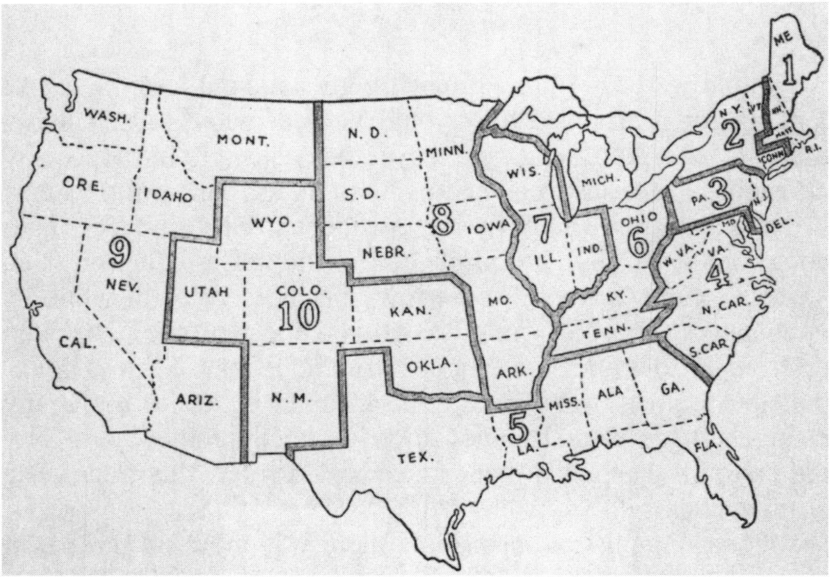

The TEN Federal Judicial Circuits in 1937. (*Federal Supplement,* 1937, Vol. 10 [Washington, D.C.: G.P.O., 1937])

The scheme found a powerful ally in Keenan, who was charmed by the "pork-barrel" compromise. In a long after-dinner conversation, Keenan at first tried to convince Andrews of the wisdom of the original bill. Instead, Andrews won Keenan over to the merits of his own plan, whereupon Keenan began pushing it at the White House. Corcoran and Jackson detested its "pork-barrel" flavor and opposed it strenuously.[28] Robinson objected even more strongly to Andrews's proposal. The circuit that included Arkansas also included Minnesota, which was already represented on the Court by Justice Butler. Andrews's scheme would have thus made Robinson ineligible for an appointment until Butler died or retired. Upon receiving a confidential memo from Roosevelt rejecting it, Robinson had little trouble burying it.[29] Instead, he promoted a Hatch-Logan compromise empowering the president to appoint one coadjutor jus-

[28] Alsop and Catledge, *The 168 Days,* 160, 196.

[29] FDR to Robinson, June 11, 1937, Robinson Papers, UAL. The *Nation* reported that the president feared to oppose Robinson's wishes in the matter. This is unlikely. At the time, as most commentators were agreed, the president was opposed to any compromise until it became absolutely necessary. Robert S. Allen, "Roosevelt's Defeat: The Inside Story," *Nation* 145 (July 31, 1937), 124.

tice a year for every justice on the Court over the age of seventy-five who failed to retire within six months.

After the Wagner Act decisions on April 12, Roosevelt may have already been looking for a way out of his dilemma, but he resisted any talk of compromise, and Robinson blocked any scheme that precluded the likelihood of his appointment to the bench. Farley credits Robinson with finally convincing Roosevelt that a compromise was essential to win passage of any judiciary reform and with persuading him to endorse the Hatch-Logan compromise over the Andrews scheme.[30]

In seeking an end to the court problem, Wheeler and Robinson tried to keep the lines of communication between the two sides open so that, once a bill passed or was defeated, senators would still be talking to one another, able to overcome the animosities created by the struggle. This placed a heavy burden on Robinson.[31] Years of stress, hearty living, and insufficient exercise had taken their toll on his health, and his new responsibilities taxed not only his skills as a deal maker but his stamina as well. The strain of the court fight, combined with Washington's sweltering summer heat, was wearing him down, and there was no letup in sight. By the beginning of July he was complaining openly of feeling unwell, suffering from chest pains.[32]

At the end of a Friday cabinet meeting in June, Vice President Garner announced, without prior warning, that he was leaving for Texas on a fishing trip and would be gone for some time. Newspapers played up the exit as the result of a rift with FDR over the court bill. Garner had planned the vacation back in January when given Roosevelt's assurance that his legislative program would not keep Congress in session beyond June. With the court fight "needlessly prolonged," as Garner put it, he could wait no longer. In more than thirty years, he had never left Washington while Congress was in session.

In addition to being strongly opposed to the court plan, Garner

[30] Allen, "Roosevelt's Defeat," 124; *Jim Farley's Story,* 87.

[31] Leonard Baker, *Back to Back,* 251.

[32] Ibid. Cf. Davis, *Into the Storm,* 92; on Robinson's health problems, see Dr. Henry J. Rutherford, "Case History," Bernard Baruch Papers, Princeton University.

was dismayed over Roosevelt's refusal to take a stand on the wave of sit-down strikes then plaguing industry. He knew that Roosevelt was reluctant to alienate organized labor while the Senate was fighting over the court bill. The press played up the vice president's departure as an act of desertion in the midst of a constitutional crisis, a contemptuous turning of his back on the president that would reduce the already precarious chances for passage of any kind of court reform. FDR's secretary, Grace Tully, reported: "It was believed that Garner left Washington because he wished to escape the requirement of voting against the court plan."[33]

Roosevelt bristled at Garner's lukewarm attitude, if not increasing hostility, toward his policies. Borrowing, spending, and sit-down strikes, Garner later complained, were more important to the country's welfare than the appointment of six additional justices to the Supreme Court. Garner predicted that eventually the Court would have adjusted itself: "Those black robes and life tenure have their effect on men. No President can control the Court. But let the sit-down strikes become established as an American custom and recognized in law, and it will change our entire theory of property ownership and government."[34]

Garner's hostility to the court fracas was genuine, and in the summer of 1937 his opposition was fully exploited by the press. Had he remained at his post, Roosevelt felt, he might have exerted persuasion on his cronies in the Senate, especially on southern conservatives, but the vice president refused to use any of his clout to advance judicial change. His ill-timed departure caused a deep rift with Roosevelt.[35] In the midst of Garner's "vacation," Jim Farley, over lunch at the White House, found Roosevelt seething with anger at the vice president's absence. "Why

[33] *Time* 29 (June 21, 1937), 15. On the linkage between Roosevelt's battle for his court bill and his labor policy, see Davis, *New Deal Years,* 87–91; Bascom N. Timmons, *Garner of Texas* (New York: Harper and Bros., 1948), 216–21; Cummings, Secret Diary, June 11, 1937; *Jim Farley's Story,* 83–86; Grace Tully, *F.D.R.: My Boss* (New York: Scribner, 1949), 225.

[34] Bascom N. Timmons, "John Garner's Story," *Collier's* 121 (March 20, 1948), 23; the link established between the court fight and Roosevelt's relief and labor policies is further explored in Ickes, *Secret Diary,* 2:102. See also Garner to FDR, June 20, 1937, PPF 1416, FDRL.

[35] Early to FDR, June 21, 1937, PSF 188, FDRL.

in hell did Jack have to leave at this time. . . . I'm going to write him and . . . suggest he come back. This is a fine time to jump ship. What's eating him?" When Farley tried to give him a few reasons, FDR countered: "Well, he's got to come back." Steve Early later informed Ray Clapper that "the Garner situation is at the bottom of a lot of White House trouble now. . . . It must be remembered that he is a millionaire and . . . has his goats and nut trees—is in fact a plantation man."[36]

Throughout June, Senators Robinson, Hatch, and Logan labored over drafts of amendments to the court bill, eventually settling on the Hatch proposal, to which the White House agreed. Two of Sumners's related bills were then before Congress. Logan prepared amendments to the first of them, which allowed direct intervention by the attorney general in private suits involving the constitutionality of a federal law, and to the second, which allowed direct appeals to the Supreme Court from district courts when the constitutionality of an act of Congress was at issue. Hatch drafted the amendment allowing appointment of a coadjutor for each sitting justice who refused to retire within six months after reaching the age of seventy-five, with no more than one such appointment in any calendar year.

Borrowing from Sumners's bills, Logan wove their content and Hatch's proposal into the compromise, along with other procedural provisions from the original bill. They held frequent conferences with Roosevelt, Reed, and Cummings, along with constant redrafting, revising, and deletions. While they were busy at the drafting boards, Robinson worked on waverers, trying to get them to vote for a revised bill. The undertaking was awkward for a man in waiting to be notified of appointment to the Supreme Court. When no word came from the White House, he grew restless and embittered. Members of FDR's inner circle

[36] Clapper Diary, August 3, 1937, Clapper Papers, LC; *Jim Farley's Story,* 84; Burns, *Roosevelt,* 307; related news clippings are in Scrapbook 13, John Nance Garner Papers, University of Texas, Austin; Lionel Patenaude, "Garner, Sumners, and Connally: The Defeat of the Roosevelt Court Bill," *Southwestern Historical Quarterly* 74 (July, 1970): 48. Roosevelt never forgave Garner for his desertion at this crucial time. See also Thomas L. Stokes, "Garner Turns on F.D.R.," *Nation,* June 26, 1937, 722.

supposedly harassed him, warning that if he failed to get a bill passed, he could expect no seat on the Court.[37] Senators were infuriated by the shabby treatment of a colleague by the president, whose behavior only strengthened their resolve to oppose any substitute for a scheme which they opposed in the first place.[38]

Logan, Hatch, and Reed met with FDR almost daily in June. Cummings frequently sat in on the drafting sessions. With Corcoran, Cohen, and Jackson out of the picture, his presence was no longer a problem. Roosevelt believed his attorney general "had done the big job well," but those around the president held Cummings in the same low regard they had from the start. The original bill, they contended, was a monument to his shrewdness. By the second half of June the substitute bill was still incomplete. Cummings joined Logan and Hatch to revise the wording. Hatch's proposal contained confusing legal terminology they found difficult to reduce to unambiguous language. Robinson, while attending as many meetings as possible, tried to heal the widening breach dividing congressional Democrats. The president, though still popular, had lost much of his prestige. Senators were in no mood to go down the line for a bill on his mere say-so if they thought it politically safe to resist. This situation was positively appalling for a politician like Robinson, for whom party regularity was an article of faith.[39]

The hammer blow that left Roosevelt's forces reeling fell on June 14, 1937, when the Senate Judiciary Committee filed its majority report. Those sitting in the visitors' gallery that day would not have known that anything of consequence was taking place on the Senate floor unless they had very good ears and a thorough understanding of procedure. It was all over within minutes. Shortly after noon, portly Senator McCarran rose from his seat on the Democratic side of the aisle, holding in his hand the forty-eight-page document, to make the routine announcement that he

[37] Alsop and Catledge, *The 168 Days,* 235.
[38] Ibid., 223–25; Alsop Notes, Box 53, Alsop Papers, LC.
[39] Alsop and Catledge, *The 168 Days,* 235 and passim.

was sending the report to the desk. A page rushed down the aisle to take it from his hand.[40]

Chairman Ashurst sat at his desk writing, as if unconcerned with the proceedings. McCarran strolled over and sat down beside Robinson, chatting and laughing over some private joke. Ashurst rose briefly to mutter something about "this Janus-faced verbal monstrosity," but he hardly got the words out of his mouth before the senators moved on to other routine business. No one objected to the fact that the bill's supporters filed no minority report, and Ashurst made no mention of the fact that one had been offered by Corcoran and Keenan.

Taking advantage of defections by leading Democrats, the Senate Judiciary Committee had appointed McCarran and O'Mahoney, along with Republicans King and Borah, to a subcommittee to draft the report. There was input from other senators, including Burke, Van Nuys, and Wheeler, who was not a member. Their draft, recast and polished by O'Mahoney, was divided into four sections: an analysis of the original bill, dissected provision by provision; a review of bits of relevant judicial history, going back to the records of the Constitutional Convention of 1787; the bill's likely effect on the constitutional system; and a plea for an independent judiciary. A closing flourish, probably a Borah touch, quoted excerpts from George Washington's "Farewell Address," with its warning against "usurpations."[41]

Nearly all of O'Mahoney's draft went into the final version word for word.[42] The result was a savage document. It was a stinging condemnation of the proposal and a personal humiliation for Roosevelt, inextricably identified with it. In cold logic and plain English, it was a harsh, even brutal censure of the court

[40] Senate Committee on the Judiciary, S. 1392, Reorganization of the Federal Judiciary, Senate Report no. 711, 75th Cong., 1st sess. (1937).

[41] "Farewell Address," September 17, 1796, in James D. Richardson, ed., *A Compilation of the Messages and Papers of the Presidents, 1789–1897,* 10 vols. (Washington, D.C.: By Order of Congress, 1899) 1:217.

[42] A typescript of the draft, dated June 10, 1937, is in O'Mahoney's personal papers. It substantiates that he was the report's chief author. Joseph T. O'Mahoney Papers, Western History Research Center, University of Wyoming, Laramie; cited in Gressley, "O'Mahoney, FDR, and the Supreme Court," 198; Alsop and Catledge, *The 168 Days,* 229.

plan, carving away at FDR's entire case for judicial reform, leaving it in shreds. O'Mahoney later called it "Roosevelt's Runnymede." It drew the lines of disagreement between the administration and Congress so sharply that any compromise seemed a forlorn hope.

Packed into its pages were many of the arguments raised in the hearings against the bill. The majority rejected it for the following six reasons:

> 1. The bill does not accomplish any one of the objectives for which it was originally offered.
>
> 2. It applies force to the judiciary and in its initial and ultimate effect would undermine the independence of the courts.
>
> 3. It violates all precedents in the history of our Government and would in itself be a dangerous precedent for the future.
>
> 4. The theory of the bill is in direct violation of the spirit of the American Constitution and its employment would permit alteration of the Constitution without the people's consent or approval; it undermines the protection our constitutional system gives to minorities and is subversive of the rights of individuals.
>
> 5. It tends to centralize the Federal district judiciary by the power of assigning judges from one district to another at will.
>
> 6. It tends to expand political control over the judicial department by adding to the powers of the legislative and executive departments respecting the judiciary.

Roosevelt's message, accompanying the court bill, discussed the evils of conflicting decisions by the inferior federal courts on constitutional questions and alleged abuses of the injunctive power. Yet, as the authors of the report charged, the bill before them contained not a line or a sentence dealing with either of these problems.[43]

The report examined the originally stated objectives of the plan (an increase in the personnel of the federal courts of up to fifty new judges to expedite cases; prompt hearing of appeals; invigorating the courts by the infusion of new blood, etc.). At that time there were twenty-four federal judges over seventy, but they were among the most efficient men on the bench. The report attacked the idea of roving judges ("flying squadrons" of itiner-

---

[43] Senate Report no. 711, 3.

ant judges, to be appointed to districts or circuits where there was alleged congestion) as being of doubtful effectiveness. The bill offered no advantage to litigants in reducing the law's delays. Noting that the measure contained no provision for the "continuous" infusion of new blood into the courts, the report's authors asked: "What, then, does the bill do? The answer is clear. It applies force to the judiciary."[44]

Thrown back at the attorney general were words he uttered at the hearings when he said that, if the Supreme Court justices felt that the addition of six judges would be harmful to the Court, they could avoid it by resigning.[45] The report's authors listed three separate invitations made to justices on the Supreme Court over seventy to get off the bench—first, by the bill; second, by the president's message; and third, by the attorney general's testimony—and this despite all the talk of increasing personnel in the judiciary to expedite the disposition of cases and remedy the law's delays. "Can reasonable men," the report asked, "by any possibility, differ about the constitutional impropriety of such a course?"[46]

Going to the heart of the constitutional issue involved, a powerful passage emphasized that, under the organic law (Article III of the Constitution), judges hold office for life during good behavior:

> By this bill another and wholly different cause is proposed for the intervention of executive influence, namely age. Age and behavior have no connection; they are unrelated subjects. By this bill, judges who have reached 70 years of age may remain on the bench and have their judgment augmented if they agree with the new appointee, or vetoed if they disagree. This is far from the independence intended for the courts by the framers of the Constitution. This is an unwarranted influence accorded the appointing agency, contrary to the spirit of the Constitution. The bill sets up a plan which has . . . the changing will or inclination of an agency not a part of the judicial system. Constitutionally, the bill can have no sanction. The effect of the bill, as stated by the Attorney General

[44] Ibid., 3–8.
[45] *Hearings,* I:33.
[46] Senate Report no. 711, 8.

> to the committee, and . . . by the President in both his message and speech, is in violation of the organic law.[47]

No amount of sophistry could disguise this fact. "The effect of this bill is not to provide for an increase in the number of Justices composing the Supreme Court. The effect is to provide a forced retirement or, failing in this, to take from the Justices affected a free exercise of their independent judgment." FDR's accusation, in his fireside chat of March 9, that the Supreme Court had exceeded the bounds of its jurisdiction and invaded that of the legislative branch was characterized as at best "opinion only." FDR had been forced to acknowledge that neither speed nor "new blood" in the judiciary was the bill's real object. Its aim was to effect change in the decisions of the Court, subordinating the views of the justices to those of the executive and legislative branches. This was to be brought about by forcing justices off the bench or by increasing their number to cancel out their vote.[48]

The document stunned Washington. Its stinging invective provided much of its force. Two columnists wrote: "The fury with which President Roosevelt's fellow Democrats on the Senate Judiciary Committee damned the . . . court plan today amazed this politically sophisticated capital. . . . Unexpected was the revelation that a group of Democratic senators would scourge themselves into an emotional frenzy to denounce a head of their party who had carried 46 out of 48 states in November."[49] It was the harshest, most unrestrained indictment of a presidential proposal that had ever reached the Senate floor from a committee in which a ruling party had a commanding numerical majority. Of the ten senators in the majority on the committee report, seven were Democrats. If Roosevelt's name had been substituted for references to his bill (in many minds the two were one), the report would have constituted an unprecedented personal condemnation of him. Clapper wrote: "Bitter document, extremely rough. It reads almost like a bill of impeachment."[50]

---

[47] Ibid.

[48] Ibid., 9–10.

[49] John O'Donnell and Doris Fleeson, "Capitol Stuff," *New York Daily News*, June 15, 1937.

[50] June 14, 1937, Clapper Diary, Box 8, Clapper Papers, LC.

Although the report did not directly accuse Roosevelt of being another Hitler, it drew attention to conditions abroad and maintained that any attempt to impair the independence of the judiciary leads ineluctably to autocratic domination—"the very thing against which the American colonists . . . revolted, and to prevent which the Constitution was framed." If passed, the report warned, the bill would subjugate the courts to the will of Congress and the president and destroy the independence of the judiciary, "the only certain shield protecting individual rights." It was designed to force a certain judicial interpretation of the Constitution, a rationale totally in conflict with the deceitful and intricate form of the originally stated rationale for the bill, evidently designed to obscure its real purpose.[51]

Administration insiders considered the report's harsh language and tone inappropriate and unwise. Roosevelt was aroused to an impotent fury he found difficult to conceal.[52] Historian and constitutional expert Burton J. Hendrick observed: "The gentlemen who wrote this report give the President little credit for sincerity. . . . The accusation of deliberate deceitfulness is one of the most formidable ever framed against an American President."[53] A correspondent observed that history-minded persons, delving into the records, would not discover a single instance in which a president had been so scathingly indicted in a congressional committee report plainly charging that he had practiced deceit.[54]

The bill, said the report, violated "every sacred tradition of American democracy" and would make its government "one of men rather than one of laws." It was condemned as "a needless, futile and utterly dangerous abandonment of constitutional principle." In phrases that found their way into nearly every newspaper in the land, its authors concluded: "We recommend the rejection of this bill. . . . It is a measure which should be so emphatically rejected that its parallel will never again be presented to the free representatives of the free people of America."[55]

---

[51] Senate Report no. 711, 11–15 and passim; *New York Times,* June 15, 1937, 1; Davis, *Into the Storm,* 91 and passim.

[52] Alsop and Catledge, *The 168 Days,* 233–34.

[53] *Saturday Review of Literature,* June 26, 1937, 7.

[54] *Detroit News,* June 15, 1937, 1.

[55] Senate Report no. 711, 23.

The committee's report—a bill of particulars condemning the court bill—was signed by William H. King, Frederick Van Nuys, Patrick McCarran, Carl A. Hatch, Edward R. Burke, Tom Connally, Joseph C. O'Mahoney, William E. Borah, Warren H. Austin, and Frederick Steiwer. The last three were Republicans. Appended to it was a concurring statement titled "Individual Views of Mr. Hatch":

> In filing this separate brief statement on S. 1392 it is not intended to depart in any degree from the recommendation of the majority report for the committee to the effect that S. 1392 should not pass. In that recommendation I join.
>
> It should be noted that the recommendation and the arguments advanced by the majority are directed against the bill in its present form. It has been my thought that the principal objections set forth in the majority report can be met by proper amendments to the bill; that with sufficient safeguards, it can be made a constructive piece of legislation, not designed for the immediate present, but to provide a permanent plan for the gradual and orderly infusion of new blood into the courts. Such a plan, intended to aid in the better administration of justice and to enable the courts to discharge their judicial function more efficiently, but so safeguarded that it cannot be used to change or control judicial opinions, is within both the spirit and the letter of the Constitution.
>
> Intending to offer amendments which it is believed will accomplish this purpose, I desire . . . this additional statement to accompany the majority report.[56]

Hatch had been involved in countless discussions on a compromise ever since the beginning of June, if not earlier. He believed the administration's bill could be remedied by a proposal he had made in the Judiciary Committee, which Senator Robinson seemed to favor. In his daily column, Clapper commented: "Senator Hatch signed the report, but straddled the issue by offering a bob-tailed edition of the Roosevelt plan as a compromise."[57]

If Senator O'Mahoney's aim was to turn out an explosive historic state paper, he succeeded. His tight reasoning, unequivocal language, and effective style made the document easy to understand. Some of Borah's and Wheeler's most biting passages pro-

[56] Ibid., 24.
[57] *Washington Daily News,* June 15, 1937.

vided extra punch. Every sentence dealt harsh and intentional blows. O'Mahoney was inundated with congratulatory letters and telegrams, among them a wire from Joseph Tumulty, President Wilson's secretary and close confidant: "You, my dear Joe, have saved America."[58]

The report so savagely attacked FDR's purpose that it made waverers nervous. The president was not spared biting sarcasm and cruel innuendo. Arthur Krock in an editorial commented: "Since there are two ways of writing the report, the personal excoriation of the President is accepted by politicians here as a deliberate choice." It was possible at least for the seven Democrats who voted against Roosevelt to have conceded some merit in certain parts of his bill, and the fact that none was admitted was taken for willingness on the part of deserters and those whom they represented to make a clean break, party-wise, with Roosevelt.

Krock concluded that the sum of much experienced Washington opinion was that a large group of Democratic senators who were opposed to many of the later extensions of the New Deal were determined to take back control of their party in 1940. The columnist made it a matter of public record "that the real issue was not the future of the Supreme Court, but the future of the Democratic party."[59] Of one thing everyone could be certain: the seven Democrats who joined the majority in attacking Roosevelt's motives and refusing to concede any merits in his bill could expect reprisals. For Roosevelt was not one to forgive or forget.

To ensure the report's wide circulation, Frank Gannett, having obtained an advance copy three days before it was released, airmailed it to every daily newspaper in the country. The Methodists, hostile as a body to the court bill, sent out copies to over 100,000 clergymen. The Government Printing Office found itself with a best-seller on its hands; 20,000 copies were sold to the public within weeks; congressmen and senators ordered another 70,000 for free distribution under their frank.[60]

---

[58] June 30, 1937, O'Mahoney Papers.

[59] *New York Times,* May 19, 1937, 18; Baker, *Back to Back,* 230.

[60] William E. Leuchtenburg, "F.D.R.'s Court-Packing Plan: A Second Life, a Second Death," *Duke Law Journal* (June–September 1985): 675; for Gannett's

By mid-June, Robinson thought he had forty-five votes "pretty sure pro" and thirty-nine "pretty sure no," with the remaining twelve divided between the "unknown" and "unknown, but apparently might go along." As a journalist reported, however, "a vote count is only as good as the people doing the counting."[61] Robinson's count depended on whether senators like James Hamilton Lewis of Illinois were on side. It soon became clear that neither Robinson nor Keenan had an accurate tally. Keenan claimed the administration's figures were inflated, and with help from James Roosevelt he tried to produce a more reliable list, but they never succeeded in getting one.

Keenan worked closely with Robinson on the substitute bill. Three days after the adverse report was released, Reed, Cummings, and Robinson discussed the Hatch-Logan compromise in great detail. A draft was typed up that afternoon and hurried over to the White House to show to Roosevelt. Reed's discovery that part of the original bill's "flexible feature" (by which the number of justices to be appointed was to be governed by the age of the sitting justices) had been omitted caused mild consternation. There were suspicions that it had been left out on purpose, but after a few hurried phone calls it turned out that a section had been accidentally omitted by a typist.[62]

They took a final look at a resort to a constitutional amendment, the approach favored by Reed. The president reiterated that he was not foreclosing the idea of a constitutional amendment, but had decided that none was needed. In its original form, S. 1392, with the Logan substitute, said:

> Section 215. of the Judicial Code is amended to read as follows: The Supreme Court of the United States shall consist of a Chief Justice and eight Associate Justices, two-thirds of whom shall constitute a quorum. The number of Justices may be temporarily increased by the appointment of an additional Justice for each Justice who has passed the age of seventy-five years; but not more than

---

publicity campaign, see Samuel T. Williamson, *Frank Gannett: A Biography* (New York: Duell, Sloan and Pearce, 1940), 194.

[61] Copy of Robinson's tally sheet, dated June 17, 1937, PSF, Box 165, FDRL. The original is in Robinson's papers. For the journalist's quote, see Leonard Baker, *Back to Back,* 233–34.

[62] Alsop and Catledge, *The 168 Days,* 235–36.

one such additional Justice shall be appointed in one calendar year.[63]

By June 17, however, the Logan-Hatch substitute had burgeoned into a more ambitious and complex bill than this original draft. It included most if not all the provisions included in a revised draft of the Sumners bill—H.R. 2260, which the attorney general had already submitted to the Senate Judiciary Committee. Senator Logan took the Sumners bill and wove into it the rest of the story.[64] In spite of all the conferences and drafting sessions, the end result did not satisfy Reed. He sent Cummings a long memo in which he pointed out numerous flaws in the substitute, in whose preparation he had participated.

Reed underscored the problems Robinson now faced. "The [original] proposal was obstructed by the fact, which seemed all-important to the political opposition, that if as many as six judges failed to avail themselves of retirement privileges, the President would be given the power to appoint immediately six new and additional members of the Court." The facts of the present situation, he warned, could no longer be ignored. "An unfair and unsound public opinion, which should have been or could have been avoided, must be dealt with as a fact when it exists." Public opinion, in his view, would not sanction the appointment of several justices, no matter how carefully or wisely that power was exerted. The integrity of the president's action would be under suspicion. Clear indication of Reed's disappointment with the Hatch-Logan substitute appeared in the following passage: "In order to assure that the Court should always maintain an enlightened view of the Constitution [presumably the New Deal view] and that neither the legislative nor executive branch should exert any unconstitutional control over the judicial branch, some plan

---

[63] Draft Proposal by Senator Logan, n.d., ibid. The rationale accompanying the draft said it was "a re-statement of position" intended to put an immediate end to the Supreme Court controversy by legislation "absolutely assured of wide support and wholly consistent with maintaining the President's fundamental position." Without compelling retirements or enlarging the Supreme Court, "this program would in practical effect result in the voluntary retirement of at least three and probably four Justices within one or, at most, two years. It would also serve to hold a majority of five or six to a liberal position."

[64] Alsop Notes, June 17, 1937, Box 53, Alsop Papers, LC.

has to be evolved which would provide for the permanent composition of the Supreme Court and an automatic reinvigoration of its personnel."[65]

The six-page memo with critical analysis and suggestions indicated Reed's obvious dissatisfaction with the Logan draft, which omitted an earlier requirement that justices, to be augmented, must have served for ten years. This omission, Reed thought, would make it theoretically possible for a president, by appointing a seventy-six-year-old judge to the Court, to be given an indefinite number of additional appointments. "However," he added, "the provisions for only one appointment a year and limiting the Court to fifteen should satisfy the most captious."[66]

Noting that the draft's language contained "some degree of ambiguity," Reed said that, in the form it then took, the substitute would limit new appointments filling Supreme Court vacancies to those circuits that were not already represented. This was Senator Andrews's proposal, to which Roosevelt and Robinson objected. "The disadvantages of limiting choices of justices to unrepresented circuits are as obvious as are the advantages," Reed wrote. In the final draft this provision was eliminated.[67] He complained about the lack of provision for "flying squadrons" of judges to be assigned to circuits or districts experiencing congestion: "With the elimination of the power of the Chief Justice to order judges of inferior courts to other districts and circuits, the permanent increase of district and circuit courts because of age of judges becomes much more difficult to defend." So it was back to the drawing board for the weary and frustrated drafting team.

Robinson, meanwhile, went ahead interviewing waverers each morning, meeting with supporters and opponents on the Democratic side. It was a painstaking approach, exacerbated by strong doubts about the outcome. Jesse Jones, "czar" of the New Deal's credit establishment as chairman of the Reconstruction Finance Commission, left this account of Corcoran's strategy during the latter stages of the court fight:

---

[65] Memo, Reed to Cummings, June 18, 1937, Box 165, FDRL.
[66] Re: Judicial Bill substitute, 1, ibid.
[67] Ibid., 6.

> When it began to appear that he would not get his way, the President sent Thomas G. Corcoran (Tommy the Cork) to ask me if I would sound out some of my friends in the Senate as to whether it would be possible to increase the Court by two members. I had no sympathy with the plan to pack the Court, but went up to the Hill and saw some of my friends. They made it clear to me that, had the President in the beginning asked for only two additional members for the Supreme Court, he probably could have got them, but as the score then stood, with everyone embittered, the Senate would not authorize any increase.[68]

If any bill had a chance of winning Senate approval, and that was very unlikely, Roosevelt squashed it by his tactics and by creating an embittered sentiment in Congress. Whatever good feelings remained were allowed to evaporate. FDR's approach was marked by repeated miscalculations and bad timing, compounded by a refusal to swallow the bitter pill of appointing Robinson to the Van Devanter vacancy. Precious weeks were frittered away while keeping "old Joe" at arm's length. The estrangement made Robinson's job impossible and Roosevelt's cause hopeless. Opponents seized the opportunity presented by the ill feelings and growing doubts to win firm commitments from more senators to vote against the substitute and to harden the determination of those already on side. The time when compromise seemed to some at least a slight possibility had slipped away, and Robinson was left burdened with a wearying, thankless task.[69]

Some writers speculated that, given a Robinson appointment, the senatorial mood might have softened and resulted in assent to some compromise measure on court reform. But Roosevelt dithered, expecting the problem to go away. Tensions between the White House and Capitol Hill intensified, killing all hope for passage of a substitute.[70] As a matter of fact, the substitute was even worse than the original bill. "Of course, the so-called compromise is a complete illusion," asserted Harvard's Erwin Griswold. "It is no compromise at all." Under it, FDR would still have had three appointments in less than six months. Contem-

---

[68] Jesse Jones, *Fifty Million Dollars: My Thirteen Years with the RFC* (New York: Macmillan, 1951), 263.

[69] Alsop and Catledge, *The 168 Days,* 226.

[70] MacColl, "Supreme Court and Public Opinion," 432.

plating that prospect, Griswold asserted that the compromise "is just as wrong in principle as the first bill, since its only purpose is the subjugation of the judiciary."[71]

Echoing this view, Frank Gannett sent out massive mailings, pleading with senators not to surrender before FDR's "compro-

The president at his Hyde Park estate, July 4, 1937, less than a month before the defeat of his court bill in the Senate. (Franklin D. Roosevelt Library, Hyde Park, N.Y.)

[71] As quoted in Leonard Baker, *Back to Back,* 234–35.

mise," which "is no less dishonest, reprehensible and dangerous than the first bill." It was identical to the original proposal in purpose, Gannett said, but slower in accomplishment. He urged senators to filibuster the substitute so it would eventually be defeated "by overwhelming popular opinion." Senators were assured that "the American public will uphold you in a filibuster."[72] Toward that end, his National Committee to Uphold Constitutional Government stepped up its campaign and mailings.

By the end of June, the final details of the substitute had been worked out and Robinson approached Roosevelt with an idea to smooth the way for its reception in Congress. He suggested that its introduction be preceded by what he called "a grand Democratic harmony party." The president liked the idea, believing it would give him an opening for direct personal contacts to assuage any ill feelings. A three-day outing was arranged at the 34-acre Jefferson Island Club, a Democratic sanctum with a clubhouse and a 136-acre duck-hunting preserve in Chesapeake Bay, some twenty miles southeast of Annapolis.[73] All 407 congressional Democrats and male cabinet members were invited there for an old-fashioned political picnic. Senator Robinson was that year's president of the club. The three-day frolic was intended to make congressmen, many of whom had grown restive, feel that they and the president were unified on major policies. FDR and Robinson ultimately hoped to clinch the few votes needed to put over the substitute bill.

Most lawmakers critical of the bill and administration policies attended, since failure to appear, barring a good excuse, would have been considered tantamount to a break with the party. Absent were Glass, Gerry, George, Burke, Shepherd, Copeland, King, Donahey, Holt, and Bilbo. Guests were transported to the island in groups of 130 each day by four retired submarine chas-

[72] Ibid. For background to this, see Williamson, *Frank Gannett,* 193–97.

[73] A former bootleggers' hideout, the club had been remodeled by ninety wealthy men (Breckenridge Long, Winthrop W. Aldrich, Owen D. Young, and FDR among them) as a bachelor club for duck shooting, fishing, and escape from the Washington heat. Any club member could take the place over to throw a party. *Time* 30 (July 5, 1937), 7–8.

ers based at Annapolis. With prearranged schedules, seating was drawn by lot. A newspaper noted that "a cloud of gloom spread over one motor launch when Senators Adams, Clark, Van Nuys, Byrd, and Bailey all arrived together."[74]

The guests swam, fished, went trapshooting, and feasted on Maryland crab, cold cuts, salad, and beer or stronger drink. The president, serene and relaxed, sat in an armchair under the shade of a large locust tree, dressed casually, eager to converse amiably with each and every caller. He showed no sign of hurt feelings or animosity toward signers of the Senate Judiciary Committee's majority report, but no one could be sure what he was thinking. Republican Senator McNary, who was not invited, sarcastically described FDR's effort as a "weekend charm school."[75] The dramatization the president pulled off was so slick that his audience may have momentarily been persuaded to forget his faults and recall only his virtues.

Appraisals differed on the results of this transparent attempt to end the rancor among divided Democrats. A few may have begun to have second thoughts about whether to butt heads with their leader or give in to his wishes. He seemed magnanimous, despite the acrimonious indictment of his bill. But the divisions within the ranks in some cases were too deep to be healed by a love feast. No one could divine whether the event had realigned any members or restored party harmony. Roosevelt's foes still viewed him as a man consumed by ambition and a voracious appetite for revenge.

It would appear, in fact, that neither side on the controversial bill had been conciliated. Krock reported that while Roosevelt may have shown no sign of hurt feelings, few if any Democrats in the opposition camp were charmed out of rebellion.[76] Senator Logan believed his insurgent colleagues were out to break the influence of the president, rendering him powerless to name his

---

[74] *New York Times,* June 27, 1937. Cf. MacColl, "Supreme Court and Public Opinion," 455; "Parley Called by Democrats to Heal Breach," *Washington Post,* June 17, 1937, 1; Robinson to Bernard Baruch, July 12, 1937, Robinson Papers, UAL.

[75] *Time* 30 (July 5, 1937), 7–8.

[76] *New York Times,* June 29, 1937. Leuchtenburg takes a more positive view in *Supreme Court Reborn,* 147–48; cf. Burns, *Roosevelt,* 307–8; MacColl, "Supreme Court and Public Opinion," 455; Ickes, *Secret Diary,* 2:156.

successor in 1940.[77] Two more weeks went by, during which Robinson tried to convince himself that the usual bitterness and acrimony over the troublesome substitute bill had subsided.

With the promise of a compromise he hoped Democrats could live with, Robinson thought he could pull enough senators over to assure a majority. Outwardly he seemed cheerful, but that may have been a pose. He now claimed to have fifty-one "sure" for the Logan-Hatch compromise, boasting in a letter to Garner: "I have enough votes pledged to pass it."[78]

That statement raises the question whether he really had the votes "sewed up," as he claimed. With Keenan, he had drawn up what they considered their first reliable list, showing a majority for the new measure. But how reliable was it? And where was it? The only remnant bearing Robinson's guesswork on the Senate lineup is a typed account of senators' names dated June 17, copies of which can be found in Robinson's and FDR's papers. That Robinson failed to leave an updated list is no proof that he did or did not have one recording the votes that would spell success. It was a characteristic trait of his to record very little information of that sort. He kept the figures in his head because certain senators wanted their vote kept confidential, never to be revealed, even to the White House. But around this time he made this enigmatic remark: "It's too bad you can never tell a president of the United States the truth."[79]

The issue that for five tumultuous months had held Congress and the nation in a state of suspense was brought a decisive step closer to resolution in early July. Robinson was sole deputy of Roosevelt, whose original plan was hopelessly bogged down, to formulate a compromise on enlarging the Supreme Court. Having made his final choice, the senator trotted it out before the full Senate for a final showdown.[80]

The Hatch-Logan substitute for S. 1392 was formally intro-

[77] *Washington Post,* July 4, 1937.

[78] Robinson to Garner, July 2, 1937, quoted in Leonard Baker, *Back to Back,* 233–34.

[79] Alsop and Catledge, *The 168 Days,* 243–45.

[80] *Time,* July 12, 1937, 14.

duced by Senator Logan on July 2. The job facing Robinson and the bill's supporters was to pass it, allowing Roosevelt to save face. But before debate could begin, Robinson, after a talk with Roosevelt, insisted on one last attempt to eliminate the opposition's strongest weapon. If their Democratic opponents could be persuaded to remain quiet and content themselves with merely voting against the bill, that perhaps would clear the way to victory. But to achieve this, it would be necessary to deal with Senator Wheeler, who so far had resisted all efforts to bring him in for a talk with FDR. The intermediary this time was Senator Homer T. Bone, a western liberal and close friend of Wheeler's. He urged Roosevelt to invite the senator in for a talk, but FDR preferred to make it seem that, without any personal overture, visitors would come to him. Rarely would he bring himself to issue a personal invitation, especially to a "turncoat" like Wheeler. On the morning of July 6, the invitation was extended by Bone, telephoning from the White House. At first, Wheeler said he was too busy preparing for the Senate debate, scheduled to open that afternoon. But when Bone pleaded with him, he finally agreed to come over. It was his first meeting with FDR since the court fight had begun.

The president, like the sunny Oval Room, was the soul of cheerfulness, amiability, and charm, but according to Wheeler the atmosphere was "heavily charged." FDR first wanted to acquaint him with a "little background information." He said he had gone into this fight because, while he thought the Supreme Court would "cooperate" with him, it had not done so, and instead had blocked his social and economic reforms. He thought it was his prerogative to bring the Court into line. After all, he added soothingly, his court plan was nothing for old friends to fight over. A workable judicial system—like the English one, flexible and swift—was all he really wanted.

Wheeler heatedly told him that packing the Supreme Court was something else again. He later charged that Roosevelt showed "a gross ignorance" not only of the Supreme Court's function, but also of the Court's workings, of the founders' intent in establishing the judiciary as one of the three independent branches of government, and of the built-in system of checks and balances.[81]

An incensed Senator Wheeler lashed out at Roosevelt. How could any president, he demanded to know, be so cruel to the eighty-year-old Justice Brandeis, one of the best friends the New Deal had ever had? FDR replied that there were times when the pressure of circumstances did not permit consideration of personalities. In fact, he was still stung by the assistance Brandeis had given Wheeler in producing the Hughes letter for the Senate hearings. It had not only discredited his contentions about old age and delays, but sent signals publicly to progressives and liberals alike that the revered Brandeis disapproved of his bill.

Brandeis had always seen dangers, as well as certain benefits, in the course Roosevelt was charting. But the court bill offended him personally as well as constitutionally. Brandeis had been deeply wounded by Roosevelt's remarks. He believed that the Court's independence, prestige, and integrity were at stake. Although he was one of its staunchest progressives, he was also its oldest member. The plan aroused resentment in him for its emphasis on the advanced age of justices and, in particular, the insinuation that judges over seventy suffered from declining vigor and ability to do their work.[82] Privately, Brandeis observed that age had nothing to do with a "conservative mentality."

The court fight forced Brandeis to reflect ruefully on the inevitability of his approaching retirement. In 1937 and 1938, his last two full years on the Court, he produced fewer than half as many opinions as in earlier years. The prospect of leaving the Court affected him in a particularly personal and distressing way. Roo-

---

[81] Years later, Francis Biddle, FDR's third attorney general, lodged a related but milder criticism: "Like most vigorous Presidents, Roosevelt was not very much concerned with the Court, as long as it did not interfere with his plans. He had never had sufficient training as a lawyer to understand that the art of judging required skill, although he must have appreciated that the quality of judges had some relation to the country's direction." Biddle failed to mention how severely limited was Roosevelt's conception of an independent judiciary. Alsop and Catledge, *The 168 Days,* 251–53; Biddle, *In Brief Authority,* 92–93; Alsop and Catledge, "The 168 Days: The Story behind . . . ," *Saturday Evening Post* 210 (October 16, 1937), 19.

[82] Pusey, *Hughes,* 2:753; Jackson, *Struggle for Judicial Supremacy,* 190; Mason, *Brandeis,* 624–25.

sevelt's bill implicitly identified him, the oldest of the nine justices, as the one who should most appropriately and promptly retire. He recognized the impatience of Roosevelt and his supporters to remake the Court and resented the mounting pressure on him to resign, especially because it came from many of those he regarded as old friends and supporters.

But then none of the justices except Van Devanter had any intention of leaving, especially under pressure. Brandeis now realized that he had only a short time left, and fewer chances to realize an ambition he had worked assiduously over a long period to achieve—a reversal of the 1842 decision in *Swift v. Tyson.* As it turned out, he stayed on the Court long enough to experience his two greatest triumphs: the defeat of Roosevelt's hated court bill in 1937 and the overthrow of *Swift* by *Erie Railroad v. Tompkins* in 1938.[83]

In the interview with Wheeler, Roosevelt eventually came to the main point by asking: "Why not let the Republicans do all the fighting?" Wheeler asked why he had not consulted with some Senate liberals before launching his plan, but he got no reply. "We need a liberal Court, Burt," FDR shouted, and realizing that Wheeler would refuse to budge, he exclaimed: "Well, I *want* it, and *I'm going to get it.*" There the interview ended. As Wheeler was leaving, he turned to face the president and warned, "This will kill your popularity."[84]

That same afternoon, the curtain went up on the final act of the court-packing drama. As Wheeler was leaving the White House, Robinson was opening the historic Senate debate, ushering in one of the angriest sessions ever seen in that chamber. Spectators were lined up four abreast, stretching far along the corridors, waiting outside every glass-paneled door leading into the spectators' gallery, hoping to be admitted. They came to witness a political fight among titans, the bitterest in a generation. The battle

[83] The definitive history of the emergence of *Erie* is recounted in Purcell, *Brandeis and the Progressive Constitution.* On the court bill and Brandeis, see Leonard Baker, *Brandeis and Frankfurter,* 333–36; Bruce Murphy, *Brandeis-Frankfurter Connection,* 179–84; and Ickes, *Secret Diary,* 2:124, 471, 539–40.

[84] MacColl, "Supreme Court and Public Opinion," 459.

over what was to be done with the Supreme Court was finally joined on the Senate floor.

Anticipating fierce opposition, Robinson launched the attack. He held the floor for part of two days with a long, impassioned speech favoring the substitute for a bill he had once termed "pretty raw." Angry colleagues dogged him with frequent interruptions and posed hostile questions. He roared back at them, attacking the Court, defending the president, threatening his opponents, and fighting them off ruthlessly. But again and again they returned to the attack. Threatening vengeance, he warned that ways would be found to meet their obstruction. "It will not be tolerated," he shouted.[85]

The next day the tirade became even more unrestrained, more violent. As Robinson continued to speak, the veins in his thick neck were throbbing. His booming voice resounded throughout the chamber, assuring everyone in it that the bill was going to pass. Senator Burke needled him with more questions, causing him to fly into another rage. To his opponents in general, he shouted: "You know you have not the votes to defeat the bill, and therefore you are starting out with a filibuster."[86]

As the opposition riddled Robinson with questions, his face grew redder, and occasionally he gasped for air, his brow glistened with perspiration. Finally, his voice gave out. It was obvious that he was unwell, but his colleagues did not know what to make of it. They could not have known how ill and utterly exhausted he was. As the strain on him took its toll, his color deepened to purple. Senator Royal S. Copeland of New York, a medical doctor, crossed the aisle and whispered to him: "Joe, the cause you're fighting for isn't worth your life. For God's sake, calm down." Pausing, Robinson turned to Copeland and muttered: "I know, but those fellows make me so damned angry

---

[85] Davis, *Into the Storm,* 92. Steve Early wrote to a friend, Ambassador Joseph Davies: "The debate on the Supreme Court bill opens today in the Senate. There are signs and threats and declarations of a filibuster. However, it will not be a repetition of the League of Nations proceedings, unless I am sadly mistaken. I expect to see the Boss prove his mastery again." July 6, 1937, Box 3, Early Papers, FDRL.

[86] *Congressional Record,* 75th Cong., 1st sess., July 6–7, 1937, Vol. 81:6789, 6796, 6788–98.

"The Motive Power." "Driving the Senate Majority Leader." A cartoon by Orr, in the *Chicago Tribune,* n.d., 1937.

with their questions." Throwing up his hands, he bellowed: "That's all. No more questions today. Good-bye." And with that he stalked off the floor toward the cloakroom.[87]

For three days, Robinson, Hatch, Guffey, Minton, and Logan, all supporting the substitute, held the floor. Sharply, incessantly, the opposition baited them. When Senator Guffey tried to speak, his hecklers made it impossible for him to continue. The debate went on uninterrupted throughout the week. There was very little reference to the bill under debate. Guffey called the chief justice a consummate politician, desperately trying to defeat the New Deal. Logan deplored the harsh language in the Judiciary Committee's report on the original bill, accusing the seven Democrats who signed it of ingratitude. Honing in on ingratitude, Wheeler, in rebuttal, said: "Those of you who rode in on the coat tails of the President will ride out on the coat tails of the President, if that is the only reason you are here."[88]

Returning to the Senate on July 8, Robinson relied heavily on his parliamentary skills and congressional friendships for support. At his behest, Senator Pittman, who was presiding, raised a point of order. Through a series of such maneuvers, long-neglected rules limiting floor debate were eventually invoked. The acerbity of the rhetoric was sharpened less by persistent ad hominem arguments than by Robinson's efforts to break some of the unwritten rules of the Senate—meaning that its written rules were to be strictly enforced. Insisting on this was something lawmakers had not experienced for decades. There was more talk among the bill's opponents of a filibuster to prevent its passage, but Robinson had begun using anti-filibuster tactics well before any real filibuster could begin.

Under the new regime, no one was allowed to interrupt a speaker who had the floor without his consent, and then only for a question. No other business could be conducted by anyone except by unanimous consent, and no senator could speak more

---

[87] Before Robinson finished his opening speech, he was so riddled with questions and agitated by the heat of the debate that he took a cigar from his pocket and struck a match to light it on the floor of the Senate chamber. Catching himself just in time, he threw away the match and roared: "I'm through." *Time* 30 (July 19, 1937), 10.

[88] Ibid.

than twice on the same subject on any one "legislative day." The Senate was not allowed to adjourn, but went into recess each evening, thereby extending the same "legislative day" until there could be a vote on the measure being debated. Under this regimen, a "legislative day" could last for two weeks or longer, depending on a ruling from the chair. In the midst of the searing heat wave, Robinson even threatened to go into all-night sessions.

Senators in both parties fumed, objecting vociferously as Robinson and Pittman plowed over them like a bulldozer. They tried challenging the newly enforced rules, but president pro tem Pittman, a Roosevelt supporter, upheld the majority leader, hoping to end debate before it could degenerate into a brawl, and trying to kill any chance for a filibuster. If Vice President Garner, a firm observer of the Senate's unwritten rules, had been presiding, Robinson might not have had so much success, but with Pittman in the chair all rulings were decided in favor of backers of the substitute.[89] The verbal attacks continued. Robinson fought on, arguing, pleading, at times begging for support, until his waning strength finally gave out.

Day in and day out, the heat wave continued. By the end of a long, tiring week on Saturday, July 10, most of the arguments for the bill had been made; those against it had just begun. But a weekend of rest failed to restore Robinson's strength. By invoking long-forgotten Senate rules, he became a target for what one writer termed "such vast and general wrath" that the angry reaction became a new source of agitation for him. The tactics he used probably lost votes for the bill.[90] Robinson thought he had at least fifty senators for the modified plan, but during the week of debate, men on whom he counted began slipping away. The opposition argued that if it was wrong to pack the Court with

[89] Ibid. When Wheeler, for instance, interrupted Logan to charge that one of his statements was untrue, Robinson invoked a point of order stating that, under the generally ignored rules of the Senate, a member "may yield for a question. But he may not yield to other Senators for speeches." Snapped Wheeler: "I don't know anybody on this floor who violates that rule more often than the Senator from Arkansas."

[90] Davis, *Into the Storm,* 92.

six justices, to pack it with one was just as wrong.[91] On Monday, July 12, Robinson began to falter under stabbing chest pains.

O'Mahoney took the floor, followed by Josiah Bailey, one of the court bill's bitterest foes. Regarded as a notoriously ineffective speaker, on this occasion he delivered a cogent, tightly reasoned argument that held his surprised listeners enthralled. Some considered it a speech worthy of the great constitutionalist, Borah at his best.[92] Back in February, Bailey had led a group of southern Democrats to declare their open opposition to the president's plan. O'Mahoney and Bailey were especially embittered toward Robinson for authorizing changes in the Senate rules, and they accused him of attempting to throttle debate. During an angry exchange, Charles Michelson feared that O'Mahoney and Robinson would come to blows.[93] Bailey accused the administration of applying undue pressure, threatening reprisals, and bribing the faithful with rewards. "I will not divulge the identity of any personalities on the Senate floor," he asserted, but then he went on to accuse Senator Minton of "debasing the debate."[94]

Toward midafternoon, Robinson, by then racked with severe pain, left the chamber. On the verge of collapse, he slumped into a wicker chair on the Capitol portico, gasping for breath. From his office he phoned Keenan to tell him that Bailey was inside making a great speech. "He's impressing a lot of people, and I tell you I'm worried." Sending for his close colleagues, Robinson told them he was leaving for the day. He informed Minton: "I've got a terrible pain . . . it hurts so, I can hardly stand it. Go in and tell . . . Barkley to take over for the rest of the day."[95] While Bailey continued to argue passionately against tampering with the Supreme Court, Robinson left the Senate.

---

[91] *Time* 30 (July 26, 1937), 10. Robinson needed forty-nine votes for a clear majority, but by then scarcely fifty were left and he could not be sure of them.

[92] Ibid. Turner Catledge of the *New York Times* called it one of the outstanding Senate orations in recent years. Bailey's points brought cheers from all parts of the chamber.

[93] *Congressional Record,* 75th Cong., 1st Sess., Vol. 81, 7033–34; Michelson, *The Ghost Talks,* 183.

[94] *Congressional Record,* 7054.

[95] Alsop and Catledge, *The 168 Days,* 263–63.

He spent most of the next day alone in his small, un-airconditioned apartment in the Methodist building, directly opposite the plaza from the Capitol and across Maryland Avenue from the Supreme Court. His wife was at their home in Little Rock. Too ill to go anywhere, he remained anxious and fretful, too weak to be in the Senate where the fight was going badly. Reports brought to him indicated that the debate went worse for them that day. Bailey's powerful speech seemed to have persuaded some waverers to join the opposition.

Over in the House, Hatton Sumners was launching into a speech on what he called "the state of the nation." Instead of the usual handful of listeners, more than three hundred members were assembled to hear him. He stated flatly that his Judiciary Committee would not report out a court bill, even if the Senate passed one. He was applauded enthusiastically, and when the speech ended he received a standing ovation. Robinson, resting at home, knew of none of this. By nightfall, he was brought to the brink of a crushing despair. Sometime around midnight his heart stopped beating. The next morning, July 14, a maid found his pajama-clad body sprawled on the bedroom floor, a copy of the *Congressional Record* in his hand and his glasses at his side. A massive heart attack ended his life. A few hours before he expired, a group of undecided senators met to lay plans to desert the administration.[96]

On June 13, while Royal Copeland was addressing the Senate, two men seated in the freshman row where Democrats sat behind Republicans fell into conversation. Prentiss Brown and Edward Johnson, both waverers, were swayed by Bailey's address. Brown announced that he could not go along with his colleagues and intended to vote for recommittal of the bill to the Judiciary Committee. Johnson joined him. They decided to go as a delegation to FDR the next day, tell him in forthright terms of their decision, warn him that he was fighting a losing battle, and plead with him to give in gracefully.

To strengthen their position, they invited two Democrats, Gary

[96] *Congressional Record,* 75th Cong., 1st Sess., Vol. 81, 7033–39; "Congress: The End of Strife," *Time* 30 (July 26, 1937), 10–13; *New York Times,* July 15, 1937, 1:13; Burns, *Roosevelt,* 308. On Robinson's near despair, see Davis, *Into the Storm,* 92–93.

Gillette and Charles Andrews, who sat near them in the Senate, to join the delegation. Gillette was already on record in opposition, but Andrews was considered a possible Robinson convert. The evening papers carried news of the four-man cohort and for the first time predicted outright defeat for the president. The next morning Robinson was found dead.[97] He died knowing nothing about this final blow, enough in itself to kill all his hopes and dreams.

How Roosevelt took the news of Robinson's death is impossible to determine. According to reports, he reacted privately with bitterness, regretting what it meant for his court plan as much as for the loss of a stalwart and faithful friend. Evidence of his black mood was borne out by his actions over the next days as he saw all hope fade for the passage of any bill touching the Supreme Court. The fragile coalition Robinson had supposedly built crumbled. Whatever pledges he may have won from waverers or whatever IOUs he may have been able to call in were canceled. Most of the senators who may have given him pledges did not want the bill. Robinson's death doomed any remnant of court-packing and left the president's forces leaderless. Robinson had won the admiration of senators, many of whom thought he was a soldier worthy of a better leader. FDR later told Farley: "Joe's death was a heavy loss. . . . I appreciated his splendid service. He was wonderful in the court fight. I was going to put him on the Supreme Court for it." But was he? Analysts and commentators ever since have wondered whether Roosevelt would actually have honored the promise to put Robinson on the bench.[98]

There was a funeral service at the Capitol in Washington, attended by the president, but despite urgings from close advisers, he refused to accompany the funeral train on the journey to Little Rock for the funeral and burial. His decision irritated many of the dead leader's friends, who accused the president of ingratitude toward a man who had served him so faithfully, and for

---

[97] Alsop and Catledge, *The 168 Days,* 265.

[98] *Jim Farley's Story,* 89; Charles Michelson speculated that FDR would have kept the promise to Robinson. *The Ghost Talks,* 178; Arthur Schlesinger, Jr. concurs with his assumption; Grace Tully drew the same conclusion in *F.D.R.: My Boss,* 224.

whose death he could, in part, be held responsible. In extenuation, FDR maintained that the trip would create a bad precedent, although he had boasted about breaking precedents many times since 1933. A president, he argued, should only make funeral trips for the vice president, the Speaker of the House, or members of the cabinet.[99]

It infuriated Roosevelt when, on the afternoon of July 15, Wheeler, on the floor of the Senate, demanded that the president withdraw the bill "lest he appear to fight against God."[100] As a psychological weapon, the charge cut deeply. At that juncture FDR was peculiarly vulnerable. He reacted bitterly to the insinuation in private talks. Wheeler aroused court plan die-hards by making this declaration on the Senate floor. Although he was criticized in some circles for being self-righteous and insensitive, he was merely giving expression to what many others were thinking—that had it not been for Roosevelt's stubborn insistence on getting a court bill, Robinson might still be alive. Many senators, now completely at liberty to oppose the bill, were still angry over the way Robinson had been treated by the president and blamed FDR for the senator's untimely death. At the services in Little Rock, the elderly J. G. Burlingame, judge of Pulaski County, remarked to Senator Robert Bulkley of Ohio: "Yes sir, that court bill is responsible for the funeral we're having today. Joe was leading a losing fight and he knew it. It was the first fight he ever lost in the Democratic party, and that's what killed him."[101]

While Wheeler was addressing the Senate, the four Democratic "turncoats" (formerly pledged to Robinson) presented themselves at the White House to break the news to FDR of their intention to oppose his compromise bill. They urged him to give up the battle, but they got nowhere. The president insisted that Congress knew what he wanted, and he fully expected to get it

[99] *Jim Farley's Story,* 84; Davis, *Into the Storm,* 93–94; Alsop and Catledge, *The 168 Days,* 273. FDR delegated Farley, Keenan, Cummings, and West to represent him.

[100] *New York Times,* July 15, 1937, 1 and 13:8; Burns, *Roosevelt,* 308.

[101] Alsop and Catledge, *The 168 Days,* 278. Wheeler's words, as quoted in the *New York Times,* July 18, 1937, were: "Joe Robinson was a political and personal friend of mine. Had it not been for the court bill he would be alive today. I beseech the President to drop the fight lest he appear to fight against God."

in some form. Every liberal Democrat would be obliged to follow him as unquestioningly as Joe Robinson had. The sermon lasted for half an hour. Distressed, the four left him to report the results of the meeting to their leaders.[102]

In his office, Senator Barkley, the acting majority leader, was conferring with Senators Schwellenbach and Minton to determine how they were going to proceed. The news that Brown and the others brought fell like a bombshell on their deliberations. They protested, shouted, and cajoled, but all they could get from Andrews was an agreement not to vote for recommittal of the bill until it became certain that the White House would offer no other substitute. If not, they agreed that they would not vote directly against the substitute and the president, but they would vote to send the bill back to committee. Their support gave the opposition a decisive majority.[103]

After they left, Barkley conferred with Roosevelt by telephone, asking advice on the course of action to follow in the Senate. Word was to go out that the president was still for the substitute bill, along with the charge that southern and western senators were using it as a "punching bag" to prevent passage of the wages and hours bill. Democratic representative Fred Vinson favored both court reform and passage of the administration's wages and hours bill, but he predicted that the labor legislation would make a great deal of trouble among lawmakers. Indeed, he believed that the linkage of the wages and hours bill with the court bill in the minds of many congressmen had much to do with stiffening the opposition against it. He thought it might easily have been the turning point in the entire matter. But then there had been so many other turning points that it became impossible to distinguish one from another.

On the afternoon of July 15, the day before the Robinson funeral in Arkansas, FDR released what is known as his "Dear Alben" letter. The hastily composed document, written only a few hours before his meeting with the group of freshman senators, was addressed to Senator Barkley as acting majority leader.

[102] *New York Times,* July 16, 1937.

[103] MacColl, "Supreme Court and Public Opinion," 463; *New York Times,* July 15, 16, 1937; *New Republic* 91 (July 28, 1937), 333.

The two rivals for Robinson's mantle as Senate majority leader were Senators Harrison and Barkley, and by choosing, at that moment, to write to Barkley, Roosevelt gave the impression that he was taking sides in the contest about to be held, interfering in an internal Senate matter. Both had supported the court bill from the outset. Harrison's supporters were well aware that White House aides had been lobbying the Senate, pressuring members to vote for Barkley. Therefore White House protestations of neutrality in the matter rang hollow. The letter, replete with defiance and undertones of bitterness, conveyed the writer's unspoken determination that "they can't use Joe Robinson's death to beat me. I'll show them." The charge that the court battle was responsible for Robinson's sudden death cut deeply, making Roosevelt at that moment peculiarly resentful. He reacted by releasing the letter on July 15.

My dear Alben:

I am glad you called my attention to certain events of yesterday and today. Lest there be any misunderstanding in regard to judicial reform, please let me clarify the situation.

Since the untimely death of our Majority Leader, I had hoped with you that at least until his funeral services had been held a decent respect for his memory would have deferred discussion of political and legislative matters.

It is, therefore, with regret that I find that advantage is being taken of what, in all decency, should be a period of mourning.

Because of this situation, however, I am compelled in the public interest, though against every inclination, to write to you. I do this because you are the Acting Majority Leader in the Senate.

Over four years ago it became apparent to the American people and to the leadership of the new Administration . . . and . . . Congress that grave problems of many kinds called for great reforms. . . .

The Congress and the Administration effected during the first four years many of these reforms. The reform of the processes of justice, the need for which was nothing new, was recommended by me on February fifth of this year. The time had come to act.

In my Message to Congress I set forth objectives. With these objectives the overwhelming majority of the people of this country were in accord. With these objectives the overwhelming majority of the Congress were in accord.

Proposed tentative legislation was drawn at that time to facilitate discussion of methods in both Houses of the Congress and discussion commenced immediately in the Congress and throughout the country.

Let me make clear once more the objectives. They constituted improvements in the process of justice in all Federal courts, from the lowest to the highest. Those improvements included systematic addition of younger judges to all such courts in which there were judges beyond retirement age who had not taken advantage of retirement privileges—for the dual purpose of helping the older judges give a maximum of justice in a minimum of time, and of keeping the social viewpoints of the courts abreast of changing conditions. Those improvements also contemplated adequate machinery for supervision by the Supreme Court of the expeditious dispatch of business by the lower courts, and for getting constitutional questions to the Supreme Court without delay.

These were the objectives. At no time have I or any member of my Administration insisted that the method or methods originally proposed be sacred or final except to point out that action was of immediate necessity and, therefore, that the process of constitutional amendment was an impossibility if the objective was to be attained within a reasonable time. It is, of course, clear that any determined minority group in the nation could, without great difficulty, block ratification by one means or another in at least thirteen states for a long period of time.

Objectives can be obtained by constitutional legislation and both the original bill and Senator Robinson's bill were clearly constitutional.

There was the other reason for action by legislation rather than by constitutional amendment. The situation of the civilized world has been, for several years, at the point of extreme danger. This has been caused by three factors—aggression and armament, economic crisis and major social needs.

The United States is happily free from any thought of aggression . . . but the people of the United States have called for economic security and for major social improvements. National safety demands them.

About a month ago Senator Robinson advised me that some new form or forms of method were called for if the objectives of judicial reform were to be attained. I told him that in my judgment the bill he proposed would be a satisfactory method of attaining such objectives. I told him further what I had told to all others who have asked my opinion—that on the Congress of the United States falls the primary responsibility for the adoption of methods but that on the President falls the responsibility of recommending objectives. This is in accordance with the Constitution.

To abandon any reform of the judicial processes at this session of the Congress means an abandonment of the objectives.

An abandonment of judicial reform, including, of course, all the Federal Courts, because of the inability of a majority of Senators or a majority of Representatives to agree on method and reach a vote, places the responsibility squarely on the Congress of the United States.

May I, therefore, tell you very simply once more that the objectives of the President, and, I believe of the great majority of our citizens, remain the same, and that I believe that it is the duty of the Congress, and especially of the members of the majority party in the Senate and the House of Representatives, to pass legislation at this session to carry out the objectives.

Very sincerely yours,[104]

Roosevelt's decision a few hours after loyal Senator Robinson's death to omit attending the funeral at Little Rock did not sit well with a good many members of Congress. They said nothing publicly, but when he came out before the funeral train's departure with his "Deal Alben" letter, not only taking up the politics involved immediately, but at the same time accusing others of their failure to observe a decent period of mourning, the anger among Robinson's colleagues rose to even greater heights. And it was not assuaged by what senators considered an unwarranted effort to boost Senator Barkley as Robinson's successor. Instead of healing the Democratic split, he only widened it sorely. The death of Robinson had become not only a grief, but a turning point in New Deal politics. Only for Robinson did it mean "the end of strife."[105]

Roosevelt was fully aware of the inherent risk in sending this letter to Barkley, anticipating that it would be interpreted as an attempt to determine Robinson's successor.[106] The letter's release

---

104 *PPA,* 1937 volume, 306–8.

105 "Congress," *Time,* July 26, 1937, 12.

106 Roosevelt admitted as much to his postmaster general, as reported by him in *Jim Farley's Story,* 87.

introduced another disturbing element into an already indescribably confused situation on Capitol Hill. Now there would be not only a fight over a court bill, but a bitter internecine struggle over the Senate leadership.

Shortly after the letter's release, Minton, Pittman, Barkley, and Schwellenbach paid an evening call on Roosevelt to deliver a gloomy prognosis. Besides providing an update on the freshman senators who had been to see him and Barkley, Minton brought news that three or four more senators were ready to desert the administration. The outlook seemed hopeless. Unaware of all the implications in the problem they faced, the four were cajoled into believing that hope for the measure was still alive. They left Roosevelt with assurances that they would try and might yet be able to cobble together some kind of agreement enabling them to carry on the fight.[107]

Before the funeral train left for Arkansas, Roosevelt called Harrison in for a talk. Aides advised him to do this, bluntly reminding him that it was the height of foolishness to alienate any member of the Senate when they needed every bit of support they could get. FDR tried clumsily to mollify Harrison, and to assure him that he was neutral in the contest, "absolutely neutral," but he only further enraged the already angry senator with these glaring mendacities. Harrison said he resented his "Dear Alben" letter as a virtual White House endorsement of Barkley. Blandly, FDR again denied he had any personal preference between the two aspirants and even accused Harrison of misinterpreting the "tone" of his letter. In no uncertain terms, the irate senator made it clear that he disliked presidential interference in the leadership fight, in spite of the assertion that neither FDR nor his lieutenants would interfere "in any way" with a distinctly internal Senate affair. Roosevelt repeated denials of trying to influence the outcome of the Senate contest and asked Harrison to make a public statement of his denial and assertion. Both were promptly published, but the statement fooled no one, nor did it do much to allay the tense feelings on the funeral train.

---

[107] Alsop and Catledge, *The 168 Days,* 272, recounts that on the day Robinson died, Senator Ashurst, at a meeting at which they were still trying to nail down amendments to the original bill, said: "Anyone of his aides who gives the President the idea that he can win out on this is doing him a grave disservice."

Roosevelt's denial was recognized for what it was, a deliberate falsehood. He had consulted on the matter of the leadership with several senators, including James Byrnes, on May 18, the day Van Devanter announced his retirement. Harrison's supporters were enraged by FDR's letter and lies—a sure indication that he was backing Barkley. The incident reinforced an already widely pervasive image of the president as deceitful and untrustworthy. Observers viewed the intervention as "an extreme assertion of executive strength against the independent position of Congress."[108]

While the president lectured senators on their failure to observe a decent period of mourning for their fallen leader, and professed neutrality in the leadership fight, behind the scenes he exerted all the influence at his command to ensure Barkley's selection. He phoned Farley and told him to contact Boss "Ed" Flynn of the Bronx to put pressure on Senator Dieterich of Illinois. When Farley refused, Roosevelt got Harry Hopkins to execute the task.[109] Farley, however, did put in a call to Kansas City Boss Pendergast, then vacationing in Colorado Springs, asking him to "line up Harry [Truman] on 'the right side.'" Pendergast phoned the senator, urging him to vote for Barkley. Truman replied: "No, Tom, I can't . . . I've made up my mind to vote for Pat Harrison . . . I'm going to do it."[110] And he did.

On the funeral train bound for Little Rock, the Pullman cars were a beehive of political activity. Farley described the atmosphere as "one continual bicker." Before leaving Washington, Roosevelt's emissaries were instructed to work out and accept any compromise they could get so long as it did not appear as a defeat for the administration.[111] When Keenan boarded the train, he was reportedly under instructions to push for a new proposal advanced by Senator Millard Tydings, at Wheeler's behest. It had been dreamed up a day or two before Robinson's death. If true, this was one of the most bizarre developments in the entire affair,

[108] Edward Canham, *Christian Science Monitor,* July 20, 1937.

[109] *Jim Farley's Story,* 92.

[110] Frank McNaughton and Walter Hehmeyer, *This Man Truman* (New York: Harper and Row, 1945), 81–82.

[111] *New York Times,* July 16, 1937.

because both men were adamantly opposed to any compromise. At the last minute, it appears they suffered a loss of confidence, uncertain that they could muster more than the forty-two "sure votes" Wheeler counted. They knew nothing at that time of the freshman Democrat desertions to their side. Hiram Johnson, who fought bitterly against any kind of court bill, expected the administration to have the edge when it came to a final showdown. "They have the votes to put it over," he wrote a friend,[112] but that was before Robinson's death.

After lying in state in the well of the Senate, the body of Joe Robinson rode back to Arkansas with a congressional delegation that included thirty-eight senators, twenty-three representatives, and four thousand floral offerings, including wreaths from the Jefferson Island Club and one from the mother of the president. In almost every compartment lawmakers spent most of the time discussing either the court bill or the leadership contest. In his lobbying activities, Keenan learned by nightfall on July 17, before the train even reached Little Rock, that there was no support for the Tydings proposal or any other.

Mrs. Ewilda Gertrude Robinson, who had made the tiring journey to Washington, rode the special train back to Little Rock. As they pulled into the station on Sunday morning, Bernard Baruch and Harvey C. Couch detrained to escort the senator's widow to her home. She had barely finished breakfast when she was inundated by messages from friends and local politicians, wanting to know her views on who would succeed to her husband's seat in the Senate. Mrs. Robinson would herself have been a possible choice for the vacancy were it not for the fact that the junior senator from the state was Hattie Caraway, the only woman to hold a Senate seat.

Waiting for the train on the platform that morning was Vice President Garner, who had rushed up from Uvalde, Texas. On June 28 he had written Robinson that there were only two people in the world who could entice him back to Washington: "One of them is you, and the other is the 'Chief.'"[113] Garner boarded the

---

[112] Johnson to Garrett W. McEnerney, July 7, 1937, quoted in Leuchtenburg, "Roosevelt's Supreme Court Packing Plan," 103.

[113] June 28, 1937, Robinson Papers, UAL.

special train carrying the delegation back to Washington the next day. En route he held conferences with colleagues on both sides of the court issue, assessed their relative strengths, and found the opposition far stronger than support for the bill. He had watched the Democratic Party slowly disintegrate during the long fight and wanted to do what he could to prevent a complete debacle. Making a shrewd assessment of the situation, and doing the arithmetic, he concluded that the administration cause was lost. Keenan, who returned by night plane to Washington, briefed the president on what he could expect to hear from Garner and the others when they returned.

As the train rumbled through West Virginia on July 20, news reached its passengers of a letter printed that day in the *New York Times* in which Governor Herbert Lehman of New York, writing to Senator Robert Wagner, attacked Roosevelt's court plan and asked the senator to vote against it. The letter reiterated views Lehman had conveyed to FDR in a letter of February 19, but his letter had not then been released to the public.

On July 19, Roosevelt was having one of his worst days since entering the White House. It began with reading Hugh Johnson's acerbic anti–New Deal column, which stated that Joe Robinson's death had in at least one respect been fortunate, for it spared the senator the knowledge that the president, with all his promises, had no intention of putting him on the Supreme Court. Roosevelt's guilt feelings may have increased the cold fury that came over him after reading it. He summoned Johnson to his office to read the column aloud to the red-faced, embarrassed old New Dealer. Then, in a voice laden with contempt, FDR asked: "Hugh, do you know what fine, loyal old Joe would have said to you if you had written that while he was still alive?" "No," he replied. "He would have said, Hugh, you are a liar, a coward and a cad." Then he repeated the words slowly. Johnson muttered, "Sorry, sorry Mr. President, very sorry," and broke down and wept.[114]

The next morning's front pages carried Governor Lehman's letter. Judge Irving Lehman of the New York Court of Appeals advised his brother on many matters. Judge Lehman adamantly

[114] Davis, *Into the Storm,* 94.

opposed the court bill and told his brother that no man had a right to stand aside in what he regarded as a great crisis if he could help materially in averting it. Both were liberal Democrats with impeccable credentials, and FDR had once considered the governor a close political ally, if not a personal friend. The letter's publication just at that critical stage outraged FDR, but it caused no real surprise at the White House.

Intensely stirred by the court fight, with the outcome still in doubt, Judge Lehman believed that his brother, Herbert, as governor of a great state, had to raise his voice in protest. Almost every other leader had spoken out. Governor Lehman explained: "Now, I thought that we were getting to the critical point, and unless I released the letter, it would be useless for me to do anything." It said, in part: "I believe that the orderly and deliberate processes of government should not be sacrificed merely to meet an immediate situation." From the standpoint of the public interest, whatever immediate gain might be achieved by the proposed change would, in his opinion, be "far more than offset by a loss of confidence in the independence of the courts and in government procedure."

For some months Governor Lehman had contemplated speaking his mind about the Court. When it was released to the press, his letter caused a stir. Roosevelt's irritation was heightened by the extensive coverage it was given in the press. Editorials were almost unanimous in commending it, and public sentiment was highly favorable. After speaking by phone to his old friend Justice Cardozo, Judge Irving Lehman informed the governor: "He was greatly pleased—and that is putting it very mildly."[115]

Not all the reaction to the letter was positive. Some Roosevelt supporters were stunned. Two of Lehman's oldest friends, David Dubinsky and Samuel Untermyer, criticized it sharply, and Governor Earle of Pennsylvania denounced it. Senator Wagner contented himself with a noncommittal reply to Lehman (although Garner reportedly had phoned from Washington, warning him not to answer the letter). Frankfurter wrote FDR one of his fawn-

[115] *New York Times,* July 20, 1937, 1; Nevins, *Lehman,* 193–93. This account is based on material in the Herbert Lehman Papers in the New York Public Library.

ing letters which read in part: "Some things just aren't done—they violate the decencies of human relations and offend the good taste and decorum of friendship."[116]

When the funeral train returned to Washington, Roosevelt summoned Garner, Barkley, Pittman, and Harrison to a staff conference at the White House. The exchange between Garner and FDR went as follows:

"How did you find the Court situation, Jack?"

"Do you want it with the bark on or off, Cap'n?" was the reply.

Roosevelt said he did not know what was meant by that "down-country" phrase, Garner explained that when Texans wanted the naked truth, they asked for it with the bark off. If they wanted it sugarcoated, they asked for it with the bark on. Laughing, FDR said he wanted it "the rough way." He got it. Garner relayed the talk among senators of determined and bitter opposition to the revamped bill. He counted seven freshman senators reportedly preparing to desert and vote for recommittal to the Judiciary Committee.

Garner told him: "You are beat. You haven't got the votes."[117] Roosevelt seemed to take the bad news calmly. Outwardly, at least, he maintained his composure, offering no objection to the vice president's appraisal of the situation, and when Garner proposed to spend the day on the Hill, sizing up the situation, he agreed. Garner promised to return later that afternoon with Pittman, Barkley, and Harrison to lay plans for their next move.

Garner knew how much FDR loathed the idea of surrender. He was also unimpressed by the pep talks the president had been receiving from radical freshman New Dealers Lewis Schwellenbach and Sherman Minton, who were reportedly urging him to

---

[116] Nevins, *Lehman,* 192–93; Alsop and Catledge, *The 168 Days,* 282; Frankfurter's letter is quoted in Davis, *Into the Storm,* 95. Some have speculated that Senator Wagner, wishing to be relieved of any obligation to support the substitute court bill, quietly urged Lehman to write the letter to provide him with an excuse for voting against the bill. In the 1936 election in New York Lehman had failed to poll as many votes as Roosevelt. Since then, Roosevelt and Lehman were no longer on friendly terms. Patronage favors did not flow so liberally in New York's direction. *Time* 30 (July 26, 1937), 9.

[117] Burns, *Roosevelt,* 308.

carry on the fight. He was determined to hamstring the bitter enders in the administration and force FDR to accept his betrayal by fellow Democrats as a fait accompli. With the other senators, he returned that evening to find FDR agreeable to compromise, the terms of which were left vague. Garner left the White House feeling more powerful than he had in a long time. Whether his chief liked it or not, he was now in command of the final outcome.

In his office the next day, Garner waited while Democrats gathered in the caucus room of the old Senate Office Building to elect the new majority leader. Voting was by secret ballot. With all but one ballot to go, the count stood at thirty-seven apiece for Barkley and Harrison. A tense few moments later the final ballot to be opened was for Barkley. When this news reached Garner, he went directly to Senator Wheeler, greeted him warmly, and said: "Burt, you can write your own ticket."[118]

Accompanied by Senator Bailey, Wheeler, on Josiah Bailey's advice, wandered back to Garner's office to find out precisely what was meant by his vague directive. Garner played a little cat-and-mouse game with them for awhile, uncertain what to tell them. Finally, he assured them that he meant just what he had said, adding, "But for God's sake and the sake of the party, be reasonable." Anything relating to the Supreme Court—that is, additional appointments, provision for roving judges, a proctor—all of it was to be left out. They agreed on a motion to recommit the bill immediately. But Garner first wanted a full meeting of the Senate Judiciary Committee the next morning.

According to one journalist, it was Garner, after summoning Wheeler, and with the full connivance of Senator Clyde Herring of Iowa, who engineered a meeting of the seven Democratic fence-sitters. They decided to join the opposition in shelving the Logan substitute, sending it back to committee and demanding the administration agree to abandon all provisions affecting the Supreme Court and lower courts. In other words, complete surrender.[119]

---

[118] Timmons, "Garner of Texas," *Collier's* 121 (February 28, 1948), 81; MacColl, "Supreme Court and Public Opinion," 466–67; Alsop and Catledge, *The 168 Days,* 279–80.

[119] Allen, "Roosevelt's Defeat," 123–24.

Garner asked Senator Ashurst to arrange an extraordinary meeting of his committee. Invited to sit down in Garner's office, Ashurst told him: "I'm tired of all this foolishness. I think the best thing to do is throw this damn discredited thing out the first window we come to." Garner responded: "All we want you to do, Henry, is act as undertaker." Roosevelt, meanwhile, made clear to Barkley that he wanted the court bill, S. 1392, left on the Senate calendar. Barkley, now finding himself in the unenviable position Robinson had once occupied, offered to do his best and stood ready to hold out to the bitter end.

Final arrangements for the funeral of the 1937 court bill were made the following day, July 22, which dawned bright and hot. It was day 168 of the legislative battle. The Senate Judiciary Committee, with invited guests (including Wheeler, Keenan, Barkley, and Garner), met at 10 o'clock. Garner opened with a plea for party harmony, asking the senators to bury their animosities with the court bill as quickly as they could for the good of the country and the Democratic Party. He told them what they already knew—that the court bill was dead. The president was licked, and he knew it. "But don't bloody his nose on top of it," he pleaded. "Let's get together and be brothers again."

What about political reprisals? demanded Senator McCarran (who had good reasons for asking). "There will be none of that," Garner assured him (as if he could). "I can promise you that I will do everything I can to prevent it." With an enigmatic smile, Senator Borah observed: "I am sure that the Republicans will be glad to help you." The opposition still wanted airtight assurances that "the Supreme Court was out of it," and when Barkley brought up the issue of keeping bill S. 1392 on the Senate calendar, he was shouted down by those around the table. Even faithful administration supporters like Logan were opposed, anxious to end the struggle that had fruitlessly occupied them for so many months. Garner had not yet recovered from the shock of FDR's interference on behalf of Barkley in the leadership race. After that vote, Senator Logan, the substitute bill's cosponsor, became so thoroughly disgusted that he announced he was ready to give up the fight: "I'm sick and tired of the court issue."[120]

[120] *New York Times,* July 23, 1937.

It was agreed by the majority, over protests from Barkley and other Democrats, to strip the bill of all provisions relating to the Supreme Court and to provide any additional judges for the lower federal courts on the basis of need. When Garner began to show irritation with Barkley, the Kentuckian grew strangely silent. Senator Burke brought all the discordant voices, shouting at once, to attention when he called for their approval for a motion requesting the Senate to recommit bill S. 1392. The motion was approved by acclamation. Barkley refused the request to introduce the motion, so Marvel Logan was deputized to bring it up on the Senate floor later that afternoon. At that point, reporters and cameramen were allowed into the room and captured smiles and handshakes all around. But there were no smiles in the White House.

The Judiciary Committee meeting ended just before noon. Minutes later, the Senate convened for its July 22 session. Senator Logan had to face a delay in taking the floor while another motion was before them to override a presidential veto of a measure to continue low interest rates on federal farm mortgages. Debate on the issue lasted for several hours, and when it ended, the Senate voted overwhelmingly to override FDR's veto in favor of their farmer constituents.

Roosevelt's major setback was still to come. As the afternoon wore on, the ornate Senate chamber began to fill up and tension mounted. Representatives in hordes came over from the other side of the Capitol and sat down on couches lining the chamber walls to watch the final act in the drama unfold. The galleries were packed. The Washington crowd seems to have had a "vulture-like" propensity for being in on the kill.[121]

Action began when Senator Logan rose from his seat to address the chair. Recognized immediately by Garner, he said: "Mr. President, I rise to ask unanimous consent to make a motion to recommit to the Committee on the Judiciary bill S. 1392 to reorganize the judicial branch of the government, with all the amendments thereto." He explained that at the committee meeting that morning, he had been instructed to introduce his motion with the understanding that the committee was to report out a new bill to reform the judiciary within ten days, should the mo-

[121] Alsop and Catledge, *The 168 Days,* 291.

tion prevail. He asked unanimous consent to so move "at this time." Garner asked: "Is there objection?"

Barkley stood to pose a technical question regarding Logan's motion, and there ensued a procedural squabble in which Senator McNary joined. Logan was finally allowed to introduce his motion, and Garner put the question. But at that point, Senator Austin of Vermont, suspicious of the motives of Logan and his fellow Democrats, wanted clarification, and asked if the legislation to be produced by the Judiciary Committee was to be "a bill to reform the federal judiciary" or "a bill for reform of judicial procedure." As a member of the Judiciary Committee, Austin knew perfectly well the nature of the agreement that had been reached among its members that morning. His question was coldly calculated to produce the admission by Logan that in any future bill, the Supreme Court would not be affected. Grasping the drift of Austin's query, Logan tried to dodge the issue, arguing that he had shown his motion to Senator Burke and had obtained his approval. Austin let it go at that.

But this exchange precipitated the high point in the afternoon's drama. Those in the crowded galleries, it seemed, expected that something in the way of a climax was about to take place. Senator Hiram Johnson, a veteran of the 1919 League of Nations fight (he was a charter member, with Borah, of the "battalion of death"), rose to his full height, determined to clear away the deliberate obfuscation and smoke out the true nature of whatever "cozy agreement" he suspected had been reached that morning by Democrats on the Judiciary Committee. It was Johnson who took the opportunity to drop the last bombshell by uttering the forbidden words: "Mr. President, I desire to know what the term 'judicial reform' refers to. Does it refer to the Supreme Court or to the inferior courts?"

Logan continued to bluster, stumbling through yet another account of the committee's efforts that morning to try and spare the president any further humiliation, now that he had been so badly beaten. He might have known that a veteran of as many wars as Senator Johnson would not be denied, and finally he had to acknowledge that the terms accepted by both sides at that morning's session "did not refer to the Supreme Court." He added, for emphasis, that the Supreme Court was not to be considered at all. But Johnson was implacable. Again, his voice, cracking with emotion, shattered the deadly silence.

"The Supreme Court is out of the way?"

"The Supreme Court is out of the way," Logan replied solemnly.

"Glory be to God!" exclaimed Hiram Johnson, speaking more to himself than to anyone else, but the triumphal words echoed from one end of the chamber to the other. After less than a second's silence, the crowd in the gallery and on the floor burst into wild applause. Garner allowed it to continue for as long as it lasted, and when there was a slight lull, he seized the opening to shout: "The question is on agreeing to the motion of the Senator from Kentucky." McNary asked for the yeas and nays, and the clerk began calling the roll.

The ayes were seventy; the nays were twenty. Five senators cast no vote. The twenty "bitter enders" or "die-hards," as they were called, were Bilbo, Black, Bone, Bulkley, Caraway, Chavez, Ellender, Green, Guffey, Hatch, Hitchcock, Hughes, La Follette, Lundeen, McKellar, Neely, Schwartz, Schwellenbach, Smathers, and Truman. Not voting were John H. Bankhead of Alabama, Berry, Hayden, Norris (who was ill), and Pittman. The numerical results were handed up to the rostrum, and Garner shouted them out. "The court bill was dead," commented the *Jackson (Miss.) Daily News,* "dead as a salt mackeral shining beneath the pale moonlight. As dead as the ashes of Moses, the world's first law giver."

The motion to recommit carried overwhelmingly. In the *New York Times,* Arthur Krock wrote that it was one of the most far-reaching political reverses ever suffered by a great party leader. In the aftermath, Senator Ashurst took the floor and promised that his committee would work "with zeal and fidelity" to report out, within ten days, a new bill incorporating the features of the Garner-Wheeler agreement. The bill would be a hodgepodge of procedural changes that went largely unnoticed. Some of them were already on the statute books. When the new bill was eventually presented to the Senate in August, Garner rammed it through to passage in just fifty-seven minutes.[122]

---

[122] Ibid., 291–94; for the *Jackson Daily News* quote, see "The Court and the Press," *Current History* 46 (September 1937): 19; see also *New York Times,* July 23, 1937.

15

Aftermath

> The long, protracted legislative battle over the Court-packing bill blunted the momentum for additional reforms, divided the New Deal coalition, squandered the political advantage Roosevelt had gained in the 1936 election, and gave fresh ammunition to those who accused him of dictatorship. . . . When the dust settled, FDR had suffered a humiliating political defeat at the hands of . . . the administration's Congressional opponents.
>
> Michael E. Parrish, "The Great Depression, the New Deal, and the American Legal Order," *Washington Law Review* 59 (1984), 737.

Writing to a friend, Ben Cohen said he found it difficult to know "whether we should laugh or cry about the denouement." He was referring to the one-sided Senate vote on July 22, 1937, to recommit the president's court bill to the Judiciary Committee. The administration, he said, had started out attempting to get a more liberal interpretation of the Constitution from a more liberal Court. "The old Court," he charged, "has turned a triple somersault" in order to give a more liberal interpretation. The process of retirement having commenced with Justice Van Devanter, opponents of the court proposal predicted that another justice (Sutherland) would depart "as soon as the firing ceases." He concluded: "The real test will lie in the quality of the new Supreme Court appointees."[1]

When Cohen wrote this, the severe setback sustained by the

[1] Cohen to Leon Green, Dean of Northwestern Law School, July 29, 1937, Box 13, Benjamin Cohen Papers, LC. Green had testified for the original court plan before the Senate Judiciary Committee. Cohen agreed with him that Dean William Clark of the Yale Law School would make an admirable choice for the Van Devanter vacancy.

administration still rankled. The defeat was the most damaging blow to his prestige and leadership Roosevelt ever experienced as president, and the wounds it inflicted were still open and festering. The end of the drama was anticlimactic—some would even say macabre. FDR's treatment of the late Senator Robinson had inflamed an already heated atmosphere in the Senate, and to some extent in the House, turning it into a deadly battleground.

The defeated Hatch-Logan compromise had authorized the naming of a coadjutor justice for sitting justices past the age of seventy-five who failed to retire or resign. Appointments were to be limited to one in any calendar year. When district and circuit court judges reached the age of seventy, additional judges were to be provided for, to a limit of twenty.[2] Appointment of a proctor was included—but to be made by the chief justice, not the president—in order to regulate district and circuit court dockets and give detailed information on the volume, character, and status of litigation. These provisions would have permitted assignment of judges to courts other than the ones to which they were commissioned in order to alleviate congestion in overburdened circuits, thus expediting cases.[3]

The measure authorized the government to introduce evidence and take part in Supreme Court reviews in any suit between private parties in which the constitutionality of a federal statute was at issue in any federal court. In such cases the government was to be given notice. Roosevelt's message of February 5, 1937, had recommended that "no decision, injunction, judgment or decree on any constitutional question be promulgated by any federal court without previous and ample notice to the Attorney General and an opportunity for the United States to present evidence and be heard."

Writing to a friend, constitutional historian Charles Warren said that, in general, he was "in most hearty accord" with this

[2] A memo of June 10, 1937, prepared by Alexander Holtzoff, listed the names of federal judges having life tenure who would be seventy-five or over as of July 1, 1937. They included Chief Justice Hughes, Justices McReynolds, Brandeis, and Sutherland, three judges on the Third and Tenth Circuit, two on the U.S. Court of Appeals for the District of Columbia, three district judges, and one each on the Court of Claims and U.S. Customs Court. Supplementary Series 1, Box 11–114, Robinson Papers, UAL.

[3] Cummings to Robinson, July 2, 1937, Box 201, Cummings Papers, ALDL.

proposal. He agreed that the attorney general should intervene, file briefs, and take appeals in such cases, which would be expedited and promptly determined.[4] On November 10, 1935, he had talked informally with "one of the Supreme Court justices" (Harlan Fiske Stone) on this subject, and had written him the following day, pointing out the undesirability of having the Supreme Court decide any case involving the constitutionality of a federal statute without requiring a government attorney to be heard on behalf of the general public. In the 1895 income tax case *Pollock v. Farmers' Loan and Trust Company,*[5] to which the government was not a party, the attorney general had argued "by leave of the Court" as *amicus curiae.* To Warren it seemed unfortunate that cases involving such important federal statutes as the 1894 Wilson-Gorman Tariff Act, establishing an income tax on earnings over $4,000, or the 1934 Farm Mortgage Act, invalidated on "Black Monday," should have been decided without the government being heard.[6]

As for allowing the attorney general to appear in the lower federal courts, Warren considered some provision of that kind desirable, but drew attention to two considerations that needed more thought. The Justice Department would in the future require a considerable additional force because the volume of cases in the inferior federal courts, where constitutional questions are raised, was already very large. The new requirement would result in even further delays in such cases. Ordinarily, the Justice Department moved slowly in deciding whether to intervene, and it would require more time to prepare briefs and arguments after notification by the Supreme Court.

The agreed-upon strategy, mapped out on July 21 and 22,

---

[4] Charles Warren to William Z. Ripley, June 1, 1937, Box 13, Cohen Papers, LC. Professor Ripley, a Harvard economist, was lobbying Cohen, Warren, and others at that time to obtain congressional appropriations to provide the Supreme Court with a research service, enabling it to obtain better information as to the factual situation of state and federal laws whose constitutionality was being challenged in the courts. For FDR's February 5, 1937, Message, see *PPA,* 1937 volume, 58.

[5] 157 U.S. 429 (1895).

[6] The farm mortgage case was *Louisville Bank v. Radford,* 295 U.S. 555 (1935). Warren to Ripley, June 1, 1937, 2, Box 13, Cohen Papers, LC; Warren to Hon. Harlan Fiske Stone, November 11, 1935, and Stone to Warren, November 12, 1935, Box 30, Stone Papers, LC.

called for recommittal of the original bill, S. 1392, with the Hatch-Logan amendment incorporating a draft of amendments to Hatton Sumners's bill (H.R. 2260), which had passed the House. Assurances were given that no changes would be made to the Supreme Court. Administration members in the House were to be effectively prevented from taking any action on their own.[7]

In the Senate Judiciary Committee's executive session of July 22, Marvel M. Logan had submitted in writing to Senator Burke the motion he later offered on the floor of the Senate—that S. 1392, with all amendments, be re-referred to the Judiciary Committee with instructions to report out a bill on judicial reform within ten days.[8] Senator O'Mahoney had hastily scribbled out the majority's terms: "The Supreme Court out of it, no roving judges, no Supreme Court proctor." A photo of his memo, on five-by-seven scratch paper, was sent out over the wire services.[9]

Outwardly, FDR appeared to accept defeat with equanimity, but beneath the facade he remained defiant. Roosevelt was not one to let bygones be bygones, nor would he give up the determination to reform the judiciary. The day after the Senate vote, he wrote a friend: "You and I have had to keep on trying for objectives many times in the past, even though we did not at first succeed. Judicial reform is coming just as sure as God made little apples."[10]

The president was furious at rebels in his party, and mystified because the vote killing the substitute bill was so overwhelming.

---

[7] *Time* 30 (August 2, 1937), 11.

[8] *Congressional Record,* 81:9572.

[9] Ibid., 9572–73. When Chairman Ashurst announced that his committee would assemble the following Monday morning to begin work on a bill, colleagues objected. Senator Borah reminded him that the job expected of them in ten days required that they get to work immediately. Ashurst then gave notice that they would meet the following day. On the O'Mahoney memo, see Gressley, "O'Mahoney, FDR, and the Supreme Court," 200–201. The original is in the O'Mahoney papers.

[10] Krock in the *New York Times,* July 23, 1937; FDR to Senator Theodore F. Green, July 23, 1937, Box 1123, Green MSS., quoted in James T. Patterson, *Congressional Conservatism and the New Deal: The Growth of the Conservative Coalition in Congress, 1933–1939* (Lexington: University Press of Kentucky, 1967), 124n. Cf. Burns, *Roosevelt,* 316; and MacColl, "Supreme Court and Public Opinion," 470.

Only twenty Democrats remained loyal.[11] Feeling that he had been double-crossed by men whose support he counted on, he was now determined to get even. Many regulars, members of the Democratic leadership, and sincere New Dealers voted with the majority because they knew Garner had arranged for the final tactical approach with Wheeler. Veteran Democrats deserted the New Deal fold for the first time on this vote. Party unity, as reflected in the "Grand Coalition" of 1936, was in tatters.[12]

The Senate Judiciary Committee, in its allotted time, put together a bill "for Procedural Reform of the Federal Judiciary," incorporating features of the Garner-Wheeler agreement. Procedural improvements were made in the lower federal courts, embodying provisions Progressives had supported for three decades. In the aftermath of the six-month battle, however, they seemed not only inconsequential, but humiliating.

The new court bill had four main provisions. The revised H.R. 2260 provided that the attorney general be given notice by the Supreme Court of constitutional questions involved in litigation before the Court between private parties, and afforded the government the right to intervene in these private suits to defend federal statutes challenged on constitutional grounds. Provision was made for expediting appeals in such cases: direct appeal to the Supreme Court was to be permitted. This was designed to curtail "the reckless granting by lower courts of injunctions" restraining government officials in enforcement of federal statutes.

A single district judge was precluded from issuing injunctions against enforcement of federal statutes involving constitutional challenges. In such suits, which could result in setting aside acts of Congress, frustrating the public policy of the government, the new provision required three judges to sit in cases involving the constitutionality of federal acts. Roosevelt had long resented the practice by which one federal district judge could grant injunctions, at times permitting his political views to influence the decision on the constitutionality of federal legislation. The measure

---

[11] For various reasons, including illness, Bankhead, Berry, Hayden (the lone Independent), Norris, and Pittman did not vote.

[12] See at end of chapter 14 the names of the twenty loyalists. *Congressional Record,* July 22, 1937, 81:9573; Patterson, *Congressional Conservatism,* 124.

eliminated the power of the chief justice to order judges of inferior courts to other circuits and districts. Federal courts were denied jurisdiction to "enjoin, suspend, or restrain" the collection of state taxes if there was a "plain, speedy, and efficient" remedy available under state law.[13]

The essence of Roosevelt's original proposal for judicial reform was missing entirely from the bill, which cleared both houses in mid-August after a brief Senate debate. Garner boasted to Senator Barkley: "Well, Alben, you told me to do it, and by George, I did it." What he did was end in less than an hour the bitter Senate wrangle that had tied up U.S. legislation for the previous six months. Applying the steamroller tactics he had learned as Speaker of the House, Garner rammed the modified court bill through without a dissenting vote. Only about twenty senators were on the floor when Senator McCarran stood up to introduce the bill that "was a ghost of FD's high-flown plan to enlarge the Supreme Court."

Illinois senator Hamilton Lewis attacked the bill, challenging its sponsor to make a reply. But the vice president cut him off, snapping: "Are there amendments?" "Yes," shot back McCarran, evidently referring to an amendment to Sumners's bill (H.R. 2260), which had previously passed the House. Garner intoned: "Without objection, the bill, as amended, is passed." Under Senate rules, a lone "I object" could have stopped him, for only one was enough to prevent unanimous consent. But strangely, not one of the surprised senators could find the words on the tip of his tongue. Thus ended the bitterest U.S. legislative battle in decades.

There were of course repercussions. Senator Guffey pounded his desk, shouting "Mr. President! Mr. President! I want to be recorded as voting against the bill." Laughter drowned out Guffey's shouting. Garner shouted back that his statement would go in the *Record* as sufficient proof that he was recorded against it. Others had speeches prepared, but they were cut off. At 2:26 P.M.,

[13] Purcell, *Brandeis and the Progressive Constitution,* 36–37; *PPA,* 1937 volume, 338–42; U.S. Congress, Senate Report no. 963 (1937); 50 Stat. 751 (1937); 50 Stat. 738 (1937); Memo of Stanley Reed to the Attorney General, June 18, 1937, Cummings Papers, ALDL; Cummings to FDR, August 17, 1937, OF 41 A, Box 117, FDRL.

less than an hour after McCarran had taken the floor, "the job the Senate had been trying to do since February was finally, forcefully, and completely done."[14]

Roosevelt asked the attorney general for comments on the new bill. Cummings sent his analysis to Alexander Holtzoff and the president. It stated that the bill recently passed was not without deficiencies. It dealt "in a very limited way" with certain aspects of procedural reform growing out of proposals submitted to Congress with the president's message of February 5. "Measured against the objectives you outlined in that message and in other communications to the Congress," Cummings wrote, "it is but a meager performance." Nevertheless, within the limits of the subject it treats, he wrote, "it presents meritorious provisions of a minor character." He could not find in it anything objectionable, but added: "It is a shadowy reminder of the effective plan you originally proposed. The challenge to which it is open is that of feebleness and inefficiency." Under the circumstances, he concluded, "I recommend its approval with the suggestion that an explanatory statement might profitably accompany your action in the matter."[15]

In his letter to FDR, Cummings acknowledged that the bill contained some of the president's recommendations in a modified degree. Amendments made to the bill on the floor and in conference, he wrote, "relieved it of a few of its absurdities and of some of its manifest and obvious faults, thereby giving rise to the question as to whether it would not be more desirable to approve the bill, rather than veto it *in toto.*" This indicates that Roosevelt was evidently considering a veto of the bill. He added that, should the measure become law, it could be made "the basis of further reforms at some future session of Congress. Intensive study could be given to the subject . . . especially along the following lines: a) Supreme Court b) personnel of Circuit and Dis-

[14] *Time* 30 (August 16, 1937), 8.

[15] Swisher, ed., *Selected Papers,* 170. In the introduction to his public papers for 1937, written in 1941, Roosevelt still spoke of the necessity for "a high degree of cooperation among the three coordinate branches of the government." *PPA,* 1937 volume, 338–42; Cummings to Holtzoff, August 16, 1937, includes the analysis sent to FDR. Box 201, Cummings Papers, ALDL.

trict courts and c) Problem of aged and infirm judges who refuse to retire." With reluctance, Roosevelt signed the bill on August 26, 1937, while reciting its deficiencies in an accompanying statement, as suggested by Cummings.[16]

In August 1937, Roosevelt was obliged to accept a bill that ignored his cardinal reform. Writing to a judge on the Third Circuit Court of Appeals, Roosevelt had to admit: "The original bill was, of course, pretty drastic, but at least it served to focus attention on real needs. The bill passed the other day by the Senate is a tiny step in the right direction, and when you get a chance to read it, I think you will agree with me that it is a very small step."[17]

The fallout from the court fight continued to hang over the administration like a pall. Neither the presidency, the Congress, nor the judiciary could escape the effects. Roosevelt's letter to the judge makes one wonder whether he ever had any expectation that the bill he considered "pretty drastic" would pass, no matter what revisions were made. Perhaps, as some have speculated, he used it as a prod in a vain attempt to bring the Court around to his "modern approach" to national affairs.

The personal attacks hurled at him in the heat of the fierce struggle left burning scars. Rebel Democrats, flushed with their success, were under no illusions about FDR's sunny smile. They were not fooled by newspaper accounts relating that the president was taking his defeat philosophically. FDR could put on a good show, but he had not forgiven a thing and would retaliate at the first opportunity.

Relations between the president and the vice president would never be the same. Whatever influence Garner once wielded at the White House had been destroyed when he opposed the court plan. During the final stages of the fight, FDR had told Garner to get him the best deal he could, while still preserving party har-

---

[16] Public Act no. 352, 50 Stat. 751, August 26, 1937. See "Notes for Statement," August 21, 1937, and Memo re: Judicial Reform, Cummings to FDR, n.d., Box 210, Cummings Papers, ALDL. For Roosevelt's statement and enumeration of the bill's deficiencies and merits (Memorandum of Approval for Bill for Judicial Reform), see Swisher, ed., *Selected Papers,* 170.

[17] FDR to J. Warren Davis, August 11, 1937, "Supreme Court" file, PSF, Box 186, FDRL.

mony. To administration leaders present at that meeting, this could only have meant recommittal. But Roosevelt later insisted he had told Garner to obtain a compromise. The vice president said he could recollect no such order, but admitted that, had it not been for intervention by the White House in the Senate leadership contest, he might have "wangled a better deal."[18]

In Ickes's version, Garner, on returning to Washington, saw the president, received his approval to undertake a compromise, and then went to the Hill for conferences. He returned to the White House with "a suggestion." Ickes understood that it would have meant enlarging the Supreme Court to eleven by statute and adoption of a joint resolution for a constitutional amendment providing for a justice from each of the ten circuits. Garner supposedly tried to make a bargain, offering to put a compromise over if Roosevelt would agree to his terms with respect to labor policy and relief spending. Rebuffed by his chief, Garner then went back to Capitol Hill "and ditched the whole program."[19]

Whichever version is correct, Roosevelt, who never trusted him, believed Garner had made no attempt to salvage some of the main elements of the court bill, and instead had abjectly surrendered to Wheeler and the opposition. With other southern conservatives, Garner detested FDR's efforts to tamper with the Supreme Court. The vice president had other differences with the administration as well: he was opposed to its efforts to undermine the foundations on which the American government was built and considered FDR a precedent-breaker. Few presidents were ever placed in the humiliating position Roosevelt faced when he was forced to send a pleading letter to Texas, urging Garner to return to the capital at a crucial stage in the court fight.[20] Garner was compared by two columnists to a latter-day John C. Calhoun, a vice president who worked openly with and covertly against his chief.[21]

[18] MacColl, "Supreme Court and Public Opinion," 467.

[19] Ickes, *Secret Diary,* 2:171.

[20] Burns, *Roosevelt,* 307–8; the full text of the president's two-page letter to Garner of July 7, 1937, is in PSF 188, FDRL.

[21] Joseph Alsop and Robert Kintner, *Washington Star,* January 6, 1939, A-9, quoted in Patterson, *Congressional Conservatism,* 292. Labor unrest at one time infuriated Garner and Byrnes, whom Garner had supported for Senate majority leader. At a cabinet meeting, according to an insider, Garner became so angry

By late summer, Congress was beyond Roosevelt's or anyone else's control. Three days before Robinson died, there was a mild quake in the Senate with the public announcement of defection by Senator Pat McCarran. He had defied them all, saying: "Let them throw me out . . . I think this cause is worthy of any man's life." This was the first major Senate speech the Nevada lawmaker had made since 1935. He was just then recovering from a dangerous illness that had almost killed him, and according to one reporter, "he showed it." Members of the House came over to listen as, in a high-pitched voice, trembling with emotion, the senator rambled on. But his vehement remarks that day proved highly effective.[22]

While the roll call on recommittal was being taken in the Senate, Sumners was attacking Roosevelt's bill in the House, calling on all Democrats in Congress to establish a new party leadership from among their own ranks. By implication, he was reading the president out of the Democratic Party. It was an amazing performance. House Leader Rayburn sat through his fellow Texan's ferocious tirade, listening mutely. John J. O'Connor, chairman of the powerful House Rules Committee, seemed to be encouraging the speaker, plying him intermittently with friendly questions. Not a single Democrat in the House leadership came to the defense of the president. Nothing quite like it had occurred in that body for a long time.[23]

To congressmen, overworked and on edge from the sweltering heat and strain of the long session, the events of July seemed to sound a grave warning. Many of the senators were no longer young, and in their mind's eye they pictured themselves sprawled out dead on a bathroom floor from heart ruptures. In the brief period since the session began, two senators had died; two others had undergone treatment at Washington's naval hospital, and Senator Norris had already left the capital a very sick man. Pres-

---

with Roosevelt and Frances Perkins that he rose, stood behind his chair, and gave Perkins so much hell that she began to cry. Roosevelt abruptly ended the meeting. Clapper Diary, December 28, 1937, Clapper Papers, LC. (His source was Emil Hurja.) See also Henry M. Hyde, "White House no-Man (Garner)," *Saturday Evening Post* 210 (June 25, 1938), 23, 49–51.

[22] Edwards, *McCarran,* 77–78; *Congressional Record,* July 10, 1937, 81:7022.

[23] "Washington Notes," *New Republic* 91 (July 28, 1937), 333.

sure was brought to bear on incumbents from wives, families, and physicians to speed up their work and get out of the capital. Ickes complained: "Everything on the Hill seems to be at sixes and sevens."[24]

Still angered by FDR's treatment of Robinson, senators hurled recriminations about with abandon. At cabinet meetings, Roosevelt sent pointed barbs in Garner's direction. In those final, fretful weeks of the session, there were times when he lost his usual poise. Steve Early was reprimanded for putting out a statement about the court bill that was garbled in the press, and FDR lost his temper at a session with the White House press corps. Ickes was criticized for announcing at a press conference that he favored a constitutional amendment, a remark that went out over the news wires. He learned that "Missy Le Hand is very nervous and sensitive these days, because she is so close to the President," and he hurried to see Corcoran about her "in great distress."[25]

A memo dictated by Roosevelt to Cummings said that he wanted Barkley to make a statement on the floor of the Senate clarifying the agreement he had reached with Garner and Wheeler. FDR alleged it contained the administration's objective of rallying behind a bill for judicial reform on which all Democrats could agree. The next step was to have been a personal appearance by the attorney general before the Senate Judiciary Committee, seeking the same end. Cummings had to agree to the motion to recommit, but he later insisted that he did not agree to any other language:

> No matter what members of the Judiciary Committee may have agreed amongst themselves, no matter what they told me they proposed to do in relation to the Supreme Court, the Proctor, or any other feature of the matter, the fact is that I was bound to nothing except the wording of Senator Logan's motion as originally stated by him to the Senate.
>
> Therefore, I wish to make it clear that, in my judgment, no Senator is bound—actually or by implication—by any alleged agree-

[24] *New York Times,* July 15, 1937; Leuchtenburg, *Supreme Court Reborn,* 152; Ickes, *Secret Diary,* 2:172–74.

[25] Burns, *Roosevelt,* 316; Ickes, *Secret Diary,* 2:172–73.

> ment relating to the Supreme Court, the Proctor, roving judges, or any other specific features of the bill. How far members of the Judiciary Committee feel bound by agreements amongst themselves is for them to determine.[26]

One of the purposes behind the effort to get out the administration's version of its position was implicit in a Cummings memo to Holtzoff: "I rather imagine that the Judiciary Committee will seek to sabotage the essential provisions dealing with the proctor, the flexible features of the [original] act, and the method of appointing additional judges. It would be desirable to watch the situation as closely as we can and be prepared, should an appropriate occasion offer, to submit additional suggestions in support of the original plan."[27] The committee proceeded as Cummings suspected it would. Any other outcome was hopeless.

The court fight's resolution was entangled in the struggle over the Democratic leadership in the Senate. Once the furor over that died down, Roosevelt had to work on regaining leadership of his party and trying to rescue what was left of his legislative program. He told members of the cabinet that Congress had to take responsibility for what was done and what was left undone. When lawmakers went to the White House to discuss such matters with him, they almost always were given some hint that those who had opposed the court bill might be in for trouble. FDR made clear to Garner that Democrats in Congress who had rejected his court bill "might expect to be defeated at the polls in 1938." He warned him privately that, having brought a lot of congressmen in on his coattails in 1936, he might openly oppose "rebel Democrats" who went against his bill or other pending measures. In any case, he predicted, if farm prices continued to fall, a good many Democrats would go down to defeat in the next election.[28]

The president did not seem grim about the matter, and, in fact, turned it into a laughing game. Over lunch at the White House with Farley, he chortled over the uneasiness he was causing in

---

[26] Memo, August 2, 1937, Box 201, Cummings Papers, ALDL.
[27] July 24, 1937, ibid.
[28] Burns, *Roosevelt,* 305, 310.

congressional minds. "I've got them on the run, Jim," he boasted happily. "They go out of here talking to themselves, memorizing the lines to repeat up on the Hill. I'd like to see their faces sag over my mumbo-jumbo. They have no idea what's going to happen and are beginning to worry. . . . They'll be sorry yet."[29]

Under FDR's prodding, Congress had passed the new Guffey-Vinson Coal bill, replacing the earlier law invalidated in *Carter v. Carter Coal Company* (1936). The new bill provided regulations in marketing, price controls, and trade practices, but the labor provisions of the voided act were omitted. Also enacted were a farm tenancy bill, a new Reciprocal Trade Agreements Act, and a revised Neutrality Act. By the end of July, several other measures Roosevelt wanted passed still awaited action by Congress. Included were Black's Fair Labor Standards Act (formerly called the wages and hours bill), Wagner's housing bill, FDR's proposal for reorganization of the executive department, a new farm bill, and a measure creating seven regional agencies modeled on the TVA. Of these and other measures, only the housing bill cleared both houses before Congress went into recess in late August.

Housing had been Wagner's major concern for a long time, but his bill received only lukewarm backing from Roosevelt. Nevertheless he pressed ahead on it, aided by housing enthusiasts, social workers, and lobbyists, to loan municipalities funds for slum clearance and construction of low-cost housing. In the final version, expenditures on construction costs in urban areas were slashed by crippling amendments. Stalled by delaying tactics in the House, the bill finally became law in late August.[30] From the outset, Wagner had avoided involvement in the court controversy, fearing it would jeopardize passage of his bill.

There was added significance in Wagner's lone legislative achievement in the waning days of the congressional session. It was attributable far more to his indefatigable labors than to the

[29] Mooney, *Roosevelt and Rayburn,* 104.

[30] Patterson, *Congressional Conservatism,* 155; Robert S. Allen, "The New Deal Fights Back," *Nation* 145 (August 28, 1937), 187–88. A southern and western bloc of senators representing rural constituencies was hostile to the growing federal expenditures on urban areas, an increasingly important Democratic base. They succeeded in loading the bill with crippling amendments.

president's. Why did the rest of Roosevelt's program fail? The president had originally calculated that the court bill would have a better chance of passage if other major bills were postponed in its favor. Later, he shifted to a different view, deciding that at least one prized measure—Black's wages and hours bill—should be brought up. He believed it would prove to be so popular that it would unify Democratic ranks that had been divided over court reform. Both calculations turned out to be wrong.[31]

It was becoming clear that the court fight solidified a bipartisan bloc of conservatives in both houses who now stood in the way of passing the remaining parts of the president's program. The acid test would come when new bills came up for a vote. Blocking of the wages and hours bill—introduced by Senator Black in May and given Roosevelt's full support, with an accompanying message vigorously urging its passage—showed how extensive the fractures had already become in the "Grand Coalition" that had made possible Roosevelt's electoral triumph in 1936.[32] The Black bill failed to overcome the objections of congressional opponents and had to be recommitted, in the same way that the court bill had been.

Forced, after long and stubborn resistance, to abandon his battle for judicial reorganization, Roosevelt turned to retribution. Nothing illustrates the blow dealt to his political prestige better than the paltry legislative record of that congressional session. It gave strong indication that his influence and his ideas had passed their apex. By mid-August Roosevelt appeared ready to give up the fight for the rest of his program. Serious doubts clouded the minds of reformers about what, if anything, would emerge from the struggle for progressive legislation.

What was the effect of the court bill's defeat on the Supreme

---

[31] Burns, *Roosevelt,* 311.

[32] Ibid. Congressman Fred Vinson thought that the wages and hours bill was so inextricably linked in the minds of congressmen with the court bill that it had much to do in the last month with the stiffening of opposition against the bill. Steve Early to Joseph P. Davies, July 6, 1937, Early Papers, FDRL. Vinson thought it might easily have been the turning point in the legislative fight. Patterson, in *Congressional Conservatism,* traces the evolution of this bipartisan coalition from its inception with measures such as the Public Utilities Holding Company Act and its "death sentence" clause to the end of Roosevelt's second term.

Court, and what would follow in the realm of further progressive legislation? For Court supporters, triumphant over what had once seemed insuperable odds, the main result of the outcome was the preservation of an independent judiciary, shielded against tampering by Congress or the executive. Partisans of the court plan argued that the independence of the judiciary had never been threatened. Referring later to the "slow and uncertain processes of the law," Roosevelt characterized his bill as an "up-building process" designed to "preserve the independence and integrity of the Judiciary, to reinforce and strengthen it as an honored and essential part of our institutions."[33] But that was not the Supreme Court's or the public's perception at the time, as reflected in the thousands of letters and telegrams flooding the Supreme Court and Congress from citizens who thought otherwise.

The impact of the long fight on the sitting justices is difficult to determine, owing to their reticence in such matters. They must have heaved a collective sigh of relief after the final vote on the substitute bill, but for them the outcome was never in doubt. More troubling was the perception—created by the administration, its supporters, and generations of liberal interpreters—that the Court, led by an able chief justice, had reversed itself on a number of important constitutional issues mainly out of fear that Roosevelt would succeed in ramming his bill through Congress. One of the chief promoters of this fiction at the time was Professor Edward Corwin. Neither he nor anyone else in 1937 could have known that Justice Roberts's vote in the Washington minimum wage case, for whatever reasons, had been cast in December 1936, two months before the court bill went to Congress. Hughes was portrayed as being far from insensitive to the strength of liberal pressure. He was even accused of changing his vote to counter the effects of the electoral landslide in 1936 and the threat to the Court posed by FDR's bill. It would have been virtually impossible to disabuse administration leaders of the notion that the court proposal had much, perhaps all, to do with the reversal in constitutional direction. Roosevelt certainly thought so. His attack on the Court in such an unprecedented and radical

[33] FDR's Memorandum of Approval of Bill for Judicial Reform, August 26, 1937, *PPA,* 1938 volume, 338–42.

way was expected to be bolstered by this assumption, fed by what he perceived to be a popular demand for a more "progressive" exercise of the federal government's powers.

Roosevelt had one more opportunity during that long session to provide the country and Congress with a final controversy, and one that would affect the Supreme Court for years to come. He had not yet filled the Van Devanter vacancy. With an eye on future decisions coming from the Court, he contemplated making his first appointment as the first step in a grand design. By making the right kind of appointment, he thought he might at least turn an uncertain five-to-four majority into a more reliable six-three.[34] He remained unconvinced that Hughes or Roberts, or both, would continue to be "enlightened," and might eventually desert their "new-found principles." Then too, Justice Sutherland was likely to retire before very long, especially after the pressure on aging justices was removed by defeat of the court bill. This would yield two appointments, and in the normal course of events FDR would have the kind of Court he wanted. Observers wondered why he had failed to act on this strategy soon after Justice Van Devanter's retirement, before the lasting bitterness of the court struggle emerged.[35]

For more than six weeks the search for a nominee went forward in secrecy. Roosevelt discussed the question with only three or four advisers. Eventually the attorney general became the sole presidential aide in narrowing the field of choice. Neither Farley nor Frankfurter was privy to the discussions. In May the *Literary Digest* published a list of probable candidates. Headed by Cummings, it included Robert Jackson, J. Warren Madden, James M. Landis, Donald Richberg, Lloyd Garrison, and William O. Douglas.[36] There were some surprising omissions.

William Draper Lewis, a founder of the American Law Institute, sent Roosevelt his list of six "liberals," all men who had "a knowledge of modern social and economic conditions" and

---

[34] "Roosevelt's Strategic Retreat," *New Republic* 91 (August 4, 1937), 347–48.

[35] Ibid., 348.

[36] Gerald T. Dunne, *Hugo Black and the Judicial Revolution* (New York: Simon and Schuster, 1977), 49; *Literary Digest,* May 29, 1937.

would be worthy of consideration for Supreme Court appointments. The list was headed by Judge Learned Hand. "I need not tell you," Lewis wrote, "that, like Cardozo, when he was Chief Judge of New York, Learned Hand is the person whose appointment to the Supreme Court the bar, without distinction of party or constitutional ideas, would acclaim as a great one."[37] This suggestion landed many times on the presidential desk from a diversity of sources but was systematically ignored.

Roosevelt never intimated when he would appoint Van Devanter's successor and seemed to relish Congress's discomfort over the uncertain timing of a selection. It was taken for granted that he would make the appointment before Congress adjourned. But, as the time drew near, what had been taken for granted became a matter of speculation. He increased it by issuing the bland statement that he had asked the attorney general for an opinion on his power to appoint a successor to Van Devanter after Congress adjourned.

Would a recess appointment be legal?[38] Did he wish to avoid having the appointment considered by the Senate during the adjournment rush? Or did he hope, by making it afterward, to seat a justice the Senate might not wish to approve, trusting that they would not be able to reject a new justice the following January, after he had already served on the bench through the fall term? The vacancy had not occurred during a Senate recess. But an appointment would "occur" if the president waited to make it until after Congress adjourned. Roosevelt told the press that the attorney general espoused the latter view, but he gave no hint of his intentions. Once again he enjoyed "his year-round sport of keeping the press [and Congress] guessing."[39]

---

[37] August 7, 1937, PSF 186, FDRL.

[38] Cummings wrote FDR: "In view of conflicting statements which have been made in various quarters concerning recess appointments and the history thereof, I caused an additional study of the matter to be made." He enclosed a memorandum prepared by Assistant Solicitor General Golden W. Bell, a summary of appointments to fill Supreme Court vacancies that became available while the Senate was in recess, and recess appointments filling vacancies made available during the previous session of the Senate. Bell's data showed that very few appointees took their seat on the bench before confirmation. Cummings to FDR, August 4, 1937, PSF, Supreme Court, Box 186, FDRL.

[39] "The Presidency," *Time* 30 (August 9, 1937), 9.

The threat of a recess appointment would give senators the unpleasant alternative of forfeiting a summer break to forestall it, or, on returning from one, facing the fait accompli of a sitting nominee. Those making departure plans were further thwarted by Cummings's announcement that all candidates for the Supreme Court vacancy would be subjected to a thorough FBI screening. As it turned out, this was an empty threat, as was the recess appointment. By early August, despite rumors to the contrary, the list of candidates had been narrowed to three: Senator Hugo Black of Alabama (Roosevelt wanted someone from the South or West), Senator Sherman Minton of Indiana, and Solicitor General Stanley Reed of Kentucky. More than coincidence placed the two senators at the top of the list. Both were longtime critics of the Supreme Court and ardent supporters of court-packing. Minton, however, considered some remarks he had made about the sitting justices during the court battle so personalized that he asked Roosevelt to name someone who would make a better colleague for the brethren. Giving the Senate the maximum amount of displeasure tipped the scales in Roosevelt's final choice—Alabama's Hugo Black.

The nominee's qualifications for the post were at best marginal. He had shown meager ability as a general law practitioner. As for judicial experience, it amounted to a year and a half as a Birmingham Police Court magistrate. In 1923 he joined the Ku Klux Klan, but he resigned membership in 1925, at the start of his first Senate campaign. In later years he claimed he had joined the Klan largely because most Alabama jurors were members. He won election to the Senate with KKK support and remained politically indebted to the Klan until the early 1930s.

Once in Congress, Black was extremely critical of the Supreme Court. He wrote a constituent: "A study of the cases [decided by the Court] has convinced me that a majority of the judges for a number of years have been usurping powers that were never intended to be given to the Courts by the Constitution. This is dangerous and jeopardizes Constitutional Government itself." In 1935, from the floor of the Senate, he called for a constitutional amendment that would require the direct election of Supreme Court justices, asking angrily: "Whose government is this?" But that was all forgotten when he went on the bench.[40]

A positivist jurisprudence permeated Black's approach to specific constitutional questions. As a New Deal senator, he had been appalled by what he termed the Supreme Court's use of substantive due process and its expansive construction of the Tenth Amendment to place a laissez-faire gloss on the Constitution's text. A few days before Roosevelt introduced his court bill, Black wrote him advocating a change in the structure of the Court. He argued that it should be expanded by two justices and said that the enlarged Court should sit in panels. After announcing his court proposal, Roosevelt wrote him: "We seemed to have been thinking along the same or else parallel lines." Black considered the Roosevelt plan a "much-needed reform of the judiciary."[41]

The senator's views were an almost perfect match for those of a frustrated president who was eager to change the makeup of the Supreme Court and the direction of its rulings. FDR did not consider Supreme Court justices important policy makers, and on court appointments political concerns dominated his thinking. But for a president seeking to transform government structures and/or policies, it might have been wise for him to perceive the Court as a necessary ally in accomplishing his agenda. Theodore Roosevelt and Ronald Reagan are two good examples of this pattern of behavior.[42]

Black was chosen because he had earnestly, wholeheartedly, and vigorously supported FDR's efforts to rein in the Court. He was ready to stand by him no matter what the outcome. Nowhere was that loyalty more conspicuously displayed than in his zeal for the court plan, which was not popular in Alabama. In fact, there was little support for it anywhere. It was seen as a crass

---

[40] Black to Hugh Mallory, March 18, 1937, Box 134, Hugo L. Black Papers, LC.

[41] Dunne, *Hugo Black,* 596; "Hugo Black," *Oxford Companion to the Supreme Court,* ed. Hall, 72–75; see also Rayman L. Solomon, "Nominations, Controversial," ibid., 595–96; Black to Hugh Mallory, March 18, 1937, Box 134, Black Papers, LC; Black to FDR, January 28, 1937, and FDR to Black, February 6, 1937, cited in Howard Ball, *Hugo Black: Cold Steel Warrior* (New York: Oxford University Press, 1996), 86–88.

[42] Solomon, "Nominations, Controversial," 596.

political gambit floated by a power-hungry president. If Black had remained in the Senate, his part in the controversy would have increased his electoral problems in 1938. Despite taking up Robinson's mantle and attempting to win a compromise bill, Black's efforts as a leader were not enough to sway fellow senators to vote for it. When the roll was called on the wreckage of Roosevelt's plan, he remained loyal to the bitter end, along with Barkley, Minton, and Truman. In his *Literary Digest* column, Ray Moley characterized Black as "F.D.R.'s terrible swift sword."[43]

On the sultry evening of August 11, Roosevelt had Hugo Black in his office and, after the customary banter, asked him to print in his name on the nominating form for a Supreme Court justice. Astonished, Black consented and they went on to discuss briefly how valuable he could be to the administration "in legislative versus judicial capacities." With an eye on future decisions coming from the Court, FDR sealed the completed form in the envelope for delivery to Capitol Hill the next day.[44] The surprise element surrounding Black's nomination was almost as great as that accompanying announcement of the court plan. Roosevelt delighted in giving the greatest discomfort he could to Senate conservatives by designating a liberal southerner his first Supreme Court nominee. At the time, he wrote: "Just now I have a discombobulated Congress, running around in circles."[45]

When Ashurst rose on the Senate floor and asked to make Black's nomination unanimous, Hiram Johnson stood up to object, refusing to allow the usual unanimity of consent. "Judging him by his disposition," he had once said, "he ought not to be made a member of the Supreme Court." As a further sign of Black's unpopularity, the Senate refused to waive hearings on his nomination, an unusual insult to one of their own. For his part, Roosevelt failed to show the Senate the customary courtesy

[43] *Literary Digest,* August 28, 1937. Unlike Black, Truman took no part in the Senate debate. A freshman senator, elected in the 1936 landslide, he was just settling in to his new responsibilities when the court plan was unveiled. David McCullough, *Truman* (New York: Simon and Schuster, 1992), 227.

[44] Dunne, *Hugo Black,* 44.

[45] FDR to Frankfurter, August 12, 1937, PPF 140, FDRL.

by simply enclosing the nomination form (with Black's name lettered in by his own hand) in a bundle of other papers brought up by messenger to Capitol Hill.

Five days later the Senate Judiciary Committee approved the nomination by a vote of thirteen-to-four, but only after a fistfight was narrowly averted. The next day, after a tumultuous six-hour debate, Black was confirmed by a vote of sixty-three-to-thirteen. Six Democrats joined seven Republicans in opposing the appointment. Amid this strained atmosphere the Senate moved to wind up its business. Roosevelt had known all along what the outcome would be. "They'll have to take him," he assured Farley.[46]

During confirmation hearings, rumors began circulating that Black had joined the Klan in the early 1920s when it was at its peak. Klan membership virtually assured the election of Democrats in the Deep South. When evidence of Black's prior membership became public after his confirmation, the news created a furor. The revelation confirmed what many had suspected all along—that naming Black to the Supreme Court was an act of revenge. Roosevelt repeatedly insisted that he knew nothing about any Klan link when he chose Black for the Court.[47]

In spite of occasional press comments on it, the Klan connection did not surface during the initial subcommittee's deliberations. What did come up, at the urging of Senator Warren R. Austin of Vermont, was the "Emoluments" provision (Section 6 of Article I of the Constitution), which forbade any member of Congress during his or her tenure (in Black's case, until January 3, 1939) to be appointed to any office in the United States, either created or whose "Emoluments" were increased during such time. The provision could have disqualified Black, but Austin's argument did not impress a majority of the subcommittee, and it had no greater effect on the full committee when it met on August 16. In that stormy session the nomination was reported out favorably.[48]

---

[46] *Jim Farley's Story,* 98; Patterson, *Congressional Conservatism,* 158.

[47] O'Brien, *Storm Center,* 59.

[48] Dunne, *Hugo Black,* 52–54.

Black and Roosevelt faced a painful dilemma. Apart from constitutional issues, there was the media and a dismayed public to deal with. Another bombshell was thrown into the controversy by Senator Borah, who from the very first day had insisted that Black was constitutionally disqualified for appointment to the Supreme Court under the terms of Hatton Sumners's 1937 retirement bill. By retiring rather than resigning, Justice Van Devanter technically remained a member of the Supreme Court. On the Senate floor, Borah asserted: "Certainly the President cannot name a successor until there is a vacancy and I challenge any lawyer here to say there is a vacancy." The only thing troubling Borah was whether or not a vacancy existed to be filled. He insisted there was none. On that point, however, he was finally forced to admit that "very few people seem to agree with me. In fact, before Black's nomination came up, practically no one agreed with me." Not the kind of man to let that change his views, however, he stuck to his position. As one of a handful of Republicans, he voted against Black's confirmation even though he believed the senator was personally qualified to sit on the Court.[49]

The Klan link posed a greater threat to the prize that seemed within Black's grasp, seriously questioned the judgment of the president, and cast doubt on the position of the administration. It seemed to some observers an episode out of the dead and supposedly buried past. Black assumed a posture of silent audacity and carried it off. Years later, with the controversy all but forgotten, he asked, apparently with honest perplexity, what all the fuss was

[49] The Sumners-McCarran bill included a provision making it possible for retiring justices to be recalled for court duty when conditions required it, and thus they remained justices or justices emeriti. Borah to R. W. Washburn, August 16, 1937, Borah Papers, LC. On the Black appointment, Borah's votes were erratic. He voted to report the nomination favorably to the floor of the Senate, not to send it back to the Judiciary Committee, and then against confirmation. Instead of remaining reticent, he stoutly defended Black in the letter to Washburn, one of his detractors. He did not regard him as a "New Deal Lunatic," partly because Black had voted against the NIRA, "the very basis of New Dealism." He had influenced his committee to rewrite the New Deal's wages and hours bill, to which Borah was opposed, but considered it saner after Black took hold of it. "Besides," he concluded, "if Black is not appointed, who will be? Some names have been suggested which would indeed make a man shiver." *Time* 30 (August 16, 1937), 11.

about on a matter which he insisted was common knowledge at the time. But during the six-hour Senate debate on his confirmation, knowledge was not that common, and Black made no effort to clear up the matter. Borah, who took a prominent role in the debate, repeatedly injected quotations by Black in which he categorically denied, then did not deny, his past Klan membership.

In the subcommittee hearings, Borah sought clarification, and there Black reportedly revealed the whole story. With lawyer-like caution, he asserted that "he was not now a Klansman" but that any senator concerned about his former membership should vote against him. A prominent newspaper editor, commenting on what had transpired in the committee, thought the senator's disclosure could scarcely have been more candid. "Without actually saying so, he let the committee understand that he had been a member. To any lawyer or politician, the delicate nuance should have been obvious." But to some it was not.[50] Black was adamant in denying that any fault lay with the president. "F.D. must have known," he said, "but he didn't ask me." After a White House conversation with FDR, Ickes wrote: "The President, when he appointed him, had no knowledge of this, and it apparently never occurred to him to ask."[51]

But the issue would not die. After Black and his wife returned from a European vacation, he went on national radio with a brief explanation but no apology for his Klan membership from 1922 to 1925. Roosevelt continued to deny having had any knowledge of the association. The performance by the two men was a good example of "lying by omission," or what the more sophisticated might call "compulsive silence." Was Black culpable? If he was, to some extent he redeemed himself with his frank radio acknowledgment of Klan membership. A pundit quipped: "Hugo won't have to buy a robe; he can dye his white one black."[52]

As a final coda to this controversial episode, many years later Black left a note in his private papers "to correct for posterity any idea about President Roosevelt's having been fooled about my membership in the Klan":

---

[50] Dunne, *Hugo Black,* 56–58.

[51] Ibid., 59; Ickes, *Secret Diary,* September 25, 1937, 2:215.

[52] One group condemned October 4, 1937, his first day on the Supreme Court bench, as "Black day." Solomon, "Black," 72.

> President Roosevelt, when I went up to lunch with him, told me there was no reason for my worrying about having been a member of the Ku Klux Klan. He said that some of the best friends and supporters he had in the State of Georgia were strong members of the organization. He never in any way, by word or attitude, indicated any doubt about my having been in the Klan, nor did he indicate any criticism of me for having been a member of that organization. The rumors and statements to the contrary are wrong.[53]

By the fall of 1937, if not earlier, Roosevelt's dissatisfaction with conservative Democrats in Congress was no secret. He had a special antipathy for those who had voted against his court bill along with other administration measures. They had disrupted party unity, poisoning the well of those liberal policies he considered part of the New Deal. On May 2, 1938, Governor Olin T. Johnston of Alabama, after holding talks with Roosevelt, announced from the White House steps his intention to contest Ellison ("Cotton Ed") Smith of South Carolina for his Senate seat that fall. It was clear, well before his announcement, that Roosevelt was contemplating a purge of conservative Democrats in his party. The idea had been supported by Ickes, Hopkins, and Corcoran. He required little encouragement. It was something he wanted to do anyway. He felt not the slightest doubt that by "going to the people" he could be successful in bringing about the defeat of candidates singled out by him. The battle lines were being drawn. "To potential victims of 1938 the prospect should have been frightening."[54] But it only hardened the resolve of conservative Democrats to withstand his attacks and intensified their determination to keep relief funds for their states out of Roosevelt's hands.

The president made a feeble effort to conceal his pique over

[53] The statement was appended to a letter to Virginia Hamilton, April 7, 1968, Box 31, Hugo Black Papers, LC. See the related materials in Box 234. The note's text is quoted in O'Brien, *Storm Center,* 70. During his tenure on the Supreme Court (1937 to 1971), Justice Black eventually compiled a liberal voting record, especially in First Amendment and civil rights cases. On his Supreme Court career, see Newman, *Hugo Black.*

[54] Patterson, *Congressional Conservatism,* 238–39; *New York Times,* May 17, 1938, 1. Farley was not alone in opposing the purge. Rayburn said privately that it was a mistake. Mooney, *Roosevelt and Rayburn,* 104.

the defeat of his court bill. As soon as the tumultuous first session of the Seventy-fifth Congress ended in late August, he boarded a train for the West to gauge his popularity. He found the trip exhilarating, but his resentment was still patent. In Montana he snubbed Wheeler; in Wyoming he tried to shut out O'Mahoney, who boarded the presidential train uninvited; in Nebraska he deliberately ignored Burke. Patronage channels mysteriously dried up for Democrats who had opposed him on the court bill. A critic described his attitude as "high school girl revenge."[55] The president gave unmistakable evidence that anger over his recent humiliation had not abated. Conservative Democrats sensed that they would face serious trouble once the primary season began.[56]

By the end of 1937, commentators were almost unanimous in predicting a purge in the upcoming primaries. If conservative Democrats were forced to go on the defensive and fight for their political lives, would they be inclined to cast aside partisanship and unite with Republicans in a common cause? And if they did, would anti–New Deal Republicans help them out, or would self-interest make conditions as difficult as ever? Only time would tell. Conservatives in both parties had long dreamed of forging a successful bipartisan coalition to harness the New Deal, but they were shaken by this new development. Few Democrats of any persuasion relished the idea of making a clean break with their party, but to conservatives it was becoming increasingly obvious that Roosevelt intended to try to force them out.

Men like Senator Bailey had wanted, if possible, to reform the Democratic Party from within. But FDR was furious at the "treachery" of Bailey, George, and Van Nuys, men he claimed accepted his support and then deserted him. By the fall of 1937, Roosevelt no longer made any effort to hide his anger. A reporter recalled: "Resentment crystallized into the desire to crush all who [had] conspired against the throne." Farley was opposed to the purge and later recalled: "For weeks and months I found him [FDR] smoldering against the members of his own party." Ac-

[55] Alva Johnston, "President Tamer," *Saturday Evening Post* 210 (November 13, 1937), 8–9.

[56] Patterson, *Congressional Conservatism,* 262.

cording to former presidential aide Stanley High, Roosevelt, as much as any conservative Democrat, was "crossing the Rubicon."[57]

Conservative strength in the Senate in late 1937 stood somewhere between thirty-five and forty. This made it necessary for them to enlist ten more members to be assured of a dependable bulwark against the New Deal onslaught. Nearly always in off-year elections, support for the majority party declines. Roosevelt needed to hold on to his huge majority and make it appear that popular support remained behind the administration. Ten seats were held by those conservative Democrats Roosevelt considered "unreliable": George, Smith, Tydings, Lonergan, McCarran, Adams, Berry, Clark, Van Nuys, and Gillette.

Senators Dieterich and Bulkley stood somewhere between the liberal and conservative sides, but Dieterich was replaced by the Democratic machine in Illinois; Congressman Scott W. Lucas would be their candidate for his seat. Of the thirty-four upcoming Senate races, twenty-one involved seats held by Democrats Roosevelt was willing to support.[58] These were seats conservatives wanted to win. Three of the remaining thirteen belonged to Republicans, while the other ten constituted the "unreliables." At the start of the primary season, most of these Democrats were either certain of renomination or immune from interference by the opposition.

In several states, close contests loomed for administration-held seats that were up for grabs. Bolstered by the decline in Roosevelt's prestige, Republicans were hoping to win them on their own in November. They were not very interested in forming bipartisan coalitions. What would be the point in electing New Deal Democrats? In one contest in Idaho, however, Republicans did intervene. There, New Deal loyalist James P. Pope was trounced in the primary on August 10. In that state Republican

[57] Creel, *Rebel at Large,* 295; *Jim Farley's Story,* 95; "Party Purge," *Saturday Evening Post* 210 (November 13, 1937), 8.

[58] Ordinarily, there would have been thirty-two Senate contests (one-third of ninety-six), but a resignation and a vacancy, filled in 1937, added two more. Twenty-two seats held by Democrats remained potential battlegrounds. Twelve of them were occupied by "reliable" administration supporters. Patterson, *Congressional Conservatism,* 263. The lone woman in the Senate at that time was Hattie Caraway of Arkansas.

and Democratic primaries were held on the same day, and voters were allowed to cross over. The victor was D. Worth Clark, Idaho's Democratic congressman since 1935. He was an isolationist, and no great enthusiast for the New Deal. With help from many Republicans who deserted their own primary, he won by a margin of some four thousand votes. Pope was the only Democratic senator to lose a primary to a more conservative opponent, and Idaho's primaries offered the only example, among all twenty-one contests, of successful bipartisanship in defeating an incumbent New Deal senator.[59]

The spotlight in 1938 was trained on ten contests involving incumbent Democrats whom Roosevelt was determined to punish. His anger at these men was fanned by revolts against his judicial reorganization bill and his tax proposal of early 1938, and it remained at white heat as the summer primary season progressed. At one time Roosevelt seriously considered moving against nine of the ten, but aides and political leaders convinced him that Lonergan, Adams, and Clark had such solid strength in their states that they could not be dislodged. The president refrained from meddling in these contests.[60] That left George, Smith, Tydings, Van Nuys, and Gillette to face the perils of a purge. McCarran would have been included in this group, but he was too strongly entrenched. Recognizing this, Roosevelt made no serious effort to interfere in the Nevada contest in which a New Dealer was slated to oppose the incumbent.

First to face a primary was Guy Gillette of Iowa. He was not much of a conservative, having supported the "death sentence" in the Holding Company bill and FDR's executive reorganization. For Roosevelt, however, the cardinal test of liberalism was the court plan, and Gillette had opposed it. That made him subject to mild intervention. But something called a "flying squadron," including Wheeler, Bailey, Van Nuys, and King, went into Iowa and rallied to the senator's defense. Gillette was too shrewd

[59] *Idaho Daily Statesman,* August 10, 11, 1938, 1; Patterson, *Congressional Conservatism,* 268–69.

[60] The tenth, George L. Berry, a 1937 appointee from Tennessee, did not need Roosevelt's interference. Edward H. Crump, Democratic boss of Memphis, was determined to defeat him. See Patterson, *Congressional Conservatism,* 270–71; and *Jim Farley's Story,* 123–24.

and hardy a campaigner for his opponent. Backed by the state's Democratic bosses, he piled up more votes than all three of his opponents combined. He refrained from attacking Roosevelt by name, but scored heavily by denouncing "this gang of political termites boring from within . . . planning on taking over . . . the Democratic party." His pledge to voters was: "I will not be a rubber stamp member of Congress." With no help from Republicans, he defeated a New Dealer all on his own.[61]

Frederick Van Nuys, as a Senate Judiciary Committee member, had signed the majority report against the court bill. That was enough for Roosevelt to target him. The powerful Indiana machine, run by Governor Paul V. McNutt and Senator Sherman Minton, also had him in its sights. Indiana law called for a state convention instead of a primary. Without much of an organization backing him, Van Nuys threatened to run as an Independent if denied the convention's nomination. He declared he would not, if offered, accept any Republican support, emphasizing his long-term loyalty as a New Dealer. His threat to run as an Independent, with the certainty of gaining at least some Republican support, was enough to induce members of the Democratic machine to reconsider. Within a week, Van Nuys was proclaimed the Democrats' candidate by acclamation. Minton sullenly went along with the switch.

The president sounded the battle cry in a fireside chat on June 24, 1938, coming out in the open in his campaign to purge the rest of the rebels. The explosive announcement came near the end of the talk. He intended, he said, to play an active part in the upcoming Democratic primary elections. He wasted no time in turning up the heat. Soon after this radio talk he boarded the presidential train (dubbed the "purge train") heading South, with the first stop at Warm Springs, Georgia.

In that summer of 1938, southern Democratic senators were Roosevelt's main targets. By then his conservative opponents were more out of favor with him than they had ever been, and he felt he had little to lose in trying to purge them. Concentrating

---

[61] *New York Times,* June 4, 1938; *Time,* June 13, 1938, 16; Patterson, *Congressional Conservatism,* 272–73. Iowa's primary laws, unlike Idaho's, did not allow crossover voters in the Democratic and Republican primaries, which were held on the same day.

on the Senate, he determined, to go after Walter F. George of Georgia, Millard Tydings of Maryland, and "Cotton Ed" Smith of South Carolina with particular zeal. Tydings, though not a southerner, shared their opposition to New Deal labor policies. FDR wanted to see all conservatives beaten. Most were southerners, and he wanted them defeated by southern votes. They chaired powerful committees, voted against his court plan, obstructed other New Deal legislation, and in some cases challenged his control of the Democratic Party. Howard W. Smith of Virginia also looked vulnerable. FDR's political lieutenants went around actively seeking a popular candidate to oppose him, along with John J. O'Connor of New York, chairman of the powerful House Ways and Means Committee.[62]

Southern Democrats in large numbers viewed the president as a troublesome meddler, interfering in their state and local affairs in the old carpetbagger tradition. Considering his wife's well-known tendencies, they feared he might go so far as to tamper with race relations and segregation in the South. In his fireside chat, Roosevelt said he felt he had every right to speak out in those few instances where there were clear-cut issues between candidates for Democratic nominations—issues involving the liberal declaration of principles set forth in the party's 1936 platform or the clear misuse of his name.[63]

In a prepared speech in Georgia, Roosevelt shared the platform with its senior senator, Walter F. George. After calling George "a gentleman and a scholar," the president announced that in no way could he be considered a liberal. He told his audience that if he were voting in the Georgia primary, he would support Lawrence Camp, his handpicked opponent to challenge the senator. That and other slurs turned erstwhile New Deal senator Richard Russell, who was not up for reelection in Georgia that year, into a staunch foe of Roosevelt and his policies.

With Governor George Rivers out of the running as a challenger to the senior senator of his state (he decided to run for reelection rather than against George), Roosevelt and his aides

[62] *Newsweek,* July 25, 1938, 5.

[63] *PPA,* 1938 volume, 391–400; *FDR's Fireside Chats,* eds. Russell D. Buhite and David M. Levy (Norman: University of Oklahoma Press, 1992), 134.

had to shop around for another candidate. They finally settled on Lawrence Camp, a federal district attorney in Atlanta. He was relatively unknown through the state but was apparently the best Roosevelt could do.[64]

The attempt to defeat Senator George backfired. When FDR asked Senator Richard Russell to lend his support to defeating George because he had opposed his plan to enlarge the Supreme Court, the junior senator's curt reply was: "I have been elected to represent and work for Georgia's interests in Washington, D.C. . . . and not Washington's interest in Georgia."[65]

Speaking at a whistle stop in Greenville, South Carolina, Roosevelt snapped and snarled so directly at Senator "Cotton Ed" Smith that Marvin McIntyre, on hearing FDR's remarks, ordered the engineer to pull the train out of the station as quickly as possible.[66] None too delicately, the president criticized "Cotton Ed" for allegedly stating that a family could live on fifty cents a day. In the case of both Smith and George, Roosevelt interfered against the advice of his political advisers.

In Maryland, he stumped for two days against the urbane Millard Tydings. Once back in Washington, FDR wrote Ickes: "I find everything all well here and as you know, I stepped on the gas in Georgia and South Carolina on my way back North and have done it again . . . in opposition to Tydings [your buddy] and John J. O'Connor."[67] He saved his heaviest ammunition for the attack on Tydings, who faced a primary fight against Representative David J. Lewis, a former coal miner who had helped frame the Social Security Act. Tydings, FDR said, "had betrayed the New Deal in the past, and will again."[68]

---

[64] Luther Herman Ziegler, Jr., "Senator Walter George's 1938 Campaign," *Georgia Historical Quarterly* 43 (December, 1959), 335. Roosevelt's secretary Marvin McIntyre is credited with having found Camp. Cf. *Congressional Digest* 17 (October, 1938), 264.

[65] Josephine Mellichamp, *Senators from Georgia* (Huntsville, Ala.: Strode, 1976), 251. Cf. Ziegler, Jr., "George's 1938 Campaign," 333–52. For political reasons of his own, Senator Richard Russell remained personally neutral, while the members of his organization supported Senator George. See Ziegler, Jr., 347.

[66] OF 200, CCC, FDRL.

[67] August 17, 1938, PPF 3650, FDRL.

[68] *Baltimore Sun,* August 17, 1938, quoted in Patterson, *Congressional Conservatism,* 280–81. Roosevelt's interference in these campaigns was unprece-

Roosevelt's careless choice of objectives and tactics in the party purge of 1938 was a costly miscalculation. If he had been the master politician many admirers thought he was, how could he have so badly misjudged the political situation? The defeat of his court bill had become an obsession. He assumed incorrectly that New Dealers and moderates in the states he targeted would line up solidly behind him. They did not. Governor George Rivers of Georgia maintained a traditional neutrality common to southern governors, and Senator Russell remained aloof, if not hostile. South Carolina's James F. Byrnes not only refused to take any part in the purge but contributed funds to Millard Tydings's campaign. Senator George L. Radcliffe of Maryland, a former Roosevelt business associate, not only refused to help the president, but served as Tydings's campaign manager.[69]

The results that November were a staggering defeat for Roosevelt. Senator George ran first in a three-man race. Camp ran third, behind demagogue and former governor Eugene Talmadge. In South Carolina, Smith received 55.4 percent of the vote to Johnston's 44.6 percent. Tydings ran far ahead of Lewis, winning a thumping 58.8 percent to his 38.5 percent. Of the nine or ten conservative Democrats marked for removal, the only casualty of the purge was New York's John J. O'Connor, who as chairman of the House Ways and Means Committee had succeeded in bottling up Black's wages and hours bill in his committee during the session of Congress that ended on August 21, 1937. All the other nine senators retained their seats.

In a chapter on the purge in his book *Congressional Conservatism,* James Patterson summarizes and analyzes the numerous reasons for the president's setback. He lists, among other things, the superior campaigns conducted by southern conservatives,

---

dented. Ancillary activity included diverting federal patronage from his conservative Democratic opponents. He sent speakers and aides into southern states to campaign against them, offering advice and money. He spoke personally for his handpicked "liberal" candidates—Camp, Johnston, and Lewis. Senator Glass angrily predicted that Roosevelt "will do what he can to beat George and Smith, and every other person who has crossed his path." Carter Glass to Senator Harry Byrd, July 5, 1938, Box 383, Glass Papers, ALDL.

[69] Patterson, *Congressional Conservatism,* 283–84; *Baltimore Sun,* August 29, 1938, 1; Clapper Diary, June 12, 1938, Clapper Papers, LC; Byrnes, *All in One Lifetime,* 102.

The Congress that was—"Patent Applied For!"

The Congress that is—"The Toy That Went Bust."

"Congress Rediscovers Its Backbone." A cartoon by Bruce Russell in the *Los Angeles Times* and Jerry Costello in the *Knickerbocker News.* (*New York Times Magazine,* section 8, April 10, 1938, p. 2)

which hurt the New Deal cause. He concludes that there was no chance the purge could have succeeded, no matter what tactics Roosevelt adopted. Most important of all, failure to oust the conservatives revealed how powerless the president was to deliver on candidates he had personally supported. More ominous for the Democratic Party's future, the attempted purge of 1938 strengthened the trend against Roosevelt and widened the liberal-conservative split within his party.[70] No other American president since Andrew Johnson during Reconstruction had ever interfered so blatantly or taken a more active part in congressional elections than Roosevelt did in 1938.

As far as the future of Roosevelt and his party was concerned, the events of 1937 and 1938 were especially remarkable for two developments. Congress, after the court bill defeat, reestablished its legislative power, but it then did very little legislating. Both developments were the result of a deep split within the Democratic Party for which Roosevelt was largely responsible. By comparison with earlier sessions, the Congress reasserted itself in dramatic fashion. But by no means was the Seventy-fifth a "do nothing" Congress. It could point to the new farm tenancy bill, Wagner's modified housing bill, a new Guffey-Vinson Coal bill, a new Reciprocal Trade Agreements Act, and a revised Neutrality Act as achievements. Roosevelt's court plan defeat revealed some previously concealed flaws in his leadership ability and in his relations with Congress. There had been, as Rexford Tugwell later admitted, incredible ineptitude on the part of White House management.[71]

---

[70] On the purge, see Patterson, *Congressional Conservatism,* especially chapter 8, in which he sums up the reasons for its failure. Unifying factors in the equation included opposition to most of the domestic program of the New Deal—for example, the expansion of federal power and the bureaucracy, deficit spending and the growing national debt, the power being accumulated by labor unions, and most welfare programs. The term "conservative" in this context was used very loosely to refer to members of Congress who opposed FDR and the New Deal on most key issues. Cf. *Jim Farley's Story,* chapters 13 and 14.

[71] *Democratic Roosevelt,* 435.

Epilogue

> Of all the effects of the legacy of the New Deal, the most baleful has almost certainly been its subversion of the Supreme Court. Without this . . . the other destructive effects of the New Deal might not have survived long after the trauma of the Great Depression and [after] the fresh memory of it had passed away.
>
> Arthur Schenfield[1]

BETWEEN THE CIVIL WAR and the advent of the New Deal, the Supreme Court rose to a position of enormous prestige. Its new building, completed in 1935, became a magnificent symbol of that prestige. Fathered by a former chief justice, William Howard Taft, it was designed by Cass Gilbert. Three years and ten million dollars were spent building it. The famous Marble Temple was constructed on a scale to match the Capitol, which it fronts. The East Wing housed palatial suites for the nine justices, but during the 1930s only three used them; all the others preferred to work at home. Its important rooms were built to accommodate nine justices and would be inadequate for additional members.

No issue in the years before World War II shook the country as did President Roosevelt's proposal to enlarge the membership of the Supreme Court. No less amazing was the manner in which most of the electorate rose up in wrathful protest against FDR's effort to "pack" the Court to ensure New Deal decisions. The demonstration in defense of the Court amounted to a popular tribute to its integrity and position, almost a vote of confidence in the Chief Justice. Meanwhile, the justices went about their

[1] "The New Deal and the Supreme Court," in *The New Deal and Its Legacy: Critique and Reappraisal* (Westport, Conn.: Greenwood, 1989), 167.

work, making no comment on the political storm whirling around them.

FDR, it seems, badly misjudged the generally held respect the people had for members of the bench, especially the high bench. Perhaps this reflected a strong streak of antipathy the president nurtured for the legal profession to which he himself belonged, but for which he developed an apparent aversion. To be sure, this antipathy was shared by others, markedly during the Progressive Era and again in liberal circles in the 1920s and 1930s. The target of this animosity was usually lawyers for large corporations. Roosevelt's attitude bore a striking resemblance to that of Brooks Adams, the nineteenth-century Boston Brahman who once tartly observed that the historic purpose of the federal judiciary seemed to be "to dislocate any comprehensive body of legislation whose effect would be to change the social status." Like FDR, he was a patrician, with undisguised contempt for "profit-hungry" captains of industry, and he revealed his bias when he remarked: "The capitalist, as I infer, regards the constitutional form of government which exists in the United States, as a convenient method of obtaining his own way against a majority."[2] Roosevelt's term for corporation magnates, which he used occasionally, mainly in private, was "fat cats." In public he coined the term "economic royalists." As for the sentiments expressed by the less famous brother of Henry Adams, he would evidently have been in complete accord with FDR.

In proposing to increase the size of the Supreme Court in 1937, Roosevelt abruptly ended an era during which the Court, though often lambasted for its activism, for propounding arguments that were termed inconsistent, or for manipulating doctrines of constitutional law, had remained immune from frontal attack. At times outraged by a few of the Court's rulings, public opinion was even more outraged by the president's proposal to pack it. For a brief interval many congressional leaders were noncommittal, waiting to hear from their constituents. Representative Hatton Sumners, chairman of the House Judiciary Committee, in announcing his intention to postpone his committee's consideration of the proposal, commented: "The visibility is poor. It's foggy.

[2] Levy, *Our Constitution,* 369.

The barometer is too low and the wind is not blowing in the right direction. I decided not to take off."[3] Almost overnight, there began a heated nationwide debate on the very fundamentals of the American system of government.

This book recounts the history of the origins of the court plan and the six-month struggle the accompanying bill faced in Congress, culminating in defeat by the Senate of a milder substitute. Some attention is given during this critical period in constitutional ferment to the mechanics of presidential leadership or lack thereof, as well as the political context in which Roosevelt acted and the Court reacted. It raises such questions as: How strong a leader was Roosevelt during this crisis? Where did he fail, and why? What were the short- and long-term consequences of this episode for American constitutional government, the presidency, and American statecraft?

During his second term, Roosevelt became enmeshed in forces he could not control and was thwarted by men he could not master. That term, according to his biographer James MacGregor Burns, constituted the most significant phase of a remarkable political career. In the court-packing episode, his performance throws a different and less flattering light on Roosevelt's political leadership, personal integrity, and character from that presented in other accounts. The narrative raises fundamental questions about the inner workings of that important executive arm of government, the Justice Department. It highlights frequent clashes between personalities and the creation of intractable problems growing out of failed leadership in frenetic efforts to reorganize the judiciary. The facts, in their totality, offer a revised estimate of Roosevelt's approach to handling the problems created by a Supreme Court majority that took a dim view of major New Deal legislative programs launched during FDR's first term. This investigation places both Court and president under the harsh searchlight of history, examining the nature of judicial resistance to prewar presidential leadership and the executive's radical reaction to the Court's obstruction of his programs and purposes.

Previous writers have found excuses in this episode for Roose-

[3] *New York Times,* February 22, 1937, 11.

velt's motives and methods. He was sorely tried, they argue, provoked beyond endurance by a recalcitrant court majority, and reacted with a proposal that they considered "rather mild."[4] But even Roosevelt's loyal lieutenant, Senate Majority Leader Robinson, thought the plan was "pretty raw," and Roosevelt himself later referred to it as "pretty drastic." The Court undoubtedly impeded certain New Deal policies, but many other critics besides judges and justices doubted the intrinsic wisdom of these policies, not to mention their constitutionality, and minimized the gravity of the Court's efforts to block the legislative process. History may one day confirm, if it has not already, that some New Deal laws were neither as efficacious nor as popular with the general public as FDR and New Dealers thought. Regardless of the effect of these laws, there was an almost total public backlash against Roosevelt's method of dealing with the Supreme Court in 1937. What his bill purported to do, and in a thoroughly disingenuous manner, lies at the heart of this study. The presentation of his plan, marked by his characteristic deviousness, severely limited the authority of such a highly placed executive officer.

---

[4] David Kennedy, *A History of the American People in the New Deal and World War II* (New York: Oxford University Press, 1999), 331. Kennedy, one of the very few who have addressed the subject, believes that given the decades-long agitation against "judicial supremacy," as one among the array of proposals prescribed at the time for judicial reform, the plan Roosevelt put forward stood out not for its boldness but for its mildness. "It defined no new constitutional role for the Court," he writes, "and thus left the time-honored system of checks and balances unperturbed." How he can deduce such a conclusion is beyond belief. He argues that the bill did not propose literally to "get rid of" the Court's sitting justices but asked merely for an expansion, under stipulated conditions, of the Court's personnel, and asked for it in the larger context of streamlining the entire federal judiciary. Obviously, Kennedy knows nothing of the collusion between Cummings and Roosevelt that resulted in their subterfuge.

Roosevelt's court plan, Kennedy concludes, was no wanton blunder. It was a "calculated risk," and not an unreasonable one. He was wagering a "modest challenge" to the tradition of an independent judiciary against the prospect of the entire New Deal's judicial extinction. But fortunately, Congress, Democrats and Republicans alike, and the public at-large knew instinctively which of these two prospects to defeat. But even Kennedy goes on to admit that from the moment it was unveiled, FDR's court plan stirred up a "nest of furies" whose destructive power swiftly swelled to awesome proportions, well beyond the president's ability to control. (For his full coverage of the court fight, see 325–40).

As for the origins and specifics of Roosevelt's court plan, perhaps one of the most significant comments was included in a letter Felix Frankfurter sent to a close friend: "What awful ignorant advice he had on that subject from those who were in on the secret."[5]

When Homer Cummings resigned in 1939 as attorney general, the *Bridgeport Evening Post,* surveying his record over the previous six years, referred to his court reform bill as representing "a black mark" on that record. By then it was generally conceded that the ideas incorporated in the bill were exclusively his. That, of course, was a misconception, as the evidence shows. Most of the provisions in the bill pertaining to the federal judiciary, with the exception of the Supreme Court, originated in a reform program for the lower federal courts, which was largely the work of Judge William Denman. He had lobbied for it a full two years before the final bill was framed and sent to Congress. Methods to curtail the power of the Supreme Court were meanwhile being exhaustively studied in the Justice Department.

The precipitate action taken by Roosevelt and Cummings in submitting their bill soon after the election was in large part a reflection of political arrogance. The strategy and tactics employed in attempting to ensure its passage represent a series of political mistakes, bad miscalculations, and failures of judgment. The arguments supporting the plan were dishonest, deliberately intended to mislead, and so transparent that they were easily knocked down almost as soon as the plan was unveiled. As a result, FDR was left with a flock of new enemies, a rebellious Congress, and a public no longer willing to take him at his word. The Democratic coalition that had made possible his 1936 landslide was in tatters. No study of the 1937 court fight would be complete without taking into account the long-term and profoundly disturbing consequences of this—the worst political defeat ever endured by a president at the pinnacle of his power.

Roosevelt must bear full responsibility for the fiasco. All the ideas and arguments Cummings and others furnished were supplied at his request and won his approval. He made all the final

[5] Frankfurter to Judge Sam Rosenman, May 27, 1952, Frankfurter Papers, LC, quoted in Liva Baker, *Frankfurter,* 191.

decisions. The age issue and inefficiency provisions regarding the sitting justices were the product of a few men working with the administration. White House aides Corcoran and Cohen prepared and submitted a somewhat different court-packing proposal a year earlier, but it was rejected. Corcoran was barred from the drafting of the final court bill at the insistence of Homer Cummings, who despised him. When the final plan was unveiled, it left Corcoran torn between two of his deepest loyalties—his devotion to FDR and his admiration for Justice Brandeis. The bill's implication that justices over seventy were less than competent was a cruel blow to his old mentor, but Corcoran did not hesitate. He waded into the battle on FDR's behalf.

At one point during the struggle for passage of the bill, as congressional resistance began to stiffen, Roosevelt asked Corcoran for his assessment of Senate sentiment. Corcoran's response was candid. He said he thought the court-packing plan was doomed. He believed at the time that Roosevelt, who had come to see himself as politically invincible, resented his pessimism. In later years, Corcoran marked that conversation as the beginning of his eventual fall from favor. He was eased out of the White House by 1940 with the aid of his chief rival, Harry Hopkins.[6] It was Corcoran's and Hopkins's ill-fortune to be closely identified with two of Roosevelt's most controversial and ultimately disastrous political ventures: the court-packing episode of 1937 and the attempted purge of conservative Democrats in 1938, an aftermath of the court fight.

One is forced to concede that Roosevelt's failures of perception and vision were responsible for this sorry chapter. President Harry Truman later blamed the failed court plan on "that growing ego of his, which notably wasn't too miniscule to start with."[7] Roosevelt, it seems, simply could not see that he was headed for a catastrophe. He listened to no one but flatterers, thus failing to perceive or even suspect what was going on all around him. The president was elitist, arrogant, and too readily dismiss-

[6] Patrick Anderson, *The President's Men: The White House Assistants of Franklin D. Roosevelt, Harry S. Truman, Dwight D. Eisenhower, John F. Kennedy, and Lyndon Johnson* (Garden City, N.Y.: Doubleday, 1968), 49.

[7] Quoted in Wilson, *Character above All,* 35.

ive of the opinions of others that ran contrary to his own, as Corcoran's experience indicates.

In a decade of ferment, the court plan and its progeny rocked the nation. The bill produced an overwhelming outpouring of public outrage before it was finally dismembered and buried. Two of the most ambitious legislative initiatives of Roosevelt's second term—the attempts to reorganize the executive and judicial departments of the government—were rejected by Congress and a suspicious public, made fearful of the president's unbridled ambitions and, as some thought, his aspirations toward a dictatorship.

In a railroad station speech at Marshalltown, Iowa, on his western tour in September 1937, FDR for the first time admitted frankly that some people who may have favored his objectives did not like his methods. He tried to sound conciliatory, with an admission that those who had opposed him on his court plan were not necessarily all "children of darkness," as a reporter for the *Pioneer Press* (September 25, 1937) phrased it. This was the president's only concession that there might have been an honest difference of opinion over his court proposal. It came as close as anything could to an apology. As for himself, he reiterated that he was not in love with any particular method, so long as the main objective could be reached. Ironically, this president, after the fact, pretended to entertain a startling indifference to a method he had fought for tooth and nail, for so long. Until it was too late, he refused even to consider replacing it with any form of compromise. The September trip, he said, was meant to discover the best way to proceed with the rest of his program. The speech foreshadowed a major shift in presidential tactics. The abandonment of his fight with the Supreme Court was to be the outcome. It was bad news only for those who wished to see the humiliated president suffer more rebuffs.

How, then, can we account for the plan's defeat? The multiple causation explanation is not apt. More plausible is the conclusion drawn by James MacGregor Burns in 1956 and, before his death, by James Roosevelt, the president's oldest son, who acted as his secretary throughout the entire court fight. They agree that the battle was lost before it began. In James Roosevelt's words, the court bill was "dead on arrival." Hopelessly flawed, it had no chance of passing. The original proposal could not command a majority in the Senate. House leaders refused to take it up. All other eventualities, planned or unplanned, such as the Hughes letter, the Court's opinions on the Wagner and Social Security Acts, Justice Van Devanter's retirement, and Robinson's demise, were but passing stages in the inevitable death of the plan, rather than causes of it. If by some miracle the bill had passed, it would certainly have been ruled unconstitutional by the same Supreme Court it was designed to humble, minus the vote of Willis Van Devanter.

In defeat, Roosevelt assumed an unreconstructed and defiant attitude. He claimed that although he may have lost the battle, he had won the war. Time and again he said his chief objective was to achieve a modernized judiciary that would look at "modern problems through modern glasses." On June 24, 1938, during a fireside chat, he declared: "In one way or another, during the sessions of this [1938] Congress, the ends—the real objectives—sought in that message [of February 5, 1937] have been substantially attained." The Court yielded; the Court changed. Those recent decisions of the Supreme Court, he announced, "are eloquent testimony of a willingness to collaborate with the two other branches of the Government to make Democracy work."[8]

Those few words encapsulated what constituted FDR's idea of an "independent judiciary." But that was not the general public's idea, nor that of the bench, the bar, or the academic community. A judiciary in "collaboration" with either or both branches of government, or with the majority on any given constitutional issue, could spell despotism.

Liberal columnist and author Max Lerner shall have the last word. In 1942, when the reconstituted Court—"the Roosevelt Court," as it was then called—was in full flower, Lerner took the occasion to recall "the great constitutional war" of New Deal days. By and large, he wrote, the Supreme Court and those who battled on its behalf were the real victors in the "war of 1937." As a result, it seemed to him that it would be difficult in the future for any group, conservative or otherwise, to attack the Su-

---

[8] *PPA,* 1937 volume, lxv; *New York Times,* June 25, 1938.

preme Court as a whole, because the Court rested on the essential judicial foundation for which the victors of 1937 fought so bitterly.

Labeling them "conservative" in this context tended to be misleading, because it suggested that the victors of 1937 were a politically homogeneous group, or that they remained one. They were not and they did not. But they constituted another "grand coalition" those many years ago, arrayed in defense of an independent Supreme Court. The interesting fact for Mr. Lerner was that a generation later, subsequent attacks on the Court, from whatever source, rested comfortably on the essential political foundations so bitterly fought for, and won, in 1937.[9]

[9] Lerner, "Great Constitutional War"; see also Alexander Bickel, *The Least Dangerous Branch: The Supreme Court at the Bar of Politics* (New York: Bobbs Merrill, 1962), 75. John P. Frank, in *The Marble Palace: The Supreme Court in American Life* (New York: Knopf, 1958), disapproved of many of the rigid barriers set up by the Supreme Court in the 1930s, and yet, "for sheer creativity," he thinks "there has never been anything like it."

Bibliography

Manuscript Collections

The following are abbreviations used in footnote documentation, identifying those manuscript collections consulted and used in the preceding chapters. Their locations are: COHC——Columbia University Oral History Collection, Butler Library, Columbia University, New York City; FDRL—Franklin Delano Roosevelt Presidential Library, Hyde Park, New York; LC——Manuscript Division, The Library of Congress, Washington, D.C.; NA—National Archives and Records Service, Washington, D.C.

Joseph Alsop Papers, LC

William E. Borah Papers, LC

Charles C. Burlingham Papers, LC; COHC

Benjamin Cohen Papers, LC

Marquis Childs, COHC

Raymond Clapper Papers, LC

Benjamin Cardozo Papers, Harvard Law Library, Cambridge, Mass.

Thomas Corcoran Papers, LC

Homer Stillé Cummings Papers, Alderman Library, University of Virginia, Charlottesville, Va.

Department of Justice Files, RG 60, NA

Stephen Early Papers, FDRL

James A. Farley Papers, LC

Jerome Frank Papers, Sterling Library, Yale University, New Haven, Conn.

Felix Frankfurter Papers, LC; Harvard Law Library, Cambridge, Mass.

Stanley High Papers, FDRL

Harry Hopkins Papers, FDRL

Charles Evans Hughes Papers, LC

Gardner Jackson, COHC
James Landis, COHC
Robert Jackson Papers, LC
Herbert Lehman Papers, New York Public Library, New York City
William Gibbs McAdoo Papers, LC
James Clark McReynolds Papers, Alderman Library, University of Virginia, Charlottesville, Va.
Basil O'Connor Collection, FDRL
Frances Perkins, COHC
Stanley Reed, COHC
Samuel Rosenbaum, COHC
Thomas Reed Powell Papers, Harvard Law Library, Cambridge, Mass.
Donald Richberg Papers, LC
Joseph T. Robinson Papers, Special Collections, University of Arkansas Library, Fayetteville, Ark.
Eleanor Roosevelt Papers, FDRL
James Roosevelt Papers, FDRL
Franklin D. Roosevelt Papers, FDRL
Judge Samuel I. Rosenman Papers, FDRL
Harold Stephens Papers, LC
Henry L. Stimson Papers, Sterling Library, Yale University, New Haven, Conn.
Harlan Fiske Stone Papers, LC
Henry Suydam Files, RG 60, NA
George Sutherland Papers, LC
Rexford Tugwell Papers, FDRL
Burton K. Wheeler Papers, Montana Historical Society, Helena, Mont.
Charles Wyzanski, COHC

Interviews

James A. Farley, New York City; Erwin Griswold, Washington, D.C.; Joseph Rauh, Washington, D.C.: James Roosevelt, Corona Del Mar, California; Arthur M. Schlesinger, Jr., New York City; Edward Wheeler, Washington, D.C.

Government Documents

Congressional Record 74th Cong., 1st Sess.; and 75th Cong., 1st Sess., Vols. 79–81. Washington, D.C.: 1935–1937.

U.S. Congress. Senate. Committee on the Judiciary. *Reorganization of the Federal Judiciary.* Judiciary. Hearings, 75th Cong., 1st Sess., on S. 1392. Washington, D.C.: 1937.

U.S. Congress. Senate. Committee on the Judiciary. *Reorganization of the Federal Judiciary.* 75th Cong., 1st Sess., Adverse Report 711 to accompany S. 1392. Washington, D.C.: 1937.

U.S. Department of Justice. *Annual Reports of the Attorney General of the United States* for the fiscal years 1913, 1914, and 1936. Washington, D.C.: 1913, 1914, 1936.

U.S. Department of Justice. Record Group 9, 60. National Archives and Records Service, Washington, D.C.

Books and Dissertations

Acheson, Dean G. *Morning and Noon.* Boston: Houghton, Mifflin, 1965.

Ackerman, Bruce. *We the People: I. The Foundations.* Cambridge: Harvard University Press, 1991.

Alfange, Dean. *The Supreme Court and the National Will.* Garden City, N.Y.: Doubleday, Doran, 1937.

Alsop, Joseph. *FDR, 1882–1945: A Centenary Remembrance.* London: Thames and Hudson, 1982; New York: Viking Press, 1982.

Alsop, Joseph, and Turner Catledge. *The 168 Days.* Garden City, N.Y.: Doubleday, Doran, 1938.

Alsop, Joseph, and Robert Kintner. *Men Around the President.* Garden City, N.Y.: Doubleday, Doran, 1939.

Anderson, James Johnston. "The President's Supreme Court Proposal: A Study in Presidential Leadership and Public Opinion." Ph.D. diss., Cornell University, 1940.

Anderson, Patrick. *The President's Men: The White House Assistants of Franklin D. Roosevelt, Harry S. Truman, Dwight D. Eisenhower, John F. Kennedy and Lyndon B. Johnson.* Garden City, N.Y.: Doubleday and Co., 1968.

Baker, Leonard. *Back to Back: The Duel Between FDR and the Supreme Court*. New York: Macmillan, 1967.

———. *Brandeis and Frankfurter: A Dual Biography.* New York: New York University Press, 1986.

Baker, Liva. *Felix Frankfurter.* New York: Coward-McCann, 1969.

Baker, Ralph. *The National Bituminous Coal Commission.* Baltimore: Johns Hopkins University Press, 1941.

Ball, Howard. *Hugo Black: Cold Steel Warrior.* New York: Oxford University Press, 1996.

Barkley, Alben W. *That Reminds Me.* Garden City, N.Y.: Doubleday, 1954.

Baskerville, Stephen W., and Ralph Willett, eds. *Nothing Else to Fear.* Manchester: Manchester University Press, 1985.

Beard, Charles A., and Mary Beard. *America in Midpassage.* Vol. 3 in *The Rise of American Civilization.* 3 vols. New York: Macmillan, 1939.

Benedict, Murray. *Can We Solve the Farm Problem? An Analysis of Federal Aid to Agriculture.* New York: Twentieth Century Fund, 1955.

———. *Farm Policies of the United States: 1790–1950: A Study of Their Origins and Development.* New York: Octagon, 1966.

Beschloss, Michael. *Kennedy and Roosevelt: The Uneasy Alliance.* New York: W. W. Norton, 1980.

Biddle, Francis. *In Brief Authority.* Garden City, N.Y.: Doubleday, 1962.

Blum, John M., ed. *From the Morgenthau Diaries: Years of Crisis: 1928–1938.* 3 vols. Boston: Houghton, Mifflin Co., 1959–1967.

Bond, James Edward. "James Clark McReynolds: I Dissent." Unpublished MS in James McReynolds Papers, Alderman Library, University of Virginia, Charlottesville, Va.

Boudin, Louis. *Government by Judiciary.* 2 vols. New York: William Godwin, 1932.

Brand, Donald R. *Corporatism and the Rule of Law: A Study of the NRA.* Ithaca, N.Y.: Cornell University Press, 1988.

Buhite, Russell D., and David W. Levy, eds. *FDR's Fireside Chats*. Norman: University of Oklahoma Press, 1992.

Burns, James MacGregor. *Roosevelt: The Lion and the Fox.* New York: Harcourt, Brace, and World, 1956.

———. *Crosswinds of Freedom.* Vol. 3 in *The American Experiment.* New York: Knopf, 1989.

Byrnes, James F. *All in One Lifetime.* New York: Harper and Bros., 1958.

Campbell, Christiana M. *The Farm Bureau and the New Deal: A Study of Making a National Farm Policy, 1933–1940.* Urbana: University of Illinois Press, 1962.

Cantril, Hadley, ed. *Public Opinion: 1935–1946,* Prepared by Mildred Strunk. Princeton: Princeton University Press, 1951.

Caplan, Lincoln. *The Tenth Justice: The Solicitor General and the Rule of Law.* New York: Knopf, 1987.

Caro, Robert. *The Years of Lyndon Johnson: The Path to Power.* New York: Knopf, 1983.

Carr, Robert F. *The Supreme Court and Judicial Review.* New York: Farrar and Rinehart, 1942.

Carter, John Franklin. *The New Dealers.* By Washington's Unofficial Observer. New York: Simon and Schuster, 1934.

Chase, Harold M. *Federal Judges: The Appointing Process.* Minneapolis: University of Minnesota Press, 1972.

Clarke, Jeanne N. *Roosevelt's Warrior: Harold L. Ickes and the New Deal.* Baltimore: Johns Hopkins University Press, 1996.

Cohen, Wilbur J., ed. *The New Deal: Fifty Years After.* Austin: University of Texas Press, 1984.

Conkin, Paul. The New Deal. Arlington Heights, Ill.: Harlan Davidson, 1975.

Connally, Tom, and Alfred Steinberg. *My Name is Tom Connally.* New York: Thomas Y. Crowell, 1954.

Conrad, David E. *The Forgotten Farmer: The Story of Share-Cropping in the New Deal.* Urbana: University of Illinois Press, 1965.

Cope, Alfred, and Fred Kinsky, eds. *Franklin D. Roosevelt and the Supreme Court.* Lexington, Mass.: D.C. Heath, 1969.

Corwin, Edward S. *The Commerce Power versus States' Rights: "Back to the Constitution."* Princeton: Princeton University Press, 1936.

———. *Constitutional Revolution, Ltd.* New York: Greenwood Press, 1977.

———. *Court over Constitution: A Study of Judicial Review as an Instrument of Popular Government*. Gloucester, Mass.: Peter Smith, 1957.

———. *The Twilight of the Supreme Court: A History of Our Constitutional Theory.* New Haven: Yale University Press, 1934.

Creel, George. *Rebel at Large: Recollections of Fifty Crowded Years.* New York: Putnam's, 1947.

———. *A Rebel in Politics*. New York: Putnam's, 1947.

Cummings, Homer Stillé, and Carl McFarland. *Federal Justice: Chapters in the History of Justice and the Federal Executive.* New York: Macmillan, 1937.

———. *Selected Papers of Homer S. Cummings*. Carl Brent Swisher, ed. New York: Charles Scribner's Sons, 1939.

Currie, David P. *The Constitution in the Supreme Court: The Second Century, 1888 to 1986.* Chicago: University of Chicago Press, 1990.

Curtis, Charles C. *Lions Under the Throne*. Boston: Houghton Mifflin, 1947.

Cushman, Barry. *Rethinking the New Deal Court: The Structure of a Constitutional Revolution.* New York: Oxford University Press, 1998.

Danelski, David J., and Joseph S. Tulchin, eds. *The Autobiographical Notes of Charles Evans Hughes.* Cambridge: Harvard University Press, 1973.

Davis, Kenneth S. *FDR: The Beckoning of Destiny, 1882–1928.* New York: Putnam's, 1972.

———. *FDR: The New Deal Years, 1932–1937.* New York: Random House, 1986.

———. *FDR: Into the Storm, 1937–1940.* New York: Random House, 1993.

Dawson, Nelson L. *Louis D. Brandeis, Felix Frankfurter and the New Deal*. Hamden, Conn.: Archon Books, 1980.

Dorsett, Lyle W. *Franklin D. Roosevelt and the City Bosses.* Port Washington, N.Y.: Kennikat, 1977.

Dunham, Allison, and Philip B. Kurland, eds. *Mr. Justice: Biographies of Twelve Supreme Court Justices.* Chicago: University of Chicago Press, 1956.

Dunne, Gerald T. *Hugo Black and the Judicial Revolution*. New York: Simon and Schuster, 1977.

———. *Monetary Decisions of the Supreme Court.* New Brunswick, N.J.: Rutgers University Press, 1960.

Eden, Robert, ed. *The New Deal and its Legacy: Critique and Reappraisal*. New York: Greenwood Press, 1989.

Edwards, Jerome E. *Pat McCarran: Political Boss of Nevada.* Reno: University of Nevada Press, 1982.

Emerson, Thomas I. *Young Lawyer for the New Deal: An Insider's Memoir of the Roosevelt Years.* Savage, Md.: Rowman and Littlefield, 1991.

Eriksson, Erik M. *The Supreme Court and the New Deal.* Los Angeles: University of California Press, 1941.

Fagin, Vernon A. "Franklin Roosevelt, Liberalism in the Democratic Party and the 1938 Congressional Elections: The Urge to Purge." Ph.D. diss., University of California, Los Angeles, 1979.

Farley, James A., *Behind the Ballots*. New York: Harcourt, Brace, 1938.

———. *Jim Farley's Story: The Roosevelt Years*. New York: Whittlesey House, 1948.

Fassett, John D. *New Deal Justice: The Life of Stanley Reed of Kentucky*. New York: Vantage Press, 1994.

Fisher, Louis. *Constitutional Conflicts between Congress and the President.* Princeton: Princeton University Press, 1985.

Fisher, Robert M. *Twenty Years of Public Housing*. New York: Harper and Row, 1959.

Fite, Gilbert C. *George N. Peek and the Fight for Farm Parity*. Norman: University of Oklahoma Press, 1954.

Flynn, Edward J. *You're the Boss*. New York: Viking, 1947.

Flynn, John T. *Country Squire in the White House*. New York: Doubleday, Doran, 1940.

———. *The Roosevelt Myth*. New York: Devin Adair, 1965.

Freedman, Max, ed. *Roosevelt and Frankfurter: Their Correspondence, 1928–1945*. Boston: Little Brown, 1967.

Friedman, Leon, and Fred Israel, eds. *The Justices of the United States Supreme Court, 1789–1969*. 5 vols., New York: Chelsea House, 1969–1978.

Friedman, Milton, and Anna Schwartz. *A Monetary History of the United States: 1867–1960.* Princeton: Princeton University Press, 1963.

Fusfeld, Daniel. *The Economic Thought of FDR and the Origins of the New Deal.* New York: Columbia University Press, 1956.

Gallup, George H. *The Gallup Poll: Public Opinion, 1935–1971.* New York: Random House, 1972.

Gerhart, Eugene C. *America's Advocate: Robert H. Jackson.* Indianapolis: Bobbs Merrill, 1958.

Graham, Otis L, and Meghan R. Wander, eds. *Franklin D. Roosevelt: His Life and Times: An Encyclopedic View.* Boston: G. K. Hall, 1985.

Hall, Kermit, ed. *The Oxford Companion to the Supreme Court.* New York: Oxford University Press, 1992.

Hanby, Alonzo L., ed. *The New Deal: Analysis and Interpretation.* New York: Weybright and Talley, 1969.

Hardeman, D. B., and Donald C. Bacon. *Rayburn: a Biography.* Austin: Texas Monthly Press, 1987.

Hawley, Ellis. *The New Deal and the Problem of Monopoly, 1933–1939.* Princeton: Princeton University Press, 1966.

Hellman, George S. *Benjamin Cardozo, American Judge.* New York: Russell and Russell, 1940.

Hendel, Samuel. *Charles Evans Hughes and the Supreme Court.* New York: King's Crown Press, 1951.

Himmelberg, Robert F. *The Origins of the National Recovery Administration . . . 1921–1933.* New York: Fordham University Press, 1976.

Hoar, Victor, ed. *The Great Depression.* Toronto: Copp Clark, 1969.

Hollingsworth, Harold M., and William F. Holmes, eds. *Essays on the New Deal.* Austin: University of Texas Press, 1969.

Hoover, Herbert. *Addresses on the American Road, 1933–1938.* New York: Charles Scribner's Sons, 1938.

Hughes, Charles Evans. *The Supreme Court of the United States: Its Foundations, Methods and Achievements.* Garden City, N.Y.: Doubleday, 1928.

———. *The Autobiographical Notes of Charles Evans Hughes,* David J. Danelski and Joseph Tulchin, eds. Cambridge: Harvard University Press, 1973.

Hyman, Harold, and Leonard Levy, eds. *Essays in Honor of Henry Steele Commager*. New York: Harper and Row, 1967.

Hyneman, Charles. *The Supreme Court on Trial.* New York: Atherton Press, 1963.

Ickes, Harold L. *The Secret Diary of Harold L. Ickes,* Vol. 1. *The First Thousand Days, 1933–1936;* Vol. 2. *The Inside Struggle, 1936–1939*. 3 vols. New York: Simon and Schuster, 1953–1954.

Irons, Peter H. *The New Deal Lawyers*. Princeton: Princeton University Press, 1982.

———. *A People's History of the Supreme Court.* New York: Viking Press, 1999.

Jackson, Robert H. *The Struggle for Judicial Supremacy: A Study of a Crisis in American Power Politics*. New York: Knopf, 1941.

Johnson, D., and K. Porter. *National Party Platforms, 1840–1972*. Urbana: University of Illinois Press, 1973.

Johnson, James P. *The Politics of Soft Coal*. Urbana: University of Illinois Press, 1979.

Jones, Jesse. *Fifty Million Dollars: My Thirteen Years with the RFC*. New York: Macmillan, 1951.

Karl, Barry D. *Executive Reorganization and Reform in the New Deal: The Genesis of Administrative Management, 1900–1939*. Cambridge: Harvard University Press, 1963.

Kaufman, Andrew. *Cardozo*. Cambridge: Harvard University Press, 1998.

Kelly, Alfred H., and Winfred Harbison. *The American Constitution: Its Origins and Development.* New York: Norton, 1963.

Kennedy, David M. *Freedom From Fear: The American People in Depression and War, 1929–1945.* New York: Oxford University Press, 1999.

Konefsky, Samuel J. *Chief Justice Stone and the Supreme Court.* New York: Macmillan, 1945.

Krislov, Samuel. *The Supreme Court in the Political Process*. New York: Macmillan, 1965.

Krock, Arthur. *Memoirs: Sixty Years on the Firing Line*. New York: Funk and Wagnalls, 1968.

Kurland, Philip, ed. *The Supreme Court and the Judicial Function*. Chicago: University of Chicago Press, 1975.

Kurland, Philip, and Allison Dunham, eds. *Mr. Justice: Biographies of Twelve Supreme Court Justices.* Chicago: University of Chicago Press, 1956.

Kurland, Philip, and Gerhard Casper, eds. *Landmark Briefs and Arguments of the Supreme Court of the United States: Constitutional Law.* Arlington, Va.: University Publications of America, 1975–1978.

Kutler, Stanley. *Judicial Power and Reconstruction Politics.* Chicago: University of Chicago Press, 1968.

Lash, Joseph. *Dealers and Dreamers: A New Look at the New Deal.* Garden City, N.Y.: Doubleday, 1988.

———, ed. *From the Diaries of Felix Frankfurter.* New York: Norton, 1974.

Lasser, William. *The Limits of Judicial Power: The Supreme Court in American Politics.* Chapel Hill: University of North Carolina Press, 1988.

Latham, Frank B. *FDR and the Supreme Court Fight, 1937.* London: F. Watts, 1972.

Lawrence, David. *Nine Honest Men.* New York: Appleton Century Crofts, 1936.

Leonard, Charles A. *A Search for a Judicial Philosophy: Mr. Justice Roberts and the Constitutional Revolution of 1937.* Port Washington, N.Y.: Kennikat Press, 1971.

Leuchtenburg, William E. *Franklin D. Roosevelt and the New Deal, 1932–1940.* New York: Harper and Row, 1963.

———. *The Supreme Court Reborn.* New York: Oxford University Press, 1995.

Levy, Beryl Harold. *Our Constitution: Tool or Testament?* New York: Knopf, 1941.

Levy, Leonard, et al., eds. *Encyclopedia of the American Constitution.* 2 vols., New York: Macmillan, 1986.

Lippmann, Walter. *The Supreme Court, Independent or Controlled?* New York: Harper Bros., 1937.

Lorant, Stefan. *The Glorious Burden: The American Presidency.* New York: Harper and Row, 1968.

———. *FDR: A Pictorial Biography.* New York: Simon and Schuster, 1950.

Lowitt, Richard C. *Norris: Triumph of a Progressive, 1933–1944.* Urbana: University of Illinois Press, 1978.

MacColl, E. Kimbark. “The Supreme Court and Public Opinion: A Study of the Court Fight of 1937.” Ph.D. diss., University of California, Los Angeles, 1953.

McCraw, John. “Justice McReynolds and the Supreme Court.” Ph.D. diss., University of Texas, Austin, 1949.

McCune, Wesley. *The Nine Young Men*. New York: Harper Bros., 1947.

McDean, Harry C. “M. L. Wilson and Agricultural Reform in Twentieth Century America.” Ph.D. diss., University of California, Los Angeles, 1969.

McDonnell, Timothy, S.J. *The Wagner Housing Act: A Case Study of the Legislative Process*. Chicago: Loyola University Press, 1957.

McFarland, Carl, and Homer Stille Cummings. *Federal Justice: Chapters in the History of Justice and the Federal Executive.* New York: Macmillan, 1937.

McNaughton, Frank, and Walter Heymeyer. *This Man Truman.* New York: Harper and Row, 1945.

Mason, Alpheus T. *Brandeis: A Free Man's Life*. New York: Viking Press, 1946, 1956.

———. *Harlan Fiske Stone: Pillar of the Law*. New York: Viking Press, 1956.

———. *The Supreme Court from Taft to Warren.* Baton Rouge: Louisiana State University Press, 1958.

———. *The Supreme Court: Vehicle of Revealed Truth or Power Groups, 1930–1937*. Boston: Boston University Press, 1953.

Mason, Alpheus T., and William Beaney. *The Supreme Court in a Free Society*. Englewood Cliffs, N.J.: Prentice Hall, 1959.

Mayer, Robert R. *The Court and the American Crisis: 1930–1952*. Millwood, N.Y.: Associated Faculty Press, 1986.

Mellichamp, Josephine. *Senators from Georgia*. Hunstville, Ala.: Strode, 1976.

Michelson, Charles. *The Ghost Talks*. New York: Putnam's, 1944.

Miller, Nathan. *FDR: An Intimate History.* New York: New American Library, 1983.

Moley, Raymond. *After Seven Years.* New York: Harper and Bros., 1939.

———. *The First New Deal*. New York: Harcourt, Brace, World, 1966.

Mooney, Booth. *Roosevelt and Rayburn: A Political Partnership.* Philadelphia: J. B. Lippincott, 1971.

Morgan, Ted. *F.D.R.: A Biography.* New York: Simon and Schuster, 1985.

Murphy, Bruce A. *The Brandeis-Frankfurter Connection: The Secret Political Activities of Two Supreme Court Justices.* New York: Oxford University Press, 1982.

Murphy, Paul L. *The Constitution in Crisis Times, 1918–1969.* New York: Harper and Row, 1972.

Murphy, Walter. *Congress and the Court: A Case Study in the American Political Process.* Chicago: University of Chicago Press, 1962

———. *The Elements of Judicial Strategy*. Chicago: University of Chicago Press, 1964.

Nevins, Allan. *Herbert H. Lehman and His Era.* New York: Charles Scribner's Sons, 1963.

Newman, Roger. *Hugo Black: A Biography.* New York: Fordham University Press, 1997.

O'Brien, David. *Storm Center: The Supreme Court in American Politics.* New York: W. W. Norton, 1986.

O'Keane, Josephine. *Thomas J. Walsh: A Senator from Montana.* Francestown, N.H.: M. Jones Co., 1955.

Parrish, Michael E. *Felix Frankfurter and His Times: The Reform Years.* New York: Free Press, 1982.

Paschal, Joel F. *Mr. Justice Sutherland: A Man Against the State.* Princeton: Princeton University Press, 1951.

Patterson, James T. *Congressional Conservatism and the New Deal: The Growth of the Conservative Coalition in Congress, 1933–1939.* Lexington: University of Kentucky Press, 1967.

Pearson, Drew, and Robert S. Allen. *The Nine Old Men.* Garden City, N.Y.: Doubleday, Doran, 1936.

Pederson, William D., and Norman W. Provizer, eds. *Great Justices of the Supreme Court: Ratings and Case Studies.* New York: Peter Lang, 1993.

Perkins, Dexter. *The New Age of Franklin Roosevelt, 1932–1945.* Chicago: University of Chicago Press, 1957.

———. *Charles Evans Hughes and American Democratic Statesmanship*. Boston: Little Brown, 1956.

Perkins, Frances. *The Roosevelt I Knew*. London: Hammond and Hammond, 1947.

Perkins, Van L. *Crisis in Agriculture: The AAA and the New Deal*. Berkeley: University of California Press, 1969.

Polenberg, Richard. *Reorganizing Roosevelt's Government: The Controversy over Executive Reorganization, 1936–1939*. Cambridge: Harvard University Press, 1966.

Purcell, Edward A., Jr. *Brandeis and the Progressive Constitution: Erie, the Judicial Power, and the Politics of the Federal Courts in Twentieth Century America*. New Haven: Yale University Press, 2000.

Pusey, Merlo J. *Charles Evans Hughes*. 2 vols. New York: Macmillan, 1951.

———. *The Supreme Court Crisis*. New York: Macmillan, 1937.

Rauch, Basil. *A History of the New Deal*. New York: Creative Age Press, 1944.

Richardson, James D., ed. *A Compilation of the Messages and Papers of the Presidents, 1789–1897*. 10 vols. Published by Authority of Congress, Washington, D.C.: 1899.

Richberg, Donald. *My Hero*. New York: Putnam's, 1954.

———. *The Rainbow*. Garden City, N.Y.: Doubleday, Doran, 1936.

Roche, John. *Courts and Rights: The American Judiciary in Action*. New York: Random House, 1966.

Rodell, Fred. *Nine Men: A Political History of the Supreme Court of the United States, 1790–1955*. New York: Random House, 1955.

Roosevelt, Eleanor. *This I Remember.* New York: Harper and Bros., 1949.

Roosevelt, Elliott, ed. *F.D.R.: His Personal Letters, 1928–1945*. 4 vols. New York: Duell, Sloan and Pearce, 1950.

Roosevelt, Franklin D. *Complete Presidential Press Conferences of Franklin D. Roosevelt*. 23 vols. New York: Da Capo Press, 1972.

———. *The Public Papers and Addresses of Franklin D. Roosevelt*. Samuel I. Rosenman, ed. 13 vols. New York: Random House, Macmillan, Harper Bros., 1938–1950.

Roseboom, Eugene H. *A Short History of Presidential Elections*. New York: Collier Books, 1967.

Rosenman, Samuel I. *Working with Roosevelt*. New York: Harper and Row, 1952.

Rowley, William D. *M. L. Wilson and the Campaign for the Domestic Allotment Plan*. Lincoln: University of Nebraska Press, 1970.

Salokar, Rebecca Mae. *The Solicitor General: The Politics of Law*. Philadelphia: Temple University Press, 1992.

Saloutos, Theodore. *The American Farmer and the New Deal*. Ames: Iowa State University Press, 1982.

Salter, John T., ed. *The American Politician*. Chapel Hill: University of North Carolina Press, 1938.

Savage, Sean J. *Roosevelt, The Party Leader, 1932–1945*. Lexington: University Press of Kentucky, 1991.

Schlesinger, Arthur M., Sr. *The New Deal in Action, 1933–1939*. New York: Macmillan, 1940.

Schlesinger, Arthur M., Jr. *The Crisis of the Old Order, 1919–1933*. Vol. 1 of *The Age of Roosevelt*. Boston: Houghton Mifflin, 1957.

———. *The Coming of the New Deal, 1933–1935*. Vol. 2 in *The Age of Roosevelt.*. Boston: Houghton Mifflin, 1959.

———. *The Politics of Upheaval, 1935–1936*. Vol. 3. in *The Age of Roosevelt*. Boston: Houghton Mifflin, 1960.

———, ed. *The History of American Presidential Elections, 1789–1968*. 5 vols. New York: Chelsea House, 1971.

Schwartz, Jordan. *The New Dealers: Power Politics in the Age of Roosevelt*. New York: Vintage Books, 1994.

Scigliano, Robert. *The Supreme Court and the Presidency*. New York: Free Press, 1971.

Sherwood, Robert. *Roosevelt and Hopkins: An Intimate History*. New York: Harper and Bros., 1948.

Steamer, Robert J. *The Supreme Court in Crisis: A History of Conflict*. Amherst: University of Massachusetts Press, 1971.

———. *Chief Justice: Leadership and the Supreme Court*. Columbia: University of South Carolina Press, 1986.

Steinberg, Alfred. *Sam Rayburn: A Biography*. New York: Hawthorn Books, 1975.

Stephenson, Donald Grier, Jr. *Campaigns and the Court: The*

U. S. Supreme Court in Presidential Elections. New York: Columbia University Press, 1999.

Sternscher, Bernard. *Rexford Tugwell and the New Deal*. New Brunswick, N.J.: Rutgers University Press, 1964.

Stokes, Thomas L. *Chip Off My Shoulder*. Princeton: Princeton University Press, 1940.

Strum, Philippa. *Louis D. Brandeis: Justice for the People*. Cambridge: Harvard University Press, 1984.

Sutherland, Arthur. *Constitutionalism in America: Its Origins and the Evolution of Fundamental Ideas*. New York: Blaisdell Co., 1965.

Swindler, William. *Court and Constitution in the Twentieth Century: The New Legality, 1932–1968*. 3 vols. Indianapolis: Bobbs Merrill, 1970.

Swisher, Carl Brent. *American Constitutional Development*. Boston: Houghton Mifflin, 1943, 1954.

———, ed. *Selected Papers of Homer S. Cummings*. New York: Charles Scribner's Sons, 1939.

Timmons, Bascom N. *Garner of Texas*. New York: Harper and Bros., 1948.

Tribe, Laurence H. *God Save This Honorable Court*. New York: Random House, 1985.

Tugwell, Rexford G. *The Democratic Roosevelt*. Garden City, N.Y.: Doubleday, 1957.

Tully, Grace. *F.D.R., My Boss*. New York: Charles Scribner's Sons, 1949.

Urofsky, Melvin. *Louis D. Brandeis and the Progressive Tradition*. Boston: Little Brown, 1981.

Urofsky, Melvin, and David W. Levy, eds. *"Half Brother, Half Son": Letters of Louis Brandeis to Felix Frankfurter*. Norman: University of Oklahoma Press, 1991.

Wheeler, Burton K., with Paul Healy. *Yankee From the West*. Garden City, N.Y.: Doubleday, 1962.

White, G. Edward. *The American Judicial Tradition: Profiles of Leading American Judges*. New York: Oxford University Press, 1976.

———. *The Constitution and the New Deal*. Cambridge: Harvard University Press, 2000.

Wiecek, William M. *Liberty Under Law: The Supreme Court*

Childs, Marquis. "The Supreme Court Today." *Harper's* 176 (May 1938): 581–88.

Churchill, Winston. "What Good's a Constitution? Our Heritage of Freedom." *Collier's* 98 (August 22, 1936): 22, 39–40.

Clapper, Raymond. "Can Congress Come Back?" *Review of Reviews* 93 (February 1936): 29–31.

———. "Leadership in Congress." *Review of Reviews* 95 (January 1937): 47–51.

———. "Along the Potomac." *Review of Reviews* 95 (March 1937): 29–31.

———. "Resentment Against the Supreme Court." *Review of Reviews* 95 (January 1937): 38–39.

Clark, Charles E. "Supreme—Court or the People?" *American Scholar* 6 (Spring 1937): 201–13.

Clark, Grenville. "The Supreme Court Issue." *Yale Law Review* 26 (June 1937): 669–88.

Corley, Roger W. "How Liberal Was Chief Justice Hughes?" In *Great Justices of the Supreme Court: Ratings and Case Studies,* edited by William D. Pederson and Norman W. Provizer. New York: Peter Lang, 1993: 167–84.

Corwin, Edward S. "The Schechter Case—Landmark or What?" *New York University Law Quarterly Review* 13 (January 1936): 151–90.

———. "Curbing the Court." *Annals of the American Academy of Political Science* 185 (1936): 45–55.

———. "Statesmanship on the Supreme Court." *American Scholar* 9 (Spring 1940): 159–63.

Creel, George. "Looking Ahead with Roosevelt." *Collier's* 96 (September 7, 1935): 7–8.

———. "Roosevelt's Plans and Purposes." *Collier's* 98 (December 26, 1936): 39–42.

———. "If the Court Please." *Collier's* 99 (May 8, 1937): 22–26.

Culp, Maurice S. "A Survey of Proposals to Limit . . . the Power of Judicial Review by the Supreme Court of the United States." *Indiana Law Journal* 4 (1928–29): Pt. 1, 386–89; Pt. 2, 474–90.

Cummings, Homer S. "The State v. Harold Israel." *Journal of the American Institute of Criminal Law and Criminology* 15 (November 14, 1924): 406–34.

———. "Immediate Problems for the Bar." Address delivered at Silver anniversary banquet of New York County Lawyers' Association, March 14, 1934. *American Bar Association Journal* 20 (1934): 212–14.

———. "Reasons for the President's Plan and the Remedy." *Law Journal* 19 (August 1954): 373–78.

Currie, David P. "The Constitution in the Supreme Court: The New Deal, 1931–1940." *University of Chicago Law Review* 54 (Spring 1987): 504–44.

Cushman, Barry. "The Secret Lives of the Four Horsemen." *Virginia Law Review* 83 (April 1997): 559–645.

———. "Rethinking the New Deal Court." *Virginia Law Review* 80 (February, 1994): 201–61.

Davis, Kenneth S. "F.D.R. as a Biographer's Problem." *American Scholar* 53 (Winter 1983–84): 100–108.

Dawson, John P. "The Gold Clause Decisions." *Michigan Law Review* 33 (March 1935): 647–84.

Dilliard, Irving. "Mr. Roosevelt and the Supreme Court. The Observations of a Citizen." *Survey Graphic* 26 (February 1937): 93–96.

Eder, Phanor J. "The Gold Clause Cases in the Light of History." *Georgetown Law Journal* 23:3 (March 1935): Part I, 359–88; (April 1935): Part II, 722–61.

Fairman, Charles. "The Retirement of Federal Judges." *Harvard Law Review* 51 (1938): 397–443.

———. "Mr. Justice Bradley's Appointment to the Supreme Court and the Legal Tender Cases." *Harvard Law Review* 54 (April 1941): Pt. 1, 977–1034 (May 1941): Pt. 2, 1128–55.

Fite, Gilbert. "The McNary-Haugen Episode and the Triple-A." *Journal of Farm Economy* 42 (December 1960): 1084–93.

Fite, Katherine, and Louis B. Rubenstein. "Curbing the Supreme Court—State Experiences and Federal Proposals." *Michigan Law Review* 35:5 (March 1937): 762–87.

Flynn, John T. "The President and the Supreme Court." *Southern Review* 3 (Summer 1937): 1–14.

Fraenkel, O. K. "What Can Be Done about the Constitution and the Supreme Court?" *Columbia Law Review* 37 (1937): 212–26.

Frankfurter, Felix. "Mr. Justice Roberts." *University of Pennsylvania Law Review* 104 (December 1955): 311–17.

———. "The Administrative Side of Chief Justice Hughes." *Harvard Law Review* 63 (November 1949): 1–26.

———. "Chief Justices I Have Known." *Virginia Law Review* 39:7 (November 1953): 883–905.

Fraser, Hugh Russell. "Attorney General Cummings." *American Mercury* 23 (December 1934): 398–406.

Freund, Paul A. "Charles Evans Hughes as Chief Justice." *Harvard Law Review* 81 (1967): 4–43.

Friedman, Richard D. "A Reaffirmation. The Authenticity of the Roberts Memorandum, or Felix the Non-Forger." *University of Pennsylvania Law Review* 142:6 (June 1994): 1892–95.

Gardbaum, Stephen. "New Deal Constitutionalism and the Unshackling of the States." *University of Chicago Law Review* 64 (Spring 1997): 483–566.

Gressley, Gene M. "Joseph O'Mahoney, FDR, and the Supreme Court." *Pacific Historical Review* 40 (1971): 183–202.

Griswold, Erwin. "Government in Ignorance of the Law: A Plea for Better Publication of Executive Legislation." *Harvard Law Review* 48 (1934–35): 198–213.

Haines, Charles H. "Judicial Review of Acts of Congress and the Need for Constitutional Reform." *Yale Law Journal* 45 (1936): 816–41.

Hart, Henry H. "The Supreme Court Carries On." *New Republic* 82 (April 3, 1935): 220–21.

High, Stanley. "Roosevelt: Democrat or Dictator?" *Harper's* 175 (November 1937): 480–87.

———. "The White House Is Calling." *Harper's* 175 (December 1937): 580–89.

———. "Whose Party Is It?" *Saturday Evening Post* 209 (February 6, 1937): 10–13.

Hoffman, Roy E. "Montana's Contribution to New Deal Farm Policy." *Agricultural History* 33 (October 1959): 164–66.

Howard, J. Woodford. "Frank Murphy and the Sit-Down Strikes of 1937." *Labor History* 1 (Spring 1960): 103–40.

Hughes, Charles Evans. “Reason as Opposed to the Tyranny of Force.” *Vital Speeches* 7 (May 1937): 458–59.

Hunter, Robert M. “Shall the Supreme Court Have New Blood?” *Ohio State University Law Journal* 3 (March 1937): 125–41.

Hyde, Henry M. “White House ‘No’ Man.” *Saturday Evening Post* 211 (June 25, 1938): 23, 49–53.

Jackson, Robert H. “Back to the Constitution.” *American Bar Association Journal* 9 (September 1939): 745–49.

Johnson, James P. “Drafting the NRA Code of Fair Competition for the Bituminous Coal Industry.” *Journal of American History* 53 (1966): 521–41.

Johnston, Alva. “White House Tommy.” *Saturday Evening Post* 210 (July 31, 1937): 6.

———. “The Dean of Inconsistency.” *Saturday Evening Post* 210 (December 25, 1937): 23.

———. “President Tamer.” *Saturday Evening Post* 210 (November 13, 1937): 8–9, 52–54.

Kens, Paul. “Lochner v. New York.” In *Oxford Companion to the Supreme Court,* edited by Kermit Hall. New York: Oxford University Press, 1992: 510.

Key, Sewall. “The Legal Work of the Federal Government.” *Virginia Law Review* 25 (1938): 165–201.

Kintner, Robert. “Joe Robinson: The New Deal’s Old Reliable.” *Saturday Evening Post* 209 (September 26, 1936): 5.

Krock, Arthur. “Nine Judges—and Nine Men, Too.” *New York Times Magazine* 7 (March 29, 1936):1–2, 15.

———. “Congress Discovers Its Own Backbone.” *New York Times Magazine* 8 (April 10, 1938):1–2, 20–21.

Kutler, Stanley. “Ex parte McCardle: Judicial Impotency? The Supreme Court and Reconstruction Reconsidered.” *American Historical Review* 72 (April 1967): 835–51.

Kyvig, David E. “The Road Not Taken: FDR, the Supreme Court, and Constitutional Amendment.” *Political Science Quarterly* 104:3 (1989): 463–81.

La Follette, Robert M., Jr. “Backing the President’s Court Proposal.” *Vital Speeches* 3 (1937): 311.

Lamb, Karl A. “The Opposition Party as Secret Agent: Republicans and the Court Fight, 1937.” *Papers of the Michigan Academy of Science, Arts, and Letters* 46 (1961): 539–50.

Langran, Robert W. "Presidents vs. the Court." *Supreme Court Historical Society Yearbook* (1977): 70–78.

Lee, Murray G. "The Supreme Court Catches Up." *United States Law Review* 71 (March 1937): 121–7; (April 1937): 199–210.

Lees, John D. "The President and the Supreme Court: New Deal to Watergate." British Association for American Studies. BAAS Pamphlets 3 (Durham, U.K.), 1980: 1–48.

Lerner, Max. "The Fate of the Supreme Court." *The Nation* 142 (March 25, 1935): 379–81.

———. "The Great Constitutional War." *Virginia Quarterly Review* 18 (1942): 530–45.

———. "Constitution and Court as Symbols." *Yale Law Journal* 46 (June 1937): 1290–1319.

Leuchtenburg, William E. "The Origins of Franklin Roosevelt's Court-packing Plan" *Supreme Court Review* (1966): 347–400.

———. "F.D.R.'s Court-Packing Plan: A Second Life, A Second Death." *Duke Law Journal* (June–September 1985): 673–89.

———. "Franklin D. Roosevelt's Supreme Court Packing Plan." In *Essays on the New Deal,* edited by Harold M. Hollingsorth and William F. Holmes. Austin: University of Texas Press, 1969: 69–115.

———. "Election of 1936." In *The History of American Presidential Elections, 1789–1968,* v. 3, (1930–1936), edited by Arthur M. Schlesinger, Jr. New York: Chelsea House, 1971: 2809–49; for the Democratic Platform of 1936, see 2851–54.

———. "Constitutional Revolution of 1937," 31–83. In *The Great Depression*, edited by Victor Hoar. Toronto: Copp Clark, 1969.

Lowitt, Richard. "Only God Can Change the Supreme Court." *Capitol Studies* 5 (Spring 1977): 9–24.

McBain, Howard L. "The Constitution and the New Deal." *Yale Review* 25 (September 1935): 114–30.

McElwain, Edward. "The Business of the Supreme Court as Conducted by Chief Justice Hughes." *Harvard Law Review* 63 (1949): 5–26.

Maddox, Robert J. "Roosevelt vs. the Court." *American History Illustrated* 4 (November 1969): 4–11.

Maidment, Richard. "The New Deal Court Revisited," 38–63,

in *Nothing Else to Fear,* Stephen W. Baskerville and Ralph Willett, eds. Manchester: Manchester University Press, 1985.

Mason, Alpheus T. "Charles Evans Hughes: An Appeal to the Bar of History." *Vanderbilt Law Review* 6 (December 1952): 1–19.

———. "Politics and the Supreme Court: President Roosevelt's Proposal." *University of Pennsylvania Law Review* 85 (May 1937): 659–77.

———. "Harlan Fiske Stone and FDR's Court Plan." *Yale Law Journal* 61: 6 (June–July 1952): 791–817.

———. "Supreme Court: Instrument of Power or Revealed Truth?" *Boston Law Review* 33 (June 1953): 279–336.

———. "Has the Supreme Court Abdicated?" *North American Review* 238 (October 1934): 353–60.

Miller, William I. "Dorothy Thompson and the Court packing Plan: Of Muse and Men." *Houston Law Review* 19 (May 1982): 695–711.

Murphy, Paul. "The New Deal Agricultural Program and the Constitution." *Agricultural History* 29 (October 1955): 160–69.

Nagel, Stuart S. "Court Packing Periods in American History." *Vanderbilt Law Review* 18 (March 1965): 925–44.

Nelson, Michael. "The President and the Court: Reinterpreting the Court-packing Episode of 1937." *Political Science Quarterly* 103:2 (Summer 1988): 267–93.

Parrish, Michael E. "The Great Depression, the New Deal and the American Legal Order." *Washington Law Review* 59 (September 1983–84): 723–50.

Patenaude, Lionel V. "Garner, Sumners and Connally: The Defeat of the Roosevelt Court Bill." *Southwestern Historical Quarterly* 74 (July 1970): 36–51.

Patterson, James T. "A Conservative Coalition Forms in Congress, 1933–1939." *Journal of American History* 52:4 (March 1966): 757–72.

Polenberg, Richard. "The National Committee to Uphold Constitutional Government, 1937–1941." *Journal of American History* 52:3 (December 1965): 582–98.

Post, Russell L. "The Constitutionality of Government Spending for the General Welfare." 22 *Virginia Law Review* (November 1935): 1–38.

Post, Russell L., and Charles H. Willard. "The Power of Congress to Nullify Gold Clauses." *Harvard Law Review* 46 (June 1933): 1225–57.

Powell, Thomas Reed. "The Next Four Years: The Constitution." *New Republic* 89 (January 13, 1937): 317–21.

Pritchett, C. Herman. "Stanley Reed." In *The Justices of the United States Supreme Court: 1789–1969,* edited by Leon Friedman and Fred Israel. New York: Chelsea House, 1969–1978: v. 3, 2373–98.

Pusey, Merlo J. "F.D.R. vs. The Supreme Court." *American Heritage* 9 (April 1958): 24–27, 105–7.

Rankin, J. Lee. "The Supreme Court, the Depression and the New Deal: 1930–1941." *Nebraska Law Review* 40 (1961): 35–62.

Ratner, Leonard G. "Congressional Power over the Appellate Jurisdiction of the Supreme Court." *University of Pennsylvania Law Review* 109 (December 1960): 157–202.

———. "Was the Supreme Court Packed by President Grant?" *Political Science Quarterly* 50 (September 1935): 343–58.

Rodell, Fred. "Justice v. Justices." *New Republic* 87 (December 23, 1936): 251.

Shenfield, Arthur. "The New Deal and the Supreme Court." In *The New Deal and its Legacy: Critique and Reappraisal,* edited by Robert Eden. New York: Greenwood Press, 1989, 167–76.

Shannon, Jasper B. "Presidential Politics in the South." *Journal of Politics* 1 (May 1939): 146–70.

Sirevag, Torbjorn. "Rooseveltian Ideas and the 1937 Court Fight: A Neglected Factor." *Historian* 33 (August 1971): 578–95.

Smith, Charles W. "President Roosevelt's Attitude Toward the Court." *Kentucky Law Journal* 31 (May 1943): 301–15.

Smith, Sylvester C. "Public Opinion Defeated the Court Bill." *Journal of the American Bar Association* 9 (September 1939): 545–82.

Sommer, F. H. "Bill for Reforming the Supreme Court." *Journal of the American Bar Association* 23 (May 1937): 347–53; 389–93.

Stern, Robert. "The Commerce Clause and the National Economy." *Harvard Law Review* 49 (May–July 1946): 645–93, 883–947.

Sternscher, Bernard. "Tugwell's Appraisal of F.D.R." *Western Political Quarterly* 15 (March 1962): 67–79.

Stokes, Thomas L. "Garner Turns on F.D.R." The *Nation* 144 (June 26, 1937), 722.

Swisher, Carl Brent. "Federal Organization of Legal Functions." *American Political Science Review* 33 (1939): 984.

———. "The Supreme Court in Transition." *Journal of Politics* 1:4 (November 1939): 349–70.

Timmons, Bascom N. "John Garner's Story," *Collier's* 121 (February 21, 1948): 11–12, 45–49; February 28, 1948, 22–23, 81–84; March 13, 1948, 22–23, 70–72; March 20, 1948: 30, 62–67.

Ward, Paul W. "Hacking to Justice with Cummings." The *Nation* 141 (July 3, 1935): 14—16.

———. "Roosevelt Will Win." *The Nation* 144 (February 20, 1937): 202.

Welch, Frances X. "Constitutionality of the Tennessee Valley Project." *Georgetown Law Journal* 23:3 (March 1935): 389–417.

Whisenhunt, Donald. "Roosevelt, McReynolds, and the Court Fight." *Artes Liberales* 5 (Fall 1977): 1–12.

White, J. Walter. "The Case of the Processors v. the People." *Virginia Law Review* 22:5 (March 1936): 546–54.

White, Michael. "Five Out of Nine Have It." *American Spectator* 4 (September 1936): 4–5.

Wickersham, Cornelius W. "NIRA from the Employers' Viewpoint." *Harvard Law Review* 48 (1934–1935): 954–77.

Wilkinson, Ignatius M. "The President's Plan Respecting the Supreme Court." *Fordham Law Review* 6 (May 1937): 179–89.

Wolfskill, George. "New Deal Critics: Did They Miss the Point?" In *Essays on the New Deal,* edited by Harold M. Hollingsworth and William F. Holmes. Austin: University of Texas Press, 1969: 49–68.

Ziegler, Luther H., Jr., "Senator Walter George's 1938 Campaign." *Georgia Historical Quarterly* 43 (1959): 333–52.

INDEX